ENVIRONMENTAL LAW

ENVIRONMENTAL LAW

JOHN D LEESON
LLB, FRSH, Barrister

PITMAN
PUBLISHING

London · Hong Kong · Johannesburg · Melbourne · Singapore · Washington DC

This book is dedicated with affection to my family, Gillian, Jonathan, Catherine and Stephanie, who according to their various talents have provided the support and encouragement to see its completion

PITMAN PUBLISHING
128 Long Acre, London WC2E 9AN
Tel: +44 (0)771 447 2000
Fax: +44 (0)771 240 5771

A Division of Pearson Professional Limited

First published in Great Britain in 1995

© Pearson Professional Limited 1995

ISBN 0 273 60496 1

British Library Cataloguing in Publication Data
A CIP catalogue record for this book can be obtained from the British Library

10   9   8   7   6   5   4   3   2

Typeset by 🖋 Tek Art, Croydon, Surrey
Printed and bound in Great Britain by
Clays Ltd, St Ives plc

*The Publishers' policy is to use paper manufactured
from sustainable forests.*

Contents

Preface

Stimulated from below by increasing public concern and from above by the demands of the European Commission, the last few years have seen the production and consolidation of legislation on a number of environmental issues. The Water Act 1989, providing for privatisation of the industry and consolidating earlier protection provisions, has itself been re-enacted in the Water Industry Act 1991 and the Water Resources Act 1991. Building on he Control of Pollution Act 1974, the strengthened licensing code for waste handling and disposal in Part II of the Environmental Protection Act 1990 is, at last, in place together with the Waste Management Licensing Regulations 1994 and the Council Regulation on the Community-wide transport of waste. The Clean Air Act 1993 consolidates the earlier smoke control legislation originating with the Act of 1956. Similarly the Radioactive Substances Act 1993 consolidates the 1960 Act and the amendments in the Environmental Protection Act 1990. Increased powers to cope with unwanted and excessive noise are now available in the Noise and Statutory Nuisance Act 1993.

There is no doubt that quality and omission standards for receiving media and discharges respectively will be continually reviewed and amended. Nevertheless there now appears to be in place a comprehensive structure of basic environmental controls for the immediate future. As an indication of, or response to, public interest there is a proliferation of courses for students at varying levels having some environmental content and a similar increase in practitioners in this field, both public and private. There are already available a number of large, and therefore expensive, multi-volume works on environmental law with updating service; and never was an up-dating service more necessary. The aim here though is to offer a source of material, with general exposition and commentary, that is more accessible in both size and cost. In providing such a source for students of the subject this work may also perhaps provide a convenient first point of reference for practitioners in the field; especially those from a non-legal background.

John D Leeson
Tonbridge
Kent

Table of cases

Table of statutes

Table of statutory instruments

Table of European Community legislation

Directive	Reference	
70/157/EEC	OJ L42 (23.2.70, p16)	320, 325
70/220/EEC	OJ L76 (7.4.70, p1)	240, 241, 247
73/350/EEC	OJ L321 (22.11.73, p33)	320, 325
74/440/EEC	OJ L84 (29.3.74, p25)	325
75/442/EEC	OJ L194 (25.7.75, p26)	343, 350, 354, 402, 406, 415, 417, 420
75/16/EEC	OJ L307 (27.11.75, p22)	282
76/160/EEC	OJ L31 (5.2.76, p1)	133, 137, 138
76/464/EEC	OJ L129 (17.5.76, p23)	133, 157, 222
77/212/EEC	OJ L66 (12.3.77, p33)	320, 322, 324, 325
78/319/EEC	OJ L84 (31.3.78, p43)	355, 435
78/611/EEC	OJ L197 (22.7.78, p19)	237
78/659/EEC	OJ L222 (14.8.78, p1)	143
78/1015/EEC	OJ L349 (13.12.78, p21)	327, 328
79/923/EEC	OJ L281 (10.11.79, p47)	144
80/68/EEC	OJ L20 (26.1.80, p43)	164, 389, 390
80/778/EEC	OJ L229 (30.8.80, p11)	123, 128, 152, 160
80/779/EEC	OJ L229 (30.8.80, p30)	229
81/334/EEC	OJ L131 (18.5.81, p6)	320, 322, 324, 325
82/176/EEC	OJ L81 (27.3.82, p29)	134
82/884/EEC	OJ L378 (31.12.82, p.15)	229
83/513/EEC	OJ L291 (24.10.83, p1)	134
84/360/EEC	OJ L188 (16.7.84, p20)	45

Directive	Reference	
	Art 12	46
	Art 13	46
84/372/EEC	OJ L196 (26.7.84, p47)	322, 324, 425
84/424/EEC	OJ L238 (6.9.84, p31)	322, 324, 325
84/631/EEC	OJ L326 (13.12.84, p31)	417, 441
	Art 10	37
85/203/EEC	OJ L87 (27.3.85, p1)	229
85/210/EEC	OJ L96 (3.4.85, p25)	238, 241
85/337/EEC	OJ L175 (5.7.85, p40)	63
85/536/EEC	OJ L334 (12.12.85, p20)	238
86/280/EEC	OJ L181 (4.7.86, p16)	134
87/217/EEC	OJ L85 (28.3.87, p40)	252
87/219/EEC	OJ L91 (3.4.87, p19)	238, 282
87/441/EEC	OJ L238 (21.8.87, p40)	238
88/347/EEC	OJ L158 (25.6.88, p35)	134
88/77/EEC	OJ L36 (9.2.88, p33)	241, 246, 247
89/235/EEC	OJ L98 (11.4.89, p1)	327
89/458/EEC	OJ L226 (3.8.89, p1)	247
90/313/EEC	OJ L158 (23.6.90, p56)	15, 61
	Art 6	16
	Art 7	18
90/415/EEC	OJ L219 (14.8.90, p49)	134
91/492/EEC	OJ L268 (24.9.91, p1)	150
92/72/EEC	OJ L297 (13.10.92, p1)	229, 230

Regulation	Reference	
EEC/259/93	OJ L30	413–24

'The truth is that the whole of our sanitary legislation is in a state which I hardly like to characterize in the language that naturally suggests itself; and the attempt to extract from the various details of the legislation a set of harmonious principles always underlying the specific provisions is, I am afraid, futile.'

per Wills J
Bradford v Mayor of Eastbourne 1896

Part One

REGULATION

1

Structure

INTRODUCTION

The growing concern with environmental issues, and their impact on general public awareness, is one of the more noticeable phenomena of the last 20 years or so. From holes in the ozone layer to the recycling of discarded cans, environmental issues affect us all at many levels. The increasing range of these concerns has generated a correspondingly comprehensive response from legislators, not only at national level but internationally and, perhaps of most immediate significance, in the European Community. Responding to these developments one increasingly finds writers in the field optimistically referring to the 'coming of age' of environmental law. To use such terms now though is to claim more than is justified.

If one is to use the analogy of human development, it is perhaps more appropriate to characterise the present stage of the discipline as precocious adolescence. There is currently rapid growth coupled with what may pass for youthful exuberance. As in all such cases, though, many of the consequences of this energy have yet to be properly integrated into and accepted by the existing structures with which environmental law will have to live. Its elders – government, industry and commerce – may smile indulgently and make encouraging comments when asked but, as with most adolescents, they often appear reluctant to seek too close an acquaintance. While the precise character and role of the maturing adult is not yet entirely clear, one can detect in its development so far indications of its eventual nature and functions. That further growth is to be expected before full maturity is attained is self-evident and, as with other living entities, inevitable. Perhaps that takes the analogy as far as is profitable.

Turning from the present to the past, the history of United Kingdom legislative control over the impact of man's activity on the environment can be divided into three broad stages. The first period, extending up to the nineteenth century and the industrial revolution, is characterised by spasmodic and ineffective attempts to deal with the more acute pollution problems. As this long period was essentially one of a rural, agricultural-based economy, the only problems sufficiently serious to stimulate action were those attaching to the larger centres of population, such as the concern in London during the reign of Charles II over the production of smoke from the burning of 'sea coal'.[1] Those measures were largely ineffective because then, as now, the specifying of legal duties and standards without providing appropriate enforcement machinery might have indicated good intentions but achieved little of a practical nature.

The second stage, prompted by the profound effects on the environment of the industrial revolution and the urbanisation of society, produced increasingly comprehensive statutory controls on the discharge of pollutants into the various receiving media. Typical of such measures was the Clean Air Act 1956. Here the objectives

1 See, e.g., John Evelyn, *Fumifugium or The Smoake of London Dissipated*, 1661.

of legislation are limited to the nature and quantity of the pollutants themselves and, in some cases, their effects on their immediate surroundings; for example, the diluting effects of receiving water in the case of effluent discharges. This stage is characterised by a general lack of concern with any deterioration in the quality of environmental media, or with the wider ranging impacts of pollutants over regions, nations or continents.

The third stage has been marked by expansion from emphasis on public health and the effects of pollutants on man to concern for the environment and the impact of pollutants on the biosphere as a whole. With this change has come a parallel extension of concern for the wider consequences of man's discharge of pollutants into the environment, currently expressed through the imposition of quality standards for the various media. The beginning of this third stage is less easy to identify but is attributable to two factors. Originating probably in the 1970s and no doubt accentuated by pictures of Earth from space, there has been an increasing awareness that the planet we inhabit is a finite entity. Further, that it is consequently more vulnerable than previously thought, if it was ever thought about, to the impact of man's activities – activities that are themselves, with the passage of time, increasing in both scale and complexity. It is therefore increasingly apparent that in the environmental context we are all our brother's keepers. The other contributory factor has been the coercive effect of the European Community on member governments. While response to national opinion would doubtless have eventually produced the same result, there can be little doubt that Community initiatives have accelerated these developments.

This evolutionary process has been characterised at each stage by certain common features. An important preliminary requirement is a learning phase while the effects on the environment of the material or process are recognised; this process being accompanied by the identification of appropriate technical and procedural remedies. Then, having understood the nature of the problem and its solution, a period of time is needed to build a sufficient weight of public concern and demand to overcome the inertia of commercial interests, established institutions and modes of thought and so to make it politically expedient to legislate for the remedy. This process occupies varying lengths of time. In acute cases the learning and execution curve is very short, as is instanced by the development of the nuclear industry. In other cases, for example water pollution, it appears to be extending over a century or more. In spite of the vast regulatory machine and detailed quality standards, water quality is not improving as it should.

While these latter stages are not complete in the sense of having achieved their objectives, it is quite apparent that they possess inherent deficiencies that make any real, comprehensive improvement unlikely. First, it is a truism that legal, and especially criminal, standards merely represent a minimum attainment level; the assumption being that if and when performance drops to that level sanctions may be applied. In the environmental context, though, where the imposed standard often represents and requires a substantial improvement on current performance, the stipulated legal standard invariably becomes the norm rather than the minimum, setting a psychological ceiling on any real or progressive improvement.

A second major defect of these present regulatory structures is the process of regulation itself. Is the evaluation in environmental terms of existing and new materials and processes even keeping pace with their rate of production? The more control that is imposed the greater is the burden of the necessary supervisory and

2 See below at p.54.

3 See below at pp.40, 45.

inspection machinery with all its attendant costs, irrespective of the expense of remedying the pollution itself. The scale charges for IPC authorisations[2] indicate not only the financial burden imposed by this procedure on industry but also the comparable costs of other forms of environmental control borne by public authorities and, through them, society as a whole. Thirdly, the standards applied to determine emission levels are invariably based on technical feasibility, as indicated by the use of such terms as 'best practicable means' and 'best available technology not entailing excessive cost'.[3] A code of law primarily devoted to the protection of the environment is founded not so much on the perceived needs of that environment as on technical and commercial expediency. That those reasons are in themselves legitimate and justifiable does not detract from their environmental irrelevance.

As a result of these inherent flaws in the present state of environmental law it may be that the most that can be expected from it is a relatively modest reduction in the more gross forms of pollution and levels of pollutants. Such improvements are of course worth having and their attainment, set against what has gone before, should not to be undervalued. A cursory examination of erstwhile industrial areas may now reveal clear skys, cleaned building facades and fish returning to rivers and canals. However, the limits of the present structure of regulation and control are also discernible, with the perceptible and increasing chronic deterioration of the biosphere. A deterioration moreover resulting either from the application of presumed tolerance levels based on, as has been said, non-environmental criteria, or due to the uncontrolled disposal of polluting material. Those local gains have to be placed in the wider context of the heating up of the atmosphere, the reduction of the ozone layer, the destruction of forests either by commercial exploitation or acid rain, and the increasing incidence of cancers and allergic reactions in the human body.

If this superficial appraisal is nevertheless realistic, protection of the environment still has a long way to go and a great deal to achieve. Following the pattern of the previous stages of development in environmental law, and being at least in part aware of the nature of the problem and of the deficiencies of earlier methods, we should now be identifying and encouraging those elements that will form the fourth stage of environmental protection. A legal textbook is not an appropriate context for prognostication, nor can one writer bring to the activity all the disciplines and skills needed to assess the range of factors impinging on the environment, much less to anticipate their individual and collective development over any particular time scale. However, a few trends may be noted as a conclusion to this introduction.

Noting the burden in costs and resources imposed by regulation and the rate at which the process and procedures are increasing, some alternative may be desirable, or indeed necessary. To emphasise this point, the machinery of regulation does not itself directly contribute to the desired objective, it only ensures that others are coerced towards its achievement. Substitution of this costly regulatory structure by some other process, if one can be found, may therefore produce the same result at a more socially economic cost. Contemplation of an alternative leads inevitably to consideration of the potential of the carrot rather than the stick. If the advantages of actively embracing environmentally sound practices sufficiently outweighed the burdens, persons and organisations would not only cease to need compulsion but the levels of achievement would progressively rise beyond legally imposed minima. Such an idea is not as fanciful as it may at first seem, a practical example being to hand. It can for instance be argued that the improvements in food retailing and catering of the last 30 or 40 years owe more to the effects of commercial competition and consumer demand than to the enforcement of legal controls.

What has applied in the food industry may also apply to similar effect in the environmental context. Indeed it is already becoming apparent, and can be expected to increase as BS 7750[4] and its requirement for routine environmental auditing is progressively adopted. Organisations are increasingly having to face and meet environmental expectations in respect of their products and practices from purchasers, suppliers, consumers and neighbours. Also, of course, it is to be remembered that the members of and workers in an organisation are in their turn, with their families, also consumers and neighbours, and thus living in the world that is the recipient of their activity in the organisation.

A second factor – which while currently more difficult to assess, will undoubtedly in the long term have a more pervasive and profound effect on man's impact on the environment – is the post-industrial restructuring of society. Just as the change from a rural to an industrial society was long, spasmodic and incomplete, so will this next phase be. In fact industrialisation is still proceeding apace in many parts of the world, its apparent association with first world affluence being too obvious to require explanation or justification. Equally, though, the move away from the industrial form of society with its apparently immutable structures and practices is under way. The requirement of industry and commerce for concentrations of power, resources and particularly labour in both time and place has produced a society and mentality shaped by and attuned to those needs. Work, and indeed education as its necessary precursor, happens at a set place at set times. Other activities happen at home and in other places and, save for the fortunate few, are the exclusive source of pleasure and satisfaction.

Technological changes, particularly in communications, are removing the necessity for such concentrations of resources and activity and the consequent compartmentalisation of life. This is not to say that a post-industrial society will revert in all its features to the earlier rural pattern. Already, though, the traditional and almost universal work patterns are being replaced by a diversity of alternatives. Work, or paid activity, is performed in increasingly flexible permutations extending beyond the standard eight-hour day and, with the aid of PCs, faxes and so on, outside the 'works'. In consequence one may expect to see increasingly, as these trends take firmer hold, reductions in commuting and in the size of industrial and commercial complexes, with a commensurate reduction in the pollutants derived from these functions. Also, when people live and work in the same area they can be expected to display an increased concern for its quality as a place in which to occupy their time.

The previous considerations may be regarded as descriptive of developments that will evolve with time from presently discernible origins, requiring therefore little innovation. The third factor, necessitating the conscious adoption of a new policy, may be through a move to what Professor Gerd Winter[5] refers to as 'soft technology'. This concept is a response to the production of increasing numbers of materials and products that are hostile to the natural environment and which, due to their resistance to assimilation by it, can be considered as hard technology. Instead of adopting a very narrow, self-interested view of the merits of some

4 Specification for Environmental Management Systems.

5 'Perspectives for Environmental Law – Entering the Fourth Phase' JEL vol. 1, no. 1, p.42. It is to be emphasised that the four stages discussed here do not equate with the four phases propounded in that article.

new technology, this approach requires a wider assessment of its acceptability in broad, holistic terms. The characteristics of such 'soft technologies' would include, in Professor Winter's view, those which:

(a) can be accepted back into nature and do not require separation from it to prevent contamination;
(b) strengthen natural forces and substances;
(c) are reversible when mistakes become apparent;
(d) are tolerant of failure;
(e) take the possibility of human error into account;
(f) utilise substances and energy sparingly;
(g) recycle instead of disposing of resources.

The underlying principle then is that the value of any new development should not be determined in the narrow isolation of its immediate, individual application. Rather, its total role in the wider scheme of things must receive consideration. One man's meat may prove to be more than one other man's poison. The wider issues that need to be considered and resolved in the context of environmental audits constitute a significant move towards that goal.

LAW AND THE ENVIRONMENT

The law that may legitimately be considered environmental is not all the law that has any bearing on or involvement with environmental issues. Many elements of the common law, for example tort, property, injunctive relief and administrative law principles and remedies, may contribute to the resolution of environmental problems. The law that may be regarded as specifically environmental is, as with other specialist areas of law, that having exclusive or predominant concern with the subject. Being a relatively new discipline, such law is to be found in legislation; although it is to be noted that a considerable body of such material, originating before present concerns with the wider environment developed, is categorised as public health law. As will be evident from the substance of this book, reflecting the transboundary nature of much pollution and therefore of environmental concerns, legislation on this issue is increasingly generated by European and international bodies.

With its origins in the civil law, proceedings were at the initiative of the person affected, and therefore to secure a personal benefit. On that basis wider questions concerning the community at large or prejudice to other than human aspects of the environment remained unanswered. Also, of course, the remedy and therefore the extent to which the polluter paid was confined to the quantifiable damage to the particular plaintiff. In these respects the gradual move to an essentially criminal law-based structure consequent upon legislative control has been of questionable advantage. The merits derive from centralised or public authority control, permitting a broader and more dispassionate approach as well as ensuring the prosecution of cases and incidents that would go unregarded if left to the action of some affected individual. In that chronic low level pollution may not affect individuals in any significant sense it may not in consequence reach the threshold of civil liability. The disadvantage is that, although statutory procedures often make provision for the remedying of the deficiency, criminal law remedies can hardly be said to require the polluter to pay in any realistic way for the damage caused, or even in the civil law sense. Fines, with notable modern improvements, are often inadequately proportionate to the scale and duration of the offence, and anyway bear no necessary relationship to the harm caused. Also the requirement to remedy the defect merely assimilates the faulty operation to the standard that others have been observing as a matter of course. The backlog of pollution is ignored.

A further characterisic of the use of criminal procedures, as also with the various forms of licensing, approval, control and so on, is that they all operate through the medium of public authorities. The power to call such authorities to account or to challenge their decisions and actions, or lack of them, is a matter for administrative law, and particularly judicial review. Through the Order 53 procedure[6] a person prejudiced by the action or decision of a public authority may obtain a remedy by the prerogative orders of certiorari, prohibition or mandamus, or by the civil law remedies of injunction or declaration, to which may be added damages. The precise grounds on which such remedies are available are not an appropriate matter for this present work, being anyway exhaustively dealt with in texts on that subject. There can, however, be no doubt that the development of and increasing resort to environmental law procedures will see a commensurate growth in the use of the controlling mechanisms of administrative law. Judicial review will prove to be an indispensable tool for the environmental lawyer and an understanding of it necessary for anyone concerned with environmental issues.

AUTHORITIES

Local authorities[7]

For most of the country for most of our history, local government in any recognisable sense has been non-existent. Many towns were granted charters giving them identity and certain powers, typically to hold fairs and collect a variety of tolls. In the other, larger rural areas such local administration as existed was in the hands of the justices at Quarter Sessions. The later eighteenth and early nineteenth centuries introduced society, rulers and ruled, the novel consequences of industrialisation and urbanisation. Environmental problems that were chronic and diffuse in a rural setting – and therefore, buttressed by familiarity, socially tolerable – became acute and concentrated in the new industrial context and, illumined by the novel situation, proved unacceptable. As each problem appeared, whether by type or locality, it was dealt with on an *ad hoc* basis, producing a plethora of central and local boards, trusts and commissions, as well as increasing the tasks of those same justices. Order was brought out of this individuality by the creation of multi-functional local authorities composed of elected representatives and having the power to levy a general rate.[8] Professor I. Jennings suggests that what converted the old municipal corporations from private to public governmental institutions was the granting of functions concerned with policing, lighting, appointment of magistrates and provision of courts, and the power to make byelaws for the good rule and government of their areas.[9] Similarly, Professor J.F.Garner identifies the characteristics of an English local authority as:[10]

(a) being a separate person in law;
(b) having governmental powers over a defined local area;
(c) being financed, at least partly, by income derived from the inhabitants of the area;

6 And see section 31 of the Supreme Court Act 1981.

7 This term is used here as referring to 'principal authorities' within section 270(1) of the Local Government Act 1972, i.e. county and district councils, metropolitan districts and also London boroughs. A district may be granted 'borough' status by Royal Charter under section 245 of the Local Government Act 1972.

8 See, e.g., Municipal Corporations Act 1835 and Local Government Act 1894.

9 *A Century of Municipal Progress*, eds Laski, Robson and Jennings, Greenwood Press, London,1978, chapter 3.

10 *Administrative Law*, Butterworth, London, 6th ed. 1985, p.326.

(d) being controlled by directly elected representatives;

(e) exercising statutorily conferred governmental functions over its area.

Subsequently local authorities at county and district level exercised between them a wide range of functions, not the least of which where those concerned with public health, the environment and planning. While administratively convenient, time and experience indicated that, for a variety of reasons, the size of such unitary authorities was not necessarily the most appropriate for the effective performance of a number of disparate activities. Obvious examples that, for their own reasons, did not fit conveniently into standard local government boundaries being policing and water supply. The modern history and experience of local authorities has therefore been one of contraction as erstwhile local government functions have been re-allocated to specially created, specialist bodies offering the prospect of greater efficiency at the cost of reduced accountability. Responsibility for and control of water supplies having been redistributed in 1973, Her Majesty's Inspectorate of Pollution now has responsibility for the range of functions subsumed within Integrated Pollution Control, and it is expected that the waste regulation function is to be transferred to the imminent Environment Agency. It may therefore be that a primary environmental function of local authorities in the future will be the monitoring, on behalf of their residents, of the performance of these new service providers.

The present structure of local government derives from the Local Government Act 1972[11] giving effect to the White Paper 'Local Government in England : Government Proposals for Reorganisation'[12] which, *inter alia*, reduced the 1385 existing authorities to 422. Responsibility for the principal environmental functions is as follows:[13]

(a) In the metropolitan areas all functions are exercised by the district councils except for the special provisions applying in south Lancashire for waste regulation and disposal.[14]

(b) In the non-metropolitan areas –
   (i) Counties are responsible for planning (exercised in association with district councils), derelict land, waste disposal and regulation;
   (ii) District councils are responsible for planning (shared functions with the county council), waste collection, some water and sewerage responsibilities, air pollution control, building regulation, cemeteries and crematoria

(c) With the abolition of the GLC on 1 April 1986, the 32 London boroughs became solely responsible for environmental functions in Greater London with the exception of those allocated to other authorities or bodies as follows[15] –
   (i) Land drainage and flood prevention – with the privatisation of the water industry by the Water Act 1989 these functions passed from the Thames Water Authority to the regional flood defence committee acting under the supervision of the NRA.
   (ii) Planning – section 5 of the Local Government Act 1985 required the London boroughs and Common Council to establish a joint planning committee for Greater London to co-ordinate and represent a collective approach on particular matters.
   (iii) Waste regulation and disposal – the London Waste Regulation Authority is responsible for that function in the Greater London area, and 21 of the 32 boroughs are combined into four areas (West, North, East and Western

11 In London, the London Government Act 1963 as amended by the Local Government Act 1985.

12 Cmnd 4584 (1971).

13 See DoE Circular 121/72.

14 See below at pp.344–5.

15 The City and the Inner and Middle Temples are responsible for certain local government functions in their areas.

Riverside) for the waste disposal function. The remaining authorities are themselves responsible for waste disposal.[16]

16 See in more detail at p.345 below.

Environmental services and pollution control are usually the responsibility of an Environmental Health Department within the authority. These functions are frequently combined with others such as housing and food control, the department being staffed by environmental health officers. The present trend, though, is towards the re-allocation of many erstwhile local government functions to specially created environmental bodies. It may have been that with a multi-purpose authority the importance and therefore the resources devoted to a particular function, being a matter of individual or local judgement, or indeed fashion, consigned some of these responsibilities to an unreasonably low priority. By transferring such functions to specially created bodies, however, while their range of activity is reduced and attention concentrated, they are generally unaccountable in any direct way to the community they purport to serve; unaccountable that is in quality and effectiveness of performance or financially. It is assumed in this criticism that the submission of an annual report to a Minister does not carry with it the same degree of detailed control as that of a monthly appearance before a locally informed committee. This development therefore raises two questions, the answers to which, it is suggested, provide complementary solutions. First, with the removal of environmental functions to unelected and therefore less accountable authorities, how are such bodies to be made responsible and responsive to the communities they serve – *Sed quis custodiet ipsos custodes?*'[17] Secondly, with the removal of ever more functions from local authorities, what, if any, environmental role will they have? Being still the primary locally elected body an obvious remaining responsibility of a local authority will be to represent the interests of its constituents in the monitoring on their behalf of the quality of performance of this increasing range of specialist bodies. Whether overtly given to them, as in the case of the water supply function[18] or, *faut de mieux*, in the absence of any effective alternative, this is a role that they could and should perform.

17 'But who is to guard the guards?' Juvenal, Satires no.6, 1. 347.

18 See section 77 of the Water Industry Act 1991 and Part VIII of the Water Supply (Water Quality) Regulations 1989.

Her Majesty's Inspectorate of Pollution

Consequent upon the individual responses to particular pollution problems as they arose, most legal controls operate in relatively isolated and piece-meal ways. That pollution of the various media – air, water and land – is interrelated was shown by the Royal Commission on Environmental Pollution in 1976.[19] The transferability of pollutants between receiving media makes an integrated approach to pollution control of fundamental importance if real, overall improvement to the condition of the environment is to be achieved.[20] The Commission therefore recommended the formation of a unified inspectorate to ensure an integrated approach to such problems at source and thus minimise damage to the total environment. It suggested that the aim of the inspectorate should be to achieve the 'Best Practicable Environmental Option' taking account of the total pollution from a process and the technical means for dealing with it.[21]

19 'Air Pollution Control: An Integrated Approach', Cmnd 6371.

20 Ibid, para. 2.63.

In response to these proposals Her Majesty's Inspectorate of Pollution (HMIP) was formed within the Department of the Environment in April 1987, combining:

21 For a consideration of BPEO see below at p.42.

- HM Radiochemical Inspectorate,
- HM Industrial Air Pollution Inspectorate,
- Hazardous Waste Inspectorate.

The obvious, serious omission is the Alkali Inspectorate, concerned with pollution control in specialised industrial processes and particularly emissions to air. They had been incorporated into the Health and Safety Executive on its formation in 1974 in spite of the latter body's primary concern with employment and the internal working environment. The Pollution Inspectorate is organised[22] under a Director and Chief Inspector who is also responsible for planning, policy and administration. The Chief Inspector also heads a Regulatory Standards Division which is broadly subdivided into sections with responsibility for the major forms of pollutants. England and Wales is divided into seven regions – North West, North East, Anglian, Southern, South West, Midlands, and Wales. The regions have responsibility for regulation, including the processing of applications, plant inspection, complaint investigation and enforcement.

The present functions of HMIP, in relation to England and Wales, may be summarised as follows:[23]

(a) provision of authoritative and independent advice to Government and industry on pollution control practices;
(b) approval, inspection and oversight of potentially polluting processes under the Health & Safety at Work etc. Act 1974 and the Environmental Protection Act 1991;
(c) registration and authorisation of premises both holding and disposing of radioactive materials under the Radioactive Substances Act 1993;
(d) regulatory oversight and audit of waste regulation authorities;
(e) research on the regulatory aspects of pollution; and
(f) operation of Integrated Pollution Control (IPC).

Elaborating on some of these matters, HMIP provides Government departments with advice on pollution issues such as acid rain deposition, the environmental impact of pollutants and incineration technology. HMIP is represented on European Community working groups, Euratom, OECD, the International Atomic Energy Agency, the Oslo and Paris Commissions, and the United Nations International Maritime Organisation. A principal duty of the inspectorate is the authorisation and control of the larger industrial manufacturing and waste recovery processes through the IPC provisions in Part I of the Environmental Protection Act 1990. Associated with that function, and to facilitate uniformity of approach and standards, is the production of Chief Inspector's Guidance Notes (CIGNs). Such guidance notes, covering each of the 200 IPC processes, are produced to anticipate the extension of the IPC procedure to the process concerned. They provide detailed guidance on best available technology, pollution abatement techniques, operating procedures and the emission standards to be achieved.

The HMIP mission statement of July 1992 says:

HMIP protects the environment by enforcing regulations to prevent pollution
We will:
Authorise, enforce, inspect and monitor under the relevant legislation
Consult openly and widely and report on our performance
Provide expert advice to government
Initiate research and development and disseminate our results
Work cost effectively and to the highest professional standards.

22 See Second Annual Report 1988-89 (HMIP).

23 Dr J. Marshall, 'IPC – Progress in Implementation' (NSCA, April 1991), as necessarily amended.

National Rivers Authority

Prior to the privatisation of the water industry the 10 regional water authorities were responsible for both the utility or service provision and the regulatory function. With privatisation of water services by the Water Act 1989, it was necessary to create a new regulatory authority for the industry. That body, created by the privatising legislation but now provided for in Chapter I of Part I of the Water Resources Act 1991, is the National Rivers Authority (NRA); an unduly modest title for a body responsible for all inland water resources and coastal waters as well as rivers.

The Authority is an independent, non-governmental, corporate body, section 1(5) of the Water Resources Act 1991 providing that 'The Authority shall not be regarded as the servant or agent of the Crown...'. However, the Secretary of State[24] and the Minister of Agriculture, Fisheries and Food exercise a considerable degree of control in that between them they appoint the members[25] and, by section 5, may issue 'Directions of a general or specific character' after consultation with the Authority. These directions, details of which have to be included in the Authority's Annual Reports,[26] indicate the close association of the Authority with government and the formation of policy. Its national structure is broadly based on the preceding regional water authorities, though now reduced to eight. Each region has a Regional Rivers Advisory Committee established under section 7 of the Water Resources Act 1991. The functions of the NRA, primarily delineated in section 2, include:

(a) resource management and abstraction licensing (Part II);
(b) control of water pollution (Part III);
(c) land drainage and flood protection (Part IV);
(d) the fishery and navigation functions of the former water authorities;
(e) promotion of conservation and recreational interests (section 16);[27]
(f) regard to the impact of the exercise of its powers on water and sewerage undertakers (section 15(1)).

The Authority's finances are provided for in Part VI of the Act. Most of its services and the issue of consents and licences, e.g. for abstraction, are charged for, while flood defence costs are recovered from the local authorities concerned. A specific matter worthy of note is the power in section 190 for the Secretary of State to make regulations specifying the matters to be included in registers maintained by the NRA for either five years from the date of entry or thereafter for as long as necessary for the exercise of their functions in respect of pollution control. The Control of Pollution (Registers) Regulations 1989[28] currently require that those registers shall include details of :

(a) notices served by the Secretary of State under section 83 of the Water Resources Act 1991 specifying water quality objectives;
(b) applications for consents under Chapter I;
(c) consents and conditions under Chapter I;
(d) samples taken by the NRA under Chapter I;
(e) certificates issued by the Secretary of State of exemption from disclosure under Schedule 10 of the Water Resources Act 1991.

Environment Agency

In July 1991, the Government declared its intention to establish an environmental agency and published a Consultation Paper in October of the same year. In

24 Secretary of State for the Environment and the Secretary of State for Wales.

25 The Authority consists of 8–15 members, two of whom are appointed by the Minister and one is designated by the SoS as chairman: section 1(2) and (3).

26 Section 187.

27 And see the Water and Sewerage (Conservation, Access and Recreation)(Code of Practice) Order 1989 (S.I. 1989 No. 1152).

28 S.I. 1989 No. 1160.

July 1992, a formal announcement was made stating that the agency's functions would include those of the present HMIP and the NRA, and the waste regulation functions of local authorities. There has been no indication that the Drinking Water Inspectorate should be included. The proposed date for the commencement of operations was 1995. The Queen's Speech opening the Parliamentary session for 1993/94 promised a 'paving bill' in that session to begin to lay down powers necessary to create the agency; a promise that remained unfulfilled. In July 1994, Lord Crickhowell told the House of Commons All Party Water Group that the establishment of the proposed agency was likely to be delayed following Treasury pressure. The earliest set-up date could be the spring of 1996. Also in July 1994, the Department of the Environment published 'Options for the geographic and managerial structure of the proposed environment agency'. The report, produced by Touche Ross, outlines five differing structures for the agency. It was stated that the Secretary of State would establish an advisory committee to oversee the agency, if and when created.

Shortly before the summer recess of 1994, the Environment Secretary, in a written answer to a Parliamentary question, stated that there would be put in place an Advisory Committee on arrangements for the proposed agency, to play a continuing role after Parliament had approved the necessary legislation creating the agency. He also considered that it would be possible to establish the agency during 1995 and incorporate the existing authorities into it by April 1996.

ROYAL COMMISSION ON ENVIRONMENTAL POLLUTION

As its title indicates, the Royal Commission is not an executive body. It has, however, a wide-ranging brief to investigate and report on environmental pollution issues, thus identifying and bringing such issues to the public attention. The dozen or so reports so far produced constitute a valuable source of material and opinion on particular problems, as subsequent areas of this present work demonstrate. For a review of the Commission and its functions it is difficult to improve on its own assessment, as expressed in its Fifth Report.[29]

29 'Air Pollution Control; An Integrated Approach' Cmnd 6371, January 1976.

The Royal Commission's Role

1.6 The Commission was constituted on 20 February 1970, as a standing body, 'to advise on matters, both national and international, concerning the pollution of the environment; on the adequacy of research in this field; and the future possibilities of danger to the environment'. Appointments to the Commission are made by Royal Warrant, on the advice of the Prime Minister. There is thus an important distinction to be drawn between the Commission's status, as an independent body not constrained by departmental boundaries, and that of an advisory committee appointed by a Minister to advise him on matters falling within his departmental responsibilities. As the first Report stated: 'We have no specific or restricted task We are authorised to enquire into any matter on which we think advice is needed, and also to enquire into any issues within our terms of reference that are referred to us by any of Her Majesty's Secretaries of State or Ministers.

1.7 To quote again from the First Report:

We regard it as our function to find out what is happening to our physical environment and to inform the British public about trends in pollution and needs for research and development. We expect to propose ways to improve the quality of the environment through education, legislation, financial measures and international agreements.

...The nation's resources for reducing pollution are limited; difficult choices will have to be made in their deployment. A standing Royal Commission, which is independent of Government, has an opportunity to give objective advice on how those choices should be made and to contribute ideas toward a comprehensive policy for safeguarding the environment.

1.8 This theme was developed in the Fourth Report, which (after noting the steady improvements in environmental protection introduced by successive governments) commented:

The existence of a standing Royal Commission with such broad terms of reference implies a judgment that pollution will continue to raise issues of such consequence to the nation as to justify on independent "watch-dog" body. Our role ... is to identify aspects of pollution that appear to call for independent enquiry, to study these in depth and to publish our conclusions. We see it as an important part of this work to inform the general public on environmental matters as well as to recommend action by Government and other agencies where we consider that this is needed. Though we are essentially a lay body, we bring a wide range of experience and expertise to the Commission, and we are in a position to take a comprehensive view of the issues raised by pollution. ... We expect ... to concern ourselves with the principles that relate to pollution control and abatement and to deal with matters which may escape the attention of official bodies having more narrowly defined responsibilities than those of the Commission, but which may nevertheless be of considerable importance for the future protection of the environment.

We believe that these statements are as valid today as when they were first written.

What is 'pollution'?

1.9 In our consultations various bodies or persons have urged us to look at topics which lie outside the general area previously covered by the Commission. It may therefore be helpful to consider what the Commission understands by environmental pollution. While we do not consider that it is either practicable or helpful to seek a comprehensive simple definition of 'pollution' to apply to every occasion, we find the following to be a useful working definition.

The introduction by man into the environment of substances or energy liable to cause hazards to human health, harm to living resources and ecological systems, damage to structures or amenity, or interference with the legitimate uses of the environment.

In practice the word 'pollution' is used both to describe the act of polluting and the consequences.

1.10 It is implicit in the above definition that pollution is not simply the presence in the environment of an alien substance or other unnatural disturbance; there must also be an unwanted effect. Substances introduced into the environment become pollutants only when 'their distribution, concentration or physical behaviour are such as to have undesirable or deleterious consequences'. For many substances whether a particular discharge or emission is considered to be pollution depends not only on the nature of the substance, but also on the circumstances in which it occurs, and often on the attitude of the people affected and on value judgments.

PROCEEDINGS

Access to Information

The availability of information on activities having environmental impact is a necessary preliminary to the application of controls or the protection of individual rights. As Ludwig Kramer says:[30]

> In order to discuss environmental matters in an open society – where governments derive their right to govern from the consent of the governed and where the setting of standards does not consist of transforming shadows of the Platonic idea of Justice into a piece of legislation, but are conceived, scheduled and accepted by way of democratic procedure – a number of conditions must be fulfilled. The first is access to environmental information ...

Such access, or rather lack of it, has in the past proved an insuperable barrier to the exercise of those rights of protection that the law affords, leaving persons actually or potentially at risk with no effective remedy, or indeed unaware that they were even exposed to any risk.

The European Community has recognised and responded to this problem in its Directive on the Freedom of Access to Information on the Environment[31] which was required to be implemented by Member States by 31 December 1992, notifying the Commission of the fact of and methods of that implementation.[32] In stating its general purpose Article 1 says that 'The object of this directive is to ensure freedom of access to, and dissemination of, information on the environment held by public authorities and to set out the basic terms and conditions on which such information should be made available.' The Directive has been largely implemented in Great Britain in the Environmental Information Regulations 1992.[33]

The Environmental Information Regulations 1992 apply to information[34] which:

(a) relates to the environment;
(b) is held by a relevant person in an accessible form and otherwise than for the purposes of any judicial or legislative functions; and
(c) is not (apart from the Regulations) either –
(i) statutorily required to be provided on request to every person who makes a request; or
(ii) contained in records statutorily required to be made available for inspection by any person wishing to inspect them.

By regulation 1(c), then, these regulations fill the gaps in existing provisions and do not, subject to the additional demands of regulation 5, supercede the specific requirements in a variety of environmental statutes that information held on registers should be available for public inspection. It may be, though, that an effect of this wide general power will be to enable access to other information held by those authorities but not on public registers. The effect of regulation 5 is to apply to other statutory duties to supply information the terms of regulation 3(2) and (4) concerned with time and cost (see below). While, with the exception of regulation 5(d), there is no specific limitation of this provision to environmental matters, the contextual inference is to that effect.

This description of the scope of the Regulations itself requires identification respectively of matters 'relating to the environment' and of 'relevant person'. The former phrase is defined in regulation 2(2), largely following the Directive, as relating to:

30 'The Open Society, Its Lawyers and Its Environment' JEL vol. 1, no. 1, p.1 at p.4.

31 90/313/EEC.

32 Article 9.

33 S.I.1992 No. 3240; made under section 2(2) of the European Communities Act 1972. See also W. Birtles, 'A Right to Know: The Environmental Information Regulations 1992' [1993] JPL 615.

34 Regulation 2(1).

(a) the state of any water or air, the state of any flora or fauna, the state of any soil or the state of any natural site or other land;
(b) any activities or measures (including activities giving rise to noise or any other nuisance) which adversely affect anything mentioned in sub-paragraph (a) above or are likely adversely to affect anything so mentioned;
(c) any activities or administrative or other measures (including any environmental management programmes) which are designed to protect anything so mentioned.

This definition includes information relating to past, present and future or potentially prejudicial activities. Its most obvious deficiency is that it is limited to the natural environment and its constituent elements, thus ignoring those circumstances exclusively affecting people, or alternatively requiring that access to information on activities harmful to the human population may only be obtained on establishing the potentiality for damage to one of the specified forms.

Department of the Environment guidance on the implementation of the Regulations amplifies this definition in the following terms:[35]

> By definition, information relating to the environment includes information on the state of water, air, flora, fauna, soil, natural sites and other land. The state should be taken to include physical, chemical and biological conditions at any moment in time (i.e. past, present or future). Water should be taken to include underground and surface waters (both natural and in man-made structures); the latter to include inland waters (i.e., rivers, canals, lakes, estuaries and seas). Air extends to the limits of the atmosphere and should be taken to include the air within buildings and other natural and man-made structures above or below ground. Fauna and flora should be taken to include species both living and dead. Land should be taken to include all land surfaces, buildings, land covered by water and underground strata. Soil should be taken to include the in situ upper layer of the mantle of rock in which plants grow. A natural site should be taken to include areas identified by reason of their flora, fauna, geological or physio-graphical features (e.g. Sites of Special Scientific Interest) or general environmental quality (e.g., Areas of Outstanding Natural Beauty).

35 Published December 1992; quoted by R. Stein, *Environmental Health*, vol. 101, no. 9, September 1993, p.293.

The scope of the Article 1 statement of principle quoted above is limited to information held by public authorities. Having regard to the re-allocation of many environmental functions and services to private and commercial bodies, that term has been replaced in the Regulations by 'relevant person', which is defined in regulation 2(3) to include:

(a) Ministers of the Crown, Government departments, local authorities and other persons carrying out public administration functions at a national, regional or local level and having environmental responsibilities; and
(b) any body having public responsibilities for the environment which does not fall within (a) above but is under the control of a person falling within that sub-paragraph.

The broader operation given to the Regulations by this definition gives effect to Article 6 of the Directive, providing that 'Member States shall take the necessary steps to ensure that information relating to the environment held by bodies with public responsibilities for the environment and under the control of public authorities is made available on the same terms and conditions as those' applicable to public authorities.

The evident limiting factor here, determining those bodies that are within this provision is the meaning and scope of 'control' by a public authority. The Department of the Environment guidance suggests that, 'Control is taken to mean a relationship constituted by statute, rights, contracts or other means which either separately or jointly confer the possibility of directly or indirectly exercising a decisive influence on a body'. The word has yet to be interpreted in this present context. Its meaning has however been extensively interpreted in relation to the imposition of vicarious liability on employers for the torts of their employees committed while at work. As the right to, and the degree of, control in this latter case determines legal liability, one may however assume that the term would be more narrowly construed than in the present context. In particular, it would seem reasonable that public authorities should for this purpose be deemed to be in control of such bodies where, as the guidance advises, the relationship is one of contract. In that case, for example, information relating to waste collection and disposal contractors would be accessible.

The general statement of principle that a relevant person holding information covered by these Regulations is to make it available to anyone requesting it is to be found in regulation 3(1); subject to the provisos, in paragraph (3), that requests that are either manifestly unreasonable or formulated in too general a manner may be refused. In complying with that duty the person concerned has also to ensure that:[36]

(a) every request is responded to as soon as possible;
(b) that the response is within two months of the request being made; and
(c) where the request is refused, the refusal is in writing and includes the reasons for the refusal.

These obligations are restricted in that the supplier of the information is only required to make it available in the form and at such times and places as are reasonable, and may make such charges as are reasonably attributable to meeting the request.[37]

The general right of access to environmental information is restricted by regulation 4 in relation to confidentiality. The regulation then interprets confidentiality, first by specifying its categories and then by stipulating the characteristics that will make information in those classes confidential.[38] First then, information may only be treated as confidential if it:

(a) relates to matters affecting international relations, national defence or public security;
(b) relates to any actual or prospective legal or other proceedings or their subject matter;
(c) relates to the confidential deliberations of any relevant person or the contents of any internal communication of a body corporate or other undertaking or organisation;
(d) is contained in a document or record still in the course of completion; or
(e) relates to matters to which any commercial or industrial confidentiality attaches or affecting any intellectual property.

Further, information must only be treated as confidential if :

(a) it is capable of being so treated and its disclosure would contravene any statutory provision or rule of law or involve a breach of agreement;
(b) it is personal information held in relation to an individual who has not given his consent to its disclosure;

36 Regulation 3(4)

37 Regulation 3(5) and (4) respectively.

38 Regulation 4(2) and (3).

(c) the information was supplied by a person who -
  (i)   had no legal obligation to supply it,
  (ii)   did not supply it in such circumstances that the relevant person is entitled apart from these regulations to disclose it, and
  (iii) has not consented to its disclosure, or
(d) its disclosure would in the circumstances increase the likelihood of damage to the environment affecting anything to which the information relates.

Article 7 of the Directive, not incorporated into the Regulations, requires that member governments 'shall take the necessary steps to provide general information on the environment by such means as the periodic publication of descriptive reports'. The British Government's response to the Directive, in a Green Paper,[39] was to declare its intention to publish at regular intervals, statistical reports covering a range of environmental data. Such reports have subsequently been published on an annual basis. On the question of access to information generally, the Green Paper says that 'The Government will propose arrangements, including registers, by which environmental information can be made available in Britain'.[40] Publicly accessible registers, of which special mention is made, are perhaps the commonest method of making information generally available. That information is publicly available, whether generally under these regulations or specifically under other legislation, does not necessarily mean that the public will use it, as has been noted by T.P. Burton.[41] His consequent criticism on that score alone is not, it is suggested, entirely justified. While those of us with a concern for the environment would wish to see that concern more widely espoused, the fact that the public at large does not generally occupy its time with environmental data is not to be regarded as the sole, or perhaps any, test of their usefulness. A range of factors, such as accessibility and comprehensibility, may influence the degree of use, as Burton notes, but the primary reason for their use is not that they are available but that someone has a question to be answered. As a resource the availability of such material has a far greater value in the potential support it may provide to persons, or their advisors, than is to be measured in the frequency of its use, particularly in its early years. Also, of course, the knowledge that the details of their operation are open to public view is likely in itself to have a salutory effect on the persons responsible for the conduct of those operations.

The extent to which information required to be made available is or is not used does, though, pose, in the context of accessibility, subordinate questions relating to location and user friendliness on the one hand and the appropriate or justifiable costs on the other. In their answer to these questions the House of Lords Select Committee on the European Communities[42] proposed a two-tier system of information. The first tier, in the form of a register, would contain basic information and a review of the material available at the second tier. With that knowledge an investigator could decide whether to proceed to the more detailed and extensive material, possibly including raw data, at the second tier. Such a system would reduce the costs of maintaining the first tier and, with the use of computer terminals and/or periodically revised disks, be relatively cheap to operate.

Consultation

Many statutory provisions conferring on the Secretary of State power to make regulations stipulate as a necessary preliminary that he shall in one form or another

39 'This Common Inheritance: Britain's Environmental Strategy' (Cm 1200), September 1990.

40 Ibid., para. 17.27.

41 'Access to Environmental Information; The U.K. Experience of Water Registers' JE vol. 1, no. 1, p.193.

42 First Report of the House of Lords Select Committee on the European Communities: Freedom of Access to Information on the Environment (HL Paper 2 Session 1989/90).

'consult', either appropriate expert organisations or those bodies, or their representatives, who will be affected by the proposed legislation. Such consultation, while being required, invariably gives the Secretary of State discretion, in some such phrase as 'as he thinks fit', over the range or identity of the consultees. In such circumstances he must exercise that choice reasonably in the *'Wednesbury'* sense. This common requirement of consultation therefore poses two questions. First, what does the duty to consult require in practice, recognising in particular that in some respects its content is a matter for the Secretary of State? Secondly, what are the consequences when the consultation process is found to be inadequate?

As to the preliminary duty, consultation requires a genuine seeking and consideration of information from appropriate consultees. In *Rollo* v *Minister of Town and Country Planning* (1948)[43] it was said that the Secretary of State ' ...with a receptive mind, must, by such consultation, seek and welcome the aid and advice which those with local knowledge may be in a position to proffer' in regard to the proposal. A more recent and detailed analysis is that of Webster J in *R* v *Social Services Secretary ex parte AMA* (1986):[44]

43 [1948] 1 All ER 13; 64 TLR 25. See also on the question of consultation *Agricultural, Horticultural and Forestry Industry Training Board* v *Aylesbury Mushrooms Ltd* [1972] 1 WLR 190.

44 [1986] 1 WLR 1 at p. 4g.

> There is no general principle to be extracted from the case law as to what kind or amount of consultation is required before delegated legislation, of which consultation is a precondition, can validly be made. But in any context the essence of consultation is the communication of a genuine invitation to give advice and a genuine receipt of that advice. In my view it must go without saying that to achieve consultation sufficient information must be supplied by the consulting to the consulted party to enable it to tender helpful advice. Sufficient time must be given by the consulting to the consulted party to enable it to do that, and sufficient time must be available for such advice to be considered by the consulting party. Sufficient, in that context, does not mean ample, but at least enough to enable the relevant purpose to be fulfilled. By helpful advice, in this context, I mean sufficiently informed and considered information or advice about aspects of the form or substance of the proposals, or their implications for the consulted party, being aspects material to the implementation of the proposal as to which the Secretary of State might not be fully informed or advised and as to which the party consulted might have relevant information or advice to offer.

The necessary features of proper consultation will therefore include the supply of sufficient information to allow consideration of the matter by the consultees, enough time for that consideration and response, and then that the consulting body should give proper consideration to the response.

The facts of the *AMA* case illustrate both the effectiveness of the consultation process and the selection of appropriate consultees. Under section 36(1) of the Social Security and Housing Benefits Act 1982, the Secretary of State was given the power to make regulations creating the housing benefits scheme and requiring him to 'consult with organisations appearing to him to be representative of the [housing] authorities concerned'. The regulations, having been made and brought into operation, were now challenged by the applicant as the representative body of a proportion of the authorities concerned alleging certain defects in the consultation process. Dealing with their expectation to be consulted, Webster J said:

> In the present case, looking at the whole 'scope and purpose' of the Act of 1982, one matter which stands out is that its day-to-day administration is in the hands of local housing authorities who bear 10 per cent of the cost of the scheme. It is common ground

that in them resides the direct expertise necessary to administer schemes made under the Act on a day-to-day basis. For these reasons, if for no other, I conclude that the obligation laid on the Secretary of State to consult organisations representative of those authorities is mandatory, not directory.

The sequence of events claimed to constitute consultation commenced with a letter of 16 November 1984 from the DHSS requesting views on proposed amendments to the regulations. The letter, received on 20 November, asked for a response by 30 November; producing a complaint from the applicant of the inadequate time and a request for an extension. On 4 December a further letter from the DHSS requested views on additional amendments, without a draft of the amendments and omitting one proposed change. On 7 December the AMA sent a response to the first letter, and on December 13 brief comments on the second. The amendment regulations were introduced on 17 December and came into operation on 19 December. This scenario clearly reveals deficiencies of information communicated and time for consideration. While, in the opinion of Webster J, such matters may be affected by urgency and indeed content, neither consideration could completely absolve the Secretary of State from his obligation to consult.

The consequences of establishing a material defect in procedure are conceptually clear and obvious, but in practice less so. An act or decision tainted by procedural irregularity is unlawful or *ultra vires* and therefore void. In Lord Diplock's words in the *Grunwick* case,[45] 'My Lords, where a statutory authority has acted *ultra vires* any person who would be affected by its act if it were valid is normally entitled *ex debito justiciae* to have it set aside'. What is self-evident in relation to a decision having limited effect has less practical logic when applied to a legislative act that may already have been applied to determine the rights and liabilities of countless other persons. In such a case, although finding for the applicant on the substantive issue, the court has a discretion to deny a remedy that will quash the regulation and thus cast doubt on earlier decisions; as indeed happened in the *AMA* case.

In appropriate cases, and depending on the particular circumstances, there may be some intermediate alternative to the all or nothing approach indicated above. A form of rescission may permit the removal of the part affected by the defective or improper procedure, leaving the lawful remainder in being. This requires of course that the remaining part unaffected by the impropriety is capable on its terms of effective separate existence and operation. The *Aylesbury Mushrooms* case[46] provides an illustration. Preparatory to setting up a Training Board the Secretary of State was required to consult with bodies representative of the industry. He confined his consultations to those representing the larger areas of activity. On complaint by representatives of the mushroom growers the Court of Appeal concluded that, not having been consulted, they could be excluded from the scheme which otherwise would remain in operation. This judicial surgery excised one of the affected bodies. In *Dunkley* v *Evans* (1981)[47] a similar approach limited the regulation's sphere of operation.

Notices

Many statutory environmental procedures, whether concerned with enforcement, licensing and authorisation or approval, require the service of notices. Apart from, in some cases, specifying that the notice is to be in writing, legislation rarely goes further in stipulating either their form or content of such notices. An example

45 *Grunwick Processing Laboratories Ltd* v *Advisory, Conciliation and Arbitration Service* [1978] AC 655 at p.695.

46 *Agriculture, Horticulture and Forestry Training Board* v *Aylesbury Mushrooms Ltd* [1972] 1 WLR 190.

47 [1981] 1 WLR 1522.

to the contrary is provided by section 21(2) of the Radioactive Substances Act 1993 which specifies matters to be included in enforcement notices. Such contents, being mandatory, will render the notice liable to challenge on grounds of invalidity if absent.[48] While any specific requirements have of course to be satisfied, in their absence the principles established in case law will be applied to make good any legislative lacunae.

The contents of a notice will finally be determined by reference to the purpose stated in the particular statutory provision. The essentials are likely to consist of identification of the person, or company, addressed and authentication, usually by signature,[49] by the person so authorised. Where, as frequently happens, the recipient of a notice requiring action is given a statutory right of appeal against the terms of the notice, that fact, together with details of the appellate body and time for the appeal, must also be stated.

When the purpose of the notice is the enforcement of a statutory duty entailing work or expense, the nature of the requirement must be specified with sufficient particularity to enable confident compliance by the addressee. Justice and fairness demand that the addressee should know what is required of him to meet his legal obligations. It therefore follows that where the specified works are ambiguous or ineffective as a remedy, the notice will be bad.[50] Accurate specification of the necessary work is also – and particularly – important where the enforcing authority may exercise default powers on the recipient's failure to comply, such powers generally being limited to the work stated in the notice.[51] This necessary work will include a statement of the defect(s) or deficiency and, as required for example by section 99(1) of the Building Act 1984, 'shall indicate the nature of the works to be executed and state the time within which they are to be executed'. The required work then is to be 'indicated' rather than demanded. It may be taken as a general principle that the specification of certain remedial work in the notice does not make that mandatory and necessarily exclude any other equally effective solution.[52] While it is important that the recipient should understand from the notice what will be regarded by the enforcing authority as sufficient to achieve the purpose, he has the freedom to achieve the same result by other means of his choosing.[53]

In relation to the stating of a time limit for the execution of work, either of two broad forms of abatement may be contemplated – either stopping the offensive activity, or the doing of remedial work. In the former case, the cessation of activity needs no period of time. In *Strathclyde Regional Council v Tudhope* (1983)[54] the notice under section 58 of the Control of Pollution Act 1974 required various noise reducing measures in connection with the use of road-breakers and that the equipment was not to be used until fitted with such effective dampers. In the absence of a date for compliance the notice was held to come into effect at midnight following the day of service and was valid. While the comparable provision in the Environmental Protection Act 1990 requires the inclusion of a time, this case supports the above proposition. A common formulation of or synonym for 'as soon as possible' is 'forthwith', which has been interpreted as meaning immediately or within a reasonable time and to be a sufficient indication of the time required to stop a prohibited activity.[55]

Where work has to be done to abate the nuisance the time allowed must be reasonable. A useful statement of principle is to be found in *Bristol Corporation v Sinnott* (1918)[56] where a notice under section 150 of the Public Health Act 1875 required the frontagers to make up the road:

48 *Miller-Mead v Minister of Housing and Local Government* [1963] QB 196 at p. 226 *per* Upjohn LJ and see below at note 53.

49 Section 284(2) of the Public Health Act 1936 states that 'In this subsection the expression "signature" includes a facsimile of a signature by whatever process reproduced'.

50 *Whatling v Rees* (1914) 84 LJ KB 1122.

51 *Carlton Main Colliery Co. Ltd v Hemsworth RDC* [1922] 2 Ch 609; and see *Nicholl v Epping UDC* [1899] 1 Ch 844.

52 See *per* Lord Goddard CJ in *McGillivray v Stephenson* [1950] 1 All ER 942 at p. 944b.

53 *Robinson v Sunderland Corporation* (1898) 78 LT 194.

54 [1983] JPL 536.

55 *Thomas v Nokes* (1894) 58 JP 672.

56 [1918] 1 Ch 62.

Where a statute provides that an authority may serve a notice requiring work to be done within a time to be therein specified, the notice must specify a time within which the work can reasonably be completed, having regard to the nature of the work and all the circumstances. The least time that can be fairly and reasonably allocated for the completion of the work being ascertained, is the least time to be inserted in the notice; there is a discretion to allow further time for the completion of the work, but not to fix a shorter time.

Supplementary to this principle, it was said in *Macclesfield Corporation* v *Macclesfield Grammar School* (1921)[57] that in considering whether the period allowed was reasonable, regard should be had to the work to be done by the particular frontagers and not to the whole work to be done on the road.

Depending on the nature and purpose of the notice, a time period may be expressed in days, weeks or months. While the first two are sufficiently specific,[58] a period of a month is variable in duration. The rule governing its determination was authoritatively stated by the House of Lords in *Dodds* v *Walker* (1981),[59] the headnote reading,

> In calculating the period of a month or a specified number of months that had elapsed after the occurrence of a specified event, such as the giving of a notice, the general rule was that the period ended on the corresponding date in the appropriate subsequent month, irrespective of whether some months were longer than others.

This approach is logical and simple but leaves unresolved those cases in which the day of service, usually the last day of a 31 day month, has no corresponding day in the month when the period is to end. To meet such situations the same judgement provides that, 'If the month on which the period expires has no corresponding date because it is too short the period given by the notice ends on the last day of that month'.

Questions of authority, form and content, together with the distinction between invalidity and nullity, were considered by Upjohn LJ in *Miller-Mead* v *Minister of Housing & Local Government* (1963),[60] concerning the issue of a town planning enforcement notice in respect of the use of land as a caravan site without planning permission. His Lordship said

> Now, I think, is the time to draw the distinction between invalidity and nullity. For example, supposing development without permission is alleged and it is found that no permission is required or that, contrary to the allegation in the notice, it is established that in fact the conditions in the planning permission have been complied with, then the notice may be quashed under section 23(4)(a). The notice is invalid: it is not a nullity because on the face of it it appears to be good and it is only on proof of facts *aliunde* that the notice is shown to be bad: the notice is invalid and, therefore, it may be quashed. But supposing the notice on the face of it fails to specify some period required by subsection (2) or (3). On the face of it the notice does not comply with the section; it is a nullity and is so much waste paper. No power was given to the justices to quash in such circumstances, for it was quite unnecessary. The notice on its face is bad. Supposing then upon its true construction the notice was hopelessly ambiguous and uncertain, so that the owner or occupier could not tell in what respect it was alleged that he had developed the land without permission or in what respect it was alleged that he failed to comply with a condition or, again, that he could not tell with reasonable certainty what steps he had to take to remedy the alleged breaches. The notice would be bad on its face and a nullity, the justices had no jurisdiction to quash it, for it was unnecessary to give them that power, but this court could, upon application to it, declare that the notice was a nullity. That to my mind is the distinction between invalidity and nullity.

57 [1921] 2 Ch 189.

58 A day is deemed to be a period of 24 hours running from midnight to midnight.

59 [1981] 2 All ER 609.

60 [1963] 2 QB 196 at p. 226, CA.

The distinction then, to summarise, is that if a notice appears on reading to be patently defective or incomprehensible it is a nullity, not a notice in law and therefore may be disregarded with impunity. Conversely, if a notice appears to be lawful and is apparently in order but is shown to be factually or legally erroneous it will be invalid. In this second case the deficiency is determined by a competent court following evidence and argument and therefore, until that determination, the notice remains effective and enforceable.

These principles were applied and illustrated in *McKay* v *Secretary of State for the Environment* (1993).[61] Cornwall County Council had served an enforcement notice on the appellant requiring him to do certain work on his land which was part of a scheduled ancient monument. He appealed to the Secretary of State on the ground of insufficient time. The inspector varied the original notice, in particular requiring that the work should be done subject to and within six months of the granting of Ancient Monument Consent. On appeal against that decision the Court, in allowing the appeal, held that the original notice had been a nullity and was therefore incapable of variation. The appellant had been required to do work affecting a scheduled ancient monument which would be unlawful without Ancient Monument Consent. Although consent might be obtained it could not be assumed and could take a considerable time, during which the appellant would be committing an offence either by failing to comply with the notice or by doing work without authorisation. The recipient of a notice must be able to understand with reasonable certainty the steps which are required of him, and that must bear on the question of whether he can in reality carry out the requirements of the notice. Applying the test of Upjohn LJ the Court considered that it was clear merely by looking at the notice that it was defective. It was not merely invalidated on the basis of external evidence.

Though silent on the question of form and content, many statutes stipulate methods of service of documents. Section 233 of the Local Government Act 1972 provides a number of rules applicable to local authorities generally in the absence of alternative provisions in the particular statute being enforced. Similarly, section 160 of the Environmental Protection Act 1990[62] provides for methods of service of documents by all enforcing authorities for the purposes of that Act, and section 102 of the Building Act 1984 has comparable effect for that statute. A comparison of those three provisions shows that not only are they broadly similar in effect but that much of the phraseology is the same. Consequently in considering below statutory provisions relating to service, those in section 160 of the 1990 Act will be used.

Although the majority of circumstances envisage notification from the public authority to the individual or company concerned, there are some cases where the reverse is true.[63] In these cases the same principles apply, though it may be expected that the courts will look more indulgently on the minor procedural deficiencies of a relatively inexperienced private individual than those of a competent, experienced public authority; particularly if in the latter case costly or punitive consequences result.

The service of a notice is often made dependent or conditional upon a preceding event or on the enforcing authority, through its delegated officer or committee, being of a certain state of mind. For example, prior to the service of an abatement notice under section 80(1) of the Environmental Protection Act 1990 a local authority is required to be 'satisfied that a statutory nuisance exists, or is

61 (1993) 7 Env Law 74.

62 Following section 285 of the Public Health Act 1936.

63 See, e.g., section 9(2) of the Environmental Protection Act 1990 concerning transfer of IPC authorisations.

likely to occur or recur'. Should it be established that any such preliminary requirement is not satisfied the notice will be invalid and may be quashed.[64] The same
result will of course accrue where the authority, being legitimately of the appropriate mind, is subsequently found on the evidence to be in error.

Service of a notice may be by delivery to the addressee, by leaving it at his proper address, or by sending it by post to him at that address. In the case of a body
corporate service may be by delivery to the secretary or clerk of that body and the
effective address for service is its registered or principal office.[65] Section 160 of
the 1990 Act provides that service 'may be by', the stipulated methods being
permissive. Consequently, if another method is used and the notice is received,
that is good service.[66] Where service by 'leaving it at his proper address' is used
'the notice must be left in a manner which a reasonable person, minded to bring
the document to the attention of the person to whom it is addressed would adopt'.[67]
The 'proper address' of a person in this context is their last known address.[68]
Generally an address which a person is known to have left is not a proper address
for service,[69] but this rule does not apply where, as here, use of the last known
address is expressly authorised.[70] Service at a last known address in England or
Wales is not good if a later address abroad is known.[71]

On the question of service by post, section 7 of the Interpretation Act 1978 provides that 'service is deemed to be effected by properly addressing, prepaying and
posting a letter containing the document and unless the contrary is proved, to have
been effected at the time at which the letter would be delivered in the ordinary
course of post.' Service by post may be effected by ordinary or registered post[72]
and therefore by implication, also by recorded delivery.

Rights of entry

Many statutes in this field containing enforcement powers also, and necessarily,
equip the officials concerned with implementation with the necessary procedures
to achieve those purposes, including rights of entry. Examples of such provisions
are:

- section 287 of the Public Health Act 1936;
- section 91 of the Control of Pollution Act 1974;
- section 95 of the Building Act 1984;
- sections 69 and 115 and Schedule 3(2) of the Environmental Protection Act 1990;
- sections 168–173 of the Water Industry Act 1991;
- sections 169–174 of the Water Resources Act 1991;
- section 56 of the Clean Air Act 1993;
- section 31 of the Radioactive Substances Act 1993.

It is stating the obvious to observe that entry onto private property without the
permission of the occupant is *prima facie* unlawful, amounting in civil law to trespass. Where it is necessary, as here, for the enforcement of statutory provisions,
any stipulated purposes and procedural requirements will therefore be strictly construed and applied by the courts. *Stroud* v *Bradbury* (1952)[73] provides an example and authority. The owner of a bungalow failed to repair a drain as required
by the local authority. When access to the premises was sought to do the work in
default it was prevented by the owner's husband. Lord Goddard put the matter
as follows:[74]

64 See *Miller-Mead* v *Ministry of Housing & Local Government* [1963] 2 QB 196 at p.226.

65 See, e.g., section 160 (3) and (4) of the Environmental Protection Act 1990.

66 *Sharpley* v *Manly* [1942] 1 KB 217; *Stylo Shoes Ltd* v *Prices Tailors Ltd* [1959] 3 All ER 901.

67 *Lord Newborough* v *Jones* [1975] Ch 90; [1974] 3 All ER 17, CA; and see *LB of Lambeth* v *Mullings* [1990] Crim LR 426 on putting a notice through a letter box.

68 Section 160(4) of the Environmental Protection Act 1990.

69 *White* v *Weston* [1968] 2 QB 647.

70 *Re Follick, ex parte Trustee* (1907) 97 LT 645.

71 *R* v *Farmer* [1892] 1 QB 637.

72 *T.O.Supplies (London) Ltd* v *Jerry Creighton Ltd* [1952] 1 KB 42; [1951] 2 All ER 992.

73 [1952] 2 All ER 76.

74 At p.77.

It was very necessary that the inspector should enter the premises to do this work and it was very necessary that the work should be done, but before the inspector could enter the premises he must comply with the statute. The statute provides by the proviso to section 287(1) '... admission to any premises not being a factory, workshop or workplace, shall not be demanded as of right unless 24 hours' notice of the intended entry has been given to the occupier...' The only document relied on as a notice justifying the entry on June 1st was a letter written on February 17th, more than three months before ... The contention that an expression of intention on February 17th to proceed under section 290(6) of the Act of 1936 on June 1st can possibly be a 24 hour notice of the intended entry is quite untenable. Therefore the appellant was not guilty of obstructing the sanitary inspector in the execution of his duty because the sanitary inspector had no right to enter the appellant's wife's premises when he did.

75 (1958) 56 LGR 239.

Senior v *Twelves* (1958)[75] emphasises that the power to enter any premises includes where necessary premises other than those on which the nuisance occurs. In that case, access was necessary to adjoining property to do work on the uninhabited premises concerned.

The other side of the power of entry coin is of course the possibility of obstruction. Provisions authorising entry are therefore invariably associated with others making the 'wilful' or 'intentional' obstruction of a person acting under statutory powers liable to summary prosecution, conviction and fine. The common requirement of some element of purpose on the part of the obstructor is to be noted.

76 [1984] 3 WLR 875.

77 [1955] 3 All ER 406; 1 WLR 1207.

Lewis v *Cox* (1984)[76] has significantly extended the scope of obstruction in this respect. Earlier authority, exemplified by *Hinchliffe* v *Sheldon* (1955),[77] had required action directed towards the person obstructed. In that case, the appellant son of the licensee returned to his father's inn at 11.17 pm and found police outside intending to enter. He called out a warning and when the police eventually gained access at 11.25 pm there was no evidence of after hours drinking. The Court found that the appellant was guilty of wilfully obstructing a constable in the execution of his duty. *Lewis* v *Cox* (1984) concerned two drunk and disorderly persons outside a public house. One was arrested and put inside a police car. The defendant then opened the car door to ask his arrested friend where he was being taken. The constable closed the door with a warning that if the defendant opened it again he would be arrested for obstruction, and got into the car preparatory to driving off. Before he could start, the defendant opened the car door again and was arrested. On appeal by the prosecution, the Divisional Court said in its judgement:

> A person wilfully obstructed the police under section 51(3) of the Police Act 1964 [and, on the same principles, other authorised officers acting under statutory powers], if he deliberately did an act which, though not necessarily 'aimed at' or 'hostile to' the police, in fact prevented a constable from carrying out his duty or made it more difficult for him to do so, and if he knew and intended (whether or not that was his predominant intention) that his conduct would have that effect; and that the motive with which the act was committed was irrelevant unless it constituted a lawful excuse for the obstruction ...

In conclusion it may be emphasised again that the question of obstruction cannot arise unless those seeking entry are acting within their legal authority, substantively and procedurally. Any stipulated requirements precedent to gaining access must be satisfied. For example, section 102 of the Public Health Act 1875 provided that a local authority or any of its officers 'shall be admitted into any premises' etc., with a penalty for obstruction. So in *Consett UDC* v *Crawford* (1903)[78]

78 [1903] 1 KB 183; and see *Wimbledon UDC* v *Hastings* (1902) 87 LT 118.

the court considered that that phraseology necessarily implied prior seeking of permission. Failure to seek such permission prevented the defendant being liable for obstruction.

TERMINOLOGY

Person aggrieved

'Person aggrieved' is an expression used in a number of environmental statutes to identify persons who have a right to challenge decisions or acts of public author-ities, usually by litigation or by appeal to the Secretary of State. The term orig-inated to describe the level of interest, or standing, required of an applicant for the prerogative writs, subsequently orders, of *certiorari* and prohibition. The scope and meaning of the term has therefore largely arisen for consideration and been developed in the context of those orders. Having acquired a sufficient weight of authority and familiarity it is now applied more generally in a variety of statutes to indicate persons entitled to question public authority activity under those pro-visions. It is to be noted, though, that the level of standing required of an applicant for judicial review now is that he must have a 'sufficient interest in the matter to which the application relates'[79] rather than being a 'person aggrieved'.

Evidently a person whose legal rights are infringed has a sufficient interest to found a complaint; that after all is the basis of civil litigation and applies equally in public law. The consequences of the exercise of public power, though, may be more diffuse, impinging on a wide range of persons at varying levels and there-fore requiring identification of the degree of interest needed over and above the concern of the general public to entitle a person to enlist the aid of the legal sys-tem to secure redress. A formulation of this necessary interest level by Lord Denning in *R v Liverpool Corporation ex parte Liverpool Taxi Fleet Operators Association* (1972)[80] was:

> The writs of prohibition and *certiorari* lie on behalf of any person who is a 'person aggrieved' and that includes any person whose interests may be prejudicially affected by what is taking place. It does not include a mere busybody who is interfering in things which do not concern him: but it does include any person who has a genuine grievance because something has been done or may be done which affects him.

A person who, though not suffering any infringement of a legal right, is never-theless prejudicially affected by the action in question will *prima facie* be a per-son aggrieved. So, for example, in the *Liverpool Taxi Fleet Operators* case itself the Corporation had a long-standing agreement to consult the Association before issuing any additional taxi licences. Subsequently, ignoring or having forgotten the arrangement, they issued an additional 50 licences without any consultation. The Association sought to enforce the agreement which, though accepted not to be contractual, was considered to confer on them a sufficient degree of interest to make them aggrieved.[81]

Another frequently quoted example is *R v Greater London Council ex parte Blackburn* (1976),[82] in which the applicant wished to challenge the GLC's oper-ation of its film censorship function. A preliminary question was whether he was entitled to do so. Lord Denning dealt with the matter in these terms: 'Mr Blackburn is a citizen of London. His wife is a ratepayer. He has children who may be harmed by the exhibition of cinematograph films. If he has no sufficient interest, no other

79 Section 31(3)of the Supreme Court Act 1981.

80 [1972] 2 QB 299.

81 See also *R v Thames Magistrates' Court ex parte Greenbaum* (1957) 55 LGR 129.

82 [1976] 3 All ER 184; 1 WLR 550, CA.

citizen has'. The other judges in the Court of Appeal considered respectively that residence in the area and being a ratepayer conferred standing in these circumstances. The authorities recognise that a ratepayer, and presumably a council tax payer, has standing to challenge the decisions and actions of his local authority, having an interest in its proper financial management.[83]

83 *R v Paddington Valuation Officer ex parte Peachey Property Corporation Ltd* (No. 2) [1966] 1 QB 380.

This broad approach has been developed by the courts to apply generally to the operation of the prerogative orders. That the term may have to be more narrowly construed in its context in particular statutes appears from the judgement of Lord Hewart CJ in *Sevenoaks UDC* v *Twynam* (1929):[84]

84 [1929] 2 KB 443.

> Now undoubtedly those words, 'a person aggrieved', have very often been considered, and, if one looked at the terms apart from their context and apart from the particular circumstances, it would have been quite easy to marshal decisions of contradictory import. But as has been said again and again there is often little utility in seeking to interpret particular expressions in one statute by reference to decisions given upon similar expressions in different statutes which have been enacted *alio intuitu*. The problem with which we are concerned is not, what is the meaning of the expression 'aggrieved' in any one of a dozen other statutes, but what is its meaning in this part of this statute?

This is in accordance with general principles of statutory construction. It does however suggest that in the predominantly statutory field of environmental law the term will not have a static or universal meaning but will need to be re-interpreted in relation to the particular purposes and objectives of the provision currently being considered. More recently Schiemann J has made the same point in the following terms:[85]

85 *R v Secretary of State for the Environment, ex parte Rose Theatre Trust Co.* [1990] 2 WLR 186 at p.202.

> Not every member of the public can complain of every breach of statutory duty by a person empowered to come to a decision by that statute ... However, a direct financial or legal interest is not required ... Where one is examining an alleged failure to perform a duty imposed by statute it is useful to look at the statute and see whether it gives an applicant a right enabling him to have that duty performed. The court will ... decide whether [the] statute gives [the applicant] expressly or impliedly a greater right or expectation than any other citizen of this country to have [the] decision taken lawfully.

The 'person aggrieved' concept has two further areas of operation that deserve particular notice in the environmental context. These are, first, its application to organisations or interest groups and, second, its application to the public authorities themselves. Accepting that a corporate body has legal and property rights capable of protection by litigation, the real issue concerns the capacity of unincorporated associations to represent and protect the interests either of their members or of the aims and objectives they are created to espouse. In this context the authorities distinguish between two circumstances.

Where a body having certain avowed aims is established and in being, it will be recognised as having the necessary standing to represent and protect those interests. A significant decision in this respect was *Covent Garden Community Association Ltd* v *Greater London Council* (1981),[86] in which the Association, consisting of 80 per cent of the residents and being formed to protect their interests, was accepted as having standing to challenge a grant of planning permission by the GLC for premises in the area.[87] A decision in the environmental context to the same effect concerned the ability of Greenpeace to question the decision to operate the THORP re-processing plant at Sellafield.[88] In according them standing the court took into account that Greenpeace has 5 million members inter-

86 [1981] JPL 183.

87 See also to the same effect, *R v Secretary of State for Social Services, ex parte Child Poverty Action Group* (1985) The Times, 8 August.

88 *R v HMIP ex parte Greenpeace* (1993) *Independent*, 30 September; (1993) 225 ENDS Report 42.

nationally; 400,000 in the United Kingdom and, of particular note, 2,500 in the Cumbria region. Also regarded was the consultative status they have in the United Nations Economic and Social Council and the Paris Convention for the Prevention of Marine Pollution (PARCOM). Summarising the position David Foulkes says[89] that:

> to establish whether an applicant has standing it will be necessary to examine the scheme in question, the rights and obligations to which it gives rise, the persons to whom it gives and on whom it imposes them, and the relation of the applicant to the scheme; the defect shown to be present in the decision challenged, its seriousness and its effect will be relevant ...

89 *Administrative Law* (London: Butterworth, 7th edn, 1990), p. 360.

Alternatively, it appears clear from the judgment of Schiemann J in *R v Secretary of State for the Environment ex parte Rose Theatre Trust Co.* (1990)[90] that a group of concerned persons, having no sufficient interest to confer standing upon them as individuals, cannot acquire it by combining together *ex post facto*. In his words, 'It would be absurd if two people, neither of whom had standing could, by an appropriately worded memorandum, incorporate themselves into a company which thereby obtained standing'. In distinguishing these cases, then, Greenpeace is a permanent campaigning organisation with a well-known record of involvement in environmental issues and with THORP from an early stage, therefore having a bona fide interest in BNFL's activities. It was described by Otton J as 'an entirely responsible and respected body with a genuine concern for the environment'. The Rose Theatre Trust was simply an *ad hoc* group.

90 [1990] 2 WLR 186 at p.201.

Litigation concerning the environment is generally initiated by persons and bodies to resist or challenge enforcement action by public authorities. In the nature of things, though, occasions arise when a public authority finds itself in the role of applicant, being faced with the need to challenge actions or decisions of another. In such cases it appears that to be 'aggrieved' an authority must be able to point to some tangible loss or burden suffered as a consequence of the subject matter of the dispute, and that mere obstruction of or inability to perform a duty is not sufficient. For example, in *R v Nottingham Quarter Sessions ex parte Harlow* (1952)[91] the local authority had required an owner of premises to provide a dustbin. The owner succeeded in his appeal to the justices. It was held that the authority could appeal to quarter sessions as a person aggrieved, because once the requirement on the owner of the premises to provide a dustbin had been avoided, the local authority itself could be compelled to perform that duty. *Ealing Borough Council v Jones* (1959)[92] reached the opposite conclusion on its facts. The magistrates' court quashed an enforcement notice served by the local planning authority under section 23 of the Town and Country Planning Act 1947. The authority succeeded in its appeal to quarter sessions. On case stated the Divisional Court held that the authority was not a 'person aggrieved' since the decision of the magistrates' court had not imposed on the authority a financial or legal burden. Lord Parker CJ said:[93]

91 [1952] 2 QB 601..

92 [1959] 1 QB 384

93 At p.391.

> It is also clear that a person is not aggrieved when that person being a public body has been frustrated in the performance of one of its public duties ... I am satisfied that a mere annoyance that what was thought to be a breach of planning control turned out not to be a breach of planning control and, equally, the mere fact that this authority, charged with certain duties under the Act, has been frustrated in the performance of what it thought was its duty, are not, of themselves, considerations sufficient to make the local planning authority an aggrieved person.

94 (1962) 60 LGR 292; see also *Phillips v Berkshire County Council* [1967] 2 QB 991.

So, in *R v Boldero and Others ex parte Bognor Regis UDC* (1962)[94] the council proposed certain sewering works under the private street works code, and objections to them were referred to the magistrates' court. The court considered the works unreasonable and quashed the resolutions. The council appealed to quarter sessions where, it being contended that the council was not a 'person aggrieved' by the decision of the justices, the court held that it had no jurisdiction and dismissed the appeal. On the council's application for an order of mandamus to compel quarter sessions to hear and determine the appeal, the Divisional Court held that since the decision of the justices quashing the resolutions cast on the council the legal burden of carrying out its duty to sewer, the council was 'aggrieved' within the section and accordingly had a right of appeal. In his judgment Lord Parker observed:[95]

95 At p.294.

> In other words, that case [*R v Nottingham Quarter Sessions ex parte Harlow*] was a case where the local authority found themselves as a result of the decision of the court of summary jurisdiction saddled with a burden from which they would otherwise have been discharged. That, as it seems to me, is the highwater mark, if I may use that expression, of the cases on the matter.

These cases may therefore be regarded as embodying and illustrating the principles governing the application of the standing requirement to public authorities.

Practicability

Many statutes in this and indeed other fields stipulate that action shall, or shall not, be taken or that a discretion may or may not be exercised, where practicable or reasonably practicable, or conversely that such a step shall not be taken where it is impracticable. Such standards therefore indicate the level of proximity required as a preliminary to action in a variety of circumstances. The scope and meaning of the phrases is obviously very close to 'best practicable means' discussed above,[96] the difference being that whereas the latter is exclusively a defence to proceedings these present terms may also be applied as the threshold standard to actions or decisions of enforcing authorities.[97] As an example, section 1(4) of the Clean Air Act 1993 provides as a defence to a charge of the emission of dark smoke that, *inter alia,* all practicable steps have been taken to minimise such emissions, section 64(1) then stating that 'practicable' means 'reasonably practicable having regard, amongst other things, to local conditions and circumstances, to the financial implications and to the current state of technical knowledge'. As well as conflating 'practicable' and 'reasonably practicable', the definition makes it clear that all the surrounding circumstances, including cost, are to be considered, thus being at one with judicial opinion.

96 See pp.40–2.

97 See, e.g., section 22(3) of the Clean Air Act 1993.

Speaking in a shipping context, Maule J said:[98]

98 In *Moss v Smith* (1850) 9 CB 94 at p.103.

> a thing is impracticable when it can only be done at an excessive or unreasonable cost. A man may be said to have lost a shilling, when he has dropped it into deep water; though it might be possible, by some very expensive contrivance, to recover it. So, if a ship sustains such extensive damage that it would not be reasonably practicable to repair her, – seeing that the expense of repairs would be such that no man of common sense would incur the outlay, – the ship is said to be totally lost.

99 In *Jayne v National Coal Board* [1963] 2 All ER 220 at p.224.

Moving from questions of cost to the assessment of risk, this time in the employment field, Veale J approached the issue in the following way:[99]

It is submitted on behalf of the plaintiff that 'impracticability' amounts almost to 'impossibility', the distinction being that 'practicable' means 'possible in the state of knowledge at the time', the only limitation being the state of knowledge at the time. I do not accept this argument. It is, I would have thought, clearly impracticable to take precautions against a danger which could not yet be known to be in existence, or to take a precaution which has not yet been invented. I think, however, that 'impracticable' means more than this. For instance if one imagines that as a result of firing a shot in a ripping a dangerous stone is exposed in the roof, it might be immediately possible to remove it by boring and firing another shot; but to do so might well cause greater danger in the surrounding roof than the stone itself. It would be, no doubt, possible to support such a stone forthwith with a support which was in use supporting the roof elsewhere. I would without hesitation hold both these possible methods of dealing with the danger to be impracticable.

Commenting on this view Buckley LJ said:[100]

> He is there saying that, if you are exposed to an unexpected danger, one possible solution which suggests itself may in fact carry within it the seeds of further disaster, and that in that case it would not be a sensibly practicable course to attempt to deal with the danger by pursuing that particular remedy.

'Cause or permit'

A number of statutes, in defining offences in the environmental field, provide that the wrong occurs when the perpetrator 'causes or permits' or alternatively 'knowingly causes or knowingly permits' the prohibited act. Such terms are to be found, for example, in a number of statutes specifying water pollution offences, as appears below. The scope of these phrases, identifying as they do the degree of proximity or relationship of the defendant to the offence, is evidently of essential importance in establishing liability.

It is accepted first that the phraseology, whatever its precise form, creates two separate offences,[101] care therefore being necessary to ensure that the appropriate limb is applied to any given situation. The meaning of 'cause' received judicial consideration in the context of section 2(1) of the Rivers (Prevention of Pollution) Act 1951, which created the offence of 'causing poisonous, noxious or polluting matter to enter a stream'.[102] The leading decision establishing the principles is *Alphacell* v *Woodward* (1972).[103] Polluted washing water from the appellants' paper factory entered two settling tanks adjoining a river which were provided with an overflow to the river and also pumps, activated when the water reached a certain level, to prevent overflow into the river. On the instant occasion, due to blockage of the pump inlets with vegetation, they failed to prevent discharge of the polluted water into the river. The appellants were convicted under section 2(1). The House of Lords rejected their appeal, Viscount Dilhorne saying[104]:

> What then is meant by the word 'caused' in the subsection? If a man intending to secure a particular result, does an act which brings that about, he causes that result. If he deliberately and intentionally does certain acts of which the natural consequence is that certain results ensue, may he not also be said to have caused those results even though they may not be intended by him? I think he can, just as he can be said to cause the result if he is negligent, without intending that result.

Lord Salmon, emphasising that the inevitable or foreseeable consequences of an action imply causation irrespective of intention, said:[105] 'It seems plain to me that

100 In *Boyton* v *Willment Bros Ltd* [1971] 3 All ER 624 at p.631.

101 See, e.g., per Lord Wilberforce in *Alphacell Ltd* v *Woodward* [1972] 2 All ER 475 at p.479.

102 The forerunner of section 107(1)(a) of the Water Act 1989 and section 85 of the Water Resources Act 1991.

103 [1972] AC 824; 2 All ER 475; 2 WLR 1320.

104 At p.483.

105 At p.490.

the appellants caused the pollution by the active operation of their plant. They certainly did not intend to cause the pollution but they intended to do the acts which caused it ...'. Finally, taking this same view a stage further, Lord Cross said:[106]

106 At p.489.

> It was not for the respondents to prove that the appellants had been negligent. The appellants having started to operate their plant on that day could only escape being held to have caused polluted effluent to enter the river if they proved that the overflow of the tank had been brought about by some other event which could fairly be regarded as being beyond their ability to foresee or control.

The Divisional Court in *F.J.H. Wrothwell Ltd* v *Yorkshire Water Authority* (1984)[107] accepted that the section 2 offence was absolute and proof of *mens rea* was not required; 'cause' not generally being regarded as a word importing a mental element as is 'possess' or, usually, 'permit'. The facts here were that the appellants poured 12 gallons of Bidicin, a concentrated herbicide, into a drain expecting it to pass via the public sewer to the treatment works. The drain was not connected to a sewer but discharged into a stream. The herbicide caused a nuisance and killed many fish. Being charged under section 2 their defence was that since the actual result of the act had been so different from that expected, it could not be said to be its natural consequence. The Court, following *Alphacell*, found that the appellants had caused the pollutant to enter the stream according to the ordinary, common sense meaning of the word.

107 [1984] Crim LR 43; and see to the same effect *NRA* v *Welsh Development Agency* [1993] EGCS 160 concerning a prosecution under the similarly worded section 107 of the Water Act 1989

In *Southern Water Authority* v *Pegrum* (1989),[108] in which the respondents were found liable when, following heavy rain and cracking to the retaining wall of a lagoon, pig effluent gained entry to a river, the Divisional Court summarised the principles as follows:

108 [1989] Crim LR 442.

(a) Where the defendant conducts some active operation involving the storage, use or creation of material capable of polluting a river should it escape, then if it does escape and pollute, the defendant is liable if he 'caused' that escape.
(b) The question of causation is to be decided in a common sense way.
(c) A defendant may be found to have caused that escape even though he did not intend that escape and even though the escape happened without his negligence.
(d) It is a defence to show that the cause of the escape was the intervening act of a third party, or an act of God or *vis major*, which are the *novus actus interveniens* defences to strict liability referred to in *Rylands* v *Fletcher* (1868) LR 3 HL 330.
(e) In deciding whether the intervening cause affords a defence the test is whether it was of so powerful a nature that the conduct of the defendant was not a cause at all, but was merely part of the surrounding circumstances.[109]

109 See also *Shave* v *Rosner* [1954] 2 All ER 280; *Lovelace* v *DPP* [1954] 3 All ER 481; *Shulton (GB) Ltd* v *Slough BC* [1967] 2 All ER 137.

The scope of the term then is very broad. It includes intentional and negligent acts and the logical consequences of acts undertaken to achieve other purposes. The need evident in these decisions for some positive act though has subsequently been disavowed, though, by the Divisional Court in *NRA* v *Yorkshire Water Services Ltd* (1993).[110] Yorkshire Water operated a sewage works, effluent entering and being discharged therefrom by gravity. An unknown party discharged a quantity of iso-octonal into the public sewer which passed naturally through the works and thence into the River Spen. It was evident, therefore, that the water company was not responsible in any active sense either for the presence of the chemical in the

110 [1994] 2 WLR 1202; (1993) *The Times*, 24 November.

sewer or for its subsequent passage through the system into the river. Discharge consents issued by the NRA to Yorkshire Water and by Yorkshire Water to its customers contained a standard condition prohibiting the discharge of iso-octon-al. In the course of his judgement Buckley J reviewed earlier authorities and con-cluded that 'cause' required neither knowledge nor negligence. A mere passive standing-by as here could, and in the view of the Court did, amount to a causing. Further, it was immaterial that other persons or causes contributed to the offence. The real significance of the judgement, though, lies in the emphasis the Court placed on the determination of 'cause' as a question of fact rather than law. Although case law may assist in interpreting its meaning and could therefore be used as a guide, courts remained free, said the Divisional Court, to reach their own decisions on the facts before them. Once the facts had been fully established, whether or not a party might be said to have caused a discharge was a matter of fact for the court to decide. The House of Lords has subsequently emphasised the same factual basis for determining causation.[111] In its view, the fact that Yorkshire Water had set up a system for collecting and treating effluent and then for delib-erately discharging the results into the river would warrant as a finding of fact that they had caused its entry.

It may be that interpretation of the particular facts contributed to the appar-ently conflicting decision in *Wychavon DC* v *National Rivers Authority* (1994)[112] concerning the entry of raw sewage into a river following the blockage of a sewer. The local council, responsible under an agency arrangement with the water author-ity, though being informed of the problem, did not secure its clearance until the following day. In allowing the council's appeal against conviction by the magis-trates the High Court noted that it had committed no positive or deliberate act that caused the discharge of the sewage,[113] Watkins LJ concluding that:

> In my judgement the facts found by the justices are not capable of establishing that the council caused the pollution by creating a nuisance or otherwise. There is nothing to point to the performance by the council of either a positive or deliberate act such as could prop-erly be said to have brought about the flow of sewage effluent into the river Avon.

This difference of approach remains to be clarified.

A further clearly established point is that the acts of an independent third party will not be attributable to the operator of the process. In *Impress (Worcester) Ltd* v *Rees* (1971),[114] for example, a trespasser entered one night and opened the valve to an oil storage tank, the escaping oil eventually reaching a river. Allowing the appeal the Divisional Court said that the action of the unauthorised person was an intervening cause of so powerful a nature that the conduct of the appellant was not a cause at all but merely part of the surrounding circumstances.

The Court of Appeal has had an opportunity to consider the meaning of 'cause' in its current statutory context in section 85 of the Water Resources Act 1991 in *CPC (UK)* v *NRA* (1994),[115] confirming the principles discussed above. The facts here were that as the result of a pipe fracture on the defendants' premises approx-imately 168 gallons of cleaning liquid escaped through a storm drain into the River Lyd in Devon. The cause of the fracture was the failure of specialist subcontrac-tors, carrying out work some nine months before CPC bought the premises, to join two pipes together properly. The defendants' survey of the premises before purchase had revealed no defect and it was accepted by the Court that the defect was truly latent. In the appeal against conviction under section 85 of the 1991 Act

111 [1994] *The Times*, 21 November.

112 [1994] 2 All ER 440; 158 LGR 181; and see to similar effect *Price* v *Cromack* [1975] 1 WLR 988; *NRA* v *Welsh Development Agency* [1993] EGCS 160.

113 Note that a prosecution for 'knowingly permitting' might have been successful.

114 [1971] 2 All ER 357; see also on similar facts, *NRA* v *Wright Engineering Co. Ltd* (1993) *Independent*, 19 November.

115 CA (Crim Div), 15 July 1994 ; ENDS Report 235, August 1994, p.41.

and section 4 of the Salmon and Freshwater Fisheries Act 1975, the NRA contended that the positive activity of the defendants was their operation of the factory with the faulty pipe. CPC argued that the installation of defective piping by the subcontractors was the true cause of the incident, and that this question had not been properly put to the jury. The Court of Appeal rejected this latter argument on the ground that the legislation did not require there to be only one cause. If satisfied that the defendants had caused the escape, 'then whatever part had been played in the history of events by their predecessor's sub-contractors was irrelevant to their guilt as a matter of law'. It is perhaps significant in relation to the conflicting decisions noted above that the NRA thought it necessary to seek for some positive activity on the part of the defendants as a 'cause'.

The Court of Appeal has further considered the scope and significance of 'causing' in Attorney-General's Reference (No 1 of 1994).[116] The circumstances giving rise to the Reference originated with the discharge of highly toxic effluent and oil through a sewerage system into a stream and thence a river, destroying fish life for a distance of about three miles. The three respondents, i.e. the collector of the waste who disposed of it into the sewerage system, the sewerage undertaker having statutory duties to provide and maintain the sewerage system, and the local authority who performed cleansing functions delegated by the undertaker were acquitted by the Crown Court of the offences under section 107 of the Water Act 1989.[117]

The three points of law referred to the Court, together with its responses may be summarised as follows:

1. Whether the offence of causing polluting matter to enter controlled waters could be committed by more than one person, i.e., where a number of different, separate acts were each instrumental in the material entering the waters? In the case of a joint enterprise the answer was obviously yes. Where, as here, different and separate acts were concerned the answer was the same. The present case illustrated the impracticability of confining causation to one party.
2. Whether the reception of polluting material and its discharge into a stream due to a defective pumping system comprised a chain of operations and therefore a positive act sufficient to constitute a 'causing' for the purposes of the section? The answer was effectively given by the decision in *NRA v Yorkshire Water Services* [1994].[118] Where a sewerage undertaker set up a plant to carry out its statutory duties, then if sewage passing through that system polluted controlled waters then the company, per Lord Wilberforce in Alphacell, had participated in the 'active operation of a chain of operations involving as the result the pollution of the stream'.
3. Whether the failure to maintain the pumping system, either negligently or in breach of a statutory duty, constituted a positive act or chain of operations sufficient to constitute 'causing'? The question, here expressed negatively, could also be formulated in positive terms: 'Is running a system in an unmaintained state sufficient to constitute 'causing'? Where a party had undertaken the day-to-day running and maintenance of a sewerage system, if it failed properly to maintain the system and ran it in an unmaintained state, that would be sufficient to entitle the jury to find that party guilty of causing pollution to controlled waters resulting from lack of maintenance.

In the reserved opinion read by the Lord Chief Justice, the Court also emphasised that 'knowingly' is not to be implied as qualifying the word 'causes' in the sec-

116 *The Times*, 26 January.

117 Now section 85 of the Water Resources Act 1991.

118 3 WLR 1202.

tion. Further that 'causes' involves some active participation and that a 'mere tacit standing by and looking on'[119] will be insufficient to amount to a causing.

The second limb of the phrase, 'permit', has received little judicial consideration in the environmental context; however, Lord Wilberforce has emphasised that the two essential features are a failure to prevent and knowledge[120]. In its turn a failure to prevent implies the ability to do so, and therefore the requisite degree of control. Concerning the requirement of knowledge, in *Impress (Worcester) Ltd v Rees* (1971), considered above, another information alleged that the defendants had 'knowingly permitted' the pollution. As the pollution had been caused by an unknown trespasser at night, and therefore outside the knowledge of the defendants, the magistrates dismissed that information.

The meaning of 'permit' received the attention of the House of Lords in *McLeod v Buchanan* (1940),[121] which followed an action against a van driver who caused a fatal accident but was unable to satisfy the judgement. This subsequent action was against the owner of the vehicle for permitting its use for private purposes without third-party insurance. There was no evidence that the owner either knew of its use for private purposes or had given such express permission. The court, however, found that the owner was liable for permitting its use, Lord Wright saying,[122]

> To permit is a looser and vaguer term [than cause]. It may denote an express permission, general or particular, as distinguished from a mandate. The other person is not told to use the vehicle in a particular way, but he is told that he may do so if he desires. However, the word also includes cases in which permission is merely inferred. If the other person is given the control of the vehicle, permission may be inferred if the vehicle is left at the other person's disposal in such circumstances as to carry with it a reasonable implication of a discretion or liberty to use it in the manner in which it was used. In order to prove permission, it is not necessary to show knowledge of similar user in the past, or actual notice that the vehicle might be, or was likely to be, so used, or that the accused was guilty of a reckless disregard of the probabilities of the case, or a wilful closing of his eyes. He may not have thought at all of his duties under the section. The Lord President in his judgement stated that both parties before the First Division expressly accepted as the test for the present case, '... did the defender know or ought he to have known that the van was being or was likely to be used by his brother for his own private purposes?' This, so far as it goes, is a compendious and practical way of stating the crucial question. If the answer is in the affirmative, a case of permission is made out.

Whereas causing requires some active involvement, then, permitting is negative and may occur where a person, having the opportunity or ability to intervene, stands by while the prohibited event occurs. The right or ability to forbid is a necessary element in establishing liability for permitting.[123] So, in *Price v Cromack* (1975)[124] the defendant allowed the adjoining factory owner to build lagoons on his land into which effluent from the factory was discharged and from which the supernatant liquid was dispersed by saturation through the defendant's land. On the breach of a lagoon wall, escaping effluent entered an adjoining stream and killed fish. The defendant's passive acquiescence in the events did not amount in the eyes of the court to 'causing'. It would, though, appear to come within the 'permitting' limb of the phrase.

119 Per Lord Widgery CJ in *Price v Cromock* [1975] 1 WLR 988.

120 In *Alphacell v Woodward* [1972] 2 All ER 475 at p.479.

121 [1940] 2 All ER 179.

122 At p.187.

123 *Goodborne v Buch* [1940] 1 KB 771; *Lloyd v Singleton* [1953] 1 QB 357.

124 [1975] 1 WLR 988.

2

Principles and Procedures

PRINCIPLES

A criticism frequently made of environmental law is that it has yet to develop principles or concepts of general application. Given its early growth by pragmatic response to disparate problems as they arose, that is perhaps not so surprising. However, with further growth and an increasing range and sophistication of application one would expect such principles to emerge here as they have in other areas of law. While such general principles have yet to appear, common phrases are to be found in legislation, from early, Victorian public health measures to European Directives; such terms usually being indicative of the degree of obligation demanded of an operator. The purpose now is to consider those general principles, which appear to fall into two broad categories dependent on their underlying assumptions, although the distinction between the two is not always clear-cut, many having certain features in common. On the one hand there is the predominently environment-centred view where remedying the pollution or preventing its occurrence is the primary aim. This category includes the concepts 'the polluter pays' and 'sustainable development'. The second approach is centred more on the economic and/or technical practicality of any remedy. Within this category are to be found 'best practicable means' and 'BATNEEC' (best available techniques not entailing excessive cost).

Polluter pays principle

Of the expressions in the first category, that having the widest currency is without doubt the general assertion that 'the polluter pays'. While as a broad statement of principle it appears to be just and valid, what the term means in its practical application is less clear. The implication seems to be that the person causing the pollution should pay the costs of that pollution. The National Society for Clean Air (NSCA)[1] suggests that this means two things, that 'the cost of preventing pollution or of minimising environmental damage due to pollution should be borne by those responsible for the pollution'. The principle is considered to have originated from the proceedings of the UN Conference on the Human Environment at Stockholm in 1972, and was included in the European Community's First Action Programme on the Environment (1973–76).

To the extent that the polluter is required to make good the deficiency giving rise to the pollution, he is only doing what the non-polluter is already doing voluntarily or is being required to do, for example, under a licence condition.[2] Further, experience suggests that the polluter, by the very fact that he has been a polluter, will apply as superficial and inexpensive a remedy as he can persuade the relevant authority to accept. It was this context that generated the acronym CATNIP – cheapest available technology not involving prosecution. As has been said, in this

1 *Pollution Handbook* (1993), p.25.

2 See, e.g., financial requirements of waste management licensing and 'fit and proper person' under section 74 of the Environmental Protection Act 1990.

sense it is the conscientious and concerned non-polluter who really pays. Nevertheless, if one considers that a function of the law, and especially the criminal law, is to bear on the minority who are unwilling to conform to generally accepted codes of conduct or behaviour, then to require payment and action to secure a pollution-free environment from those who are seeking to avoid that obligation has its own evident merit.

Turning to the second limb of the NSCA's definition, that the polluter, as well as being required to cease polluting for the future, must clear up or remove the pollution already caused, this again appears to be fair and just. Moreover it accords with the increasing trend in the criminal law generally to give courts the discretion, following a conviction, to make an award of compensation to the injured victim as well as to punish the wrong-doer.[3] There are a number of reasons why it is difficult to apply this meaning to the phrase with any degree of confidence though, at least in the light of current practice. First, in many cases the only effective and necessary remedy for past pollution is the cessation of the polluting activity. Any pollutants in the environment will then adequately be dealt with by natural processes; the polluter therefore being required to take no further action nor to incur additional costs for that purpose. This is particularly true, for example, of the pollution of water and air where natural dilution, turbulence and dissemination will, over a period of time, sufficiently neutralise existing pollution. However, by the same token, where there is no possibility of such effective dilution, as in the case of pollution of the soil, some additional remedial action is required if past pollution is to be rectified. That such action has not been taken, whether or not it has been required, is sufficiently indicated by the present concern over and difficulty of allocation of responsibility for contaminated land.

A second reason militating against the remedying of past pollution has been the lack in many cases of an appropriate or sufficiently affected, and therefore concerned, party to stimulate such action. Evidently, where pollution from A injures the property and/or activities of B, B will have a direct interest in securing compensation, by civil proceedings, for the harm done. Who, though, is to take action, and hitherto on what legal basis, where the pollution by A is confined to the premises of A, or alternatively makes a small contribution to long-term, widely disseminated and chronic pollution? The town gas works was a prime example of the first situation, and perhaps in some respects of the second. In such cases the polluter was not, or could not be, made responsible for cleaning up, which therefore generally was not done.

Following on from that second reason, the passage of time produces another, equally intractable problem. With the passing of the affected property or the contaminating source through the hands of a succession of innocent owners, where is liability now to be placed? The simplistic approach is doubtless to say, as the law does, that a prospective purchaser has the responsibility to make any necessary enquiries and investigations to satisfy himself of the condition of the property he is buying, and is not therefore, at least in law, innocent. Whether or not he does so enquire he cannot thereafter avoid his responsibilities as the owner of those premises having those characteristics. The obvious response to such an assertion, though, is to point out that a subsequent owner is not in any real sense the polluter and therefore cannot be brought within the scope of the term under consideration. Also, of course, common commercial practice does not entirely accord with those legal assumptions. Purchasers do not as a matter of course, or at least

3 See, e.g., section 28 of the Theft Act 1968.

have not, commissioned detailed and sophisticated surveys in the fear that something nasty might be revealed. The time might not be far off, though, when they may be well advised so to do. However, if this consideration is valid it would appear that the principle that 'the polluter pays', while expressing a justifiable and laudable aim, has so far left a great deal to be desired in its practical application.

While the phrase is usually applied, as in the previous discussion, to impose remedial costs on the polluter, other interpretations are possible. An example is provided in Article 10 of Directive 84/631/EEC concerned with the transfrontier shipment of hazardous waste, which states:

> In accordance with the 'polluter pays' principle, the cost of implementing the notification and supervision procedure, including the necessary analyses and controls, shall be chargeable to the holder and/or the producer of the waste by the Member State concerned ...

On this approach the polluter pays not for cleaning up the pollution, but for the administrative costs of policing the activity. One assumes that the intention here is that these costs are 'as well as', rather than 'instead of' and therefore represents an extension of the principle.

A fundamentally different meaning has been given to the principle by linking it with permissive licensing and licence payments. Recognising that some emission of pollutants is inevitable, it has been suggested that this 'acceptable' amount of pollution of a particular type could be divided up and allocated to applicants in the form of credits that would be paid for as an element in the licence fee. Where subsequently any licence-holder reduced his emission levels, his surplus credits would then be available for sale to some other licensee. As well as being a direct application of the principle, this approach has the virtue of identifying a specific maximum for a given pollutant. Its obvious disadvantage is that unless some system of review of overall emission levels is provided for there appears to be no opportunity for improvement.

A concluding aspect of this expression worthy of note is that for the principle to apply there has to be a polluter. The term is therefore limited to reactive situations where pollution has been or is occurring. With the increasing emphasis on the pro-active, for instance in relation to environmental impact assessment and the imposition of conditions upon which an activity may be permitted to be carried on, it is perhaps becoming necessary to extend the concept and the term to include the obligation on any person to conduct their affairs in an environmentally sympathetic fashion; in effect to embrace the potentially polluting activities of the conscientious operator who voluntarily conducts his concern in a non-polluting way. It is not just the polluter who pays, if indeed he does. Anyone doing anything should be aware of, and accept responsibility for, the environmental consequences of that activity.

Sustainable development

The principle of 'sustainable development' attempts to assess or quantify development in relation to the impact of its range of effects or potential effects on the local and global environmental media at risk. The environmental viability of a given activity or process may then be determined independently of or in addition to other considerations and form part of the decision whether that activity is appropriate in its proposed form in that location. More importantly, sustainable development is particularly concerned with wider national or regional trends and the longer term consequences of social and commercial developments; confronting decision-makers with choices between the more immediate, quantifiable merits of a proposed course of action and the more speculative benefits to future generations of present self-denial. A common definition of the concept[4] is 'development that meets the needs of the present without compromising the ability of future generations to meet their own needs'.

In September 1990, the Government published a comprehensive strategy for the environment in the United Kingdom in the White Paper 'This Common Inheritance',[5] including targets and objectives for policies in specific areas. Progress on these, together with new commitments, have subsequently been the subject of reports in September 1991 and October 1992.[6] This concern, also increasingly evident internationally, achieved its most notable expression to date in the United Nations Conference on Environment and Development (The Earth Summit) held in Rio de Janeiro in 1992. That conference produced four major policy aims, including Agenda 21, which was a programme of action applicable throughout the world to achieve a more sustainable pattern of development for the next century. In response, the European Community's Fifth Environmental Action Programme is closely linked to the principles and themes of Agenda 21.

International machinery was also established to follow up those agreements. A new UN Commission on Sustainable Development (CSD) was set up to monitor progress on Agenda 21, and held its first meeting in New York in June 1993. The Earth Summit recommended that individual countries should prepare strategies and action plans to give national effect to these agreements. The United Kingdom Government has accordingly produced and published a separate report on each of the four 'Rio' policy aims, including 'Sustainable Development: The UK Strategy'.[7] This latter document may therefore be regarded as the latest national review of the topic and statement of the Government's policy intentions. What follows is in consequence largely derived from that report. Agenda 21 placed great emphasis on the need for all sectors of society to participate in the formation of effective national strategies for sustainable development. While the report represents Government thinking it is based on wide consultation with a comprehensive range of bodies representing all sectors of the community. As the report makes clear, if sustainable development is to make a real impact it will require the active participation of those same interests, in alliance with Government.

In the view of central government, sustainable development does not mean having less economic development nor does it entail preservation of every aspect of the present environment at all costs. What it does require is that decisions throughout society are taken with proper regard to their environmental impact. While human health has been a primary consideration in environmental policy in the past, acute health problems in the United Kingdom are now rarely the result of environmental causes. Such health concern has now therefore moved to the effects of long-term, low-level exposure to environmental pollution where cause and effect are harder to assess and require more extensive studies to evaluate the precise dangers.

A parallel concern is to conserve natural resources, with a primary emphasis on those that are of economic value (such as land, fish stocks and diversity of species). There is also, however, a desire to protect resources, such as landscape and wildlife, that are valued for their own sake. This concern extends now beyond the im-

4 'Our Common Future', the report of the World Commission on Environment and Development (the Brundtland Commission) (Oxford: OUP, 1987).

5 'This Common Inheritance: Britain's Environmental Strategy', Cm 1200, 1990.

6 'This Common Inheritance. The First Year Report', Cm 1655; 'This Common Inheritance. The Second Year Report', Cm 2068.

7 Cm 2426, published January 1994.

mediate environment to global issues, including protection of the oceans and great forests of the world, of the stratospheric ozone layer and of the world's climate. Because, in many cases, their degradation is attributable to universal practices any remedy must likewise be a matter of collective action. To this end certain basic principles should be observed, including the following:

(a) decisions should be based on the best possible scientific information and analysis of risk;
(b) where there is uncertainty and potentially serious risks exist, precautionary measures may be necessary;
(c) ecological impacts must be considered, particularly where resources are non-renewable or effects may be irreversible;
(d) cost implications should be brought home directly to the people responsible – the 'polluter pays' principle.

It is therefore evident that the assessment and interrelation of a range of disparate factors involves judgements. To ensure that those judgements are soundly based, an important and immediate objective must be to develop better indicators and natural resource accounting, giving over time better quantification of the benefits for and damage to the environment consequent upon commercial, economic and social change.

The primary factor to which deterioration of the global environment is attributable is population growth. That of the United Kingdom is slow in comparison with many developing countries and compared with earlier periods of our history. Nevertheless the trend is still upwards. In 1992 the population of the United Kingdom was 57.6 million. Present projections of birth rates and migration trends suggest that the population might increase by 6 per cent to about 61 million in 2012 and might stabilise thereafter at about 62 million (8 per cent above present levels) around the year 2030. Though the rate of growth is low our population density is already, at 235 persons per sq km, one of the highest in the world. This national figure obscures regional variations; whereas the South East, with 746 persons per sq km, has a rapidly growing population through internal migration, Scotland, with a population density of 66 persons per sq km, is among the lowest in Europe.

An associated demographic factor is that while population growth is slow the number of households is increasing more rapidly as more people choose to live in smaller groupings or separately. On present projections the number of households in the United Kingdom is expected to increase by 14 per cent to 26 million by 2012. This leads not only to increased pressures on the housing stock and on land for development, but also to increased consumption of many goods and services that tend to be used by households rather than individuals. These projections, coupled with the generally increasing standard of living indicated by figures for economic growth, represent potential pressures on land, water, energy and other natural resources required for housing, food, employment and transport. The effective and environmentally sympathetic use of all these natural resources is therefore of paramount importance, involving among other disciplines the re-use of derelict or contaminated land and the recycling of materials.

Against this background specific aspects of the economy that may be regarded as particularly significant from the point of view of sustainable development dealt with in the report are agriculture, forestry, fisheries, minerals extraction, energy, manufacturing and services, waste, development and construction, transport, and leisure. On the other side of the balance sheet are the features of the biosphere requiring consideration as being vulnerable to the impact of those activities. They will include global atmosphere, air quality, fresh water, the sea, soil and land use, minerals, wildlife, and habitats.

Having regard to the scale of the problem, putting sustainability into practice will necessitate consensus and co-operation at many levels from, at one extreme, through international organisations and between countries to, at the other, local and community groups. Within the national context it is the Government's view that three new initiatives are desirable. First, the Government's Panel on Sustainable Development consisting of a small group of experienced and knowledgeable advisors. They would keep under review issues at national and global level, identify major problems and opportunities as they arise, monitor progress and consider questions of priority. They would have access to Ministers, be consulted by government and provide a source of authoritative and independent advice. Secondly, a UK Round Table on Sustainable Development as a forum for the main sectors or groups in the community. This would bring together representatives of the many advisory and consultative bodies already in existence to meet under the chairmanship of the Secretary of State for the Environment. Its main purpose would be to facilitate communication between people with differing responsibilities who in consequence approach common issues from different positions. Members would thus be able to compare experience on what is being done in different sectors, develop a better understanding of the problems faced by others, and see how far common perspectives might be developed. Thirdly, the report envisages a Citizens' Environment Initiative to provide a channel of communication to and from individuals and communities and to stimulate interest in the issues and activities embraced by sustainable development. Its aim is to increase general awareness of the part that personal choice can play in delivering sustainable development and to enlist individual support and commitment to its achievement.

Best practicable means

Turning to the second category of principles, the phrase 'best practicable means' has appeared in a number of public health statutes in the context of nuisance abatement.[8] Its usual use as a defence indicates that, having done what is practicable in terms of prevention or reduction, the defendant has discharged the duty imposed upon him and the nuisance or pollution may be allowed to continue. The application of this principle to existing activities therefore precludes the cessation of the business or process because of its environmental impact. In the case of new businesses, of course, such questions will come within the scope of planning approval, with or without environmental impact assessment.

The definition and interpretation of the phrase is therefore important in determining the extent of the obligation to remedy and the consequent degree of pollution permitted in a particular situation. 'Practicable' has received judicial consideration largely in the context of health and safety at work, and more often in the defence of 'reasonably practicable' which, it is recognised, is a narrower term than the more strict 'practicable' or physically possible. The distinction between the two is not entirely clear, however, nor the precise weight to be given to 'reasonably' in this context. The Clean Air Act 1956, for example,[9] provided

8 See as examples section 94(4) and (5) and section 103(3) of the Public Health Act 1936; sections 58(5) and 66(9) of the Control of Pollution Act 1974; section 80(7) and section 82(9) of the Environmental Protection Act 1990.

9 In section 34.

that 'practicable means reasonably practicable', having regard to a number of specified factors. The headnote to *Edwards* v *NCB* (1949)[10] notes, 'The risk of accident had to be weighed against the measures necessary to eliminate the risk. The greater the risk the less would be the weight to be given to the factor of cost.' To the degree or likelihood of risk one might also add as a factor, the seriousness of the consequences should they occur. Emphasising the relationship between, or the proportionality of, the remedy and the harm, Lord Atkin said, in the context of employment,[11]

> I am unable to take the view that it is reasonably practicable by any means to avoid or prevent the breach of section 55. The time of non-protection is so short, and the time, trouble and expense of any other form of protection is so disproportionate that I think the defence is proved.

The term has been defined in a number of environmental statutes incorporating judicial interpretation of the scope of 'practicable'.[12] The latest, section 79(9) of the Environmental Protection Act 1990, provides that:

'best practicable means' is to be interpreted by reference to the following provisions:

(a) 'practicable' means reasonably practicable having regard among other things to local conditions and circumstances, to the current state of technical knowledge and to the financial implications;
(b) the means to be employed include the design, installation, maintenance and manner and periods of operation of plant and machinery, and the design, construction and maintenance of buildings and structures;
(c) the test is to apply only so far as compatible with any duty imposed by law;
(d) the test is to apply only so far as compatible with safety and safe working conditions, and with the exigencies of any emergency or unforeseeable circumstances;

and, in circumstances where a code of practice under section 71 of the Control of Pollution Act 1974 (noise minimisation) is applicable, regard shall also be had to guidance given in it.[13]

It will be seen from that interpretation of the term that the determination of reasonable practicability relates to the immediate physical context, which may be taken to include topographical features and the proximity, size and use of neighbouring buildings and land. The current state of technical knowledge applicable to that process, activity or its products and waste by-products embraces the knowledge and equipment readily and commercially available rather than the sum total of knowledge including that still at the developmental stage. Financial implications relate the costs of prevention and treatment to the overall cost and profitability of the enterprise, although there appears to be no authority providing guidance on the relationship or proportion they should bear to one another. It would seem in this respect, though, that big is beautiful, the larger concern being able to provide more extensive and more sophisticated monitoring and treatment plant.

In *Wivenhoe Port* v *Colchester Borough Council* (1985)[14] the defence argued that the routine use of vacuum machinery to prevent dust nuisance would make the operation uneconomic. The Court accepted that profitability was a relevant factor but that the mere fact of increased expenditure, or even unprofitability, was not sufficient to establish the defence. This view, bearing on the acute nature of the consequences in this case, emphasises that the statutory criteria leave much to

10 [1949] 1 KB 704.

11 *Coltness Iron Co.* v *Sharp* [1938] AC 90 at p.94.

12 See, e.g., section 72 of the Control of Pollution Act 1974 and, e.g., *Adsett* v *K & L Steelfounders* [1953] 1 WLR 773

13 See also the very similar terms of section 72 of the Control of Pollution Act 1974.

14 JPL 175 (affirmed [1985] JPL 396); and see at pp.70, 83, 96.

the discretion of the Court in the particular circumstances and in relation to the changing perceptions and expectations of the times.[15]

The uncertainties inherent in the application of the principle in practice were identified as a major deficiency by the Royal Commission on Environmental Pollution[16]:

> There are, however, some defects in the system by which best practicable means are decided for an industry; for one thing, the system has sometimes appeared imprecise and inaccessible to the outsider. The judgment of costs and benefits which is implied in the determination of best practicable means requires not only technical assessment but assessment of financial, economic and scientific factors and of local circumstances. The relevant expertise must be available to the control authority and, in particular, the best practicable means for an industry should in future be determined through a more formal machinery which enables the views of amenity groups, the scientific community, local authorities and the general public to be taken into account as well as those of the industry. At the plant level, we propose that the main elements of the agreed best practicable means for each works be recorded in a local 'consents' register, and that there should be a procedure for public involvement in significant changes.

This passage reveals another perceived defect in the concept, or at least in its present operation; that the determination of what is best is made privately and by too narrow a group of people. In consequence the Report suggests that[17] 'With the use of bpm should go a recognition of the need to justify the decisions reached'.

In spite of these criticisms, however, the Commision considered that the concept had substantial merits at least in comparison with anything else on offer. They gave it their qualified imprimatur in the following terms[18]:

> ...we are satisfied that the best practicable means approach to control is inherently superior to control by nationally-fixed and rigid emission standards. The realities of pollution control require a continuing balance to be struck between the costs and benefits of pollution abatement for industry and society. The best practicable means formula provides flexibility to take account of local circumstances.

Adding later:

> We have reached the firm conclusion that the bpm system should be continued; indeed, so convinced are we of the merits of this approach to air pollution control that in a later chapter of this Report we recommend extension of this system to the control of industrial pollution of other forms. The bpm system is consistent with the realities of pollution control. In principle it provides a flexible and sensitive means of acheiving the balance of costs and benefits which should be the aim of control. We are aware, however, that precisely because of its flexibility the bpm concept can be misused. At its best the term connotes a rigorous analysis of the objectives and consequences of air pollution control. At its worst the term can be used as a catchword to conceal the absence of any such analysis.

Best practicable environmental option

'Best practicable environmental option' (BPEO) as a principle clearly owes something in its derivation to the phrase just considered, although instead of concentration on cost-effective techniques for reducing emissions it is primarily concerned to select the most appropriate or least damaging environmental alternative for the reception of the waste or polluting material. The term is wide enough, though, to include the reduction of such emissions by modification of processes and plant.

15 See also generally HMIP guidance note 'Best practicable means: general principles and practice' (BPM 1/88, January 1988).

16 Royal Commission on Environmental Pollution, Fifth Report 1976, 'Air Pollution Control: An Integrated Approach', Cmnd 6371, paragraph 17.

17 Ibid., paragraph 166.

18 Ibid., paragraphs 16 and 166 respectively.

The expression derives from the Fifth Report of the Royal Commission on Environmental Pollution, advocating the formation of a new central body to provide co-ordinated pollution control.[19] In its Tenth Report[20] the Royal Commission stated that the term meant 'The optimal allocation of the waste spatially; the use of different sectors of the environment to minimise damage overall.' Elaborating further in its Eleventh Report[21] the Royal Commission stated that the aim of BPEO

> is to find the optimum combination of available methods of disposal so as to limit damage to the environment to the greatest extent achievable for a reasonable and acceptable total combined cost to industry and the public purse,

thus retaining the 'financial implications' of best practicable means as a factor for consideration. In its Twelfth Report, devoted to BPEO,[22] the Royal Commission described its nature as follows:

> A BPEO, is the outcome of a systematic consultative and decision-making procedure which emphasises the protection and conservation of the environment across land, air and water. The BPEO procedure establishes, for a given set of objectives, the option that provides the most benefit or least damage to the environment as a whole, at acceptable cost, in the long term as well as in the short term.

Commenting on these views, Holgate[23] notes that,

> The point about BPEO is that it is a chosen pollution disposal system: an end point. It is achieved by control over processes, by adoption of the best practicable means either to generate the wastes which pose least environmental problems or to dispose of wastes in the best way.

These quotations indicate that BPEO may be regarded as a more developed treatment of the factors potentially subject to review in considering the application of the 'best practicable means' test. That alone, however, does it less than justice. Apart from the matters to be considered, the extent of its operation is significantly wider than the limited application of the older term as a defence. For example BPEO will be a relevant factor in planning consents for the location and operation of new and extended activities and processes, and in this context is one of the objectives of Environmental Impact Assessment (EIA)[24] and constitutes a factor in the issue of authorisations for IPC. The connection between EIA as a procedure and BPEO as an objective was emphasised by the Royal Commission on Environmental Pollution in its Twelfth Report[25]:

> [W]e consider that the carrying out of an EIA in respect of any project which is likely to have a significant effect on the environment will rationalise planning procedures and will contribute to the identification of a BPEO for a new project.

The DoE Consultation Paper dealing with EIA[26] also notes the connection:

> In addition to improving the quality of decision-making, the preparation of environmental assessments can help an industrial developer in his consideration of the environmental effects of a project. The compiling of the information in the assessment will bring out issues that may affect the planning decision, and the developer may be able to take such issues into account by modifying his proposals at an early stage, for example, through the identification of a better practicable environmental option.

Having introduced the concept in 1976, the Royal Commission in 1988 was driven to note that, 'The indiscriminate use of the term to describe almost any course of action which takes some account of environmental factors can only undermine

19 Ibid., p.74.

20 Tenth Report 1984 'Tackling Pollution – Experience and Prospects' Cmnd 9149 (HMSO).

21 Eleventh Report 1985 'Managing Waste : The Duty of Care' Cmnd 9675 (HMSO).

22 Twelfth Report 1988 'Best Practicable Environmental Option' Cm 310 (HMSO), paragraph 2.1.

23 M.W. Holgate, 'The Reality of Environmental Policy' (1987) *Journal of the Royal Society of Arts*, 135, pp.310-27.

24 C. Wood, 'EIA and BPEO: Acronyms for Good Environmental Planning?' 1988 JPL 310–21.

25 Twelfth Report 1988 'Best Practicable Environmental Option' Cm 310 (HMSO).

26 'Implementation of the European Directive on Environmental Assessment', Consultation Paper (DoE, 1986).

the underlying principles on which BPEO is based'. The two consequent questions therefore are, how does one arrive at a BPEO, and what are its characteristics when produced? Both questions are answered in the Commission's Twelfth Report, from which the following extracts are taken:

SUMMARY OF STEPS IN SELECTING A BPEO

Step 1: Define the Objective
State the objective of the project or proposal at the outset, in terms which do not pre-judge the means by which that objective is to be achieved.

Step 2: Generate Options
Identify all feasible options for achieving the objective: the aim is to find those which are both practicable and environmentally acceptable.

Step 3: Evaluate the options
Analyse these options, particularly to expose advantages and disadvantages for the environment. Use quantitative methods when these are appropriate. Quantitative evaluation will also be needed.

Step 4: Summarise and present the evaluation
Present the results of the evaluation concisely and objectively, and in the format which can highlight the advantages and disadvantages of each option. Do not combine the results of different measurements and forecasts if this would obscure information which is important to the decision.

Step 5: Select the Preferred Option
Select the BPEO from the feasible options. The choice will depend on the weight given to the environmental impacts and associated risks, and to the costs involved. Decision-makers should be able to demonstrate that the preferred option does not involve unacceptable consequences for the environment.

Step 6: Review the Preferred Option
Scrutinise closely the proposed detailed design and the operating procedures to ensure that no pollution risks or hazards have been overlooked. It is good practice to have the scrutiny done by individuals who are independent of the original team.

Step 7: Implement and Monitor
Monitor the acheived performance against the desired targets especially those for environmental quality. Do this to establish whether the assumptions in the design are correct and to provide feed-back for future developments of proposals and designs.

Throughout Steps 1 to 7: Maintain an audit trail

Record the basis for any choices or decisions through all of these stages; i.e. the assumptions used, details of evaluation procedures, the reliability and origins of the data, the affiliations of those involved in the analytical work and a record of those taking decisions.

Note: The boundaries between each of the steps will not always be clear-cut: some may proceed in parallel or may need to be repeated.

Paragraph 5.10 of the Report lists the 'Characteristics of a properly selected BPEO' in the following terms:

(a) it will be selected after evaluating all feasible courses of action and their effects on all environmental media.
(b) it will represent that option best for the environment as a whole, which does not incur excessive costs.

(c) it will observe the imposed standards and limits for emissions to air and discharges to water and the handling and treatment of wastes for disposal to land.

(d) it will improve upon relevant environmental standards if practicable.

(e) it will incorporate a precautionary element to overcome uncertainty about environmental impacts or their scale and reduce inadvertant pollution transfer between media.

(f) it will envisage potential for accidental damage to the environment and how it might be mitigated.

(g) it will include specification of control equipment and operating procedures when these provide an effective means of achieving the environmental objectives in the BPEO brief.

(h) it will seldom remain the best option for ever and therefore it will include provision for monitoring and review.

The steps listed above towards a BPEO are, as indicated, a summary, each being discussed in greater detail in the Report. A reading of these brief extracts and a consideration of their implications may leave one asking, as Tromans suggests,[27] 'What is the use of it all? Are there really problems of pollution which are so intractable as to need an approach from all angles (o)n all media? Surely in most cases the best disposal or management route will be glaringly obvious?'. The answer to these questions in many, particularly small scale, operations will of course be 'yes'. Identification of the BPEO will then be itself a simple and small scale process. However, there is a wide range of developments, both public and private, that will have complex and less easily discerned primary and secondary impacts on the local and distant environmental media. In such cases there is an evident need at an early stage in their planning for, as Tromans goes on to say,

27 UKELA, 'Best Practicable Environmental Option – a new Jerusalem?', ed. S.Tromans (1987), paragraph 1.8.

> sensitive and appropriate use of BPEO policy within a framework of –
>
> (a) what is economically practicable
> (b) what is scientifically and environmentally sound
> (c) what is legally achievable within the legal powers available.
>
> It is in questions of this type that BPEO will be most useful and, in solving which, could indeed become an indispensible tool.

Best available techniques not entailing excessive cost

Section 7 of the Environmental Protection Act 1991 provides that BATNEEC will be a factor in securing IPC and LAAPC[28] objectives in relation to prescribed processes of preventing or minimising the release of prescribed substances into an environmental medium, or for rendering harmless any potentially harmful substances that are to be released. In this context section 7(10) then stipulates that

28 See on these topics at p.47.

> References to the best available techniques not entailing excessive cost, in relation to a process, include (in addition to references to any technical means and technology) references to the number, qualifications, training and supervision of persons employed in the process and the design, construction, lay-out and maintenance of the buildings in which it is carried on.

The Department of the Environment (DoE)[29] points to the increasing use of this or comparable terms in international standards, with EC Directives favouring 'best available technology'.[30] 'Techniques', though, as the DoE points out and as subsection (10) quoted above stipulates, includes the technology and hardware but is also wide enough to include operational factors.

29 Draft Guidance (DoE News Release No. 271), The Meaning of BATNEEC.

30 See, e.g., EC Air Framework Directive (84/360); EC Dangerous Substances Directive (76/464) and their daughters.

General principles worthy of preliminary emphasis are that BATNEEC will be but one of a number of factors to be considered in any particular case. As the DoE guidance emphasises, and irrespective of BATNEEC, no release can be tolerated which constitutes a recognised health hazard, either in the short or long term. Further, in reducing emissions to the lowest practicable level, account will need to be taken of local conditions and circumstances, both of the process and the environment, the current state of knowledge, and the financial implications in relation to capital expenditure and revenue cost. Local conditions will of course include variable factors such as the configuration, size and so on of the individual plant. While much is therefore left to the discretion of the enforcing authority, what is BATNEEC for one process is likely to be so for other comparable processes. The following commentary on the constituent elements of BATNEEC is largely taken from the DoE guidance already referred to.[31]

31 See note 29 above.

In relation to 'best available techniques' (BAT), 'best' means the most effective in 'preventing, minimising or rendering harmless polluting emissions'. In this sense a number of processes may be equally effective and therefore be 'best'. In each case though the implication is that the effectiveness of that technique has been demonstrated. 'Available' does not necessarily imply that the technology is in general use but that it is generally accessible, including from sources outside the United Kingdom. Also, availability does not depend on a multiplicity of sources because even if equipment is available only from a monopoly supplier then, assuming it to be sufficiently accessible, it will be available for this purpose. 'Techniques', as has been said, refers both to the technology or process and how it is operated. The DoE guidance says that

> The word should be taken to mean the concept and design of the process, the components of which it is made up and the manner in which they are connected together to make the whole. It should also be taken to include matters such as staff numbers, working methods, training, supervision and manner of operating the process.

The 'not entailing excessive cost' (NEEC) element is to be considered independently in its application to new and existing processes. In relation to new processes the presumption is that the best available techniques will be used. However, where in a particular case the best process offers a relatively modest gain in efficiency over the alternative at a disproportionate cost, it may be that that additional cost should be considered excessive in this context and the alternative adopted. Judgement based on the individual circumstances will still govern the decision, though, so that if, for example, the emissions here were particularly dangerous, even the disproportionate cost would not be excessive.

In applying NEEC to existing processes the concern is with the upgrading of old processes to new standards, guidance being provided by Articles 12 and 13 of the Air Framework Directive.[32] Article 13, which applies to processes existing prior to 1987, provides that in applying measures for the gradual adaptation of existing plants in the Annex I categories, Member States shall take into account in particular:

32 84/360/EEC.

- the plant's technical characteristics,
- its rate of utilisation and length of its remaining life,
- the nature and volume of polluting emissions from it,
- the desirability of not entailing excessive costs for the plant concerned, having regard in particular to the economic situation of undertakings belonging to the category in question.

It would appear that BATNEEC should be expressed in technological terms, the enforcing authority specifying the equipment that is deemed to satisfy the requirement. However, there are advantages in seeing the concept and applying it in the form of emission or performance standards. Once such standards have been determined in respect of the appropriate BATNEEC technology or process then the expression of the authorisation in terms of those standards or figures will give the operator the freedom to choose the means to achieve that target and the flexibility to develop new and improved technology and procedures.

The European Commission is preparing technical notes on the application of BATNEEC to various processes; dealing with abatement technology options, monitoring techniques, storage and handling, and emission controls. While having no legal status the intention is that they will provide the main criteria for authorities in dealing with applications for authorisation in the future. Notes have so far been published for:

- heavy metals emissions from non-ferrous industrial plant (lead, zinc and copper) (EUR 13001),
- ammonia production (EUR 13002),
- manufacture, storage and handling of benzene (EUR 13003),
- nitric acid production (EUR 13004),
- cement manufacture (EUR 13005),
- sulphuric acid production (EUR 13006),
- hazardous waste incineration (EUR 13007).

PROCEDURES

Possibly one of the most significant changes in the approach of environmental law is the radical shift in emphasis in legislation from response to problems after they have arisen to a structure of prior control and approval with the opportunity to attach operating conditions; from the re-active to the pro-active. This development may be seen as a consequence of a century or so of experience in monitoring and responding to processes that, with such experience and increasingly sophisticated measuring and recording apparatus, can be anticipated to have ever more clearly predictable forms of impact on the environment. That being the case, the virtues of having the necessary emission standards and controls known and in place before operations commence are obvious. There have been registration and licensing requirements in some specific areas of public health, and progressively more detailed planning provisions to be satisfied. However, this major, significant change in policy, introducing a new stage in the development of environmental law, is exemplified by the establishment of Integrated Pollution Control (IPC) in Part I of the Environmental Protection Act 1990 and, in response to European Community Directives, of Environmental Impact Assessment (EIA). These two processes are now to be considered.

Integrated pollution control

The individualised operation of much pollution control has already been noted in considering HMIP and BPEO, above. The Royal Commission in its Fifth Report[33] commented on the evident deficiencies of such an approach and recommended, as has been seen, a structure to deal with the pollution of all environmental media in

33 'Air Pollution Control: An Integrated Approach', Cmnd 6371, January 1976.

an integrated way with, necessarily, a unified inspectorate to operate it. The Government's response, after 12 years' thought, was to welcome the principle[34] and, two years later, to give it expression in the IPC structure in Part I of the Environmental Protection Act 1990. It may be noticed as a preliminary that the term in fact embraces IPC by HMIP and Local Authority Air Pollution Control (LAAPC), the legal provisions, referring as they do to 'enforcing authority', applying equally to both systems.

34 'Integrated Pollution Control' DoE/Welsh Office Consultation Paper, July 1988.

The purpose of IPC and LAAPC (hereafter generally IPC) is specified in section 4 to be 'preventing or minimising pollution of the environment' due to the release of substances into, in the case of HMIP, any environmental medium and, in the case of local authorities, into the air. This aim is expanded in the DoE guide[35] as follows:

35 DoE/Welsh Office, *'Integrated Pollution Control: A Practical Guide'* (1993), paragraph 2.3 (The Green Book).

Main objectives –

(a) to prevent or minimise the release of prescribed substances and to render harmless any such substances which are released; and
(b) to develop an approach to pollution control that considers releases from industrial processes to all media in the context of the effect on the environment as a whole.

Additional aims –

(c) to improve the efficiency and effectiveness of pollution controls on industry;
(d) to streamline and strengthen the regulatory system, clarify the roles and responsibilities of HMIP, other regulatory authorities, and the firms they regulate;
(e) to contain the burden on industry, particularly by providing for a 'one stop shop' on pollution control for the potentially most serious polluting processes;
(f) to provide the appropriate framework to encourage cleaner technologies and the minimisation of waste;
(g) to maintain public confidence in the regulatory system through a clear and transparent system that is accessible and easy to understand and is clear and simple in operation;
(h) to provide a flexible framework that is capable of responding both to changing pollution abatement technology and to new knowledge on the effects of pollutants; and
(i) to provide a means to fulfil certain international obligations relating to environmental protection.

For this purpose, section 1 of the 1990 Act defines 'pollution of the environment' as

meaning pollution of the environment due to the release (into any environmental medium) from any process of substances which are capable of causing harm to man or any other living organisms supported by the environment.

Actual proof of harm or damage is not therefore required, the capacity of the substances to cause harm being sufficient. The same section also defines 'process' as

any activities carried on in Great Britain, whether on premises or by means of mobile plant, which are capable of causing pollution of the environment.

Fundamental to the objectives of pollution control noted above are the concepts of BATNEEC to determine the techniques to be applied to reduce discharges of pollutants and BPEO to identify the most appropriate receiving environmental medium.[36]

36 See above at pp.42, 45. respectively.

To achieve these objectives the operation and production of the more harmful polluting processes and substances requires approval through a system of authorisations. These processes and substances are prescribed by the Secretary of State in regulations,[37] now the Environmental Protection (Prescribed Processes and

37 Under section 2 of the Environmental Protection Act 1990.

38 S.I.1991 No. 472, as amended by the Environmental Protection (Amendment of Regulations) Regulations 1991, S.I.1991 No. 836 and the Environmental Protection (Prescribed Processes and Substances) (Amendment) Regulations 1992, S.I. 1992 No. 614; of 1994, S.I. 1994 No. 1271; and also of 1994, S.I.1994 No. 1329. The 1992 Regulations postponed the operation of the main 1991 Regulations in certain specified cases from 1.4.1991 to 1.4.1992.

Substances) Regulations 1991.[38] The processes are prescribed in Schedule 1 to the Regulations and the substances in Schedules 4, 5 and 6, applying respectively to air, water and land. What follows here retains the structure of the schedule but is a synopsis of its contents to give an indication of its scope. It will be seen that each section may be divided into Parts A and B, the latter generally being smaller scale operations or less harmful in effect. Part A processes are subject to central control by HMIP, and Part B processes discharging to air to control by local authorities.

SCHEDULE 1

Descriptions of Processes

	PART A	PART B
Chapter 1 : Fuel Production Processes, Combustion Processes (incl. power generation)		
Section 1 : 1	Gasification and associated processes	Nil
1 : 2	Carbonisation and associated processes excl. use as fuel or incineration	Nil
1 : 3	Combustion processes, i.e. energy production	Nil
1 : 4	Petroleum processes incl. handling; manufacturing processes	Nil
Chapter 2 : Metal Production and Processing		
Section 2 : 1	Iron and steel	Smaller if assoc. with another process
2 : 2	Non-ferrous metals incl. recovery	Nil
2 : 3	Smelting processes	Nil
Chapter 3 : Mineral Industries		
Section 3 : 1	Cement and lime manufacture and assoc. processes	Independent assoc. processes
3 : 2	Processes involving asbestos[39]	Industrial finishing of asbestos products
3 : 3	Other mineral fibres processing incl. glass	Nil
3 : 4	Nil	Other mineral processes, crushing, grading, screening
3 : 5	Glass manufacture and production incl. enamel	Lead glass, acid etching
3 : 6	Ceramic production incl. heavy clay goods, salt glazing	Other than Part A processes
Chapter 4 : The Chemical Industry		
Section 4 : 1	Petrochemical processes incl. manufacture and processing of olefins	Nil
4 : 2	Manufacture and use of organic cemicals specific processes not within 6 : 8	Nil
4 : 3	Acid processes incl. manufacture and/or release to atmosphere of sulphur or nitrogen oxides	Nil

39 Asbestos is defined in the Schedule as meaning actinolite, amosite, anthophylite, chrysotile, crocidolite and tremolite.

4 : 4	Processes involving halogens, i.e. production etc. of flourine, chlorine, bromine or iodine	Nil
4 : 5	Inorganic chemical processes	Nil
4 : 6	Chemical fertiliser production	Nil
4 : 7	Pesticide production[40] release to water of Schedule 5 substances	Nil
4 : 8	Pharmaceutical production incl. release to water of Schedule 5 substances	Nil
4 : 9	The storage of chemicals in bulk specified chemicals if more than stated quantity	Nil

Chapter 5 : Waste Disposal and Recycling

Section 5 : 1	Incineration specified categories and/or quantities[41]	Other incineration, human cremation
5 : 2	Recovery processes incl. oils and resins and Schedules 4, 5, 6 substances	Nil
5 : 3	The production of fuel from waste using heat but excl. charcoal	Nil

Chapter 6 : Other Industries

Section 6 : 1	Paper and pulp manufacturing processes incl. where release to water of Schedule 5 substances	Nil
6 : 2	Di-isocyanate processes incl. foams or elastomers	Excess of 5 tonnes p.a. and not within other classes
6 : 3	Tar and bitumen processes	Nil
6 : 4	Processes involving uranium excl. on premises licensed under Nuclear Installations Act 1965, section 1	Nil
6 : 5	Coating processes and printing[42] incl. shipyards, textiles and printing and painting processes producing more than 1000 tonnes special waste p.a.[43]	More than 20 tonnes waste p.a.
6 : 6	The manufacture of dyestuffs, printing ink and coating materials	Reduced quantities of Part A processes
6 : 7	Timber processes incl. chemical treatment, preservatives	Manufacture of timber products over specified quantities
6 : 8	Nil	Processes involving rubber, incl. using carbon black
6 : 9	The treatment and processing of animal and vegetable matter, unless within another scheduled process[44]	Incl. maggot breeding

40 'Pesticide' is defined in Schedule 6 of the Regulations, as 'any chemical substance or preparation prepared or used for destroying any pest, including those used for protecting plants or wood or other plant products from harmful organisms; regulating the growth of plants; giving protection against harmful creatures; rendering such creatures harmless; controlling organisms with harmful or unwanted effects on water systems, buildings or other structures, or on manufactured products; or protecting animals against ectoparasites'.

41 In this context 'exempt incinerator' means one consuming waste, including animal remains, at less than 50 kg per hour but excluding clinical waste, sewage sludge or screenings, and municipal waste.

42 Coating material includes paint, varnish, lacquer, dye, metal oxide, adhesive and elastomer, metal or plastic coating.

43 Schedule 2 provides that 'special waste' means waste subject to regulations made under section 17 of the Control of Pollution Act 1974 or section 62 of the Environmental Protection Act 1990

44 The main problem from fur processing trades is that of odour nuisance. The 1993 Amendment Regulations (see next note below) therefore exclude them from IPC/APC control, regulation now being under the Part III statutory nuisance provisions.

General guidance for the operation and interpretation of these categories is provided in Schedule 2 of the Regulations. In particular it may be noted that where one business or location includes two or more processes in the same section they are to be treated as one; however, where the processes are in different sections they will require separate authorisations.[45] Where processes within the same section fall within Parts A and B they are to be treated as all coming within Part A for the purposes of control. It is inevitable, given the very broad category descriptions, that a process may come within more than one section. In such cases the most apt description should be applied; although it is to be noted that special rules govern Chapter 4 processes.

Regulation 4 qualifies the operation of the Schedule 1 lists with a number of exceptions as follows:

(1) Subject to paragraph 6, a process is not within Part A if –

   (a) it cannot result in release into the air, except in trivial quantities, of Schedule 4 substances;
   (b) it cannot result in release into water, except at less than background concentrations, of Schedule 5 substances;
   (c) it cannot result in the release into land, except in trivial quantities, of Schedule 6 substances.

(2) Subject to paragraph 6, a process is not to be taken to be a Part B process unless it will or is likely to result in the release to air of substances in Schedule 4 in more than trivial quantities.[46]

(3) Working museums are excluded.

(4) The running and testing of engines for propelling vehicles, locomotives, aircraft etc., are excluded.

(5) Processes undertaken as domestic activities in private dwellings are excluded.

(5A) Process not to be taken to be within Section 6:4 if on a nuclear site licensed under section 1 of the Nuclear Installations Act 1965.

(6) Process not to be exempted under (1) or (2) above if it may give rise to an offensive smell noticeable outside the premises.

(7) 'background concentration' means a concentration that would be present in a release irrespective of any effect the process may have had on the composition of the release and ... includes such concentration of the substance as is present in –
   (a) water supplied to the premises where the process is carried on;
   (b) water abstracted for use in the process; and
   (c) precipitation onto the premises on which the process is carried on.

The substances referred to in regulation 4(1) and (2) above are as follows:

Schedule 4 – Release into the Air: Prescribed Substances
   Oxides of sulphur and other sulphur compounds
   Oxides of nitrogen and other nitrogen compounds
   Oxides of carbon
   Organic compounds and partial oxidation products
   Metals, metalloids and their compounds
   Asbestos (suspended particulate matter and fibres), glass and mineral fibres
   Halogens and their compounds

45 This general principle has been modified by the Environmental Protection (Prescribed Processes and Substances) (Amendment) (No. 2) Regulations 1993, S.I. 1993 No 2405, so that where a process includes two or more chemical processes within Part A of different sections of Chapter 4 of Schedule 1, they are to be authorised as a single process.

46 'Trivial' for these purposes means incapable of causing harm or having an insignificant capacity to cause harm.

Phosphorus and its compounds
Particulate matter

Schedule 5 – Release into Water: Prescribed Substances
Mercury and its compounds
Cadmium and its compounds
All isomers of hexachlorocyclohexane
All isomers of DDT
Pentachlorophenol and its compounds
Hexachlorobenzene
Hexachlorobutadiene
Aldrin
Dieldrin
Endrin
Polychlorinated Biphenyls
Dichlorvos
1,2-Dichloroethane
All isomers of trichlorobenzene
Atrazine
Simazine
Tributyltin compounds
Triphenyltin compounds
Trifluralin
Fenitrothion
Azinphos-methyl
Malathion
Endosulfan

Schedule 6 – Release into Land: Prescribed Substances
Organic solvents
Azides
Halogens and their covalent compounds
Metal carbonyls
Organo-metallic compounds
Oxidising agents
Polychlorinated dibenzofuran and any congener thereof
Polychlorinated dibenzo-p-dioxin and any congener thereof
Polyhalogenated biphenyls, terphenyls and naphthalenes
Phosphorus
Pesticides[47]
Alkali metals and their oxides and alkaline earth metals and their oxides

47 See definition at note 42 above.

Processes commencing operation after the date the scheme was introduced, 1 April 1991, are required to obtain authorisation on commencement. The DoE guide suggests that for new processes with normal characteristics and for which Chief Inspector's guidance notes have been produced, applications should be made when designs are completed but before construction commences. In the case of novel or complex processes, though, it may be appropriate for the applicant to obtain HMIP's agreement to a staged application procedure. The parties then agree a plan for the application and supporting information to be submitted in a number of tranches, as the process plans are developed. Authorisation was introduced for existing processes according to the timetable in Schedule 3. That programme has been completed except for Chapter 6 processes. The relevant date for those processes to come within IPC[48] is 1 November 1995, applications to be made between that date and 31 January 1996.

The core of the IPC process is the authorisation and its associated procedure. Section 6(1) of the 1990 Act states that no person shall carry on a prescribed process after the date determined by regulations for that description of process ... except under an authorisation granted by the enforcing authority and in accordance with any conditions. The 'carrying on' of a business, and therefore possibly of a process, is considered to require both a repetition or series of acts,[49] and that the person carrying it on has control and direction over it.[50] Section 1(9) provides that 'authorisation' means an authorisation for a process (whether on premises or by means of mobile plant) granted under section 6; and a reference to the conditions of an authorisation is a reference to the conditions subject to which at any time the authorisation has effect. The procedures for the grant of an authorisation are found in sections 6 to 8 and Schedule 1 of the Act and the Environmental Protection (Applications, Appeals and Registers) Regulations 1991.[51]

Application

The application for authorisation under section 6 is, by regulation 2(1), to be in writing and must contain:

(a) the name, address and telephone number of the applicant (if a body corporate, its registered office);
(b) except in the case of mobile plant –
   (i) the name of the local authority;
   (ii) the address of the premises where the prescribed process will be carried on;
   (iii) a map or plan showing the location of the premises;
   (iv) if only part of the premises is to be so used, a plan or other means of identifying that part;
(c) in the case of mobile plant –
   (i) the name of the local authority for the area where the applicant has his principal place of business;
   (ii) the address of his principal place of business;
(d) a description of the prescribed process;
(e) a list of prescribed substances to be used or resulting from the process;
(f) a description of mitigation techniques;
(g) details of proposed releases of substances and an assessment of their environmental consequences;
(h) proposals for monitoring the release and the environmental consequences of such substances and techniques in (f) above;
(i) matters relied on to acheive section 7(2) objectives, and an assurance that the applicant will comply with the section 7(4) general condition;
(j) any additional information the applicant wishes the enforcing authority to take into account in considering his application.

Special substituted provisions for (d) to (i) apply to applications for the burning of waste oil.[52] The section 7(2) objectives are:

48 DoE, 'Integrated Pollution Control : A Practical Guide', (1993), p.28.

49 *Smith* v *Anderson* (1880) 15 Ch D 247, CA, at pp.277 and 278.

50 *Lewis* v *Graham* (1888) 22 QBD 1, CA, at p.5.

51 S.I.1991 No. 507; and see HMIP booklet, *Application Form for an Authorisation under IPC and Guidance to Applicants for Authorisation.*

52 Regulation 2(3); defined in regulation 2(4) as 'mineral based lubricating or industrial oil which has become unfit for its intended use ... and is generated only as a result of activities carried out by the applicant on the premises where the process is to be carried on'.

(a) ensuring that, in carrying on a prescribed process, the best available techniques not entailing excessive cost[53] will be used –

    (i) for preventing the release of substances prescribed for any environmental medium into that medium or, where that is not practicable by such means, for reducing the release of such substances to a minimum and for rendering harmless any such substances which are so released; and

    (ii) for rendering harmless any other substances which might cause harm if released into any environmental medium;[54]

(b) compliance with any directions by the Secretary of State given for the implementation of any obligations of the United Kingdom under the Community Treaties or international law relating to environmental protection;

(c) compliance with any limits or requirements and achievement of any quality standards or quality objectives prescribed by the Secretary of State under any of the relevant enactments;

(d) compliance with any requirements applicable to the grant of authorisations specified by or under a plan made by the Secretary of State under section 3(5).

These objectives, to be covered in the application, are also, by section 7(1)(a), the subject matter of conditions attached to the authorisation by the enforcing authority. In many cases, therefore, a thoughtfully prepared application may, to some degree, influence the content of the final conditions. In addition to any conditions imposed by the enforcing authority, section 7(4) attaches to every authorisation the standard implied condition that,

> in carrying on the process to which the authorisation applies, the person carrying it on must use the best available techniques not entailing excessive cost –
>
> (a) for preventing the release of substances prescribed for any environmental medium into that medium or, where that is not practicable by such means, for reducing the release of such substances to a minimum and for rendering harmless any such substances which are so released; and
>
> (b) for rendering harmless any other substances which might cause harm if released into any environmental medium.

An application also requires the payment of the stipulated fees, the Secretary of State having established a charging scheme to meet the costs of 'relevant expenditure attributable to authorisations'.[55] The scheme has three categories of charges:

(a) *an application fee,* to cover the costs of considering each IPC application;

(b) *a subsistence charge,* payable annually, for the holding of each IPC authorisation, to cover the ongoing costs of inspection, monitoring and enforcement;

(c) *a substantial variation fee,* to cover the costs of considering an application for substantial variation of an authorisation.[56]

Fees are charged on a flat-rate basis related to the number of components that a process contains, thus being linked to the amount of regulatory effort involved. Failure to pay the charge due may lead, following notice, to revocation of the authorisation.

Having submitted an application, the applicant is required[57] to advertise the fact in a local newspaper circulating in the area within a period of 28 days beginning 14 days after the date of the application. The advertisement is to contain details of the application, the process to be authorised and notification of the right to make representations to the enforcing authority. Similar information relevant

---

53 See above at p.45 for an explanation of this term.

54 Section 1(2) of the Act provides that 'The environment consists of all, or any, of the following media, namely, the air, water and land; and the medium of air includes the air within buildings and the air within other natural or man-made structures above or below ground'.

55 Defined in section 8(7) of the Environmental Protection Act 1990; and see HMIP, Integrated Pollution Control Fees and Charges Scheme (England and Wales) 1992.

56 Taken from DoE 'Integrated Pollution Control: A Practical Guide' (1993), p.17 (The Green Book).

57 Regulation 5; this requirement does not apply to mobile plant or to other limited exceptions specified in the regulation

to the application, subject to the confidentiality limitation, is to be placed on a publicly accessible register. Consequent representations are to be made within 28 days of the date of the advertisement.[58]

Authorisation procedure

Following receipt of an application the enforcing authority has a period of 14 days within which to notify the statutory consultees,[59] who then have a further 28 days from receipt of the notification within which to respond.[60] The consultees are, by regulation 4(1):

(a) Health and Safety Executive in all cases;
(b) Minister of Agriculture, Fisheries and Food in the case of all processes for central control in England;
(c) Secretary of State for Wales in the case of all processes for central control in Wales;
(d) Secretary of State for Scotland in the case of all processes for central control in Scotland;
(e) NRA for prescribed processes which may result in the release of any substance into controlled waters;
(f) sewerage undertaker for prescribed processes for central control which may involve the release of any substance into a sewer vested in the undertaker or local authority;
(g) Nature Conservancy Council for –
   (i) prescribed processes for central control involving the release of any substance;
   (ii) prescribed processes for local control involving release of any substance into the air;
(h) the harbour authority in the case of all prescribed processes for central control which may involve the release of any substance into their harbour(s).

In determining the application the enforcing authority is then required to consider any representations made by persons so consulted and by those responding to the advertisement.[61]

The Secretary of State has the discretion in respect of any particular application or class of applications, to direct the enforcing authority to transmit the application to him for determination.[62] In such cases he may, or if requested by either party as provided by regulation 8 shall, either cause a local enquiry to be held or afford the parties a hearing. On determining the application the Secretary of State shall then direct the enforcing authority whether to grant the application and as to the conditions to be attached to the authorisation.

The consultation process inevitably adds to the time for consideration of an application. Generally, therefore, the period allowed, which may be extended by agreement between the parties, is four months.[63] Where the applicant claims that the application contains details affecting commercial confidentiality or national security the period will be four months from the day on which that claim was finally determined.[64] If the authority fails to determine the application within the stipulated period the applicant may, on giving notice to the authority, treat the application as having been refused, permitting him to commence the appeals procedure.

An application having been made, the enforcing authority is required by section 6(3) either to grant the authorisation subject to the section 7 conditions, dis-

58 Schedule 1, paragraph 2(6)(b).

59 Schedule 1, paragraph 2(1) and 4.

60 Schedule 1, paragraph 2(6)(a).

61 Schedule 1, paragraph 2(3) and (5).

62 Schedule 1, paragraph 3 and Regulation 8.

63 Schedule 1, paragraph 5(1).

64 Environmental Protection (Authorisation of Processes)(Determination Periods) Order 1991, S.I. 1991 No. 513; claims on these grounds may, by regulation 7 of the 1991 Regulations, apply to directions by the Secretary of State under section 21(2), notices under section 21(4), applications under section 22(2) and objections under section 22(4).

cussed below, or to refuse it. The reason for refusal, in section 6(4), is stated to be that the authority considers the applicant will not be able to comply with the conditions. The clear implication is that the conditions are to be tailored primarily to environmental objectives rather than to the circumstances of the applicant, notwithstanding the 'excessive cost' limitation. The judgment in *Gateshead MBC v Secretary of State for the Environment and Northumbria Water Group plc* (1994)[65] emphasises this approach in noting that the section 6(4) power 'did not otherwise derogate from HMIP's power to refuse authorisation if they considered that the release of a particular substance would do 'harm' as defined by the Act'.[66] The learned deputy judge found further support for this view in the section 4(2) stipulation that the functions of the chief inspector were to be exercised 'for the purpose of preventing or minimising pollution of the environment due to the release of substances into any environmental medium'.

The grant of an authorisation shall include the three categories of conditions specified in section 7(1):

(a) such specific conditions as the enforcing authority considers appropriate for achieving the subsection (2) objectives;
(b) conditions specified in directions given by the Secretary of State;
(c) any other conditions appearing to the enforcing authority to be appropriate.

In addition, the general condition in section 7(4) shall be implied into every authorisation.[67] According to the Green Book these conditions may, 'among other matters, relate to the method of operation, the training of staff and abatement techniques used to reduce the release of substances'. Tromans suggests[68] in relation to (b) above, that directions may specify conditions that are not to be included as well as those that are; the power thus being available to prevent an enforcing authority from including unjustified or irrelevant conditions. While the scope for attaching conditions is clearly very wide it may be that in some, or indeed most, cases they will not be sufficiently comprehensive to cover every possible eventuality. The inclusion of the standard implied condition requiring BATNEEC to prevent, minimise or render harmless releases into the environment is designed to meet any such prospective deficiency. Commenting on its operation, the Green Book says[69]:

> The implied condition is designed to cover the most detailed level of plant design and operation, where only the operator can reasonably be expected to know and understand what the demands of pollution control require in practice. For this reason, the Act provides that in any proceedings for an offence or failure to comply with the implied condition, the onus of proving that the operator was in fact using BATNEEC (and thus complying with the implied condition) falls on the operator himself.

The main steps in the application procedure for an authorisation are presented diagramatically in the Green Book as shown in Figure 2.1.

Subsequent changes

An authorisation having been granted, two significant changes may occur during its lifetime. Where the operation of a prescribed process is transferred to another person, section 9 of the 1990 Act requires that person to notify the enforcing authority of the fact within 21 days of the transfer. The authorisation, with the same conditions, then applies as if granted to that person under section 6. Failure to give such notice is an offence actionable summarily or on indictment.[70] The

65 [1994] JPL 255.

66 At p.261. 'Harm' is defined in section 1(4) to mean harm 'to the health of living organisms or other interference with the ecological systems of which they form part and, in the case of man, includes offence caused to any of his senses or harm to his property'.

67 For section 7(2) and (4) conditions see requirements of the application above

68 *The Environmental Protection Act 1990: Text and Commentary,* (London: Sweet & Maxwell, 1991).

69 At paragraph 6.6.

70 Section 23(1)(b) and (3)of the Environmental Protection Act 1990.

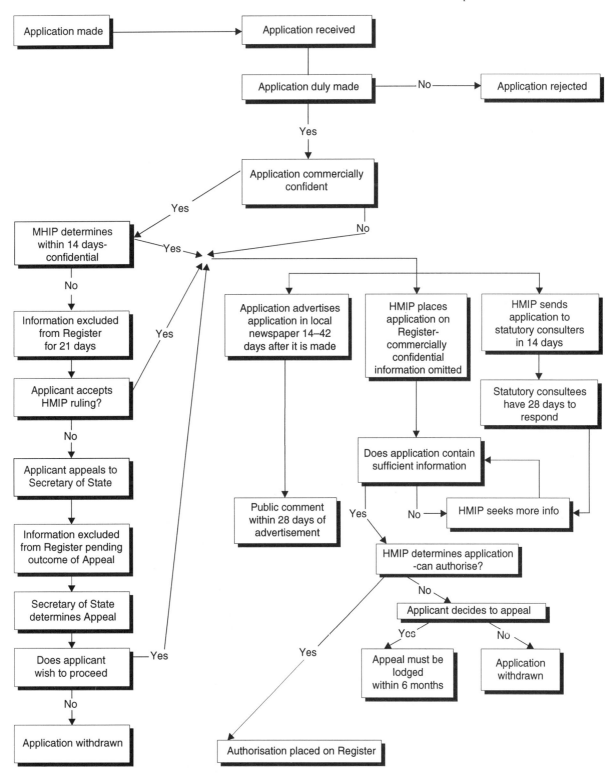

Figure 2.1 Application procedure from the Green Book

authority is given no discretion to object to the transfer, although it retains the general range of enforcement powers in the event of breach of conditions or other deficiencies in operation.

The authorisation sanctions the operation of the process in the terms of the original application. The enforcing authority has a duty, by section 6(6), to review periodically and at least every four years the conditions attaching to authorisations. Whenever the authority considers that conditions need to be changed, in particular to continue to secure compliance with the section 7 objectives, it shall serve a 'variation notice' on the holder notifying him of the proposed changes and the date or dates when they shall take effect. The notice shall also require the holder of the authorisation to notify the authority, within the stipulated time, of the action he proposes to take (if required) to meet the new requirements, and to pay any necessary fees. The enforcing authority is also required[71] to so inform the holder if it considers that the action by him to meet the terms of the variation notice will 'involve a substantial change in the manner in which the process is carried on'. Substantial change in this context 'means a substantial change in the substances released from the process or in the amount or any other characteristic of any substance so released'.[72] The DoE guide provides that, subject to any relevant guidance note 'change will generally be regarded as substantial if it results in an increase in the rate, concentration or absolute quantity of a prescribed substance released'. In such cases the provisions of Schedule 1, paragraph 6 apply requiring, as with the original application, advertising by the holder of the proposals and notification by the enforcing authority of prescribed consultees, with consideration of their responses.

The holder of an authorisation may himself seek variation of its conditions in the range of circumstances found in section 11. Where he wishes to make a 'relevant change' he may notify the enforcing authority and ask for its determination of the section 11(2) matters.[73] The authority shall then determine what effect the proposals may have on the operation of the process and on the existing authorisation conditions, and in consequence what changes, if any, should be approved. Having been notified by the authority of its conclusions the holder may then, if he chooses, apply for a variation in those terms. Alternatively, where the holder considers that a relevant change is needed requiring a variation of the authorisation conditions, he may, by section 11(6), apply to the authority for such a variation. In that case a prior determination is not required. In both cases if the authority considers that substantial change is involved necessitating changed conditions, similar steps to those required under section 10 above are required[74] preparatory to the variation.

Where a change to the conditions not involving a relevant change is considered by the holder to be necessary, he may apply for a variation under section 11(5) and the advertising and consultation requirements do not apply. A relevant change for this purpose[75] 'is a change in the manner of carrying on the process which is capable of altering the substances released from the process or of affecting the amount or any other characteristic of any substance so released'. This definition is wide enough to include all 'substantial change' within section 10(7), and in consequence requires advertising and consultation procedures comparable to those for the original procedure, which are not needed for a section 11(5) application.

Enforcing authorities have a general power in section 12(1) to revoke an authorisation, and a similar specific power in section 12(2) where they believe that the

71 By section 10(5).

72 Section 10(7); guidance on what constitutes substantial change for any particular class of process will be included in the relevant Chief Inspector's guidance note.

73 Section 11(1).

74 Schedule 1, paragraph 7.

75 Section 11(11).

authorised process has not been carried on for at least 12 months. In this latter case 28 days' notice of the revocation is required. In the operation of these powers of variation, revocation and the following powers of enforcement the Secretary of State is given powers of direction in particular cases.

Enforcement

The enforcement powers available to an authority consist of 'enforcement notices' under section 13 where the authority considers that an authorisation condition is, or is about to be, contravened and 'prohibition notices' under section 14 where the authority believes that the carrying on of a prescribed process, or the carrying of it on in a particular manner, 'involves an imminent risk of serious pollution of the environment'. Commenting on this last requirement Sir Frank Layfield QC[76] suggests that

> having regard to the definitions of 'pollution' and 'harm', in Part I, [is] whether the risk is one capable of causing harm to man or his property, other living organisms, or supporting ecological systems. The use of the word 'imminent' suggests that a high degree of urgency in the need for preventive action should be evident.

In both cases the notices shall state the authority's opinion, the contravention or the ground of the risk, the necessary remedial work and the period within which it is to be completed. In the latter case the notice shall also state that until the notice is withdrawn the authorisation shall cease to have effect to the extent specified, i.e. prohibiting the continuation of the offending part of the process. The terms of section 14 make it clear that the prohibition notice is not confined to breaches of condition. Even though a process may be operated properly and within the imposed conditions, emergency circumstances may arise, for instance the serious reduction of diluting water in a river due to drought conditions, that create the imminent risk of serious pollution warranting the issue of the notice.

Section 23 of the Act specifies a range of offences, essentially constituting failures to comply with the various obligations imposed by the IPC structure. Such offences are actionable either summarily or on indictment, and subject to the penalties stipulated in section 23(2) to (4). If the authority considers, in the case of non-compliance with an enforcement or prohibition notice, that those proceedings afford an ineffectual remedy, it may take proceedings in the High Court. Criminal proceedings may be ineffectual where, for example, the penalties would not serve as an effective deterrent or where they would entail excessive delay. The alternative is therefore civil proceedings for an injunction, including, if the circumstances require, interlocutory relief.[77]

In particular cases punishment or prohibition may not provide a sufficiently comprehensive solution to the harm[78] caused by the offence. In such cases the court is given the power, by section 26, as well as or instead of imposing any punishment, to order the person convicted of carrying on a prescribed process without authorisation or in breach of a condition, or with contravention of an enforcement or prohibition notice, to remedy those matters. The heading to the section speaks of remedying the cause of the offence. The division between the cause and the consequences of an offence may be difficult to determine, however. Is, for instance, the ponding of noxious effluent on land the cause of an offence or the consequence of it? That aside, it is to be noted that the scope of the order is limited to the subject matter of the conviction. It is also restricted to those

76 'The Environmental Protection Act 1990: the System of Integrated Pollution Control' [1992] JPL 3 at p.9.

77 For the principles for obtaining injunctions in these circumstances see *Hammersmith LBC v Magnum Automated Forecourts* [1978] 1 WLR 50; principles for the grant of interlocutory relief are to be found in *American Cyanamid Co. v Ethicon* [1975] AC 396.

78 Section 1(4) 'harm' means harm to the health of living organisms or other interference with the ecological systems of which they form part and, in the case of man, includes offence caused to any of his senses or harm to his property.

matters that it is within the power of the person convicted to remedy. This second specific restriction may envisage the use of the power to clear up the consequences of the offence, recognising, for example, that the offender will have no right to follow the pollutants onto adjoining land.

As well as this power of the court to order the remedying of such matters, section 27 gives the chief inspector the power to take reasonable steps to remedy harm derived from the same offences as covered by section 26, and to recover the costs. While the use of this power is not necessarily linked to a conviction, the recovery of costs is. The exercise of this power requires the written approval of the Secretary of State and, if to be undertaken on land in other occupation, the permission of that occupier. This section, specifically referring to the chief inspector, does not extend to local authorities, although there appears to be nothing to prevent the chief inspector from using this power to remedy harm deriving from both centrally and locally controlled processes.

These enforcement provisions necessitate extensive regulatory and policing powers by the enforcing authorities. For this purpose section 16(1) and (6) provide for the appointment of inspectors respectively by the Secretary of State for HMIP and by local authorities. Section 17 then confers wide powers on such inspectors in respect of premises on which prescribed processes are being carried on, or on which they have been carried on and the condition of which is such as to give rise to a risk of serious pollution of the environment. What is a 'serious risk' is of course a matter of fact and degree in each case. Three principal factors in this assessment are, however, likely to be the volume of pollutant emitted related to the concentration or toxicity of the polluting material and the vulnerability of the environmental medium receiving it.

Powers of inspectors, subject to specific controls and limitations in the section, include[79] power of entry on production (if required) of an authority, examination, investigation, questioning of personnel, access to records and the right to demand any necessary assistance. An inspector may also take measurements, photographs and samples. Additional powers apply to articles or substances believed to have caused or to be likely to cause pollution of the environment, governing their seizure, testing and sampling. It is specifically provided that any answers given in response to questioning within these provisions are inadmissible in evidence against that person[80] but not, it would appear, against the employer. Where an inspector finds on the premises inspected an article or a substance which he has reasonable cause to believe 'is a cause of imminent danger of serious harm he may seize it and cause it to be rendered harmless (whether by destruction or otherwise)'.[81] The scope of 'serious harm' is not explicitly restricted to the environment and may conceivably therefore extend to employees on the premises or consumers of the product. Whether the term will be given the limited construction derived from its statutory context remains to be seen. Prior to any necessary treatment, and if practicable, a sample of the material is to be given to the responsible person at the premises. After the action the inspector is to prepare a written, signed report of the circumstances and give a copy to the responsible person at the premises and, if they are different, to the owner of the substance.

Appeals

Rights of appeal to the Secretary of State are given to the operator against[82]:

79 Section 17(3)(a) to (l).

80 Section 17(8).

81 Section 18(1).

82 By section 15(1) and (2) and section 22(5).

(a) refusal of an authorisation;

(b) refusal of a variation of an authorisation;

(c) conditions attached to an authorisation;

(d) revocation of an authorisation;

(e) variation, enforcement and prohibition notices;

(f) determination that information is not commercially confidential.

Generally the exercise of a right of appeal does not affect or delay the action appealed against. The exceptions are appeals against a revocation which is suspended during the appeal[83] and appeals against a determination that information is not commercially confidential which prevents the entry of the information in the register.[84] The rules governing appeals are found in section 15 of the Act and in the Environmental Protection (Applications, Appeals and Registers) Regulations 1991.[85] By regulation 10(1) the time limits for appeals are, for (a) to (c), six months from the date of the decision; for (d), the date on which it is to take effect; for (e), two months from the date of the notice; for (f), 21 days from the date of the notice of determination.

The procedure contained in the Regulations requires the appellant to send a notice of appeal to the Secretary of State with the documents specified in regulation 9(2)(a) – (f) and to send a copy of the notice to the enforcing authority. That authority shall then notify specified 'interested parties', comparable with but not identical to the statutory consultees, and convey their responses to the Secretary of State. In making the appeal, the appellant must state his preference for its determination on written representations or by a hearing. A hearing will be held if either party asks for it, or if the Secretary of State decides that a hearing is more appropriate. The hearing procedure is specified in regulation 13, which provides[86] that the persons entitled to be heard are the appellant, the enforcing authority and the 'interested parties'. The person holding the hearing is also given the power[87] to permit 'any other person to be heard at the hearing and such permission shall not be unreasonably withheld'. Following the conclusion of the hearing the Secretary of State shall notify the appellant of his determination of the appeal and provide him with a copy of the report of the person holding the hearing.

Registers

In association with the IPC process and in accordance with the EC Directive on Freedom of Access to Information on the Environment[88] a system of public registers of information is provided for in section 20 of the Act. Registers are to be maintained by enforcing authorities and, by regulation 15 of the 1991 Regulations, shall contain all the information and contents of documents coming into the possession of the authority in connection with each authorisation or application. They may be in any form and shall be open to public inspection free of charge at all reasonable times; copying facilities are also to be available but subject to reasonable charges.

Because of their public nature there is provision for the exclusion of matters affecting national security[89] and commercial confidentiality[90] from the register. The question of what information or categories of information is or are contrary to the interests of national security is a matter for the Secretary of State, who may give directions to enforcing authorities to secure its or their exclusion. Commercially confidential information shall only be included on the register with the consent of

83 Section 15(8).

84 Section 22(5)(b).

85 S.I.1991 No. 507.

86 In regulation 13(6).

87 By regulation 13(7).

88 Directive 90/313/EEC; see above at p.15.

89 Section 21.

90 Section 22.

the person affected. What information is commercially confidential is a question initially for the enforcing authority and ultimately, on appeal, for the Secretary of State. The relevant DoE News Release[91] indicates that the Government will look sceptically at such claims. The Draft Guidance issued with the News Release stated that the Secretary of State

> will require cogent and specific evidence to substantiate the claim that disclosure would prejudice to an unreasonable degree some person's commercial interests. This would need to demonstrate that disclosure of information would negate or significantly diminish the commercial advantage that one operator has over another. ... Arguments based on general claims, for instance, that disclosure might damage the reputation of the operator and hence his commercial competitiveness, are unlikely to be given weight. Where information is withheld from the register, the register will indicate that there has been an omission.

Categories of information that may be excluded from these registers[92] are monitoring information more than four years old and any superceded information more than four years after it has been superceded.

Conclusions

In conclusion, the proposals in the Draft Directive on Integrated Pollution Prevention and Control (IPPC)[93] that are likely to have the greatest impact on United Kingdom practice may be noted. The significance, and implications, in this context of the change in nomenclature is in itself worthy of thought. Authorisations will have a 10-year review period, in contrast to the United Kingdom maximum of four years. While that shorter period may be retained, the perceived disadvantages, for instance in relation to competition, may generate pressure from industry for conformity with Community practice. United Kingdom practice gives to the enforcing authority discretion to determine 'substantial change'. The proposal is that it will hereafter relate to a formula increase of more than 5 per cent in the rate of emissions. Two entirely new proposals, rather than mere changes of scale, are the inclusion of noise emissions in the IPC process and the requirement that persons seeking authorisations shall state and explain the steps to be taken on 'the permanent cessation of the operation of the installation'. This latter requirement reflects the similar obligation on applicants for waste management licences under Part II of the Act.

Environmental Impact Assessment

As was said in the introduction to this section, with the experience of a century or so of pollution control, it is possible to anticipate that the establishment of a particular activity or operation will have certain inevitable forms of impact on its surroundings. By requiring a statement of such environmental consequences it is possible to assess their effect and therefore determine whether the project should be permitted, either in its original or in a revised form. The virtue of anticipating and, as far as practicable, resolving the environmental consequences of harmful activities before they commence is a primary reason for Environmental Impact Assessment (EIA). Its purposes, more fully, may be said to be:

(a) to ensure consideration of the likely environmental effects of possible schemes so that decisions can be made with a knowledge of their environmental consequences, including –

91 DoE News Release No. 56 (30 January 1990).

92 By regulation 17.

93 COM (93) 230; proposed operation deadline of 30.6.1995.

(i) deciding whether or not to proceed with the scheme,
(ii) identification of ways in which environmental effects could be minimised,
(iii) assessment of the importance of predicted effects,
(iv) evaluation of scope for mitigation;
(b) To allow public/statutory authorities to consider and comment on the environmental implications of the proposals.

Local planning authorities (LPAs), under United Kingdom planning law, already had the power to require information on the likely environmental effects of an application,[94] and to have regard to such matters in exercising their planning powers.[95] However, the concept of prior assessment and the principles of its operation were established as a distinct process by the implementation of EC Directive 85/337/EEC on the assessment of the effects of certain public and private projects on the environment, to be introduced by Member States by 2 July 1988. The option adopted by the United Kindom Government of linking the procedure to the existing planning process was implemented in the Town and Country Planning (Assessment of Environmental Effects) Regulations 1988,[96] regulation 4(2) providing that 'the local planning authority or Secretary of State shall not grant planning permission to an application to which these regulations apply unless they have first taken environmental information into consideration'. The regulations further state[97] that:

environmental information means the environmental statement prepared by the applicant, any representations made by any body required by these regulations to be invited to make representations or be consulted and any representations made by any other person about the likely environmental effects of the proposed development.

As Christopher Wood notes,[98] 'EIA should, therefore, be seen as an environmental management tool within the land use planning process: as an instrument for achieving an environmentally desirable goal'. While this structure has all the advantages associated with the use of an existing and familiar procedure, its obvious disadvantage is that assessment is thereby confined to those new or extended developments that require planning approval according to existing, non-environmental principles.

Assessment requirement

The requirement for an environmental statement, which may be regarded as the end-product of the EIA process, may occur in five circumstances:

(a) mandatory assessments for projects listed in Annex I of the Directive and Schedule 1 of the Regulations;
(b) assessments at the discretion of the LPA for projects listed in Annex II of the Directive and Schedule 2 of the Regulations;
(c) voluntary assessments at the discretion of the applicant;
(d) projects under other specific statutory provisions, see e.g., section 105A of the Highways Act 1980 applicable to roads and bridges;
(e) major development projects promoted through the Parliamentary Private Bill procedure.

Evidently the first two categories are the most important, if only by volume. Projects within these categories are as follows:

94 See, e.g., Town and Country Planning (Applications) Regulations 1988 (S.I.1988 No. 1812), regulation 4.

95 See, e.g., Town and Country Planning Act 1971, sections 7(3), 11, 51(1), 65(1).

96 S.I. 1988 No. 1199, amended by the Town and Country Planning (Assessment of Environmental Effects)(Amendment) Regulations 1992, S.I. 1992 No. 1494.

97 In regulation 2

98 Op. cit. at note 24, at p.313.

Annex I and Schedule 1 projects
Projects requiring an assessment:

1. Crude-oil refineries, including gasification and liquefaction of coal.
2. Thermal power stations and other combustion installations with a heat output of more than 300 megawatts, nuclear power stations and reactors.
3. Installations solely designed for the permanent storage or final disposal of radioactive waste.
4. Integrated works for the initial melting of cast-iron and steel.
5. Installations for the extraction, processing and transformation of asbestos and asbestos products; with annual maxima of –
   asbestos–cement products   20,000 tonnes of finished products
   friction material   50 tonnes of finished material
   other asbestos uses   200 tonnes of asbestos
6. Integrated chemical installations.
7. Construction of motorways, express roads, long distance railway lines and airport runways of more than 2,100m.
8. Trading ports and inland waterways and ports taking vessels of more than 1,350 tonnes.
9. Waste disposal installations for the incineration, chemical treatment or land fill of toxic and dangerous waste.

Annex II and Schedule 2 projects
Projects subject to discretionary statements; specified activities within the following categories (with a brief synopsis of each class):

1. Agriculture, including associated water-management and land reclamation from the sea; salmon farming; poultry and pig-rearing.
2. Extractive industry, including mining and quarrying operations; deep drilling; fossil fuel, mineral ores and peat extraction; coke ovens; cement manufacture.
3. Energy industry, non-nuclear thermal power stations; hydro-electric production; storage of gas and fossil fuels; briquetting of coals; movement of gas, steam or electricity; production, reprocessing, collection of nuclear fuels not within Schedule 1.
4. Processing of metals, including production, large casting and treatment of iron, steel and non-ferrous (other than precious) metals; boilermaking etc.; motor-vehicle manufacture, shipyards.
5. Manufacture of glass.
6. Chemical industry, including treatment of intermediate products; production of chemicals, pesticides, pharmaceuticals, paints, elastomers or peroxides.
7. Food industry, including slaughterhouses; manufacture or processing of oils or fats, dairy products, confectionery, industrial starch, sugar and fish-meal or oil; brewing or malting.
8. Textile, leather, wood and paper industries, including wool processing; manufacture of pulp, paper, board; fibre-dyeing; cellulose-processing; tannery.
9. Rubber industry, manufacture and treatment of elastomer-based products.
10. Infrastructure projects, including industrial estate or urban development projects; construction of road, harbour, aerodrome not within Schedule 1, dams and water storage, railways and tramways, oil or gas pipelines, yacht marina; flood relief works.

11. Other projects, including holiday or hotel complex; vehicle racing or test track; treatment or disposal of wastes; scrap iron storage; engine or reactor testing; manufacture of artificial mineral fibres; manufacture etc., of explosives; knacker's yard.

12. Modifications to development projects included in Annex I and projects in Annex I undertaken exclusively or mainly for the development and testing of new methods or products and not used for more than one year.

13. Schedule 1 processes established for up to one year and used exclusively or mainly for development or testing new methods or products.

14. A wind generator.

15. A motorway service area; and

16. Coast protection works.[99]

In those circumstances the local planning authority has the power or duty to ask for the submission of an environmental statement with the planning application. In spite of the general presumption in favour of development,[100] the decision not to ask for a statement, implying that the project will have no significant impact on the environment, does not thereby carry with it the presumption that planning permission will necessarily be granted, paragraph 38 of the DoE Circular[101] stating that a 'decision not to require assessment in a particular case carries no implication that planning permission will or should be granted for the development'.

In the case of Schedule 2 projects the exercise of the LPA's discretion relates to those that are 'likely to have significant effects on the environment by virtue of factors such as their nature, size or location'. The interpretation of 'significant' is therefore – significant. As Steven Mertz[102] points out, this concept introduces an element of circularity to the system in that while the need for an environmental statement depends on the likely significance of the project's environmental impact, a major reason for its production is to determine the significance of that impact. However, without the preliminary perception its validity could scarcely be tested by later detailed investigation. Guidance from the DoE on its meaning is very general and in seeking to clarify the original term introduces new areas of uncertainty. Paragraph 19 of the Circular relates 'significant environmental effects' to the content of Schedule 3 of the Regulations specifying the type of information that may be required in an environmental statement. The Department of Transport Manual for Roads and Bridges[103] suggests that:

'Significant' may be determined by –

(a) relative scale of importance – national, regional, county, local
(b) degree to which the environment is affected e.g. quality enhanced or impaired
(c) scale of change – land area, size of population, degree of change; and scale of change resulting from cumulative impacts
(d) temporary or permanent effect and if temporary, the duration
(e) degree of possible mitigation.

Also, in relation to 'significant effects', paragraph 20 of the DoE Circular states that an assessment will, in the Secretary of State's view, be needed for three main types of Schedule 2 projects:

(a) major projects which are of more than local importance;
(b) occasionally for projects on a smaller scale which are proposed for particularly sensitive or vulnerable locations; and

99 Town and Country Planning (Assessment of Environment Effects) (Amendment) Regulations 1994 No.677

100 See DoE Circulars 22/80, 15/84, 14/85.

101 DoE Circular 15/88, Welsh Office Circular 23/88.

102 The European Economic Community Directive on Environmental Assessments: How will it affect United Kingdom Developers? 1989 JPL p.483.

103 Volume 11, section 2, chapter 1.

(c) in a small number of cases, for projects with unusually complex and potentially adverse environmental effects.

The general nature of many of the terms used here has the potential to create as many problems as it resolves.

The broad scope of these three categories is, however, the subject of paragraphs 22–29 of the Circular. For example 'projects which are of more than local importance' will clearly include large scale operations such as mining and large manufacturing plants; for which, in fact, voluntary submissions have become increasingly common. Further guidance on the Government's approach, and incidentally its concern to reduce the costs necessarily attendant on the procedure, is to be gained from the Nottingham decision.[104] The DoE decided on appeal that no environmental statement was required for a retail park of 200,000 square feet consisting of restaurants, housing, leisure facilities, an hotel, and a car park, the LPA having considered that it amounted to an 'urban development project' within Schedule 2. It also noted its large scale and its location on a major motorway approach to the city. Further, that part was high rise (therefore having significant visual impact), it required traffic flow alterations and adversely affected geological features. The DoE accepted that the proposal amounted to an 'urban development project' within Schedule 2 but considered that there would be no sufficiently significant environmental effects to warrant the production of an environmental statement.

A further phrase used in the Regulations, in particular in Schedule 3, without definition or explanation is 'direct or indirect' effects. Paragraph 2(c), for example, requires 'a description of the likely significant effects, direct and indirect, on the environment of the development'. One is led to conclude by the very fact of the distinction that this classification is on the basis of impacts that are either immediate, that is stemming from the development itself, or at one or more places removed, that is consequential on an effect itself derived from the development. Until decisions have been made, and challenged, there is little available assistance in this jurisdiction to clarify the distinction. Experience of environmental assessment in the United States, though, extends from 1970, and the question was considered in a note in the Wisconsin Law Review in the following terms[105]:

> [s]econdary, or indirect, impacts include the socio-economic and environmental impacts of a proposed action which are not immediately realised. The construction of a highway, for example, might cause such secondary impacts as increased air pollution from automobile exhaust, increases in population density, accelerated commercial development and strains on sewer and water systems leading to increased water pollution. Socio-economic factors such as local employment levels, availability of public services and crime rates may also be affected. The primary, or direct, impact of the highway would include the immediate physical impacts of the project such as tree removal, land levelling, destruction of wet lands or interference with natural water flow.

General guidance on the approach to be adopted by LPAs in deciding on the need for a statement, in *R v Swale BC ex parte RSPB* (1991),[106] suggests that:

(a) The decision whether any particular development was or was not within the scheduled descriptions was exclusively for the planning authority in question, subject only to *Wednesbury* challenge. Questions of classification were essentially questions of fact and degree, not of law.

(b) The question fell strictly to be asked in relation to the planning application rather than the permission being granted, assuming the latter to be materially

104 *Planning*, 16–23 September 1988.

105 May/June 1986; and see Steven Mertz, *op. cit.* p.488.

106 JPL 39.

different. It would always be open to a planning authority to invite the applicants to submit a lesser application if that was all it was minded to grant and if that would then make an environmental assessment unnecessary.

(c) The question whether or not the development was of a category described in either schedule had to be answered strictly in relation to the development applied for, not any development contemplated beyond that. But the further question arising in respect of Schedule 2 development, the question whether it 'would be likely to have significant effects on the environment by virtue of factors such as its nature, size or location', should be answered differently. The proposal should not then be considered in isolation if in reality it was properly to be regarded as an integral part of an inevitably more substantial development; ... developers could otherwise defeat the object of the regulations by piecemeal development proposals.

Before concluding this consideration of the need for an environmental statement there are two special development contexts to be noted, at either end, as it were, of the 'normal' situation. Paragraph 20 of the DoE Circular referred to above expresses the view that environmental statements should be required for Schedule 2 projects 'for particularly sensitive or vulnerable locations'. Quite how this term should be interpreted is not clear. That it is not synonymous with specially designated areas is apparent from paragraph 24 of the Circular which states only 'that consideration should be given' to the need for environmental assessment where a Schedule 2 project is likely to have significant effects on the special character of a protected area or site, such as a national park or area of outstanding natural beauty. Paragraph 27 adds that there should be no automatic presumption that environmental assessment will be necessary merely because the proposal relates to such an area, emphasising that in this context they are to receive no special consideration. At the other extreme there are enterprise zones and simplified planning zones, created to stimulate development in economically depressed areas by, among other things, deregulating and simplifying planning procedures. In both types of zone individual planning applications are not required for the classes of development specified in the scheme. Nevertheless, in its relevant Circular[107] the DoE states that for special zones created since July 1988 such general approval should not be granted for any project to which EIA applies.

A prospective applicant who is in doubt about the need for an environmental statement may ask the LPA for a written opinion whether the proposed development is within Schedule 1 or Schedule 2 and, if within Schedule 2, whether a statement will be required.[108] Regulation 8 also makes provision for preliminary notification by an applicant, with certain necessary information, of his intention to submit an environmental statement with a planning application. Conversely, where LPAs receive a planning application which they consider to be within Schedule 1 or 2 and it is not accompanied by a statement, they shall within three weeks notify the applicant of the requirement 'giving their full reasons for their view clearly and precisely'.[109]

A statement being required, or volunteered, its content is a matter of discretion for the LPA, subject only to its containing sufficient information for the decision. Schedule 3, paragraph 2 of the 1988 Regulations does, however, identify the 'specified information' to be provided 'for the purpose of assessing the likely impact upon the environment of the development proposed to be carried out':

107 DoE, 'Environmental Assessment of Projects in Simplified Planning Zones', 25 November 1988.

108 Regulation 5.

109 Regulation 9(1).

(a) a description of the development proposed, comprising information about the site and the design and size or scale of the development;
(b) the data necessary to identify and assess the main effects which that development is likely to have on the environment;
(c) a description of the likely significant effects, direct and indirect, on the environment of the development, explained by reference to its possible impact on –
  human beings;
  flora;
  fauna;
  soil;
  water;
  air;
  climate;
  the landscape;
  the inter-action between any of the foregoing;
  material assets;
  the cultural heritage;
(d) where significant adverse effects are identified with respect to any of the foregoing, a description of the measures envisaged in order to avoid, reduce or remedy those effects; and
(e) a summary in non-technical language of the information specified above.

It is evident from the foregoing that a statement for even quite a modest project is no light undertaking. The assessment of the possible environmental impact of a new development will in many cases take on the characteristics of peeling an onion without, one hopes, the tears. Beneath or beyond any one level of investigation there are likely to be revealed further effects and consequences awaiting examination. In such cases a developer, as an alternative to drawing an arbitrary line that may be disputed later, is driven to investigate all those revealed levels of impact, however tenuous, long-term or distant they may initially appear. The additional costs both to the applicant and to the LPA in evaluating the result, may be considerable, even though the Circular states,[110] somewhat optimistically, that the Government's aim is 'to ensure that no unnecessary additional burdens are placed on either developers or authorities' and that 'additional costs imposed on developers ... should be kept to a minimum'. In most cases, both for the developer and the authority, a major extra expense will be the costs of engaging specialist consultants to evaluate and assess the impact effects on life forms, geology and soils, cultural and social media, as well as the aesthetic effects. Such expertise is unlikely to be found in-house in most cases.

Evaluation procedure

Having received an application with statement, the LPA has 16 weeks for consideration instead of the normal eight (regulation 16). Within that time, unless extended by agreement, it must evaluate the statement and also consult with certain 'statutory consultees' specified in Article 15 of the General Development Order 1986.[111] These include:

(a) any other principal council for the area;[112]
(b) Countryside Commission;
(c) Nature Conservancy Council;
(d) HMIP, in special cases, i.e. that involve mining, manufacturing or disposal of waste and are likely to involve –

110 Paragraph 8.

111 S.I. 1986 No. 435.

112 'Principal council' is defined in section 270(1) of the Local Government Act 1972.

      (i)   waste requiring authorisation under the Radioactive Substances Act 1993,

     (ii)   controlled or special waste, except domestic sewage,

   (iii)   consent or licence of a water authority,

   (iv)   works specified in Schedule 1 of the Health and Safety (Emissions to Atmosphere) Regulations 1983.[113]

This assessment procedure explicitly incorporates a public contribution, the scope of environmental information to be reviewed by the LPA being so defined. The Regulations[114] therefore provide two procedures for publicising the fact, details, location and availability of the relevant documents, the necessary publicity to be undertaken by the applicant. As with all such public control procedures, the Regulations provide for appeals, in this context to the Secretary of State, against the actions, inactions or decisions of the LPA.[115]

113 S.I. 1983 No. 943.

114 Regulations 12 and 13.

115 See, e.g., regulations 5(6) and 9(1).

3

Statutory Nuisances

GENERAL PRINCIPLES

'Nuisance' is a term of broad popular and narrower legal meaning. In the legal sense, to be considered in more detail below, its function is to reconcile conflicting expectations. A person has a right to live and act as he chooses until such activity impinges unreasonably on the rights of his neighbours to do likewise. In this sense the law of nuisance may be regarded as resolving after the event the problems that planning law attempts to anticipate by separating disparate or mutually irreconcilable activities. The manure manufacturer may not ply his trade next to the prestige executive housing. Where an unreasonable interference with another's property or enjoyment occurs the civil law provides a remedy by injunction and/or damages, should the complainants wish to avail themselves of it. In many cases, though, the person affected may not be able or wish to resort to the civil courts, whether for reasons of cost or otherwise. To meet this deficiency a succession of public health measures, originating with the Public Health Act 1845, has provided an alternative abatement procedure in the criminal law and usually, though not exclusively, by the local authority. The activities proscribed are the statutory nuisances.

The relevant provisions are now found in Part III of the Environmental Protection Act 1990, which identifies certain matters as statutory nuisances and specifies a summary procedure for their abatement. Although now found in a statute concerned with general environmental issues, these provisions originated in public health measures and are still confined to actions causing harm or nuisance to persons rather than to the wider environment.

'Prejudicial to health or a nuisance'

Section 79(1) of the 1990 Act lists those activities constituting a statutory nuisance, the requirement in each case being that they are 'prejudicial to health or a nuisance'.[1] Whether the incident is prejudicial to health is a question of fact to be established by evidence, although it appears that medical or other expert evidence is not necessarily required. In *London Borough of Southwark* v *Ince* (1989)[2] the defence had argued that a finding of prejudice to health did require such expert evidence. Woolf LJ concluded on the facts that the magistrates were justified in reaching a decision on the evidence of the respondent occupiers of the flats alone that the noise complained of had 'adversely and materially affected their health'. Also, in *Wivenhoe Port* v *Colchester BC* (1985), in a different context, Butler J said:

> Whilst there was no medical evidence it was elementary commonsense that dust emanating from dusty cargoes of the kind that were dealt with at the port would be likely to cause injury to health by inhalation, and by irritation of eyes or nose.[3]

1 There is currently one exception: section 141 of the Public Health Act 1936 provides that the specified matters will be a statutory nuisance where they are prejudicial to health only.

2 (1989) 21 HLR 504.

3 [1985] JPL 175 at p. 178.

4 See Public Health Acts 1848, 1860, and 1875, and the Nuisances Removal Act 1855.

The phrase 'prejudicial to health', appearing previously in section 92 of the Public Health Act 1936, replaced the term 'injurious to health' found in earlier statutes[4] and extends the scope of that term, being defined as 'injurious, or likely to cause injury to health'.[5] The phrase has however been limited, at least in its application to section 79(1)(e), to 'something which produces a threat to health in the sense of a threat of disease, vermin or the like' and not to 'inert matter merely because that inert matter may cause physical injury'.[6] On this view the prejudice to health is therefore to be interpreted in the context of a public health statute and is to be a threat to health in the nature of disease or infection rather than physical or accidental harm, of illness rather than danger. The validity of this narrow approach may now be questioned, though.

5 Section 79(7).

6 *Per* Lord Widgery CJ in *Coventry City Council* v *Cartwright* [1975] 2 All ER 99 at pp.102f and 104c.

The meaning of 'nuisance' is a matter of law. It has been argued, however, that 'nuisance' appearing in public health statutes should be coloured by that context and be confined to matters relating to health, disease and so on. For example, in *National Coal Board* v *Neath BC* (1976) Watkins J said[7] 'Not only must a statutory nuisance be either of a private or public kind at common law, but the act of nuisance itself must be such as comes within the spirit of the 1936 Act'. On this same principle, and in spite of what was said initially, it may be expected that the range of nuisance situations embraced by an environmental statute may be wider than those deemed to be within a public health measure. For a full discussion of the scope of nuisance as a legal term, reference should be made to a textbook on tort. What follows now is a brief summary of the principles.[8]

7 [1976] 2 All ER 478.

Nuisance may be public or private, although one incident may constitute both. Where, for instance, an activity that causes a public nuisance to the general population of an area affects a particular complainant, it may be a private nuisance to him.[9] It is to be noted, though, that in such cases, to establish a private nuisance, the harm must be shown to be different in kind rather than merely greater in volume or quantity. So, for example, in *Benjamin* v *Storr* (1874)[10] B ran a coffee house in Rose St, Covent Garden. In connection with his business, S kept horses and vans standing outside the coffee house all day, causing obstruction to the highway and thereby constituting a public nuisance. B alleged special damage because the vans obstructed the light to his windows necessitating the additional expense of gas lights burning all day, and because the smell from the horse manure deterred potential customers. A public nuisance is 'one which materially affects the reasonable comfort and convenience of life of a class of Her Majesty's subjects who come within the sphere or neighbourhood of its operation'.[11] The Court of Appeal in *Attorney-General* v *PYA Quarries Ltd* (1957)[12] added

8 See also for a general discussion on this area of law Steve Silvester, 'Odour Nuisance : Legal Controls II', (1986)

9 See, e.g,. *Campbell* v *Paddington BC* [1911] 1 KB 869 CR 9 CD 400

10 (1874) LR 9 CP.

11 Winfield & Jolowicz, 12th edn pp.378–9.

12 [1957] 2 QB 169.

> that the sphere to the nuisance might be described generally as the neighbourhood, but the question whether the local community within the sphere comprises a sufficient number of persons to constitute a class of the public was a question of fact in every case.

In *Attorney-General of British Columbia ex rel Eaton* v *Haney* (1963), seven neighbouring families were held to constitute sufficient members of a class. In contrast, in *R* v *Madden* (1975)[13] the defendant made a 999 call warning of the presence of a bomb in a local steel works. The telephonist taking the call notified the police, who in turn notified the security officer who instituted a search of the premises by eight security guards. After an hour the call was discovered to be a hoax. Accepting that only the stated persons had been affected, one question for the court was whether such a bogus call, being capable of being a public nuisance, was so in

13 [1975] 3 All ER 155, CA.

these present circumstances. Concluding that it was not sufficiently public, James LJ said[14] 'It is quite clear that for a public nuisance to be proved, it must be proved by the Crown that the public, which means a considerable number of persons or a section of the public was affected, as distinct from individual persons'. In consequence a public nuisance 'is one which is so widespread in its range and so indiscriminate in its effect that it would not be reasonable to expect one person as distinct from the community at large'[15] to take proceedings to stop it. The remedy is therefore by criminal proceedings instituted by the Attorney-General on behalf of the public. An individual therefore has no standing or right to take action unless:

(a) he is affected in a different way, i.e. as a private nuisance, see e.g. *Rose* v *Miles* (1815)[16] and *Harper* v *Haden & Sons* (1933);[17]

(b) by application to join the Attorney-General in relator proceedings.

While local authorities were in the same position as other persons in the requirement to proceed at the relation of the Attorney-General to secure the abatement of a public nuisance that is now no longer the case. Section 222 of the Local Government Act 1972 gives a local authority the power to act independently in its own name where it considers it expedient 'for the promotion or protection of the interests of the inhabitants of [the] area'.[18]

Private nuisance

Private 'nuisance is, as has often been observed, a tort of which the components vary so much that it is not susceptible of any comprehensive definition'.[19] It has therefore been held to include a wide range of acts and omissions of human and natural origin; although perhaps nuisances attributable to natural omissions are hard to find. The one common feature is that it involves 'unlawful interference with a person's use or enjoyment of land, or some right over it, or in connection with it'.[20] Private nuisance then protects plaintiffs as occupiers of land from external deleterious occurrences. Common examples involve noise, smell, smoke, fumes and the like. Generally a continuous or recurrent state of affairs is involved. For instance, in *Bolton* v *Stone* (1949)[21] Oliver J said that 'it must be a state of affairs, however temporary, and not merely an isolated happening'. In such cases the tendency is to regard the isolated happening as the product of a continuing nuisance situation. This was the approach adopted for instance, in *Spicer* v *Smee* (1946),[22] where defective electrical wiring in the defendant's bungalow caused a fire which destroyed the plaintiff's adjoining bungalow. Atkinson J held that there was a dangerous state of affairs on the defendant's property making him liable in nuisance. As Thesiger J said[23]:

> while there is no doubt that a single isolated escapade may cause the damage that entitles a plaintiff to sue for nuisance, yet it must be proved that the nuisance arose from the condition of the defendant's land or premises or property or activities thereon that constituted the nuisance.

So when a golf ball was sliced from a tee onto an adjoining road,[24] breaking a taxi cab window and causing the driver the loss of an eye, the siting of the tee was held to constitute a continuing nuisance.

The question of fault in establishing liability is complex and is governed by a number of factors. The general test has been expressed succinctly as:

---

14 At p.158.

15 *Per* Denning LJ in *A-G* v *PYA Quarries Ltd* [1957] 2 QB 169.

16 (1815) 4 M&S 101.

17 [1933] Ch D 298.

18 See, e.g., *Solihull MBC* v *Maxfern Ltd* [1977] 1 WLR 127; *Kent CC* v *Batchelor (No. 2)* [1979] 1 WLR 213.

19 *Per* Sachs LJ in *Radstock Co-op* v *Norton & Radstock UDC* [1968] 2 All ER 59 at p.73

20 Adopted by Scott LJ in *Read* v *J.Lyons & Co. Ltd* [1945] KB 216.

21 [1949] 1 All ER 237.

22 [1946] 1 All ER 489.

23 In *SCM (United Kingdom)Ltd* v *W.J.Whittall & Son Ltd* [1970] 1 WLR 1017 at p.1031.

24 *Castle* v *St Augustine's Links* (1922) 38 TLR 615.

the defendant is liable if his interference with his neighbour's land is of sufficient gravity to constitute a nuisance in law and if he is responsible for the interference in the sense that he knew or ought to have known of a sufficient likelihood of its occurrence to require him to take steps to prevent it.[25]

So, for example, liability has been imposed where the nuisance has been caused by the action of a trespasser but has continued with the knowledge of the occupier[26] and where the origin was a natural occurrence and the occupier's response was inadequate,[27] or where the occupier failed to take any remedial action.[28]

The key factor in nuisance is the unreasonableness of the conduct complained of. Many of the matters the subject of nuisance proceedings are intrinsically unexceptional, everyday occurrences, and indeed to be expected in a complex society. It is not therefore the act itself but the question of degree that is at issue, and the 'unreasonableness' question is resolved by balancing the competing rights and interests of the parties. In the words of Lawton LJ[29]:

> The question is whether the neighbour is using his property reasonably, having regard to the fact that he is a neighbour. The neighbour who is complaining must remember too, that the other man can use his property in a reasonable way and there must be a measure of 'give and take, live and let live'.

In this context the degree of care, or lack of it, in undertaking the activity may be a relevant consideration. Contrast, for example, *Leeman v Montague* (1936)[30] in which 750 cockerels crowing between 2 and 7 am with no attempt to rearrange the farm was held to constitute a nuisance, and *Moy v Stoop* (1909),[31] where crying children in a day nursery with no lack of care was not. However, establishing care will not exculpate a defendant where the degree of interference is excessive and beyond what a neighbour should be required to tolerate in those circumstances. In such a case, where the activity may not be carried on without causing a nuisance in law, then the activity may not be carried on.

Additional factors influencing the classification of an event as a nuisance and requiring some consideration now, are locality and utility. Where the nuisance complained of is one affecting enjoyment of land rather than causing physical damage to property the nature of the locality is relevant: 'What would be a nuisance in Belgrave Square would not necessarily be so in Bermondsey'.[32] For example, in *St Helens Smelting Co. v Tipping* (1865)[33] the plaintiff had bought an expensive country estate only to have the trees and shrubs injured by vapours exhaled by the defendant's extensive copper smelting operations. The judge asked the jury to consider whether the process was a necessary one, whether it was carried on properly and whether it was in a proper location. The jury's response was 'Yes', 'Yes' and 'No' respectively; the defendant in consequence being held liable in nuisance. Lord Westbury's speech in this case makes some helpful distinctions between nuisances affecting enjoyment of land on the one hand and causing physical injury on the other in relation to the question of location and its effect on reasonableness. In *M'Ewen v Steedman and M'Alister* [1912],[34] the Court found that vibration due to the working of a gas engine, whereby the structure of the adjoining premises was injured and the comfort of its occupants affected, constituted a nuisance which might be restrained by interdict, notwithstanding that the premises were situated in an industrial district of Glasgow.

It is in this context that the planning process impinges on nuisance, and indeed, may be said to forestall it by separating incompatible activities before they start.

25 In Winfield & Jolowicz, *op. cit.*, note 11, at p.387.

26 *Sedleigh-Denfield* v *O'Callaghan* [1940] AC 880.

27 *Goldman* v *Hargrave* [1967] 1 AC 645.

28 *Leakey* v *National Trust* [1980] QB 485.

29 In *Kennaway* v *Thompson* [1980] 3All ER 329 at p.333.

30 [1936] 2 All ER 1677.

31 [1909] 25 TLR 262.

32 *Per* Thesiger LJ in *Sturges* v *Bridgman* (1879) 11 Ch D 852 at p.865.

33 (1865) 11 HLC 642.

34 (1912) SC 156; see also *Halsey* v *Esso Petroleum Co.* [1961] 1 WLR 683.

The impact of planning on the assessment of a nuisance situation has been given a new dimension in relation to the nature of the locality in *Gillingham BC* v *Medway (Chatham) Dock Co. Ltd* (1991).[35] On the closure of the naval dockyard planning permission was given for its use as a commercial dock. This change generated a significant increase in heavy goods traffic, both during and outside working hours and on roads through residential neighbourhoods. The local authority brought an action on behalf of the local residents for a declaration that the increased traffic amounted to a public nuisance and for an injunction restraining such traffic at night. Buckley J, in deciding that the activities complained of did not amount to a nuisance, considered that although a grant of planning permission was not a licence to commit a nuisance, local authorities, through development plans and planning decisions, could alter the character of a neighbourhood. That could then result in activities that might otherwise constitute a nuisance not conferring any right of action. He thought that, in the instant case, taking into account the present character of the neighbourhood with a grant of planning permission for a commercial port, the disturbance complained of did not amount to a nuisance.

35 (1991) *The Times*, 20 October.

Clearly, over a period of time, the character of a neighbourhood may change. The quality of the Belgrave Square environment may deteriorate, just as Bermondsey may improve. Such changes will affect the legitimate expectations of the residents and the assessment of potential nuisances. In this process of change, development policy and planning will play a part. However, this judgment increases the importance of the planning approval itself. It may now be a direct factor in the assessment of the nature of the area, the consequent reasonable expectations of the occupants, and therefore of the level, intensity or duration at which a given activity will amount to a nuisance. In justifying this approach Buckley J noted that the planning process provided opportunities for objections and challenges by persons potentially affected. It may therefore seem reasonable on public policy grounds that a disappointed objector to a planning application should not be able to take a second, and subsequent, bite at the cherry by invoking the nuisance procedure. However, that, it is submitted, presents an over-simplistic view of the range of potential nuisance situations. In the sort of circumstances exemplified by the *Gillingham* facts, a planning approval by one authority in one area may produce a nuisance in quite a separate or distant area. To place upon residents, or indeed the local authority on their behalf, the obligation to monitor, as well as the prescience to anticipate, developments in other districts that may in the future impinge upon their quality of life seems to be expecting more than can be reasonably achieved.

A concluding matter from the judgment of Buckley J concerns his emphasis that the grant of planning permission was not a licence to commit a nuisance. This is, with respect, obviously right and is to be explained in the context of reasonableness. A planning permission authorises the conduct of the specified activity within parameters appropriate to that location. Just as such an approval cannot be advanced as justification for the breach of environmental standards governing, say, noise or air pollution, so it will not sanction the conduct of the permitted activity in such a way that the reasonable expectations of the neighbours, judged in relation to all the surrounding circumstances, are prejudiced.

Another factor in determining the reasonableness of the activity in question is its justification on the ground of utility, either to the locality or to the communi-

36 See, e.g., *Adams v Ursell* [1913] Ch 269.

ty at large.[36] This again is a matter of degree and will only justify injurious activity up to a certain point. The plaintiff should not be required to suffer the burden of an activity even though it benefits the community at large where such a burden would be excessive. This defence was raised in *Kennaway v Thompson*

37 [1980] 3 All ER 329, CA.

(1980)[37] to justify the continuation and growth of power boat racing with its increasing duration and volume of noise. The damage to the riparian residential occupant's enjoyment of her property was contrasted with the enjoyment of the large numbers of the public who attended the meetings; including those held at national and international level. On this ground the judge at first instance had refused an injunction to restrain the current level of operation, awarding instead damages for the nuisance already suffered and a larger sum, £15,000, under the Chancery Amendment Act 1858 (Lord Cairn's Act) for damage likely to be suffered in the future. In dealing with this issue Lawton LJ approved the statement of principle that:

> the Court (of Chancery) has always protested against the notion that it ought to allow a wrong to continue simply because the wrongdoer is able and willing to pay for the injury he may inflict. Neither has the circumstance that the wrongdoer is in some sense a public benefactor (e.g. a gas or water company or a sewer authority) ever been considered a sufficient reason for refusing to protect by injunction an individual whose rights are being persistently infringed.[38]

38 From Lindley LJ in *Shelfer v City of London Electric Lighting Co.* [1895] 1 Ch 287 at pp.315–16.

Applying this principle, the Court of Appeal replaced the damages for future loss with an injunction reducing, but not terminating, the noise.

Prejudice to health and nuisance

A consideration of the expression 'prejudicial to health or a nuisance' must include some reference to the relationship of these terms and their effect, if any, on one another. The early view, exemplified in the judgment of Cockburn CJ in *Great*

39 (1872) LR 7 QB 550.

Western Railway v Bishop (1872)[39] was that 'whether you regard public or private nuisance, still it was intended that the powers of this Act should only apply when the thing complained of was injurious to health'. The complaint was that a railway bridge over a public highway allowed water to drain from it and drip onto the road. The court thought that while the facts amounted to an ordinary public nuisance they were not susceptible to remedy under the Act. Lush J thought that the word 'nuisance' in the Act must be limited to those wrongful acts spoken of by the statute, namely, those which are "injurious to health". This view underwent a rapid change. In *Bishop Auckland Local Board v Bishop*

40 (1882)10 QBD 138.

Auckland Iron & Steel Co. (1882),[40] Stephen J, referring to his speech in an earlier case,[41] said:

41 *Malton Board of Health v Malton Manure Co.* (1879) 4 ExD 302.

> The nuisance was injurious to health, because it was found that the effluvia caused sick persons to become worse but I said in effect in my judgment that, even if the nuisance were not shown to be precisely injurious to health, yet if shown to be injurious to personal comfort, and possibly injurious to health, it would be exactly one of the nuisances to which both the old and the new Acts would apply.

Here was the halfway stage. The next and concluding step followed quickly in

42 (1881) 8 QBD 97.

Banbury Urban Sanitary Authority v Page (1881),[42] in which all three judges considered that it was an offence under the Public Health Act to keep swine so as to be a nuisance within the common law meaning of that term. It was not necessary to that offence that there should be any injury to health. Similarly, in the *Bishop*

Auckland case itself, the Court found that an offence within the section was committed where the accumulation emitted offensive smells which interfered with the personal comfort of persons living in the neighbourhood, but did not cause injury to health.

This has subsequently been the prevailing view. *Betts* v *Penge UDC* (1942)[43] though disapproved by the House of Lords on other grounds,[44] is authority that an activity will be within the statute if it is a nuisance even though it is not prejudicial to health. The 'or' in the phrase is to be read disjunctively, and bearing in mind the differing criteria to be applied to each term it is most important that any or each set of circumstances is assessed exclusively in its appropriate context. In this respect the advice given to magistrates by Lord Wilberforce[45] should be heeded by all involved with statutory nuisances. He said:

> They should in the first place ... ask themselves, after they have found the condition of the premises, the questions (1) is the state of the premises such as to be injurious or likely to cause injury to health or (2) is it a nuisance? ... And the magistrate should find specifically under which limb the case falls. If he answers either question in the affirmative he must make an abatement order.

43 [1942] 2 KB 154, DC.

44 *Salford City Council* v *McNally* [1975] All ER 860; and see below at pp.88, 93.

45 In *Salford City Council* v *McNally*, at p.864.

PROCEDURE

The reason for and purpose of the statutory nuisance concept lies in the procedure for abatement. As has been seen, it is closely related to and covers many of the same matters that are nuisances in the civil law of torts. A person affected therefore has a private right of action in the civil courts for damages and/or an injunction. However, many will have neither the resources nor the inclination to pursue such a remedy. Alternatively, therefore, this procedure provides, by a complaint to the local authority, a criminal process for the abatement of nuisances, with or without a fine and at no cost to the person affected.

Investigation and notice

Section 79(1) of the 1990 Act imposes two duties on local authorities in connection with the discovery of statutory nuisances:

(a) to cause their area to be inspected from time to time to detect any statutory nuisance which ought to be dealt with under section 80; and
(b) where a complaint is made by a resident of their area, to take reasonable steps to investigate it.

Where a local authority fails to carry out the periodic inspections required in (a) above, Schedule 3, paragraph 4 gives the Secretary of State default powers following service of an order directing the defaulting authority to perform the function as specified.

Supplementary to and in support of these duties, paragraph 2 of Schedule 3 gives authorised persons powers of entry at any reasonable time, with the proviso that 24 hours' notice be given in the case of residential property except in the case of emergencies as defined in paragraph 2(7) of Schedule 3. Where such notice would be to no purpose or would defeat the purpose of entry, a warrant may be obtained from a justice of the peace on written application, such warrant remaining valid until executed. Powers of entry are necessarily modified in relation to vehicles and machinery emitting noise in the street, especially if unattended. Section 4(5) of the Noise and Statutory Nuisance Act 1993 amends Schedule 3, enabling a properly authorised person to enter or open such vehicles or machinery, if necessary by force, or to remove them to a secure place, prior notification of the police of the intention to take that action being required. In such circumstances there is an obligation on such a person, when leaving the unattended property, to ensure that it is 'secured against interference or theft in such a manner and as effectually as he found it'. If that is not possible then it is either to be immobilised in whatever manner appears expedient or removed to a secure place. In the event of such action, the police are again to be informed.[46] The general law governing powers of entry and the associated issue of obstruction is dealt with in Chapter 1. Here specifically, paragraph 3 of Schedule 3 provides that wilful obstruction of a person acting under paragraph 2 powers will render that person liable to summary prosecution.

Where a local authority is satisfied that a statutory nuisance exists or is likely to occur or recur it shall serve an abatement notice under section 80(1) imposing all or any of the following requirements:

(a) requiring the abatement of the nuisance or prohibiting or restricting its occurrence or recurrence;
(b) requiring the execution of such works, and the taking of such other steps as may be necessary for any of those purposes;

and the notice shall specify the time or times within which the notice is to be complied with. By section 81(2) this power extends to occurrences outside the local authority area causing a statutory nuisance within it. For the purposes of subsequent litigation, the magistrates' court for the area in which the relevant act or default took place has jurisdiction.

Although the section requires that, on finding that a statutory nuisance exists, the local authority 'shall' serve a notice and therefore appears to be mandatory, that may not in fact be the case. The Divisional Court in *Nottingham Corporation v Newton* (1974)[47] recognised that the authority had in that case a choice of action either under the Public Health Act 1936 or the Housing Act 1957 and, while the 'shall' seemed to require the use of the statutory nuisance procedure it was 'not as mandatory as it appears'. On the question of recurrence Lord Widgery CJ said in *Phillips v Crawford* (1974),[48] a case concerning noisy dogs:

> Whether or not the original nuisance continued, as opposed to a new nuisance being started, will not always be an easy matter to decide, but it is essentially a question of fact, it depends on all the circumstances of the case. Was it the same sort of noise which recurred after the interval? How long was the interval? Is the extent and intensity of the noise the same? Indeed, looking at it fairly and as a layman, can it be said that all that happened is that the nuisance has been suspended for a little while, or is the fair and proper view that the nuisance was abated pursuant to the notice, and that which followed on a later date is fairly to be regarded as the start of a new nuisance?

While there is no prescribed form of notice the contents must include the time within which the nuisance is to be abated and notice of the right of appeal. It may also prohibit occurrence or recurrence of the nuisance and shall stipulate the work to be done or other action required – see section 80(1) above.[49] A right of appeal against the notice to the magistrates' court within 21 days is provided by section 80(3), and Schedule 3, paragraph (6) stipulates that the notice must include a state-

46 Section 4(3) and (6).

47 [1974] 2 All ER 760.

48 (1974) 72 LGR 199.

49 On the question of contents and service of notices generally, see Chapter 1 at pp.20–6.

ment of the right of appeal and the time limit. The form of appeal is, by Schedule 3, paragraph (1), by way of complaint for an order and the provisions of the Magistrates' Courts Act 1980 apply to the proceedings. There is a right of further appeal to the Crown Court. Additional regulations relating to appeals may, under section 81(7) and Schedule 3, paragraphs (1) and (4), be made and have been made by the Secretary of State.[50]

There is considerable authority, some of it deriving from a consideration of magistrates' nuisance orders, on the requirement to specify the necessary work, but much of it inevitably bears on the particular statutory provision concerned and is therefore of limited value. In particular, the preceding provision in section 93 of the Public Health Act 1936 required the local authority to state what work was to be done or other steps taken to secure abatement. Until there is direct authority on the present section 80(1), the following approach seems to the author to be derived from the wording and existing principles. The present flexibility to include a statement of the required work or not, is not a matter for the unfettered discretion of the enforcing authority. Whether work should be specified will depend upon the nature of the nuisance and therefore the remedy required. For example, in the case of the emission of black smoke from a steam tug, it was considered that an 'abatement or prohibition order was not bad because it did not specify the works to be executed'[51]. However, where remedial works are required, rather than the mere changing of procedures or methods of work, the recipient of the notice is entitled to know what works the local authority regards as suitable and sufficient to abate the nuisance. In *R v Horrocks* (1900)[52] Darling J said:

> he does not know what the Justices intended him to do, and it may well be that, having done what he himself thought sufficient to abate the nuisance, he has not succeeded in taking any of the steps the Justices intended him to take or considered necessary; and that he will still be liable to fresh proceedings.

Justice and fairness demand that the defendant should know, with sufficient particularity, what is required of him. It therefore follows that where the specified works are ambiguous or ineffective as a remedy, the notice will be bad.[53] Further, the fact that particular remedial work is specified in the notice does not make that mandatory and necessarily exclude any other equally effective solution.[54]

Person responsible

The person on whom an abatement notice is to be served is, by section 80(2), the person responsible for the nuisance. Such person is defined in section 79(7) as the person to whose act, default or sufferance the nuisance is attributable. It will be seen that these three terms trace a declining level of responsibility. There seems to be no authority suggesting that they are to be applied in that sequence, but it would appear to be the proper course. The point is that whether that person has caused the nuisance or merely allowed it to continue, he will be responsible within these provisions. As commentary on 'default' see *Neath RDC v Williams* (1951) in the treatment of section 259 of the Public Health Act 1936.[55] As an example of sufferance, in *Clayton v Sale UDC* (1926)[56] the owner was held liable to abate a nuisance due to flooding following breach of a flood bank that he was under no obligation to repair. On the question of liability in such circumstances it has been said that:

50 The Statutory Nuisance (Appeals) Regulations 1990, S.I. 1990 No. 2276.

51 *Tough* v *Hopkins* [1904] 1 KB 804.

52 (1900) 69 LJ QB 688; and see *Perry* v *Garner* [1953] 1 All ER 285.

53 *Whatling* v *Rees* (1914) 84 LJ KB 1122.

54 See *per* Lord Goddard CJ in *McGillivray* v *Stephenson* [1950] 1 All ER 942 at p.944b.

55 See in Chapter 4 at note 67.

56 [1926] 1 KB 415; [1925] 1 All ER 279.

The occupier continues a nuisance if with the knowledge or presumed knowledge of its existence, he fails to take reasonable means to bring it to an end, though with ample time to do so.[57]

57 Per Lord Romer in
Sedleigh-Denfield v
O'Callaghan [1940] AC 880 at
p.913.

On the question of presumed knowledge, Viscount Caldecote LCJ said, in *Leanse* v *Lord Edgerton* (1943),[58]

58 [1943] 1 All ER 489 at
p.490.

The fact that Lord Edgerton lived either somewhere else in London or in the country ... and did not know of the damage to the house, does not in my judgement, prevent him from having what is called 'presumed knowledge'.

The defendant owned an empty house which was damaged in an air raid. Before repairs could be carried out the plaintiff was struck on the head by a piece of broken glass. The Court considered that the defendant was liable for continuing the nuisance. However, reasonable action by the person responsible, even though not successful, may be enough to exclude liability on this ground. In *London Borough of Southwark* v *Ince* (1989),[59] concerning action against the local authority owner for failing to insulate flats against traffic noise, Woolf LJ said[60]:

59 (1989) 21 HLR 504, and
see at note 2 above.

60 At p.516.

If the situation was one where the flats had been properly constructed and adequately insulated to exclude noise but notwithstanding that noise still penetrated into the flat, which interfered with the enjoyment of those flats by the occupants, that would certainly not be a situation which is the same as that which is revealed here. In particular in a situation of that sort it would be difficult to see how the local authority could be regarded as a person whose act, default or sufferance caused the nuisance to arise or continue.

This general requirement, of action against the person responsible in however tenuous a way, is subject to two provisos. Where the nuisance arises from any defect of a structural character the notice is to be served on the owner of the premises and, where the person responsible for the nuisance cannot be found or the nuisance has not yet occurred, it is to be served on the owner or occupier of the premises. In the first case liability is clearly related to responsibility for and right to have access to and work on the building(s) or land. It may be assumed, therefore, that the distinction between structural and non-structural matters is likely to be influenced by landlord and tenant principles relating to fixtures. This view is supported by *Warman* v *Tibbotts* (1922)[61] which concerned action against the owner to repair a defective kitchen range. Other cooking facilities were available, the Court therefore finding that while the defect was annoying to the tenant it was not injurious or dangerous to health. Lord Hewart CJ said that 'liability of the landlord depends *inter alia* on the defect being of a structural character. Here the defect was to a fixture.' The absolute liability of the owner for structural matters has, however, been mitigated by the Divisional Court in *GLC* v *Tower Hamlets London Borough* (1983).[62] The GLC were the owners of a flat affected by severe condensation, dampness and mould growth, being exposed on three sides and below to the air. The fireplace had been blocked up and the tenant used three oil fires and an electric fire for heating. In dismissing the GLC's appeal against the magistrate's order, because they had taken no remedial action, the Court did say that if the landlord had done everything reasonable and the cause of the continuing condensation was that the tenant was unwilling to use the heating provided then the landlord could not be held responsible for the state of the premises.

61 [1922] All ER Reps 725.

62 (1983)15 HLR 57.

While the present Act does not include a definition of 'owner', the 1936 Act definition was[63] 'the person receiving the rackrent of the premises, whether on his own

63 Section 343.

account or as agent or trustee for any other person'. In default of other authority it may be that the sizeable body of case law on the scope of the word in the earlier Act will be retained for present purposes. It is not proposed to deal in detail with the authorities but, by way of illustration, *Midland Bank Ltd* v *Conway Corporation* (1965)[64] may be noted. The owner of the property concerned lived in Peru. The tenant paid the rent to the local branch of the bank who also paid the rates. The local authority served the abatement notice on the bank who, the court now said, was not the owner. Such a person, to be an owner, had to be constituted an agent to receive the rent and not merely a person who handled the rent money, whether or not they knew it was rent. In the case of a bank something more than the normal banker–customer relationship was required before the bank could be an agent for this purpose. This is of course an exceptional situation, which is why it has been selected. A bank may legitimately be handling a customer's money without being an agent for any particular purpose. Generally, however, other persons, in receiving the rent, will be acting, either expressly or by implication, as agents for that purpose.

    A case of particular interest bearing on the question of ownership and allied responsibility is *Pollway Nominees* v *London Borough of Havering* (1989).[65] A flat owned as lessees by the appellants was affected by rising damp due to defects in the outside wall. The outside walls were not included in the lease. Pollway Nominees now appealed against the magistrate's abatement order. In dismissing the appeal the Court made the following points:

(a) Premises means the premises that are prejudicial to health – in this case the flat and not the outside wall.
(b) Proviso (a) to section 93 (i.e. requiring the notice to be served on the owner) is not limited to structural defects arising in the premises. Where structural defects are the cause of the nuisance it is the owner of the premises who is to be served with the notice, irrespective of whether or not he is responsible for causing the statutory nuisance in question.

This of course presents obvious problems to the owner concerned. He is responsible in law for matters over which he may have no control, and possibly on another's property to which he has no right of access. In his judgement, Sackville J dealt with this problem in the following ways:

(a) Such a person would have a 'reasonable excuse' for non-compliance within section 95; substantially re-enacted in section 80(4).
(b) He would be a person aggrieved by the nuisance within section 99 (now section 82) and thus be able to institute proceedings against the person by whose act or default the nuisance arose. The precise basis of his grievance is not made clear. Obviously the occupant of the flat is affected by the physical condition of the premises. The lessee landlord may be regarded as aggrieved by the consequential deterioration of his property or its reduced marketability due to the dampness. Alternatively, he may be aggrieved by the abatement proceedings instituted against him by the local authority. If this is the real basis of the grievance, though, such proceedings, or the threat of them, are a necessary precondition to action by the lessee.
(c) A person served with an abatement notice may ask the magistrates under section 290 to make a contribution order against the owner or occupier of any other premises to be benefitted. See also on this matter the Statutory Nuisance (Appeals) Regulations 1990, and in particular regulations 2(2)(i) and 2(6).[66]

64 [1965] 1 WLR 1165, DC.

65 (1989) 21 HLR 462.

66 S.I. 1990 No. 2276.

(d) In a case such as the present the defendants may or would have a contractual remedy against the owners of the outside wall under the terms of their lease.

While the owner is liable for defects of a structural character, section 80(2)(c) further provides that he or the occupier is to be served where the person responsible for the nuisance cannot be found. Commenting on the similar provision in an earlier statute, the Divisional Court in *Rhymney Iron Co. v Gelligaer DC* (1917)[67] considered that the phrase extended to the case where the actual cause of the nuisance could not be identified or was unattributable. Recognising that this had the effect of imposing liability on persons who were not in fact responsible, Lord Coleridge J noted that,[68]

> ... the object of the Act is to give power to secure abatement of nuisances with as much dispatch as possible in the public interest ... The question of ultimate liability can be raised, if disputed, before the magistrates, and the person served can obtain his remedy against the local authority if he succeeds.

The ability now to take action in respect of noise from vehicles or machinery in the street, possibly unattended, raises new issues concerning the person responsible and the appropriate recipient of the notice. Where the nuisance is occurring or has occurred and the person responsible can be found, then, as in other cases, action is to be taken against the person responsible as defined.[69] Where, however, the nuisance has yet to occur or the appliance emitting the noise is unattended, a new section 80A(1) and (2)[70] provides that, first, if the person responsible can be found then the notice is to be served on that person. Where he cannot be found, or the local authority decides that this provision should apply, the notice is to be fixed to the vehicle or equipment.[71] Noise originating in these circumstances may be attributable to a number of people, any one of whom may not themselves be causing a nuisance. In that case a new section 81(1A) provides that within section 80(2)(a) the notice may be served on any one of those persons, presumably meaning each of them. The removal of or interference with a notice fixed to a vehicle in these circumstances, unless by the person responsible for the vehicle or with his authority, is a summary offence.

Enforcement

Failure to comply with an abatement notice without reasonable excuse is an offence and, by section 80(5), renders the person concerned liable to a fine following summary proceedings and conviction. The consent of the Secretary of State is required before a local authority institutes summary proceedings under section 79(1)(b), (d) or (e) if proceedings may be instituted under either Part l of the Alkali etc. Works Regulation Act 1906 or section 5 of the Health and Safety at Work etc. Act 1974.[72] Fine levels are specified in section 80 (5) and (6). It is in this part of the procedure that the new Act has simplified and improved the Public Health Act process, replacing two court hearings with one. Under the earlier legislation failure to comply with an abatement notice required summary proceedings to obtain from the magistrates a nuisance order. Failure to comply with the nuisance order then constituted an offence necessitating a further prosecution to obtain a fine. The present procedure has dispensed with the need to obtain a nuisance order as the first stage. Now, failure to comply with the terms of the abatement notice itself constitutes the offence for which summary proceedings may be instituted. This change no doubt reflects common practice. The courts had emphasised that under the 1936

67 [1917]1 KB 589.

68 at p.597.

69 See section 79(7).

70 Enacted in section 3(6) of the 1993 Act.

71 Where the notice is attached to the vehicle etc., by resolution of the authority and the person responsible can be found, a copy is to be served on that person as well.

72 Section 79(10).

Act procedure, magistrates were not bound by the terms of the local authority's abatement notice and could, indeed had a duty to, issue the nuisance order in the terms that they considered proper.[73] In practice, however, the terms of the order invariably closely reproduced those of the original notice. This new procedure recognises and formalises that practice and thereby gives greater importance to the local authority's view: a change that not only reflects common practice but in consequence recognises the increasing experience and competence of local authorities and their officers.

The defence of 'reasonable excuse' for failure to comply with the notice was considered in *Saddleworth UDC* v *Aggregate and Sand* (1970).[74] It was argued that an expert had advised certain works to be carried out but funds were exhausted before the work was completed. The Divisional Court held that lack of finance was not a reasonable excuse and that it would be difficult to rely on the advice of an independent expert as a defence when that advice had not been followed. The distinction between the defence of 'reasonable excuse' and matters of mitigation arose in *Wellingborough BC* v *Gordon* (1990),[75] where a birthday party was not accepted as a reasonable excuse for excessive noise produced by reggae music, air horns and whistles.

A further general defence available with certain exceptions is that although the nuisance has occurred, 'the best practicable means' have been used to prevent or counteract the effects of the nuisance.[76] Section 80(8) lists the exceptional cases where this defence is not available, i.e. to nuisances within section 79(1) in the following categories:

(1) (a) premises (d) dust, steam, smell or effluvia (e) accumulation or deposit (f) animals (g) noise; except where the nuisance arises on industrial, trade or business premises;
(2) (b) smoke, except where emitted from a chimney;
(3) (c) fumes or gases, and (h) any other matter.

In short, therefore, the defence may be available to defendants in the commercial context. It is not available in the non-commercial situation – domestic, residential, recreational and so on.

Interpretation of the term 'best practicable means' is provided by section 79(9), which states:

(a) 'practicable' means reasonably practicable having regard among other things to local conditions and circumstances, to the current state of technical knowledge and to the financial implications;
(b) the means to be employed include the design, installation, maintenance and manner and periods of operation of plant and machinery, and the design, construction and maintenance of buildings and structures;
(c) the test is to apply only so far as compatible with any duty imposed by law;
(d) the test is to apply only so far as compatible with safety and safe working conditions, and with the exigencies of any emergencies or unforeseeable circumstances.

The subsection further provides that in the case of noise, regard shall be had to the guidance contained in any code of practice under section 71 of the Control of Pollution Act 1974. Currently such codes include:

Audible intruder alarms	S.I. 1981 No. 1829
Ice cream van chimes	S.I. 1981 No. 1828
Model aircraft	S.I. 1981 No. 1830

73 See *McGillivray* v *Stephenson* [1950] 1 All ER 942.

74 (1970) 114 SJ 931.

75 (1990) *The Times*, 9 November.

76 Section 80(7).

Construction and open sites (Scotland)   S.I. 1982 No. 601
Construction and open sites   S.I. 1984 No. 1992
                                S.I .1987 No. 1730[77]

77 These codes of practice are summarised in Chapter 12 in their appropriate context.

78 [1985] JPL 175.

The financial aspect of best practicable means arose for consideration in *Wivenhoe Port v Colchester BC*(1985).[78] The nuisance in this case was caused by dust produced by the handling of soya meal at the docks. The defendants installed new machinery which reduced the quantity of dust produced. However, they argued that to use the new machinery for all dusty cargoes would cause so much extra expense that the company's operation would become unprofitable and have to cease. In response, and commenting on the magistrate's approach, Butler J in the Crown Court said[79]:

79 At p.179.

> the court accepted that it was probable that the use of the vacuum machinery would cause the company to be less profitable than it was. And profitability was a relevant factor; see section 110(2)(b) of the 1936 Act. But how much less profitable was by no means clear, and it was certainly not established, even on a balance of probability that the operations would go from profit to loss, or become so uneconomic that the company could not profitably continue if the new machine were to be used at all times. The court therefore rejected the defence based on section 94(5) of the Act ...

ie. best practicable means.

Apart from finance the test of best practicable means concerns the particular standard to be applied in a given case. That the standard is not necessarily that common in the industry or area was established as long ago as 1855 in *Scholefield v Schunk*,[80] which concerned injury to the plaintiff due to unfenced machinery in the defendant's mill. On appeal the court found that the jury, acting under a misdirection from the judge, had found for the defendant because his fencing was not less secure than that of his neighbours. This, as the court pointed out, had the effect of making the manufacturers in the district the judges of the degree of protection to be afforded. The test applied by the House of Lords in a different context but, it is submitted, nevertheless relevant to the determination of best practicable means is 'inevitability', relating both to design and installation on the one hand and operation on the other. In *Manchester Corporation v Farnworth* (1930)[81] the respondent farmer brought proceedings for nuisance, including damage to plant foliage, caused by emission of sulphur fumes from the chimneys of the appellant's electricity generating station. Lord Dunedin said[82]:

80 (1855) 19 JP 84.

81 [1930] AC 171.

82 At p.183.

> When Parliament has authorised a certain thing to be made or done in a certain place, there can be no action for a nuisance caused by the making or doing of that thing if the nuisance is the inevitable result of the making or doing so authorised.

Is, then, the nuisance complained of really the inevitable consequence? In the same case Viscount Sumner said[83]:

83 At p.200.

> As it is the appellants have never put themselves in a position to say that a nuisance by sulphur is necessarily incidental to the emission of fumes nor that prevention is only possible by some extraordinary means or at the price of defeating the enterprise ...

On the question of original or structural defects and also the impact of subsequent improvements, he said[84]:

84 At p.202.

> the authority to erect and work the plant and the obligation in both respects to use reasonable care and precautions are correlative and erection cannot be so severed from

use and maintenance as to enable the undertakers to go on permanently using a plant with all its original imperfections unremedied, merely on the ground that original faults in construction must be deemed to be irremediable in subsequent use. Reasonableness applies not merely to construction but also to improvement.

This case concerned an operation under statutory authority. The same principles and approach would appear to apply to the carrying on of any activity. Having regard to the nature of the process, the state of technical knowledge (including progressive developments) and cost, is the consequence complained of the inevitable result of engaging in that undertaking?

Those principles were approved and applied by the House of Lords in *Allen* v *Gulf Oil Ltd* (1981)[85] which concerned the construction and operation of an oil refinery under a private Act. Lord Wilberforce said[86]:

> the establishment of an oil refinery etc., was bound to involve some alteration of the environment and so of the standard of amenity and comfort which neighbouring occupiers might expect. To the extent that the environment has been changed from that of a peaceful unpolluted countryside to an industrial complex ... Parliament must be taken to have authorised it. So far, I think, the matter is not open to doubt. But in my opinion the statutory authority extends beyond merely authorising a change in the environment and an alteration of standard. It confers immunity against proceedings for any nuisance which can be shown (the burden of showing being on the appellants) to be the inevitable result of erecting a refinery upon the site ... however carefully and with however great a regard for the interest of adjoining occupiers it is sited, constructed and operated.

Lord Edmund-Davies returned to the question of cost, saying[87]:

> it would be for the defendant to establish that any proved nuisance was wholly unavoidable and this quite regardless of the expense which might necessarily be involved in its avoidance, whereas he will clear himself of negligence if at the end of the day it emerges that any discomfort suffered by the plaintiff arose despite his exercise of reasonable care.

Where an abatement notice is not complied with, and whether or not the local authority takes proceedings under section 80(4), it may abate the nuisance itself and do whatever may be necessary in execution of the notice.[88] The authority may then recover its reasonable expenses from the person by whose act or default the nuisance was caused, or the owner of the premises as appropriate, and the court may apportion expenses between the persons responsible.[89] An interesting commentary is provided on the use of a similar power in section 4(3) of the Public Health (London) Act 1891 by Lord Coleridge CJ in his judgement in *Conservators of the River Thames* v *Port Sanitary Authority of the Port of London* (1894).[90] That provision gave a similar power to the authority where the person causing the nuisance could not be found and the owner or occupier was not at fault. His Lordship said:

> I do not construe 'may' as 'must'; but I have no doubt that, if a state of things arose in which the person creating the nuisance could not be found, and in which the continuance of the nuisance was not in the least degree owing to the act, default or sufferance of the particular person served with the notice, in such a case, if the sanitary authority did not perform the duty they were empowered to do, they could be compelled to fulfil it by indictment.

If the same view may be taken of the present section 81(3), it places the local authority in the position of a long stop with the duty, on behalf of its citizens, to

85 [1981] AC 1001.

86 At pp.1013h–1014b.

87 At p.1015.

88 Section 81(3)

89 *Watney Coombe & Reid & Co. v Westminster (City) Council* (1970) 214 EG 1631.

90 [1894] 1 QB 647 at p.654.

remedy those nuisances for which noone else can be held responsible. It may be that that is Parliament's intention.

Where the local authority's expenses in remedying the nuisance could not be immediately recovered, the old section 291(1) of the Public Health Act 1936 provided *inter alia*, that the sums would be a charge on the premises. That power was not retained in the Environmental Protection Act 1990 but has been re-introduced in a new section 81A by section 10 of the Noise and Statutory Nuisance Act 1993, allowing recovery of expenses and interest in this way. It may be assumed that 'expenses' for this purpose means those reasonably incurred, implying for example the use of competitive tendering and the prompt execution of the work. The procedure requires service of a notice on all persons who to the knowledge of the local authority have an interest in the property capable of being affected by the charge, stating the amount claimed, the rate of interest and the effect of subsections (1) and (4)–(6). There is a right of appeal to the county court within 21 days of service of the notice, and the charge applies 21 days from the service of the notice or from final determination of the appeal and until the total sum, expenses and interest, has been recovered. The local authority as proprietor of the charge is required to register it, section 7 of the Local Land Charges Act 1975 providing that 'charges take effect when registered as if they are created by a deed of charge by way of a legal mortgage but without prejudice to matters of priority'. Failure to register may not always affect enforceability, however.[91] Section 81A(8) provides that the local authority's powers to enforce the charge are those of a mortgagee under the Law of Property Act 1925. Section 101 of that Act specifies the remedies, including power of sale, which may be in priority to earlier mortgages.[92] A new section 81B gives local authorities the additional power to declare expenses and interest to be payable by instalments within a specified period up to 30 years from date of service of the notice. The sums are recoverable from the owner or occupier for the time being, i.e. the liability runs with the land. Where the occupier is charged, he may deduct the sums paid from rent.

Where a local authority is satisfied that summary proceedings afford an inadequate remedy, it may, by virtue of section 81(5) take proceedings in the High Court 'for the purpose of securing the abatement, prohibition or restriction of the nuisance', i.e., for an injunction. The wording of the subsection indicates that these proceedings in the High Court are to be preceded by the preliminary stages applicable to summary proceedings i.e., service of an abatement notice etc. As has been noted earlier,[93] local authorities have a general power under section 222 of the Local Government Act 1972 to institute similar proceedings in the High Court in their own name where they 'consider it expedient for the promotion or protection of the interests of the inhabitants of their area'. However, this, or indeed any other procedure to secure the abatement of a statutory nuisance is implicitly excluded by the provision of a procedure in the statute specific to the wrong. This is a principle of long standing. See, for example, Lord Tenterden in *Doe* v *Bridges* (1831),[94] 'where an Act creates an obligation and enforces the performance in a specified manner, we take it to be a general rule that performance cannot be enforced in any other manner'.

A leading authority and a useful illustration of the use and value of the injunctive procedure is provided by *Hammersmith LBC* v *Magnum Automated Forecourts Ltd* (1978).[95] A 24-hour 'taxi care' centre was established at a filling station in a residential street. Under section 58(1) of the Control of Pollution Act 1974, the

91 See section 10 of the Local Land Charges Act 1975.

92 *Paddington BC* v *Finucane* [1928] Ch 567.

93 See p.72 above.

94 (1831) 1 B & Ad 847 at p.859. See also per Lord Halsbury LC in *Pasmore* v *Oswaldtwistle UDC* [1898] AC 387 at p. 394; followed by Maugham J in *Clark* v *Epsom RDC* [1929] 1 Ch 287.

95 [1978] 1 WLR 50; and see also *Stafford BC* v *Elkenford Ltd* [1977] 1 WLR 324 in the Sunday trading context.

local authority required cessation of operations between 11.00 pm and 7.00 am. The company appealed to the magistrates' court. Regulations provided that the notice was not suspended pending appeal but the company nevertheless continued operations. The local authority decided to apply to the High Court for an injunction under section 58(8) rather than to prosecute under section 58(4). At the appeal hearing the magistrates were told of the pending High Court proceedings and so adjourned their hearing to await the High Court decision. In the High Court the injunction was refused on the ground that the statutory procedures had not been exhausted and the magistrates should decide. In allowing the appeal the Court of Appeal said that the company had made no effort to comply and therefore the local authority was entitled to apply for an injunction under section 58(8) rather than bring a prosecution under section 58(4). Interlocutory relief would be granted pending trial of the action or determination by the magistrates. Lord Denning MR said[96]:

96 At p.55c.

> It shows that when defendants are committing a clear breach of the law, a local authority can come to the High Court for an injunction without waiting for the decision of the magistrates' court or for finality anywhere. The High Court has inherent power to secure by injunction obedience to the law by everyone in the land – whenever a person with a sufficient interest brings the case before the Court.

Private action

Section 82 of the 1990 Act gives a person aggrieved by a statutory nuisance a similar right of action to secure abatement on his own account without complaint to the local authority or where the authority decides not to proceed. This retains the similar power in section 99 of the Public Health Act 1936. The meaning of 'person aggrieved' has received much consideration by the courts in the public law context.[97] Clearly a person whose health is prejudiced or whose reasonable enjoyment of their property is materially affected by the activity complained of will be a 'person aggrieved'. In contrast, a council tenant in a block of flats who complained of a statutory nuisance affecting the block in general but not his flat, was held not to be a 'person aggrieved'.[98] In *Sandwell MBC v Bujok* (1990)[99] it was argued on behalf of the local authority defendant that a tenant who had not given notice of the defect to the landlord was not a 'person aggrieved' within the meaning of section 99. In response Lord Griffiths said[100]:

97 See above in Chapter 1 at p26.

98 *Birmingham DC v McMahon* (1987) 151 JP 709, DC.

99 [1990] 3 All ER 385.

100 At p.391.

> I am satisfied that an individual who is adversely affected by a statutory nuisance is a 'person aggrieved' within the meaning of the section whether or not he has given notice of the nuisance to the proposed defendant.

As Tromans notes,[101]

101 'Environmental Protection Act 1990', Current Law Statutes Annotated Reprints, pp.43 – 164

> It appears that the important consideration is to relate the grievance to the existence of the relevant category of statutory nuisance and the interpretation to be placed on the qualifying words in section 79(1) (a)-(g) prejudicial to health or a nuisance.

The procedure differs in certain respects from that in section 80, applicable to action by local authorities. The private complainant may not take action to prevent the occurrence of a nuisance, presumably because not yet aggrieved by something that has yet to happen. Neither is he required to serve an abatement notice,[102] although it has been held that the information under section 99 should disclose, at least in summary form, the same details as would have been contained in the

102 *R v Newham JJ ex parte Hunt* [1976] 1 All ER 839.

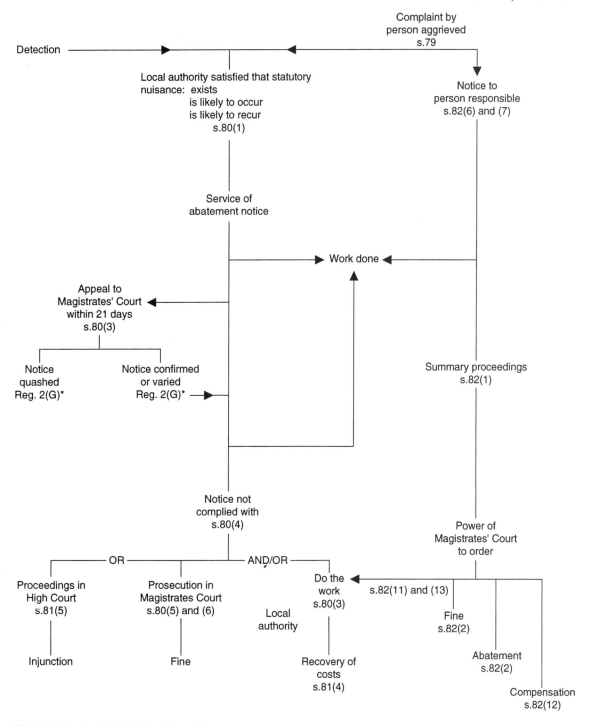

* Statutory Nuisance (Appeals) Regulations 1990

Figure 3.1 Statutory nuisance procedure: Part III Environmental Protection Act 1990

abatement notice.[103] The subsequent powers of magistrates approximate to those in the 1936 Act. Where they are satisfied that the nuisance exists or is likely to recur they shall make an order requiring abatement, the execution of any necessary works and/or prohibiting recurrence and requiring any preventative work.[104] The magistrates have a wide discretion as to the terms of the order and , in particular, are not bound by the terms of any prior notification.[105] Additionally, section 82(3) gives them the power, where they consider that the nuisance renders the premises unfit for human habitation, to prohibit the use of the premises for that purpose until, to the satisfaction of the court, they are made fit. In *Morgan* v *Liverpool Corporation* (1927)[106] broken sash cords had caused a window sash to fall, injuring the tenant's hands. Atkin LJ in a dissenting judgment considered that such a defect could render a house unfit and said[107]:

> ... if the state of repair of the house is such that by ordinary user damage may naturally be caused to the occupier, either in respect of personal injury to life or limb or injury to health, then the house is not in all respects reasonably fit for human habitation.

In *Summers* v *Salford Corporation* (1943),[108] as Lord Atkin, he followed his judgement in the earlier case and also said that habitable repair was the same as reasonably fit for human habitation. He also approved the view of Alderson B[109] that fit for human habitation meant that 'the premises might be used and dwelt in not only with safety, but with reasonable comfort, by the class of persons by whom and for the sort of purposes for which, they were to be occupied'. In *Hall* v *Manchester Corporation* (1915)[110] Lord Parker took the matter a stage further in holding that a house could be unfit due to extrinsic causes, for instance the impairment of ventilation by neighbouring buildings. He said, 'The sole question in every case is whether the house is as a fact fit for human habitation and not in any case the cause of the unfitness'. So in *Birchall* v *Wirrall UDC* (1953),[111] a shed on a camping ground had been converted into a permanent residence. In connection with proceedings for a demolition order the question of its unfitness within section 188(4) of the Housing Act 1936, related to disrepair and sanitary defects, was in issue. Holding that it was a matter of fact and evidence in each case and finding that the building was in fact clean and sanitary, the Court of Appeal concluded that it was not unfit. The criteria for unfitness are now to be found in section 604(1) of the Housing Act 1985,[112] which provides that premises shall be deemed to be unfit if, and only if, they are so far defective in one or more of the specified matters that they are not reasonably suitable for occupation in that condition. The matters are repair, stability, freedom from damp, internal arrangement, natural lighting, ventilation, water supply, drainage and sanitary conveniences, and facilities for the preparation and cooking of food and for the disposal of waste water. However, this standard is specifically applicable to Housing Act purposes. The determination of unfitness under this present Act may therefore still be a matter of assessment according to the general principles noted above.

As well as requiring the execution of work, the court may also impose a fine. For this reason the old procedure was held to be criminal in nature and therefore to be commenced by information and summons rather than by complaint.[113] The present 1990 provision, as originally drafted retained 'complaint' and omitted any reference to a fine; clearly indicating civil proceedings. However, during the third reading in the Lords the power to impose a fine was reintroduced with the intention of 'criminalising' the procedure. The reason, as Lord Byron explained in mov-

103 *Warner* v *Lambeth LBC* (1984) 15 HLR 42.

104 Section 82(2).

105 See, e.g., *Nottingham Corpn* v *Newton* [1974] 1 WLR 923; *Salford City Council* v *McNally* [1976] AC 379. On precision and clarity of the order, see *R* v *Fenny Stratford JJ ex parte Watney Mann (Midlands)* [1976] 1 WLR 1101.

106 [1927] 2 KB 131.

107 At p.145.

108 [1943] AC 283.

109 In *Belcher* v *M'Intosh* (1839) 2 M & Rob 186 at p.189.

110 (1915) 84 LJ Ch App 732 at p.742.

111 (1953) 117 JP 384, CA.

112 Re-enacting section 4 of the Housing Act 1957.

113 See *Northern Ireland Trailers* v *Preston Corpn* [1972] 1 All ER 260.

114 [1947] 2 All ER 537; and
see also *Scarborough
Corporation* v *Scarborough
Sanitary Authority* (1876) 1 Ex
D 344.

115 [1990] 3 All ER 385.

ing the amendment, was to enable magistrates to make an award of compensation under section 35 of the Powers of Criminal Courts Act 1973 if they think
it necessary.

It is now well established that this procedure is available against a local authority as against any other defendant, the argument to the contrary being based on
the primary role of local authorities in enforcing these provisions. The Divisional
Court in *R* v *Epping (Waltham Abbey) JJ ex parte Burlinson* (1947)[114] found no
inconsistency in the two roles. Lord Goddard CJ considered that the preceding
section 99 applied in two cases: (1) where the local authority is alleged not to have
carried out its duty, i.e. to secure abatement, and (2) where the local authority
itself is alleged to have caused the nuisance. Returning now to *Sandwell MBC* v
Bujok (1990),[115] the prosecuting council house tenant, advised by a private self-
help group, had taken action in the magistrate's court under section 99 with no
prior warning to or communication with the local authority. There was no evidence that the local authority otherwise knew of the defects to the premises and,
being now informed, it had completed the work before the hearing. The Court
decided that under section 99 an individual could commence proceedings without first requiring the person concerned to abate the nuisance, although some preliminary notification should be given. In fact their Lordships condemned in very
strong terms the failure to give any prior warning, leading, through a late amendment to the Bill, to the requirement in section 82(6) and (7) of written notice to
the proposed defendant of the intention to bring proceedings. In the case of noise
(section 79(1)(g)), not less than three days' notice is required, and in all other cases
not less than 21 days' notice.

By section 82(8), failure to comply with the terms of the order constitutes an
offence and, following summary proceedings and conviction, renders the defendant liable to a fine and daily penalty. Where a person is convicted of an offence
under subsection (8) the court may also, after hearing the local authority, direct
the local authority to carry out any or all the terms of the order.

4

Statutory Nuisance Content

SCOPE OF STATUTORY NUISANCES

The matters stated by section 79(1) of the Environmental Protection Act 1990 to be statutory nuisances are:

(a) any premises in such a state as to be prejudicial to health or a nuisance;

(b) smoke emitted from premises so as to be prejudicial to health or a nuisance;

(c) fumes or gases emitted from premises so as to be prejudicial to health or a nuisance;

(d) any dust, steam, smell or effluvia arising on industrial, trade or business premises and being prejudicial to health or a nuisance;

(e) any accumulation or deposit which is prejudicial to health or a nuisance;

(f) any animal kept in such a place or manner as to be prejudicial to health or a nuisance;

(g) noise emitted from premises so as to be prejudicial to health or a nuisance;

(ga) noise that is prejudicial to health or a nuisance and is emitted from or caused by a vehicle, machinery or equipment in a street;[1] or

(h) any other matter declared by any enactment to be a statutory nuisance.

1 Added by section 2(2) of the Noise and Statutory Nuisance Act 1993.

The 'other matters' coming within section 79(1)(h) are, in the following sections of the Public Health Act 1936:

(a) an insanitary well, tank, cistern or water-butt used for water for domestic purposes which is so placed, constructed or kept as to render the water therein liable to contamination prejudicial to health (section 141);

(b) any pond, pool, ditch, gutter or watercourse which is so foul or in such a state as to be prejudicial to health or a nuisance (section 259(1)(a));

(c) any part of a watercourse (not navigated) which is so choked or silted up as to obstruct or impede the proper flow of water and thereby cause a nuisance, or give rise to conditions prejudicial to health (section 259(1)(b));

(d) a tent, van, shed or similar structure used for human habitation –

    (i) which is in such a state, or so overcrowded, as to be prejudicial to the health of the inmates; or

    (ii) the use of which, by reason of the absence of proper sanitary accommodation or otherwise, gives rise whether on the site or on other land, to a nuisance or to conditions prejudicial to health (section 268(2)).

And in the Mines and Quarries Act 1954 unfenced, abandoned and disused mines and quarries.

These matters will be dealt with in turn.

Premises

'Premises' are defined by section 79(7) and (12) to include land and vessels other than those powered by steam reciprocating machinery. Houseboats and other vessels on inland waterways will therefore be included. Tents, caravans and other mobile accommodation are not brought within this subsection, however, being dealt with as statutory nuisances under section 268 of the Public Health Act 1936. Section 109 of the Public Health Act 1936 excluded mines and smelting works from the scope of premises, but that exclusion has not been carried over to this present statute.

Streets also appear to be included in premises if *Attorney-General v Kirk* (1896)[2] is still good authority, an interlocutory injunction being granted to restrain the defendant from allowing the street to remain in such a state as to create a nuisance or become injurious to the public health. Its validity may be questioned, however, in the light of the reasoning adopted in *London Borough of Tower Hamlets v Manzoni and Walder* (1984)[3] holding that 'noise emitted from premises' did not cover noise from streets or public places. As section 93 of the Public Health Act 1936, which is substantially re-enacted in section 80(2)(c) of the Environmental Protection Act 1990, provided that 'Where a local authority are satisfied of the existence of a statutory nuisance they shall serve a notice on the person by whose act, default or sufferance the nuisance arises or continues ... or if that person cannot be found, on the owner or occupier of the premises on which the nuisance arises,' it was considered that such phraseology necessarily excluded streets.

However, 'premises' for the purpose of these provisions do not include either public sewers (*Fulham Vestry v LCC* (1897)),[4] or sewage works (*R v Parlby* (1889)),[5] although Professor Cross justifiably doubts the reasoning in the former case; a similar approach being adopted in the second, the decision seeming to turn on the public ownership rather than the nature of the premises. In the first case Day J said[6]:

> What are contemplated are nuisances arising from the acts of owners of property, as distinguished from anything which may be caused by the construction of great public works, which are entrusted to the County Council.

The defence of either statutory authority or public benefit to justify the commision of a statutory nuisance except in unavoidable circumstances, has long since been discarded.

Nevertheless, the definition of 'premises' is wide. While in practice the emphasis inevitably falls on residential property, the application of these provisions, where appropriate, to other categories should be noted. It is in the context of premises, and in particular domestic premises, that the distinction between the prejudicial to health limb and the nuisance limb of the section 79 criteria is of most significance and has tended to be obscured. The confusion on this point, particularly evident in the earlier cases, was exacerbated by the legislative wording. While this procedure for abating nuisances was introduced in the Public Health Act 1845, it was only with the 1936 Act that such nuisances were identified as 'statutory' nuisances. The four earlier Acts spoke of matters that are injurious to health or a nuisance being a nuisance. The consequent uncertainty over whether, when talking of nuisance in this context, the statutory or common law form is intended is often difficult to determine. The impression also given is that the distinction is not always apparent to the author of the judgement. The interpretation and application of such earlier judgements has carried this uncertainty over into the post-1937 period.

2 (1986) 12 TLR 514.

3 (1984) 148 JPR 123.

4 [1897] 2 QB 70.

5 (1889) 22 QBD 520.

6 At p.78.

The question is now clear, though. Where premises are prejudicial to the health of the occupants they will constitute a statutory nuisance, whereas to be a statutory nuisance within the second, 'nuisance' limb they must amount to a common law nuisance, in the sense discussed in the previous chapter, to the occupiers of other premises. Conversely, to be a nuisance as a private nuisance, the form most applicable to the occupation of premises, the activity affecting premises or their enjoyment has to come from elsewhere. While defects to premises may render them prejudicial to the health of the occupants and so actionable as a statutory nuisance, if they merely constitute a nuisance to the occupants of the same premises they will not amount to a nuisance at law and therefore also not a statutory nuisance; a distinction illustrated by *Springett* v *Harold* (1954).[7] The walls and ceilings to the first floor rooms were stained, dirty and flaking and in need of decorative repair but were not damp, verminous or injurious to health. The court found that mere want of decorative repair did not constitute a nuisance within the meaning of section 82(1)(a) of the Public Health (London) Act 1936 even if it did cause discomfort and inconvenience.

This emphasis on the scope of the nuisance is evident in *Turley* v *King* (1944).[8] The main roofs of the defendant's properties were found to be in such a state of dangerous disrepair as to amount to a nuisance. However, as their condition was due to war damage the defendant claimed relief under the Landlord and Tenant (War Damage) Act 1939, section 1. The editorial note in the All England Law Reports reads:

> The principle upon which this case is decided is that the duty upon every person who is an owner of property to avoid committing a statutory nuisance, and to abate one when ordered to do so, is something quite different from his duty as a landlord towards his tenant. Therefore, the fact that he is in a position to plead statutory relief from liability to repair, as against his tenant, is no answer to proceedings to abate a nuisance.

The landlord's respective duties on the one hand to his tenants under the lease and on the other to his neighbours in nuisance are clearly distinguishable. If the damaged roof had been categorised as prejudicial to health, though, as it could justifiably have been, the persons owed the respective duties under the lease and under the statutory nuisance provisions then become the same, that is the occupants. Presumably the same principle would then apply, denying the tenant any remedy under the lease but allowing a solution under the statutory nuisance provisions.

So in *National Coal Board* v *Neath BC* (1976),[9] premises owned by the appellants had two defective windows, no stop end to a rainwater gutter and a defective skirting board. The justices held that although the premises were not in such a state as to be prejudicial to health the defects constituted a nuisance in that they interfered with the personal comfort of the occupiers. In allowing the appeal the Divisional Court said:

> The word nuisance in section 92(1) [now section 79(1) of the 1990 Act], meant either a public or a private nuisance at common law, i.e. an act or omission materially affecting the comfort or quality of life of a class of the public or an interference for a substantial period with the use and enjoyment of neighbouring property. Accordingly a nuisance could not be said to have arisen on premises if what had taken place only affected the person or persons occupying those premises.

In this context the approach in *Betts* v *Penge UDC* (1942)[10] is instructive. The tenant of a flat had not paid rent or responded to a notice to quit. The landlord

7 [1954] 1 All ER 568.

8 [1944] 2 All ER 489.

9 [1976] 2 All ER 478.

10 [1942] 2 All ER 61.

removed window sashes and the door. Both the magistrates and the Divisional Court found that although not prejudicial to health the lack of windows and door interfered with the personal comfort of the tenants and therefore constituted a nuisance, following *Bishop Auckland Local Board* v *Bishop Auckland Iron & Steel Co.* (1882).[11] In that case offensive smells from accumulations of waste at a steel works interfered with the personal comfort of persons living in the neighbourhood. Though not injurious to health they were held to constitute a nuisance within section 91 of the 1875 Act. So in *Betts* v *Penge UDC*,[12] both courts, finding that the lack of windows and door interfered with the personal comfort of the tenants held that it too constituted a nuisance. However the two cases are clearly distinguishable. In the earlier case the cause of the nuisance, the offensive smells, came onto the premises from elsewhere, as required in the case of a private nuisance at common law. In *Betts*, on the other hand, the cause of the nuisance originated on those premises and could not therefore amount in law to a nuisance. The fact that both interfered with the personal comfort of the occupants obscures and cannot compensate for this fundamental difference. For this reason the decision in *Betts* v *Penge UDC* was disapproved by Lord Wilberforce in *Salford City Council* v *McNally* [1975][13] His Lordship said[14]:

11 (1882) 10 QBD 138.

12 See note 10 above.

13 [1975] 2 All ER 860.

14 At p.864.

> A similar confusion occurs in some of the cases through the use of the words 'personal comfort'. These words are appropriate enough in the context of what is a 'nuisance' for the purposes of the Public Health Act 1936 ... but they are quite inappropriate in relation to the other limb 'prejudicial to health'. Health is not the same as comfort and interference with the latter does not bring a case within the 'health' limb of the 1936 Act. In my opinion *Betts* v *Penge UDC.* is guilty of this confusion and was wrongly decided.

If this analysis reveals an apparent lacuna in the law to the detriment of occupiers of residential premises, the main class on the face of it who require protection, it is to be remembered that housing legislation provides a range of appropriate remedies for that very group.

For premises to constitute a statutory nuisance they must be in 'such a state' as to be prejudicial to health or a nuisance. The sense is that it is the inherent characteristics or condition of the property rather than the activities carried on that are at issue. In *Metropolitan Asylum District* v *Hill* (1881)[15] it was said that premises that are only a nuisance because of the use to which they are put are not a statutory nuisance, and Wills J in *R* v *Parlby* (1889)[16] confined premises as a statutory nuisance to their condition. So in *London Borough of Lambeth* v *Stubbs* (1980)[17] Waller LJ applied the principle in the following way to the abatement of a statutory nuisance. He said:

15 (1881) 6 App Cas 193.

16 (1889) 22 QBD 520 at p.525.

17 (1980) *The Times*, 15 May.

> As it seems to me the original finding was that the premises were in such a state as to be prejudicial to health, and if the tenants are removed nothing has been done to alter the state of the premises. They remain prejudicial to health even if nobody goes and lives in those premises. ... As it seems to me in order to abate the statutory nuisance, something must be done to the house ... Prohibiting occupation simply avoids actual injury to health the danger remains and therefore the nuisance is not affected.

18 [1981] 2 All ER 184.

In both this case and *Coventry City Council* v *Doyle* (1981)[18] there are however *dicta* suggesting that if occupation is effectively prevented, e.g. by boarding up and disconnection of services, that may be sufficient to constitute abatement for the purposes of the Act.

An interesting application of this principle is provided by *London Borough of Southwark* v *Ince* (1989).[19] The prosecutors were occupants of premises converted into flats by the local authority, and were alleging that due to lack of any or adequate sound insulation the flats were prejudicial to their health due to severe noise penetration from neighbouring road and rail traffic. The magistrates found in their favour ordering the local authority to provide sound insulation. The appeal by the local authority was now dismissed by the Court of Appeal. The following points arise from the judgment of Woolf LJ:

19 (1989) 21 HLR 504.

(a) The building was not itself a nuisance. It could not be a public nuisance as the tenants of the building could not be described as a class. It could not be a private nuisance as there was no interference by one owner or occupier with the use or enjoyment of other property.
(b) The question was not whether the noise was a nuisance but whether the premises were in such a state as to be prejudicial to health. Woolf LJ said:

> "that may be the case for a whole variety of external factors, be they weather, noise, incursion of sewage or anything else. The fact that there is legislation dealing with those responsible for some of those external factors does not suggest that the Public Health Act is inappropriate to premises which are in such a state as to be prejudicial to health by reason of the external factors for which others may be responsible.

This is an unusual and, as Woolf LJ notes in his judgement, a unique application of the principle in the existing authorities. He therefore returns to the question and the statement of principle in the following paragraph[20]:

20 At p.515.

> Before leaving this topic, there was some debate in front of us as to whether a distinction could be drawn between an external factor such as noise and other external factors such as, for example, rain. It was suggested at one stage that there could be a distinction drawn which would assist the respondents in this case. Suffice it to say that having thought as carefully as I can about it, I can see no valid distinction between the two. In each case there is an external factor which, when applied to the premises in question, may enable it to be said that the premises are in such a state as to be prejudicial to health by reason of that factor.

(c) The magistrates were justified in finding that the premises were in such a state as to be prejudicial to health since they found that they were not properly insulated against noise and therefore allowed the ingress of noise.

The significance and therefore the potential of this case is self-evident. The actual cause of the statutory nuisance was a host of vehicles in, as far as the complainants were concerned, anonymous ownership. Being unable to tackle the source of the problem any amelioration could only be sought in preventing its access to their premises. Therefore, and adopting Woolf LJ's analogy, if the procedure applies to keep rain out, why should it not in logic keep noise out as well?

Smoke

Previously, section 101 of the Public Health Act 1936 declared certain 'smoke nuisances', essentially from industrial premises to be statutory nuisances. This limited provision was extended by section 16 of the Clean Air Act 1956 and re-enacted in section 1 of the Control of Smoke Pollution Act 1989 before being consolidated in the present section 79 and again extended, in particular to apply to 'premises' as widely defined for the purposes of this section. While now therefore including domestic premises, this provision is still more likely to be used in connection with commercial or industrial activity, save possibly for the ubiquitous garden bonfire.

Section 79(3) retains some of the exclusions of the earlier provisions, i.e.:

(a) smoke emitted from a chimney of a private dwelling house within a smoke control area;

(b) dark smoke emitted from a chimney of a building or a chimney serving the furnace of a boiler or industrial plant attached to a building or for the time being fixed to or installed on any land;

(c) dark smoke emitted otherwise than as mentioned above from industrial or trade premises.

None of these occurrences is a statutory nuisance, being actionable under other provisions on proof of the discharge and without the need to establish either prejudice to health or nuisance. By virtue of section 79(7) the definition of 'dark smoke' in section 34(2) of the Clean Air Act 1956 as 'smoke that is as dark as or darker than shade 2 on the Ringelmann Chart' applies. Section 79(3)(iii) also excludes from these provisions smoke emitted from a railway locomotive steam engine. Although it might be questioned whether such smoke is actually emitted from premises, the position is now clarified for the benefit of the various railway preservation societies who operate such locomotives.

The definition of 'smoke' in section 79(7) is imported from the Clean Air Act 1956 and 'includes soot, ash, grit and gritty particles emitted in smoke'. Any or all of these may commonly be found as constituents of smoke. They may therefore be dealt with under this subsection only where they originate in a combustion process and form part of the products of combustion. This view is supported in that dust, defined in section 79(7) as excluding dust emitted from a chimney as an ingredient of smoke, is otherwise dealt with in section 79(1)(d); see, for example, *Wivenhoe Port v Colchester BC* (1985).[21]

While smoke control legislation has concentrated on visible smoke, that limitation does not apply here. The products of combustion may be either prejudicial to health or a nuisance whether visible or invisible and, depending on the constituents, irrespective of quantity. In this respect it is to be noted that, in common with section 79(1)(g) noise, there may be applicable standards, discharge or emission levels and imposed by statute or regulation, or the subject of a condition attached to a consent or licence, or so on. The determination of whether a particular incident is a statutory nuisance is independent of such specific standards. While the achieving of the standard may bear on the defence of best practicable means in appropriate cases, the assessment of the emission as prejudicial to health or a nuisance is based on other criteria as discussed above. This is not to say that enforcement by an alternative specific procedure that does not necessitate proof of prejudice to health or nuisance may not be more appropriate. As an example one may instance the nuisances caused by stubble burning and the controlling regulations made under section 152 of the Environmental Protection Act 1990; currently the Crop Residues (Burning) Regulations 1993.

Fumes or gases

This is a category of statutory nuisance newly included by the Environmental Protection Act 1990 and, by section 79(4), is restricted to private dwellings. It is difficult to see what prompted or is intended to be aimed at by this provision.

Perhaps it is included here to apply this procedure as a remedy, *inter alia*, for occupants of dwellings affected by the seepage of radon gas.

Section 79(7) defines 'fumes' as airborne solid matter smaller than dust, and 'gas' as including vapour and moisture precipitated by vapour. Also, by virtue of the same subsection, terms common to this section and the Clean Air Acts 1956 and 1968 shall have the same meaning in this section as under those Acts. So:

(a) 'grit' is defined in the Clean Air Act (Emission of Grit and Dust from Furnaces) Regulations 1971 as particles exceeding 76 microns in diameter;
(b) 'fumes' are defined in section 13 of the Clean Air Act 1968 as airborne solid matter smaller than dust;
(c) British Standard BS3405 defines 'dust' as small solid particles between 1 and 75 microns in diameter.

Dust, steam, smell or other effluvia

This provision re-enacts that in section 92(1)(d) of the Public Health Act 1936, but in slightly broader terms. In particular, where the earlier provision covered dust or effluvia 'caused by' etc., it is now enough that the prohibited effluvia merely arises on the stipulated premises, whatever its cause or origin. Section 79(5) again excludes steam emitted from a railway locomotive engine. The dust in this category is that emitted otherwise than as a constituent of smoke, which would be actionable under section 79(1)(b) above.

The stipulated emissions may be dealt with under this subsection only where they arise on 'industrial, trade or business premises'. This term is defined in section 79(7) to include premises used for such purposes, or where they are used for the purpose of any treatment or process as well as manufacturing. 'Trade' has been defined judicially in the following terms:

> No doubt in many contexts the word 'trade' indicates a process of buying and selling, but that is by no means an exhaustive definition of its meaning. It may also mean a calling or industry or class of skilled labour.[22]

A trade is an organised seeking after profits as a rule with the aid of physical assets.[23]

'Business' appears to be a wider term than 'trade', although it must be construed in its context. It has been said to mean, 'almost anything which is an occupation, as distinguished from a pleasure – anything which is an occupation or duty which requires attention is a business'.[24] So professional activities would be included,[25] but purely domestic or recreational activities would not,[26] and neither would an isolated transaction undertaken with no intention that it be repeated.[27]

The judgement of Butler J in *Wivenhoe Port v Colchester BC* (1985)[28] deals with the scope of this nuisance in the context of dust. The issue concerned dust generated by the discharge of grab from moored vessels and the handling and loading of soya meal into lorries within the premises. The court accepted that the dust was prejudicial to health. Butler J dealt with the question of nuisance in the following terms[29]:

> To be within the spirit of the Act [i.e. the Public Health Act 1936] a nuisance to be a statutory nuisance had to be one interfering materially with the personal comfort of the residents, in the sense that it materially affected their well-being although it might not be prejudicial to health. Thus, dust falling on motor-cars might cause inconvenience to

22 *Skinner v Jack Breach* [1927] 2 KB 220.

23 *Aviation & Shipping Co. v Murray* [1961] 1 WLR 974.

24 *Rolls v Miller* (1894) 27 Ch D 71 at p.88.

25 See, e.g., *Re Wilkinson* [1922] 1 KB 584, P 587; *R v Breeze* [1973] 1 WLR 994.

26 See, e.g., *Abernethie v Keiman* [1970] 1 QB 10; *Town Investments v Dept of the Environment* [1976] 3 All ER 479 at p.496, CA.

27 See, e.g., *Re Griffin ex parte Board of Trade* (1890) 60 LJ QB 235 at p.237.

28 [1985] JPL 175, affirmed [1985] JPL 396.

29 Ibid. at p.178.

their owners; it might even diminish the value of the motor-car: but it would not be a statutory nuisance. In the same way dust falling on gardens or trees, or on stock held in a shop would not be a statutory nuisance. But dust in eyes or hair, even if not shown to be prejudicial to health would be so as to interfere with personal comfort.

The line between inconvenience and discomfort is clearly hard to draw, and perhaps even more so in the case of other forms of statutory nuisance. In the passage quoted the learned judge is, as he says, mindful of the context of a public health measure and its qualification of the scope of the nuisance. A question for consideration now is the extent to which that limitation should be relaxed as a consequence of the wider scope of an environmental statute. What now of the dust falling on gardens and trees?

A different type of dust was at issue in *Pwllbach Colliery Co. Ltd v Woodman* (1915).[30] The respondent butcher operating a slaughterhouse and sausage factory, successfully complained of the coal dust emitted from the appellant colliery company's adjoining screening and breaking operations and contaminating his premises and processes. The early case of *Malton Board of Health v Malton Manure Co.* (1879)[31] concerned the effluvia produced in the manufacture of artificial manures, involving the crushing and dissolving of bones and coprolites by sulphuric acid. The resulting effluvia was wind borne into the adjoining town. In finding for the Board, Kelly CB said, 'The question is whether on the facts before us, it appears that the effluvium from this place is a nuisance or injurious to the health of any of the inhabitants of the district'. This case therefore seems to offer an example of a statutory nuisance founded on public rather than private nuisance criteria.

Accumulation or deposit

This provision reproduces section 92(1)(c) of the Public Health Act 1936, and therefore cases thereunder, of which *Coventry City Council v Cartwright* (1975)[32] is now without doubt the principal authority, are relevant. The facts of that case were that the local authority owned a plot of vacant and unfenced land on which indiscriminate tipping occurred, including builder's rubble, scrap iron, broken glass, tin cans and household refuse. The local authority periodically removed the household and putrescible matter. The principal question for the Divisional Court was whether the remaining material could be a statutory nuisance, particularly as persons, including children, going on the land might hurt themselves on the iron, broken glass, tin cans and so on. Lord Widgery dealt with the matter in the following terms[33]:

> [*Counsel*] says, and I agree with him, that the real question here is whether that which the justices found to exist was an accumulation prejudicial to health, and on that approach to the matter he says that the possibility of physical injury from cuts and the like is sufficient to justify the assertion that this deposit or accumulation was prejudicial to health.
>
> For my part, I think that that is taking too wide a view of the section. The words are obviously very wide, and one should hesitate, in construing the section in proceedings such as the present, to lay down boundaries which may in another case prove to be unsuitable. But I think that the underlying conception of the section is that that which is struck at is an accumulation of something which produces a threat to health in the sense of a threat of disease, vermin or the like.

This, of course, accords with its context in a statute concerned with public health matters, and produced a similar result when applied to another contention of the

30 [1915] AC 634.

31 (1879) 4 Ex D 302.

32 [1975] 2 All ER 99.

33 At p.102e, f.

complainant, that the appearance of the site and contents could amount to a nuisance within section 92 of the 1936 Act. Lord Widgery said, on that question[34]:

> it seems to me, first, that there is no justification for [*the justices'*] view that visual impact might be a nuisance within the meaning of this section. I think that is going a very very long way beyond whatever limits could properly be imposed on the meaning of this provision. It is quite remote and utterly different from the other type of mischief which the Act is aimed at.

While this second statement of principle is undoubtedly right, the conclusion of the first is more open to question. Having regard to the extension of this statutory nuisance procedure by section 151 of the Mines and Quarries Act 1954 to protect against physical injury, even though without reference to prejudice to health or nuisance, the view that the procedure is confined to the suppression of disease and the like and is not to extend to circumstances involving physical injury may require reconsideration.

Nevertheless, on current authority this clause is primarily concerned with accumulations of rotting and decomposing organic matter, whether produced in conjunction with a business – *Draper* v *Sperring* (1861),[35] where sheep droppings on a pavement constituted a nuisance under the Nuisances Removal Act 1855; *Smith* v *Waghorn* (1863),[36] where the respondent kept stable manure in an open yard so as to be a nuisance to the appellant and others under the Tunbridge Wells Improvement Act 1846 – or domestically – *Flight* v *Thomas* (1839),[37] where a mixen (dung heap) on the defendant's land 'cause(d) divers stenches and smells necessarily and unavoidably to arise rendering the plaintiff's premises uncomfortable, unhealthy and unwholesome and unfit for habitation'. In *Bland* v *Yates* (1914)[38] a pile of garden manure which gave off smells and collected large numbers of flies was a nuisance.

That accumulations of inorganic material may also come within this paragraph is illustrated by *Bishop Auckland Local Board* v *Bishop Auckland Iron & Steel Co.* (1882),[39] where fumes and offensive smells given off by piles of waste from the works interfered with the personal comfort of persons living in the neighbourhood though not causing injury to health. Also the accumulation may be a natural occurrence, for instance of seaweed on the foreshore, as in *Props. of Margate Pier and Harbour* v *Town Council of Margate*.[40] In his judgement Lush J said:

> I have no doubt, whatever, that it is the duty of the appellants to prevent the accumulation of seaweed so that it shall not become a nuisance, and that, whether produced by natural or artificial causes, they are bound to remove all matter in the harbour which is a nuisance or injurious to health.

The reference to 'natural or artificial causes' was no doubt prompted by evidence that the accumulation of seaweed was encouraged or facilitated by the positioning of the steel piers on which the pier was constructed.

It is to be noticed that in many cases the nuisance produced by an accumulation or deposit is in the form of noxious fumes or smells. The question therefore arises whether it should be dealt with as fumes or effluvia under either section 79(1)(c) or (d) as appropriate, or as an accumulation or deposit here. The answer, it is submitted, is indicated in the terms of section 80(1) which requires the local authority to serve an abatement notice requiring 'the execution of such works, and the taking of such other steps, as may be necessary'. By considering the action

34 At p.104b.

35 (1861) 10 CB (NS) 113.

36 (1863) 27 JP 744. The judgement of Wightman J reads, in total: 'The case says the dung was allowed to accumulate. Does not that amount to a nuisance?'

37 (1839) 10 Ad & El 590.

38 (1914) 58 SJ 612.

39 (1882) 10 QBD 138.

40 (1869) 20 LT (NS) 564.

to remedy the nuisance the true source will be indicated as will the appropriate category within section 79(1).

Animals

41 [1955] 1 All ER 380.

This provision reproduces in the same words section 92(1)(b) of the Public Health Act 1936. The leading authority here is without doubt *Galer* v *Morrisey* (1955).[41] The case actually concerned a prosecution under a county council byelaw for keeping noisy animals; in this case, greyhounds. The defence sought to show that the byelaw was *ultra vires* in that it dealt with a matter already covered by statute. In holding that the byelaw was valid, Lord Goddard CJ confined the scope of this statutory provision to smell and the like. He said: 'It is the conditions under which the animal is kept that create the nuisance. The subsection does not deal with noisy animals'. This is with respect, no doubt right so far as the manner in which the animals are kept is concerned. However, it is submitted that 'place' may incorporate nuisances due to noise. That it did not include noise at that time is implied by Lord Goddard CJ in these words[42]:

42 At p.381.

> What puts this matter beyond doubt is that you find this provision in Part III of the Public Health Act 1936, which is headed 'Nuisances and Offensive Trades' and there is a fasciculus of sections, all of which deal with factories, houses unfit for habitation and smoke nuisances – all matters which come from insanitary or defective premises.

43 See below, section 79(1)(g).

44 See section 84 of the Environmental Protection Act 1990.

45 In *Coventry City Council* v *Cartwright* [1975] 2 All ER 99 at p.103.

46 [1950]1 All ER 942.

47 [1963] CLR 839.

48 (1895)59 JP 571.

Since that statement there have been two changes to the statutory context. Noise has been brought within the scope of statutory nuisances,[43] and control over offensive trades as such has gone.[44] It may therefore be that noisy animals are now brought within this provision. Lord Widgery CJ thought that they were within the earlier term, saying,[45] 'I would have thought for my part that a noisy animal could as much be prejudicial to health as a smelly animal'. However, because noise is now within the section in its own right the distinction is not now so important. Noise, and/or the animal making it may both be statutory nuisances.

As the classic animal nuisance, *McGillivray* v *Stevenson* (1950)[46] concerned smelly pigs. In *R* v *Walden-Jones ex parte Coton* (1963)[47] C kept a large number of cats in her bungalow; the court finding that if straying cats caused a nuisance they were within the Act. *R* v *King* (1895),[48] held that harmless snakes from the defendant's house appearing in the adjoining premises constituted a nuisance under the Public Health (London) Act 1891. There was medical evidence that the discovery by Mrs Taylor (the neighbouring occupant) of a snake in her bed might prove fatal. It might also, in the view of the court, injure the health of anyone.

49 (1889) 24 QBD 357.

In conclusion *R* v *Brown* (1889),[49] though not concerned with these particular provisions, is authority that poultry are animals.

Noise

50 On aircraft noise generally, see sections 5, 6, 78 and 79 of the Civil Aviation Act 1982 and the Rules of the Air and Air Traffic Control Regulations 1985.

Noise was not included as a statutory nuisance in the earlier statutes, concerned as they were with what might be regarded as primary public health matters deriving from the industrialisation and urbanisation of the nineteenth century. Section 1 of the Noise Abatement Act 1960 first declared noise to be a statutory nuisance. Those provisions were re-enacted in sections 58–59 of the Control of Pollution Act 1974 and now appear in this present form. By section 79(7) of the 1990 Act, noise includes vibration, and section 79(6) excludes noise created by aircraft other than model aircraft.[50] Section 80(9) provides certain defences where a local authority institutes proceedings following failure to comply with an abatement notice. These are:

(a) that the alleged offence is covered by a notice served under section 60, or a consent given under sections 61 or 65 of the Control of Pollution Act 1974 (construction sites);

(b) where the premises are subject to a noise reduction notice under section 66 of the Control of Pollution Act 1974, that the level of noise emitted did not contravene that notice;

(c) when a noise level fixed under section 67 of the Control of Pollution Act 1974 applied to the premises, that the level of noise emitted at that time did not exceed that level.

These defences reproduce those in section 58(6) of the Control of Pollution Act 1974 and are based on the principle that it is unreasonable for the local authority to institute proceedings under these provisions when it has, under other powers, given consent to a particular level of noise and the person concerned is complying with those requirements.

To come within this subsection noise need not be a public nuisance. It is sufficient if it interferes with personal comfort.[51] Whether noise constitutes a nuisance therefore is a question of degree,[52] although if it is caused maliciously that will be a relevant factor.[53]

R v Fenny Stratford JJ ex parte Whatney Mann (Midlands) Ltd (1976)[54] concerned noise from a juke box in the appellant's public house which was situated in a building containing residential flats. The justices in making a nuisance order, had imposed a limit of 70 decibels on the noise. On appeal, while finding that the nuisance existed, the Divisional Court found that as the order did not specify where the noise level was to be recorded its terms were so imprecise as to be void for uncertainty. On the question of location Watkins J said[55]:

> the place for determining whether a nuisance exists is not to be ascertained, in the case of noise, by standing in the place from which the noise emanates, but by standing in the nearest of the dwelling places and listening to the noise flowing into that place.

In the same case Lord Widgery CJ made the following general observations in his judgement[56]:

> This case does throw up for the first time the very interesting question whether the introduction by modern science of the decibel cannot be used for the purposes of precision in cases such as the present. I agree with Watkins J that it can and should. It seems to me that if the justices take the trouble to hear evidence which translates noise into a decibel reading and satisfy themselves that any emanation of noise in excess of a certain level is a nuisance, they can as well describe that which is to be done as a reduction of noise volume to below so many decibels instead of using the time-honoured formula of 'abate the nuisance'. I think that we should try to use the advantages which scientific development gives us rather than reject them, and I think here there is an opportunity of using a scientific approach to what has always previously been a somewhat haphazard assessment.

Cooke v *Adatia* (1989)[57] suggests that, in relation to evidence, it may be sufficient to present the evidence of decibel levels from an environmental health officer without calling neighbouring occupiers to testify as to interference with their reasonable comfort or enjoyment.

51 *Betts* v *Penge UDC* [1942] 2 KB 154, DC.

52 *Gaunt* v *Fynney* (1872) 8 Ch App 8.

53 *Christie* v *Davey* [1893] 1 Ch 316.

54 [1976] 2 All ER 888.

55 At p.892e.

56 At p.892j – 893b.

57 (1989) JP 129.

58 *Sedleigh-Denfield* v
O'Callaghan [1940] AC 880.

59 (1984) 148 JP 123; [1984]
JPL 436.

60 (1989) 153 JP 597; (1989)
153 LG Rev 831.

61 (1907) 21 HLR 504.

62 Published by the DoE in
1990. See also DoE
Consultation Paper, published,
1992.

63 (1985) 83 LGR 72.

Generally a private nuisance presupposes the possession and control of the land from which the nuisance proceeds.[58] This principle has been applied in holding that these provisions do not apply to control noise in the street. In *London Borough of Tower Hamlets* v *Manzoni and Walder* (1984),[59] the respondents and other members of the public demonstrated noisily against the sale of pet animals in a street market, using megaphones and other amplification devices. On action by the local authority under section 58(1) of the Control of Pollution Act 1974, the Divisional Court found that the section was concerned only with noise emitted or likely to be emitted from premises. While this limitation still applies, 'premises' is sufficiently wide now to include land and therefore streets (see also below). However, in support of their reasoning the Court noted the requirement of section 93 of the Public Health Act 1936, substantially re-enacted in section 80(2)(c), that the local authority shall 'serve a notice on ... or if that person cannot be found, on the owner or occupier of the premises on which the nuisance arises'. The members of the public participating in the demonstration in the instant case could in no sense be regarded as occupiers of the premises. Notice that noise originating outside the premises was considered in *London Borough of Southwark* v *Ince* (1989)[60] to render the premises prejudicial to health and therefore to impose a duty on the owners to insulate against noise.

In conclusion, *Lyttelton Times Co.* v *Warners* (1907)[61] warrants some reference although it was concerned with civil tort proceedings rather than, as here, criminal actions. The parties agreed that the appellant's property be rebuilt with an engine house and printing machine on the ground floor. The upper floor was to be let to the respondents to be used for bedrooms in connection with their adjoining hotel. Though the machinery caused unexpected vibration the appellant was only doing what both parties had contemplated he should. The Court therefore implied a reservation of a right to do it, notwithstanding that it caused a nuisance to the respondents. Such an agreement may apply in the civil law context. The question is whether such an agreement may be a bar to criminal proceedings under environmental legislation. In the absence of authority it is submitted that it is not. Even though the agreement may be binding on the parties to it, it cannot displace the statutory duty imposed on the local authority to take action when it becomes aware of the existance of a statutory nuisance.

Street Noise

This addition to the list of statutory nuisances by the Noise and Statutory Nuisance Act 1993 appears to have been prompted by the *Manzoni and Walder* situation considered above, and is a limited response to the many recommendations of the Report of the Noise Review Working Party.[62] The limited range of this ground of nuisance is however emphasised in that, by section 2(3), street noise derived from traffic or political or other campaigning demonstrations is excluded. The same section also excludes noise from the military forces of the Crown or visiting forces. To accommodate these particular circumstances the scope of 'person responsible', hitherto the person to whose act, default or sufferance the nuisance is attributable, is extended to include the registered owner of the vehicle and the driver and operator of the machinery or equipment. A definition of 'street' is also added to section 79(7), being a highway and any other road, footway, square or court that is for the time being open to the public. In *Tower Hamlets LBC* v *Creitzman* (1985)[63] it was said that an open space beneath a building used and attended by the public for a Sunday market could be regarded as a street, being open to the public and in the nature of a square.

The defence of best practicable means in section 80(7) of the 1990 Act is not available to this head of nuisance unless the machinery or equipment is being used for industrial, trade or business purposes.[64] While such purposes are not defined, section 79(7) of the principal Act offers a description of 'industrial, trade or business premises' which includes with manufacturing, the operation of any treatment or process. The defences in section 80(9) of the 1990 Act, that the noise was authorised by a notice served under section 60 or a consent given under sections 61 or 65 of the Control of Pollution Act 1974, are applied to noise from streets by section 3(5).

64 Section 3(4) of the Noise and Statutory Nuisance Act 1993.

Other matters

As indicated above, there are currently four other such provisions specifying statutory nuisances. These are as follows:

(a) Section 141 of the Public Health Act 1936 covers:

> Any well, tank, cistern or water-butt used for the supply of water for domestic purposes which is so placed, constructed or kept as to render the water therein liable to contamination prejudicial to health.

> As was noted at the beginning of this chapter, this statutory nuisance is uniquely limited to the stipulated matters being prejudicial to health only. There appears to be no authority or judicial commentary on this provision and therefore presumably, no litigation, at least in the higher courts. As there are now express quality standards for private water supplies monitored by local authorities, this provision may now be effectively regarded as obsolete.[65]

65 The Private Water Supplies Regulations 1991, S.I. 1991 No. 1790; see in Chapter 6 at p.155.

(b) Section 259(1) of the Public Health Act 1936, provides:

> The following matters shall be statutory nuisances –

> (a) any pond, pool, ditch, gutter or watercourse which is so foul or in such a state as to be prejudicial to health or a nuisance;
> (b) any part of a watercourse, not being a part ordinarily navigated by vessels employed in the carraige of goods by water, which is so choked or silted up as to obstruct or impede the proper flow of water and thereby cause a nuisance, or give rise to conditions prejudicial to health;

> Provided that in the case of an alleged nuisance under paragraph (b) nothing in this section shall be deemed to impose any liability on any person other than the person by whose act or default the nuisance arises or continues.

The two parts of this provision deal with nuisances deriving from two distinct causes. In paragraph (a) the nuisance derives from the condition of either the channel or the water contained in it and, unlike paragraph (b), includes commercial canals. So in *R v Bradford Navigation Co.*[66] the defendant company was held liable in public nuisance for taking into its canal 'large quantities of foul, liquid filth, sewage and polluted water'. Paragraph (b) is concerned with nuisances deriving from the obstruction of the flow of the stream.

66 (1865) 6 B&S 631.

The significance of the proviso is that, unlike statutory nuisances attributable to other causes, liability will not arise through 'sufferance' alone. The Divisional Court took this view in *Neath RDC v Williams* (1951),[67] holding that the mere

67 [1951] 1 KB 115; [1950] 2 All ER 625, DC.

failure by a landowner to keep a natural stream flowing through his land free from an obstruction brought about by natural causes was not an 'act or default' within the meaning of the proviso to section 259(1). In his judgement Lord Goddard CJ limited the scope of the default in this respect, saying :

> I do not think that in this case 'default' could mean merely doing nothing, unless an obligation to do something is imposed by the Act. There is no act of the defendants which caused the obstruction either to arise or continue. I can well understand that there might be a case where it might be said that a person who failed to do something which he ought to have done, such for instance, as failing to prevent obstructive matter from going into a river from his own premises, had caused an obstruction by his default.

(c) Section 268 of the Public Health Act 1936 provides that:

(1) The provisions of [*inter alia*] Part III, shall apply in relation to tents, vans, sheds and similar structures used for human habitation as they apply in relation to other premises and as if a tent, van, shed or similar structure used for human habitation were a house or a building so used.

(2) For the purposes of the said Part III, a tent, van, shed or similar structure used for human habitation –

(a) which is in such a state, or so overcrowded, as to be prejudicial to the health of the inmates; or

(b) the use of which, by reason of the absence of proper sanitary accommodation or otherwise, gives rise, whether on the site or on other land, to a nuisance or to conditions prejudicial to health, shall be a statutory nuisance, and the expression 'occupier' in relation to a tent, van, shed or similar structure shall include any person for the time being in charge thereof.

(3) Where such a nuisance as is mentioned in paragraph (b) of the preceding subsection is alleged to arise, wholly or in part, from the use for human habitation of any tent, van, shed or similar structure, then, without prejudice to the liability of the occupants or other users thereof, an abatement notice may be served on, and proceedings under Part III of this Act may be taken against the occupier of the land on which the tent, van, shed or other structure is erected or stationed;

Provided that it shall be a defence for him to prove that he did not authorise the tent, van, shed or other structure to be stationed or erected on the land.

Section 151(2) of the Mines and Quarries Act 1954 provides:

For the purposes of Part III of the Public Health Act 1936 each of the following shall be deemed to be a statutory nuisance that is to say –

(a) a shaft or outlet of an abandoned mine (other than a mine to which the proviso to the foregoing subsection applies) or of a mine (other than as aforesaid) which, notwithstanding that it has not been abandoned, has not been worked for a period of twelve months, being a shaft or outlet the surface entrance to which is not provided with a properly maintained device such as is mentioned in that subsection;

(b) a shaft or outlet of a mine to which the proviso to the foregoing subsection applies, being a shaft or outlet with respect to which the following conditions are satisfied, namely –

(i) that its surface entrance is not provided with a properly maintained device such as is mentioned in that subsection; and

(ii) that, by reason of its accessibility from the highway or a place of public resort, it constitutes a danger to members of the public; and

(c) a quarry (whether in course of being worked or not) which –

    (i) is not provided with an efficient and properly maintained barrier so designed and constructed as to prevent any person from falling into the quarry; and

    (ii) by reason of its accessibility from a highway or a place of public resort constitutes a danger to members of the public.

Definitions of 'mine' and 'quarry' appear in section 180 of the Act as follows:

> 'Mine' means an excavation or system of excavations made for the purpose of, or in connection with, the getting, wholly or substantially by means involving the employment of persons below ground, of minerals (whether in their natural state or in solution or suspension) or products of minerals.
>
> 'Quarry' means an excavation or systems of excavations made for the purpose of, or in connection with, the getting of minerals (whether in their natural state or in solution or in suspension) or products of minerals, being neither a mine nor merely a well or bore-hole or a well and bore-hole combined.

In relation to the working of a mine or quarry, section 182(3) provides that:

(a) the working of a mine shall be deemed to include the operation of driving a shaft or outlet therefore;

(b) the working of a quarry shall be deemed to include the operation of removing the overburden thereat;

(c) a mine or quarry shall be deemed to be worked notwithstanding that the only operations carried on thereat are operations carried on with a view to abandoning the mine or quarry ...

Both sections 151(2)(b)(ii) and (c)(ii) use the terms 'accessibility' and 'public resort'. The former has been held to mean the capability of access without reasonable let or hindrance.[68] The latter includes places to which the public have access even though not of right. In *Kitson* v *Ashe* (1899)[69] an unenclosed building site bounded by streets was frequented by bookmakers and others for betting. Lawrence J said:

> No doubt these persons have not a right to go there, and the owner may turn them out whenever he pleases; but at present they can in fact go there just as freely as to any other place within the borough. In these circumstances I have no doubt that this piece of ground has been properly held to be a 'place of public resort'.

Of the term 'deemed' it has been said that its primary function is to bring in something which would otherwise be excluded.[70]

    Contemplation of this provision and the type of statutory nuisance aimed at prompts two questions. First, in the past the view has been that, being found within public health legislation, the statutory nuisance concept and procedure is concerned with matters that are dangerous to health in the sense of disease, infection, vermin and the like, and not matters of physical danger or injury; see especially in this respect the views of Lord Widgery CJ, in *Coventry City Council* v *Cartwright* (1975).[71] In clear contrast, however, section 151(2) is aimed at physical danger, essentially attendant upon falling into a hole. What effect then should this have on the interpretation of the scope of statutory nuisance? Does it not at least provide grounds to argue for an extension of 'prejudicial to health' to physical injury? If the procedure is here made available to protect people from falling down the face of a quarry, may it not logically be used in a similar way to protect people from falling out of or into dilapidated premises? In *Pontardawe RDC* v *Moore-Gwyn* (1929)[72] the Court considered that though rocks falling from a steep slope

68 *Henaghan* v *Rederiet Farangirene* [1936] 2 All ER 1426.

69 [1899] 1 QB 425.

70 See *Barclay's Bank Ltd* v *IRC* [1961] AC 509 at p.523, [1960] 2 All ER 817 at p.820; *Public Trustee* v *IRC* [1960] AC 398, 1 All ER 1 at p.10.

71 [1975] 2 All ER 99 at p.102f.

72 [1929] 1 Ch 656.

might be dangerous, they were not 'premises in such a state as to be a nuisance'. Noting that 'premises' are defined to include land, may not the effect of this legislative extension of the scope of statutory nuisance be to change such a decision?

The second question arises from the evident lack of litigation under this section, at least in the appellate courts. Considering the number of mines and quarries throughout the country, many on or adjacent to land to which the public has access, and the statutory duty on local authorities to inspect for and remedy such nuisances, lack of more recent proceedings is surprising. As an example of action in this context, see *Attorney-General v Roe* (1915),[73] in which summary proceedings were taken under the Public Health Act 1875 to abate a nuisance under section 3 of the Quarry (Fencing) Act 1887, and requiring the owner to fence a worked out limestone quarry adjoining a road and causing subsidence.

Conclusion

In considering the range of matters dealt with by this statutory nuisance procedure the most significant omission is artificial light. Since the House of Lords removed light pollution from the Environmental Protection Bill because of the low incidence of the problem, complaints to local authorities have increased sufficiently to suggest that light in the 1990s may prove to be the social problem that noise was in the 1980s. A survey of local authorities conducted in 1993 by the Institution of Environmental Health Officers at the request of the Department of the Environment[74] revealed that 216 authorities[75] had received 1,271 complaints. Recognising that lack of any effective remedial procedure may both discourage complaints and deter the recording of all those that are made, it can be presumed that this number does not accurately reflect the real magnitude of the problem. Half the complaints related to domestic security lighting, while others concerned commercial and industrial sources and the floodlighting of sports grounds and golf driving ranges. Street lighting itself attracted few complaints. Of the complaints received two-thirds were assessed as nuisances, that is a greater proportion than in the case of noise complaints. It is apparent from this survey, and the assumption that the problem with its causes is likely to increase, that its recognition and remedy as a statutory nuisance should not be long delayed. The objection that difficulties of magnitude and duration will arise in determining nuisance thresholds is not a legitimate ground for inactivity. The question, and assessment, of reasonableness is an issue in all nuisance situations, whether private or statutory, and is resolved on evidence and argument.

73 [1915] 1 Ch 235, and see *Coupland v Hardingham* 3 Camp 398.

74 *Environmental Health*, vol. 102/04, April 1994, p.90.

75 Of the 307 authorities responding, i.e., a response rate of 63%.

Part Two

WATER

5

The Water Industry

STRUCTURE OF THE WATER INDUSTRY

Water as a service affects most people in two distinct though connected ways: the provision of a wholesome supply, and the removal and disposal of contaminated liquid wastes. That the latter returns to and may pollute the sources from which the former is drawn, requiring control of both functions, was a major factor generating the public health reforms of the nineteenth century and the creation of multi-purpose local authorities. Those authorities retained that dual responsibility until the logic of structuring the industry on the basis of hydrogeological rather than political boundaries was given effect in the Water Act 1973. That Act created nine regional water authorities for England, essentially related to the catchment areas of the main river basins, with an additional national authority for Wales, and gave them, as public bodies, the dual functions of utilities and regulatory authorities.

The next major changes were those attendant upon privatisation introduced by the Water Act 1989 and preceded by a succession of policy and discussion papers.[1] The utility or service provision is privatised, now being delivered by private companies appointed as water and sewerage undertakers. Their respective powers and responsibilities are now to be found in the consolidated Water Industry Act 1991 and are dealt with in the body of this chapter. The first undertakers were appointed under an Instrument of Appointment by the Secretary of State and succeeded to a proportionate division of the assets and liabilities of the predecessor water authorities under a transfer scheme approved by the Secretary of State under Schedule 2 of the Water Act 1989. The conditions of appointment of each undertaker provide a basic regulatory structure governing prices, performance standards and other aspects of their relationship with their customers, and providing an important parallel set of regulatory requirements supplementary to those contained in legislation.

The procedure for flotation in Part II of the 1989 Act reflected that of earlier privatisations, with a notable exception. The successor companies being the appointed undertakers are wholly owned by holding companies. It is only shares in the holding companies that are available for public purchase. The reason for this two tier structure, it is suggested,[2] is, by distancing the holding companies from the statutory regulation necessarily attendant upon the delivery of the core utility services, to facilitate their diversification into other business activities, possibly through a range of subsidiary companies (such as overseas services, land development and recreation). This division between the core functions of a water or sewerage undertaker on the one hand and the non-core activities of business ventures on the other will doubtless be an area of uncertainty and concern for the industry and its.regulators. Undertakers are now seen therefore to be subject to statutory regulatory

1 See, e.g., White Paper, 'Privatisation of the Water Authorities in England and Wales' (Cmnd 9734, February 1986), 'The Water Environment: the next steps' (DOE/WO Consultation Paper, April 1986). 'The National Rivers Authority ; the Government's proposals for a public regulatory body in a privatised water industry' (DOE/Ministry of Agriculture, Fisheries and Food and Welsh Office, July 1987).

2 By Macrory, (1990) 53 MLR 78.

control as public utilities, and also to the same company and stock exchange controls as other public limited companies. In this respect, and in the interests of the users of an essential service, undertakers are not allowed to commence voluntary winding-up proceedings, and proposed mergers will also be viewed strictly from a public interest viewpoint.

Regulation

Regulation of the industry is divided between a number of authorities, having at their head 'the Secretary of State'. This term may imply any one of Her Majesty's Principal Secretaries of State,[3] but for the purposes of this Act the functions are allocated to the Secretary of State for the Environment and the Secretary of State for Wales. Similarly, references in the legislation to 'the Minister' mean the Minister for Agriculture, Fisheries and Food.

3 Interpretation Act 1978, Schedule 1.

Water is abstracted from natural sources by water undertakers for purposes of supply, and eventually returned to those same sources by sewerage undertakers. Between these two functions, and linking them, the management of natural water resources in all their forms with the necessary associated regulatory powers, was given to a new national body created by the 1989 Act, the National Rivers Authority (NRA). Its structure and powers are now provided for in the consolidated Water Resources Act 1991 and are dealt with in Chapter 1. Detailed control over the water industry is given to the Director General of Water Services (the Director) as head of the Water Services Office, a post created by the Water Act 1989 and the appointment being made by the Secretary of State. What follows is an indication of his range of functions rather than a comprehensive catalogue.

Section 2 of the Water Industry Act 1991 requires that, in carrying out their powers and duties under the Act, both the Secretary of State and the Director are to have regard to two primary and a number of secondary principles. The two primary objectives, which necessarily take precedence over the secondary, are to ensure that the functions of undertakers are properly carried out and that they are able to finance the proper performance of those functions. The secondary principles, all, on general rules of statutory interpretation, being of equal importance, are to:

(a) ensure that customer's interests are protected in relation to –
  (i) rural areas,
  (ii) equality of charge fixing,
  (iii) terms of service provision,
  (iv) disposal of protected land
(b) promote economy and efficiency in the performance of functions;
(c) facilitate effective competition;
(d) ensure that the interests of the disabled and pensioners are taken into account.

These stipulated principles provide the basic objectives against which the performance of the Director is to be judged and by which he is to assess the operations of the undertakers. Further, they will constitute the criteria used by the High Court in determining the validity or reasonableness of decisions or actions challenged by judicial review. It is therefore difficult to over-emphasise the importance of these section 2 duties in establishing the foundation or underlying principles against which the performance of the industry is to be measured.

Section 3(2) imposes on the Secretary of State and Director the obligations:

(a) consistently with their section 2 duties so to exercise such powers as to further the conservation and enhancement of natural beauty and the conservation of flora, fauna and geological or physiographical features of special interest;

(b) to have regard to the desirability of protecting and conserving buildings, sites and objects of archaeological, architectural or historic interest; and

(c) to take into account any effect which the proposals would have on the beauty or amenity of any rural area or on any such flora, fauna, buildings sites or objects.

Section 3(3) then requires that due consideration be given to the preservation of freedom of access to and availability of such amenities.

Thus environmental considerations are of fundamental importance in the performance by undertakers of their core functions, and also generally to their land management. It is to be expected that those factors will be applied by the Director in overseeing the performance of undertakers and may be enforced by section 18 enforcement notices.[4] Against this, however, it has to be noted that, where there is a conflict, the section 2 duties are of primary importance and override any others, including these environmental objectives.

In relation to these environmental responsibilities, section 3 uses the phrases 'conservation and enhancement' and 'protecting and conserving'. While these terms have yet to receive judicial consideration in this present context, the comparable expression 'preservation and enhancement', which appears in section 277(8) of the Town and Country Planning Act 1971 dealing with conservation areas, has been considered by the House of Lords in *South Lakeland DC v Secretary of State for the Environment* (1992).[5] Lord Bridge, with whom all the other law lords agreed, expressly approved[6] the statement of principle by Mann LJ in the same case in the Court of Appeal.[7] He said :

> Neither 'preserving' nor 'enhancing' is used in any meaning other than its ordinary English meaning. The court is not here concerned with enhancement, but the ordinary meaning of 'preserve' as a transitive verb is 'to keep safe from harm or injury, to keep in safety, save, take care of, guard;' O.E.D. In my judgement character or appearance can be said to be preserved where they are not harmed. ... The statutorily desirable object of preserving the character or appearance of an area is achieved either by a positive contribution to preservation or by development which leaves character or appearance unharmed, that is to say, preserved.

The Director has a duty under section 27 to keep under review the activities of water and sewerage undertakers and to collect information regarding the discharge of their functions. The model instrument of appointment contains a number of conditions requiring undertakers to supply information to the Director, and section 203 provides the Director with wide powers to obtain information from undertakers relating to enforcement orders under section 18. Section 27(3) permits the Secretary of State to give general directions to the Director indicating the matters to which he should give consideration in exercising certain specified powers and duties under the Act.

Where a complaint is made to the Director which is not concerned with appointment conditions or duties enforceable under section 18, or requiring investigation by the Director under section 181, he is required, by section 30, to consider whether he should deal with it himself or refer it to the customer service committee. The Director must also consider whether a complaint relating to appointment con-

4 See below p.113.

5 [1992] 2 WLR 204.

6 At p.209h.

7 [1991] 1 WLR 1322 at pp.1326h–1327b.

ditions or breach of section 18 requirements should be referred to the Secretary of State. Responsibilities in connection with fair trading and competition are given to the Director General of Fair Trading by the Fair Trading Act 1973. By section 31 of the Water Industry Act 1991, he may request the Director to exercise his functions under Part III of that Act relating to conduct which may be detrimental to the interests of consumers in relation to the supply of water and the provision of sewerage services. These consumer interests are not confined to economic considerations and may include health, safety and other matters. Also, in relation to the monopoly situations existing in connection with the supply of these services, both Directors, by section 31(2), are entitled to exercise concurrently the functions under sections 44, 45, 50, 52, 53, 86, and 88 of the Fair Trading Act 1973. The Director may therefore, in particular, under section 31(2)(b), make a reference to the Monopolies and Mergers Commission under section 50 of the 1973 Act. He may also undertake preliminary investigations into anti-competitive practices and, as an alternative to a reference as above, obtain an undertaking in respect of such practices.

As with other privatised services, a structure of, in this case up to 10, customer service committees is provided,[8] to one of which each water and sewerage undertaker is allocated. Each committee consists of a chairman and 10–20 members appointed by the Director. In making appointments the Director must have regard to the experience of prospective committee members of the functions of undertakers and the desirability that at least one person has experience of work in respect of the special needs of disabled persons. On the general composition of the committees, the Minister during the Committee Stage of the 1989 Act said[9]:

[8] By section 28 of the Water Industry Act 1991.

[9] Standing Committee D, col. 511, 1989.

> ... there will be a three-way balance between industrial, commercial and farming consumers, domestic consumers and local authorities. ... [the Director] will need to ensure that there is effective consumer representation if he is to obtain the advice that he requires from customer service committees for the proper protection of customers.

These committees differ from the old consumer consultative committees[10] in that local authorities have lost their automatic right of representation, and maintaining such committees is no longer a matter solely for the undertaker companies. The committees are subject to the Public Bodies (Admission to Meetings) Act 1960.

[10] Under section 24(a) of the Water Act 1973.

The duties of the committees in relation to the companies allocated to them are, by section 29, to:

(a) review matters affecting customers' interests;
(b) consult on such matters;
(c) make representations to companies on such matters.

By section 29(2) they also have the duty to investigate any complaint by a customer or potential customer relating to the functions of an undertaker, unless the complaint appears to be vexatious or frivolous, or the complaint is of a type which must be referred to the Director. Such complaints relate to contravention of appointment conditions or duties enforceable under section 18. Complaints relating to an undertaker's right to lay pipes etc., on private land under section 159 must also generally be investigated by the Director under section 181.

These present investigative powers are more formalised than those under the Water Act 1983, and are of special significance because undertakers are no longer within the jurisdiction of the Local Government Ombudsman. Investigation of maladministration by undertakers is now therefore a matter for these committees. While they are given no special statutory powers of investigation, conditions in the model instrument of appointment place important requirements on undertakers in relation to such investigations. In particular they are required to meet their committee at least once a year and at other times as reasonably required by the committee, and to consult with the committee on their codes of practice concerning disconnections and the liability of metered customers for leakages.

Enforcement procedures

Compliance by undertakers with their conditions of appointment and their statutory duties is secured through the issue of section 18 enforcement orders by the Secretary of State or the Director, or by the imposition of a special administration order through High Court proceedings.[11]

Enforcement orders under section 18 are the means provided to enforce a range of duties under the Act. While this specific remedy against undertakers in the performance of their duties owed to the public excludes any other individual rights of action,[12] for example by judicial review, such rights presumably remain to enforce the supervisory duties of the Director and Secretary of State. In most cases a particular duty is stated to be enforceable exclusively by either the Secretary of State or the Director, but some general functions, e.g. section 37 (general duty to maintain a water system) and section 94 (general duty to maintain a public sewerage system) are enforceable by either. Further, section 213(2) provides that the Secretary of State may secure the performance of functions imposed by regulations made under the Act by section 18 orders enforceable by either or both himself and the Director. In all cases the issue of an order by the Director requires the authorisation of the Secretary of State.

Where a contravention exists the appropriate authority must generally make an order, there being no discretion.[13] The ability to enforce such a duty would require a sufficient degree of interest to give the applicant standing. In this respect it may be questioned whether any individual member of the public would have a sufficient interest to enforce the general duties imposed by the Act; for example, those in sections 37 and 94 referred to above. The general duty to issue an order is qualified in three cases by section 19(1), having the effect of converting the duty to a discretion in these cases:

(a) Trivial contraventions – there is no guidance in the Act or elsewhere on the scope of 'trivial', which is therefore a matter of judgement. During the Committee Stage of the 1989 Act the Minister said that 'it is very unlikely that circumstances giving rise to danger to health could properly be regarded as trivial'.

(b) Undertaking given by companies to secure compliance – a compliance undertaking to remedy the contravention may be accepted by the authorities in lieu of serving a section 18 order. While the terms of such an undertaking may in the event approximate closely to the terms of a possible order, the burden of production is placed on the undertaker and probably therefore is intended to take account of the possible large capital cost or investment programme that may be needed to secure compliance. An undertaking, having been accepted, operates as an exception to section 18 proceedings only as long as it is complied with. Subsequent failure will result in the statutory enforcement action.[14] A copy of the undertaking is required to be placed on the Director's public register.[15]

11 Section 23.

12 Section 18(8), and see to the same effect *Passmore* v *Oswaldtwistle UDC* [1898] AC 387 and *R* v *Kensington LBC ex parte Birdwood* (1976) 74 LGR 424.

13 Section 18(1).

14 Section 19(2).

15 Section 195(2)(d).

(c) Overriding duties under Part I of the Act precluding the making of an enforcement order – in deciding whether to make a section 18 order the Secretary of State or the Director is required to have regard to the overriding requirement that undertakers' functions are properly carried out and adequately financed, and to the environmental duties under section 3. Where such factors prevail section 19(1)(c) provides a discretion not to make an order.

Enforcement orders may be provisional or final. Provisional orders would be appropriate where loss or damage due to a serious contravention is likely before the procedures for a final order could be completed.[16] Such orders take immediate effect but have a maximum duration of three months[17] unless confirmed in accordance with section 18(4). Final enforcement orders must satisfy the procedural requirements of section 20. As a preliminary to such procedure, and where either the Secretary of State or Director considers that an undertaker has contravened a condition or duty imposed by section 18, they are empowered by section 203 to obtain information from that undertaker. Notice of the making of a final order or the confirmation of a provisional order, which removes its temporary status, must be served on the undertaker[18] and must specify, *inter alia*, a minimum period of 28 days within which representations or objections may be made.[19] The notice must be placed on the Director's public register[20] and be published in a manner likely to bring it to the attention of persons likely to be affected by the issues dealt with.[21] The same requirements, except that relating to wider publicity, apply to modifications of the original order and to its revocation.

An enforcement order may be challenged by an aggrieved recipient in the High Court within 42 days[22] on the grounds either of *ultra vires* or of procedural error. A challenge on the *ultra vires* ground appears easier in the case of final orders than provisional orders. In the latter case the person making the order may make such provision 'as appears to him requisite for the purpose of securing compliance with the condition or requirement in question',[23] implying assessment on *Wednesbury* principles. Conversely, in the case of final orders, the absence of any reference to the authority's opinion or judgement indicates an objective test to determine the appropriateness of the provisions. A provisional order will have taken effect within the appeal period and an application to the Court does not suspend its operation. In the absence of any express provision in the Act it would also seem that a final order will take effect and remain operative until held otherwise by a court.[24]

Section 22 provides three sanctions for non-compliance with an enforcement order. First, either the Secretary of State or the Director may bring proceedings for an injunction or other relief in the case of a contravention or apprehended contravention.[25] Secondly, contravention or likely contravention of a final order or a confirmed provisional order is one of the grounds for applying for a special administration order under section 24. Thirdly, anyone affected by the breach of an order may bring a civil action for consequent loss or damage.[26] In such proceedings section 22(3) gives an undertaker the due diligence defence.

Whereas enforcement orders provide a general administrative remedy to secure performance by undertakers of their statutory functions, special administration orders are limited to five specific situations and are judicial in nature. The five grounds warranting the making of a special administration order are, as specified in section 24(2):

16 Section 18(3).

17 Section 18(7).

18 Section 20(1)(b).

19 Section 20(1)(c).

20 Section 195(2)(c).

21 Section 20(2)(a).

22 Section 21.

23 Section 18(2).

24 See *Hoffman-La Roche & Co. v Secretary of State for Trade and Industry* [1975] AC 295.

25 Section 22(4).

26 Section 22(4).

(a) There has been or is likely to be a contravention of the undertaker's principal duty with respect to water supply (section 37) or sewage services (section 94). In this case the procedure is an alternative to enforcement orders.

(b) Other duties under the Act enforceable by the section 18 procedure where there has been or is likely to be a sufficiently serious contravention of a final or confirmed order as to warrant the undertaker losing his appointment.

(c) The undertaker is or is likely to be unable to pay his debts.

(d) It would have been appropriate to wind up the undertaker's business under section 440 of the Companies Act 1985 following an inspector's report but for the effect of section 26 of this Act.

(e) The undertaker is unable or unwilling to participate in arrangements for termination certified as necessary by the Secretary of State or Director following notice of termination in accordance with its appointment conditions.[27] Condition O of the model instrument of appointment requires at least 10 years' notice.

27 Section 7(4)(c).

A principal use for this procedure, then, is consequent upon the terminal financial difficulty of an undertaker. In this context section 26 prohibits the winding up of a company holding an appointment under this Act, or the making of an administration order under Part II of the Insolvency Act 1986 or, thirdly, action by anyone to enforce any security over the company's property without notifying the Secretary of State or the Director. Under this alternative special administrative order procedure the High Court, on the application of the Secretary of State or the Director, may make an order appointing a special administrator to run the company's business, thus ensuring that there is no disruption in the supply of water or sewerage services. The administrator carries on the business, if necessary with the injection of Government grants or loans under section 153, allowing time for the transfer of sufficient of the undertaking as a going concern to a replacement appointee or appointees to enable continuation of those functions. In this context, condition K of the model instrument of appointment (Ring Fencing) is significant in that it requires undertakers to have sufficient rights and assets (other than financial resources) to enable a special administrator on appointment to manage the business. This duty is enforceable either by section 18 enforcement orders or by an injunction under section 22(4).

Schedule 3 of the Act modifies the provisions of the Insolvency Act 1986 in their application to special administration orders. Following the making of the order and the identification of the replacement appointee, Schedule 2 provides for transitional arrangements, including transfer of property, rights and liabilities to the new company. A consequence of this procedure is that the creditors of such an undertaker are likely to be in a worse position than those of failed commercial companies. While the administrator is required to have regard to the respective interests of the members and creditors of the company,[28] the purpose of the order and therefore his primary concern is the carrying out of the core functions of the undertaker.[29]

28 Section 23(1)(b).

29 Section 23(2)(b).

Drinking Water Inspectorate

This review of the structure of the water industry may be concluded by a reference to section 86, providing a power for the Secretary of State to appoint persons as technical assessors in relation to, by section 86(1), the powers and duties conferred on him by sections 67–70 and 77–82 and 'other powers and duties in relation to the quality and sufficiency of water supplied by a water undertaker'. This section forms the basis for the appointment of the staff of the Drinking Water Inspectorate who monitor, investigate and report to the Secretary of State. Water undertakers have a duty under section 86(3) to provide such inspectors with assistance and information to enable them to perform those functions; breach of the duty being a criminal offence.[30]

The prospective role of the Inspectorate was succinctly indicated by Lord Hesketh during the passage of the Water Act 1989,[31] in the following terms:

> The Inspector's main job will be to carry out a thorough technical audit of each undertaker's compliance with the water quality regulations. They will monitor the progress of improvement programmes. They will of course check for failures to comply with standards. They will also check for deterioration in quality. They will have to assess the adequacy of the undertaker's sampling and analysis arrangements and the quality of laboratory results. If they are not satisfied on any of these counts they will obviously need to discuss corrective action with the undertaker. They will advise the Secretary of State on the use of his enforcement and prosecution powers. They will also need to produce regular published reports on their assessments.

WATER SUPPLY

The supply of water involves, and therefore may be considered in, three separate stages:

(a) abstraction of supplies from natural sources;
(b) provision of delivery and supply mains;
(c) supply of water, with attendant powers of control over misuse.

Abstraction

The right to take water from any surface source[32] and probably from some underground sources, is qualified by the common law rights in the flow of water of others downstream. No one, therefore, including those providing a public service, has an unrestricted right to use natural waters. The legislation governing such rights of use is now found in Chapter II of Part II of the Water Resources Act 1991, which reproduces the provisions of the Water Resources Act 1963 as amended by the Water Act 1989 which transferred the licensing function from individual water authorities to the NRA.

By section 24(1) of the Act, the abstraction of water from surface or underground sources, either directly or by another, is prohibited without a licence from the Authority, as also, by subsequent sections, is the doing of any associated construction or boring work, the installation of machinery, or the increase in quantity taken. For this purpose abstraction 'in relation to water contained in any source of supply, means the doing of anything whereby any of that water is removed from that source of supply, whether temporarily or permanently, including anything whereby the water is so removed for the purpose of being transferred to another source of supply',[33] and includes the turning of a valve or tap to remove water from a reservoir.[34] The discharge of water from an overflow does not constitute abstraction, however. Section 25 similarly prohibits the impounding of inland waters or any associated works unless authorised by a licence and in accordance with any conditions. 'Impounding', means the construction of a dam, weir

30 Section 86(6).

31 *Hansard*, HL, vol. 508, col. 1209.

32 See Ch.7 at p.158.

33 Section 221(1).

34 Decision Letter WS/3471/521/13, 10 April 1969.

or other similar works on inland waters, or any associated works for diverting the flow of such waters.[35] 'Source of supply', by section 221(1), means:

35 Section 25(8).

(a) any inland waters except discrete waters; or
(b) any underground strata in which water is or at any time may be contained.

Section 221(3) further provides that water contained in underground strata excludes water in a sewer, pipe, reservoir or other tank constructed in such strata but does include water in any well, borehole or similar work, adit, passage or excavation where the level of water in the excavation depends on water entering it from those strata.

This general licensing requirement is subject to a number of exceptions where unlicensed abstraction may occur:

(a) navigation requirements and operations connected with the functions of harbour and conservancy authorities;[36]
(b) abstraction of small quantities;[37]
(c) land drainage purposes;[38]
(d) abstraction of underground water in connection with mining, quarrying, engineering or building operations;[39]
(e) abstraction by a vessel for use on a (i.e., that or another) vessel;[40]
(f) firefighting purposes, including training and testing of equipment;[41]
(g) exploration for water, with the Authority's consent.[42]

36 Section 26.

37 Section 27.

38 Section 29(1).

39 Section 29(2).

40 Section 32(1).

41 Section 32(2) and see Fire Services Act 1947.

42 Section 32(3) and (4).

While these exceptions are logical and largely self-explanatory, some comment is required in particular cases.

A 'small quantity' for the purposes of section 27 means up to 5 cubic metres may be abstrated without consent as long as it is an individual operation and is not part of a series of abstractions, or 20 cubic metres, individually or in aggregate, may be abstracted with the consent of the Authority. These maxima may be exceeded in two cases where, by sections 27(3)–(5), up to 20 cubic metres may be abstracted in each period of 24 hours:

(a) the occupier of land contiguous to the point of abstraction uses the water on that land for domestic or agricultural purposes, excluding spray irrigation;[43]
(b) abstraction by or on behalf of an individual from underground strata for the domestic purposes of his household.

43 See definition in section 221(1) and the Spray Irrigation (Definition) Order 1965, S.I. 1965 No. 1010.

Within these limits the persons concerned have a right to the use of water. Recognising the potential conflict in the exercise of such rights of abstraction by a number of neighbouring occupiers of holdings of differing sizes, the NRA has the power, in section 28, to restrict by notice the area of the holding (the relevant part) on which the water may be used.

The removal of water for land drainage purposes is rather to move it from that location than to take it out of the environment for use; its removal being incidental to other purposes and not the primary objective. The expectation is therefore, and in spite of the very wide definition of abstraction, that it will shortly be restored to one or other natural source. Land drainage operations generally, and the abstraction of water where it is necessary to prevent interference with, or damage to, works or activities in (d) above, do not require licensing. For these purposes 'land drainage' is widely defined to include the protection of land against erosion or encroachment by inland waters or the sea. To the extent that these activities include the construction of a well or borehole to protect underground works, prior notice of such work is to be given to the Authority.[44] The Authority may then serve a conservation notice specifying reasonable measures for the conservation of the water that do not interfere with the protection of the underground works. It is to be noted that such mining or engineering activities may constitute a change of land use requiring planning permission[45] and also, in some cases, entailing environmental impact assessment.[46]

Licences may be for either abstraction or impounding, or for both functions,[47] and the licensing process and documents are governed by regulations made by the Secretary of State.[48] Applicants are restricted by section 35, broadly to persons having some interest in the land concerned. In relation to inland waters they must be either the occupier of land contiguous to the water, or persons who have or will have a right of access to such land.[49] In the case of underground water strata, the applicant is to be the occupier of the land consisting of or comprising those strata or, if the water is in an excavation, it is to be derived from those strata. 'Occupier' here includes persons who are in the process of acquiring title, including by compulsory purchase.[50]

The licensing procedure is to be found in sections 37–43 of the Act. Application details are to be published and are to include, by section 37(4), where the application may be seen and the right to make objections. To accommodate any objections a decision on the application shall not be taken before either 25 days from the date of publication in the *London Gazette* or 28 days from publication in some other newspaper. In granting an abstraction licence a major consideration for the Authority will be the consequences of the removal of the particular quantity of water from that source. To that end, section 39 requires that in granting a licence the Authority shall not derogate from any persons' protected rights, except with their consent. Protected rights within the Act are considerably narrower than the general common law rights of a riparian owner, being limited to persons having a right to abstract small quantities under section 27(6) and other licence holders under section 48(1). It is not clear whether common law rights are superceded by the creation of these narrower statutory protected rights, or whether the latter are merely identified as a licensing consideration. In the absence of any clear and unequivocal indication of intention to the contrary, it is submitted that, in accordance with general principles of statutory interpretation, the existing rights of riparian owners and occupiers remain in being. The next succeeding section, section 40, also concerns the volume of water, requiring the Authority in granting a licence to have regard to a minimum acceptable flow for that stream where such a minimum has not already been determined under Chapter I of Part II.[51]

Generally the licensing authority is the NRA, but the Secretary of State has power to call in applications, either in particular cases or of a class, for his decision.[52] His powers in relation to such applications are the same as the Authority's,[53] with the added discretion to hold a local enquiry or a hearing.[54] If requested by either party an enquiry or hearing must be held.[55] The Secretary of State has no power himself to grant a licence, his decision so to do acting as a direction to the Authority to grant the licence. As well as this power to determine applications, the Secretary of State is, by section 43, the appellate body against decisions of the Authority.

Where occupation of the whole of the land subject to a licence changes, the new occupier will become the licence-holder subject to the requirement to notify the

44 Section 30(1).

45 Section 57 Town and Country Planning Act 1990.

46 Assessment of Environmental Effects Regulations 1988, S.I. 1988 No. 1199, regulation 4(2).

47 Section 36.

48 Section 34 and see Water Resources (Licences) Regulations 1965, S.I. 1965 No. 534.

49 Section 35(2).

50 Section 35(4).

51 See sections 22 & 23.

52 Section 41.

53 Sections 38–40.

54 Section 42; section 250 of the Local Government Act 1972 applies to local enquiries under this section.

55 Section 42(2).

Authority within 15 months of the change.[56] Failure to notify the change will cause the licence to lapse. It is to be noticed that the requirement here is merely of a notification. A new application is not required and the Authority has no discretion to refuse to amend the licence. This section is limited to cases where all the land changes occupation. Evidently, if subdivision of the land carried with it comparable rights to the use of water, unreasonable proliferation would ensue. The transfer of licence rights following succession to part of the land is governed now by the Water Resources (Succession to Licences) Regulations 1969,[57] made by the Secretary of State under section 50.

57 S.I. 1969 No. 976.

Drought Orders

The right to abstract water from natural sources, and, even more, the ability to do so, depends on the availability of water in the first place. Where natural supplies diminish rights of abstraction are illusory and in practice need to be curtailed or rationalised among a number of users or demands. In this context the Secretary of State may exercise the necessary control powers through drought orders made under sections 73–81 of the Water Resources Act 1991. These powers are modelled on those introduced by the Drought Act 1976, amended to take account of privatisation.

Under section 73(1), the Secretary of State, following an application by either the NRA or a water undertaker in the area, may make an ordinary drought order if he 'is satisfied that by reason of an exceptional shortage of rain, a serious deficiency of supplies of water in any area exists or is threatened'. There are therefore two criteria on which the Secretary of State is to be satisfied on ordinary *Wednesbury* principles. Where the NRA applies, it will be bound by its general duty under section 15 to have particular regard to the service duties of water and sewerage undertakers. The procedure for making an order is to be found in Schedule 8 and includes publication of the application in local newspapers and that (depending on the proposed provisions of the order) local authorities, specified public bodies and persons be given the opportunity to make representations to the Secretary of State.[58] Section 74(1) and (2) respectively list the possible contents of orders made on the application of the NRA or an undertaker, but broadly cover:

58 Where a local enquiry is held (see paragraph 2(1)), the Drought Order (Inquiries Procedures) Rules 1984, S.I. 1984 No. 999 apply.

(a) prohibition, limitation or conditions attaching to the taking of water from any source;
(b) authority for the discharge of water;
(c) variation of existing conditions relating to the taking, discharge, supply or treatment of water;
(d) suspension or variation of effluent discharge consent conditions.

The effects of limitation of water use by a drought order may be applicable to consumers generally, or to specified persons or classes. Where a water undertaker is given power to prohibit or limit water use, it is required to publicise notice of the restriction in local newspapers and to the persons affected.[59] Any such prohibition or limitation will only come into effect 72 hours after the date of such publication.

59 Section 76(1)(b).

By section 74(3), the period of validity of any authorisation, prohibition, suspension etc., imposed under the order is six months from the date of operation of the order, not that is from the coming into effect of any condition or restriction made under the order, subject to a power of extension in the Secretary of State.

Drought order restrictions have, as they must, very wide effect, overriding any rights of abstraction derived from statute, agreement or ownership of land.[60] Section 77 also provides for modification of drought order provisions in respect of canals and inland navigations. Where the exercise of a power under a drought order restricts the discharge of effluent by a sewerage undertaker, it may similarly modify any consents or agreements for discharge by others of trade effluents that are necessary to enable compliance with the drought order.[61] It is to be noted generally, though, that the powers to modify or override existing consents and conditions may themselves be restricted by obligations imposed by EC Directives.

Taking, using or discharging water contrary to any drought order restriction is made an offence by section 80. Conversely, Schedule 9 provides for the payment of compensation in respect of the effects of drought orders, section 79(2) stating that those provisions are in place of and exclude any other liability for loss or damage due to any act or omission in pursuance of a drought order. Compensation is payable if the damage sustained by the claimant was the natural and reasonable consequence of the order and if it was not too remote. This may allow recovery of expenditure incurred before the order came into operation.[62] Claims under Schedule 9, paragraph (2) must be made within six months after the relevant provision in the order ceased to have effect and, in the absence of agreement, the amount of compensation will be determined by the Lands Tribunal. Any authorised or necessary work in connection with a drought order has deemed planning permission,[63] avoiding the delays attendant upon the need to obtain such approval.

Emergency drought orders under section 73(2) are subject to the same basic procedure and criteria, except that in addition the Secretary of State is to be further satisfied that the deficiency is such as to be likely to impair the economic or social well-being of persons in the area. An emergency may last for a maximum of three months with a power of extension by the Secretary of State for a further two months. Powers under an emergency order are the same as those under general drought orders, with the additional power of water undertakers to prohibit or limit the use of water for any purpose they think fit, instead of for the purposes specified by the Secretary of State,[64] and to supply water by means of stand pipes or water tanks.[65]

Provision of Mains

The general duty of water undertakers in this context is imposed by section 37 of the Water Industry Act 1991, which provides that:

(1) It shall be the duty of every water undertaker to develop and maintain an efficient and economical system of water supply within its area and to ensure that all such arrangements have been made –
   (a) for providing supplies of water to premises in that area and for making such supplies available to people who demand them; and
   (b) for maintaining, improving and extending the water undertakers water mains and other pipes
   to meet its obligations under this Part.

This statutory obligation, which is enforceable by special administrative order[66] without using the enforcement procedure, is developed in detail in the subsequent sections. The very general terms of the section 37 duty may be given greater detail in regulations made by the Secretary of State. These may specify performance stan-

60 Section 77(2).

61 Section 77(5).

62 *Bateman v Welsh Water Authority* (Ref/84/1985) (1986) 27 RVR 10.

63 See Pt 15, Class A and Pt 17, Class E of Schedule 2 to the General Development Order 1988, S.I. 1988 No. 1813.

64 Section 75(2)(b).

65 Section 75(2)(c).

66 See section 24 and p.114. above.

dards, failure to meet which will amount to breaches of section 37, including performance standards in relation to individual consumers with penalties for failure. Currently the Water Supply and Sewerage Services (Customer Service Standards) Regulations 1989[67] apply and provide, *inter alia*, for daily penalties for failure to keep a domestic appointment or to respond to account queries within specified time limits.

When required by notice to do so a water undertaker has a duty under section 41 to provide a water main for buildings or proposed buildings. The persons who may require such provision are restricted, being confined primarily to the owner or occupier of the premises or the local authority. Such provision is also conditional, except in the case of local authorities, on the financial undertakings in section 42. The main is to be provided within three months of the relevant day, subject to extension by agreement or, if necessary, by arbitration.[68] The relevant day is either the date of receipt of the section 42 financial undertakings, or of the identification of the connection points. The location of the main is a matter of agreement or, failing that, arbitration; section 44(3) providing that it is 'to be t he places at which it is reasonable, in all the circumstances, for service pipes to premises in the locality in question to connect with the water main'.

Taking these provisions together, it will be seen that what constitutes a water main for these purposes, as well as its length and location, will determine the financial contribution that can be required from the person requesting it. The question has come before the courts on two occasions. Section 37(1)(a) of the Water Act 1945 gave a similar power to require contributions towards the expense of providing any 'necessary mains'. In *Cherwell DC* v *Thames Water Authority* (1975)[69] the local authority, proposing to build houses on two sites, asked the Authority to indicate the contribution required for the main. Because the existing source of supply was becoming inadequate for the needs of the area the Authority proposed taking water by a 27 inch trunk main from the Thames to the service reservoir. They now included in the contribution the main from the service reservoir to the dwellings and a proportion of the cost of the trunk main. In rejecting this second head of cost the House of Lords held that:

> 'necessary' applied to new mains and service reservoirs provided for the purpose of conveying water from a point to which it was presupposed that a supply of water in bulk was already being brought in existing works belonging to the undertakers to points at which it would be practicable at reasonable cost to connect the proposed new buildings by service pipes, and for no other purpose; ... since in the instant case the 27 inch trunk main, when completed, would serve to supply water to the general body of consumers as well as the proposed new buildings it was not a necessary main within section 37.

In his judgement, Lord Diplock notes[70] that

> the section presupposes that there will be a supply of water in bulk capable of being brought to the new mains by the undertakers which if it is not already available to them it is their duty to procure without demanding from the requisitioner any contribution to the cost of doing so.

It appears, then, that contributions may only be levied for the cost of providing what may be called 'distribution mains' conveying water from a point at which a supply is already available in existing works or should be, to a point at which it is practicable to connect the proposed building by service pipe. So, in *Royco Homes Ltd* v *Southern Water Authority* (1979),[71] the appellants were building an estate

67 S.I. 1989 No. 1147, amended by the Water Supply and Sewerage Services (CSS) (Amendment) Regulations 1989, S.I. 1989 No. 1383.

68 Section 44.

69 [1975] 1 WLR 448, HL.

70 At p.455e.

71 [1979] 1 WLR 1366.

of 700 houses which required the construction of a new main 3.5 kilometres from an existing main of sufficient capacity to supply the estate. The appellants' contention that they were liable only for the costs of the distribution mains on the site and to the nearest main off the site was rejected by the Court, confirming their liability for a contribution of £115,000 for the entire length.

Where the owner or occupier of a building or proposed building serves a connection notice, a water undertaker has a duty to connect those premises by a service pipe to its water main for the purpose of providing a supply of water for domestic purposes at the expense of the person serving the notice.[72] 'Premises' are not defined for the purposes of this section. However, in *West Mersea UDC v Fraser* (1950)[73] it was said that premises referred to property with a sufficient degree of permanency on the site it occupies and therefore could include a permanently moored houseboat. In *Slaughter v Sunderland Corporation* (1891)[74] it had been said that a building should normally be understood to signify a construction or erection capable of enclosing some area of ground.

This section 45 duty is limited to the supply of water for domestic purposes, which, by section 218, means 'drinking, washing, cooking, central heating and sanitary purposes for which water supplied to those premises may be used and include washing of vehicles and watering of gardens without the use of a hosepipe' but excludes:

(a) a bath of greater capacity than 230 litres;
(b) a laundry business;
(c) the business of preparation of food and drink for consumption off the premises.

This definition or description has clearly been compiled from the considerable body of case law on the subject; which also establishes that domestic purposes include the operation of a boarding house[75] and a school,[76] including a boarding school,[77] but exclude the sanitary conveniences at a railway station.[78]

The duty to connect is also subject to compliance with any conditions imposed by the undertaker under sections 47–50.[79] These may include:

(a) security for costs;
(b) payment of any disconnection charges, if applicable;
(c) provision of a meter;
(d) plumbing complies with requirements for installing a meter;
(e) separate service pipes are provided to each house or building or separately occupied part;
(f) provision of a cistern and float-operated ball valve under section 66;
(g) compliance with any regulations under section 74, i.e. for preventing contamination and waste etc.;
(h) compliance with any requirements of a notice under section 75, i.e. to prevent damage, contamination or waste.

Supply of water

Turning now to the obligations of water undertakers in connection with the delivery of a supply of water and their concomitant powers of regulation, the Water Industry Act 1991, sections 52–65, specify the duties attaching to supply for various purposes; sections 68–70 impose additional responsibilities relating to the

72 Section 45.

73 [1950] KB 119.

74 (1891) 60 LJ MC 91.

75 *Pidgeon v Great Yarmouth Waterworks Co.* [1902] 1 KB 310.

76 *S.W.Suburban Water Co. v St Marylebone Union* [1904] 2 K3 174.

77 *Frederick v Bognor Water Co.* [1909] 1 Ch 149.

78 *MWB v London, Brighton and South Coast Rly* [1910] 2 KB 890.

79 Section 45(2)(b).

quality of supplies; and sections 73–75 contain powers for the control of contamination, waste and misuse. Ancillary to these provisions, sections 77–85 give local authorities general duties of oversight on behalf of their citizens and, in particular, in relation to private supplies.

The general obligation to provide a supply of water for domestic purposes is contained in section 52, which provides:

(1) The domestic supply duty of a water undertaker in relation to any premises is a duty –
   (a) to provide a sufficient supply of water for domestic purposes; and
   (b) to maintain the connection by which that supply is provided to those premises.

This duty, which is owed to the consumer,[80] applies where connection has followed the procedure in sections 45–51 or where a supply was provided immediately before 1 September 1989.[81] The conditions that may be imposed upon an applicant for a supply of water are those in the above list under sections 47–50 at (b), (d), (f), (g) and (h).[82] It will be seen below that the duty under section 55 to supply water for non-domestic purposes is limited and conditional on this primary obligation to provide for demands for 'domestic purposes'. The definition and scope of this term, discussed above,[83] is therefore important in determining the precise obligations of undertakers.

Water undertakers are of course responsible not only for quantity but also for meeting the quality standards considered in the following chapter.[84] To that end section 68 provides that:

(1) It shall be the duty of a water undertaker –
   (a) when supplying water to any premises for domestic or food production purposes to supply only water which is wholesome at the time of supply; ...

That final phrase is emphasised in section 68(2), which states that water is not to be regarded as unwholesome at the time of supply where it has ceased to be wholesome only after leaving the undertaker's pipes. This gives statutory effect to the decisions in *Milnes* v *Huddersfield Corporation* (1886)[85] and *Barnes* v *Irwell Valley Water Board* (1939)[86] that the statutory duty of a water undertaker was limited to securing a wholesome supply at the point where it passes from its mains to the pipes of the premises. This limitation is however relaxed by section 68(3) where the water is still under mains pressure after leaving their pipes and the unwholesomeness is due to a forseeable risk that the undertaker should have guarded against.[87] This uncertainty as to the precise limits of responsibility may in part be attributable to an endeavour to secure conformity with Article 12 of the EC Directive[88] requiring that monitoring is to take place 'at the point where it is made available to the consumer,' a point which is not defined but could be either the connection with the consumer's service pipe or the tap. In addition to this specific statutory liability undertakers may also be liable under the Consumer Protection Act 1987 where injury or damage to property has occurred and liable in negligence; see e.g. *Read* v *Croydon Corporation* (1937).[89]

Subordinate to section 68 and to secure compliance with it, the Secretary of State may, under section 69, make regulations imposing specific duties on undertakers, and in particular for monitoring and recording the wholesomeness of water supplies for domestic and food production purposes and the quality of water from the sources of supply for such purposes. The regulations may also provide for the use by undertakers of any processes, substances and associated products that might

80 Section 54.

81 Section 52(2).

82 Section 53.

83 See p.122; and see Report on the consolidation of the legislation relating to water, Law Commission Report No. 198, Cmnd 1483, p.15 at paragraph 21.

84 See at p.152.

85 (1886) 11 App Cas 511.

86 [1939] 1 KB 21.

87 See regulation 24 of the Water Supply (Water Quality) Regulations 1989, and below.

88 80/778/EEC.

89 (1937) 37 LGR 53.

affect water quality, including the prohibition, restriction or regulation of the use of any such materials. This section gives the Secretary of State a very wide power to specify in detail what is required of water undertakers in relation to their general duty to supply wholesome water. As these regulations amplify the section 67 duties, their provisions would be enforceable by section 18 enforcement orders, but they may also provide for criminal sanctions.[90]

The current regulations under this section are the Water Supply (Water Quality) Regulations 1989;[91] Part VI dealing with water treatment. Regulation 23 requires that raw water shall be disinfected before supply and, in the case of surface water, shall undergo such further treatment as is necessary to secure compliance with Directive 75/440/EEC. Further treatment to eliminate or reduce the risk of metallic contamination from water pipes is required by regulation 24 where there is such a risk. For the same purpose, and if appropriate, the undertaker is to remove any of its lead pipes.

Lastly, for present purposes, regulation 25 prohibits the introduction of any substance or product into water, subject to three exceptions:

(a) where approved by the Secretary of State; or
(b) if the water undertaker is satisfied that it is unlikely to affect water quality or can demonstrate that for 12 months prior to the Regulations it has been applied or introduced by a water authority to water supplied for domestic purposes; or
(c) the substance or product was, before the commencement of the Regulations listed on the 15th Statement of the Committee on Chemicals and Materials of Construction for Use in Public Water Supply and Swimming Pools.

These duties governing water quality are buttressed by the publicity provisions in Part VII. These require water undertakers to maintain specified records for each water supply zone[92] and to make them available for inspection and copying.[93] By regulation 33 local authorities are required to make arrangements for water undertakers to notify them of the records and information kept under the Regulations. They are also given the power to take and analyse samples of water supplied to premises in their area.

To conclude this review of duties relating to domestic supplies, section 70 of the Act provides that where a piped supply to premises is unfit for human consumption the undertaker may be liable to summary or indictable proceedings. Such liability is subject to the defences that either the undertaker had no reasonable grounds for suspecting that the water would be used for human consumption, or that all reasonable steps were taken and all due diligence exercised for securing that the water was so fit on leaving its pipes, or that it was not used for human consumption. This offence has been created to provide criminal sanctions in the case of serious incidents and as a result of the major contamination of water supplies at Camelford, Cornwall in 1988. 'Unfit for human consumption' is not defined for the purpose of this section but is presumably not the same as 'unwholesome' in section 67 which indicates a less serious or harmful level of contamination. It seems probable that this is to be regarded as a strict liability offence.[94]

The controversial power of a water undertaker to disconnect a supply for non-payment of charges is contained in section 61. This power, which faced strong criticism during the passage of the Water Act 1989, is subject to two restrictions.

90 Section 69(4)(f).

91 S.I. 1989 No. 1147, amended by the Water Supply (Water Quality) (Amendment) Regulations 1989, S.I. 1989 No. 1384.

92 Regulation 29.

93 Regulation 30.

94 See *Maidstone BC v Mortimer* [1985] 3All ER 552.

By section 61(2) and (3), where a customer disputes liability the undertaker may only disconnect either with a court judgment or following breach of a settlement anticipating litigation. Secondly, the undertaker is bound by the conditions of its instrument of appointment relating to disconnection. These include provision for a code of practice to be approved by the Director.[95] Essentially this requires the undertaker to obtain a court judgement for arrears of debt in all cases before exercising these disconnection powers; unless that is, the occupier was already in breach of a previous court judgment for non-payment of water charges.

The supply obligations of undertakers for non-domestic purposes are to be found in sections 55 and 57 of the Act. Section 55 provides that there is a duty to supply, on request, water for non-domestic purposes, but subject to the conditions in section 56 on not entailing unreasonable expenditure and, by section 55(3), to the overriding duty to discharge domestic supply obligations. These limitations apply to 'new' supplies or requests and do not therefore appear to affect existing arrangements. Between these two situations, however, there is the question of what increase in quantity constitutes a new or additional supply for these purposes. By section 57, water authorities have a duty to allow the use of water for fire-fighting and to fix fire hydrants at such convenient places as are requested by the fire authority.

Underlying these duties is the responsibility, in section 65, to maintain water in all mains and other supply pipes for domestic purposes, or to have fire hydrants affixed at constant supply and sufficient pressure to reach the top storey of buildings in the area; subject, that is, to gravitation from service reservoirs. Again this duty is enforceable by the section 18 enforcement order procedure and also, by section 65(10), its breach is made a criminal offence. Performance of this duty to provide water under pressure was held, in *Department of Transport v North West Water Authority* (1984),[96] to exclude liability for nuisance consequent upon a burst main under a street, even though section 18(2) of the Public Utilities Street Works Act 1950 expressly imposed such liability. It was said that section 18(2) imposes liability in relation to the exercise of a power and not the performance of a duty.

Control of misuse

Associated with the duties imposed on water undertakers concerning supply are a number of powers to control the misuse of water. Principally, section 73 creates the summary offences of contaminating, wasting and misusing water. The first two offences are limited to causation due to defective water fittings, being therefore the liability of the owner or occupier of the premises, whereas any person may be liable for misuse if they use water, other than to extinguish fire, for a purpose other than one for which it was supplied to the premises. In most cases, therefore, the purposes for which water is supplied to premises, to determine misuse, will be the uses specified in the definition of 'domestic purposes' in section 218 of the Water Industry Act 1991.[97] The criteria in section 73(1) for contamination and waste are that a water fitting is so defective, constructed, adapted or used that:

(a) the water in the undertaker's supply system or any pipe connected therewith is or is likely to be contaminated by the return of any substance from the premises to such mains or pipes; or

95 See condition H of the model instrument of appointment.

96 [1984] AC 336.

97 See above at p.122.

(b) water supplied for use on the premises is or is likely to be contaminated before use; or

(c) water so supplied is or is likely to be wasted, misused or unduly consumed.

In the normal course of things contamination of water that is used on the premises, in (b), is more likely than the contamination of water in the mains and supply pipes from those premises. The duty on undertakers in section 65 to maintain a positive pressure in their supply system, as well as being necessary for the delivery of water, has the ancillary benefit of reducing the risk of ingress of such contaminants.

Where misuse under section 73(2) has occurred, and in addition to any other penalties, the undertaker is entitled to recover the reasonable cost of the water improperly consumed. Further, by section 75(1), where an undertaker has reason to believe that any of the offences in section 73 is occurring or may occur, it may:

(a) in an emergency, disconnect the service pipe or otherwise cut off the supply;

(b) in other cases, serve a notice on the consumer requiring the action specified in the notice to prevent damage, contamination, waste, misuse or undue consumption.

Where the emergency powers in (a) are used, the water undertaker must notify the consumer of the steps to be taken to remedy the defect before the supply will be restored.[98] There is also a power to disconnect where the premises appear to be unoccupied and the notice in (b) is not complied with. Section 75(9)(b) gives the undertaker power to do the work specified in the notice itself in default and recover the costs. Action under this section necessarily suspends the duty in section 52(7) to supply water for domestic purposes.

[98] Section 75(3).

The Secretary of State is given the power to make regulations providing in more detail for the range of offences in section 73(1), and in particular specifying materials, workmanship and testing of water fittings in order to reduce contamination, undue consumption and misuse of water.[99] Enforcement powers may be conferred by the regulations on either or both a water undertaker or local authority as also may default work powers. Section 76 gives a water undertaker the power to introduce a temporary hosepipe ban where it considers that a serious deficiency of water exists.

[99] Section 74.

Local authority powers and duties

Prior to the Water Act 1973, local authorities were the regulatory authorities for the industry, and in many cases the utilities as well, providing water supplies through municipal undertakings. As has been seen in the introduction to this Part, that has changed. However, local authorities still retain some general and a few specific powers and duties on behalf of their residents, now largely to be found in sections 77–85 of the Water Industry Act 1991. These functions fall into two broad categories: those providing for the oversight of piped supplies provided by water undertakers, and in particular the quality and fitness of such supplies; and their regulatory function in relation to private supplies.

Before considering their powers and duties under that water legislation, it is to be noted that the building control function of local authorities necessarily includes as an aspect of the fitness of dwellings for habitation, the provision of an adequate water supply. Section 25(1) of the Building Act 1984 provides that a local authority is to reject the plans of a house unless satisfactory provision is made for the supply of wholesome water sufficient for the domestic purposes of the occupants:

(a) by connecting to a supply in pipes provided by the water undertaker; or
(b) if that is unreasonable, by otherwise taking a piped supply to the house; or
(c) if that is unreasonable, by providing a supply within a reasonable distance of the house.

If after being approved the necessary provision is not actually made, section 25(3) requires that the local authority, by notice to the owner, shall prohibit the occupation of the house until it certifies that the required provision has been made. The issue of a section 25(3) certificate is therefore a necessary prerequisite to the occupation of a newly constructed house, the person liable in default being the owner. Section 69 of the same Act gives a local authority similar powers to secure an effective water supply to existing houses. The person responsible is the owner, with default powers in the local authority who may recover costs up to £300 per house.

Local authorities are required by section 77(1) and (2) of the Water Industry Act 1991 to keep themselves informed as to the quality of water supplies in their area, both public and private, and to comply with any directions from the Secretary of State governing the performance of that duty. Sections 77(3) & (4) provide for and specify the matters about which the Secretary of State may make regulations in respect of local authorities' water supply functions. Current regulations under this section are the Water Supply (Water Quality) Regulations 1989, Part VIII.[100] In particular, regulation 33 provides that, in carrying out its section 77 duties, a local authority has the power to arrange with the water undertaker for the supply to it of copies of the records and information kept by the undertaker under regulation 30(6). Also, it may take and analyse samples of water supplied to premises in its area. Regulation 30(6) requires a water undertaker to notify the local authority and District Health Authority of any event which threatens water supplies by giving rise to a significant health risk.

Section 78 applies in those cases where information acquired under section 77 reveals some deficiency and provides for the local authority response. Having no direct powers of enforcement, the section requires the local authority to notify the water undertaker by written notice, where it appears to it that:

(a) a supply from the undertaker for domestic purposes or food production is, has been or is likely to become unwholesome or insufficient;
(b) that such deficiency is, was or is likely to cause a danger to life or health; or
(c) that the section 68(1)(b) duty on water undertakers has been contravened so as to affect the water supply to the area.

The meaning of 'wholesomeness' is considered below in relation to the quality of domestic supplies.[101] Section 68(1)(b) requires water undertakers to ensure that there is no deterioration in the quality of water supplied for domestic purposes or food production from their sources of supply. If the local authority is not then satisfied that the appropriate remedial action is taken by the undertaker, it is to inform the Secretary of State of the contents of its original notification.

100 S.I. 1989 No. 1147.

101 See p.150.

In cases where it is not economically practicable for a piped supply to be provided for domestic purposes, section 79 imposes reciprocal duties on the local authority and undertaker. If the authority is satisfied that the existing supply is dangerous to life or health because of its insufficiency or unwholesomeness, and that the water undertaker can at reasonable cost provide an unpiped supply, it shall require the undertaker so to do.[102] Then, where those criteria are satisfied and the authority has notified the undertaker of the danger to life and health and required a supply, the undertaker has a duty to provide an unpiped supply to the premises for the period specified by the local authority.[103] The undertaker's charges under Chapter I of Part V for such supply are recoverable from the local authority, who may recover the costs from the owner or occupier of the premises concerned. This duty of the undertaker under section 79(3) is enforceable by the Secretary of State using the section 18 enforcement procedure.

Where a local authority considers that remedial action is required in relation to a private water supply it is empowered to take necessary enforcement action by section 80. Subordinate thereto, section 81 details the procedure and effects of private supply notices and section 82 is concerned with their enforcement.

The enforcement powers of a local authority under section 80 apply where the authority is satisfied that any water supplied to premises from a private supply for domestic purposes or food production is, was or is likely to be unwholesome or insufficient. It may then serve a 'private supply notice' on one or more of the relevant persons. The relevant persons are, by section 80(7), the owners and occupiers of the premises and persons having powers of management or control over the source of the supply, including the owners and occupiers of those premises, thus giving the authority a wide discretion in apportioning responsibility. Section 80(2) and (3) specify the matters that respectively shall and may be included in such notices. A private supply notice must:

(a) specify the deficiency;
(b) specify the necessary remedial action;
(c) notify a 28-day period for representations or objections;
(d) notify the effect of section 81(2) and (3).

Those two subsections provide that where a written representation or objection is received the notice is to be submitted to the Secretary of State for confirmation, and delineate the powers of the Secretary of State relating to confirmation, including where appropriate the holding of a local enquiry, thereby creating in effect an appeals system. Section 80(3) lists the range of action that the authority may require of the recipient; including action to be taken by the authority or another relevant person to be paid for by the person on whom the notice is served. The notice will not take effect until after the 28-day period for objections.[104]

The general duty in section 68 on water undertakers to supply wholesome water does not apply to private suppliers, but by this section local authorities are given a discretion to ensure that such supplies meet those same standards. The standards defining wholesomeness are contained in the Water Supply (Water Quality) Regulations 1989.[105] Local authorities are given the power to authorise a relaxation of the standards in line with the permissible derogations under EC Directive 80/778/EEC relating to the quality of water intended for human consumption, provided that no threat to public health is involved. Where the supply concerned serves more than 500 people the authority must first consult with the Secretary of State.

102 Section 79(2).

103 Section 79(3).

104 Section 81(1).

105 S.I. 1989 No. 1147 and see below at p.152.

Local authorities are given default powers by section 82, with the concomittant power to recover the costs of any necessary work. The terms of a private supply notice shall be registered as a local land charge and bind successive owners and occupiers of the premises.[106] There is also of course power in the local authority, by a subsequent notice, to modify or revoke the terms of the original notice.

106 Section 82(5).

6

Water Quality

NATURAL WATERS

The quality of water has been of most concern to most people at the time of supply for consumption, whether from natural sources or by piped supply and either with or without treatment. The standards for such waters are now the subject of detailed regulations implementing EC Directives and are dealt with below.[1]

1 See pp.150–6 below.

While the general quality of water in the natural environment has been of less immediate concern, its protection has a long, if more fragmented, history, being evidenced in legislation at least from 1388. This, and most subsequent attempts to maintain the purity of natural waters have concentrated exclusively on preventing or controlling the discharge into such waters of polluting effluents. The condition of the receiving waters has, on this approach, either been presumed to be satisfactory or else to be adequately safeguarded by limiting the quantity or the harmful contents of individual emissions. Experience demonstrates that this approach alone is no longer capable of answering the problem. There is an increasing, observable discrepancy between the contributions of identifiable discharges of effluent and the quality of the receiving water. This is in large measure attributable to contamination from diffuse, unidentifiable sources which therefore cannot be effectively controlled. Among such are to be included the leaching into waters of contaminants in or on land, ranging from the residues of past industrial processes and contents of land fill sites to the application of agricultural chemicals for various purposes.

Just as individual discharges need to be and are individually controlled so the quality of the receiving water also requires monitoring. Such supervision not only serves to discover any changes of quality, but the revealed condition of the water will also assist in determining any conditions to be attached to discharge consents and identify the purposes for which a given water may be suitable. Ancillary to this last point, of course, where a particular water is required for a certain use any shortfall in the appropriate quality and consequent improvement can be determined and rectified.

Although the quality of natural waters has been of implicit statutory concern in relation to the operation of particular water-based activities or uses for some time,[2] the identification of general objectives is a relatively new development. The initial scheme, voluntarily adopted by water authorities in 1978, was for the classification of inland surface waters into five quality categories:

2 See, for instance, a succession of Salmon and Freshwater Fisheries Acts from 1923.

Good Quality – 1A	Water of high quality suitable for potable supply; game or other high class fisheries; high amenity value.
Good Quality – B	Water of less high quality than Class 1A but used for substantially the same purposes.
Fair Quality – 2	Waters suitable for potable supply after advanced treatment; supporting reasonably good coarse fisheries; moderate amenity value.

Poor Quality – 3   Waters which are polluted to such an extent that fish are absent or only sporadically present; may be used for low grade industrial abstraction purposes; considerable potential for further use if cleaned up.

Bad Quality – 4   Waters which are grossly polluted and likely to cause a nuisance.

This classification was based on periodic sampling and the requirement that 95 per cent should achieve the requisite standard for a particular grade based on the assessment of dissolved oxygen content and biochemical oxygen demand.

This first tentative and voluntary step has been overtaken by the demands of the European Community. It is perhaps an indication of the rapid growth of environmental consciousness that the seminal document of the Community, the Treaty of Rome 1957, makes no mention of environmental matters. While the view was taken that the wording of Articles 100 and 235 permitted an interpretation that allowed the development of environmental policies, the Treaty has now been specifically amended by the Single European Act 1987 to include, *inter alia*, environmental objectives, i.e., to preserve, protect and improve the quality of the environment; to contribute towards protecting human health; to ensure a prudent and rational utilisation of natural resources.[3] The co-ordination of the Community's environmental policy objectives has been through the production of a series of Action Programmes. The first Action Programme for the Environment was adopted in 1973[4] and identified the principal objectives for subsequent legislation, including the prevention of pollution at source rather than dealing with the consequences later and the principle that the polluter should pay. Subsequent Action Programmes have followed at approximately five-yearly intervals. The draft Fifth Action Programme, 'Towards Sustainability',[5] includes as policies for the period to 2000:

(a) prevention of pollution of fresh and marine surface waters and ground water;
(b) restoration of natural ground and surface waters to an ecologically sound condition.

Specific Community-wide environmental regulation is by Directives. A Directive itself has no authority but each Member State, by virtue of membership, is required to enact national legislation giving it effect. It is the practice in Britain to implement EC Directives by statutory instruments. The power to enact such regulations governing water quality is given to the Secretary of State in Chapter I of Part III of the Water Resources Act 1991. The individual sections provide as follows.

Section 82 of the 1991 Act empowers the Secretary of State to prescribe by regulations a system for classifying the quality of any description of controlled waters according to any specified criteria. 'Controlled waters' are defined in section 104(1) as:

(a) relevant territorial waters, i.e., waters extending three miles seaward from specified baselines;[6]
(b) coastal waters, which includes waters to the landward side of those baselines up to the limit of the highest tide or up to the freshwater limit of any relevant river or watercourse together with any enclosed dock adjacent to such waters;
(c) inland fresh waters, that is any relevant lake, pond or relevant river or watercourse above the fresh water limit;
(d) ground waters, i.e., waters in any underground strata.

3 Article 130R(1) as amended.

4 1973 OJC 112 p.1.

5 COM (92) 23 final.

6 The baselines from which the territorial waters are measured are established by the Territorial Waters Order in Council 1964 (dated 25 September 1964) as amended by the Territorial Waters (Amendment) Order in Council 1979 (dated 23 May 1979).

Although UK territorial waters were extended to 12 miles by section 1(1) of the Territorial Sea Act 1987, the three mile limit under the Control of Pollution Act 1974 has been retained here. However, the Secretary of State may by order under section 104(4) extend jurisdiction to other areas of territorial waters. Paragraph (c) refers to 'relevant lake or pond' which, by section 104(3), means lakes or ponds that discharge into any other relevant waters, excluding in effect discrete bodies of water. The Secretary of State has, however, the power under section 104(4)(b) to bring any specified lake or pond within the scope of the definition by order, and, by the Controlled Waters (Lakes and Ponds) Order 1989,[7] has brought reservoirs not communicating with relevant waters within the definition.

7 S.I. 1989 No. 1149.

Section 82 gives the Secretary of State a wide discretion not only in relation to the standards to be applied but also to the categories of waters to be classified. The standards may relate not only to the characteristics of the type of water but also to its specified or intended purpose. The making of classification regulations under this section involves no formal consultative or other procedural requirements and the classifications so specified have in themselves no legal effect. They do, however, form the basis for the establishment of 'water quality objectives' under section 83. Where such objectives are to be established or varied the review procedure in section 83(4) is to be followed.

Founded on and following classification as above, section 83(1) provides that

> For the purpose of maintaining and improving the quality of controlled waters the Secretary of State may ... establish the water quality objectives for any waters of a description prescribed for the purposes of section 82.

The classification of any description of water under section 82 is then a necessary preliminary to the establishment of quality objectives for those waters. The aim of the procedure and the scope of the Secretary of State's power is to improve controlled waters, apparently generally rather than specifically. The wording seems wide enough to permit a downgrading in a particular case, although the burden on the Secretary of State to demonstrate that this would produce some other or general improvement would be heavy. Improvement under this section also envisages periodic review and varying of objectives, either at a minimum of five-yearly intervals or on the request of the NRA following consultation with the water undertakers concerned. The procedure to establish or vary objectives is specified in section 83(4), and includes three months' notice of that intention for any representations or objections, and their consideration if made. The notification of proposed action is to be served on the Authority and must be placed on the public register maintained under section 190. All concerned, whether potential dischargers or members of the public, will thus be able to determine the statutory water quality objective applicable to any particular body of water.

The third and final section concerned with water quality objectives, section 84(1), places responsibilities both on the Secretary of State and the NRA to ensure so far as is practicable that any water quality objectives specified in a section 83 notice are achieved at all times. In order to perform this function the Authority has the ancillary duty under section 84(2) to monitor the extent of pollution in controlled waters. As these powers are exercised, classification regulations for various categories of water issued and water quality objectives established for specific bodies of water, the criteria thus established will serve as a standard against which subsequent decisions will be taken and discharge consents, and their conditions, will be issued. The NRA has published proposals for the protection of ground-water from pollution under section 84.[8]

As has been said, a (or the) main purpose of this part of the Act is to provide a procedure for the implementation of EC Directives relating to water quality. This is implicit in the wording of section 82, which gives the Secretary of State a broad discretion in the exercise of his powers under the section and, unusually, makes no provision for consultation. While unusual in the context of the making of national regulations, though, such a feature is not only reasonable but inevitable when related to the implementation of Community legislation.

To date these powers have been used on four occasions, although additional water quality standards giving effect to Community requirements for other waters are to be expected.[9] The current provisions are:

- Surface Waters (Classification) Regulations 1989,[10] giving effect to the Drinking Water Directive (75/440/EEC)
- Surface Waters (Dangerous Substances)(Classification) Regulations 1989,[11] giving effect to the Dangerous Substances Directive (76/464/EEC) and others
- Surface Waters (River Ecosystems)(Classification) Regulations 1994[12]
- Bathing Waters (Classification) Regulations 1991,[13] giving effect the Bathing Waters Directive (76/160/EEC)
- Implementation of Council Directives for Freshwater Fish and Shellfish Waters.

These regulations will now be considered in turn.

SURFACE WATERS (CLASSIFICATION) REGULATIONS 1989

These regulations specify criteria to determine the suitability of inland waters for abstraction by water undertakers for supply, and for ascertaining the treatment to which the water is to be subjected before supply for public use in accordance with Part VI of the Water Supply (Water Quality) Regulations 1989. The Schedule to the regulations provides for three classifications of such waters with their respective criteria, DW1, DW2, and DW3, reflecting the mandatory values assigned by Annex II of Directive 75/440/EEC as follows. These classifications are also relevant for setting water quality objectives for rivers, lakes and other inland waters under section 83 of the Water Resources Act 1991.

Criteria for the classification of waters

The limits set out below are maxima

No. in Annex II to 75/440/EEC	Parameters		DW1	DW2	DW3
2	Coloration (after simple filtration)	mg/1 Pt Scale	20	100	200
4	Temperature	°C	25	25	25
7	Nitrates	mg/1 NO_3	50	50	50
8(1)	Fluorides	mg/1 F	1.5		
10	Dissolved iron	mg/1 Fe	0.3	2	
12	Copper	mg/1 Cu	0.05		
13	Zinc	mg/1 Zn	3	5	5
19	Arsenic	mg/1 As	0.05	0.05	0.1
20	Cadmium	mg/1 Cd	0.005	0.005	0.005

8 'Policy and Practice for the Protection of Groundwater – Draft for Consultation', November 1991.

9 'Proposals for Statutory Water Quality Objectives' (NRA, 1991).

10 S.I. 1989 No. 1148.

11 S.I. 1989 No. 2286.

12 S.I. 1994 No. 1057.

13 S.I. 1991 No. 1597.

The limits set out below are maxima (*continued*)

No. in Annex II to 75/440/EEC	Parameters		DW1	DW2	DW3
21	Total chromium	mg/1 Cr	0.05	0.05	0.05
22	Lead	mg/1 Pb	0.05	0.05	0.05
23	Selenium	mg/1 Se	0.01	0.01	0.01
24	Mercury	mg/1 Hg	0.001	0.001	0.001
25	Barium	mg/1 Ba	0.1	1	1
26	Cyanide	mg/1 Cn	0.05	0.05	0.05
27	Sulphates	mg/1 SO_4	250	250	250
31	Phenols (phenol index) paranitraniline 4 aminoantipyrine	mg/1 C_6H_5OH	0.001	0.005	0.1
32	Dissolved or emulsified hydrocarbons (after extraction by petroleum ether)	mg/1	0.05	0.2	1
33	Polycyclic aromatic hydrocarbons	mg/1	0.0002	0.0002	0.001
34	Total pesticides (parathion, BHC, dieldrin)	mg/1	0.001	0.0025	0.005
39	Ammonia	mg/1 NH_4		1.5	4

Note The value given is an upper limit set in relation to the mean annual temperature (high and low).

SURFACE WATERS (DANGEROUS SUBSTANCES)(CLASSIFICATION) REGULATIONS 1989/1992

These regulations provide a system for classifying inland, coastal and relevant territorial waters[14] according to the presence in them of concentrations of substances listed in the Schedules, i.e. certain Black List substances. They are therefore additional to and must be considered in association with the classification system in the Surface Waters (Classification) Regulations 1989 considered above. The classification DS1 applies to inland waters and DS2 to coastal and territorial waters, and reflect the quality objectives in:

Annex II to Directive 82/176/EEC – mercury and its compounds
Annex II to Directive 83/513/EEC – cadmium and its compounds
Annex II to Directive 84/491/EEC – hexachlorocyclohexane
Annex II to Directive 86/280/EEC – carbon tetrachloride, DDT, and pentachlorophenol

and Directive 88/347/EEC which amends the 1986 Directive by adding quality objectives for a range of other insecticides. The two exceptions to the Black List requirements are the concentrations of cadmium and mercury in DS2. The Directive specifies annual mean concentrations of less than 5 and 0.5 microgrammes per litre respectively in esturial waters, while DS2 requires the more stringent annual mean of less than 2.5 and 0.3 respectively. The 1992[15] amending regulations implement the quality standards in Directive 90/415/EEC for ethylene dichloride, trichloroethelyne, perchloroethylene and trichlorobenzene in establishing classi-

14 By section 104(a) of the Water Resources Act 1991, relevant territorial waters are waters extending seaward for three miles.

15 S.I. 1992 No. 337.

fication DS3 for territorial waters for up to three miles off shore, coastal waters and inland fresh waters. They also require the Secretary of State to take action to implement that standard, and where he is so acting the regulations dispense with the requirements of section 83(4) and (5) concerning representations and objections.

The Schedules to the 1989 Regulations are as follows:

SCHEDULE 1

CLASSIFICATION OF INLAND WATERS (DS1)

Substance	*Concentration in microgrammes per litre (annual mean)*
Aldrin, Dieldrin, Endrin & Isodrin	(i) 0.03 for the four substances in total;
	(ii) 0.005 for endrin
Cadmium and its compounds	5 (total cadmium: both soluble and insoluble forms)
Carbon tetrachloride	12
Chloroform	12
DDT (all isomers)	0.025
para-para-DDT	0.01
Hexachlorobenzene	0.03
Hexachlorobutadiene	0.1
Hexachlorocyclohexane (all isomers)	0.1
Mercury and its compounds	1 (total mercury: both soluble and insoluble forms)
Pentachlorophenol and its compounds	2

SCHEDULE 2

CLASSIFICATION OF COASTAL WATERS AND RELEVANT TERRITORIAL WATERS (DS2)

Substance	*Concentration in microgrammes per litre (annual mean)*
Aldrin, Dieldrin, Endrin & Isodrin	(i) 0.03 for the four substances in total;
	(ii) 0.005 for endrin
Cadmium and its compounds	2.5 (dissolved cadmium)
Carbon tetrachloride	12
Chloroform	12
DDT (all isomers)	0.025
para-para-DDT	0.01
Hexachlorobenzene	0.03
Hexachlorobutadiene	0.1
Hexachlorocyclohexane (all isomers)	0.02
Mercury and its compounds	0.3 (dissolved mercury)
Pentachlorophenol and its compounds	2

The Schedule to the 1992 Regulations is as follows:

CLASSIFICATION OF RELEVANT TERRITORIAL WATERS, COASTAL WATERS AND INLAND FRESHWATERS (DS3)

Substance	Concentration in microgrammes per litre (annual mean)	Reference method of measurement
1,2-Dichloroethane	10	Gas chromatography with electron capture detection after extraction by means of an appropriate solvent or gas chromatography following isolation by means of the 'purge and trap' process and trapping by using a cryogenically cooled capillary trap. The limit of determination is 1µg/1. (see Note)
Trichloroethylene	10	Gas chromatography with electron capture detection after extraction by means of an appropriate solvent. The limit of determination is 0.1µg/1. (see Note)
Perchloroethylene	10	
Trichlorobenzene	0.4 (but there must be no significant increase over time in the concentration of trichlorobenzene in sediments and/or molluscs and/or shellfish and/or fish).	Gas chromatography with electron capture detection after extraction by means of an appropriate solvent or, when used to determine the concentration in sediments and organisms, after appropriate preparation of the sample. The limit of determination for each isomer separately is 10µg/1 for the water environment and 1µg/kg of dry matter for sediments and organisms. (see Note)

Note. The accuracy and precision of the method must be plus or minus 50% at a concentration which represents twice the value of the limit of determination.

SURFACE WATERS (RIVER ECOSYSTEM)(CLASSIFICATION) REGULATIONS 1994

Unlike the earlier regulations which, it will have been seen, established quality objectives for particular purposes or uses, these regulations provide a system for classifying the general quality of inland waters, provided that they are 'relevant rivers or watercourses'. We now have, for the first time, a national standard by which inland waters, as part of the natural environment and irrespective of use, can be assessed and compared. Further, of course, and perhaps more importantly, variations in the quality of any particular body of water, whether for better or worse, may be monitored. The system, consisting of five classes in order of decreasing quality from RE1 to RE5, will be used to establish water quality objectives under section 83 of the Water Resources Act 1991.[16] Regulation 2(2) provides that:

The criteria for each of the classifications RE1 to RE5 are that the following requirements are satisfied by a series of samples of water taken and analysed in accordance with regulation 3, that is to say –

(a) the 10 percentile of the saturation of dissolved oxygen shall not be less than the value specified in respect of that classification in column 2;

(b) the 90 percentile of the biochemical oxygen demand shall not exceed the value specified in respect of that classification in column 3;

(c) the 90 percentile of the concentration of total ammonia shall not exceed the value specified in reaspect of that classification in column 4;

16 Compliance with the standard is determined in accordance with the procedure and principles in the document 'Water Quality Objectives: Procedures used by the National Rivers Authority for the purpose of the Surface Water (River Ecosystem)(Classification) Regulations 1994', dated 30 March 1994.

(d) the 95 percentile of the concentration of un-ionised ammonia shall not exceed the value, if any, specified in respect of that classification in column 5;

(e) the 5 percentile of the pH value shall not be less than the lower value, if any, specified in respect of that classification in column 6, and the 95 percentile of the pH value shall not exceed the higher value, if any, so specified;

(f) the 95 percentile of the concentration of dissolved copper shall not exceed the value, if any, which is specified in respect of that classification in column 8 by reference to the hardness of the water as described in column 7; and

(g) the 95 percentile of the concentration of total zinc shall not exceed the value, if any, which is specified in respect of that classification in column 9 by reference to the hardness of the water as described in column 7.

Regulation 3 states that the frequency, location, methods of sampling, samples to be used or rejected, analysis and methods of determining percentile values are those determined by the NRA and set out in the document entitled 'Water Quality Objectives: Procedures used by the National Rivers Authority for the purpose of the Surface Waters (River Ecosystem) (Classification) Regulation 1994'.

SCHEDULE
RIVER ECOSYSTEM CLASSIFICATIONS

1 Class	2 Dissolved Oxygen % saturation 10 percentile	3 BOD (ATU) mg/1 90 percentile	4 Total Ammonia mg N/1 90 percentile	5 Un-ionised Ammonia mg N/1 95 percentile	6 pH lower limit as 5 percentile; upper limit as 95 percentile	7 Hardness mg/1 C_aCO_3	8 Dissolved Copper µg/1 95 percentile	9 Total Zinc µg/1 95 percentile
RE1	80	2.5	0.25	0.021	6.0–9.0	≤10	5	30
						>10 and ≤50	22	200
						>50 and ≤100	40	300
						>100	112	500
RE2	70	4.0	0.6	0.021	6.0–9.0	≤10	5	30
						>10 and ≤50	22	200
						>50 and ≤100	40	300
						>100	112	500
RE3	60	6.0	1.3	0.021	6.0–9.0	≤10	5	300
						>10 and ≤50	22	700
						>50 and ≤100	40	1000
						>100	112	2000
RE4	50	8.0	2.5	–	6.0–9.0	≤10	5	300
						>10 and ≤50	22	700
						>50 and ≤100	40	1000
						>100	112	2000
RE5	20	15.0	9.0	–	–	–	–	–

BATHING WATERS (CLASSIFICATION) REGULATIONS 1991

17 See above, footnote 14.

These regulations provide a system of classification of relevant territorial waters,[17] coastal waters and inland waters that are bathing waters, to establish quality objectives under section 83 of the Water Resources Act 1991. The definition of 'bathing water' appears in Article 1.2 of Directive 76/160/EEC and 'means all running or still fresh waters or parts thereof and sea water, in which:

- bathing is explicitly authorised by the competent authorities of each Member State, or
- bathing is not prohibited and is traditionally practised by a large number of bathers.'

Water used for therapeutic purposes or in swimming pools is excluded from the definition.

The Directive offers no guidance to the meaning of either 'traditionally' or 'large numbers', it being left to Member States to devise their own criteria. The Department of the Environment adopted two, using a 'commonsense assessment' rather than a 'scientific or rigorous' definition or analysis:

(a) some time in the bathing season there should be at least 500 people in the water all at once (regardless of the length of the stretch of water in question);
(b) waters where the number of bathers was assessed at more than 1,500 per mile would be classified as bathing waters; and they might be where it was between 750 and 1,500 per mile.

In the 1993 season three new bathing waters were identified, bringing the total designated in England and Wales for the purposes of Directive 76/160/EEC to 419.[18]

18 'Bathing Water Quality in England and Wales – 1993' NRA Annual Report (HMSO).

ANNEX
QUALITY REQUIREMENTS FOR BATHING WATER

	Parameters		G	I	Minimum sampling frequency	Method of analysis and inspection
	Microbiological:					
1	Total coliforms	/100 ml	500	10 000	Fortnightly (1)	Fermentation in multiple tubes. Sub-culturing of the positive tubes on a confirmation medium. Count according to MPN (most probable number) or membrane filtration and
2	Faecal coliforms	/100 ml	100	2 000	Fortnightly (1)	culture on an appropriate medium such as Tergitol lactose agar, endo agar, 0·4% Teepol broth, subculturing and identification of the suspect colonies. In the case of 1 and 2, the incubation temperature is variable according to whether total or faecal coliforms are being investigated.
3	Faecal streptococci	/100 ml	100	–	(2)	Litsky method. Count according to MPN (most probable number) or filtration on membrane. Culture on an appropriate medium.
4	Salmonella	/1 litre	–	0	(2)	Concentration by membrane filtration. Inoculation on a standard medium. Enrichment – subculturing on isolating agar – identification.
5	Entero viruses	PFU/10 litres	–	0	(2)	Concentrating by filtration, flocculation or centrifuging and confirmation.
	Physico-chemical:					
6	pH		–	6 to 9 (0)	(2)	Electrometry with calibration at pH 7 and 9.

	Parameters	G	I	Minimum sampling frequency	Method of analysis and inspection
7	Colour	–	No abnormal change in colour (0)	Fortnightly (1)	Visual inspection or photometry with standards on the Pt.Co scale.
		–	–	(2)	
8	Mineral oils mg/ litre	–	No film visible on the surface of the water and no odour	Fortnightly (1)	Visual and olfactory inspection or extraction using an adequate volume and weighing the dry residue.
		≤0·3	–	(2)	
9	Surface-active substances mg/litre reacting with (lauryl- methylene blue sulphate)	–	No lasting foam	Fortnightly (1)	Visual inspection or absorption spectrophotometry with methylene blue.
		≤0·3	–	(2)	
10	Phenols mg/litre (phenol indices) C_6H_5OH	–	No specific odour	Fortnightly (1)	Verification of the absence of specific odour due to phenol or absorption spectrophotometry 4-aminoantipyrine (4 AAP) method.
		≤0·005	≤0·05	(2)	
11	Transparency m	2	1 (0)	Fortnightly (1)	Secchi's disc.
12	Dissolved oxygen % saturation O_2	8 to 120	–	(2)	Winkler's method or electrometric method (oxygen meter).
13	Tarry residues and floating materials such as wood, plastic articles, bottles, containers of glass, plastic, rubber or any other substance. Waste or splinters	Absence		Fortnightly (1)	Visual inspection
14	Ammonia mg/litre HN_4			(3)	Absorption spectrophotometry, Nessler's method, or indophenol blue method.
15	Nitrogen Kjeldahl mg/litre N			(3)	Kjeldahl method
	Other substances regarded as indications of pollution				
16	Pesticides mg/litre (parathion, HCH, dieldrin)			(2)	Extraction with appropriate solvents and chromatographic determination
17	Heavy metals such as:				
	– arsenic mg/litre As – cadmium Cd – chrome VI Cr VI – lead Pb – mercury Hg			(2)	Atomic absorption possibly preceded by extraction

	Parameters		G	I	Minimum sampling frequency	Method of analysis and inspection
18	Cyanides	mg/litre Cn			(2)	Absorption spectrophotometry using specific reagent
19	Nitrates and phosphates	mg/litre NO$_3$ PO$_4$			(2)	Absorption spectrophotometry using specific reagent

G = guide

I = mandatory.

(0) Provision exists for exceeding the limits in the event of exceptional geographical or meteorological conditions.

(1) When a sampling taken in previous years produced results which are appreciably better than those in this Annex and when n new factor likely to lower the quality of the water has appeared, the competent authorities may reduce the sampling frequenc by a factor of 2.

(2) Concentration to be checked by the competent authorities when an inspection in the bathing area shows that the substance ma be present or that the quality of the water has deteriorated.

(3) These parameters must be checked by the competent authorities when there is a tendency towards the eutrophication of the water

Classification BW1 reflects the mandatory standards in the Annex to that Directive. The schedules set out below establish the criteria and sampling requirements. Schedule 1, paragraph 3 gives the Secretary of State power, by notice to the NRA, to modify or dispense with the requirements in any particular case, although he is prohibited from exercising this power so as to permit a risk to public health. Subject to the following provisions of this Schedule, the criteria for the classification BW1 are that:

(a) at least 95 per cent of samples of the waters taken and tested in accordance with Schedule 2 must conform to the parametric values specified in Schedule 3;

(b) no sample of the waters taken in accordance with Schedule 2 which when tested for compliance with the phenols parameter by the absorption method or with the transparency parameter fails to comply shall have a value which deviates from the relevant parametric value for that parameter specified in Schedule 3 by more than 50 per cent;

(c) consecutive samples of the waters taken in accordance with Schedule 2 at statistically suitable intervals shall not when tested deviate from the relevant parametric values specified in Schedule 3.

These sampling requirements may be relaxed in the event of abnormal weather when excessive volume and turbulence can be expected to produce distorted results. In those circumstances, and subject to the agreement of the Department of the Environment, the sample following the abnormal weather event is excluded from the compliance calculations. While there is no official definition of what constitutes 'abnormal weather' the Department of the Environment consider that generally a '1 in 5 year storm event' can be regarded as exceptional weather; that is a storm that is statistically likely to occur only once in every five years.

The sampling requirements in Schedule 2 include a sampling period in any year between 1 May and 30 September, and the duty to take additional samples where there are indications that the water quality is deteriorating for any reason or is likely to do so as a result of any discharge. Samples are to be taken at the same point which is where the daily average density of bathers is at its highest and, generally, 30 centimetres below the surface.

SCHEDULE 3

QUALITY AND ADDITIONAL SAMPLING REQUIREMENTS

Parameter	Parametric value	Minimum sampling frequency	Methods of analysis and inspection
Micro-biological:			
Total coliforms	10,000/ 100ml	Fortnightly (see Note 1)	Fermentation in multiple tubes. Sub-culturing of the positive tubes on a confirmation medium. Either counting according to MPN (most probable number) or membrane
Faecal coliforms	2,000/ 100ml	Fortnightly (see Note 1)	filtration, culturing on an appropriate medium, subculturing and identification of the suspect colonies.
			The incubation temperature is variable according to whether total or faecal coliforms are being investigated.
Salmonella	Absent in 1 litre	(see Note 2)	Membrane filtration, culturing on an appropriate medium, sub-culturing and identification of the suspect colonies
Entero viruses	No plaque forming units in 10 litres	(see Note 2)	Concentration (by filtration, flocculation or centrifuging) and confirmation.
Physico-chemical:			
pH	6 to 9	(see Note 2)	Electrometry with calibration at pH 7 and 9.
Colour	No abnormal change in colour	Fortnightly (see Note 1)	Visual inspection or photometry with standards on the platinum cobalt scale
Mineral oils	No film visible on the surface of the water and no odour	Fortnightly (see Note 1)	Visual and olfactory inspection.
Surface active substances reacting with methylene blue	No lasting foam	Fortnightly (see Note 1)	Visual inspection.
Phenols (phenol indices)	No specific odour	Fortnightly (see Note 1)	Olfactory inspection.
	<0.05 mg/litre (C_6H_5OH)	(see Note 2)	Absorption spectrophotometry 4-aminoantipyrine (4 AAP) method.
Transparency	1 metre	Fortnightly (see Note 1)	Secchi's disc.

Notes 1. Samples may be taken at intervals of four weeks where samples taken in previous years show that the waters are of an appreciably higher standard than that required for the classification in question and the quality of the waters has not subsequently deteriorated and is unlikely to do so.

2. Samples must be taken in relation to this parameter when there are grounds for suspecting that there has been a deterioration in the quality of the waters or the substances are likely to be present in the waters.

Water quality, then, is determined by reference to a number of physical, chemical and microbiological measurements, for most of which mandatory or guideline values are given. The Directive, being concerned solely with water quality, has no reference to the cleanliness of beaches. The designated bathing waters complying and not complying on the basis of coliform results for 1993 are tabulated in the latest NRA annual report as follows:

NRA Region	Number of Bathing waters	Complying		Non-complying	
		Number	%	Number	%
Anglian	33	28	84.8	5	15.2
Northumbria & Yorkshire	56	46	82.1	10	17.9
North West	33	13	39.4	20	60.6
Southern	67	58	86.6	9	13.4
South Western	175	142	81.1	33	18.9
Thames	3	3	100.0	0	0
Welsh	51	42	82.4	9	17.6
Total	418	332	79.4	86	20.6

The Commission were given a mandate at the 1992 European Summit in Edinburgh to review water quality Directives 'in the light of scientific knowledge and technical progress', one aim being to devolve responsibility for standard setting to national and local level in accordance with the principle of subsidiarity. The new, draft Bathing Water Directive was submitted to the Council of Ministers[19] in the summer of 1994 and, if adopted, would be implemented on 31 December 1995. The draft makes significant changes to the microbiological parameters with E. coli, faecal streptococci, enteroviruses and bacteriophages in place of the former categories. Also of particular significance, the proposed twelfth parameter covers tarry residues, waste or splinters and floating materials. Depending on interpretation, this last would seem to have a direct bearing on the cleanliness of beaches. Member States would be permitted to set values for all, or individual, beaches, with discretion to set more stringent values and to add further parameters. Following identification of a bathing area the Member State would have three seasons to ensure conformity with the minimum Directive values. In the absence of such compliance the competent authority would be obliged to identify the cause of failure and take the necessary action to secure compliance as soon as possible. This action would be buttressed by notification of the Commission of the reasons for non-compliance, the action needed and the timetable for remedy.

The test of compliance with the standards would be based on the number of samples failing the standard for each parameter, as specified in the draft Directive:

up to 19 samples   0 failures
20–39 samples   1 failure

19 COM (94) 36 final – 94/0006 (SYN). Proposal for a Council Directive concerning the quality of bathing water, OJ c 112. 22.04.94. See *Environmental Health*, vol. 102, no. 07, July 1994.

| 40–59 samples | 2 failures |
| over 59 samples | 5% failures |

A new requirement imposed on Member States by the Directive would be the duty to ensure that adequate information on bathing water quality was prominently displayed at each bathing area, stating:

(a) whether the bathing water complied with Directive requirements in the previous season;
(b) most recent information on bathing water quality in the current season;
(c) information, and timetable, on any remedial work in progress or planned.

There are also modified proposals for sampling frequency and requirements relating to the identification of pollution sources. Member States would have an annual reporting obligation, the Commission undertaking to publish within four months of their receipt a Community report on implementation of the Directive.

In addition to the formal system of designated bathing waters and compliance standards under Directive 76/160/EEC there are two informal, voluntary schemes to grade bathing waters and beaches. Although they are not strictly relevant to a consideration of the law the context warrants a brief reference. The European Blue Flag Scheme is organised by the Federation of Environmental Education in Europe and is administered in the United Kingdom by the Tidy Britain Group.[20] A Blue Flag is awarded on the basis of compliance with the G values of the Directive for the microbiological parameters total and faecal coliforms and faecal streptococci of samples for the previous season. The award also requires compliance with certain land-based criteria. The Seaside Award scheme, also administered by the Tidy Britain Group, was introduced in 1992. It is intended to complement the Blue Flag Awards and aims to recognise resorts and beaches which attain high standards of facilities and management, beach cleanliness and water quality (again based on samples taken during the previous season). The scheme has two categories, Resort and Rural. The Resort award applies to managed tourist resorts and is given to beaches which achieve high water quality standards and comply with 28 land-based criteria such as public access and information, dog control and hygiene, beach management and safety. The Rural category applies to smaller beaches with limited facilities whose attraction lies in their undeveloped character. The award is based on the water quality standards and the attainment of 8 land-based criteria.

20 An independent registered charity, partly funded by the DoE.

FRESHWATER FISH AND SHELLFISH WATERS

Council Directive 78/659/EEC provides for 'the quality of fresh waters needing protection or improvement in order to support fish life', such waters being designated by Member States. The aim of the Directive, as stated in Article 1.3,

is to protect or improve the quality of those running or standing fresh waters which support or which, if pollution were reduced or eliminated, would become capable of supporting fish belonging to:

– indigenous species offering a natural diversity, or
– species the presence of which is judged desirable for water management purposes by the competent authorities of the Member States.

Waters in natural or artificial fish ponds used for intensive fish-farming are excluded.

The physical and chemical parameters applicable to the waters designated by Member States are listed in Annex I and reproduced below, there being an obligation to 'respect the values in column G'[21]. Member States may set more, but not less, stringent standards than those in the Directive. In interpreting the Annex, 'salmonid waters shall mean waters which support or become capable of supporting fish belonging to species such as salmon, trout, grayling and whitefish'. Similarly, 'cyprinid waters shall mean waters which support or become capable of supporting fish belonging to the cyprinids, or other species such as pike, perch and eel'.[22] Implementation of the Directive in the United Kingdom is through discharge consents under section 88(1)(a) of the Water Resources Act 1991. To ensure protection of fish that may be affected by discharges (whether into designated waters or otherwise) all applications for a consent to discharge trade or sewage effluent to estuarial or coastal waters must be sent to the Minister by the NRA.[23] Water quality objectives may also be set under section 83 of the Water Resources Act 1991 to achieve the purposes of the Directive.

21 Article 3.2

22 Both definitions are to be found in Article 1.4.

23 As to called in applications, see S.I. 1989 No. 1157, Schedule 2; and S.I. 1989 No. 1151, regulation 4(1).

ANNEX I
LIST OF PARAMETERS

Parameter	Salmonid waters		Cyprinid waters		Methods of analysis or inspection	Minimum sampling and measuring frequency	Observations
	G	1	G	1			
1. Temperature (°C)	1. Temperature measured downstream of a point of termal discharge (at the edge of the mixing zone) must not exceed the unaffected temperature by more than:				Thermometry	Weekly, both upstream and downstream of the point of thermal discharge	Over-sudden variations in temperature shall be avoided
		1·5°C		3°C			
	Derogations limited in geographical scope may be decided by Member States in particular conditions if the competent authority can prove that there are no harmful consequences for the balanced development of the fish population						
	2. Thermal discharges must not cause the temperature downstream of the point of thermal discharge (at the edge of the mixing zone) to exceed the following):						
		21·5 (0) 10 (0)		28 (0) 10 (0)			
	The 10°C temperature limit applies only to breeding periods of species which need cold water for reproduction and only to waters which may contain such species						
	Temperature limits may, however, be exceeded for 2 % of the time						

Parameter	Salmonid waters		Cyprinid waters		Methods of analysis or inspection	Minimum sampling and measuring frequency	Observations
	G	1	G	1			
2. Dissolved oxygen (mg/1 O_2)	50 % ≥ 9 100 % ≥ 7	50 % ≥ 9 When the oxygen concentration falls below 6mg\1, Member States shall implement the provisions of Article 7 (3). The competent authority must prove that this situation will have no harmful consequences for the balanced development of the fish population	50 % ≥ 8 100 % ≥ 5	50 % ≥ 7 When the oxygen concentration falls below 6mg/1, Member States shall implement the provisions of Article 7 (3). The competent authority must prove that this situation will have no harmful consequences for the balanced development of the fish population	Winkler's method or specific electrodes (electro-chemical method)	Monthly, minimum one sample representative of low oxygen conditions of the day of sampling However, where major daily variations are suspected, a minimum of two samples in one day shall be taken	
3. pH		6 to 9 (0) ([1])		6 to 9 (0) ([1])	Electrometry calibration means of two solutions with known pH values, preferably on either side of, and close to the pH being measured	Monthly	
4. Suspended solids (mg/1)	≤ 25 (0)		≤ 25 (0)		Filtration through a 0·45 µm filtering membrane, or centrifugation (five minutes minimum, average acceleration of 2 800 to 3 200g) drying at 105°C and weighing		The values shown are average concentrations and do not apply to suspended solids with harmful chemical properties Floods are liable to cause particularly high concentrations
5. BOd_5 (mg/1 O_2)	≤ 3		≤6		Determination of O_2 by the Winkler method before and after five days incubation in complete darkness at 20 ± 1°C (nitrification should not be inhibited)		

Parameter	Salmonid waters		Cyprinid waters		Methods of analysis or inspection	Minimum sampling and measuring frequency	Observations
	G	1	G	1			
6. Total phosphorus (mg/1 P)					Molecular absorption spectrophotometry		In the case of lakes of average depth between 18 and 300 m, the following formula could be applied: $$L \leq 10\frac{Z}{Tw}(1+\sqrt{Tw})$$ where: L = loading expressed as mg P per square metre lake surface in one year; Z = mean depth of lake in metres; Tw = theoretical renewal time of lake water in years. In other cases limit values of 0·2 mg/1 for salmonid and of 0·4 mg/1 for cyprinid waters, expressed as PO_4, may be regarded as indicative in order to reduce eutrophication
7. Nitrites (mg/1 NO_2)	≤0·01		≤0·03		Molecular absorption spectrophotometry		
8. Phenolic compounds (mg/1 C_6H_5OH)		(2)		(2)	By taste		An examination by taste shall be made only where the presence of phenolic compounds is presumed
9. Petroleum hydrocarbons		(3)		(3)	Visual / By taste	Monthly	A visual examination shall be made regularly once a month, with an examination by taste only where the presence of hydrocarbons is presumed
10. Non-ionised ammonia (mg/1 NH_3)	≤0·005	≤0·025	≤0·005	≤0·025	Molecular absorption spectrophotometry using indophenol blue or Nessler's method associated with pH and temperature determination	Monthly	Values for non-ionised ammonia may be exceeded in the form of minor peaks in the daytime
	In order to diminish the risk of toxicity due to non-ionised ammonia, of oxygen consumption due to nitrification and of eutrophication, the concentrations of total ammonium should not exceed the following:						
11. Total ammonium (mg/1 NH_4)	≤0·04	≤1 (4)	≤ 0·2	≤1 (4)			

Parameter	Salmonid waters		Cyprinid waters		Methods of analysis or inspection	Minimum sampling and measuring frequency	Observations
	G	1	G	1			
12. Total residual chlorine (mg/1 HOCl)		≤0·005		≤0·005	DPD-method (diethyl-*p*-phenylenediamene)	Monthly	The I-values correspond to pH = 6. Higher concentrations of total chlorine can be accepted if the pH is higher
13. Total zinc (mg/1 Zn)		≤0·3		≤1·0	Atomic absorption spectrometry	Monthly	The I-values correspond to a water hardness of 100 mg/1 CaCO₃ For hardness levels between 10 and 500 mg/1 corresponding limit values can be found in Annex II
14. Dissolved copper per (mg/1 Cu)	≤0·04		≤0·4		Atomic absorption spectrometry		The G-Values correspond to a water hardness of 100 mg/1 CaCO₃ For hardness levels between 10 and 300 mg/1 corresponding limit values can be found in Annex II

(1) Artificial pH variations with respect to the unaffected values shall not exceed ± 0·5 of a pH unit within the limits falling between 6·0 and 9·0 provided that these variations do not increase the harmfulness of other substances present in the water.
(2) Phenolic compounds must not be present in such concentrations that they adversely affect fish flavour.
(3) Petroleum products must not be present in water in such quantities that they:
 – form a visible film on the surface of the water or form coatings on the beds of water-courses and lakes,
 – impart a detectable 'hydrocarbon' taste to fish,
 – produce harmful effects in fish.
(4) In particular geographical or climatic conditions and particularly in cases of low water temperature and of reduced nitrification or where the competent authority can prove that there are no harmful consequences for the balanced development of the fish population, Member States may fix values higher than 1 mg/l.

General observation:

It should be noted that the parametric values listed in this Annex assume that the other parameters, whether mentioned in this Annex or not, are favourable. This implies, in particular, that the concentrations of other harmful substances are very low.
Where two or more harmful substances are present in mixture, joint effects (additive, synergic or antagonistic effects) may be significant.
 G = guide.
 I = mandatory.
(0) = derogations are possible in accordance with Article 11.

24 Cmnd 9149, February 1984, 'Tackling Pollution – Experience and Prospects', paragraphs 4.74 and 4.75.

Quality standards for shellfish waters are specified in Council Directive 79/923/EEC. The Directive applies to coastal and brackish (estuarine) waters designated by Member States as needing protection or improvement in order to support shellfish (bivalve and gastropod molluscs) life and growth and thus to contribute to the high quality of shellfish products directly edible by man. It is therefore for each Member State to identify and designate its own waters, with subsequent revisions as appear necessary. Member States may also set their own values which may be more stringent than those in the Directive but not less so; the Annex to the Directive specifies both mandatory and guideline values. Within six years of designation the waters must conform to the values set.

The Royal Commission on Environmental Pollution noted in its Tenth Report[24] the confusion over whether the Directive is designed solely as an environmental quality measure to encourage shellfish growth, or whether it is concerned with protecting human health by reducing contamination of shellfish. The interpre-

ANNEX

QUALITY OF SHELLFISH WATERS

	Parameter	G	I	Reference methods of analysis	Minimum sampling and measuring frequency
1.	pH pH unit		7–9	– Electrometry Measured *in situ* at the time of sampling	Quarterly
2.	Temperature °C	A discharge affecting shellfish waters must not cause the temperature of the waters to exceed by more than 2 °C the temperature of waters not so affected		– Thermometry Measured *in situ* at the time of sampling	Quarterly
3.	Coloration (after filtration) mg Pt/1		A discharge affecting shellfish waters must not cause the colour of the waters after filtration to deviate by more than 10 mg Pt/1 from the colour of waters not so affected	– Filter through a 0·45 μm membrane Photometric method, using the platinum/ cobalt scale	Quarterly
4.	Suspended solids mg/1		A discharge affecting shellfish waters must not cause the suspended solid content of the waters to exceed by more than 30% the content of waters not so affected	– Filtration through a 0·45 μm membrane, drying at 105 °C and weighing – Centrifuging (for at least five minutes, with mean acceleration 2 800 to 3 200 g), drying at 105 °C and weighing	Quarterly
5.	Salinity ‰	12 to 38 ‰	– ≤ 40 ‰ – Discharge affecting shellfish waters must not cause their salinity to exceed by more than 10 % the salinity of waters not so affected	Conductimetry	Monthly
6.	Dissolved oxygen Saturation %	≥ 80 %	– ≥ 70 % (average value) – Should an individual measurement indicate a value of less than 60 % unless there are no harmful consequences for the development of shellfish colonies	– Winkler's method – Electrochemical method	Monthly, with a minimum of one sample represen- tative of low oxygen conditions on the day of sampling. However, where major daily vari- ations are suspected, a minimim of two samples in one day shall be taken

	Parameter	G	I	Reference methods of analysis	Minimum sampling and measuring frequency
7.	Petroleum hydrocarbons		Hydrocarbons must not be present in the shellfish water in such quantities as to: – produce a visible film on the surface of the water and/or a deposit on the shellfish, – have harmful effects on the shellfish	Visual examination	Quarterly
8.	Organohalogenated substances	The concentration of each substance in shellfish flesh must be so limited that it contributes, in accordance with Article 1, to the high quality of shellfish products	The concentration of each substance in the shellfish flesh must not reach or exceed a level which has harmful effects on the shellfish and larvae	Gas chromatography after extraction with suitable solvents and purification	Half-yearly
9.	*Metals* Silver Ag Arsenic As Cadmium Cd Chromium Cr Copper Cu Mercury Hg Nickel Ni Lead Pb Zinc Zn mg/1	The concentration of each substance in shellfish flesh must be so limited that it contributes in accordance with Article 1, to the high quality of shellfish products	The concentration of each substance in the shellfish flesh must not exceed a level which gives rise to harmful effects on the shellfish and their larvae The synergic effects of these metals must be taken into consideration	Spectrometry of atomic absorption preceded, where appropriate, by concentration and/or extraction	Half-yearly
10.	Faecal coliforms /100 ml	≤ 300 in the shellfish flesh and intervalvular liquid[1]		Method of dilution with fermentation in liquid substrates in at least three tubes in three dilutions. Subculturing of the positive tubes on a confirmation medium. Count according to MPN (most probable number). Incubation tempeature 44 °C ± 0·5 °C	Quarterly
11.	Substances affecting the taste of the shellfish		Concentration lower than that liable to impair the taste of the shellfish	Examination of the shellfish by tasting where the presence of one of these substances is presumed	
12.	Saxitoxin (produced) by dinoflagellates)				

Abbreviations:
G = guide
 I = mandatory
(1) However, pending the adoption of a Directive on the protection of consumers of shellfish products, it is essential that this value be observed in waters in which live shellfish is directly edible by man.

tation adopted by the United Kingdom Government is that it is purely an environmental measure and that no element of public health protection is involved. At the time of the report the United Kingdom had designated 29 shellfish waters, all being waters that either already met the standards or would do so within six years of designation; the implementation of the Directive thus having no immediate or direct effect on the quality of shellfish waters in the United Kingdom.

It may also be noted that Council Directive 91/492/EEC specifies the health conditions for the production and the placing on the market of live bivalve molluscs.[25] While this Directive is concerned with shellfish quality at point of sale and therefore with their commercial handling, the conditions in which they grew are also of importance. Chapter 1 of the Annex therefore deals with the conditions for production areas, as reflected in the levels of contamination in the shellfish flesh.

25 Implemented by Food Safety (Live Bivalve Molluscs and Other Shellfish) Regulations 1992, S.I.1992 No. 3164.

ANNEX II

PARTICULARS REGARDING TOTAL ZINC AND DISSOLVED COPPER

Total zinc

Zinc concentrations (mg/1 Zn) for different water hardness values between 10 and 500 mg/1 $CaCO_3$:

	Water hardness (mg/1 $CaCO_3$)			
	10	50	100	500
Salmonid waters (mg/1 Zn)	0·03	0·2	0·3	0·5
Cyprinid waters (mg/1 Zn)	0·3	0·7	0·1	2·0

Dissolved copper

Dissolved copper concentrations (mg/1 Cu) for different water hardness values between 10 and 300 mg/1 $CaCO_3$:

	Water hardness (mg/1 $CaCO_3$)			
	10	50	100	300
mg/1 Cu	0·005 (1)	0·022	0·04	0·112

(1) The presence of fish in waters containing higher concentrations of copper may indicate a predominance of dissolved organo-cupric complexes.

DOMESTIC SUPPLIES

A consideration of water quality for domestic use inevitably requires some review of the concepts of purity and wholesomeness. One or other of those terms appears in a long succession of statutes relating to water supplies, initially with little or no definition. That has now changed and, driven in part by EC Directives, the scope of 'wholesomeness' is delineated with ever increasing precision. Some basic and general principles deriving from a leading Privy Council judgement are worth noting as an introduction to the topic, however. It may also be that, depending on the interpretation to be placed on the wording of the regulations, these principles to determine wholesomeness may not be entirely or wholly displaced by the legislative code.

In New Zealand, section 240(1) of the Municipal Corporation Act 1954 empowered councils to construct waterworks for the supply of pure water for the use of the inhabitants of the district. Apparently water in that country is generally low in natural fluoride, having barely measurable quantities, thus rendering its population and particularly children, liable to dental caries. The Lower Hutt City Corporation decided to install equipment to raise the level of fluoride in their water supply to 1ppm by the addition of sodium silico-fluoride. The appellant relators in *Attorney General of New Zealand* v *Lower Hutt City Corporation* (1964)[26] contended that while section 240 allowed the removal of impurities it did not sanction the addition of a food or medicine. The following points of note appear from the judgement of the Court delivered by Lord Upjohn[27]:

> No one has suggested that the phrase 'pure water' means pure H2O distilled of all other ingredients. It would, indeed, be a most unappetising and unsatisfactory liquid.
>
> The phrase must be construed in relation to the background that 'water' in the section refers to a natural liquid obtained from the earth through artesian wells (as in this case) or rivers, or streams, and as such it must have within it many substances in solution which it has collected in the course of its percolation through the earth's crust. These substances will differ greatly according to the nature of the earth through which the water passes on its way to the point where it is finally collected by the local authority, be it by artesian well, or from rivers, streams or reservoirs to form the basic supply for the distribution of water to the local inhabitants. But the authority, exercising its powers under section 240, may not be entitled to deliver that water in its natural condition for it may contain many ingredients highly deleterious and harmful to human beings who desire to use it for drinking and domestic purposes. It must supply 'pure water'. For this purpose, therefore, it must be empowered to add to the natural water content substances such as chlorine to counteract toxic bacilli; to take the necessary steps by the addition or extraction of constituents, to prevent cloudiness or discolouration, to make the taste more acceptable and 'potable' and so on.

His Lordship then went on to add:

> Their Lordships are of opinion that an Act empowering local authorities to supply 'pure water' should receive a fair, large and liberal construction. ...They are of opinion that as a matter of common sense there is but little difference for the relative purpose between the adjectives 'pure' and 'wholesome' ... The water of Lower Hutt is no doubt pure in its natural state, but it is very deficient in one of the natural constituents normally to be found in water in most parts of the world. The addition of fluoride adds no impurity and the water remains not only water but pure water, and it becomes a greatly improved and still natural water containing no foreign elements.

From the two basic principles that no naturally pure water is chemically pure and that treatment of various sorts may be necessary before water can be delivered for consumption, we see developed here the concept of what might be called a notional pure water with a range of common or relatively common characteristics. While a water from any particular source may require the removal of certain natural characteristics to make it pure, so evidently, others may require the addition of factors naturally lacking to bring them up to a common standard of purity or wholesomeness. It would appear therefore that, while artificially added, such substances are nevertheless to be regarded as natural constituents of water.

26 [1964] AC 1469, PC.

27 At pp.1481and 1484.

Turning now to the statutory provisions, section 93(1) of the Water Industry Act 1991 provides that 'wholesome and such cognate expressions shall be construed subject to the provisions of any regulations made under section 67 above'. Section 67 gives the Secretary of State power to make regulations specifying standards of wholesomeness of water supplies and prescribing, *inter alia,* purposes for which water is suitable, requirements as to substances that are to be present in or absent from the water, concentrations of substances required to be in water, other characteristics of water and the necessary ancillary sampling procedures to determine such requirements. Regulations under this section are the Water Supply (Water Quality) Regulations 1989.[28] These regulations incorporate the standards in the EC Directive with further national standards and are applicable to all samples of water, although Part III of the regulations authorises relaxations in certain circumstances, largely but not entirely of an emergency nature. Waters then that comply with regulation 3(2) and the standards in Schedule 2 are deemed to be wholesome for the purposes of Part III of the Water Industry Act 1991. The wording of section 67 allows the Secretary of State to specify criteria for the determination of wholesomeness and unwholesomeness. Regulation 3(2), however, confines itself to specifying standards which, if satisfied, shall be 'deemed to satisfy' the wholesomeness requirement. The implication therefore being that, legally, wholesomeness may also be satisfied on other criteria. This view is supported by regulation 3(7) which provides that where water supplies contain substances in excess of the concentrations prescribed in Table C of Schedule 2 they are to be regarded as unwholesome. Failure to meet the other specified standards is not similarly stipulated necessarily to render the water impure. This statutory formulation of wholesomeness is one, but apparently not the only, standard.

Regulation 3 states that:

(2) Subject to paragraph (7), water supplied to any premises for such domestic purposes as consist in or include drinking, washing or cooking[29] shall be regarded as wholesome for the purposes of Chapter II, as it applies to the supply of water for those domestic purposes, if the requirements of paragraph (3) below are satisfied; and, where the water has been softened or desalinated and is to be supplied for drinking or cooking, the requirements of paragraph (4) are also satisfied.

(3) The requirements of this paragraph are –
  (a) that the water does not contain any element, organism or substance (other than a parameter) at a concentration or value which would be detrimental to public health;
  (b) that the water does not contain any element, organism or substance (whether or not a parameter) at a concentration or value which in conjunction with any other element, organism or substance it contains (whether or not a parameter) would be detrimental to public health;
  (c) subject to paragraphs (5) and (6) below, that the water does not contain concentrations or values of the parameters listed in Tables A to C in excess of the prescribed concentrations or values;
  (d) that samples taken in respect of the parameters listed in Table D from water supplied to the water supply zone in question have established that the average concentrations or values of those parameters over the preceding 12 months did not exceed those specified in that Table; and
  (e) that samples taken from water supplied to the water supply zone in question have established that the average concentrations over the three preceding months of trihalomethanes (being the aggregate of the concentrations of trichloromethane, dichlorobromomethane, dibromochloromethane and tribromomethane) did not exceed 100µg/1, or where (by virtue of regulation 13(3)) less than four samples

28 S.I. 1989 No. 1147; implementing EC Directive 80/778/EEC relating to quality of water intended for human consumption; amended by the Water Supply (Water Quality) Regulations 1991.

29 The Water Supply (Water Quality) Regulations 1991 (S.I. 1991 No. 1837) add to these activities, and thereby extend the 1989 Regulations to food production, giving effect to Council Directive 80/778/EEC and to the decision in *M.W.B. v Avery* [1914] AC 118.

are taken in any year, no sample contained a concentration of trihalomethanes in excess of 100µg/1.

(4) The requirements of this paragraph are that the water's hardness or its alkalinity is not below the relevant minimum specified in Table E.

A parameter is defined in regulation 2 as meaning a property, element, organism or substance listed in the second column of the tables in Schedule 2 or the first column of Tables 1–4, 6 and 7 in Schedule 3. In effect a parameter is a characteristic or constituent of water that is assessed in determining its wholesomeness. The parameters, with their concentrations, listed in Schedule 2 are as follows:

Table A

Item	Parameters	Units of Measurement	Concentration or Value (maximum unless otherwise stated)
1.	Colour	mg/1 Pt/Co scale	20
2.	Turbidity (including suspended solids)	Formazin turbidity units	4
3.	Odour (including hydrogen sulphide)	Dilution number	3 at 25°C
4.	Taste	Dilution number	3 at 25°C
5.	Temperature	°C	25
6.	Hydrogen ion	pH value	9.5 5.5 (minimum)
7.	Sulphate	$mg/SO_4/1$	250
8.	Magnesium	mg Mg/1	50
9.	Sodium	mg Na/1	150
10.	Potassium	mg K/1	12
11.	Dry residues	mg/1	1500 (after drying at 180°C)
12.	Nitrate	$mg NO_3/1$	50
13.	Nitrite	$mg NO_2/1$	0.1
14.	Ammonium (ammonia and ammonium ions)	$mg NH_4/1$	0.5
15.	Kjeldahl nitrogen	mg N/1	1
16.	Oxidisability (permanganate value)	$mg O_2/1$	5
17.	Total organic carbon	mg C/1	No significant increase over that normally observed
18.	Dissolved or emulsified hydrocarbons (after extraction with petroleum ether); mineral oils	µg/1	10
19.	Phenols	$µg\ C_6H_5OH/1$	0.5
20.	Surfactants	µg/1 (as lauryl sulphate)	200
21.	Aluminium	µg Al/1	200
22.	Iron	µg Fe/1	200
23.	Manganese	µg Mn/1	50
24.	Copper	µg Cu/1	3000
25.	Zinc	µg Zn/1	5000
26.	Phosphorus	µg P/1	2200
27.	Fluoride	µg F/1	1500
28.	Silver	µg Ag/1	10 (i)

Note: (i) If silver is used in a water treatment process, 80 may be substituted for 10.

Table B

Item	Parameters	Units of Measurement	Maximum Concentration
1.	Arsenic	µg As/1	50
2.	Cadmium	µg Cd/1	5
3.	Cyanide	µg CN/1	50
4.	Chromium	µg Cr/1	50
5.	Mercury	µg Hg/1	1
6.	Nickel	µg Ni/1	50
7.	Lead	µg Pb/1	50
8.	Antimony	µg Sb/1	10
9.	Selenium	µg Se/1	10
10.	Pesticides and related products:		
	(a) individual substances	µg/1	0.1
	(b) total substances (i)	µg/1	0.5
11.	Polycyclic aromatic hydrocarbons (ii)	µg/1	0.2

Notes: (i) The sum of the detected concentrations of individual substances. (ii) The sum of the detected concentrations of fluoranthene, benzo 3.4 fluoranthene, benzo 11.12 fluoranthene, benzo 3.4 pyrene, benzo 1.12 perylene and indeno (1,2,3-cd) pyrene.

Table C

1.	Total coliforms	number/100ml	0
2.	Faecal coliforms	number/100ml	0
3.	Faecal streptococci	number/100ml	0
4.	Sulphite-reducing clostridia	number/20ml	≤1 (i)
5.	Colony counts	number5/1ml at 22°C or 37°C	No significant increase over that normally observed

Note: (i) Analysis by multiple tube method.

Table D (i)

1.	Conductivity	uS/cm	1500 at 20°C
2.	Chloride	mg Cl/1	400
3.	Calcium	mg Ca/1	250
4.	Substances extractable in	mg/1 dry residue	1
5.	Boron	µg B/1	2000
6.	Barium	µg Ba/1	1000
7.	Benzo 3,4 pyrene	µg/1	10
8.	Tetrachloromethane	µg/1	3
9.	Trichloroethene	µg/1	30
10.	Tetrachlorothene	µg/1	10

Note: (i) See regulation 3(3)(d).

Table E

Item	Parameters	Units of Measurement	Maximum Concentration (i)
1.	Total hardness	mg Ca/1	60
2.	Alkalinity	mg HCO_3/1	30

Note: (i) See regulation 3(4).

The tables are specific and self-explanatory. It will be seen that Table A deals with physical characteristics and dissolved chemicals generally, and in addition Table E is concerned with two major physical properties that will be of most concern in general use. Table B establishes limits for a range of potentially harmful chemicals and chemical compounds likely to be found in waters, and Table C deals with indicators of sewage or other faecal contamination.

Part IV of the Regulations, supplemented by Schedule 3 which tabulates frequency of sampling at different locations having regard to the parameter to be tested for and the size of the population supplied, contains detailed provisions governing the sampling of water in each water supply zone. In particular, regulation 21(2) specifies the 'appropriate requirements' to be borne in mind when taking, handling, transporting, storing and analysing samples; essentially that the sample is:

(a) representative;
(b) not contaminated during sampling;
(c) subsequently handled and stored to avoid material alteration.

For the purposes of these Regulations, and by regulation 2, a water supply zone is an area designated by the water undertaker in which not more than 50,000 people reside.

30 S.I. 1991 No. 2790.

Similar provisions having the same purposes in relation to the quality of water from private supplies for drinking, washing, cooking or for food production are contained in the Private Water Supplies Regulations 1991.[30] They were made under the same statutory provision as those just considered in relation to public supplies and give effect to the same Council Directive. Private supplies are those not provided by a water undertaker, i.e. not connected to a mains supply. Responsibility for maintaining à register of such supplies and monitoring their quality belongs to the local authority. For this purpose private supplies are divided into two categories: Category I is water supplied for domestic purposes and not within Category II; Category II is water supplied for food and drink businesses for consumption on the premises, to staff canteens, hospitals and nursing homes etc., hostels, boarding schools, camp and caravan sites providing holiday and short-term accommodation. These categories are subdivided into classes for monitoring purposes relating to the volume used or the estimated number of persons served daily.

The parameters and standards applicable to private supplies are the same as those for public; see Tables A–E above. In any particular case the frequency of sampling and the parameters to be tested for vary according to the category and class of supply as indicated below. Schedule 5 provides a scale of charges for sampling.

	Class	No. of persons	Daily cubic metres
Category 1 classes	A	>5000	>1000
	B	501–5000	101–1000
	C	101–500	21–100
	D	25–100	5–20
	E	<25	<5
Category II classes	1		>1000
	2		101–1000
	3		21–100
	4		2–20
	5		<2

It will be noted, therefore, that in reading the Regulations, classes denoted by letters apply to Category I waters, while classes identified by numerals apply to Category II waters. There is no need to reproduce the table of sampling frequencies in Schedule 3 to the Regulations applying to all the parameters. The annual sampling requirement for classes A and B and 1 and 2 ranges from none in the case of some parameters to a highest incidence of 24 for faecal bacteria, physical characteristics and some metals. Guidance on water sampling programmes, techniques and the handling of samples is to be found in BS 6068.[31] Where a sample does not meet the specified criteria the local authority must ensure that appropriate remedial action is taken.

A consideration of domestic water quality must necessarily include reference to the power of a water undertaker to add fluoride to such supplies; now found in sections 87–90 of the Water Industry Act 1991. The addition of fluoride, or its cessation, for any specified area of supply must be preceded by an application from the District Health Authority. Before making either application that Authority must advertise its proposals in the local press on two occasions at least three months before the application, and notify and consult with the local authority for the areas concerned,[32] proceeding with the application only after considering the results of that exercise. The wording of section 87 suggests that following an application based on or reflecting such widely canvassed opinion the undertaker has the final discretion in meeting that demand; a discretion based on other, possibly operating criteria. That cost may be a factor here is indicated by the power in section 90 for the Secretary of State, with Treasury approval, to indemnify a water undertaker for the costs of fluoridation.

Where fluoridation is undertaken the District Health Authority has the further duty to ensure, with the undertaker, that the concentration of fluoride is maintained so far as is practicable at 1 milligram per litre.[33] By section 87(4) the permitted fluoridation agents for this purpose are hexafluorosilicic acid (H_2SiF_6) and disodium hexafluorosilicate (Na_2SiF_6), although the Secretary of State may vary these by order.[34] Where a water undertaker supplies fluoridated water to an area it may supply it to consumers in any other area if it considers it necessary for the purpose of dealing with any serious deficiency in supply, or in connection with the carrying out of any works; that is, in exceptional emergency situations.

31 Section 6.5 (1991).

32 Section 89. Local authorities for this purpose includes county councils; community health councils are added by virtue of the Community Health Council Regulations 1985 (S.I. 1985 No. 304).

33 Section 87(5).

34 Section 88.

7

Pollution prevention and control

MEANING OF 'POLLUTION'

Before considering the law applicable to water pollution, some consideration of the meaning of the term may be useful. A particular problem in attempting to assess or identify pollution in naturally occurring waters is that, as Lord Upjohn emphasised in the *Lower Hutt City Corporation* case,[1] in its natural state water is never pure. It will, for example, contain in solution or suspension the various chemical constituents of the rock formations through which it has passed and the fine particulate organic matter entrained in its flow. One has only to note the turbidity of a stream in spate, or see the confluence of two rivers from different catchment areas to be aware of the burden of entrained material that may be present in natural waters.

1 See Chapter 6, note 26 above.

In this context the identification and assessment of pollution presents obvious difficulties. Accepting that as well as contamination from a variety of sources, both natural and man-made, natural waters have a range of self-cleansing and regenerative processes, the two essential features of pollution in the environmental context would seem to be that it is of human origin and excessive in quantity having regard to the toxicity of its contents and those naturally occurring powers of regeneration. Against this background the following definitions or descriptions of pollution may be noted:

> 'Pollution of the environment' means pollution of the environment due to the release (into any environmental medium) from any process of substances which are capable of causing harm to man or any other living organisms supported by the environment.(Environmental Protection Act 1990, section 1(3))

> [Water] pollution means the discharge by man, directly or indirectly, of substances or energy into the aquatic environment, the results of which are such as to cause hazards to human health, harm to living resources and to aquatic ecosystems, damage to amenities or interference with other legitimate uses of water. (Dangerous Substances Directive, 76/464/EEC, Article 1(2)(c))

> The pollution of water is characterised as the human modification of water which renders it less suitable for a particular use than that water would be in its original state. (Professor W. Howarth, *Water Pollution Law*)[2]

2 (Dartford: Shaw and Sons,1988), at p.33.

These definitions, coming after a century or more of experience with pollution, are wide-ranging and extend beyond the demands of people either individually or collectively.

The common law view of water pollution has developed from the nineteenth-century cases dealing with the consequences of industrialisation and urbanisation, and in the context of the legal consequences of characterising a given emission as pollution. It is also founded on the legal rights of riparian owners to that water.

These features are evident in the following extract from the judgement of Lord McNaghten in *John Young & Co.* v *Bankier Distillery Co.* (1893)[3]:

> Every riparian owner is thus entitled to the water of his stream in its natural flow, without sensible diminution or increase and without sensible alteration in its character or quantity. Any invasion of this right causing actual damage, or calculated to found a claim which may ripen into an adverse right, entitles the party injured to the intervention of the court.

On this basis the limit of what is a tolerable interference with the quality or quantity of the contents of a stream is determined by reference to the rights of the riparian owners further down the watercourse. A further noteworthy matter is Lord McNaghten's association of quantity of flow with quality. Apart from the legitimate expectation that a river will contain water, and that in its accustomed quantity, a significant reduction in volume will reduce the ability of the stream to take and neutralise potentially polluting discharges.

The passage, betraying its civil law origins, also indicates that at that time pollution *per se* was not actionable, but only if it resulted in quantifiable damage to an interest of the plaintiff. On that basis pollution is not a matter of objective assessment but is to be determined in relation to the particular rights alleged to be infringed; as is illustrated by the facts of that case. The respondent distillers used water from the stream in question for their business. The appellant mine owners pumped large quantities of water from underground sources into the river upstream of the distillery. While the water was pure and fit for most purposes it was hard and altered the quality of the water in the river, making it unsuitable for distilling. The House of Lords considered that the distillers were entitled to receive the river water without alteration of its natural character and were not required to receive the additional water from the underground source that would never naturally have reached their land.

The particular needs and expectations of the plaintiff were also influential in *Dell* v *Chesham UDC* (1921).[4] To allay dust nuisance the local authority sprayed tar onto its roads. Later frost broke up the tar and road water containing tar acid drained into the plaintiff's watercress beds, destroying them. Although the local authority's action was then the only effective process for that purpose, and although the run-off was essentially surface water, it was held to be 'noxious' for the purposes of section 17 of the Public Health Act 1875, and the local authority was consequently liable. Conversely, in *Durrant* v *Branksome UDC* (1897)[5] surface water drainage from roads discharged large quantities of sand and silt into a stream 'The Bourne' requiring increased cleansing of the stream bed. The Court of Appeal decided that the water and sediment was not 'foul' or noxious matter such as would affect or deteriorate the purity and quality of the water in such stream or watercourse within the same section 17; as Lopes LJ said,[6] 'All that is carried according to the evidence is sand and silt, the natural belongings, as it were, to water in a soil like this'. The significance of this view lies in its seeming acceptance that mere quantity cannot constitute pollution if the material is naturally occurring.

The issue in *Attorney-General* v *Birmingham etc. District Drainage Board* (1908)[7] concerned the discharges from the defendant's sewage treatment works into the River Tame. An overflow from the settlement tanks emitted grossly contaminated and polluting effluent while the far larger quantity, after treatment in the bacteria beds, was comparatively innocuous. In its defence the Board argued

3 [1891–94] All Eng Reps 439 at p.441.

4 [1921] 3 KB 427.

5 [1897] 2 Ch D 291, CA.

6 At p.303.

7 [1908] 2 Ch 551.

that the river was already greatly polluted and that the overall effect of its discharges was to improve its quality. The Court refused to accept this trade off, holding that the legislation prohibited the discharge at any one point of polluting material,[8] Kekewich J declaring that,[9] 'the standard of quality is the standard of the stream at that point, not some arbitrary standard nor an overall general standard for the stream as a whole'.

A similar approach was used to respond to the defence of a number of polluters of the Derwent, that as each was only one among several contributors they could not individually be held liable. In this case, *Pride of Derby Angling Association Ltd v British Celanese Ltd* (1953),[10] the pollution included insufficiently treated effluent from the local authority sewage works, heated effluent with suspended matter discharged by the first defendants and heated water from the electricity authority generating station. In his judgement Sir Raymond Evershed MR said[11]:

> He [*the trial judge*] rejected the proposition that, since all defendants were individually polluting, none could be made liable, a proposition that seems to bear some analogy to the principle that a man armed with several umbrellas must be taken to have no umbrella at all.

Heated water was accepted in the Pride of Derby case as one among several pollutants. This follows from *Tipping v Eckersley* (1855),[12] where an injunction was granted to prevent the discharge of water from a steam-engine causing a rise in the temperature of the receiving river water to the prejudice of the plaintiff's use of it as condensing water.

The natural rights of use and quality expectations in respect of surface water sources were considered to have been applied to groundwater in *Ballard v Tomlinson* (1885).[13] In that case rubbish deposited in a well had caused contamination of groundwater and consequent damage to an adjacent landowner's rights of abstraction. Brett M.R. stated that

> although nobody has any property in the common source, yet everybody has the right to appropriate it … in its natural state.

A principle amplified by Lindley LJ. to the effect that

> 'the right of a man to get water from his well is to get the water as nature supplies it, and if anyone contends that he has a right to pollute the natural supply he must establish such a right.'

In the application of this principle distance or relative location, subject to the evidential question, is immaterial, Brett M.R. saying

> Neither does it matter that the parties are not contiguous neighbours. If it can be shewn in fact that the Defendants have adulterated or fouled the common source it signifies not how far the Plaintiff's land is from their land.

This view of the law was approved and applied by the Court of Appeal in *Cambridge Water Co v Eastern Counties Leather plc* (1994).[14] Perhaps because of the consequences of attaching such strict liability in a time of increasingly rigorous media quality standards the House of Lords, in the speech of Lord Goff with whom the other law lords agreed, has however imposed a foreseeability requirement as a prerequisite to liability.

The facts were that Eastern Counties Leather plc (E.C.L.) had been manufacturing leather at their Sawston works since 1879. The de-greasing of pelts involved

8 See to the same effect *Attorney-General v Cockermouth Local Board* (1874) LR 18 Eq 172.

9 At p.557.

10 [1953] 1 All ER 179 CA; see to same effect *Blair and Sumner v Deakin* (1887) 52 JP 327.

11 At p.148e.

12 (1855) 69 ER 779; see also *Mason v Hill* (1833) 110 ER 692; *Wood v Waud* (1849) 154 ER 1047.

13 29 Ch. D115.

14 2 WLR 53; 1 All ER 53; and see *Cambridge Water Co. v Eastern Counties Leather plc*: diluting liability for continuing escapes. David Wilkinson (1994) 57 MLR 799

the use of organochlorines, at least since the early 1950s. Two such materials had been used, trichloroethene (T.C.E.) up to the 1960s and then perchloroethene (P.C.E) until 1991. The amount used per year varied between 50,000 and 100,000 litres; approximately 25,000 litres being stored on the premises at any one time. Until about 1976 the material was delivered to the site and handled there in 40 gallon drums but thereafter was delivered in bulk and stored in a tank from which it was piped to the de-greasing machines. During the earlier period the drums were moved by fork-lift truck, tilted and their contents poured into a reservoir serving the machines. The first instance judge said

> It is difficult to believe that drum after drum could be emptied in that way without acci-
> dents and regular spillages. Because P.C.E. is less viscous than water it could escape
> through the finest fissure in the concrete: equally a small amount could escape at the point
> of storage from supposedly empty drums.

Such spillages must have occurred before 1976. Being a volatile liquid the assump-
tion would have been, if thought about at all, that it would evaporate into the air. It was not to be expected that it would or could soak into the ground and thence gain access to groundwater.

The Cambridge Water Co (C.W.C.) was created by statute in 1853 and, fol-
lowing the Water Act 1989, is a licensed supplier of water to some 275,000 people in the Cambridge area. To meet increasing demand, in September 1976 the company purchased a borehole at Sawston Mill, about 1.3 miles downstream from E.C.L.'s premises. Both before and after purchase, until 1983, regular sampling and chemical analysis showed that the water was wholesome and fit for public supply purposes. In August 1982 in response to an EEC Directive,[15] Department of the Environment Circular 20/82 required that as from 18 July 1985 drinking water containing more than 1 µg/1 of T.C.E. or P.C.E. would not be regarded as wholesome for public supply purposes. Subsequent regulations[16] have increased the maximum concentration values to 30 µg/1 and 10 µg/1 respectively to harmonise with the W.H.O. Tentative Guideline Values.

Samples of water from the area taken in August 1983 showed average P.C.E. concentrations of 38.5 µg/1. As the result of investigations the Sawston Mill bore-
hole was taken out of commission and the source of contamination traced to E.C.L.'s works. A replacement borehole at Hinxton Garage upstream from E.C.L.'s works was developed at a cost of £956,937; which sum, less the residual value of Sawston Mill of £60,000, was claimed as damages by C.W.C.

Having abandoned their original claims in negligence and nuisance the plain-
tiff's appeal to the House of Lords was on the basis of the rule in *Rylands* v *Fletcher*. In a preliminary consideration of *Ballard* v *Tomlinson* (1885) Lord Goff noted that if there is a natural right to surface water running in a defined channel, there is no similar right to percolating ground water. The judgements in that case, he said,[17] indicate that the defendant's liability for the contamination of the source of water supplying the plaintiff's well is determined by the law of tort, i.e., by the principle's of nuisance or of the rule in *Rylands* v *Fletcher*; necessitating a consideration of both.

Following a review of the development of the law of nuisance and omitting those cases concerned with actions for injunctions and nuisances arising from natural causes or due to the actions of trespassers, Lord Goff adopted the reasoning and statement of principle of Lord Reid in The Wagonmound[18] that

15 80/778/EC relating to the quality of water intended for human consumption.

16 Water Supply (Water Quality) Regulations 1989 No 1147.

17 At p.72c.

18 *Overseas Tombship (UK) Ltd* v *Miller Steamship Co. Pty* (The Wagonmound (No. 2)) [1967] 1 AC 617, at p.64.

> It is not sufficient that the injury suffered by the respondents' vessels was the direct result of the nuisance if that injury was in the relevant sense unforeseeable

adding that

> foreseeability of harm is indeed a prerequisite of the recovery of damages in private nuisance, as in the case of public nuisance.

Turning to *Rylands* v *Fletcher*, there is the apparent difficulty of relating foreseeability to the strict liability nature of the tort. The classic statement of the principle by Blackburn J., it is to be noted, makes many references to the state of mind, knowledge or expectations of the tortfeasor. Lord Goff therefore continues,[19]

19 At p.776.

> The general tenor of his statement of principle is therefore that knowledge, or at least foreseeability of the risk, is a prerequisite of the recovery of damages under the principle; but that the principle is one of strict liability in the sense that the defendant may be held liable notwithstanding that he has exercised all due care to prevent the escape from occurring.

20 At p.796.

He therefore concludes,[20]

> Accordingly since, following the observations of Lord Reid when delivering the judgement of the Privy Council in The Wagonmound (No 2) [1967] I A.C. 617, 640, the recovery of damages in private nuisance depends on foreseeability by the defendant of the relevant type of damage, it would appear logical to extend the same requirement to liability under the rule in Rylands v Fletcher.

Two further matters of note appear from the judgement of Lord Goff in this case. It being accepted that the pools of neat P.C.E. are still in existence at the base of the chalk aquifer under E.C.L.'s premises and that dissolved P.C.E. will continue to escape into the groundwater in the future, i.e., after the damage has become foreseeable by E.C.L., should they not be held liable for the future damage caused by the continuing escape on the principles now established? Lord Goff rejected this argument firstly on the ground that when E.C.L. created the conditions that led to this situation they could not then have foreseen that damage of the type complained of could have resulted and secondly because the P.C.E. was now irretrievably beyond their control.

Lord Goff also emphasised that this case concerned historic pollution in the sense that it had occurred before the relevant legislation had come into force and that the current philosophy was that statutory liability should not be imposed in such circumstances.[21] That being the case it would be improper for liability for such pollution to be imposed under a common law principle. In a similar context he noted the increasing general concern with environmental pollution given expression to in well-informed and carefully structured legislation to promote the protection of the environment and make the polluter pay for the damage for which he is responsible. Consequently it is probably unnecessary and undesirable for the courts to develop common law principles for the same purpose.

21 See, e.g., the Council of Europe's Draft Convention on Civil Liability for Damage Resulting from Activities Dangerous to the Environment (Strasbourg 26 January 1993) Art. 5.1.

The common law, then, by way of summary, considers that the right of a user to the water in a stream is a right to the water in its natural state substantially unchanged in quality or quantity. That state will necessarily include the natural constituents and contents of the water but not the unnatural. It may be that, as with the distillery, the particular characteristics of the original water initially determined the location of that business or process. Further, the pollutant is to be judged on its effect on the receiving water at the point of entry, irrespective of what is happening elsewhere, either by improvement or through the discharge of other pollutants.

INLAND WATERS

The legislative controls on pollution, now to be considered, are largely found in Chapter II of Part III of the Water Resources Act 1991. Section 85[22] specifies the major pollution offences together with remedies for contravention. Section 86 provides for the addition to that statutory list of discharges prohibited by notice by the NRA or by regulations. Section 87[23] deals with discharges of sewage effluent from public sewers or sewage disposal works. The control of groundwater pollution from landfill sites under regulation 15 of the Waste Management Licensing Regulations 1994 is dealt with in Chapter 14 in the context of waste management licences.[24]

Water pollution offences

Section 85 of the 1991 Act, in its first five subsections, specifies a number of pollution offences constituting contravention of the section. By section 85(6), such contravention may lead to either summary proceedings with sentencing maxima of three months' imprisonment ,or a fine of £20,000 or both, or to trial on indictment and imprisonment for up to two years, or a fine or both. The earlier subsections provide that a person contravenes the section if he causes or knowingly permits:

(a) any poisonous, noxious or polluting matter or any solid waste matter to enter any controlled water;

(b) any matter, other than trade or sewage effluent, to be discharged into controlled water from a drain or sewer in contravention of a section 86 prohibition;

(c) any trade or sewage effluent to be discharged into any controlled waters or, through a pipe into the sea outside the seaward limits of controlled waters;

(d) any trade or sewage effluent to be discharged in contravention of any section 86 prohibition from any building or fixed plant –
  (i) on or into any land, or
  (ii) into any waters of a lake or pond which are not inland fresh waters;

(e) any matter to enter any inland fresh waters so as to tend to impede the proper flow of the waters leading to, or likely to lead to, substantial aggravation of –
  (i) pollution due to other causes, or
  (ii) the consequences of such pollution.

There is here a comprehensive code of pollution offences. The first three provisions deal with discharges into controlled waters, in which the prohibition is total. In contrast, section 85(5) ((e) above) only prohibits the discharge or placing into inland fresh waters of matter where it will or may aggravate other pollution. As most inland fresh waters are also controlled waters it would seem that the total prohibition in section 85(1) will generally apply and be easier to enforce. The section 85(5) offence, with its heavier level of proof, will apply of necessity to those inland fresh waters that are not controlled waters. All these offences require that the person charged 'causes or knowingly permits' their occurrence, a phrase the meaning of which is considered in Chapter 1 above.[25]

22 Substantially re-enacts section 31 of the Control of Pollution Act 1974 which, in turn re-enacted section 2 of the Rivers (Prevention of Pollution) Act 1951.

23 Re-enacting section 32 of the Control of Pollution Act 1974.

24 See at p.389.

25 See at p.30.

The concept of controlled waters applies to most of the pollution control measures in this Part of the Act. Its meaning appears in section 104(1), which provides:

> (1) References in this Part to controlled waters are references to waters of any of the following classes –
>> (a) relevant territorial waters, that is to say, subject to subsection (4) below, the waters which extend seaward for three miles from the baselines from which the breadth of the territorial sea adjacent to England and Wales is measured;
>> (b) coastal waters, that is to say, any waters which are within the area which extends landward from those baselines as far as –
>>> (a) the limit of the highest tide; or
>>> (b) in the case of the waters of any relevant river or watercourse, the freshwater limit of the river or watercourse together with the waters or any enclosed dock which adjoins waters within that area;
>> (c) inland fresh waters, that is to say, the waters of any relevant lake or pond or of so much of any relevant river or watercourse as is above the fresh water limit;
>> (d) ground waters, that is to say, any waters contained in underground strata; and accordingly, in this Part 'coastal waters', 'controlled waters', 'ground waters', 'inland fresh waters' and 'relevant territorial waters' have the meanings given by this subsection.

Although United Kingdom territorial waters were extended to 12 miles by section 1(1) of the Territorial Sea Act 1987,[26] the three-mile limit under the Control of Pollution Act 1974 has been retained here, but the Secretary of State may, by order under section 104(4), extend jurisdiction to other areas of territorial waters. Section 85(3)(b) also extends the jurisdiction of the NRA in the case of pipes discharging effluent beyond the three-mile limit. Coastal waters include estuarine waters up to the fresh water limits of rivers and watercourses. For the purposes of these provisions, therefore, there is little distinction between coastal and inland waters, although the section 90 offence relating to deposits and vegetation applies only to inland waters. Section 104(1)(c) refers to inland fresh waters, the distinction being made with inland waters applicable to other Parts of the Act and, being derived from section 135 of the Water Resources Act 1963 (as amended), includes tidal rivers, estuaries and arms of the sea.

Inland fresh waters, by section 104(3), excludes lakes or ponds that do not discharge into other relevant waters. The Secretary of State has, however, under section 104(4)(b), the power by order to bring any specified lake or pond within the scope of the definition and, by the Controlled Waters (Lakes and Ponds) Order 1989,[27] has brought reservoirs not communicating with relevant waters within the definition. Such lakes and ponds are also within the scope of section 87 prohibiting the discharge of trade or sewage effluent and, where appropriate, will be within the statutory nuisance provisions of Part III of the Environmental Protection Act 1990 by virtue of section 259(1) of the Public Health Act 1936. Relevant river or watercourse extends to underground or artificial forms but excludes sewers and drains. This distinction between watercourse and sewer is not always as clear as it might at first seem.[28] The inclusion of groundwater emphasises the increased recognition of the effects of pollution on such water sources. The Control of Pollution Act 1974 required such waters to be specified by the water authority if they were to be subject to control. Following the implementation of EC Directives such limitations no longer apply, groundwater being there defined as 'all water

26 The baselines from which the territorial waters are measured are established by the Territorial Waters Order in Council 1964 (dated 25 September 1964) as amended by the Territorial Waters (Amendment) Order in Council 1979 (dated 23 May 1979).

27 S.I. 1989 No. 1149.

28 See, e.g., *BRB v Tonbridge & Malling DC* (1981) 69 LGR 565; *Hutton v Esher UDC* [1973] 2 All ER 1123, 2 WLR 917, and below at p.194.

which is below the surface of the ground in the saturation zone and in direct contact with the ground or subsoil'.[29] All groundwater is now therefore controlled.

The primary prohibition in section 85(1) refers to 'poisonous, noxious or polluting' matter,[30] terms that have never been statutorily defined; an omission perhaps attributable to the recognition that the precise consequences of many discharges are more appropriately left to the judgement of the court. The consequent lack of certainty, however, creates obvious problems for a prospective discharger of effluent. This uncertainty and its basis appears clearly in the following passage from Newsom and Sherratt[31]:

> But the poisonous character of an effluent must be affected by the amount of the poison and the volume of the dilutant. 'Polluting' presumably means that which pollutes or is capable of polluting and again must be interpreted in the context. A discharge of a very good effluent may well be incapable of polluting a large clean river, while the discharge of an effluent of the same size and quality into a brook near the top of a watershed may be capable of polluting, and may in fact pollute, the brook into which it is discharged to the extent of creating even a public nuisance. 'Noxious' in its dictionary meaning means no more than 'hurtful' or 'injurious' and appears to add nothing to the other adjectives. Thus there seems to be a good deal of scope for argument whether a given discharge taken by itself, is within the words of this part of the subsection.

This passage considers each term individually, a generally accepted view based on the conclusion that their separate inclusion in the statute so requires. It also appears that, at least in the environmental context, the terms appear in a declining order of harm, Lumley's *Public Health Law*, for example, saying that[32]:

> 'poisonous' implies destruction of life, human or animal; 'noxious' is lower in degree and signifies some injury; 'polluting' will include both the other qualities and also what is foul and offensive to the senses.

Professor J.F. Garner considers that the phrase is wide enough to include matter that is harmful to fauna, or possibly flora, even though harmless to man.[33] This view has been adopted by the courts in finding that discharges of substances innocuous to human beings have had such a damaging effect upon the receiving aquatic environment that they have come within the meaning of the phrase. In *Severn Trent River Authority* v *Express Foods Group Ltd* (1989),[34] for example, the Divisional Court upheld the magistrate's decision that the discharge of milk processing waste into rivers constituted a breach of consent conditions under section 34 of the Control of Pollution Act 1974. Similarly, in *NRA* v *Appletise Bottling Co. Ltd* (1991),[35] the court took the view that the discharge of concentrated apple juice came within the phrase.

A significant distinction between 'poisonous' and 'noxious' derives from the interpretation of those terms in the Offences Against the Person Act 1861. Section 58 of that Act makes it an offence to administer a poison or other noxious thing with intent to procure the miscarrige of any woman. Cases under the section, exemplified by *R* v *Cramp* (1880),[36] suggest that for the purposes of that offence 'poisonous' relates to the intrinsic nature of the substance while 'noxious' is to be determined by a consideration of the effect of the substance in the particular circumstances. A water pollution case adopting this view of 'poisonous' is *R* v *Justices of Antrim* (1906)[37] in which mill owners were prosecuted for having caused 'deleterious or poisonous' liquid to flow from their works. In his judgment Gibson J said[38] that the offence:

29 See Article 1(2)(a) of the EC Directive on The Protection of Groundwater Against Pollution Caused by Certain Dangerous Substances (80/68/EEC).

30 See Professor W. Howarth, 'Poisonous, Noxious or Polluting' (1993) 56 MLR 171.

31 *Water Pollution* (Manchester: John Sherratt & Son, 1972), p.30, n.2 on the preceding section 11(3) of the Rivers (Prevention of Pollution) Act 1951.

32 12th edn (London: Butterworth, 1954),vol.V, p.5158, note e.

33 *Control of Pollution Act 1974* (London: Butterworth, 1975), p.17.

34 [1989] CLR 226.

35 (1991) 16 *Water Guardians*, April.

36 (1880) 5 QBD 307.

37 [1906] 2 IR 298.

38 At p.319.

forbids the doing of the specified act without reference to the intent of the offender, or the consequences of the act done. It applies to all rivers, large and small, irrespective of the volume of water they discharge. The object was no doubt to protect fish and river animals, but the section excludes from the Magistrate's consideration any question of the results of the prohibited act, which in the case of several contributory riparian wrong-doers might involve a perplexing and uncertain enquiry. If the act would be criminal in fair weather when a river was low, it does not become innocent because rainfall causes a flood.

It is evidently the inherent nature of the discharge rather than its effect on the receiving medium that is the determining factor.

Conversely, illustrating the primacy of the effect in relation to 'noxious' is *Attorney-General* v *Birmingham etc District Drainage Board* (1908),[39] where the Board was charged with discharging into a stream water 'not freed from ... noxious matter'. Kekewich J said that[40]

> it is impossible to conclude that there has been an offence against the prohibition unless that special purity and quality (of the watercourse) have been shown to be deteriorated [and] in judging the effect of their operations one must regard this stream as a whole, and that if, regarded as a whole, the water in the stream or watercourse has not been deteriorated, no offence has been or can be established.

In his discussion of these terms and their relationship, Professor W. Howarth concludes[41]:

> it may be suggested that, within the formulation of the criminal offence, 'poisonous' serves as an emission standard whilst the term 'noxious' serves as an ambient standard, and an excess on either count is an element in the offence of water pollution.

The concluding question is, and having regard to the respective spheres of the first two terms, what is the scope and therefore the contribution of 'polluting'? An answer from the Crown Court in *NRA* v *Egger (UK) Ltd* (1992),[42] is that, like 'poisonous', it is a characteristic of the discharge or emission itself. Effluent discharged from the defendant's premises produced a turbid plume in the River Tyne of 5 metres width and 100 metres length. The effluent was contaminated surface water from their formaldehyde resin plant having an excessive concentration of suspended solids and a high biochemical oxygen demand. The company was found guilty of an offence under what is now section 85(1)(a), Bryant J saying on the question of 'polluting':

> One looks at the nature of the discharge and one says, 'is that discharge capable of causing harm to the river, in the sense of causing damage to uses to which a river might be put', ... One looks at that test in relation, it seems to me, to a natural, unpolluted river, and if the discharge is capable of causing such harm then the offence is made out; the material amounts to polluting matter. It is, in my view, wholly unnecessary to prove that damage was, in fact, caused.

'Polluting' therefore is to be determined, at least in part, on the same criteria as 'poisonous'; that is on its inherent qualities rather than its effects. This seems to bring the two terms confusingly close together. However, the assimilation is, it is submitted, more apparent than real, their essential characteristics providing sufficient distinction. A poisonous substance is intrinsically harmful in the toxic or debilitating sense. The harm from a polluting material lies in its capacity to reduce or destroy the natural quality or characteristics of the recipient water. If this view

39 [1908] 2 Ch 551.

40 At p.556.

41 (1993) 56 MLR 171 at p.184.

42 Unreported, Newcastle-upon-Tyne Crown Court, 15-7 June 1992.

is right one may identify pollutants that are not poisonous – heated cooling water from a power station, for example. In short, while a poisonous substance will necessarily be a pollutant, the converse may not be true.

Returning to section 85, subsection (1) also prohibits any solid waste matter from entering controlled waters, whether it is poisonous, noxious or polluting, or merely inert. Concern here is with its physical obstruction of the flow, either alone or as a focus of accumulation of other matter. The emissions covered by section 85(2) and likely to be discharged from a sewer or drain that are not trade or sewage effluent, are surface or groundwater. Such discharge is not in itself an offence but will be when in breach of a section 86 prohibition. Section 85(3) places a total prohibition on the discharge of trade or sewage effluent into controlled waters. Effluent is very widely defined, section 219(1) providing that it 'means any liquid, including particles of matter and other substances in suspension in the liquid'. Characteristics, nature or source are irrelevant in this determination. Consequently the treated effluent from sewage treatment works discharged, as it usually will be, to controlled water will potentially constitute a breach of section 85 and will therefore require a validating discharge consent under section 88(1)(a) with appropriate conditions.

Section 85(3) also extends to piped outfalls of effluent discharging to the sea. Effluent dumped at sea is dealt with by licensing provisions in Part II of the Food and Environment Protection Act 1985, as amended.[43] Section 85(4) is limited to trade and sewage effluent which may indirectly contaminate water supplies through discharge onto land in contravention of a section 86 prohibition. Treatment of agricultural land with sewage effluent is of course not uncommon but is not discharged from a building or fixed plant. It is therefore likely to be of a spasmodic nature rather than giving rise to persistent, chronic pollution of the soil and subsoil water. This offence would, however, include, for example, discharges from septic tanks, being fixed plant, through land drains. As to the scope of the word 'discharge' itself, in *Smeaton* v *Ilford Corporation* (1954)[44] Upjohn J said that 'discharge' is caused or permitted while 'escape' is involuntary.

Subordinate to the general range of offences in section 85 and considered above, section 86 gives the NRA power to prohibit specific discharges, a contravention of the prohibition then being an offence within section 85(2). Under section 86(1) the offence is a contravention by the person notified, of the terms of a notice either prohibiting a discharge or permitting it subject to conditions. The subsection (2) offence is the discharge of effluent containing either a prescribed substance, or a prescribed concentration of a substance or a derivative of such a substance, and in this case a notice is not necessary. In effect, therefore, the purpose of this section is to extend the range of the section 85 pollution offences in two areas; first to the discharge of such substances or strengths as may be prescribed by regulation and, secondly, in any specific case, to a prohibition notified by the NRA. In this latter case it is to be noted that the question of overt standards or reference to codes of acknowledged harmful substances does not apply.[45] The Authority appears to have unrestricted discretion, without any right of appeal, to apply the penalty provisions of section 85 to any discharge it chooses.

A consideration of section 86 requires reference to the confusion that exists in subsections (4) to (6) relating to the notice. These provisions appear to expect that, except in the case of an emergency, the recipient shall be given a minimum of three months' warning before the terms of the notice take effect; time within

43 See p.182 below.

44 [1954] 1 All ER 923 at p.927.

45 But see 'Inputs of Dangerous Substances to Water: Proposals for a Unified System of Control' (DoE/Welsh Office, July 1988).

which to take the necessary action to secure compliance. Similarly, if during the three months, he applies for a consent for the discharge, the notice will not take effect until and subject to the result of the application. That appears to be the logical intention, apart that is from the use of the word 'expire' in those subsections, which has the effect of applying their terms to the termination of the notice rather than to its commencement. The consequence is not only to produce confusion but also to ensure that the notice has a minimum duration of three months. The purpose of such a stipulation is hard to see, and it is therefore suggested that for these reasons the word 'expire' in subsections (4) and (6) should be read as 'come into operation'.

Section 87 of the 1991 Act extends the liability of sewerage undertakers under section 85(3) and (4) to discharges of sewage effluent where they did not cause or knowingly permit the discharge but were bound to receive the matter included in the discharge either unconditionally or subject to conditions that were observed. Discharges into natural waters of untreated or inadequately treated domestic sewage have been a major contributory factor in the general deterioration in water quality. Sewerage undertakers, having a statutory duty to receive such effluent and having control of the plant for its treatment and disposal, are liable for any discharge, whether having actual knowledge or responsibility or not. In this instance, therefore, not only is the performance of a statutory duty no defence, the responsibilities consequent on the performance of that duty impose a stricter degree of liability. The defences open to an undertaker where such a discharge is in breach of any consent conditions are that, in section 87(2):

(a) the contravention is attributable to a discharge into the sewer or works which another person caused or permitted;
(b) the undertaker was not bound to receive the discharge or was bound to receive it subject to conditions which were not observed; and
(c) the undertaker could not reasonably have been expected to prevent the discharge into the sewer or works.

The undertaker is therefore exonerated where the actual fault lies with another. To emphasise this apportioning of responsibility section 87(3) provides that such a person will not be guilty of an offence where the discharge into the sewer was either one that the undertaker was bound to take or complied with any conditions. In short, if what goes into the sewer is unlawful or unauthorised the person responsible for discharging it will be liable. If, however, what goes in is proper and permissible, the undertaker will be responsible in law, by the combined effect of sections 85 and 87, for what comes out, whether responsible in fact or not.

This section 87(2) defence was relied on, unsuccessfully, in *National Rivers Authority* v *Yorkshire Water Services Ltd* (1994).[46] The summary conviction of the water company for discharging effluent containing iso-octonal from a sewage treatment works into the River Spen had been overturned by Wakefield Crown Court, against which decision the NRA now appealed to the Divisional Court. A standard condition in all consents granted by Yorkshire Water for the discharge of effluent into their system was the prohibition of the discharge of iso-octonal. On 13 May 1990, unknown persons made a single discharge of iso-octonal into the sewer, some of which passed through the treatment process and was present in the discharge into the river. On the principles discussed above the company was found to have 'caused' the pollution by allowing the chemical to pass through its system, even though it had been put into the sewer by a third party who could therefore also be said to have caused the pollution. In rejecting the section 87(2) defence the Court decided that as it applied on its terms to the contravention of consent conditions, the defence was applicable to a charge under section 86(1) of a breach of such a condition but not to one under section 85 of causing etc., any poisonous, noxious or polluting matter to enter any controlled water. Many, if not all, cases of discharge of toxic material in breach of a consent condition will come within the terms of section 85. This apparent invitation to prosecutors in such cases, by tactical selection of the offence to deprive the defence of the protection of section 87(2) has been resolved by the House of Lords in the same case.[47] Finding that all the elements of the defence were satisfied, they held it was applicable regardless of the precise choice of charge. While this is the logical inter-pretation and protects the undertaker who is doing all that he reasonably can it has the effect, as in the instant case, of leaving the environment exposed to pollution without a remedy. With the actual polluter being unidentifiable and the exoneration of the person who, albeit without fault, is identified as having caused the discharge there is in such cases a significant gap in the operation of these pollution prevention provisions.

Sampling

Before leaving consideration of these pollution offences, and in particular pro-cedural matters, some reference should be made to the associated sampling require-ments. Water samples, and the results of analysis, may form an important item of evidence in any later prosecution. It is therefore of the utmost importance that such samples are collected and subsequently dealt with in a proper manner; mean-ing essentially that the sample is and remains until analysis a fair and accurate representation of the water quality at the time it was taken and that the person responsible for the pollution is sufficiently informed not to be prejudiced in his eventual defence.

In this regard, section 209(1) of the Water Resources Act 1991[48] stipulates the necessary sampling procedure:

the result of the analysis of any sample taken on behalf of the Authority in exercise of any power conferred by this Act shall not be admissible in any legal proceedings in respect of any effluent passing from any land or vessel unless the person who took the sample –

(a) on taking the sample notified the occupier of the land or the owner or master of the vessel of his intention to have it analysed;
(b) there and then divided the sample into three parts and caused each part to be placed in a container which was sealed and marked; and
(c) delivered one part to the occupier of the land or the owner or master of the vessel and retained one part, apart from the one he submitted to be analysed, for future comparison.

The Court of Appeal has had an opportunity in *CPC (UK) v NRA (1994)*[49] to consider this procedure, emphasising as a general principle that the purpose of the provision is to protect both the defendant and the prosecuting authority against subsequent arguments concerning the sample's validity. The preliminary and self-evident principles that nevertheless deserve emphasis are, first that this is a manda-tory exclusionary rule. Failure to comply with this procedure will prohibit production of the sample in later legal proceedings. Secondly, these requirements

47 [1994] *The Times*, 21 November and see at Chap 1 111.

48 These provisions originally appeared in section 113(2) of the Water Resources Act 1963

49 (1994) Crim Div 15 July 1994; and see Attorney-General's Reference (No. 2 of 1994) Court of Appeal, 27 Jul 1994' *The Times*, 4 August. Though not relevant to this issue the facts of this case are to be found in Chapter 1 at p.32.

are confined to samples taken by the Authority. The products of routine sampling by the plant operator and the results would be admissible without satisfying these principles.

The section is concerned with the result of 'the analysis of any sample'. While the Act is silent on the interpretation of 'sample' the question arose in the CPC case over the admissibility of pH level readings derived from a static monitoring device, water being continuously diverted from the river. The Crown Court had taken the view that as no samples were taken, the section did not apply. In agreeing with this view the Court of Appeal, in the absence of any statutory guidance, noted that of the *Oxford English Dictionary* defined 'sample' as a small, separated part of something. In the Court's view, separation was essential:

> This implies that the part must be separated physically from the whole and in the case of water that the part which becomes a sample must be isolated in some form of container. We do not consider that a 'sample' of the water comes into existence unless and until this is done.

This procedure is only obligatory where evidence is based on analysis of a sample. If no analysis is involved section 209 will not apply. The leading case on the scope of analysis is *Trent River Board* v *Wardle* (1957),[49] where exposing fish to a sample of effluent was held not to amount to an analysis. Now, though, 'analyse' is defined in the Act[50] to include, in relation to any sample of land, water or effluent, 'subjecting the sample to a test of any description'. This is a very broad definition given the possible scope of 'test', including as it appears to, ad hoc visual or olfactory examination.

The other aspect of the statutory sampling procedure considered in the judgements was that of time. Section 209 stipulates that 'on taking the sample' the occupier is to be notified of the intention to have it analysed, and, when the sample has been taken it must 'there and then' be divided into three parts. The Court of Appeal adopted a more relaxed, or pragmatic, approach to this requirement than had the Crown Court. They considered that 'on taking the sample' should be interpreted to mean on the occasion of taking the sample, implying some degree of latitude, rather than at the precise time the sample was removed from its parent body of water. They found no necessary requirement of advance notification. The whole tenor of the procedure suggests that the occupier is likely to be present or represented at the time of sampling. That is usually the case, indicating prior notification in practice. However, the Court also noted that a general duty to give prior notification could frustrate the purpose of sampling, which was to detect possible pollution, since the occupier would then have an opportunity temporarily to stop the discharge.

Normal sampling procedure, according with statute, entails its division into three parts at the time it is taken. Again, though, the Court was prepared to interpret 'there and then' in a more relaxed way as implying that it should be done at or proximate to the site of the sample and 'on the occasion' of taking the sample. Conversely, removing the sample container to a laboratory for division there or at a later time, thus interrupting the continuity of the operation, would not be acceptable. In the instant case the NRA officer had taken the sample in a bucket to the boot of his car where, a few minutes after taking the sample, he had divided it. In their formal answers to the questions referred by the Attorney-General, the Court of Appeal decided that:

49 [1957] Crim LR 196.

50 Section 221(1).

(i) notification pursuant to the section did not necessarily have to precede the taking or division of the samples;

(ii) 'there and then' in the section ... meant at or proximate to the site where the subject was taken on the occasion of taking the sample.

Discharge consents

Where a person would have been liable to proceedings under section 85 for a discharge into any waters, such liability shall be excluded under section 88(1) where the emission is the subject of:

(a) a consent under this Chapter;

(b) a prescribed process authorisation under Part I, Environmental Protection Act 1990;

(c) a waste management or disposal licence;[52]

(d) a licence under Part II, Food and Environment Protection Act 1985;

(e) section 163 of this Act or section165 of the Water Industry Act 1991 (discharges for works purposes);

(f) any local statutory powers of discharge;

(g) any prescribed enactment.

It is therefore possible for a person to obtain in advance approval or authorisation for what would otherwise constitute a pollution offence while the Authority has knowledge of and, through consent conditions, control over these activities. Such 'discharge consents' are generally issued by the NRA and are, as defined in section 91(8), 'a consent for any discharge or description of discharges given for the purposes of section 88(1)(a) either on application or by virtue of Schedule 10, paragraph 5, without application'. The Authority therefore may issue a consent on its own initiative under this provision where it considers that a discharge would otherwise be a contravention of section 85(3) or a prohibition under section 86. The Secretary of State may give directions to the Authority for the granting or modifying of consents[53] and may call in any, or any class of, application for his decision with or without a public enquiry or private hearing.[54]

As exceptions to the general powers of the NRA above, there are two cases where consents are issued by the Secretary of State. First, the Control of Pollution (Consents for Discharges etc.) (Secretary of State Functions) Regulations 1989[55] enable an applicant to request, and specify the procedure for, the transfer of his application to the Secretary of State. Secondly, where the discharges are by the NRA itself, consents must be sought from the Secretary of State and Schedule 10 is modified accordingly.[56] By section 91, appeals also lie to the Secretary of State against refusal of a consent or against any conditions, revocation of a consent or modification of conditions. Section 131 gives the NRA power to make a charging scheme for applications for consents, such schemes requiring the approval of the Secretary of State.

Discharge of effluent not covered by a consent, or in breach of a consent condition, is not of course of itself an offence. Absence of such approval does, however, remove the protection of section 88(1)(a) and so render the person responsible liable to proceedings for a pollution offence under section 85. In addition to these statutory powers, it appears that private prosecutions for breach of consent conditions may also be possible. In *Wales v Thames Water Authority* (1987)[57] details

52 See section 5 of the Control of Pollution Act 1974 below.

53 Section 91(5).

54 Schedule 10, paragraph 4.

55 S.I. 1989 No. 1151.

56 Control of Pollution (Discharges by National Rivers Authority) Regulations 1989, S.I. 1989 No. 1157.

57 Unreported, Aylesbury Magistrates' Court; see [1987] *Environmental Law*, vol. 1, no. 3.

from the Authority's register showed a failure to comply with consent limits. On prosecution by the Anglers Co-operative Association and in spite of improvements to the sewage works to meet the increased demand and satisfy the consent limits, the Authority was fined £1,000 for each of six offences.

Being authority to do what would otherwise be unlawful, it appears that consents and their terms will be strictly construed. In *Yorkshire Dyeing and Proofing Co. Ltd* v *Middleton BC* (1953),[58] the appellants had a consent to discharge trade effluent from their dye works into the local authority's sewer. They then acquired the adjoining premises as a new dye house. The effluent from the new premises was drained into the existing premises and mixed with effluent produced there before discharge. It was accepted that the resulting discharge was not greater in quantity or rate of emission. The Court dismissed their appeal against conviction on the ground that 'the trade effluent being discharged was not being produced at the same premises ... since it was now the effluent of two premises and not one'. The Court also found that the discharge from the new premises was into the public sewer even though it was indirect.

8 [1953] 1 WLR 393, DC.

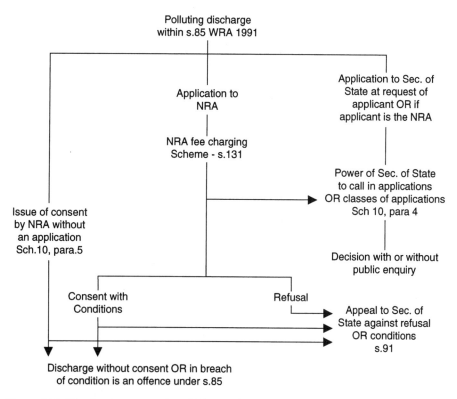

Figure 7.1 Discharge consents within section 88(1)(a)

Agricultural Sources of Pollution

Having created a range of statutory offences in Chapter II, the Water Resources Act 1991, in Chapter III of Part III, gives the Secretary of State additional powers and duties exercised through delegated legislation, relating to precautions against pollution. Section 92[59] gives the Secretary of State a regulation making-power:

9 Re-enacting section 31(4) of the Control of Pollution Act 74.

(a) prohibiting the custody or control of poisonous, noxious or polluting matter subject to specified works or precautions to prevent their entry into controlled waters;

(b) requiring a person having such control to undertake designated work or precautions for that purpose;

(c) empowering the NRA to enforce such regulations.

The scope and meaning of 'poisonous, noxious or polluting' have already been considered.[60] The precautionary measures aimed at are primarily concerned with preventing spillages entering water, and during the Committee Stage of the 1989 Act in the House of Lords, the Government indicated that the initial regulations would cover construction standards for silage and slurry stores and for oil facilities. To date, regulations under the section are the Control of Pollution (Silage, Slurry and Agricultural Oil Fuel) Regulations 1991.[61] In deciding whether to exercise its powers the NRA is required to take into account whether there is or is likely to be a Code of Good Agricultural Practice approved under section 97.[62]

As the title of the Regulations indicates, they deal respectively with the three named potential sources of water pollution from farms, referred to in the regulations as 'relevant substances', the material or liquid discharges produced from these activities being particularly concentrated and noxious.

The making of silage is governed by regulation 3 and Schedule 1, the former prohibiting the

custody or control of any crop which is being made into silage unless –

(a) it is kept in a silo in relation to which the requirements of Schedule 1 are satisfied or which is exempt; or

(b) it is compressed in the form of bales which are wrapped and sealed within impermeable membranes ..... and are stored at least 110 metres from any inland or coastal waters which effluent escaping from the bales could enter.

The unwrapping of silage bales is also restricted in a similar way to prevent pollutants entering water.

Schedule 1 requires that the design and construction of silos complies either with BS 5061: 1974 specifying the standard on cylindrical forage tower silos, or with the provisions of the Schedule. As would be imagined the purpose of those provisions is to ensure a liquid-proof structure, providing (in outline) that:

(a) the base of the silo shall extend beyond its walls;

(b) the base shall be provided with drainage channels discharging to an effluent tank;

(c) the capacity of the effluent tank shall be in stated proportion to the silo;

(d) the silo base, drainage channels and tank shall be impermeable and resistant to attack by silage effluent;

(e) the silo is to be sited at least 10 metres from any waters that the effluent could enter if it escaped;

(f) if possessing retaining walls, they are to satisfy minimum loading standards;

(g) the structure is to be capable of satisfying these requirements, to the extent that it is below ground without maintenance, for a period of at least 20 years.

Slurry storage is provided for in regulation 4 and Schedule 2, slurry meaning:[63]

(a) excreta produced by livestock whilst in a yard or building; or

60 See above at p.164.

61 S.I. 1991 No. 324.

62 See below at treatment of section 97.

63 Regulation 2.

(b) a mixture consisting wholly or mainly of such excreta, bedding, rainwater and washings from a building or yard used by livestock or any combination of these,

of a consistency that allows it to be pumped or discharged by gravity at any stage in the handling process.

Such slurry is to be stored in a storage system satisfying the requirements of Schedule 2, unless it is either exempt or is temporarily stored in a transporter with a capacity not exceeding 18,000 litres.

Being designed to achieve the same purposes as those considered above for silage, the Schedule 2 provisions governing the construction of slurry storage tanks have many features in common with them. They provide (in outline) that:

(a) the structure is to be impermeable and protected against corrosion in accordance with paragraph 7.2 of the code of practice for agricultural buildings in BS 5502: Part 50: 1989;
(b) the structure of the storage tank and reception pit shall be capable of withstanding the loadings in paragraph 5 of the code of practice, and be of adequate capacity having regard to the method of disposal;
(c) temporary storage facilities shall have a minimum two day storage capacity;
(d) no part of the system shall be within 10 metres of waters which slurry could enter if it were to escape;
(e) the system shall be so designed and constructed that, with proper maintenance they are likely to satisfy the construction requirements for a period of at least 20 years;
(f) discharge pipes from tanks shall be fitted with two valves in series, each capable of shutting off the flow and each being kept shut and locked when not in use.

Where fuel oil in excess of 1,500 litres is stored on a farm it is, by regulation 5, to be stored in one of the following ways:

(a) in a fuel storage tank complying with Schedule 3;
(b) in drums within such a storage area;
(c) temporarily in a tanker used for transporting fuel;
(d) in an exempt fuel storage tank;
(e) in an underground fuel storage tank.

The Schedule 3 requirements governing fuel oil storage areas on farms are inevitably comparable with those applicable to the storage of fuel oil in other circumstances, providing (in outline) that:

(a) the storage area is to be surrounded by a bund capable of retaining either 110 per cent of the capacity of the one or largest tank in the area or 25 per cent of the total volume of all the tanks in the area whichever is the greater, or 25 per cent of capacity where the oil is not stored in tanks;
(b) the bund and the base of the storage area are to be impermeable and so constructed that with proper maintenance they are likely to remain so for at least 20 years;
(c) every part of every fuel storage tank is to be within the bund;
(d) taps or valves through which fuel oil can be discharged are to be within the bund, to discharge vertically downward and be shut and locked in that position when not in use;

(e) similar provisions apply to flexible fuel delivery pipes;

(f) no part of the storage area shall be within 10 metres of any waters which fuel could enter if it were to escape.

Exemptions generally relate to facilities constructed and in use before 1 May 1991, and where a notice under regulation 9 has been served, its terms have been complied with or it has been substantially enlarged or reconstructed since that date. Further, by regulation 7(2), the exemption under that regulation will apply only where notice has been given to the Authority before 1 September 1991, and anyway only up to 1 September 1996. Any person proposing to store any relevant substance in any such structures that are constructed or substantially enlarged or reconstructed after 1 September 1991 shall notify the Authority at least 14 days before such storage is to commence.

The control provisions in regulation 9 empower the Authority to serve a notice on the person having custody or control of the relevant substance requiring him to carry out such works and to take such precautions and other steps as it considers appropriate, having regard to the contents of the schedules. The notice may be served where the Authority, under regulation 9(1), is satisfied that there is a significant risk of pollution of controlled waters as a result of :

(a) the use of an exempt structure for the storage of a relevant substance; or

(b) the making of silage in circumstances in which the exemption conferred by regulation 7 applies.

Regulation 10 provides for a 28-day right of appeal by notice to the Secretary of State.

Water protection zones

Section 93 of the 1991 Act provides for the making, by order, of water protection zones and the prohibiting or restricting therein of any designated activities. The power to make an order is conditional on the Secretary of State being satisfied that prohibiting or restricting the operation of such activities in the area is appropriate in preventing or controlling the entry into controlled waters of any poisonous, noxious or polluting matter;[64] with the exclusion of nitrates derived from agriculture.[65] The expectation is that implementation of such orders will be by the NRA and that a contravention will be a criminal offence subject to the same penalties as a breach of section 85 above. The purpose of these orders is to anticipate and prevent water pollution arising from activities which are unsuited to control by licensing of direct discharges.

Nitrate sensitive areas

The exclusion of agricultural nitrates from control under the above provision is explained and remedied by the express power under section 94 of the 1991 Act for the Minister to designate any land as a nitrate sensitive area.[66] The purpose of such designation is to prevent nitrates used for agricultural purposes from entering controlled waters. Where the Minister considers it necessary to achieve that purpose he may, either in the initial designation order or in a subsequent order following designation, prohibit or restrict the carrying on of any specified activities on agricultural land in the area.[67] Subordinate to these provisions section 95 provides for agreements in designated nitrate sensitive areas by which, in consideration of pay-

64 Section 93(2) and see above at p.164.

65 Section 93(3).

66 In July 1994 the Minister of Agriculture, Fisheries and Food announced the creation of 22 new NSAs to cover 28 separate water sources where nitrate levels exceed or are expected to exceed the EC limit of 50mg/litre. This will add 35,000 to the existing 10,500 hectares of the pilot scheme.

67 Section 94(3).

ments by the Minister the freeholder, or another with his consent, accepts obligations with respect to the management of the land. Such agreements are binding on successors in title but not on subsequent tenants who are not such successors.

Clearly the powers to create water protection zones and nitrate sensitive areas have very similar aims, but also have significant differences apart from the fact that the latter are the responsibility of the Minister of Agriculture, Fisheries and Food rather than the Secretary of State for the Environment. Water protection zones are confined to prohibiting and restricting activities, whereas orders in nitrate sensitive areas may require positive action from farmers. A second major distinction is that with nitrate sensitive areas financial compensation may be payable in respect of obligations consequent on the designation.

Sections 94 and 95 are drafted to give wide flexibility, but broadly they envisage three types of nitrate sensitive area:

68 Section 95(2) and (3).

(a) Voluntary areas[68] in which, building on arrangements in the Wildlife and Countryside Act 1981, management agreements may be entered into voluntarily by farmers in return for compensation. This is expected to be the initial approach.

69 Section 94(3)(a) and (4)(a).

(b) Mandatory areas without compensation[69] in which specified activities may be required, prohibited or restricted and contraventions subject to criminal sanctions.[70]

70 Section 94(4)(d).

71 Section 94(3)(b).

(c) Mandatory areas with compensation.[71]

The procedure for making an order designating a nitrate sensitive area is specified in Schedule 12 to the Act. The initiative rests with the NRA to make an application to the relevant Minister to make an order, although either the Secretary of State or the Minister of Agriculture, Fisheries and Food may direct the Authority to apply.[72] The criteria for such an application are that nitrate pollution is occurring or is likely to occur as a result of agricultural activities and other provisions are not sufficient to deal with the problem.

72 Section 5(1)(b).

Codes of practice

Following consultation with the NRA the Ministers may, by order under section 97, approve any code of practice, whether issued by themselves or others, that gives guidance on good agricultural practice relating to controlled waters and promotes good practice to avoid or minimise pollution of such waters. Compliance with a Ministerial Code of Good Agricultural Practice was a statutory defence under the Control of Pollution Act 1974. Following strong criticism that is no longer the case, and neither will non-compliance in itself give rise to criminal or civil liability.[73] In common with codes of practice in general, though, the standards advocated will be of evidential value in determining the reasonableness of any given act or process. Also, and more specifically, the Authority, by section 97, is required to have regard to compliance or non-compliance with the Code in two cases:

73 Section 97(2).

(a) before issuing a relevant prohibition notice under section 86(1), having the effect of applying pollution controls to discharges of effluent on to land or into land-locked ponds; and

(b) when exercising powers in regulations made under section 92 requiring preventative precautions to be taken in respect of the storage of potentially harmful materials such as silage.

Currently the Water (Prevention of Pollution) (Code of Practice) Order 1991[74] approves the Code of Good Agricultural Practice for the Protection of Water issued on 1 July 1991 by the Minister of Agriculture, Fisheries and Food and the Secretary of State for Wales. The scope of the Code is stated to be:

(a) to give practical guidance to persons engaged in agriculture with respect to activities that may affect controlled waters; and

(b) to promote what appear to them to be desirable practices by such persons for avoiding or minimising the pollution of any such waters.

Direct Action by the NRA

Supplementary to the powers of control and enforcement to secure good practice by others, the NRA is given the power, by section 161,[75] to take direct action itself to prevent or remedy the pollution of controlled waters and recover the reasonable costs of such action from the person responsible.[76] Where the Authority considers that any poisonous, noxious or polluting matter or any solid waste is likely to enter, or to be or to have been present in, any controlled waters,[77] it is entitled to carry out works and operations to prevent such entry or to remove, dispose of, remedy or mitigate any pollution so caused. Also, so far as is reasonably practicable, it may restore the waters, including flora and fauna, to their state immediately before the pollution. Section 161(2) exempts from these powers any discharges pursuant to a consent under Chapter II of Part III of the Act, even if causing or likely to cause pollution. In such cases the appropriate action would be to seek a revocation or variation of the consent.[78]

Under section 161(1) the preventative action is available where such matter 'appears likely to enter' any controlled waters. This is a matter of fact and judgement but implies an appropriate degree of proximity, in both time and space. These powers are not expressly stated to be of an emergency nature. However, the absence of any prior notification requirement, coupled with the right to recover costs, indicates that a factor in the judgement may be the anticipated inadequacy, either because of lack of time or co-operation, of other enforcement action.

The wide powers of pollution control in this statute are amplified by two sections of the Water Industry Act 1991 that may be dealt with conveniently here. Section 71 of that Act makes the waste or unreasonable abstraction of water from underground strata through a well, borehole or other work a criminal offence. Abstraction in excess of reasonable requirements will presumably be assessed by reference to the terms of the abstraction licence issued by the NRA.[79] There are the necessary exceptions to this general prohibition in respect of testing for quantity or quality, cleansing and maintenance, and also where the water interferes with any underground working.[80] Breach of this provision is a summary offence and, on conviction, the court may in addition to a fine, make an order requiring the sealing of the well, borehole etc., or with such other terms as appear necessary to prevent the waste.[81] Should such an order not be complied with, the NRA, on its own application, may be authorised to do the work and recover its costs as a civil debt.

Section 72 of the Water Industry Act 1991 makes it a criminal offence for a person by act or neglect to cause the water in any waterworks intended or likely to be used for domestic purposes or human consumption to be or likely to become polluted. 'Waterworks' is very widely defined for this purpose and extends, on the

74 S.I. 1991 No. 2285.

75 Modelled on section 46(4) – (7) of the Control of Pollution Act 1974.

76 Section 161(3).

77 Comparable criteria to section 85; see p.162. above.

78 Schedule 10, paragraphs 6 and 7.

79 See section 24 of the Water Industry Act 1991, and above at p.116.

80 Section 71(2) and (3).

81 Section 71(5).

82 Section 72(5).

one hand, to wells, springs, and adits, and on the other to service reservoirs, mains and pipes.[82] The exceptions under this section[83] include the consequences of land cultivation if in accord with good husbandry; and the reasonable use of oil or tar on public highways if the highway authority takes reasonable steps to prevent the pollution of water.

83 See sections 72(2) & (3).

Pollution control registers

In concluding this review of pollution control measures it is to be noted that section 190 of the Water Resources Act 1991 requires the NRA to maintain pollution control registers in accordance with regulations of the Secretary of State. The registers shall contain particulars of :

(a) any notices served under section 83;
(b) applications for consents under Chapter II of Part III;
(c) consents as in (b) above, with any conditions;
(d) certificates issued under Schedule 10, paragraph 1(7);[84]
(e) samples taken under this Act and any resulting action;
(f) any matters under section 20 of the Environmental Protection Act 1990 required by the chief inspector.

84 Discharge consents – certificates of exemption from disclosure.

Such registers are to be available for free public inspection and for copying at reasonable cost. The Secretary of State has made, under section 190(1), the Control of Pollution (Registers) Regulations 1989.[85]

85 S.I. 1989 No. 1160.

Fish protection

As well as these extensive general powers of pollution control the NRA, as the successor to water authorities, is given similar specific powers directed to the protection of fish and their habitats in the Salmon and Freshwater Fisheries Act 1975. Section 4(1) provides that

> ...any person who causes or knowingly permits to flow, or puts or knowingly permits to be put, into any waters containing fish or into any tributaries of waters containing fish, any liquid or solid matter to such an extent as to cause the waters to be poisonous or injurious to fish or the spawning grounds, spawn or food of fish, shall be guilty of an offence.

The meanings to be attached to 'causes or permits' and 'poisonous' have been discussed in Chapter 1 and in connection with the section 85 offences above.[86] The requirement that the waters contain fish is a matter of fact and does not depend on the knowledge or belief of the defendant. This element of the offence will have increasing significance as water quality improves and fish return to previously lifeless waters. Such improvements may be protected against subsequent degradation caused by the discharge of pollutants.

86 See at pp.30–4 and 164.

A general defence is provided in section 4(2) for activities performed either in the execution of a legal right or in continuation of a method in use in relation to those premises before 18 July 1923. In both cases, though, the right is qualified by the need to satisfy the court that the best practicable means, within a reasonable cost, were used to prevent matter from injuring fish, spawning grounds, spawn or food of fish. While the assumption is that the enforcing authority will usually be the NRA, proceedings may also be instituted by a person certified by the Minister as having 'a material interest in the waters alleged to be affected'.[87]

87 Section 4(3).

Rights of access to implement these provisions are of two types. By section 32, a water bailiff or other officer under a special order in writing[88] from the authority has the power to

> enter, remain upon and traverse any lands adjoining or near to waters within the water authority area, other than –
>
> (a) a dwelling house or curtilage of a dwelling house;
> (b) decoys or lands used exclusively for the preservation of wild fowl.

Alternatively, by section 33, a warrant of 24 hours maximum duration may be obtained from a justice of the peace to enter premises where there is reason to suspect that any offence against the Act is being or is likely to be committed. Parts I and II of Schedule 4 apply to the prosecution and punishment of offences under the Act together with the procedure for such prosecutions. Offences under section 4 may be subject to summary or indictable proceedings with, in the first case, fines of £400 and £40 per day on which the offence continues after conviction and, in the second, two years' imprisonment, or a fine or both.

MARINE POLLUTION[89]

Dumping of waste

Because of their vast volume there has in the past been a tacit assumption, when the matter has been thought about at all, that the seas and oceans of the world were capable of receiving the relatively modest amounts of waste and polluting matter discharged into them without detriment. Indeed, this characteristic has made them positively attractive as a means of disposal, as was noted for instance by the Royal Commission on Environmental Pollution:

> The sea is a powerful and effective scavenger of many pollutants ... In the North Sea the strong currents, the high winds and the shallow waters together give a high degree of aeration and good mixing, which provide good conditions for the assimilation of degradable effluents such as domestic sewage and certain industrial wastes.[90]

It is now increasingly recognised that man's capacity to exhaust this previously perceived inexhaustible tolerance cannot proceed unchecked. The increasing range and sophistication of man's activities is having a discernible impact on the marine environment and, without regulation, will effect an escalating and eventually irreversible deterioration.

Apart from their size, the other peculiar characteristic of the oceans is that much of them belongs to no one, and the small proportion that does involve ownership may be used by all for various purposes. It is a truism, in this context as in others, that what is the concern of all is the responsibility of none. Where individual attempts to give expression to that concern have been made they have tended to be defeated by the general inertia of indifference or the opposition of self-interest. While there have been such individual and spasmodic attempts to tackle aspects of marine pollution, therefore, the effective regulation of a world-wide problem necessarily awaited international organisations capable of formulating and implementing effective remedies. While that second stage has yet to be reached and implementation remains a matter for individual nations, international bodies are achieving sufficient consensus to produce measures and procedures to control marine pollution.

88 Such written orders have a maximum duration of 12 months, implying that they are dated.

89 I am indebted to Professor W. Howarth, Water Pollution Law (Shaw & Sons, Dartford: 1988), for the background and structure of this topic.

90 Royal Commission on Environmental Pollution, Third Report (1972), paragraphs 6 and 7.

91 Cmnd 8941.

92 Article 2.

93 Meaning 'use your property so as not to injure that of your neighbour'. As an example of its operation in customary law, though in the context of air pollution, see the Trail Smelter arbitration between the United States and Canada (1940) 3 RIAA 1905.

94 Article 1(5).

Probably the widest ranging and most comprehensive code of rules governing marine pollution so far is that contained in the United Nations Convention on the Law of the Sea III 1982 (UNCLOS III).[91] The historical jurisdiction for three miles out to sea is extended by UNCLOS III to 12 miles from a baseline which is generally low water mark and which includes the air above and the land below.[92] This 12-mile jurisdiction is now, by section 146 of the Environmental Protection Act 1990, extended to 'UK controlled waters' which are defined by section 146(7) as 'any part of the sea within the limits of an area designated under section 1(7) of the Continental Shelf Act 1964'. The effect is that Britain, in partnership with other parties to the Oslo Convention, has powers extending to the whole area of the continental shelf. Within this territorial sea a nation has authority to regulate by law the control of pollution and the preservation of the environment; regulation which governs ships passing through those waters. Extending beyond that limit, a state may adopt 'exclusive economic zones' up to 200 nautical miles from the same baselines. Within such zones a state has jurisdictional control over the marine environment.

While the code embodied in the Convention will not come into operation until ratified by 60 Member States – a process still well short of completion – provisions relating to the protection of the environment may still prove influential, for example, through individual adoption. The Convention, when implemented, is intended to augment and rationalise rather than usurp existing agreements; specifically providing that its provisions are without prejudice to obligations relating to the protection and preservation of the marine environment assumed by states under previously concluded conventions and agreements. UNCLOS III embodies the *sic utere tuo ut alienum non laedas* principle,[93] usually abbreviated to '*sic utere*', or rendered as 'the good neighbourliness principle'. Its application to environmental issues is clear. Article 194, for example, stipulates that pollution generated within a state is not to spread beyond its boundaries so as to cause environmental damage to other states. More specifically, Article 195 provides that, in acting to restrict pollution of the marine environment, a state is not to transfer, directly or indirectly, damage or risk of damage from one area to another or transform one type of pollution to another. Articles 195–210 deal specifically with marine pollution from vessels or land-based sources, or by dumping, providing for co-operation between states in research and assessment of pollution and its consequences. The protection of the seas is deemed to require the agreed formulation, either regionally or world-wide, of national legislation and procedures to prevent and control pollution of all types. In particular, Articles 198 and 199 impose duties on the occurrence of pollution. The former requires that, on becoming aware of pollution that has or is likely to cause damage to the marine environment, the state concerned is to notify others who might be affected. The latter then requires all states affected to co-operate so far as possible to eliminate its effects and prevent or minimise the damage.

A particular source of marine pollution is the intentional dumping of waste. The sea as a means of disposal has obvious attractions, as was noted earlier. These attractions have increased as controls over disposal on or into land have become progressively more restrictive. UNCLOS III defines the dumping of waste at sea as[94]:

(1) any deliberate disposal of wastes or other matter from vessels, aircraft, platforms or other man-made structures at sea;
(2) any deliberate disposal of vessels, aircraft, platforms or other man-made structures at sea.

The Article then excludes from the scope of dumping:

(1) the disposal of wastes or other matter incidental to, or derived from the normal operations of vessels, aircraft, platforms or other man-made structures at sea, operating for the purpose of disposal of such matter or derived from the treatment of such wastes or other matter on such vessels, aircraft, platforms or structures;

(2) placement of matter for a purpose other than the mere disposal thereof, not contrary to the aims of this Convention.

The United Kingdom's obligations in respect of dumping at sea derive from its participation in two Conventions: the Oslo Convention for the Prevention of Marine Pollution by Dumping from Ships and Aircraft of 1972[95] and the London Convention for the Prevention of Marine Pollution by Dumping of Wastes and Other Matter of 1972.[96] As may be expected, these Conventions, close in time as they are, are very similar in content. Their most significant difference is that while the London Convention is world-wide in scope, the Oslo Convention is confined to the north-east Atlantic and the North Sea. Being regional in operation its provisions are also regarded as being more detailed and stringent than the London Convention's can afford to be, applying as they do to more national authorities. Before considering the United Kingdom's statutory implementation of its provisions, a brief review of the Oslo Convention itself follows.

95 Cmnd 4984.

96 Cmnd 5169.

The Oslo Convention came into operation in April 1974 following ratification by sufficient signatory states. A principal and important feature of the Convention was the creation of a Standing Commission of representatives of the parties to the Convention – the Oslo Commission. The duties of the Commission are set out in Article 17 of the Convention as follows:

(1) To exercise overall supervision over the implementation of the Convention;

(2) To receive and consider the records of permits and approvals issued and of dumping which has taken place and to define the standard procedure to be adopted for this purpose;

(3) To review generally the condition of the seas within the area to which the Convention applies, the efficiency of the control measures being adopted, and the need for any additional or different measures;

(4) To keep under review the contents of the Annexes to the Convention, and to recommend such amendments, additions or deletions as may be agreed;

(5) To discharge such other functions as may be appropriate under the terms of the Convention.

The Oslo Convention establishes a classification of pollutants in three grades according to toxicity. The most detrimental are those on the 'Black List' in Annexe I. The dumping of such substances is prohibited unless in an emergency, or where they appear only as trace elements in other waste which may be classified in another category. The Black List substances are:

(a) Organohalogen compounds and compounds which may form such substances in the marine environment, excluding those which are non-toxic, or which are rapidly converted in the sea into substances which are biologically harmless;

(b) Organosilicon compounds and compounds which may form such substances in the marine environment, excluding those which are non-toxic, or which are rapidly converted in the sea into substances which are biologically harmless;

(c) Substances which have been agreed between the Contracting Parties as likely to be carcinogenic under the conditions of disposal;

(d) Mercury and mercury compounds;

(e) Cadmium and cadmium compounds;

(f) Persistent plastics and other persistent synthetic materials which may float or remain in suspension in the sea, and which may seriously interfere with fishing or navigation, reduce amenities, or interfere with other legitimate uses of the sea.

The second category, of less harmful substances, are on the 'Grey List' in Annexe II paragraph (1). Under Article 6 the dumping at sea of any of these materials requires a permit from the national authority. In granting a permit for the dumping of large quantities of these substances consideration must be given to the possible presence of similar wastes. Disposal in deep water is required for the substances in paragraph 1(b), which means a depth of at least 2,000 metres and a distance from land of at least 150 nautical miles. Grey List substances are:

(a) Arsenic, lead, copper, zinc and their compounds, cyanides and fluorides, and pesticides and their by-products not covered by the provisions of Annexe 1;

(b) Containers, scrap metal, tar-like substances liable to sink to the sea bottom and other bulky wastes which may present a serious obstacle to fishing or navigation;

(c) Substances which, though of a non-toxic nature, may become harmful due to the quantities in which they are dumped, or which are liable to seriously reduce amenities.

The third category, the 'White List', consists of all types of waste not falling within the two earlier categories. The dumping of waste within this category is subject to the approval of the appropriate national authority and, in the United Kingdom, comes within the licensing provisions of Part II of the Food and Environment Protection Act 1985.[97] The granting of approval for the dumping of both Grey and White List substances is subject to the terms of Annexe III which requires consideration, in granting approval, of the characteristics both of the waste and the location to be used, the method of deposit, its impact on other uses and activities, and possible alternative means of disposal. By Article 19(1) 'dumping' means the deliberate disposal of substances and materials into the sea by or from ships or aircraft other than:

(a) any discharge incidental to or derived from the normal operation of ships and aircraft and their equipment;

(b) the placing of substances and materials for a purpose other than the mere disposal thereof, if not contrary to the aim of this Convention.

It has been seen that a function of the Commission is to monitor the operation of the Convention. To facilitate this duty all parties to the Convention are required to keep and supply to the Commission records of the nature, quantities, times and locations of wastes dumped with their approval together with the methods of disposal. In Article 13 the parties to the Convention have also agreed to co-operate in monitoring the distribution and effects of pollutants in the area covered by the Convention.

A Protocol of July 1983[98] has extended the Oslo Convention to cover the disposal of waste at sea by incineration. While the Protocol has yet to be ratified it has been given effect to in United Kingdom law. The assumption in the Protocol

97 See below at p.359.

98 Cmnd 8942.

is that this practice is a temporary substitute until effective land-based methods of disposal are developed. To this end, 1 January 1990 was identified as the date before which the parties were to meet to agree a final date for termination of incineration at sea.

The United Kingdom implemented the provisions of the two Conventions in the Dumping at Sea Act 1974. Subsequent developments, for example concerning incineration at sea and the scuttling of ships, meant that the Act was inadequate for its purpose. To meet these and other deficiencies the 1974 Act was repealed and replaced by the extended terms of Part II of the Food and Environment Protection Act 1985. Control under the Act is based on a system of licensing of the range of activities leading to pollution of the marine environment by dumping.

Section 5 requires a licence:

(a) for the deposit of substances or articles in the sea or under the sea bed in UK waters or UK controlled waters;
(b) for the deposit of substances or articles anywhere in the sea or under the sea bed from British vessels etc.;
(c) for the scuttling of vessels in UK waters or UK controlled waters or anywhere at sea if controlled from a British vessel etc.;
(d) for the loading of a vessel etc., in the UK or UK waters with substances or articles for deposit anywhere in the sea or under the sea bed;
(e) for the loading of a vehicle in the UK with substances or articles for deposit as in (a); or
(f) for the towing or propelling from the UK or UK waters of a vessel for scuttling at sea.

In addition, section 6 requires a licence:

(a) for the incineration of substances or articles on a vessel or marine structure in UK waters or UK controlled waters or anywhere at sea on a British vessel or marine structure;
(b) for the loading of a vessel or marine structure in the UK or UK waters with substances or articles for incineration anywhere at sea.

The activities subject to these licensing provisions can be seen to fall into two broad categories: (i) those occurring in British waters irrespective of who the operators are or where they come from, and (ii) those involving British vessels etc., wherever in the world they are operating. There is of course a third class of activity covered here and attributable to the relative ease of supervision of land-based rather than sea-going operations, i.e. the preparatory loading. The craft from which these activities may be conducted, and therefore the subject of the section 5 powers, include vehicles, vessels, aircraft, hovercraft, marine structures, floating containers etc. 'Incineration' in section 6 means the combustion of substances and materials for the purpose of their thermal destruction. 'Scuttling' is not defined in the Act but may be described as the intentional sinking of ships, usually by opening the sea-cocks. The different powers applicable to United Kingdom waters and others makes this distinction of fundamental importance. By section 24(1) 'United Kingdom waters means any part of the sea within the seaward limits of UK territorial waters', and by section 146(7) of the Environmental Protection Act 1990, 'United Kingdom controlled waters means any part of the sea within the limits of an area designated under section 1(7) of the Continental Shelf Act 1964'.

Territorial waters extend for a distance of 12 nautical miles from low water mark. Controlled waters, synonymous with continental shelf limits, are defined by international law for jurisdiction for the purposes of sea deposits. The waters so defined replace the British fishery limits originally specified in the 1985 Act. Hitherto these provisions governed British vessels etc., engaged in these activities anywhere, any dumping etc., in British territorial waters and the dumping within the continental shelf limits by a foreign vessel loaded in a British port. Control is now extended by the section 146 amendments to dumping etc., within the continental shelf limits by any foreign vessel. The Ministers may by statutory instrument exempt specified operations from the licensing requirement.[99]

The licensing authority is the Minister of Agriculture, Fisheries and Food, and section 8 and Schedule 3 contain the licensing provisions. In deciding whether to issue a licence the authority is to have regard to:

(a) the protection of the marine environment, especially in relation to its living resources and human health;
(b) preventing interference with legitimate uses of the sea;
(c) availability of alternative methods of disposal.

and in granting a licence may include conditions, especially in relation to (a) and (b) and also specifying the site of the operation and the use of automatic recording equipment. An applicant may be required to provide information and permit such examinations and tests as the authority may consider necessary to determine the matter.[100] Fee levels for licences are to be settled after consultation with relevant representative organisations and may be levied to cover administrative expenses, initial examination and testing and subsequent monitoring of operations.[101] Once issued a licence may be varied or revoked for any relevant reason and, in particular, for breach of condition, changes in the circumstances relating to the marine environment or increase in scientific knowledge.[102] Schedule 3 provides, *inter alia*, that an applicant is to be given, on request, written notice of reasons for refusal, variation or revocation of a licence, or for the inclusion of any provision in the licence.

The duty of a licensing authority to maintain public registers of information with respect to licences is contained in a new section 14 substituted by section 147 of the Environmental Protection Act 1990. The information is to include particulars of applications, licences, later variations or revocations, convictions for offences and any remedial action under section 10. This last permits the Ministers to undertake emergency action at the cost of the person in default to protect the marine environment from the consequences of a breach of licence or condition, in addition to any other sanctions. Being a register open to public inspection and copying, matters prejudicial to national security or a person's commercial interests may, at the discretion of the Minister, be excluded.[103] Licensing offences within section 9 include the doing, or causing or permitting another to do, without a licence any of the activities for which a licence is required, and also knowingly or recklessly making a false statement to obtain a licence or for any other purpose. These are considered to be strict liability offences, neither the absence of *mens rea* nor mistake being a defence. Proceedings generally require the prior consent of the Attorney-General and may be summary or indictable. It is a defence to a charge of carrying out an unlicensed activity to prove that it was necessary either for the safety of the vessel or for the saving of life, and that the Ministers were informed

99 Section 7; and see the Deposits at Sea (Exemption) Order 1985, S.I. 1985 No. 1699.

100 Section 8(5).

101 Section 8(7)–(9).

102 Section 8 (10) and (11).

103 Section 14.

of the details within a reasonable time. Even so, the defence will not be available where the necessity arose through the fault of the person relying on the defence. A further defence to unlicensed dumping, scuttling or incineration from a British vessel, but not in United Kingdom waters, is that it is within the law of another state that is party to the London and Oslo Conventions. Further general defences under section 22(1) are that the person concerned took all reasonable precautions or exercised all due diligence to avoid commission of the offence. These provisions impose both individual and corporate liability,[104] and vicarious liability according to general principles may be incurred.[105]

An offence under section 9 will occur where a person does, or causes or permits another to do, any of the prohibited acts. The ability to 'cause' implies a sufficient degree of dominance or control over the actor, or some express or positive authority, while the ability to 'permit' necessarily requires knowledge of the facts and the capacity to forbid.[106] For a corporate body to be liable for 'causing' or 'permitting' it must be shown that a person for whose criminal acts the corporation would be liable caused or permitted the commission of the offence. Knowledge on the part of an ordinary employee is not sufficient; it must be that of someone exercising a controlling mind or influence over the company's affairs.

Oil pollution

If the dumping of waste in all its forms constitutes the most widespread and pernicious pollution of the marine environment, it is without doubt pollution by oil that attracts the most attention, if only through the acute impact of oil spills. Even in the context of marine oil pollution such disasters contribute only a small proportion of oil spillage or discharge into the seas, the Royal Commission on Environmental Pollution finding that[107]

> ... 60 per cent of oil reaching the sea consists of discharges from the land, for example by means of effluents in rivers, or by means of the direct deposition of hydrocarbons in the atmosphere (originating for example in motor vehicle exhausts). Tanker operations, either accidents or deliberate discharges account for about 20 per cent of the oil reaching the sea. The remaining 20 per cent appears to come largely through natural seepages and from discharges resulting from general shipping operations.

It is, however, tanker disasters that have concentrated the mind and stimulated action. In consequence, and in spite of the figures quoted above, legal control, in the United Kingdom as elsewhere, is directed to oil pollution from shipping. As with the dumping of waste, United Kingdom law governing oil pollution gives effect to international convention provisions and should therefore be considered in that context. Further, the legal controls operate in both criminal and civil law, providing penalties for infringement and a system of compensation for consequent damage.

Dealing first with the criminal law, it is sufficient for present purposes to go back no further in reviewing the international structure than 1954 and the International Convention for the Prevention of Pollution of the Sea by Oil (OILPOL) produced by the International Maritime Organisation.[108] The purpose of the Convention was to control the discharge of 'persistent oils' from tankers and other shipping over specified capacities. Persistent oils are crude, fuel, heavy, diesel and lubricating oils. These provisions were given effect to in the United Kingdom by the Oil in Navigable Waters Act 1955. The *Torrey Canyon* disaster in 1967 empha-

104 Section 21(6).

105 See esp. *Mousell Bros Ltd v London & Western Rly Co.* [1917] 2 KB 836; *Gardner v Akeroyd*

106 See discussion of these terms in Chapter 1 at p.30–4.

107 Eighth Report (1981), paragraph 11.3.

108 Cmnd 395.

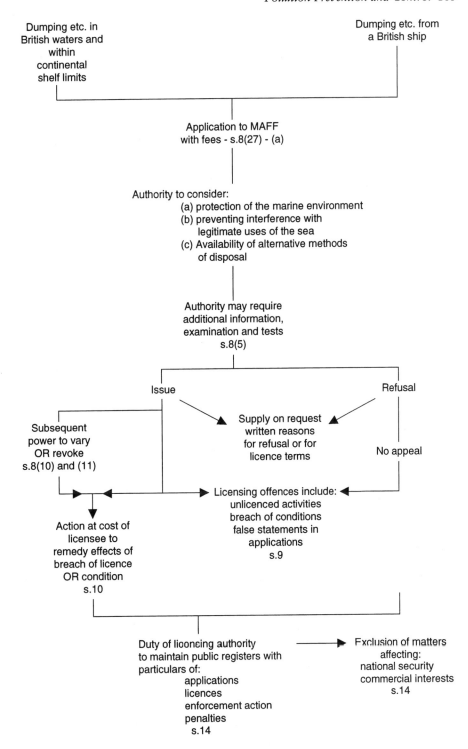

Figure 7.2 Licensing of Dumping at Sea: Food and Environment Act 1985, section 5

sised the legal difficulties of state intervention and action in such a situation to initiate remedial action and to protect the environment.

The response was the International Convention Relating to Intervention on the High Seas in Cases of Oil Pollution Casualties 1969, 'The Intervention Convention'. This permits a coastal state to intervene where a shipping accident poses a grave and imminent danger of pollution to its territorial waters or coastline. The degree of intervention is limited to that necessary to deal with the pollution danger, and consultation with the flag state of the vessel concerned is required. This Convention was given effect to by the Prevention of Oil Pollution Act 1971, which also consolidated earlier statutes and is therefore now the principal statute governing the subject. Section 20 of the Merchant Shipping Act 1979 creates a power by Order in Council to implement international conventions relating to pollution from ships. That section has been amended by sections 2 to 4 of the Merchant Shipping (Salvage and Pollution) Act 1994, the last of which adds a new section 20A to the 1979 Act. By that section effect may be given, by Order in Council, to 'any provision of the United Nations Convention on the Law of the Sea 1982[109] ... for the protection and preservation of the marine environment from pollution by matter from ships'.

The growth in numbers and size of tankers, with the consequent increase in the magnitude and consequences of oil spills, revealed inadequacies in the OILPOL Convention and led to the International Convention for the Prevention of Pollution from Ships of 1973 (MARPOL).[110] This Convention dealt with pollution from ships by oil, chemicals and sewage, and required design changes, for example to bulkheads, and equipment provision on ships to monitor and control discharges of oil. It also designated 'special areas' where oil discharges were absolutely prohibited, and inspection and detention powers of states were strengthened. MARPOL has yet to be ratified, many states considering that its provisions would be too difficult to implement. The necessary amendments to the 1971 Act to give effect to the Convention have however been made by the Merchant Shipping (Prevention of Oil Pollution) Regulations 1983.[111] It now remains to deal with these United Kingdom provisions.

The discharge of oil into non-territorial waters from a UK registered ship and into UK waters from any ship are offences under, respectively, sections 1 and 2 of the Prevention of Oil Pollution Act 1971. The former provides that if specified categories of oil are discharged into non-territorial waters from a British registered ship, either the owner or the master shall be guilty of an offence. The prohibited oils are, by section 1(2), crude, fuel, lubricating and heavy diesel oils. These are the heavier, less volatile oils, and therefore less easily dispersed in the natural environment. The Secretary of State may add to these categories by regulation to implement any Conventions to which Britain may be a party.

Section 2(1) contains a number of offences relating to the discharge of oil into United Kingdom territorial waters. For the purposes of this section, 'oil' is not restricted as in section 1 and therefore includes all oils and oil mixtures. Territorial waters include all waters within the 12-mile limit navigable by sea-going ships, including a dry dock, even when emptied.[112] The specified persons will be liable in the event of discharges, including escapes,[113] of oil as follows:

(a) from a vessel, the owner or master;

(b) from a vessel during transfer to or from another vessel or place on land and due to the act or omission of any person in the other vessel or place, the other owner or master or occupier as the case may be;

109 Cmnd 8941.

110 Cmnd 5748.

111 S.I. 1983 No. 1398, amended by the Merchant Shipping (Prevention of Oil Pollution) (Amendment) Regulations 1993 No. 1680.

112 *Rankin v De Coster* [1975] 2 All ER 303.

113 Section 29(3).

(c) from a place on land, the occupier;

(d) from a place on land and caused by a trespasser, that person;

(e) otherwise than in (a) to (d) above and due to the exploration or exploitation of the natural resources below the sea bed, the person carrying on those operations.

Section 2(3) extends the scope of 'place on land' to include, inter alia, things in or on the sea if anchored to the shore or sea bed, other than vessels. As with section 1, offences are actionable summarily or on indictment and require the consent of the Attorney-General or, if in a harbour, of the harbour authority.[114] Liability attaching in these sections to the 'owner or master' is not to be taken as indicating alternatives. Both may be prosecuted for the same offence in appropriate cases.[115] Defences, in section 5, are that the discharge was necessary either for the safety of the vessel or for the saving of life.

Sections 10 and 11 create ancillary offences relating to harbours. Section 10 prohibits the transfer of oil to or from a vessel in a harbour in the United Kingdom unless notice has been given to the harbour master between three and 96 hours previously. A general notice of such transfers for a period up to 12 months may be given. The exceptional circumstance is where the transfer is required by a fire brigade. By section 11, the owner or master of the vessel or the occupier of the premises concerned has a duty to report to the harbour master or harbour authority the discharge or escape of oil into a United Kingdom harbour from a vessel or a place on land. Failure so to do is punishable summarily. Regulations under section 4 may require the fitting of equipment in British ships to prevent or reduce discharges of oil into the sea.

The Secretary of State is given special emergency powers in sections 12–15 to deal with oil spills arising from shipping accidents in territorial waters. These powers do not apply to foreign ships, incidents outside territorial waters, or to Royal Navy or government ships, although they may be extended to the first two by Order in Council.[116] The criteria for the use of these powers are that, by section 12(1):

(a) a shipping accident has occurred; and

(b) large scale pollution will or may be caused; and

(c) use of the powers is urgently needed.

While (a) is a matter of fact, (b) and (c) are made matters of opinion for the Secretary of State. On general principles, though, such opinion must be justified by the circumstances and is not a matter of an arbitrary and unsupported decision[117]. Where these requirements are satisfied and 'for the purpose of preventing or reducing oil pollution or the risk of oil pollution',[118] the Secretary of State may give directions concerning the ship or its cargo to the owner or master, or to the salvor or anyone else in possession of the ship or in charge of the salvage operation. Such directions may require the recipient to do or refrain from doing anything and specifically govern:

(a) the movement of the ship to or from a specified place; or

(b) prohibition of its movement, or over a specified route; or

(c) any oil or other cargo is or is not to be unloaded or discharged; or

(d) specified salvage operations are, or are not to be taken.

Should the Secretary of State consider that these powers of direction are inadequate for the purpose, i.e., for prevention etc., of pollution, he may, himself or

114 Section 19.

115 See *Davies* v *Smith* 1983 SLT (notes) 644.

116 Section 16(1).

117 See, e.g., *Padfield* v *MAFF* [1968] AC 997; 1 All ER 694

118 Section 12(2)

by authorising another, take any necessary action, and in particular:

(a) any action for which he may give a direction;
(b) sink or destroy the ship, or a part of it, not being within the means of a person to whom he may give a direction;
(c) take over control of the ship.[119]

119 Section 12(4) and (5).

There is of course an overriding obligation in any circumstances to avoid risk to human life, and the defences to proceedings under section 14, as well as due diligence, include the belief on reasonable grounds that compliance with the direction would have involved a serious risk to human life. Section 13 provides that if the action under section 12 was not reasonably necessary to deal with the oil pollution, or the benefit was disproportionate to the demands made then compensation is recoverable from the Secretary of State.

The Secretary of State's powers considered above are restricted to response to emergency situations arising from shipping accidents. His role has been considerably extended by the Merchant Shipping (Salvage and Pollution) Act 1994, section 8(1) providing first that 'The Secretary of State shall continue to have the functions of taking, or co-ordinating, measures to prevent, reduce and minimise the effects of, marine pollution'. Section 8(2) then specifies the particular functions embraced by that generality, including:

(a) the acquisition, maintenance, use and disposal of ships, aircraft, equipment and other property;
(b) the provision of services, including research, training and advice;
(c) the giving of assistance to any other State or international institution under any international agreement relating to the prevention, reduction or control of marine pollution; and
(d) any other functions exercisable on his behalf at the commencement of this section by the Marine Pollution Control Unit.

Where practicable, assistance under section 8(2)(c) is to be given subject to reimbursement of the cost. For the purposes of this section, section 8(5) defines 'marine pollution' as meaning 'pollution caused by ships, offshore installations or submarine pipelines affecting or likely to affect the United Kingdom or United Kingdom waters or controlled waters' and an 'offshore installation' to mean 'any installation which is maintained for underwater exploitation or exploration to which the Mineral Working (Offshore Installations) Act 1971 applies'.

Enforcement

Machinery for the enforcement of these substantive provisions is provided in sections 17 to 19 of the Prevention of Oil Pollution Act 1971. Section 17(1) gives the Secretary of State power to make regulations requiring United Kingdom registered ships to carry oil record books recording operations relating to the:

(a) loading of oil cargo;
(b) transfer of oil cargo during a voyage;
(c) discharge of oil cargo;
(d) ballasting of oil tanks, discharge of ballast and cleaning;
(e) separation of oil from water or other mixture;
(f) disposal of oil from any of the above operations;

(g) disposal of other oil residues;

(h) emergency discharge of oil or oil mixtures.

By section 17(2) regulations may also require the keeping of records of transfers of oil to or from vessels in United Kingdom territorial waters. Such books and entries are admissible as evidence in proceedings and failure to keep any required records, or the falsifying of or the making of misleading entries are criminal offences.

The Secretary of State is empowered by section 18 to appoint inspectors to report to him on:

(a) compliance with the Act;

(b) any measures, other than statutory, to prevent escape of oil;

(c) the adequacy of oil reception facilities at harbours;

and surveyors of ships are deemed to be so appointed. The powers of inspectors under section 729 of the Merchant Shipping Act 1894 apply to such inspectors and, in section 18(6), additional inspection powers are given to harbour masters.

Proceedings for offences under the Act are generally to be brought by or with the consent of the Attorney-General. Offences under sections 2, 10, 11, 17 or 18 in or relating to a harbour are actionable by the harbour authority.[120] Section 19 has been amended by paragraph 3 of Schedule 14 of the Environmental Protection Act 1990, so that where the harbour master has reason to believe that a vessel has discharged oil, or a mixture containing oil, into the waters of the harbour contrary to section 2(2A) he may detain the vessel.[121] Subsequent subsections govern procedures, prosecutions, security payments and release of the vessel.

The Merchant Shipping (Prevention of Oil Pollution) Regulations 1983 are concerned with the physical integrity of vessels and the control of pollution in particular circumstances. The Regulations specify construction standards for new tankers, existing tankers and for oil discharge connections on tankers. They also require annual surveys and certification of British registered ships, being oil tankers of more than 150 gross registered tonnage (GRT) and other vessels of 400 GRT, and above. The Regulations contain provisions controlling operational pollution, the discharge of oil into the sea, and also special provisions to prevent oil pollution from ships in special areas, i.e., the Mediterranean, Baltic, Black and Red Seas and the Gulf area.

The 1983 Regulations have been amended by the Merchant Shipping (Prevention of Oil Pollution) (Amendment) Regulations 1993,[122] giving effect to amendments to Annex I to the International Convention for the Prevention of Pollution from Ships 1973. The amendments (in the form of amendments to the 1978 Protocol relating to the Convention) were adopted by the Marine Environment Protection Committee (MEPC) of the International Maritime Organisation at its 30th, 31st and 32nd sessions. The main purposes of the amendments are:

(a) the designation of the Antarctic as a special area;

(b) the introduction of a requirement for ships to carry oil pollution emergency plans;

(c) an increase in the stringency of discharge criteria;

(d) enhancement of the design criteria for new oil tankers; and

(e) modification of the survey and construction requirements for existing tankers.

Concerning (b) above, a substituted regulation 31A requires that:

120 Section 19.

121 Section 692 of the Merchant Shipping Act 1894 relating to the enforcing of the detention of a ship applies.

122 S.I. 1993 No. 1680, made by the Secretary of State for Transport under Article 3(1) of the Merchant Shipping (Prevention of Pollution) Order 1983, S.I. 1983 No. 1106.

(1) Oil tankers of 150 GRT and above and every other ship of 400 GRT and above shall carry on board an approved shipboard oil pollution emergency plan, although if built before 4th April 1993 it is not required to carry such a plan until 5th April 1995. The plan is to be in accordance with the guidelines for the development of shipboard oil pollution emergency plans adopted by the MEPC on 6th March 1992 and is to include at least[123] –

    (i) procedure to be followed by the master or other persons having charge of the ship to report an oil pollution incident as required by the Merchant Shipping (Reporting of Oil Pollution Incidents) Regulations 1987;[124]

    (ii) the list of persons (including national and local authorities) to be contacted in the event of an oil pollution incident;

    (iii) a detailed description of the action to be taken immediately by persons on board to reduce or control the discharge of oil following an incident; and

    (iv) the procedures and point of contact on the ship for co-ordinating shipboard action with national and local authorities in combatting the pollution.

Regulation 4 of the 1993 Regulations substitutes a new regulation 14 dealing with discharges. All ships between 400 and 10,000 GRT are required to provide for 'oil filtering equipment and oil discharge monitoring and control systems'. Additional requirements apply if ballast water is carried in bunker fuel tanks. Essentially no discharge into the sea is to occur without filtering and all such discharges are to be entered in the Oil Record Book.

Civil liability

Turning to the question of civil liability, it was again the *Torrey Canyon* incident in 1967 that revealed inadequacies in contemporary legal provision for compensation for states suffering the consequences of oil spills. The first response was voluntary, the Tanker Owner's Voluntary Agreement Concerning Liability for Oil Pollution (TOVALOP), which came into operation in 1969. The basis of this scheme, which though voluntary covered a high proportion of tankers, committed owners and charterers to reimburse governments on a strict liability basis for expenses reasonably incurred in remedying the effects of pollution of coastlines by persistent oil discharged from tankers. The liability is covered by insurance. This scheme was extended in 1971 to cover additional circumstances and to increase levels of compensation by the Contract Regarding an Interim Supplement to Tanker Liability for Oil Pollution (CRISTAL). This supplement also provided for a form of indemnity by which the costs of cleaning up pollution were more equitably distributed between tanker owners and cargo owners, i.e. the oil companies.

The operation of these voluntary schemes has been largely overtaken, at least as far as the United Kingdom is concerned, by international conventions and their implementation in national law. The principal agreements in this field are the International Convention on Civil Liability for Oil Pollution Damage 1969 (the Liability Convention)[125] and the International Convention on the Establishment of an International Fund for Compensation for Oil Pollution Damage 1971 (the Fund Convention).[126] These Conventions now govern the signatory states, while for others the voluntary agreements retain their effect.

The purpose of the Liability Convention is essentially to establish a legal structure for liability in place of TOVALOP. Shipowners are thereunder made liable for the losses incurred through oil pollution damage and for the costs of reasonable preventative and remediable measures. As with the voluntary agreement, liabi-

123 Regulation 31A(2).

124 S.I. 1987 No. 586.

125 Cmnd 4403.

126 Cmnd 7383.

lity is strict and oil cargos over a specified size are to be compulsorily insured. A notable simplification of the compensation under the Convention is that a claimant may sue the insurance company directly without proceeding against the shipowner. The provisions of the Liability Convention are enacted in the United Kingdom in the Merchant Shipping (Oil Pollution) Act 1971. Section 1(1) of the Act imposes liability on a shipowner where persistent oil carried in bulk as a cargo is discharged or escapes, for:

(a) resulting damage in any area of the United Kingdom;
(b) the cost of any reasonable measures to prevent or reduce the damage;
(c) any damage caused in any area of the United Kingdom by such measures.
Where two or more vessels are involved the owners are liable jointly.

The creation of this form of strict liability by the Act excludes any other remedies, whether or not liability is actually incurred under section 1.[127] Section 4 enables an owner, in the absence of fault, to limit his total liability to 2,000 gold francs per ton of the ship's tonnage with a maximum of 210 million gold francs. On the occurrence of a discharge the court, on the application of the ship's owner, will then determine the sums due, the time for payment in and the apportionment to persons affected.[128] The Act also requires[129] that all oil cargo carrying ships entering or leaving a United Kingdom port or oil terminal are to have a certificate of insurance issued by the Secretary of State or under the authority of another Convention country.[130] A shipowner has a defence to liability under section 1 if he is able to prove, by section 2, that the discharge or escape:

(a) resulted from an act of war, hostilities, civil war, insurrection or an exceptional, inevitable and irresistible natural phenomenon; or
(b) was due wholly to anything done or left undone by another person, not being a servant or agent of the owner, with intent to do damage; or
(c) was due wholly to the negligence or wrongful act of a government or other authority in exercising its function of maintaining lights or other navigational aids for the maintenance of which it was responsible.

The strict liability attaching to bulk oil carriers under the 1971 Act has now been extended to the discharge or escape of persistent oil 'from a ship other than a ship to which section 1 of this Act applies' by section 6 and Schedule 3 of the Merchant Shipping (Salvage and Pollution) Act 1994, adding new sections 1A, 2A and 3A to the former statute. The first two new sections are in substantially the same terms as the originals with only minor amendments. Section 3A, however, introduces some significant changes and defines more specifically the persons affected. The amount of liability is limited by section 3A(3) to any resulting loss of profits and the cost of any reasonable measures of reinstatement actually taken. These two categories of liability are related by the subsection to 'any impairment of the environment' within section 1A, a new phrase which appears to qualify 'damage caused ... by contamination' in section 1A(1) but which is not defined. Its precise meaning in any given case would appear to be a matter of fact and argument, particularly as to the scope of 'any'. Having been introduced the interest now is whether and to what extent the term will be adopted and applied in other contexts.

Section 3A also provides that, whether or not the shipowner is liable, the categories of persons listed in subsection (2) will incur liability only for acts or omis-

127 Section 3.

128 Section 5.

129 In section 10.

130 The Convention is the International Convention on Civil Liability for Oil Pollution Damage (Brussels, 1969).

sions done with intent to cause 'damage or cost or recklessly and in the knowledge that any such damage or cost would probably result'. Such persons include:

(a) the ship owners servant or agent;
(b) any person employed or engaged in any capacity on board the ship to perform any service for the ship;
(c) any charterer, manager or operator of the ship;
(d) any salvor operating with the consent of the owner or on the instructions of a public authority;
(e) any person acting to prevent or minimise damage resulting from a discharge or escape of oil;
(f) any servant or agent of a person falling within paragraph (c), (d) or (e).

The meaning of 'recklessness' in the criminal law context has received much and differing consideration. The statement of the principle by Lord Diplock in *R v Caldwell* (1982) may now though be regarded as authoritative for this present purpose.[131] He said:

> In my opinion, a person charged with an offence under section 1(1) of the Criminal Damage Act 1971 is 'reckless as to whether any such property would be destroyed or damaged' if he (1) does an act which in fact creates an obvious risk that property will be destroyed or damaged and (2) when he does the act he either has not given any thought to the possibility of there being any such risk or has recognised that there was some risk involved and has nonetheless gone on to do it.

While, as has been said, this test is framed for the purposes of the criminal law and the present concern is with civil liability for damages, the requirement of intent as an element of such liability may nevertheless give the test a relevance in this context.

The Fund Convention, analogous to CRISTAL, is posited on the principle that the costs attendant on damage from oil pollution fall on the ship and cargo owners rather than on those suffering the harm, applying in this context 'the polluter pays principle'. To this end the Convention established the International Oil Pollution Compensation Fund financed by levies on the importers of oil into the Contracting States. Payments from the Fund make good any deficiency where the Liability Convention either fails to meet the full loss or, in exceptional circumstances, where it does not apply at all. In certain circumstances the Fund may also indemnify shipowners for part of their costs in clearing oil spills. Each Contracting State is required to maintain a list of persons liable to contribute to the Fund and the amount of contributions is determined by the Assembly for each calendar year, having regard to past and estimated future expenditure on claims. The Fund Convention is given effect to in the United Kingdom in Part I of the Merchant Shipping Act 1974, section 2 dealing with contributions to, and section 4 with the liability of, the Fund.

Section 2 of the 1974 Act requires contributions to the Fund in respect of any oil brought into the United Kingdom by sea, whether or not it is being imported or whether or not contributions for it have been paid on a previous occasion. The reasonable implication here is that the risks attendant upon its carriage by sea are the same whatever the motive or reason for its shipment. Similar contributions are required to the Fund when oil is first received into an installation in the United Kingdom, and also when it is discharged at a port or terminal in a non-Fund

131 [1982] AC 341 at p.354f; [1981] 1 All ER 961 at p.967.

132 Section 2(3).

133 Section 2(4).

134 The Secretary of State for Transport may, by regulations, require security for payment; no regulations have as yet been made.

135 Section 4(7).

136 Section 4(8).

Convention country.[132] Where oil is imported into the United Kingdom payment is by the importer, and in other cases by the person receiving the oil,[133] subject to a remission of payment where the annual total imported is less than 150,000 tonnes. The amount of contributions and times for payment are determined by the Assembly of the Fund under Articles 11 and 12 of the Fund Convention, as are rates of interest on late payment.[134]

By section 4(1) of the 1974 Act the Fund is liable for pollution damage if the person suffering damage has been unable to obtain full compensation from the Liability Convention because the discharge or escape that caused the damage arose through various specified exceptional extrinsic causes or through intentional acts, or because the owner or guarantor is unable to meet his obligations in full. The concern with commercial accidents is emphasised by the exclusion of acts of war and pollution by warships,[135] and also of negligent or intentional damage.[136] For these purposes section 1(3) provides a wide definition of pollution damage, including 'damage caused outside the ship carrying oil by contamination resulting from the escape or discharge of oil from the ship, wherever occurring' and the cost of preventative measures and further damage caused by preventative measures. Preventative measures are also defined in the same section as meaning 'any reasonable measures taken by any person after the occurrence to prevent or minimise pollution damage'.

8

Drainage and Sewerage

DEFINITIONS

The treatment of this subject must necessarily begin with some consideration of the terms 'drain' and 'sewer'. Both words are in common use and have broad, and therefore imprecise, general meanings. They are, however, subject to specific legal definition and differentiation. As will be seen, the reason for such precise classification and its importance, reflected in the voluminous case law on the subject, relates to ownership and consequent responsibility for maintenance and repair. It is also worth noting as a preliminary principle that the basis of classification is therefore use or function rather than construction, size or any other physical characteristic. This view is emphasised by section 219(2) of the Water Industry Act 1991, which provides that

> references to a ... drain or sewer, shall include references to a tunnel or conduit which serves or is to serve as the pipe in question and to any accessories for the pipe.

It is what it does rather than what it is that is the determining factor.

The definitions of 'drain' in section 343(1) of the Public Health Act 1936 and section 219 of the Water Industry Act 1991 are identical, both providing that:

> drain means a drain used for the drainage of one building or of any buildings or yards appurtenant to buildings within the same curtilage.

Those same provisions also define 'sewer' in terms that are sufficiently similar to have the same effect, section 219(1) providing that:

> sewer includes all sewers and drains (not being drains within the meaning given by this subsection) which are used for the drainage of buildings and yards appurtenant to buildings.

The two definitions are therefore, and necessarily, complimentary and comprehensive. If a given length of pipe is not a drain it must be a sewer. It is however to be noted that the comprehensive nature of the definitions, and therefore the scope of the attendant legislation, is restricted in two respects. Both definitions are expressly confined to buildings and associated yards and also, by implication, include both foul and surface water. They do not therefore extend to systems of pipes provided for agricultural or land drainage. In consequence, for example, a natural underground watercourse did not become a sewer when the owner of the land piped it.[1] Secondly, natural rivers and streams cannot be or become sewers. In his judgement in *George Legge & Son* v *Wenlock Corporation* (1938)[2] Lord Maugham said that while prior to the Public Health Act 1875 a natural stream could have become a sewer it was no longer possible for such to be the case. The discharge of effluent into a natural watercourse, including those that have been improved or modified, will not convert them into sewers but will constitute a pollution offence.[3]

1 *Shepherd* v *Croft* [1911] 1 Ch 521.

2 [1938] AC 204.

3 See section 85 of the Water Resources Act 1991, and at p.162. above

The distinction between a sewer and a natural watercourse was in issue in *British Railways Board* v *Tonbridge and Malling DC* (1981).[4] On the construction of a railway embankment in the nineteenth century three natural water courses had been diverted into a culvert through the embankment. Due to subsequent residential development upstream the flow of surface water through the culvert had increased substantially. The British Railways Board now contended that the culvert, as a sewer, was the responsibility of the water authority. The Court of Appeal agreed with the first instance view that the question turned on function. Oliver LJ, as he then was, noted that the culvert taking the redirected natural watercourses in consequence of the embankment did not thereby become a sewer. The later addition of surface water from the housing estate did not affect that. Conversely, in *Hutton* v *Esher UDC* (1973),[5] the Court of Appeal, on comparable but sufficiently different facts, came to the opposite conclusion. The local authority proposed to construct a large pipe to take flood water from a river to prevent serious flooding. In addition the pipe would drain several miles of road and drain surface water from houses, shops, offices etc. The pipe was to cross the plaintiff's land necessitating the demolition of his bungalow. The question for the Court was whether the pipe was a public sewer within section 15(1)(1) of the 1936 Act, thus giving the local authority, subject to procedural requirements, power to undertake the demolition. In holding that it was a public sewer, Russell LJ said[6]:

> Undoubtedly the function of draining this very large number of houses, shop and offices etc., of their surface drainage does or would qualify it for the title of 'public sewer', and the fact that it also for convenience will absorb drainage from several miles of road and also for convenience will take water directly out of the river in times of flood, cannot really sensibly be said to deprive it of that title.

The distinctions between these cases leading to their respective results are instructive. In the first place, it is evident that in *Hutton* a, although not the only, purpose in constructing the pipe was to take surface water drainage from buildings. This clearly brings it within the definition of a sewer, and the other intended uses do not detract from that. In the *Tonbridge and Malling* case the original culverting of the natural watercourses did not change their function or their nature. They, or subsequently it, remained a watercourse. The later discharge of surface water into the culvert either by run-off from paved areas or through drains cannot, on the basis of the decision in *George Legge and Son* v *Wenlock Corporation*, above, alter that.

The essential distinction between a drain and a sewer is that a drain serves one property and for purposes of ownership and responsibility is part of that property; whereas a sewer serves several and is therefore the responsibility of several, or of the relevant sewerage authority. The change in identity, from drain to sewer, is therefore the point of junction of one drain with others. In *Beckenham UDC* v *Wood* (1896)[7] it was said that

> a pipe or line of pipes receiving the drainage of more than one building ... although a sewer from and below the point where it receives the drainage of more than one such building is a drain and not a sewer ... above that point.

So in *Holland* v *Lazarus* (1897)[8] a drain taking rainwater from a house roof and being connected, without authority, into the drain of the adjoining property, converted it into a sewer from the point of connection. On the basis of, it has to be

4 (1981) 79 LGR 565, CA.

5 [1973] 2 All ER 1123; 2 WLR 917.

6 At p.1129.

7 (1896) 60 JP 490.

8 (1897) 66 LJ QB 285.

said, rather special reasoning a majority of the Court of King's Bench, in *Poplar Board of Works v Knight* (1858),[9] decided that a wall was a sewer.

A line of pipes remains a drain even though draining a number of buildings if they are within the same curtilage. The meaning of 'curtilage' has received considerable judicial consideration in the contexts of planning and property valuation and rating as well as drainage. However, a consideration of the term may begin with two closely associated Court of Appeal decisions in the drainage context: *Vestry of St Martin in the Fields v Bird* (1895)[10] and *Pilbrow v St Leonards Shoreditch Vestry* (1895).[11] Both cases involved the development of land by the owner who subsequently leased the properties to tenants. In both cases the properties drained into a main drain running under the central passage or yard into a public sewer. The judgment of Rigby LJ in the second case, though he dissented on the facts, establishes that the curtilage is not merely a fence or boundary, that while it belongs to a messuage it cannot be associated with or common to two or more messuages and that the boundary includes and encloses the buildings and curtilage. It also appears that a building itself does not have a curtilage, but if located on a site including additional ground such as yards or gardens it does. This also appears to follow from Lord Esher's statement in the first case[12]:

> If there is any curtilage at all it must be the passage and that only, and the houses of the arcade are not within the passage, but at its side; so that the definition in the section, 'premises within the same curtilage' has no application.

Applying these principles to the two sets of facts the Court came to different conclusions. The former case concerned the Lowther Arcade, a roofed central passage with houses and shops on either side and used, though without any right, by the public as well as the tenants. As the complex consisted of many properties held by different persons, the Court unanimously found that the main pipe down the central passage taking their drainage was a sewer. The central passage could not be regarded as the curtilage specific to any of the individual properties. The development in the second case consisted of two blocks of buildings containing 46 apartments separated by a 20 yard wide yard or causeway, all within a boundary wall with one entrance from the street. The majority decided that the whole unit was intended to be used as one, i.e., for the purpose of letting out on short tenancies. The use of parts of the buildings, stairs, yard and so on in common by the tenants and the effective exclusion of others also influenced the decision. Lord Esher MR, on the interpretation of the term, said[13]:

> the question [depends] on considerations relating to the mode of building, the object with which the buildings have been erected, and the manner in which they have been used

and concluded that as the owner had clearly constructed and used the properties as a commercial, profit-making enterprise it would be wrong to impose on the local authority responsibility for the drainage. The central pipe in this case therefore remained a drain.

It remains to state what is implicit in the foregoing, that a curtilage consists of one integral plot or area of land. This appears from the judgement in *Methuen-Campbell v Walters* (1979),[14] a 'right to buy' case under the Leasehold Reform Act 1967, holding that:

> Whether land fell within the curtilage of other land was a question of fact and although the house and paddock were demised and occupied together, and the paddock provid-

9 (1858) E. B. & E. 408.

10 [1895] 1 QB 428.

11 [1895] 1 QB 433.

12 At p.431.

13 At p.437.

14 [1979] QB 525; 1 All ER 606.

ed a valuable amenity or convenience for the occupant of the house, since at all material times the paddock had been physically separated from the house, it was not within the curtilage of the house.

5 At pp.543–4

6 [1988] 3 WLR at p.219.

In his judgement Buckley LJ,[15] in a statement adopted by the Court of Appeal in *Dyer* v *Dorset CC* (1988),[16] said:

> In my judgement, for one corporeal hereditament to fall within the curtilage of another, the former must be so intimately associated with the latter as to lead to the conclusion that the former in truth forms part and parcel of the latter. There can be very few houses indeed that do not have associated with them at least some few square yards of land, constituting a yard or a basement area or passageway or something of the kind, owned and enjoyed with the house, which on a reasonable view could only be regarded as part of the messuage and such small pieces of land would be held to fall within the curtilage of the messuage. This may extend to ancillary buildings, structures or areas such as outhouses, a garage, a driveway, a garden and so forth. How far it is appropriate to regard this identity as parts of one messuage or parcel of land as extending must depend on the character and the circumstances of the items under consideration. To the extent that it is reasonable to regard them as constituting one messuage or parcel of land, they will be properly regarded as all falling within one curtilage; they constitute an integral whole ...

7 See especially the
dgements of the House of
ords in *Weaver* v *Family
ousing Association (York)
td* (1975) 74 LGR 255.

8 [1979] JPL 305.

Returning to the definition, then, a drain drains, on the one hand, one building and, on the other, a number of buildings if they are used in common and are on the same plot or piece of land. What constitutes 'one building' is closely related to the meaning of 'curtilage' and, as a question of fact, is determined, *inter alia*, by structural integrity, use and ownership.[17] In *Cook* v *Minion* (1979),[18] Walton J, applying *Weaver* (below) and earlier authorities, found that two contiguous cottages in the same ownership but separately occupied were a single building, and that therefore the two water closets in the gardens were within the curtilage of the building. This seems, with respect, an unsatisfactory application of the principles. In particular, it appears to over-emphasise ownership as opposed to use as a determining factor. Although the application of principle may be doubtful the result is clearly right when applied to drainage, the burden of repair and maintenance being cast on the owner rather than the local authority.

Consideration of the scope of 'drain' and 'sewer' next requires attention to the head of the system. At what point does a pipe discharging from a building become a drain? The general assumption is that pipes above ground are not drains; a view supported by the wording of section 59 of the Building Act 1984 and section 27 of the Local Government (Miscellaneous Provisions) Act 1982, both, in relation to the enforcement of remedial action, deeming it necessary to specify above ground apparatus as well as drains. If, as has been said, the definition is related to responsibility for repair and maintenance, the issue is only likely to become a matter for dispute when the pipe is underground and out of sight; the dispute intensifying with distance from the particular premises. Conversely, where the pipes are fastened to or contained within the structure they will self-evidently be as much the responsibility of the building owner as any other part of the structure.

However, this clear distinction loses its precision where, for example, a horizontal system of pipes, instead of being underground, is suspended in the basement or sub-basement of a building. In most cases, and for the reasons already given, whether one chooses to call it a drain or soil or waste pipe will be immaterial; as it is conveying effluent from the building in question, the building owner will be responsible in any event. The issue becomes important, though, where such a pipe conveys drainage from buildings in different ownership. Though being within a building, and though apparently indistinguishable from other pipes, regard being had to the function performed, the statutory definition is to be applied in finding that it is a sewer. So the House of Lords found in *Weaver* v *Family Housing Association (York) Ltd* (1975),[19] holding that a six inch pipe running through the cellar of a terrace house in York and draining the whole terrace was a public sewer and not a drain.

The statutory definitions of both drain and sewer, being related to function, are expressed in terms of use. What non-use, if any, will take them outside the definition? The question was answered by Stamp J in *Blackdown Properties Ltd* v *Minister of Housing and Local Government* (1965).[20] The plaintiffs had constructed a housing estate with a sewer in accordance with the requirements of and with the consent of the local authority. Following a change of plan, and after a few months' use, part of the sewer was sealed off in 1960. On 23 July 1962 the local authority, pursuant to section 17(1) of the Public Health Act 1936, notified its intention of making a declaration vesting the whole sewer in itself. The question was whether the sealed up part was a sewer for the purposes of section 17. Deciding that it was, the judge approached the matter in the following way:

> Once it is conceded that a sewer is a pipe to drain buildings, it becomes a sewer and in my judgement remains a sewer in this case notwithstanding that the actual user has ceased ...The question is not whether the pipe is performing the function of a sewer but for what function it was constituted and exists. The test is not whether the article is performing functions, but whether it can be still described as an article for performing them. As I have indicated, a mower being a machine used for mowing lawns remains in my judgement such a machine notwithstanding that one finds it in a museum of agricultural and garden machinery.

The same reasoning would presumably also apply to a sewer constructed as such but not so far used at all. That does not necessarily mean that once a sewer always a sewer; its use, and therefore classification, may change, as recognised in *Kershaw* v *Alfred John Smith & Co. Ltd* (1913),[21] where a sewer, as a result of alterations, became a drain.

Turning now to a consideration of sewers and their subdivision into public and private, one may commence with the observation of Buckley J in *Pakenham* v *Ticehurst RDC* (1903)[22] that they

> must be in some form a line of flow by which sewage or water of some kind such as would be conveyed through a sewer, should be taken from a point to a point and then discharged. It must have a *terminus a quo* and a *terminus ad quem*. There must be a line of flow from one to the other. It was decided in *Meader* v *West Cowes Local Board* (1892) 3 Ch 18, that if you have a thing which conveys sewage, but has no outfall at all, but simply terminates in a pit on the land of the person who lays the pipe, that is not a sewer.

He went on to add that a sewer, even if wrongly laid, for instance without proper authority, would still be a sewer. So, as an example, in *Clark* v *Epsom RDC* (1929)[23] a private estate was constructed, initially without drainage. In 1912 a private drainage system was provided and maintained by the owners without any reference to or approval of the local authority. It drained the houses into a septic tank and filter bed and then via a ditch, into the river Mole. Subsequently

19 (1975) *The Times*, 18 December 1975; and see to the same effect *Travis* v *Uttley* [1894] 1 QB 233.

20 [1965] 2 All ER 345 at p.348g.

21 [1913] 2 KB 455.

22 (1903) 67 JP 448 at p.449.

23 [1929] 1 Ch 287.

in 1914 the filter bed, having ceased to function, was disconnected and the efflu-ent discharged over adjoining land. The Court considered that when constructed the system comprised a sewer.

In distinguishing between public and private sewers, one may commence by noting that a private sewer is defined simply as 'a sewer which is not a public sewer'. The present definition of 'public sewer' in section 219(1) of the Water Industry Act 1991 is:

> a public sewer means a sewer for the time being vested in a sewerage undertaker in its capacity as such, whether vested by virtue of a scheme under Schedule 2 to the Water Act 1989 or Schedule 2 to this Act or under section 179 above or otherwise, and a pri-vate sewer is to be construed accordingly.

Section 179(1) and (7) provide that when a sewerage undertaker lays a sewer it shall vest in the undertaker. The definition is however at pains to make clear that not all pipes owned by a sewerage undertaker are thereby sewers. As with any other owner of property, the pipes serving it will be either drains or private sew-ers according to the same criteria as apply to persons generally.

The significance of the distinction between private and public in this context was indicated by Lord Russell of Killowen in *Bradford* v *Mayor of Eastbourne* (1896).[24] He said that private

> means a drain originally constructed for the drainage of one or more houses, as distin-guished from a drain or sewer which any member of the public may have a right to use by connecting with it the drain from his own house.

The issue here, as in many other such disputes, concerned the ability of the local authority to recover the costs of repair, in this case under section 40 of the Public Health Act 1875, which may be done in the case of private but not public sewers. The other important distinction adverted to by Lord Russell is that the public at large has a right of connection to a public sewer.[25]

25 See section 106 of the Water Industry Act 1991 and at p.215 below.

Sewers may be vested in an undertaker in various ways, now to be considered, but broadly they divide into two categories – new and existing. New sewers pre-sent few conceptual or identification problems. They are either sewers construct-ed by a sewerage undertaker under powers conferred by sections 158 and 159 of the Water Industry Act 1991 which automatically vest in them, or they are sew-ers constructed by another and subsequently adopted by the undertaker. Section 102 of the same Act gives a sewerage undertaker power to adopt any sewer or sewage disposal works constructed after 1 October 1937, the date of commence-ment of the Public Health Act 1936. The procedure, by vesting declaration, is specified in the section and provides for notice to the owners and right of appeal to the Secretary of State. In most cases, and especially in the case of new devel-opment, the expectation will be that, as with roads, the sewers constructed by the developer and to the undertaker's requirements will be adopted on completion and thereafter be the responsibility of the undertaker. To this effect section 104 provides for a prior agreement between the person proposing to construct a sewer and the authority that the latter will make a vesting declaration following com-pletion of the work and subject to its construction in the manner specified in the agreement. The sewer then vests in the authority, i.e., becomes a public sewer, from the date of the declaration. Such vesting does not affect or reduce any exist-ing rights of use and any person entitled to use the sewer before that date is entitled to do so to the same extent after.

Some reference may be appropriate here to the meaning of 'vesting' in this context, it being generally regarded as synonymous with the transfer of ownership. That that is not the case, and that it signifies something less than the passing of title is apparent from, for example, Lord Russell of Killowen in *Bradford* v *Mayor of Eastbourne* (1896)[26]:

26 [1896] 2 QB 205 at p.211.

> It has been clearly held that vesting is not a giving of the property in the sewer and in the soil surrounding it to the local authority, but giving such ownership and such rights only as are necessary for the purpose of carrying out the duties of a local authority with regard to the subject matter.[27]

27 See also *Coverdale* v *Charlton* (1878) 4 QBD 104; *Rolls* v *Vestry of St George, Southwark* (1980) 14 Ch D 785.

Existing sewers present a more complex picture consequent upon their legislative history. They are sewers which, being previously vested in a former water authority, became vested on the Transfer Date (1 September 1989) in the successor sewerage undertaker. What sewers were so vested requires a consideration of the law governing the question prior to 1989, but they may be initially classified as follows:

(a) sewers constructed by or vested in the water authority including those within section 20 of the Public Health Act 1936, i.e.
    (i)   sewers within the Public Health Act 1875,
    (ii) combined drains constructed before 1 October 1937,
    (iii) sewers and sewage disposal works constructed or acquired by a local authority,
    (iv) sewers and sewage disposal works subject to a vesting declaration under the 1936 Act;
(b) sewers constructed under Part IX of the Highways Act 1959.

With regard to (a) above, it is clear that sewers constructed after the date when the 1973 Act came into operation and water authorities were created, i.e., 1 April 1974, are in a similar position to the new sewers considered above and constructed by water undertakers after 1 September 1989. This in effect moves the scope of 'new public sewers' back to 1 April 1974. The 'vested' category referred to above is more complex. Prior to the creation of water undertakers by the 1973 Act, local authorities, i.e., district or London Borough councils, were the drainage and sewerage authorities for their areas. At the change over, by an arrangement under section 15, sewers vested in local authorities became vested in their successor water authorities. Where no such arrangements were made, a minority of cases, the sewers remained vested in the local authority. The antecedent question is, then, what sewers were vested in the local authorities? It is first to be noted that the present local authorities acquired by transfer, under the Local Government Act 1972,[28] the sewers vested in their predecessors. That earlier vesting occurred under section 20 of the Public Health Act 1936, which contained the five categories listed above. Its provisions concerning the sewering of streets may now be regarded as subsumed within the highways legislation. It now remains to consider the four elements of section 20 listed above.

28 See sections 68, 181(2) and 254.

As to (i) above, the definition of 'sewer' in section 4 of the Act is related to the associated definition of 'drain' but can perhaps be succinctly paraphrased as a pipe serving more than one building or premises not within the same curtilage. That latter term has been considered above. Section 13 was the vesting provision and provided that, 'All existing and future sewers within the district of a local authority ... shall vest in and be under the control of such local authority'. The four exceptions appearing in the omitted text were sewers constructed:

(a) for private use or profit; or
(b) used for land drainage; or
(c) under the authority of the Crown; or
(d) by any other agency with statutory authority to construct sewers.

29 *Southstrand Estate Development Co. v East Preston RDC* [1934] Ch 254.

30 [1893] 2 QB 135.

31 See also *Pinnock v Waterworth* (1887) 3 TLR 563; *Vowles v Colmer* (1895) 64 LJ Ch 414; *Solihull RDC v Ford* (1932) 30 LGR 483; *Bonella v Twickenham Local Board* (1887) 18 QBD 577.

32 See, e.g., *Ferrand v Hallas Land and Building Co.* [1893] 2 QB 135; *R v Godmanchester LB* (1886) LR 1 QB 328 .

33 *The Law of Sewers and Drains*, Professor J.F. Gower. Shaw & Sons: Dartford, 7th edn, June 1991 p.30.

The interpretation of 'profit', though said to be a matter of fact,[29] presents difficulties, not the least of which is that most construction work is done for profit. In *Ferrand v Hallas Land and Building Co.* (1893),[30] though, the Court considered that where a builder had constructed a private housing estate for sale the associated sewer had not been constructed for profit within this exception.[31] In conclusion, in the second exception it appears that the wording may be taken to mean 'exclusively used for ...', the discharge into a land drain of effluent making it thereafter a sewer.[32]

With regard to (ii) above, from the point where the drain from an individual property joins another or others it may be said to be a combined drain or private sewer. For practical purposes the terms are virtually synonymous. Such a line of pipes, taking drainage from two or more properties and designated before the operative date of the 1936 Act a combined drain, by this provision becomes a public sewer. A similar line of pipes constructed after that date is a private sewer.

The category set out in (iii) above covers what Professor J.F. Garner refers to as 'sewers properly so called',[33] and includes sewers constructed by the authority or its predecessors and in any capacity, for example as owner of a housing estate. In this latter case a declaration by the local authority was necessary to constitute the sewer as a public sewer. This widely drawn class is subject to two exceptions: first, where the local authority constructs a sewer at the expense of some other person, that is under section 36 or 275 of the Public Health Act 1936, it does not vest under this provision and therefore remains a private sewer. Secondly, where a local authority constructs a sewer after 1 April 1974, the operative date of the Water Act 1973, it will not become a public sewer unless or until adopted by the sewerage undertaker.

Under (iv) above, the sewer vests in the sewerage undertaker from the date of the declaration and existing rights of use are not affected. An owner may apply for a declaration to be made under section 102 of the Water Industry Act 1991.

The classification in (b) above covers all sewers constructed under Part IX of the Highways Act 1959, except sewers associated with a road maintained by the highway authority. This category relates to streets made up at the expense of frontagers under Part XI of the Highways Act 1980. That provision enables a highway authority to require a private street to be sewered, paved, repaired etc., to its satisfaction. A sewer, having been constructed under these provisions, vested in the local authority, subsequently the sewerage undertaker, as a public sewer.

In conclusion, the significance and consequences of the distinction between drain, private sewer and public sewer, already referred to, require consideration. The difference may be succinctly expressed as responsibility. A drain, draining one premises in the same occupation and use, is as much a part of the building as any other structural element and is therefore equally the reponsibility of the owner. This responsibility extends for the full length of the drain; that is until it joins with another drain or sewer. Enforcement action, for example under sections 59 or 60 of the Building Act 1984, is therefore taken against the owner of the building, or, in some cases, the occupier.

In the case of private sewers, responsibility for the necessary works of maintainance and repair and for the cost rests with the owners, and in some cases the occupiers, of the properties using that particular length of sewer.[34] This broad division of responsibility applying in the majority of cases may be displaced in two circumstances: (i) where the person causing the damage can be identified, and (ii) in the case of an emergency, where the authority may do the necessary remedial work and then recover the costs from the owners. Responsibility for public sewers, both physical and financial, rests of course with the sewerage undertaker.

DRAINAGE

New buildings

As with other aspects of new building provision, including alterations and extensions, the adequacy of its drainage is a matter for control under the Building Regulations 1991.[35] Section 21(1) of the Building Act 1984[36] provides that where plans are submitted to the local authority for approval under the Regulations they must be rejected unless:

(a) the plans show that satisfactory provision will be made for the drainage of the building or of the extension, as the case may be; or
(b) the local authority is satisfied that in the case of the particular building or extension it may properly dispense with any provision for drainage.

The effectiveness of the drainage here relates exclusively to the needs of the building concerned and not, for example, to the condition of the receiving sewer or other factors.[37] This general principle is, however, subject to two qualifications. The authority may not require a drain to connect to a sewer unless the sewer is within one hundred feet, measured horizontally,[38] of the building concerned; that is, of the building itself and not the curtilage.[39] The levels must also permit connection and there must be a right of drainage through any intervening land. Where, in spite of these restrictions, the local authority insists on connection it is required to 'bear so much of the expenses reasonably incurred in constructing the drain as may be attributable to the fact that the distance of the sewer exceeds' one hundred feet.[40] Secondly, if the local authority requires that drain to differ from the applicant's proposals in relation to size, depth, fall etc., so that it shall form part of a general sewerage system, it may require him, subject to a right of appeal, to construct it according to its requirements.[41] In such cases the local authority shall reimburse 'the extra expenses reasonably incurred by him in complying with their requirements'.

Returning to the Building Act 1984, section 22(1) provides that where plans for the separate drainage of buildings are submitted, the authority may require them to be drained in combination through a private sewer constructed either by the owners under the direction of the authority, or by the authority on behalf of the owners. This power is available to the local authority only when the drains are first laid. On subsequent occasions, such as alterations or extensions, drainage in combination requires the agreement of the owners. Further, the authority may insist on such combined drainage only where it appears to the authority that it is

34 See, for example, section 27 of the Local Government (Miscellaneous Provisions) Act 1982.

35 S.I. 1991 No. 2768.

36 Re-enacting section 37 of the Public Health Act 1936.

37 See *per* Lord Goddard CJ in *Chesterton RDC v Ralph Thompson Ltd* [1947] 1 All ER 273.

38 Interpretation Act 1978, section 8.

39 *Meyrick v Pembroke Corporation* (1912) 76 JP 365.

40 Section 21(5).

41 Section 19 of the Public Health Act 1936. A similar power is given to sewerage undertakers by section 112 of the Water Industry Act 1991.

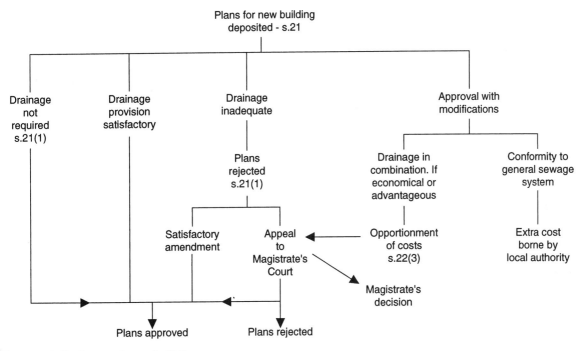

Figure 8.1 Drainage of new buildings

more economical or advantageous. The authority must then fix the proportions to be borne by each owner of the costs of construction, maintainance and repair and notify such determination to them.

A detailed treatment here of the Building Regulations 1991 would not be appropriate to the purpose of this work, nor is it necessary. There are exhaustive commentaries on the effect and operation of the Regulations for use by those engaged in the industry.[42] A series of 'approved documents' has been produced to accompany the Regulations which provides practical guidance in meeting the regulation requirements, their status and contents being advisory. Drainage is dealt with in Chapter 17 of the Regulations, supported by approved document H.[43] The Schedule to the Regulations containing the detailed provisions, deals in Part H with drainage in:

- H1 Sanitary pipework and drainage
- H2 Cesspools, septic tanks and settlement tanks
- H3 Rainwater drainage

There follows a brief review of those provisions:

Under H1, a drainage system conveying foul water from a building must be adequate.

'Foul water' means waste from:

(a) sanitary conveniences;
(b) other soil appliances;

42 See, e.g., Building Regulations Explained; John Stephenson, pub., (E & FN Spon) Chapman & Hall, London, 4th edition, 1993 – from which this synopsis is taken with approval.

43 See also BS 8301: 1985, code of practice for building drainage.

(c) water which has been used for cooking or washing.

The approved document indicates performance levels for sanitary pipework and drainage to minimise risks to health and safety, requiring that it must:

(a) carry all the foul water to a foul outfall which may be a sewer, cesspool, septic tank or settlement tank;
(b) not allow foul air from the drainage system to enter a building under working conditions;
(c) be ventilated;
(d) minimise risk of blockage or leakage;
(e) have access for removing blockages should they occur.

H2 requires that cesspools, septic tanks and settlement tanks are to be:

(a) of adequate capacity;
(b) impermeable to liquids;
(c) adequately ventilated;
(d) sited and constructed in such a way that they –
    (i)   are not prejudicial to the health of anyone,
    (ii) will not contaminate any underground water or water supply,
    (iii) will have adequate means of access for emptying.

The approved document indicates acceptable performance levels as follows:

(a) Cesspools are to be large enough to hold foul water from a building until they can be emptied.
(b) Septic and settlement tanks are to be large enough to enable breakdown and settlement of solid matter in the foul water.
(c) Cesspools, septic tanks and settlement tanks are to be so constructed that the do not leak contents into the surrounding soil or allow groundwater to enter the tank. They are to be adequately ventilated.
(d) Cesspools, septic tanks and settlement tanks must not be constructed in a position which will give rise to conditions prejudicial to health, or contaminate water supplies.
(e) There is to be satisfactory access for emptying.[44]

44 And see BS 6297: 1983, code of practice for design and installation of small sewage works and cesspools.

H3 requires that any system carrying rainwater from the roof of a building must be adequate for that purpose. The approved document sets levels of performance, in order that danger to the health and safety of people in the building will not be a risk. A rainwater drainage system must:

(a) convey the flow of rainwater to an outfall;
(b) minimise the possibility of blockage or leakage;
(c) have facility for clearing blockages should they arise.

Existing buildings

As has been seen above, a local authority has building control powers to ensure that new drainage conforms to the general system in the area. A similar power is given to sewerage undertakers under section 113 of the Water Industry Act 1991 in relation to existing drainage; section 113(1) providing that where the drain or sewer communicating with a public sewer or cesspool, though sufficient for the effectual drainage of the premises, is not adapted to the general sewerage system of the district, or is in the opinion of the authority otherwise objectionable, the authority may, at its own expense, provide an equally convenient drain or sewer and close the existing drain or sewer and fill up the cesspool, if any. There is of course, in section 113(2), the general requirement of notice to owners and a right of appeal to the magistrates' court.[45] 'Sewer' in this context is limited to private sewers. This power is limited to use in those cases where the existing provision is adequate for its purpose but does not comform to the authority's requirements. A common application will doubtless be the conversion of property using cesspools to main drainage.

45 Subsequent appeal to the Crown Court.

Powers are given to require disconnections of disused drains under the following sections of the Building Act 1984. Where the use of a drain is discontinued the local authority may, under section 62, require the owner to disconnect and seal it at such points as it may reasonably require. Secondly, in connection with the demolition of a building, sections 81 and 82 of the Act give the local authority power by notice to require 'the persons engaged in the demolition' to disconnect and seal any drain or sewer in or under the building at such points as it may reasonably require and/or to remove such conduit and seal any connecting sewer or drain. Such persons, by section 81(1), include:

(a) a person served with a demolition order under the Housing Act 1957 (now see Part IX of the Housing Act 1985);
(b) a person who appears not to intend to comply with an order under section 77 (dangerous building) or a notice under section 79 (ruinous and dilapidated buildings and neglected sites);
(c) a person who appears to have begun or to be intending to begin a demolition to which section 80 applies (intended demolition of whole or part of a building).

In both cases 48 hours' notice of compliance is required and failure to do the work is an offence punishable by fine, the local authority having, under section 82, the necessary default powers. The limitation in the exercise of these powers is that in neither case may a person be required to do work on land where they have no such rights. However, the presence of a private drain on another's land may generally be taken to carry with it an easement not only to drain through the land but also a reasonable right of access to the drain.

Where the drainage provision to a building is unsatisfactory local authorities have a range of remedial powers specific to the particular defect. The widest provision is section 59 of the Building Act 1984,[46] section 59(1) providing that: If it appears to a local authority that in the case of a building –

46 Re-enacting section 39 of the Public Health Act 1936.

(a) satisfactory provision has not been, and ought to be, made for drainage as defined in section 21(2) above,
(b) a cesspool, private sewer, drain, soil pipe, rain-water pipe, spout, sink or other necessary appliance provided for the building is insufficient or, in the case of a private sewer or drain communicating directly or indirectly with a public sewer, is so defective as to admit subsoil water,
(c) a cesspool or other such work or appliance as aforesaid provided, for the building is in such a condition as to be prejudicial to health or a nuisance, or
(d) a cesspool, private sewer or drain formerly used for the drainage of the building, but no longer used for it, is prejudicial to health or a nuisance, they shall by notice require the owner of the building to make satisfactory provision for the drainage of the building ...

'Insufficient' in (b) appears to have a very wide meaning, including not only inadequate appliances but also those that, though adequate, are defective in some way.
This is to be inferred from the phraseology of section 59(1) giving the authority
power to 'require either the owner or the occupier of the building to do such work
as may be necessary for renewing, repairing, or cleansing ...'. The concern in the
final clause of paraagraph (b) is not that a defective sewer or drain will leak foul
effluent into the surrounding ground but that, having regard to basic principles
of hydrology, it will act as an agricultural or land drain and unnecessarily increase
the burden on the treatment works. The terms 'prejudicial to health' and 'nuisance' have the meanings discussed in the context of statutory nuisances.[47]

47 See p.70.

Subordinate to section 59, section 60 is concerned with unsatisfactory ventilation of drains, specifically providing that:

(a) No pipe for conveying rainwater from a roof shall be used for the purpose of conveying the soil or drainage from any sanitary convenience;
(b) The soil pipe from every watercloset shall be properly ventilated;
(c) No pipe for conveying surface water from any premises shall be permitted to act as
a ventilating shaft to any drain or sewer carrying foul water.

Remedial action under both sections is by notice to the person responsible, either
the owner or occupier, although only the owner can be required to provide drainage.
On failure to comply, the local authority may do the work in default and recover the costs as a contract debt in the county court or High Court.[48] If the person
debited is the owner of the premises, the costs may rank as a charge on the premises and therefore be registrable as a local land charge. The local authority may
also, or alternatively, institute summary proceedings for a fine.

48 Building Act 1984, section
107.

Enforcement procedures under the above sections including service of notice,
and expiration of the stipulated period of time before the local authority is able
to do the work in default may, if involving an unco-operative owner or the co-
ordination of several, incur unreasonable delay before an urgent problem is resolved.
In such emergency situations the Local Government (Miscellaneous Provisions)
Acts 1976–82 provide more expeditious procedures. Section 35 of the 1976 Act
gives a local authority the power to deal with obstructed private sewers and can
therefore be regarded as a co-ordinating measure, the authority being able to identify and secure the co-operation of a number of persons in less time than would
be the case if they were left to their own devices. The authority serves notices on
the owners or occupiers requiring the removal of the obstruction within a specified time, subject to a minimum period of 48 hours from service of the notices.
On default the local authority may do the work and recover its expenses from the
persons served with the notices. The position and, if discoverable, the cause of the
obstruction will assist in determining which of the owners and occupiers of the
properties draining into the sewer are to be served and, in consequence, charged
for clearance. The notice under section 35(3) for recovery of costs is to specify the
other persons served and the apportionment of costs; such apportionment having
regard, *inter alia*, to any agreement between the parties. That notice also carries
with it a right of appeal within six weeks to the county court, the emergency at
this stage having been resolved.

The Local Government (Miscellaneous Provisions) Act 1982, in section 27, substitutes a new section 17 for sections 17 and 18 of the Public Health Act 1961. Those
sections gave a local authority power respectively to deal with stopped up drains

and sewers and to secure their repair. Section 17(3) empowers a local authority by notice to require the owner or occupier of any premises, within 48 hours, to remedy a stopped-up drain, private sewer, water closet, waste pipe or soil pipe. It will be noticed that unlike section 35 of the 1976 Act above, dealing with a number of properties, this section provides a more prompt remedy to deal with a property in one ownership. Where the owner defaults the local authority may do the work and recover the costs, although these may be remitted if less than £10.

Repair is dealt with in section 17(1), which provides that a local authority may, after giving seven days' notice, cause a drain, private sewer, water closet, waste pipe or soil pipe to be repaired and recover the costs reasonably incurred up to £250, where it considers that such appliance:

(a) is not sufficiently maintained and kept in good repair; and
(b) can be sufficiently repaired at a cost not exceeding £250.

49 See *R v Epsom Union* (1863) 8 LT 363.

50 (1905) 93 LT 605.

51 At p.609.

The subsection is at pains to limit its operation to 'repair', which is to be distinguished from reconstruction.[49] What constitutes reconstruction was considered by Lord Alverstone CJ in *Agar v Noakes* (1905);[50] the question arising because a byelaw required the deposit of plans for the reconstruction of a drain but not for its repair. His Lordship said[51]:

> I think it is quite clear, as counsel for the respondents very properly put it, that the mere putting of one or more new pipes into an old drain would not be reconstruction of the drain. On the other hand, work of this kind done to a drain does not, in my judgement, cease to be reconstruction because the respondents in doing the work which they did do in this case used the old pipes and gully. In my opinion we ought to look at the real and substantial work that has been done. The drain has been pulled up; concrete has been put in as a foundation, and new pipes have been laid upon that foundation; one old pipe and one old gully have been used, and that seems to me to be entire reconstruction of the drain.

The persons on whom notice may be served are, by section 17(2), in relation to a water closet or waste or soil pipe, the owner or occupier of the premises, and in relation to a drain or private sewer, the owner of any premises drained by it. In litigation to recover expenses the court may consider whether the local authority's action was justified and also whether any apportionment of expenses was fair. As to the former issue, as was stated earlier, this section provides emergency powers and is specifically stated to be without prejudice to section 59 of the Building Act

52 Subsection (15); see above at p.205.

1984.[52] Being urgent the section curtails the normal right of persons affected to challenge the validity of the authority's action. It must therefore be able to justify the use of this emergency procedure in preference to other powers.

Where any work is to be done on an underground drain communicating with a sewer or receptacle for drainage, section 61 of the Building Act 1984 requires that a minimum of 24 hours' notice be given to the local authority. There are limited exceptions to this requirement, in particular in relation to emergency situations, although in such cases the provision applies to the covering in of the pipe in question. Where the relevant authority believes that a sanitary convenience, drain, private sewer or cesspool is in such a condition as to be prejudicial to health or a nuisance, or a drain or private sewer communicating with a public sewer is

53 As amended by Schedule 8, paragraph 29 of the Water Act 1973, and see section 141 of the Water Industry Act 1991.

so defective as to admit subsoil water, it has the power, under section 48 of the Public Health Act 1936,[53] to examine it and for that purpose to open up and/or apply a test. The power of entry for this and other purposes of the Act is con-

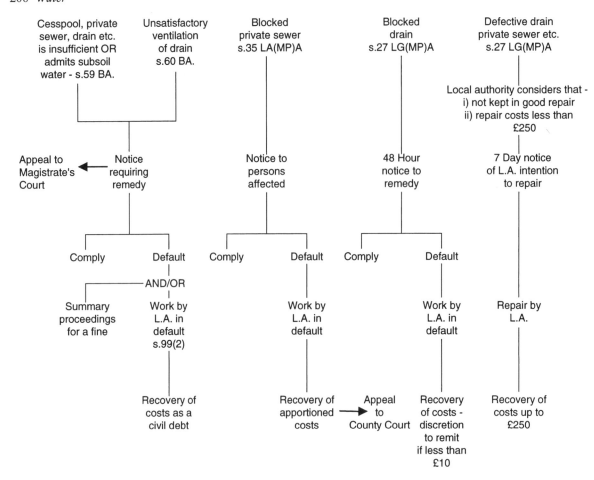

Figure 8.2 Defective drainage to existing buildings

tained in section 287. Where the appliance concerned is connected to a public sewer the relevant authority is the sewerage undertaker, and in other cases the local authority. The section is silent on the question of recovery of costs of examination or testing which therefore presumably fall on the authority.

In conclusion a reference to cesspools is necessary. In practice a cesspool is a tank or container for the reception and storage of sewage pending periodic removal for disposal, being generally used where the premises served cannot be connected to main drainage. The statutory definition,[54] however, is that a 'cesspool includes a settlement tank or other tank for the reception or disposal of foul matter from buildings', which therefore embraces cesspools as described above and septic tanks which provide a basic level of treatment before discharging the effluent. In this case removal of the resulting sludge is necessary, though at longer intervals than with cesspools that, theoretically, have no outlet. The following provisions should

54 Public Health Act 1936, section 90(1) and Building Act 1984, section 126.

55 As amended by Schedule 8, paragraph 40 of the Water Act 1973.

be read with this wider definition in mind. Section 50(1) of the Public Health Act 1936[55] empowers a local authority by notice to require the person by whose act, default or sufferance the contents of any cesspool soak or overflow therefrom to do such work as may be necessary to prevent the occurrence. The proviso to the subsection excludes tanks designed to treat sewage where the effluent is of such a character and so disposed of that it is not prejudicial to health or a nuisance. On failure to comply with the notice, where works are required the local authority may do the work in default and recover costs. In other cases the penalty is a fine following summary conviction.

SANITARY CONVENIENCES

General legislation governing the provision and adequacy of sanitary conveniences is contained in the Public Health Act 1936 and the Building Act 1984. Scales of provision for specialised categories of buildings and activities are to be found in the relevant controlling statutes and subordinate regulations; for instance in the case of employment, in the Health and Safety legislation. It is not proposed to deal with such codes here, there being a large body of material and commentary available elsewhere.[56] While the provisions now to be discussed may appear to be primarily concerned with residential premises, it should be borne in mind that the terminology in a particular case and in the absence of exclusionary clauses may be wide enough to include other classes of buildings.

56 See, for example, in that area, Redgrave, Fife and Machin, *Health and Safety*, 2nd edn (London: Butterworth & Co., 1993).

Definitions of terms in this context are to be found in section 90(1) of the Public Health Act 1936 and section 126 of the Building Act 1984, and are as follows:

> 'closet' includes privy;
> 'earth closet' means a closet having a moveable receptacle for the reception of faecal matter and its deodorisation by the use of earth, ashes or chemicals, or by other methods;
> 'sanitary conveniences' means closets and urinals;
> 'water closet' means a closet which has a separate fixed receptacle connected to a drainage system and separate provision for flushing from a supply of clean water either by the operation of mechanism or by automatic action.

It will be seen that the definition of 'earth closet' is wide enough to include chemical closets. Some uncertainty exists over the scope of the term 'closet' and whether, in consequence, the provisions governing repair, reconstruction etc., are confined to the appliance or extend to include the enclosing room or structure. Professor J.F. Garner notes[57] that the essential meaning of the word 'is that of a small room or retiring chamber'. He therefore argues that it should be so interpreted unless the particular context necessarily points to the more restricted meaning of the sanitary appliance itself.

57 *Op. cit.*, note 33, p.170, n.7.

The law requiring the provision of sanitary accommodation in new buildings approximates very closely to that already discussed above governing drainage. Section 26 of the Building Act 1984 provides that where plans for a building or extension to a building are deposited under the Building Regulations the local authority must reject the plans unless:

(a) the plans show that sufficient and satisfactory closet accommodation consisting of one or more water closets or earth closets, as the authority may approve, will be provided; or

(b) the authority is satisfied that in the case of the particular building or extension it may properly dispense with the provision of closet accommodation.

This provision applies to buildings generally, and the authority may require water closets only where a sufficient water supply and sewer are available. The availability of a sewer for this purpose is governed by section 125(2) of the Building Act 1984, which provides that it is to be within one hundred feet of the proposed building and the owner has a right of access through any intervening land. This distance may be exceeded where the local authority undertakes to bear the costs attributable to the additional distance. Section 26(3) gives a limited right of appeal against the local authority requirements, including whether the proposed closet accommodation is 'sufficient and satisfactory'. There is no statutory definition of this term and its interpretation would seem to be a matter of fact in the context of changing social attitudes and expectations. For example, in *Clutton Union* v *Ponting* (1879)[58] the Court agreed with the appellant that the provision of a separate closet or privy for every house could not be required. Such a decision would be inconceivable now.[59] Such changing social attitudes and expectations will in a similar way have rendered other authority deriving from the nineteenth century of little current practical value.[60]

The corresponding power to remedy deficiencies of provision in existing buildings is contained in section 64 of the Building Act 1984,[61] subsection (1) of which provides that if it appears to a local authority:

(a) that a building is without sufficient closet accommodation; or

(b) that a part of a building, being a part that is occupied as a separate dwelling, is without sufficient closet accommodation; or

(c) that any closets provided for or in connection with a building are in such a state as to be prejudicial to health or a nuisance and cannot without reconstruction be put into a satisfactory condition,

the authority shall by notice require the owner of the building to provide such additional or substituted closets as may be necessary. The authority may not insist on any particular type where that proposed is sufficient and satisfactory – *Robinson* v *Sunderland Corporation* (1898)[62] – nor require replacement of an earth closet unless a sewer and water supply are available as discussed above.

The operation of section 64(1)(c) is dependent upon the condition of the closet being such that reconstruction is necessary. Having regard to what was said above concerning the scope of 'closet', it is suggested that this subsection would apply where replacement of the sanitary appliance itself is required as well as structural work to the closet chamber. On the meaning of 'reconstruction', see Lord Alverstone CJ in *Agar* v *Noakes* (1905).[63]

Where reconstruction is not necessary and repair or cleansing will prove sufficient, section 45 of the Public Health Act 1936 will apply. This section provides that if it appears to a local authority that any closets provided for or in connection with a building are in such a state as to be prejudicial to health or a nuisance, but that they can without reconstruction be put into a satisfactory condition, the authority shall by notice require the owner or occupier to execute such works as may be necessary for that purpose. The nature of the work required will determine whether the owner or occupier is the appropriate recipient of the enforcement notice, cleansing and other work of a non-structural character being required of the occupier. By section 45(3) the defendant may question the reasonableness of the local authority's decision to proceed against either the owner or the occupier as the case may be.

58 (1879) 4 QBD 340.

59 See especially section 64(1)(b) of the Building Act 1984, below.

60 See, e.g., *R* v *Clutton* (1879) 4 QBD 340; *Wood* v *Widnes* [1898] 1 QB 463; *Clerkenwell Vestry* v *Feary* (1890) 24 QBD 703.

61 Re-enacting with amendments section 44 of the Public Health Act 1936.

62 (1898) 78 LT 19.

63 See note 50 above.

In the absence of any defects or insanitary conditions, section 66 of the Building Act 1984 gives a local authority the power to require that a water closet be substituted for a closet of any other type provided for, or in connection with, the building. The notice may require the owner to do the work, or notify that the local authority proposes to do the work itself. In either case the owner and the authority share the cost equally. Alternatively, where the owner initiates the action, the authority may, if it thinks fit, agree to bear half the cost of replacement.[64]

Emergency powers to deal with stopped-up drains in section 27 of the Local Government (Miscellaneous Provisions) Act 1982 extend also to water closets.[65]

SEWERAGE

The privatisation of the water industry by the Water Act 1989 provided for the appointment of private companies as sewerage undertakers to supply this service in place of local authorities. Their functions, now to be found in the Water Industry Act 1991, are the product of a long process of consolidation, re-enactment and refinement extending back to the public health legislation of the nineteenth century. While responsibility for these services now rests on sewerage undertakers, performance may be undertaken by agreement by the local authority for the area.[66] Such delegation, which may extend to the general statutory functions of a sewerage undertaker with the exception of sewage disposal,[67] does not prejudice any remedies against the undertaker for any failure or inadequacy of performance, whether by the undertaker, a local authority or any further delegatee;[68] delegation extending only to the discharge of, but not responsibility for, the function at least as far as the customer is concerned.

This division between performance and responsibility was emphasised by the Court of Appeal in *R* v *Yorkshire Water Services Ltd* (1994).[69] The company as sewerage undertakers had appointed Scarborough Borough Council as their agents; the arrangement being that the company decided matters of policy and programmes of work, while the day to day running of the sewerage system was delegated to the local authority. Sewage was discharged into controlled water contrary to section 107 of the Water Act 1989.[70] Having pleaded guilty, the appeal was against sentence, leading to a significant reduction in fines. In its reserved judgement the Court observed that even where the day to day management of sewers was undertaken by agents, water companies must be made to realise that the responsibility was still theirs and that they had to use their powers of instruction and supervision to ensure that discharges of effluent into controlled waters did not occur.[71]

Part IV of the Water Industry Act 1991 consists of three chapters:

Chapter I — General Functions of Sewerage Undertakers
Chapter II – Provision of Sewerage Services
Chapter III – Trade Effluent

There now follows a review of these provisions.

General functions of sewerage undertakers

The general broad scope of a sewerage undertaker's responsibility is established by section 94(1) of the 1991 Act, which imposes the duty:

64 Section 66(4).

65 See p.206 above.

66 Water Industry Act 1991, section 97.

67 See especially section 6(2) of the Water Industry Act 1991.

68 Local Government Act 1972, section 101.

69 (1994) *The Times*, 19 July.

70 Now section 85 of the Water Resources Act 1991.

71 In fact of course such discharges are inevitable and, to be lawful, must be authorised by a discharge consent under section 88(1)(a) of the Water Resources Act 1991.

(a) to provide, improve and extend such a system of public sewers ... and so to cleanse and maintain those sewers as to ensure that that area is and continues to be effectively drained; and

(b) to make provision for the emptying of those sewers and such further provision ... as is necessary ... for effectually dealing, by means of sewage disposal works or otherwise, with the contents of those sewers.

The wording of the section indicates that the duty is owed to persons with a right to drain into the system and does not extend, for example, to liability for loss or damage caused by sewer flooding. Such liability will therefore depend on proof of negligence by the undertaker according to general principles. In *Smeaton* v *Ilford Corporation* (1954),[72] for example, the existing sewer constructed in 1898 was overloaded by new developments. It was properly cleansed, but in time of heavy rain when the main sewers surcharged, back pressure in that sewer caused displacement of a manhole cover and flooding of the plaintiff's property. The Court found, *inter alia*, that the flooding was caused by overloading which was not due to any act of the defendants because, under section 34(1) of the Public Health Act 1936, they were bound to permit occupiers to discharge into the sewers and therefore the defendants had not created or continued the nuisance within section 31. Compliance with this duty is now secured by a section 18 enforcement order issued by the Secretary of State or, with his consent, by the Director.[73]

Subordinate to these broad duties, sections 95 and 96 give the Secretary of State, on a written application from the Director, power to make regulations specifying matters that will constitute a breach of section 94 and standards of performance for the provision of any sewerage service, together with financial penalties for failure. In making an application the Director must state his reasons and identify the undertaker(s) affected. The procedure then includes opportunity for representations and objections by the Director or any affected undertaker. The assumption is that such regulations are only likely to be used where informal advice or pressure to conform will be inadequate. The contents of any regulations made under these powers become part of the performance standards and are enforceable under section 94(3).[74] In carrying out these section 94 functions an undertaker is 'to have regard to' its obligations for the reception and disposal of trade effluent and also the present and possible future needs of its area.

This section re-enacts the duties previously found in section 23 of the Public Health Act 1936, and commenting on that section Professor J.F.Garner[75] suggests that 'cleanse' includes the clearance of obstructions, and 'maintain' includes all ordinary works of repair. The duty to maintain is restricted to the care of existing provision for current purposes and excludes improvement or extension, a distinction of less significance now in the context of the wider terms of the present section. Further, per Ungoed-Thomas J in *Radstock Co-operative and Industrial Society* v *Norton-Radstock UDC* (1967)[76]:

> I fail to see that the statutory obligation to 'maintain' the sewer includes any such extended obligation to maintain lands or conditions outside the sewer, as the plaintiffs suggest, or that it involves obligations to third parties like the plaintiffs who are complete strangers to the sewer.

The public sewer in this case had been constructed in part in the bed of a river. With time the river bed was washed away exposing the sewer, which caused eddies in the river flow that eroded and damaged the plaintiff's property.

72 [1954] Ch 540.

73 Enforcement orders and their procedure are dealt with in the introduction to this part at p.113.

74 Current regulations are the Water Supply & Sewerage Services (Customer Service Standards) Regulations 1989 (S.I. 1989 No. 1159) and the Water Supply & Sewerage Services (Customer Service Standards) (Amendment) Regulations 1989 (S.I. 1989 No. 1383).

75 *Op. cit.*, note 33, p.80.

76 [1967] Ch 1094 at p.1118.

The duty to empty public sewers would seem to include a duty to provide and maintain a proper outfall and to cause the contents to flow in the direction of the outfall. In *R v Tynemouth RDC* (1896)[77] a developer proposed to construct an estate of houses with drainage to the middle of the proposed new streets. The local authority required the provision of sewers connecting the drains and discharging to a main outfall sewer. The Court of Appeal, confirming the decision of the Queen's Bench Division, found that the authority was not entitled to make such a condition. A.L. Smith LJ said[78]:

77 [1896] 2 QB 451, CA.

78 At p.454.

> when these house drains have run the house drainage into the sewer in this street, and the sewer is run down to the edge of Lord Hasting's estate, then the obligation is cast upon the Tynemouth DC, within their district, of taking the whole of the sewage away and carrying it to a proper outfall.

As has already been emphasised in other contexts, these duties are irrespective of the location of the sewer and, for these purposes, a sewerage undertaker is given the necessary powers of entry by section 171.

The duty of sewerage undertakers to maintain, cleanse etc., is by section 67(4) enforceable by the Secretary of State or, with his consent, by the Director-General of Water Services. Sections 20 and 21 provide for the procedure and consequences of such enforcement action. Where a sewerage undertaker fails to comply with such an enforcement order, whether provisional or final, 'any person who may be affected by the contravention' and who suffers loss or damage thereby is given, in section 22, a right of action. The same section gives the undertaker a defence that he 'took all reasonable steps and exercised all due diligence to avoid contravening the order'.[79] In association with its duty to maintain, cleanse etc., a sewerage undertaker, as the owner of public sewers, may institute proceedings for damages or an injunction in the event of injury to those sewers.

79 See generally on enforcement orders in Chapter 5 at p.113.

Provision of sewerage services

Following the general terms of Chapter I, Chapter II of the 1991 Act, again largely derived from earlier statutes, makes provision for specific obligations. Section 98 imposes on an undertaker the duty to provide a public sewer for the drainage of premises for domestic purposes where a person entitled to the provision so requires by notice. The limiting criteria are that the premises do or shall contain buildings and the section 99 requirements concerning payment of or security for the costs of such provision are satisfied. Where these requirements are met, section 101(1) gives the undertaker six months from service of the notice to make the provision before being in default. The persons entitled under this section are the owner and occupier of any premises in the area served and the local authority. The phraseology indicates that the duty extends to the drainage of domestic effluent from non-domestic premises, and in this context 'domestic purposes' means[80] the domestic purposes specified in relation to those buildings in the requirement. For the purposes of Chapter II generally 'domestic sewerage purposes' means:

80 By section 98(5) of the Water Industry Act 1991.

(a) the removal from buildings and associated land, of the contents of lavatories;
(b) the removal, from buildings and such land, of water which has been used for cooking or washing; and
(c) the removal, from buildings and such land, of surface water, but excludes water used for the business of a laundry, or for the preparation of food or drink for consumption otherwise than on the premises.

The exception for laundry businesses gives statutory effect to the decision of the Court of Appeal in *Thames Water Authority* v *Blue & White Launderettes* (1980)[81] concerning the recovery of charges under section 14(1) of the Public Health (Drainage of Trade Premises) Act 1937 and therefore whether the effluent from the launderette came within the exception of 'domestic sewage', being consequently exempt from such charges. The Court said that:

> although the liquid discharged from washing machines in a launderette was identical to the liquid discharged from domestic washing machines, the purpose for which the activity was carried on was relevant, and accordingly, since all the effluent produced at the launderette was directly produced in the course of the trade or business of the launderette, it did not come within the exception of domestic sewage.

The significance of this statement of principle, of course, lies in its emphasis on the purpose for or within which the effluent was produced as well as its composition in determining the category into which it falls.

The general power to adopt sewers and sewage disposal works by declaration is given to a sewerage undertaker by section 102, ownership then being vested in the undertaker. An owner may request that such a vesting declaration be made, or the initiative may come from the undertaker. Two months' notice of intention to make the declaration is to be given to the owner or owners affected and no action shall be taken until either that time has elapsed without any appeal to the Secretary of State under section 105, or until any appeal has been determined. In deciding to make a declaration under this section an undertaker is, by subsection (5), required to consider all the circumstances, and in particular:

(a) whether the works may form part of the general sewerage system for the area;
(b) whether they are constructed under an existing or proposed street;
(c) the number of buildings and the likelihood of the addition of other buildings;
(d) the method of construction and state of repair; and
(e) where the owner objects, whether the making of the declaration would be seriously detrimental to him.

Having regard to an undertaker's powers of entry and power to prevent building over sewers, adoption should not be refused solely because the sewer is on private land.[82] Within subsection (5)(c) there is no minimum figure of buildings to be served, each case to be treated on its merits.[83] Within subsection (5)(e), on an owner's objection, the decision is on the basis of serious detriment. This may include, for example, increased likelihood of the sewer overflowing on his land or the possibility of a structural failure. Generally, however, adoption is likely to be regarded as beneficial to the owner.[84] A declaration will not affect any person's pre-existing rights of use of the sewer and, lastly, by subsection (7), is excluded for any sewer completed before 1st October 1937. This was the operative date of the Public Health Act 1936, and by section 20 of that Act such sewers automatically vested in the local authority as public sewers.

Section 104 applies similar principles to those just considered to proposed sewers or sewage disposal works. Where the work is or is to be done 'to comply with' the undertaker's requirements, for which purpose it may request reasonable information, the undertaker may agree to make a vesting declaration. Such an agreement is then enforceable against the sewerage undertaker and there is a right

81 [1980]1 WLR 700; see also *Met Water Board* v *Avery* [1914] AC 118.

82 DoE appeal decision, Westfield Drive, Bolton-le-Sands; 15 October 1987; W.S. 5523/AB/17.

83 DoE appeal decision, Portman Close, Dartford; 5 February 1987; W.S. 5274/AB/1.

84 DoE appeal decision, Stennet Ave., Spalding Re; 8 October 1987; W.S. 5530/AB/22.

of appeal by a person aggrieved to the Secretary of State against a decision or requirement of the undertaker.[85]

It has been seen that under section 98 persons have a right to require the provision of public sewers to receive domestic effluent from their premises. Section 106 provides the concomitant right of connection, giving an owner or occupier of premises or the owner of a private sewer an entitlement for his drains or sewer to communicate with the public sewers of the undertaker. This right is however limited[86] in that it does not include the right to discharge foul water into a surface water sewer nor, except with the approval of the undertaker, surface water into a foul water sewer. Further, this section gives no right to discharge trade effluent[87] or any other statutorily prohibited effluent into a public sewer. A person seeking connection must give notice to the undertaker, who may refuse, within 21 days, on the sole ground that the construction or condition of the drain makes such connection prejudicial to the sewerage system. The undertaker may not refuse to allow the connection on the ground that the system is inadequate to take the extra flow resulting from the connection,[88] the adequacy of the sewerage system being a matter for the undertaker. Neither may the undertaker, as a condition of the consent, require the applicant to pay its supervisory costs.[89] The undertaker has the power to require the drain to be opened up to determine its condition and an owner is given a right of appeal to the magistrates' court on the reasonableness of the undertaker's decision or of any requirements. Where such connection requires access through intervening land belonging to another, the consent of that other must first be obtained.[90]

On receiving notice under section 106, the sewerage undertaker may, within 14 days of such notice, notify the applicant of its intention to undertake the connection, which will include all ancillary work such as the opening up of the street. Having so notified the applicant, there is no duty on the undertaker to do the work until payment or security for payment of the reasonable estimate of costs has been received. Following notification of the undertaker's intention, it is a criminal offence liable to summary proceedings for the applicant to make the connection himself. Where the sewerage undertaker does not use its section 107 power to make the connection itself, the owner or occupier will have the same powers, as necessarily modified by Part VI, in relation to their drain as the undertaker has under sections 158 and 161(1), i.e., to lay pipes in the street etc. In doing the work they are required to notify the undertaker as it may require and to provide reasonable facilities for supervision.[91] Irrespective of criminal proceedings, section 109 also allows the undertaker to close the connection and recover its costs, although acquiescence in the connection may stop such action.[92]

Sections 111 to 116 give a sewerage undertaker a number of powers for the protection and effective operation of the sewerage system. First, and for that purpose, section 111 qualifies the general right of an owner under sections 98 and 106 to discharge drainage into the public sewers, prohibiting the discharge into a drain or sewer connecting with a public sewer:

(a) any matter likely to injure the sewer or drain, to interfere with the free flow of its contents or to affect prejudicially the treatment and disposal of its contents; or

(b) any chemical refuse or waste steam, or any liquid of a temperature higher than 110°F, being a prohibited substance under subsection (2); or

(c) any petroleum spirit or carbide of calcium.

85 Section 105.

86 Section 106(2).

87 See section 118(3) and (4).

88 *Smeaton v Ilford Corporation* [1954] Ch 450.

89 *R v Greenwich Board of Works* (1884) 1 Cab & E 236.

90 *Wood v Ealing Tenants* [1907] 2 KB 390.

91 Section 108.

92 *Clegg v Castleford Local Board* (1874) WN 229.

Section 111(2) then provides that the matters specified in section 111(1)(b) will be prohibited substances if they are, or in the case of the liquid when so heated if it is:

(a) dangerous;
(b) the cause of a nuisance;or
(c) injurious, or likely to cause injury, to health.

This provision is in addition to the controls on the discharge of trade effluent in Chapter III,[93] which have a different objective. The purpose here is to protect the structure of the sewers and disposal works, the free flow of the contents and the treatment process. The proscribed substances therefore include:

> [93] See below at p.220 and especially section 118(3)(b).

(a) those that are likely to have any of these undesired effects, the burden of establishing the necessary level of harm being on the undertaker;
(b) three classes of material that either inherently or in combination with other sewer contents exhibit the subsection (2) characteristics; and
(c) two specified substances that are self-evidently dangerous.

An illustration of the effect of the combination of two individually innocuous substances is provided by *St. Helens Chemical Co. v St Helens Corporation* (1876).[94] Discharges in separate outlets from the appellant's premises included muriatic acid and sulphur. While they were inoffensive in the appellant's drains, they combined in the sewer to produce sulphuretted hydrogen gas which escaped, causing a nuisance. Enforcement proceedings may be summary or on indictment and the court may also, as well as a penalty, stipulate the time within which any directions are to be satisfied.

> [94] (1876)1 Ex D 196.

The next two sections allow an undertaker to secure the conformity of drainage to the general system of the area. By section 112, it may require the construction of a proposed drain or sewer to form part of a general sewerage system, and to that end may specify different materials, size, depth, fall, direction, outfall etc. Subject to a 28-day right of appeal to the Secretary of State by the person aggrieved, there is a duty to comply with such requirements but the undertaker is to pay the extra expenses reasonably incurred in so complying. It may be expected that this provision would be used in conjunction with section 104. Where a drain or sewer is 'sufficient for the effectual drainage of the premises', but is not adapted to the general sewerage system of the area or is otherwise objectionable, section 113 empowers an undertaker to close it up at its own expense and to provide an equally convenient alternative. A wider power to discontinue the use of a public sewer either completely or for either foul water or surface water is provided by section 116. Again, persons having a right of use are to be provided with an equally effective replacement and the work is to be done at the undertaker's expense.

Lastly, section 114 gives an undertaker a general power to examine, test or open up any drain or sewer connecting with a public sewer that it reasonably believes to be injurious or likely to cause injury to health, or to be a nuisance or that is so defective as to admit subsoil water. The terminology is very similar to that of section 48 of the Public Health Act 1936 and gives a sewerage undertaker the powers given by that earlier provision to local authorities.

In order to carry out these duties a sewerage undertaker has power to lay public sewers under, respectively, streets and other land. In relation to street works, section 158 empowers a relevant authority:

(a) to lay a relevant pipe in, under or over any street and to keep it there;

(b) to inspect, maintain, adjust, repair or alter any relevant pipe in, under or over any street;

(c) to carry out any works necessitated by or incidental to any of these purposes, including in particular –

   (i) breaking up or opening the street,

   (ii) tunnelling or boring under it,

   (iii) breaking up or opening a sewer, drain or tunnel, and

   (iv) moving or removing earth or other material.

This and the following sections are expressed in terms sufficiently broad to apply to both water and sewerage undertakers, both being within the definition of relevant authority.[95] 'Relevant pipe' is defined by section 158(7) to include, *inter alia,* references to any sewer or disposal main. The definitions of 'street' under the earlier 1936 Act[96] and the Public Utilities Street Works Act 1950 make the term synonymous with 'highway', i.e., a way over which members of the public have a right to pass and repass. This definition applies whether the street or highway is made up or not, and whether its maintenance is a private or public responsibility. When working in or under streets the authority is governed by the street works code contained in the 1950 Act above, as are other public utilities. This essentially involves liaising with and meeting the requirements of the highway authority. If the sewer is properly laid, constructed and maintained any action arising from the presence of the sewer in the highway will fail on the defence of statutory authority. However, any deficiency of construction or maintenance amounting to negligence will render the authority liable to the persons thereby prejudiced.

Section 159 gives a sewerage undertaker the power in respect of land not in, under or over a street:

(a) to lay a relevant main, above or below the surface;

(b) to inspect, maintain, adjust or alter a relevant main; or

(c) to carry out works requisite for or incidental to any such works.

In respect of access for maintenance, repair and so on, it was said in *Birkenhead Corporation* v *L & NW Railway Co.* (1885)[97] that where a sewer is vested in an authority, the duty to maintain carries an implied right of access to private land as may be reasonably necessary; but not necessarily the most convenient. Reasonable notice of intention to enter for those purposes must be given to the owner and occupier of the land concerned, except in the case of an emergency or where the undertaker is responding to a notice under section 98 to provide a public sewer for domestic drainage. 'Reasonable notice' means, in the case of a new sewer, three months and in the case of the alteration of an existing pipe, 42 days.[98] *Hutton* v *Esher UDC* (1973)[99] is authority that this power includes, if necessary, the demolition of buildings on the land concerned. Exercise of this power does not of course involve acquisition of the land which remains in the ownership and possession of those previously enjoying such rights. Nevertheless, works of this nature may reduce the value of the land or affect its subsequent use. Section 180 therefore provides for compensation equivalent to such depreciation in value and for damage consequent on the work. Compensation disputes are within the jurisdiction of the Lands Tribunal[100] and section 181 provides for complaints to the Director with respect to the exercise of works powers on private land.

95 Section 219(1).

96 Section 343(1).

97 (1885) 15 QBD 572.

98 Section 159(5).

99 [1973] 2 All ER 1125.

100 Schedule 12, paragraph 3.

Although compensation provisions apply generally, it may be noted in relation to the reduction in value and restriction on the later use of land in which sewers have been laid, that sewerage undertakers must give their consent for the construction of any new building over a sewer or drain shown on the sewer map.[101] The local authority is required to reject such plans unless, with the sewerage undertaker's guidance, it may properly consent to the proposal.[102] Any work done without such approval may be removed by the local authority at the building owner's expense.[103] The evident purposes of this provision are to prevent damage to sewers and to ensure that adequate access is retained. On this basis it was suggested in *Urban Housing Co. Ltd* v *City of Oxford* (1939)[104] that:

> a building to be within the section must be one which by reason of its weight or otherwise, may cause an injury to the sewer over which it is built, or one which, by reason of its size or otherwise, prevents access being gained to the sewer.

In contrast to the power of a sewerage undertaker to affect the use of private land in this way, there is a countervailing power in section 185 of the Water Industry Act 1991 for a person having an interest in the land to require the removal or alteration of a sewer etc., if it is necessary to facilitate a proposed development of the land. Improvement includes development and changes of use, and the undertaker is required to comply unless the demand is unreasonable. Where a sewerage undertaker does work to comply with such a notice it will be entitled to recover its costs from the person requiring the change.[105]

Where a sewerage undertaker engages in work on private land under section 161(2), there is a right of complaint either to the Director-General of Water Services or to the local Customer Service Committee,[106] following a complaint to and failure of effective action by the sewerage undertaker itself. In the event of such a complaint the Director-General is generally required to investigate and may demand from the undertaker such information and assistance as may be reasonably required for the purposes of the investigation.

Where a sewerage undertaker is providing 'necessary' sewerage in a rural locality it may obtain a financial contribution from central government funds under the Rural Water Supplies and Sewerage Acts 1944–71. What constitutes a rural locality and what will be regarded as necessary, together with a contribution formula, are dealt with in Ministry of Housing and Local Government Circular 75/67.

In concluding this section on the provision of public sewers, there are three supplementary powers deserving reference. Work or proposed work carries with it powers of entry for authorised personnel at reasonable times and subject to seven days' notice.[107] This power carries with it the right to make experimental borings and to take and analyse samples of soil, water, effluent etc. This statutory power of entry is separate from and without prejudice to the power under Schedule 6, Part I to obtain a warrant from a justice of the peace authorising entry in certain specified circumstances; essentially where a seven-day notice would be to no effect or would defeat the purpose of entry.

Sewerage undertakers are required by section 199(1) to keep records and maps of the relevant particulars of all sewers, drains or disposal mains vested or to be vested in them. The relevant particulars are specified in section 199(2) and include the status of the pipe, the nature of its contents and whether it is vested or not. Regularly updated records are to be supplied to the local authorities within the undertaker's area and are to be available free of charge for inspection by mem-

101 See below.

102 Building Act 1984, section 18 and the Building Regulations 1985.

103 Building Act 1984, section 36.

104 [1939] 3 All ER 839 at p.850.

105 Section 185(5).

106 Section 181.

107 Water Industry Act 1991, section 171.

bers of the public at the offices of both the sewerage undertaker and the local authority in the form of a map.

Thirdly and lastly, section 155 provides a compulsory purchase power for undertakers for the carrying out of their functions. The exercise of the power requires authorisation by the Secretary of State and the provisions of the Acquisition of Land Act 1981 apply. Compensation is governed by the Compulsory Purchase Act 1965 as modified by Schedule 9 of this present statute.

Charges for sewerage services

Chapter I of Part V of the Water Industry Act 1991, sections 142–150, provide the statutory structure for charges by both water and sewerage undertakers. These provisions must be read in association with the terms of the instrument of appointment of the undertaker under section 6. In particular, therefore, what appear to be discretionary powers in the Act may in effect have quasi-contractual status under the conditions of the instrument of appointment and be enforceable by a section 18 order or injunction under section 22(4).

An undertaker has the power under section 142(1)(a) 'to fix charges for any services provided in the course of carrying out its functions' including its trade effluent functions. However, this apparently wide discretion is circumscribed by condition B of the model instrument of appointment which provides a formula for the calculation of the increase of charges for water and sewerage services and trade effluent disposal. The formula (RPI+K) limits increases to the percentage change of the retail price index plus an adjustment factor – K. The adjustment factor is reviewable by the Director General of Water Service generally at five to 10 year intervals, with a right of appeal to the Monopolies and Mergers Commission. The basis of review is to ensure that undertakers are able to finance the performance of their functions and also to secure a reasonable return on capital. Exceptionally, more frequent reviews may be necessary as a result of 'interim K determinations' including unexpected cost increases, caused, for example, by new EC requirements. However, not all cost increases, such as those arising from improvident management, may be passed on. Condition C provides a simpler mechanism for controlling increases to what are called infrastructure charges under section 146, i.e., charges for connections and highway drainage.

Charges are recoverable under section 142(1)(b) 'from any persons to whom the undertaker provides services or in relation to whom it carries out trade effluent functions'. That person, subject to any contrary agreement,[108] will usually be the occupier of the premises served. Section 143 gives undertakers the power to establish a charges scheme, including trade effluent charges. While the power is discretionary, condition D of the model instrument of appointment requires undertakers to have in force at all times a charges scheme for domestic water supplies and sewerage services, which is to be available on request to customers. The scheme will not override the power of undertakers to enter into individual agreements with trade effluent dischargers under section 143(5).

Undertakers are given, under section 142(4), a wide discretion in relation to the matters on which charges may be based; a scheme making different charges in different areas and therefore relating to different circumstances. Again, though, this broad provision is limited by the instrument of appointment, condition E requiring that no undue preference or discrimination is shown in respect of any class of customers. The general duties of the Secretary of State and the Director General

108 Section 144(1).

under section 2(3)(a) also refer specifically to the protection of the interests of customers and potential customers in rural areas.

Charges for new connections may be made under section 146. Although such connections themselves may impose no direct costs on the undertaker, increased capital expenditure on improving or enlarging the infrastructure may be necessary. Previously, before the Water Act 1989, provision for such costs was made in the calculation of their standard charges by water authorities, existing customers thereby subsidising the new. An alternative scheme now retained under section 106 of the Town and Country Planning Act 1990 as amended,[109] allows for an agreement between a developer and the local planning authority for the payment of capital sums to the undertaker. The limitations on these section 106 agreements are that they cannot be imposed on an unwilling developer. Also it may now be that a public sector planning authority may be less concerned with or sympathetic to the needs of an undertaker as a private company. In this context section 146 permits the undertaker to charge for domestic connections, with a maximum charge level imposed by condition D of the model instrument of appointment.

[109] By section 12 of the Planning and Compensation Act 1991.

Trade effluent

It has been seen that sewerage undertakers have a statutory duty to provide without cost for the disposal of domestic effluent. In the case of trade effluent, however, reception into the sewerage system and consequent treatment and disposal is only with the undertaker's consent. Such consent may be subject to a range of conditions, including payment. The distinction between domestic and trade effluent is therefore of considerable importance. By section 141(1) of the Water Industry Act 1991, trade effluent:

(a) means any liquid either with or without particles in suspension, which is wholly or partly produced in the course of any trade or industry carried on at trade premises; and

(b) in relation to trade premises means any such liquid which is so produced in the course of any trade or industry carried on at those premises; but does not include domestic sewage. For the purposes of this definition, 'trade premises' means 'any premises used or intended to be used for carrying on any trade or industry'.

In relation to any particular premises, therefore, trade effluent is that produced in the course of a trade or industrial process. Those premises will also in the nature of things produce domestic sewage. It is therefore the source or reason for production as much as the physical characteristics that determine its classification. This was the approach taken by the Court of Appeal in *Thames Water Authority v Blue and White Launderettes* (1980).[110] Accepting that a commercial activity may produce both trade and domestic effluent, the former originates only from a trade or industry. 'Trade' has been judicially described in the following terms:

[110] [1980] 1 WLR 700; and see quotation at p.214 above.

> the word trade indicates a process of buying and selling, but that is by no means an exhaustive definition of its meaning. It may also mean a calling or industry or class of skilled labour[111]

and:

[111] *Skinner* v *Jack Breach* [1927] 2 KB 220.

> A trade is an organised seeking after profits as a rule with the aid of physical assets.[112]

[112] *Aviation and Shipping Co* v *Murray* [1961] 1 WLR 974.

While the reason for its production is therefore important in classifying the effluent, the reason for the distinction lies in the nature or content of the trade effluent. Such characteristics as its toxicity, quantity, temperature, volatility (either alone or in combination with other sewer contents) and the consequent additional burden imposed in its treatment and disposal make it of primary importance that the undertaker should know with some degree of certainty what he is receiving. Section 119 therefore provides for an application by the owner or occupier of trade premises for consent for the discharge of trade effluent into a public sewer. The application, by notice, shall state the composition, the maximum daily quantity and the highest proposed rate of discharge. It is evident from the sense of this section that a given premises, having a range of production processes, may produce a number of different trade effluents and therefore require multiple consents. By section 118 the consent of the sewerage undertaker is a necessary precondition to the discharge of trade effluent, an unauthorised discharge being actionable either summarily or on indictment. Where the effluent includes substances prescribed under section 2 of the Environmental Protection Act 1990,[113] the undertaker, in considering the application, is required to consult HMIP.

113 See in Chapter 1 at p.48; and see 'Trade Effluent Discharges to Sewers' (DoE/Welsh Office, April 1988).

The terms of the consent, by section 121(1) and at the discretion of the sewerage undertaker, reflect the details required in the application, specifying the composition of the effluent together with the maximum daily quantity and the highest rate of discharge. In addition, the undertaker may specify the sewer into which the effluent is to be discharged. Section 121(2) lists in more detail matters that may be the subject of conditions:

(a) times of the day during which trade effluent may be discharged;
(b) the exclusion of condensing water;
(c) the elimination or diminution of any specified constituent in cases within sub-section 3;
(d) the temperature, acidity or alkalinity at time of discharge;
(e) payment by the occupier for the reception and disposal of the effluent;
(f) provision of access for sampling;
(g) provision of meters to measure volume and rate of discharge;
(h) provision of apparatus to determine the nature and composition of the trade effluent;
(i) the keeping of records, including readings of meters and other apparatus; and
(j) the making of returns and giving of information to the sewerage undertaker.

Accepting that the volume of flow in a sewer fluctutates during the course of a day, the undertaker may impose time limits to take advantage of such variations, e.g., for the purposes of dilution. Conditions (b), (c) and (d), on the one hand, and (e) on the other, are in a sense complementary. The applicant may be required to undertake some specified treatment to modify the effluent before discharge, or pay the undertaker for that function. In particular cases, of course, both treatment and payment may be demanded. In determining the amount of payment, the undertaker is to have regard to[114]:

114 Section 121(4).

(i) the nature, composition, volume and rate of discharge of the effluent;
(ii) any additional expense likely to be incurred in connection with its reception and disposal; and
(iii) any revenue likely to be derived from the trade effluent.

The remaining conditions all govern the provision and maintenance of appropriate monitoring and recording procedures to ensure compliance with consent conditions.

The special circumstances bringing a case within section 121(3) as stipulated in (c) above are that the constituent in question would:

(a) injure or obstruct the sewers or make treatment or disposal specially difficult or expensive; or
(b) in the case of outfall into a harbour or tidal water, cause injury or obstruction to navigation on, or use of, such water.

As with all these public control procedures there is a right of appeal[115] by the person aggrieved by a refusal of consent, a delayed consent (i.e., over two months) or any consent condition. The appeal is to the Director General of Water Services who has the power to substitute his own consent or conditions.

A consent having been granted, the undertaker has the power subsequently by direction 'to vary the consent conditions relating to the discharge of the trade effluent into a public sewer'.[116] Generally a minimum of two years must elapse between changes of condition,[117] though this period may be reduced by consent[118] or where a change is necessary 'to provide proper protection for persons likely to be affected by the otherwise lawful discharges'.[119] Unless this latter change was due to unforeseeable circumstances, compensation is payable.

Within the context of trade effluent control there are provisions governing 'special category effluent', which is defined in section 138 as meaning:

(a) substances prescribed under this Act present or present in prescribed concentrations; or
(b) effluent derive[d] from a prescribed process or a process using prescribed substances in excess of the prescribed amounts.[120]

This definition is not in itself very enlightening. Its purpose, and the intrinsically obscure wording, is to give the Secretary of State power to implement EC Directives in this area. Currently the Trade Effluent (Prescribed Processes and Substances) Regulations 1989[121] give effect to Article 3.2 of the Aquatic Environment Directive,[122] and in Schedule 1 enacts List 1 of the Directive, the so-called Red List, i.e.:

Mercury and its compounds	Dieldrin	Tributyltin compounds
Cadmium and its compounds	Endrin	Triphenyltin compounds
gamma-Hexachlorocyclohexane	Carbontetrachloride	Triflourolin
DDT	Polychlorinated biphenols	Fentrathion
Pentachlorophenol	Dichlorvos	Azinphosmethyl
Trichlorobenzene	1,2-Dichloroethane	Endosulphon
Hexachlorobenzene	Malathion	
Aldrin	Atrazine	
	Simazine	

Regulation 3 of the 1989 Regulations provides that section 138 applies to trade effluent where any of those Schedule 1 substances is present in concentrations greater than the background concentration. Regulation 4, applying to the second part of the definition, further provides that section 138 shall apply to trade effluent deriving from a process in Schedule 2 if either asbestos or chloroform is present in the effluent in a concentration greater that the background concentration.

Section 120 provides that on an application under section 119 in respect of a Red List substance the undertaker may refuse consent.[123] However, where a refusal

115 In section 122.

116 Section 124.

117 Section 124(2).

118 Section 124(3).

119 Section 125(1).

120 See also DoE Consultation Paper, 'Inputs of Dangerous Substances to Water' (1988).

121 S.I. 1989 No. 1156.

122 Directive 76/464/EEC. See also Schedule 2, giving effect to Article 3 of Directive 87/217/EEC regarding the prevention and reduction of environmental pollution by asbestos.

123 Section 120(3).

is not contemplated the undertaker must refer to the Secretary of State the questions:

(a) whether the discharges should be prohibited; and
(b) whether, if not, what if any conditions should be imposed.

The decision to refuse or the reference to the Secretary of State is to be made within two months of the application, and a copy of the reference is to be served on the applicant. Section 127 specifies the further powers of the Secretary of State in relation to 'special category effluent'. In particular, and subject to minimum time limits of generally two years, the Secretary of State may review consents 'with a view to prohibiting, restricting or controlling the emission'. The emphasis, therefore, in respect of these particularly harmful effluents, is progressively to reduce their permissible use and in no case to relax approval. The powers and procedure for Secretary of State reviews, including the right to a hearing, representation etc., are contained in section 132.

Sewage treatment and disposal

As well as placing a duty on a sewerage undertaker to make effective provision for the drainage and sewerage of its area, statute also and necessarily requires it, by means of sewage treatment works or otherwise, to make provision for effectively dealing with the contents of those sewers. Section 94(1)(b) of the Water Industry Act 1991 specifically requires sewerage undertakers to

> make provision for the emptying of those sewers and such further provision ... as is necessary from time to time for effectually dealing, with the contents of those sewers. This duty is enforceable by the Secretary of State or the Director by the section 18 enforcement order procedure.

In carrying out this duty the undertaker is required to have regard to current and likely future demands for the reception and disposal of trade effluent. The Secretary of State also has power under section 95 to make regulations to define obligations under this Part of the Act, or to establish overall standards of performance in relation to the provision of sewerage services, including individual standards of performance. Such regulations are made on the application of the Director under section 96. As in the case of sewers, though less likely in practice, a sewerage undertaker may by declaration adopt any sewage disposal works serving its area, either on its own initiative or at the request of the owners.

The section 94 duty carries with it the power to construct sewage disposal works on land lawfully acquired or appropriated for the purpose. Sewage disposal works are defined in section 90(4) of the Public Health Act 1936 as 'including a reference to the machinery and equipment of those works and any necessary pumping stations and outfall pipes'. The definition is silent about inlets, the presumption therefore being that public sewers so continue up to the point of discharge into the treatment process. Sewerage undertakers have a general power in section 155 of the Water Industry Act 1991, and subject to authorisation by the Secretary of State, 'to purchase compulsorily any land anywhere in England and Wales which is required ... for the purposes of or in connection with, the carrying out of its functions', the procedure being that in the Acquisition of Land Act 1981. This power of compulsory acquisition does not of course exclude the general ability to obtain either land or existing works by agreement, nor does the imposition of a statutory duty exclude or reduce the requirement of conformity with planning controls.[124] As well as constructing new works, a sewerage undertaker will have acquired from its predecessor water authorities on the transfer date (1 September 1989) the works vested in them. In many cases these will in their turn have been acquired from the constituent local authorities.[125]

As well as the duty to receive and treat the contents of the sewerage system, a sewerage undertaker has a comparable obligation to dispose of the contents of privies and cesspools of private dwellings delivered to it by a collection authority.[126] The authority may make a reasonable charge for emptying any non-domestic cesspools or privies that it agrees to empty.

The performance of these functions does not carry with it the right to cause, nor does it justify, causing a nuisance. *Bainbridge* v *Chertsey UDC* (1915)[127] concerned an allegation of nuisance by smell caused to the plaintiff's house by the defendant's sewage farm approximately 800 yards away. In granting an injunction the Court adopted the standard of Knight Bruce V-C[128]:

> ... ought this inconvenience to be considered in fact as more than fanciful, more than one of mere delicacy or fastidiousness, as an inconvenience materially interfering with the ordinary comfort physically of human existence, not merely according to elegant and dainty modes and habits of living, but according to plain and sober and simple notions among the English people?

In *Cornford* v *Havant & Waterloo UDC* (1933)[129] a sewage works again caused a nuisance by smell on the plaintiff's property. The works were vested in Petersfield RDC but were in the area of and operated by Havant & Waterloo UDC; the injunction in this case therefore being granted against them but not against Petersfield.

Just as a sewerage undertaker is subject to the same common law sanctions as others, so the same statutory controls apply to the discharge of the treated effluent from sewage works into controlled water. The definition of 'effluent' for this purpose in section 219(1) of the Act is 'any liquid, including particles of matter and other substances in suspension in the liquid'. In consequence all discharges from undertakers' sewage works will amount to offences under section 85 of the Water Resources Act 1991 unless protected by a discharge consent under section 88(1)(a) of the same Act.

124 See especially section 65 of the Town and Country Planning Act 1990, and the Town and Country Planning (General Development) Order 1988, S.I. 1988 No. 1813.

125 See section 20 of the Public Health Act 1936 and its treatment in relation to public sewers at p.200.

126 Section 45(5) and (6) of the Environmental Protection Act 1990; see section 30(3) for the definition of 'waste collection authority'.

127 (1915) 84 LJ (Ch) 626.

128 Quoted at p.627.

129 (1933) 31 LQR 142.

Part Three

THE ATMOSPHERE

9

Air Pollution

INTRODUCTION

Within reasonable limits people may choose when and what to eat and drink. No such choice exists with breathing. For better or worse, and irrespective of the air quality, we must continually breathe. What applies to man in this respect applies also to most other terrestrial life forms. The condition of the air around us is therefore of direct and continuing concern. That polluted air is detrimental to human health, and especially to the respiratory system, has been amply chronicled.[1] Atmospheric air has a relatively standard composition, but even in its natural state will contain fine particulate matter and gases from a variety of sources. In addition to widely fluctuating levels of water vapour the atmosphere will be affected from time to time by the products of volcanic eruptions, forest fires and dust and sand storms; in exceptional cases having more than local effect. While in some cases indistinguishable from the impact of human activities, these natural phenomena do not cause pollution in the accepted sense. As the Royal Commission on Environmental Pollution pointed out[2]:

> Pollution occurs when, as a result of man's activities, enough of a substance is present in the environment to have harmful effects. Many substances which can become pollutants are present naturally in the environment in lesser amounts, and may be beneficial or even essential to it.

Pollution may therefore be said for present purposes to be generated by man and to be excessive in quantity. Section 1 of the Environmental Protection Act 1990 defines pollution of the environment as:

> meaning pollution of the environment due to the release (into any environmental medium) from any process of substances which are capable of causing harm to man or to any other living organisms supported by the environment.

Most pollutants of the air, though by no means all, are produced by combustion; whether for power generation, heating, production processes or for transport. As these activities are an unavoidable counterpart to modern living their continuation, irrespective of any environmental consequences, is equally unavoidable. However, changes in policy and improvements in technology may lead to their more efficient and therefore less polluting operation.[3] The widespread burning of coal for most of those purposes, and particularly in the inefficient domestic grate, was an accepted feature of life for a century or more, being documented by Dickens and producing the 'pea-soup' smogs that were then a familiar characteristic of city life. 'Smog' consisted of fog grossly contaminated by the products of the inefficient combustion of coal, i.e., smoke, being produced in its acute form, and therefore largely in winter, by a meteorological temperature inversion.

Such occurrences were a common feature of urban, and especially industrial, life throughout the United Kindom and abroad. Notable air pollution disasters of

1 See, e.g., C. Holman, *Air Pollution and Health* (London:Friends of the Earth, London 1991); *Estimating Human Exposure to Air Pollutants,* WHO Offset Publication No. 69, (Geneva: WHO, 1987); R. Harrison (ed.), *Pollution: Causes, Effects and Control* (Cambridge: Society of Chemistry, 1990, 2nd edn).

2 Fifth Report, 'Air Pollution Control: An Integrated Approach', Cmnd 6371, January 1976, paragraph 25.

3 An example is provided by the introduction of Smoke Control Areas, essentially to reduce the contribution to air pollution of domestic heating.

this type were recorded, for example, over three days in December 1930 in the Meuse area of Belgium during which 60 persons died and several thousand suffered respiratory symptoms; and in October 1948 in Donora, Pennsylvania resulting in 20 deaths. December 1952 saw the great London smog lasting in its acute stage for five days and overall for 10 days. First casualties were among prize cattle brought to London for the Smithfield Show, of which one died and 12 had to be slaughtered. It is also recorded that at Sadlers Wells Theatre an opera performance had to be stopped after the first act as the audience could not see the stage.[4] More seriously, it was estimated to have been directly responsible for an additional 4,000 deaths. As a consequence of the general public reaction and possibly also because it occurred in London while Parliament was sitting, a Committee on Air Pollution under the chairmanship of Sir Hugh Beaver was set up with terms of reference 'to examine the nature, causes and effects of air pollution and the efficacy of present preventive measures; to consider what further measures are practicable; and to make recommendations'. Its second and final report was issued in 1954, the recommendations being largely enacted in the Clean Air Act 1956. That Act is entitled to be regarded as one of the most effective pieces of environmental legislation yet produced. Its implementation has replaced the dirty, smoke laden atmosphere of our cities and industrial areas, and the associated begrimed buildings and vestigial plant life, with the clear skies, clean building facades and regenerated parks and gardens enjoyed today.

4 See NSCA Pollution Handbook (1994), p.50.

It is not within the scope of this present work to examine the wide range of physical and other effects of air pollution. The Fifth Report of the Royal Commission on Environmental Pollution[5] briefly reviews the effects on human health, agriculture and crop yields, building materials and finishes, the economy and amenity. It is significant as indicative of the speed of evolution in thinking to notice that even in 1976, concern with the environment as such is not only subordinated to the requirements of human health but also to commercial interests. Nevertheless, against this background the Commission offers a definition of the aim of air pollution control in the following terms[6]:

5 See note 2 above.

6 See note 2 above, paragraph 41.

> The aim of air pollution control should be to reduce and when necessary eliminate hazards to human health and safety, taking into account both the magnitude and the certainty of the risks, including the susceptibilities of critical groups, and the resulting costs to the community; to reduce damage to amenity, property and plant and animal life to a minimum compatible with the wider public interest (which will take into account such factors as economics, employment and trade); and to prevent irreversible damage to the natural environment.

INTERNATIONAL DIMENSION

Each of the environmental media has its individual characteristics; that of the air being its general and widespread mobility. Air currents are international in their effects. This feature in the past made the disposal of pollutants into, and their dispersal by, air currents particularly attractive. Now this characteristic imposes upon polluters of the atmosphere additional and wider responsibilities. The concern, for example, of north European countries over the adverse environmental effects of the long range movement of pollutants, especially sulphur dioxide and nitrogen oxides, has been instrumental in the production of the Convention on Long-Range Transboundary Air Pollution by the UN Economic Commission for Europe.

This requires the countries concerned to 'endeavour to limit and, as far as possible, gradually reduce and prevent air pollution, including long range transboundary pollution'. Also the European Community itself has taken a leading role in applying controls on emissions to improve air quality throughout the region. More recently the global problems of climate change and depletion of the ozone layer have influenced Community policy-making. Developments of particular significance initiated by the EC concern:

- Air quality standards,
- Depletion of the ozone layer,
- Carbon dioxide emissions.

Air quality standards

Chapter 3, p.130.

As has been noted in relation to water,[7] the United Kingdom approach to pollution, hitherto exclusively by control over discharges into the medium, has had to expand to adopt general quality standards embodied in European Directives. It should be noted, though, that opinion was already moving in that direction.

Op. cit., note 2, at aragraph 22.

The Royal Commission on Environmental Pollution, in its Fifth Report[8] saying, albeit somewhat tentatively:

> We are satisfied that the enforcement of rigid air quality standards would be generally impracticable and unnecessary. However, we believe the time has come to focus attention more explicitly and openly on air quality, and we recommend a system of air quality guidelines for major pollutants.

While the standards applicable to air are as yet limited in their scope, the practice having been adopted, expansion is inevitable. Currently EC Directives specify limit values in the atmosphere for:

- sulphur dioxide and suspended particulates   80/779/EEC
- lead   82/884/EEC
- nitrogen dioxide   85/203/EEC
- ozone   92/72/EEC

S.I. 1989 No. 317.

Each Directive also specifies standard measuring and sampling procedures. These provisions are given effect to in the United Kingdom by the Air Quality Standards Regulations 1989.[9] In respect of each pollutant the Regulations apply the limit values contained in the relevant Directive. The limit values for sulphur dioxide and suspended particulates (smoke) are as follows:

Reference period	*Smoke*	*Sulphur dioxide*
One year (median of daily values)	80 µg/m³	120µg/m³ if smoke less than 40µg/m³ 80µg/m³ if smoke more than 40µg/m³
Winter (median of winter values)	130µg/m³	180µg/m³ if smoke less than 60µg/m³ 130µg/m³ if smoke more than 60µg/m³
Year, peak (98 percentile of daily values)	250 µg/m³	350µg/m³ if smoke less than 150µg/m³ 250µg/m³ if smoke more than 150µg/m³

Guide values	
24-hour mean	100–150 µg/m³
One year mean	40–60 µg/m³

Measuring stations are to be established in accordance with Annexes III – V, and in particular regulation 3(2) provides that:

> the measuring stations shall be established where pollution is thought to be greatest and where the measured concentrations are representative of local conditions and in particular ... in zones where the limit values are likely to be approached or exceeded.

Regulations 4 and 5 govern lead in air, regulation 4 providing that the Secretary of State is to

> take necessary measures to ensure that the mean annual value of concentrations of lead in air, measured in accordance with regulation 5 does not exceed 2 micrograms of lead per cubic metre expressed as an annual mean concentration.

The calculation of such values is to be in accordance with the terms of the Annex to the Directive, regulation 5 stating that :

> sampling stations are to be installed at sites where individuals may be exposed to lead in air continually for a long period and where, in the opinion of the Secretary of State, the limit value in regulation 4(1) is likely to be exceeded.

Nitrogen dioxide is dealt with in regulation 6, again requiring that the Secretary of State is to ensure that concentrations in the atmosphere, measured in accordance with regulation 7, do not exceed the limit values defined in the Annex to the Directive. Those limit values are:

	Reference period	*Nitrogen dioxide*
Limit value	One year (98 percentile of 1 – hour means)	200 µg/m³
Guide value	One year (50 percentile of 1 – hour means)	50 µg/m³
	One year (98 percentile of 1 – hour means)	135 µg/m³

Regulation 7 in its turn provides that the Secretary of State is to

> ensure that measuring stations are established at sites selected in accordance with paragraphs 1 – 3 of Annex III and in particular in zones where the limit value referred to in regulation 6 is, or is likely to be exceeded.

The final Directive, on Air Pollution by Ozone,[10] was to be implemented by Member States by 21 February 1994. The threshold limits, based on World Health Organisation recommendarions, are as follows:

10 92/72/EEC.

		µg/m³	*(ppb)*
Health protection	8 hour mean	110	55
Vegetation protection	1 hour mean	200	100
	24 hour mean	65	32.5
Population information	1 hour mean	180	90
Population warning	1 hour mean	360	180

The Directive provides for a monitoring network, exchange of information and for a warning system to operate when concentrations exceed the limits at which a risk to human health is deemed to exist. When the population thresholds are exceeded information is to be made available 'on a sufficiently large scale as soon as possible to enable the population concerned to take all appropriate preventive protective action'. The information to be made available is to include the area affected, forecast of the length of the episode and whether ozone levels are likely to increase; also advisable health precautions should be publicised.

The United Kingdom has yet to implement that Directive, relating to ozone. However, the Department of the Environment is available to the general public through an air quality telephone line.[11] The information is also supplied to the media for inclusion in weather bulletins. The air quality guidelines referred to above are as follows:

	Nitrogen dioxide	Sulphur dioxide (ppb, 1 hour mean)	Ozone
Very good	<50 (<95 µg/m³)	<60 (<160 µg/m³)	<50 (<100 µg/m³)
Good	50–99 (95–190 µg/m³)	60–124 (160–330 µg/m³)	50–89 (100–178 µg/m³)
Poor	100–299 (191–570 µg/m³)	125–399 (332–1,061 µg/m³)	90-179 (180–358 µg/m³)
Very poor	>=300 (>=557 µg/m³)	>=400 (>=1,064 µg/m³)	>=180 (>=360 µg/m³)

The 1980 Directive dealing with sulphur dioxide and suspended particulates is currently under review by the Commission. Further, its Fifth Action Programme 'Towards Sustainability' commits the Commission to a review and amendment of the Air Quality Directives before 1995. The Air Quality Framework Directive, now being drafted, is intended to replace all the existing Directives and include limit and guideline values for a wider range of pollutants. Below are the air quality categories used in the Department of the Environment bulletins. The figures are ppb (ug/m).

	Very Good	Good	Poor	Very Poor
NO₂	<50 (<96)	50–99 (96–190)	100–299 (192–575)	>300 (>577)
SO₂	<60 (<158)	60–124 (158–326)	125–399 (329–1,050)	>400 (>1,053)
Ozone	<50 (<100)	50–89 (100–178)	90–179 (180–358)	>180 (>360)

Depletion of the Ozone Layer

Depletion of the ozone layer, essentially through the discharge of chlorofluorocarbons (CFCs) into the atmosphere, has been a recent and developing concern, being expressed in the Vienna Convention for the protection of the ozone layer. The Montreal Protocol[12] to the Convention is directed to the reduction in the use of CFCs of 50 per cent by 1999. The European Community has broadly imple-

1 Freephone 0800 556677.

Dated 11 September 1987; me into force 1 January '89; subsequently amended in '90 and 1992.

mented these international initiatives, though to a narrower time scale.[13] The current EC proposals, in COM (93) 202, for the phasing out of ozone depleting chemicals are[14]:

1. **Chlorofluorocarbons** (11, 12, 113, 114, 115): using 1986 as a base level, 50 per cent reduction on production, supply and use from 1 January 1993, 85 per cent reduction from 1 January 1994 and ban from 1 January 1995.
2. **Other Fully Halogenated CFCs** (13, 111, 112, 211, 212, 213, 214, 215, 216, 217): using 1989 as a base level, as for other CFCs.
3. **Halons:** freeze on production, supply and use at 1986 levels from 1 January 1993 and ban from 1 January 1994.
4. **Carbon Tetrachloride:** using 1989 as a base level, 50 per cent reduction in production, supply and use from 1 January 1993, 85 per cent reduction from 1 January 1994 and ban from 1 January 1995.
5. **1,1,1-trichloroethane:** using 1989 as a base level, freeze on production, supply and use from 1 January 1993, 50 per cent reduction from 1 January 1994 and ban from 1 January 1996.
6. **Methyl Bromide:** using 1991 as a base level, freeze on production from 1 January 1995 and 25 per cent reduction from 1 January 1996.
7. **Hydrobromofluorocarbons:** ban on production from 1 January 1996.
8. **Hydrochlorofluorocarbons:** the limits refer to use and supply; from 1 January 1995 freeze at 2.5 per cent of maximum authorised consumption of CFCs and total HCFC consumption in 1989. Using 1996 as a base level, 25 per cent reduction from 1 January 2000, 60 per cent from 1 January 2004, 80 per cent reduction from 1 January 2008 and ban from 1 January 2014. In addition their use will be banned six months after implementation of the Regulation except as a solvent, refrigerant, for plastic foams, research and development and to protect human life. As from 1 January 1995 their use would be banned except for a few specified uses such as aerosols, cooling equipment, etc.

In the case of the first four substances listed above, limited production for essential uses will be allowed after the phase out dates. Criteria to be taken into account in deciding whether a use is essential include:

(a) the use must be necessary for the health and safety of society or critical for its functioning;
(b) there are no alternatives which are technically and economically feasible and which are acceptable on health and safety grounds;
(c) insufficient recycled material, both in terms of quantity and quality, is available.

Carbon Dioxide Emissions

Carbon dioxide is recognised as the major greenhouse gas, that is it is the principal contributor to global warming. Without some control it is estimated that emissions within the Community area are likely to increase by about 12 per cent. In accordance with commitments made at the Earth Summit at Rio de Janeiro in June 1992, therefore, the European Community has decided that emissions should be stabilised at 1990 levels by the year 2000.

The Commission has proposed a number of methods to achieve this objective in a strategy document COM (92) 246,[15] including:

13 EEC Regulations 594/91 and 3952/92. COM (93) 202 proposes the consolidation of the 1991 and 1992 Regulations.

14 Taken from 1994 Pollution Handbook with approval; pub National Society for Clean Air and Environmental Protection ed. Loveday Murley, pp. 58/9

15 See note 13 above.

(a) *Reducing energy demand*. This would implement Specific Actions for Vigorous Energy Efficiency (SAVE) and could be expected to reduce growth in CO_2 emissions by approximately 25 per cent. Methods suggested in the proposed Directive on Energy Efficiency include –

    (i) regular inspections of cars and boilers;

    (ii) energy audits for businesses;

    (iii) thermal insulation for new buildings;

    (iv) certification of CO_2 emissions related to energy consumption in buildings.

(b) *Carbon tax*. Proposals in COM(92) 226 for a Directive for a tax on carbon fuels are at a level of $3 per barrel of oil equivalent in 1993, rising by $1 per year to a maximum of $10 by 2000. The intention is to encourage a switch from coal and oil to natural gas and nuclear energy, and reduce growth of CO_2 emissions by 25 per cent. The implementation of such a tax, which would add 14p to a gallon of petrol by the year 2000, has been made conditional by EC Member States on other industrialised nations introducing similar measures.

(c) *Monitoring*. CO_2 emissions Monitoring is regarded as an integral part of national programmes and is given effect to in Council Decision 93/389 providing for the monitoring of CO_2 and other Greenhouse Gas emissions. It would be for individual Member States to evaluate the effect of reduction measures and to report on and publicise their policies and actions to limit emissions.

MOTOR VEHICLE POLLUTION

One of the more significant social phenomena of the last forty years has been the growth in travel. People and goods move about more than they have done in the past. The structure of daily living for large numbers of people now necessitates lengthy journeys, whether it be for work, shopping or leisure. Further, policy decisions are confirming and accentuating that characteristic; planning for example, ensuring that the various components of people's daily living are scattered over ever greater distances. The energy to power that activity is almost entirely derived from the combustion of fossil fuels. The consequences are beneficial and increasingly recognised to be burdensome to us all. An analysis of the purpose and mode of such travel appears in the 18th Report of the Royal Commission on Environmental Pollution[16]: as reproduced in Table 9.1.

With the removal of the major particulate pollutants from the atmosphere consequent upon the implementation of the Clean Air Act 1956 the continuing contamination of the air, particularly in urban areas, was apparent and attributed at least in part to the exhaust products of the internal combustion engine. This source is now accepted as a major contributor to the pollution of air and thereafter, through precipitation, of the soil, plants and water. Current estimates[17] are that road traffic contributes to the major atmospheric pollutants in the following proportions:

Hydrocarbons	36%
Nitrogen oxides	51%
Carbon monoxide	89%
Lead, approx.	70%
Black smoke	42%
Carbon dioxide	19%

16 Transport and the Environment, Cm 2674 1994; table 2.1.

17 DoE Digest of Environmental Protection and Water Statistics, No. 15 (1992).

Table 9.1 Why people travel *percentages (rounded to nearest whole number)*

Proportion of journeys	Proportion of distance travelled		on foot	by car: driver	by car: passenger	by car (total)	by local bus	by rail	in other ways	
						proportion of journeys for each purpose made wholly or mainly				
29	40	leisure	12	37	37	74	6	2	6	100
23	15	other personal business	7	52	31	83	6	1	3	100
20	20	to and from work	5	58	14	72	10	5	8	100
19	11	shopping	10	43	27	70	16	1	3	100
5	11	business	3	81	11	92	3	3	3	100
4	2	education	18	6	32	38	21	3	10	100
100	100	all purposes	9	46	28	74	9	2	6	100

This analysis excludes journeys of less than a mile and distances travelled outside Great Britain.

Source: 18th Report of the Royal Commission on Environmental Pollution[16]

Table 9.2 Airborne pollutants from transport: estimated emissions in the UK (1992) *thousand tonnes*

	road	rail	air	shipping	total emissions from transport	transport as % of UK emissions from all sources[a]
carbon monoxide	6029	12	11	19	6071	90 (91)
nitrogen oxides	1398	32	14	130	1574	57 (61)
Volatile organic compounds	949	8	4	14	975	38 (48)
particulates	215	not reported	1	3	219	48 (48)
sulphur dioxide	62	3	3	60	128	4 (7)

[a]Figures in parentheses include transport-related emissions from oil refineries and power stations

Source: Royal Commission on Environmental Pollution

As a commentary on the situation revealed by the figures in Tables 9.1 and 9.2, the Royal Commission, in paragraph 3.43, says[18]

18 See footnote 16; para 3.43.

> We are concerned that the present use of road vehicles may be causing serious damage to human health by triggering or exacerbating respiratory symptoms and by exposing people to carcinogens from vehicle emissions. The situation should therefore be regarded as unsustainable. Despite the many uncertainties about the effects of transport pollutants on human health and the environment, there is a clear case, on the basis of what is already known, for increasing the precautionary action taken to improve air quality. It is especially important to reduce concentrations of particulates and nitrogen oxides.

The current solution, of improving emission standards, has obvious limits technologically, some waste products being the inevitable consequence of burning fuel to generate power. Whatever limited improvement is secured in the performance of individual engines will therefore be more than nullified by the projected increase in the number coming into use. The current 24 million road vehicles in Great Britain is forecast to increase by 115 per cent to 51 million by 2025.[19] The European Commission adopted a Green Paper in 1992 on the Impact of Transport on the Environment[20] which offered forecasts of expected growth in all forms of transport with consequent increases in pollution from those sources, and outlined a strategy for 'sustainable mobility'. Its expectations are that by 2010 the volume of private cars will increase by 45 per cent, goods traffic by 42 per cent and total vehicle mileage by 25 per cent. In consequence it concludes that the Community's projected programme on emission limits and standards will not be enough to contain the likely damage from these increased levels of transport growth.

19 Road Traffic Statistics Great Britain (HMSO, 1993).

20 COM (92) 46 final.

Emissions from motor vehicles can be regulated by controlling the composition of fuel, or by setting standards for vehicle design and construction. Current national controls, enacting Community Directives, are directed to both of these matters; the content of fuels and the efficiency of the combustion process in the engine and consequent emission standards. This latter issue is approached in two ways. A new model of vehicle is required to satisfy certain standards, including those relating to pollution emissions, and to receive Type Approval before being introduced into production. Secondly, vehicles are required to comply with construction and use standards throughout their operational life. These matters are now dealt with in turn.[21]

21 Transport and the Environment, Cm 2674, Fig. 3.1.

Fuel Content

Regulations governing the composition of fuel for motor vehicles are made under section 30 of the Clean Air Act 1993[22] which provides in subsection (1) that:

22 Re-enacting section 75(1) of the Control of Pollution Act 1974.

> To limit or reduce air pollution, the Secretary of State may by regulations –
>
> (a) impose requirements as to the composition and content of any fuel of a kind used in motor vehicles; and
> (b) where such requirements are in force, prevent or restrict the production, treatment, distribution, import, sale or use of any fuel which in any respect fails to comply with the requirements.

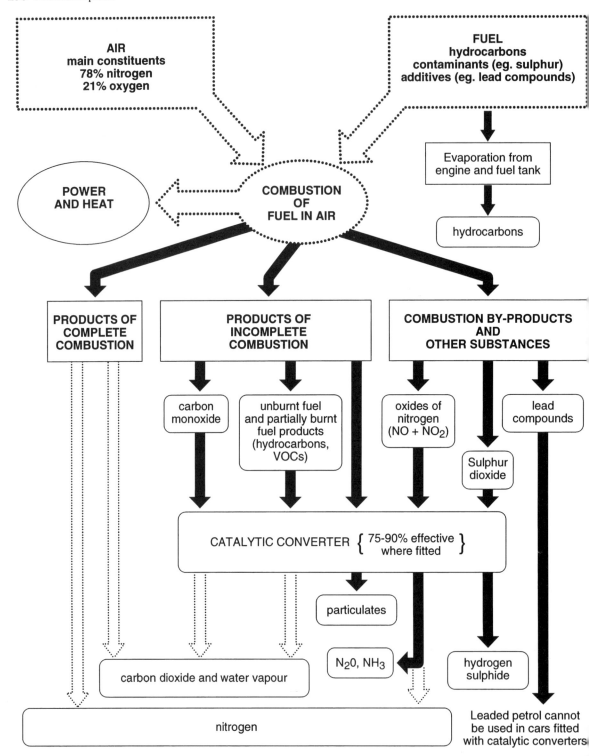

Figure 9.1 Pollutants emitted by petroleum-powered vehicles[21]

23 See Chapter 1 on 'consultation'

There is a requirement on the Secretary of State in making the regulations of prior consultation with interested parties.[23] Breach of the regulations is, by section 30(2), actionable either summarily or on indictment, subject to the terms of the regulations, and enforcement is by the weights and measures authority for its area. For this purpose, specified provisions of the Trade Descriptions Act 1968 apply relating to powers of entry, sampling and testing.[24] Section 58 of the 1993 Act also gives local authorities power, by notice, to require 'any person' to provide information which the authority reasonably considers that it needs for the purpose of any function conferred on the authority by Part IV of the Act.[25]

24 Section 30(4).

25 See also on the operation of section 30 and Part IV generally, DoE Circular 7/76.

Current regulations, implementing the relevant Community Directives, govern respectively the lead content of petrol and the sulphur content of gas oil (diesel fuel). Before considering the regulations it is to be noted that in *Budden* v *B.P. Oil and Shell Oil*; *Albery-Speyer* v *B.P. Oil and Shell Oil* (1980)[26] the Court of Appeal considered that complying with the regulations was a sufficient defence to a claim based on the adverse impact on child health of exposure to vehicle emissions in the inner city. However, Megaw LJ qualified this principle in saying that:

26 [1980] JPL 586.

> this is not to say that the courts are bound to hold, where a limit has been prescribed in the interests of safety by statute or statutory regulations, that one who keeps within these limits cannot be guilty of negligence at common law.

In this same context local authorities have the power to promote guide values within European Community limits, indicating circumstances where there may be an enforceable duty of care to observe emission levels below those specified in legislation.

Dealing with the lead content of petrol first; petrol itself is, for the purpose of the regulations, stated to be 'petroleum spirit as defined in section 23 of the Petroleum (Consolidation) Act 1928 of a kind used as fuel in motor vehicles'.[27] Section 23 states that 'petroleum spirit means such petroleum as when tested in the manner set forth in Part II of the Second Schedule to this Act gives off an inflammable vapour at a temperature of less than 73°F'. Schedule 2 in its turn provides a detailed description of the apparatus and method applicable to the test.

27 Motor Fuel (Lead Content of Petrol) Regulations 1981, regulation 2(2).

The relevant regulations are the Motor Fuel (Lead Content of Petrol) Regulations 1981, the Motor Fuel (Lead Content of Petrol)(Amendment) Regulations 1985 and the Motor Fuel (Lead Content of Petrol)(Amendment) Regulations 1989.[28] The 1981 Regulations consolidate the 1976 and 1979 Regulations with some amendments. Of particular note is the reduction in regulation 4 of the maximum permitted lead content after 31 December 1985, from 0.45 grammes to 0.15 grammes per litre when tested according to BS 5657:1978. This is the lowest permitted level under the Community equalisation provisions of Directive 78/611/EEC.

28 Respectively S.I.1981 No. 1523; S.I. 1985 No. 1728 and S.I. 1989 No. 547.

An amended regulation 5 provides that:

No person shall –

(a) produce, treat, distribute, import, sell, offer for sale, or have in his possession for sale any petrol the lead content of which exceeds the maximum permitted amount under Reg 4 if he knows or has reason to believe that it does so exceed that amount.
(b) use, cause or permit to be used such petrol if he knows or has reason to believe that the lead content does so exceed the permitted amount.

The significant change here is that the phrase 'if he knows or has reason to believe', which did not appear in the preceding regulation 5(a), has been added. Both regulation 5 offences now therefore require proof of the necessary state of mind. Regulation 6 specifies a number of exemptions including, as examples, the production, use etc., of such petrol for testing and experiment and for its use in aircraft and hovercraft.

The 1985 Regulations retain the maximum lead content for leaded petrol, and add a maximum level for unleaded petrol of 0.013 grammes per litre when tested by the method specified by the American Society for Testing and Materials.[29] In both cases the results are to be interpreted in accordance with BS 4306;1968.[30] The specific penalty provisions in earlier regulations are revoked thereby restoring those in the parent Act[31] which provide for summary or indictable proceedings. Lastly, the 1989 amendment, in regulation 3, applies a revised standard test for the lead content of leaded petrol, i.e., that prescribed by BS 5657:1988.[32] Regulation 4 also applies Directives 85/536/EEC and 87/441/EEC with revised standard specifications for leaded and unleaded petrol on the use of substitute fuel components (oxygenates). The revised specification for leaded petrol also limits the benzene content of the fuel to 5 per cent by volume in accordance with Directive 85/210/EEC. A new regulation 7 applies the latest standards for the marking of petrol pumps; in the case of leaded petrol in accordance with BS 4040:1988, and for unleaded petrol BS 7070:1988.

The sulphur content of diesel fuel is dealt with in the Motor Fuel (Sulphur Content of Gas Oil) Regulations 1976 as amended by the Motor Fuel (Sulphur Content of Gas Oil)(Amendment) Regulations 1990,[33] made under the same section 30 of the Clean Air Act 1993. For the purpose of these Regulations 'gas oil' is defined as liquid petroleum product produced for diesel engines of which at least 85 per cent by volume, including distillation losses, is distilled at a temperature of 350°C when tested in accordance with BS 2000: Part 123: 1985 (February 1985 revision). Regulation 4 of the 1976 Regulations stipulates that the maximum permitted amount of sulphur per 100 gms of gas oil, when tested by the method prescibed in BS 5379: 1976 EN 41 and the results interpreted in accordance with BS 4306: 1968, is 0.3 grammes. Regulation 5, as the punitive provision, essentially reproduces that applying to the lead content of petrol, stating that:

No person shall –

(a) produce, treat, distribute, import, sell, offer for sale, or have in his possession for sale any gas oil the sulphur content of which exceeds the maximum permitted amount under regulation 4 if he knows or has reason to believe that it does so exceed that amount,

(b) use, cause or permit to be used any gas oil the sulphur content of which exceeds the permitted amount.

It appears that, unlike the provisions governing lead, the strict liability nature of the offence in regulation 5(b) has yet to be amended. The amendments in the 1990 Regulations implement Directive 87/219/ EEC and principally apply the maximum sulphur content of 0.3 gms to all diesel engined road vehicles, including agricultural, engineering and works vehicles. Also, the exemptions in regulation 6 are amended to cover fuel imported in the tank of vehicles entering from non-EC states only.

Type approval

As well as compliance with the requirements applicable to vehicles in their day to day operation and considered below, new models must satisfy certain standards

29 Under ref. ASTM.D 3237 – 79; address – 1916 Race Street, Philadelphia, Pennsylvania 19103, USA.

30 Revised 1981 (ISO 4259:1979).

31 See section 32(2) of the Clean Air Act 1993.

32 ISO 3830:1981 – the iodine monochloride method.

33 Respectively S.I.1976 No. 1989 and S.I.1990 No. 1097.

before they are introduced into production; the production vehicles of that type then having to conform to those approved criteria. The provisions governing type approval are to be found in the Road Traffic Act 1988, sections 54–59. Section 54 gives the Secretary of State the power, without prejudice to section 41 of the Act (considered below), to prescribe by regulations type approval requirements with respect to the design, construction, equipment and marking of vehicles and vehicle parts of any class used on a road, and section 61 specifies the structure and content of such regulations including examination, certification, fees and the authorisation of examiners. Clearly the matters covered by type approval are far wider than the question of exhaust emissions, which is the present concern.

By section 55(1), where the Secretary of State is satisfied on application to him by a manufacturer of a vehicle of a class to which the above regulations apply, and after examination:

(a) that the vehicle complies with the relevant type approval requirements; and
(b) adequate arrangements have been made to secure that other vehicles of that type will conform in all respects in the relevant aspects of design, construction etc., or with permitted variations,

he may approve that vehicle as a type vehicle.

On such approval section 55(2) then requires the Secretary of State to issue a 'type approval certificate' stating the fact of compliance, the permitted variations from the type vehicle and the design weights for vehicles so conforming in all respects and for vehicles so conforming with any such variations.[34] A certificate may be issued where one or more but not all type approval requirements are satisfied, allowing for the subsequent issue of further certificates as appropriate.

Section 56, dealing with conditions, cancellation or suspension of certificates provides that a type approval certificate may be issued subject to conditions with respect to:

(a) inspection by officers of the Secretary of State of vehicles purporting to conform with the type vehicle, and of parts and equipment and right of entry to premises where they are manufactured;
(b) notification by the manufacturer of differences of design, construction etc., which might affect approval requirements or design criteria.

A type approval certificate having been issued, the manufacturer, by section 57, may then issue in respect of each vehicle produced and conforming to the type vehicle in the aspects mentioned in the certificate, a certificate of conformity:

(a) stating that it does so conform; and
(b) specifying the design weights for the vehicle,

and must, in relation to goods vehicles of prescribed classes specify in the certificate the plated weights for such vehicles. 'Plated weights means such weights as are required to be marked on a goods vehicle in pursuance of regulations under this section by means of a plate'.[35]

Separate series of regulations have been issued under section 54 for private and goods vehicles respectively.[36] Dealing with private vehicles first, the applicable regulations are the Motor Vehicle Type Approval (GB) Regulations 1984 amended by the Motor Vehicle (Type Approval (GB)(Amendment) Regulations 1988 and 1989 and the Motor Vehicle (Type Approval)(GB)(Amendment)(No. 2) Regulations

34 In the case of goods vehicles the comparable document, by section 58, is a 'Minister's approval certificate'.

35 Road Traffic Act 1972, section 40(7).

36 These are the Motor Vehicle (Type Approval)(GB) Regulations 1984, S.I. 1984 No. 981, as amended by S.I.s 1984/1401, 1984/1761, 1985/1651, 1986/739, 1987/1509, 1988/1522; and the Motor Vehicles (Type Approval for Goods Vehicles)(GB) Regulations 1982, S.I. 1982 No. 1271, as amended by S.I.s 1984/697, 1984/1402, 1985/46, 1986/1089, 1987/1508, 1988/1523.

1990.[37] The regulations apply to every motor vehicle manufactured on or after 1st October 1977 and first used on or after 1 August 1978 that is constructed for carrying passengers and their effects. Regulation 2(2) of the 1984 Regulations lists a number of exemptions including, for example, ambulances, motor caravans and vehicles from abroad temporarily in the United Kingdom.

The 1984 Regulations specify detailed requirements for the form and content of a written application for type approval and the response of the Secretary of State notifying arrangements for the examination, the subsequent application for issue of the certificate and appeals under the Act. Regulation 11 then requires the manufacturer to keep a record of every certificate of conformity issued under section 57, identifying the certificate, the type approval certificate and the vehicle or part, authorised persons being given a right of inspection.

Schedule 1 to the 1984 Regulations specifies the applicable type approval requirements by reference to Annexes I and II of the Community Directives.[38] The principal Directive governing this issue is 70/220/EEC[39] which applies to vehicles, defined in Article 1 of Directive 83/351/EEC as meaning 'any vehicle with a positive ignition engine or with a compression ignition engine intended for use on the road ... having at least four wheels, a permissible maximum mass of at least 400kg and a maximum design speed equal to or exceeding 50km/h', excepting vehicles which run on rails, agricultural tractors and machines and public works vehicles. Annex 1 of the 1970 Directive then applies its terms to tail-pipe emissions, evaporative emissions and emissions of crank-case gases and the durability of anti-pollution devices for all motor vehicles equipped with positive ignition engines.

The emission levels in the Directive for stated pollutants are expressed in chart form as set out in Table 9.3. The Directive provides that an increase of any one

37 Respectively S.I. 1984 No. 981; S.I.1988 No. 1522; S.I. 1989 No. 1580 and S.I. 1990 No. 1839.

38 These are 70/220/EEC, 74/290/EEC, 77/102/EEC, 78/665/EEC and 83/351/EEC.

39 Amended by Directives 74/290, 77/102, 78/665, 83/351, 88/76, 88/436.

Table 9.3 Directive 70/220/EEC: vehicle emission levels

Category of vehicle		Reference mass	Limit values		
			Mass of carbon monoxide	Combined mass of hydrocarbons and oxides of nitrogen	Mass of particulates
		RW (kg)	L_1 (g/km)	L_2 (g/km)	L_3 (g/km)
M_2		all	2.72	0.97	0.14
N_1	Category I	RW ≤ 1.250	2.72	0.97	0.14
	Category II	1.250 ≤ RW ≤ 1.700	5.17	1.4	0.19
	Category III	1.700 < RW	6.9	1.7	0.25

M_2 is defined in Annex II of Directive 70/156/EEC as including vehicles used for the carriage of passengers and comprising no more than 8 seats in addition to the driver's seat.

N_1 is also defined as meaning vehicles used for the carriage of goods and having a maximum mass not exceeding 3.5 tonnes.

Reference mass means the mass of the vehicle in running order less the uniform mass of the drive of 75kg and increased by a uniform mass of 100 kg.

pollutant of up to 10 per cent is acceptable provided that the mean of the three results is below the prescribed mean.

Directive 85/210/EEC makes provision for unleaded petrol, Article 1 defining the two categories of petrol as follows:

(b) unleaded petrol shall mean any petrol the contamination of which by lead compounds calculated in terms of lead does not exceed 0.013 g Pb/l;

(c) leaded petrol shall mean petrol other than unleaded petrol. This shall have a maximum permitted lead compound content, calculated in terms of lead, of not more than 0.40g Pb/l and not less than 0.015g Pb/l.

Article 1 further imposes a duty on Member States to ensure the availability and balanced distribution within their territories of unleaded petrol from 1 October 1989, with certain savings for up to four-month periods with the agreement of the Commission if supplies are unobtainable. The 1988 amending regulations implementing Directive 88/76/EEC, require that all petrol engines be capable of using unleaded fuel. The 1990 Regulations amend the 1989 Regulations by removing small passenger vehicles with spark ignition engines of less than 1,400cc from their requirements.

Diesel engined vehicles are defined in Article 1 of Directive 72/306/EEC in very similar terms to the definition for petrol engined vehicles, the term meaning:

any vehicle with a diesel engine, intended for use on the road ... having at least four wheels and a maximum design speed exceeding 25km/h; excepting vehicles which run on rails, agricultural tractors and machines and public works vehicles.

Annex I in paragraph 5 then provides that:

The components liable to affect the emission of pollutants shall be so designed, constructed and assembled as to enable the vehicle, in normal use, despite the vibration to which it may be subjected, to comply with the provisions of this Directive.

The limits specified in Annex VI to that Directive have now been superceded, with effect from 1 October 1995, by the emission levels in Annex I to Directive 88/77/EEC[40] as follows[41]:

Carbon monoxide,	g/k Wl	4.0
Hydrocarbons,	g/k Wl	1.1
Nitrogen oxides,	g/k Wl	7.0
Particulates,	g/k Wl	0.15

The comparable rules governing goods vehicles are to be found in the Motor Vehicle (Type Approval for Goods Vehicles)(GB) Regulations 1982 as amended by the Motor Vehicles (Type Approval for Goods Vehicles)(GB) (Amendment) Regulations 1984, 1988, 1989, and 1992.[42] These regulations apply to goods vehicles, tractor units of articulated vehicles and bi-purpose vehicles with certain stated exemptions. The provisions governing applications for type approval, issue of the approval certificate, appeals and the keeping of records are comparable with those for private vehicles. Also, as in the case of private vehicles, Schedule I to the 1982 Regulations applies as type approval requirements the Annexes to Community Directives 70/220/EEC, 72/306/EEC, 74/290/EEC, 77/102/EEC and 78/665/EEC, those in the first two listed having been dealt with in the context of petrol engined vehicles above.

40 Implemented, with 88/436/EEC, in the 1989 amending regulations; see note 34 above. These regulations also changed the terminology from references to 'exhaust emissions' to 'smoke emissions'.

41 See also S.I.s 1990 No. 94 and 1990 No. 1839.

42 Respectively S.I. 1982 No. 1271; S.I. 1984 No. 697; S.I. 1988 No. 1523, S.I. 1989 No. 1579 and S.I. 1992 No. 25.

The 1988 amendment implements Directive 88/76, Annex I, paragraph 6 requiring operation with unleaded petrol. The 1989 amendment implements Directives 88/76 and 88/77 changing 'exhaust emissions' to 'smoke emissions' and introducing emission standards for diesel engines. The 1992 amendment removes the exemption for vehicles of unladen weight less than 1,525 kg. Regulation 4 further requires that vehicles of 7.5 tonnes or more are either to have a speed of less than 60 mph or be fitted with a speed limiter.

It is significant to note in this context that the regulations, instead of reproducing the provisions in the Directives merely state that they shall apply. This is possibly to be explained in that the Directives themselves do not always specify emission levels, providing instead that the 'Council is to consider, following Commission recommendations, further reductions of limit values'. The implication is that as the Council periodically produces new limit values they will take effect without the issue of new Directives or regulations.

Vehicle Construction and Testing

The legal controls in this area have a number of objectives, not the least of which is of course road safety. However, only those provisions relating to exhaust pollutants are of present concern. Enabling powers for the governing regulations are found in Part II of the Road Traffic Act 1988, sections 41 to 59, and provide for general standards of construction and use applicable to the operation of such vehicles, and type approval requirements for private and goods vehicles respectively.

By section 41(1), the Secretary of State has power to make regulations governing the use of motor vehicles and trailers on roads, their construction, equipment and the conditions under which they are used, including, under section 41(2)(b), the emission or consumption of smoke, fumes or vapour and the emission of sparks, ashes and grit. 'Motor vehicle' is defined in section 185 as meaning, subject to section 20 of the Chronically Sick and Disabled Persons Act 1970 (which makes special provision in respect of invalid carriages), a mechanically propelled vehicle intended or adapted for use on roads. Section 42 makes non-compliance with regulations an offence, subject to the defences specified in section 42(2),[43] to the temporary exemptions in section 43 and to the section 44 authorisations for use on the roads of special vehicles. The Secretary of State has power to authorise the relaxation of regulations made under this section for purposes relating to the control and conservation of energy.[44]

The regulations concerned with exhaust emissions are the Road Vehicle (Construction and Use) Regulations 1986 as amended by the Road Vehicle (Construction and Use)(Amendment)(No 6) Regulations 1988, the Road Vehicle (Construction and Use)(Amendment)(No 2) Regulations 1990 and the Road Vehicle (Construction and Use)(Amendment) Regulations 1991.[45] The extensive regulation 61 of the 1986 Regulations requires consideration. It provides, in paragraph (1), that, subject to paragraph (4), every vehicle shall be constructed and maintained[46] so as not to emit any avoidable smoke or visible vapour. By paragraph (4), instead of complying with the paragraph (1) requirement, a vehicle may at the time of its first use comply with specified European Community Directives. Paragraph (2) deals with the use of solid fuel and therefore may, for present purposes, be omitted. Paragraph (3) requires that wheeled vehicles of a class specified in column 2 of Table I shall be so constructed as to comply with the requirements in column 3. Table I is set out opposite.

43 These defences relate exclusively to weight and loading and are therefore of no direct environmental concern.

44 Energy Act 1976 section 4(2) and Schedule 1, paragraph 1.

45 S.I. 1986 No. 1078; S.I. 1988 No. 1524; S.I. 1990 No. 1131 and S.I. 1991 No. 1526 respectively.

46 'Maintained' added by the 1991 Regulations.

Table I
(regulation 61(3))

1 Item	2 Class of vehicle	3 Requirements	4 Exemptions

1	Vehicles propelled by a compression ignition engine and equipped with a device designed to facilitate starting the engine by causing it to be supplied with excess fuel.	Provision shall be made to ensure the device cannot readily be operated by a person inside the vehicle.	(a) a works truck;
			(b) a vehicle on which the device is so designed and maintained that–
			  (i) its use after the engine has started cannot cause the engine to be supplied with excess fuel, or
			  (ii) it does not cause any increase in the smoke or visible vapour emitted from the vehicle.

2	Vehicles first used on or after 1 April 1973 and propelled by a compression ignition engine.	The engine of the vehicle shall be of a type for which there has been issued by a person authorised by the Secretary of State a type test certificate in accordance with the British Standard Specification for the Performance of Diesel Engines for Road Vehicles published on 19 May 1971 under number BS AU 141a: 1971. In the case of an agricultural motor vehicle (other than one which is first used after 1 June 1986 and is driven at more than 20mph), an industrial tractor, a works truck or engineering plant, for the purposes of that Specification as to the exhaust gas opacity, measurements shall be made with the engine running at 80% of its full load over the speed range from maximum speed down to the speed at which maximum torque occurs as declared by the manufacturer of the vehicle for those purposes.	(a) a vehicle manufactured before 1 April 1973 and propelled by an engine known as the Perkins 6.354 engine; (b) a vehicle propelled by an engine having not more than two cylinders and being an agricultural motor vehicle (other than one which if first used on or after 1 June 1986 and which is driven at more than 20mph), an industrial tractor, a works truck or engineering plant.
3	Vehicles first used on or after 1 January 1972 and propelled by a spark ignition engine other than a 2-stroke engine.	The engine shall be equipped with means sufficient to ensure that, while the engine is running, any vapours or gases in the engine crank case, or in any other part of the engine to which vapours or gases may pass from that case, are prevented, so far as it reasonably practicable, from escaping into the atmosphere otherwise than through the combustion chamber of the engine.	(a) a two-wheeled motor cycle with or without a sidecar attached; (b) [deleted by 1990 amending regs] (c) a vehicle to which any item in Table II applies.

Subordinate or in addition to these detailed requirements, regulation 61(5) and (6) stipulate that:

(5) No person shall use, cause or permit to be used, on any road any motor vehicle

(a) from which any smoke, visible vapour, grit, sparks, ashes, cinders or oily substance is emitted if that emission causes or is likely to cause, damage to any property, or injury or danger to any person who is, or who may reasonably be expected to be, on the road;

(b) which is subject to the requirement in Item 2 of Table I if any part of the propulsion equipment has been altered or adjusted so as to increase the emission of smoke; or

(c) which is subject to the requirement in Item 1 of Table I if the device mentioned in column 2 is used while the vehicle is in motion.

(6) No person shall use, or cause or permit to be used, on a road a motor vehicle to which Item 3 of Table I applies unless it is so maintained that the means specified in column 3 are in good working order.

The 1988 amendment introduces a new regulation 39A to the 1986 Regulations requiring petrol engined vehicles first used on or after 1 April 1991 to be designed and constructed to run on unleaded petrol, while a new Schedule 3A provides for specific exclusions from these requirements for older vehicles. The 1990 amendment adds a new regulation 61(3A) to the effect that:

A motor vehicle to which Table II applies shall be so constructed as to comply with the requirements relating to conformity of production models set out in the provisions specified in that Item in column (4) of that Table.

A new paragraph (7) to regulation 61 specifies certain limited exceptions to these Table II requirements. Table II is set out below.

Table II
(regulation 61 (3A) and (7))

(1) Item	(2) Class of vehicle	(3) Date of first use	(4) Design, construction and equipment requirements		(5) Vehicles exempted from requirement	(6) Emitted Substances
			(a) Instrument	(b) Place in Instrument where requirements are stated		
1	Vehicles propelled by a spark ignition engine	1 October 1982	Community Directive 78/665, or ECE Regulation 15.03.	Annex 1 paragraphs 3 and 5 Paragraphs 5, 8 and 11.	(a) A vehicle whose maximum gross weight exceeds 3,500 kg; (b) A vehicle which complies with the requirements of items 2, 4, 5 or 8; (c) A vehicle whose maximum speed is less than 50 km/h; (d) An exempt vehicle.	Carbon monoxide, hydrocarbons and oxides of nitrogen

2	All vehicles	1st April 1991	Community Directive 83/351, or ECE Regulation	Annex 1, paragraphs 5, 7 and 8.	(a) A vehicle propelled by a compression ignition engine and whose maximum gross weight exceeds 3,500 kg;	Carbon monoxide hydrocarbons and oxides of nitrogen.
				Paragraphs 5, 8 and 12.	(b) A vehicle which complies with the requirements of items 4, 5, 6 or 8; (c) An industrial tractor, works truck or engineering plant; (d) A vehicle whose maximum speed is less than 50 km/h; (e) An exempt vehicle.	
3	Industrial tractors, works trucks and engineering plant propelled in each by a compression ignition engine.	1 April 1993	ECE Regulation 49.	Paragraphs 5 and 7.	A vehicle which complies with the requirements of item 6.	Carbon monoxide, hydrocarbons and oxides of nitrogen.
4	Passenger vehicles which– (1) are constructed or adapted to carry not more than 5 passengers excluding the driver, and (2) have a maximum gross weight of not more than 2,500 kg, not being in either case, an off-road vehicle and (a) are propelled by a spark ignition engine with a capacity of–		Community Directive 88/76.	Annex 1, paragraphs 5, 7 and 8.	(a) A vehicle which complies with the requirements of item 8; (b) A vehicle whose maximum speed is less than 50 km/h; (c) An exempt vehicle.	Carbon monoxide, hydrocarbons and oxides of nitrogen.
	(i) not less than 1,400 cc and not more than 2,000 cc,	1 April 1994				
	(ii) more than 2,000 cc, or	1 April 1993				
	(b) are propelled by an indirect injection compression ignition engine with a capacity of not less than 1,400 cc, or	1 April 1994				
	(c) are propelled by a direct injection compression ignition engine with a capacity of–					
	(i) not less than 1,400 cc and nor more than 2,000 cc, or	1 April 1997				
	(ii) More than 2,000 cc.	1 April 1994				

5	Vehicles which are not of a description specified in this column in items 4 and 8 but which– (a) are propelled by a spark ignition engine, and whose maximum gross weight is (i) not more than 2,000 kg, or (ii) more than 2,000 kg. (b) are propelled by a compression ignition engine and whose maximum gross weight is (i) more than 3,500 kg, or (ii) not more than 3,500 kg.	 1 April 1992 1 April 1994 1 April 1991 1 April 1994	Community Directive 88/76.	Annex 1, paragraphs 5, 7 and 8.	(a) A vehicle within the meaning given by Article 1 of Community Directive 88/77 and which complies with the requirements of item 6; (b) An industrial tractor, works tractor or engineering plant; (c) A vehicle whose maximum speed is less than 50 km/h; (d) An exempt vehicle.	Carbon monoxide, hydrocarbons and oxides of nitrogen.
6	All vehicles propelled by compression ignition engines.	1 April 1991	Community Directive 88/77.	Annex 1, paragraphs 6, 7 and 8.	(a) A vehicle whose maximum gross weight is less than 3,500 kg, is first used before 1 April 1994 and which complies with the requirements of item 2; (b) A vehicle which complies with the requirements of items 4 or 5; (c) A fire appliance which is first used before 1 October 1992; (d) An industrial tractor, works truck or engineering plant; (e) An exempt vehicle.	Carbon monoxide, hydrocarbons and oxides of nitrogen.
7	Passenger vehicles which– (a) are constructed or adapted to carry not more than 5 passengers excluding the driver, and (b) have a maximum gross weight of not more than 2,500 kg, which are propelled by a compression ignition engine of (i) the indirect injection type, or (ii) the direct injection type.	 1 April 1991 1 April 1997	Community Directive 88/436.	Annex 1, paragraphs 5, 7 and 8, as far as they relate to particulate emissions	(a) A vehicle whose maximum speed is less than 50 km/h; (b) An off-road vehicle. (c) An exempt vehicle.	Particulates

| 8 | Passenger vehicles propelled by an engine with a capacity of less than 1,400 cc which–
(a) are constructed or adapted to carry not more than 5 passengers excluding the driver, and
(b) have a maximum gross weight of not more than 2,500 kg. | 31 December 1992 | Community Directive 89/458. | Annex 1, paragraphs 5, 7 and 8. | (a) A vehicle whose maximum speed is less than 50 kmh;
(b) An off-road vehicle.
(c) An exempt vehicle. | Carbon monoxide, hydrocarbons and oxides of nitrogen. |

The 1991 amendment adds a new regulation 61(10A) making it unlawful for a vehicle with a 4-stroke spark ignition engine first used after the stated date, to be used if, when the engine is idling the carbon monoxide and hydrocarbon content of the exhaust emissions exceed the following limits:

(a) carbon monoxide content, after 1 August 1983, 4.5%;
(b) hydrocarbon content, after 1 April 1975, 0.12%.

These provisions may be summarised as follows:

(1) The 1986 Regulations in regulation 61 –
   (a) implement Directives 70/220/EEC, 74/290/EEC, 77/102/EEC and 78/665/EEC and ECE Regulation 15.03 and 15.04;
   (b) prohibit the emission of avoidable smoke and visible vapour;
   (c) prohibit the use of vehicles whose emissions may cause damage to property or injury to persons;
   (d) to secure compliance with those general objectives Table I makes specific stipulations governing vehicle engines relating to:
      (i) the manual choke operation of diesel engines,
      (ii) the requirement of a relevant type test certificate for new diesel engined vehicles after 1973,
      (iii) the requirement that after 1972 new petrol engined vehicles are to consume their crank case gases.
(2) The 1990 Regulations amend the 1986 requirements by introducing:
   (a) compulsory compliance with limits on gaseous emissions from cars and light vans set by Directive 83/351/EEC and ECE Regulation 15.04;
   (b) more stringent limits on gaseous emissions from cars and light vans set by Directives 88/76/EEC and 89/458/EEC;
   (c) new limits on gaseous emissions from diesel engined vehicles over 3,500kg gross weight set by Directive 88/77/EEC;
   (d) the technical requirements set by ECE Regulation 49 for diesel engined industrial tractors, works trucks and engineering plant;
   (e) new limits on particulate emissions from diesel engined cars set by Directive 88/436/EEC; and
   (f) prohibitions on the use of a vehicle which fails to meet such applicable requirements where:
      (i) the failure results from an alteration to the engine or exhaust system;
      (ii) the requirements would be met or the emissions could be materially reduced if the vehicle were to undergo a normal periodic service; or
      (iii) the failure is due to equipment on the vehicle specifically designed to reduce emissions not being in good and efficient working order.

These provisions are enforced through the operation of the Motor Vehicle (Tests) Regulations 1981 as amended by the 1991 (Amendment) Regulations.[47] The 1981 Regulations repeal and re-enact the 1976 Regulations governing vehicle testing and bring within their scope public service vehicles. The matters covered by the test include the exhaust emissions as considered above from vehicles of the following classes:

Class I   light motor cycles
      II   other motor cycles
      III   light motor vehicles
      IV   motor cars not within classes III, V or VI
      V   large passenger carrying vehicles and public service vehicles

to which the 1991 Regulations added –

Class VII goods vehicles of gross weight 3,000–3,500 kg.

47 Respectively S.I.1981 No. 1694 and S.I. 1991 No. 1525.

Conclusion

When all that can be done to render petrol and diesel powered internal combustion engines efficient and clean in operation they will still, because of their number, constitute a major source of the pollutants considered earlier. Further improvement, therefore, can only be achieved by a reduction in the number and use of vehicles so powered. To that end, policies and initiatives espoused by central and local government will be of primary importance. The assumptions upon which society is organised and the consequent patterns of living require rethinking. In particular the relationship between, and the interaction of, transport and land use needs to be reassessed in this context.

The Royal Commission on Environmental Pollution emphasises this issue in relation to the application of PPG 13 (Planning Policy Guidance 13), saying:

9.41 PPG 13 advises how local authorities should integrate transport and land use planning. It emphasises the need to reduce growth in the number and length of motorised journeys, encourage more environmentally friendly means of travel and reduce reliance on the private car. The specific measures it advocates are broadly consistent with those which we endorsed above. It rightly recognises that, although the number of new developments each year is relatively small, they contribute to patterns which will endure long into the future and therefore have a potential to influence – for good or ill – the long-term effectiveness of policies to reduce the environmental effects of transport.

9.43 Planning policies are a necessary instrument for reducing travel demand but in isolation they will not suffice. The effectiveness of the new measures will depend crucially on the transport policy context as a whole and on the ability of local planning authorities to achieve the necessary shifts in policy, when it is not always clear that they have the powers to do so. To move towards more sustainable land use patterns will not be easy, and it will be necessary for the Department of the Environment to support consistently the aims of PPG 13. For this reason we welcome the Department's plan of producing a good practice guide to demonstrate practical ways of implementing appropriate policies. We welcome this and recommend both that the results be made public and that any shortcomings which are revealed be corrected without delay. Further long-term work may be needed to understand fully the effects of planning decisions on travel behaviour.

In concluding an exhaustive review of the impact of transport on the environment, the Royal Commission identifies the objectives that in its view should govern and inform future policy. In relation to pollution from vehicle exhaust emissions they are:

Objective A   To ensure that effective transport policy at all levels of government is integrated with land use policy and gives priority to minimising the need for transport and increasing the proportion of trips made by environmentally less damaging modes.

Objective B   To achieve standards of air quality that will prevent damage to human health and the environment.

Objective C   To improve the quality of life, particularly in towns and cities, by reducing the dominance of cars and lorries and providing alternative means of access.

Objective D   To increase the proportion of personal travel and freight transport by environmentally less damaging modes and to make the best use of the existing infrastructure.

AGRICULTURAL POLLUTION

The contribution made by agriculture to air pollution, apart from odours, derives from the burning of stubble and other crop residues after harvesting. This once common practice has been subjected to increasing criticism on a number of grounds in addition to pollution. The large volumes of smoke produced at ground level may constitute a hazard to traffic on adjacent roads, and fires, having been started, may continue and spread in unexpected ways. The seriousness of the problem was recognised by the Royal Commission on Environmental Pollution in its Tenth Report in 1984.[48] It recommended in consequence a total ban on the practice within five years and more research into alternative uses for straw. Power to control the practice is exercised through regulations made by the Secretary of State or the Minister of Agriculture, Fisheries and Food under section 152 of the Environmental Protection Act 1990. It is also to be noted that the production of smoke in such circumstances may constitute a statutory nuisance within the terms of section 79(1)(b) of the Environmental Protection Act 1990.[49]

The current regulations under section 152 are the Crop Residues (Burning) Regulations 1993.[50] They are intended to replace existing local authority byelaws on the subject and Schedule 15, paragraph 21 repeals section 43 of the Criminal Justice Act 1982 providing that byelaw-making power. The definition of 'crop residues' in the Regulations is narrower than that in the Act, being stated to 'mean straw, stubble or any other crop residue *remaining on the land after harvesting of the crop grown thereon'*. The portion in italics appears in the Regulations but not in the Act and is clearly intended to confine their operation to the burning of such residues on the land where they are produced; that of course being the problem. Where the waste material is removed for incineration elsewhere, either on or off the premises on which it is produced, it will be subject to control under either the IPC or LAAPC provisions of Part I of the Environmental Protection Act 1990,[51] or Part I of the Clean Air Act 1993 dealing with dark smoke,[52] or the waste control and disposal provisions in Part II of the Environmental Protection Act 1990[53] or the statutory nuisance provisions of Part III of the Environmental Protection Act 1990. The formulation of the definition appears to envisage only other crop residues that are *eiusdem generis* with straw and stubble. This view is supported

48 'Tackling Pollution: Experience and Prospects', Cm 9149, 1983, paragraphs 2.7-2.11.

49 See in Chapter 4 at p.94 above.

50 S.I. 1993 No. 1366, revoking S.I. 1991 No. 1590.

51 See section 5.1 of Schedule 1 of the Environmental Protection (Prescribed Processes and Substances) Regulations 1991, S.I. 1991 No. 472; and see Chapter 4, p.90-4.

52 See p.256.

53 See p.365.

by the opinion of the Parliamentary Secretary to the Minister of Agriculture, Fisheries and Food expressed during the Commons debates on the Bill that 'fruit pruning, clipping and heather are not crop residues and are not covered by the clause'.

The Regulations impose a general ban on burning, subject to specific limited exceptions, regulation 4 providing that:

> No person engaged in agriculture shall, on any agricultural land, burn any crop residues of a kind specified in Schedule 1 unless burning is for the purpose of –
>
> (a) education or research;
> (b) disease control or elimination of plant pests where a notice has been served under article 22 of the Plant Health Order 1993;[54] or
> (c) the disposal of straw stack remains or broken bales.

54 S.I. 1993 No. 1320.

Article 22(2) of the Plant Health Order 1993 gives an inspector, on suspecting on reasonable grounds the presence or likely presence on any premises of certain stipulated plant pests, the power to require by notice in writing on the occupier or the person in charge of the premises or the particular articles, *inter alia,* the treatment, destruction or disposal of the affected material as specified in the notice. This may include destruction by burning.

In the exceptional cases where burning is permitted it is to be undertaken in accordance with the terms of regulation 5 that:

> No person engaged in agriculture shall on agricultural land, burn –
>
> (a)   any crop residue of a kind specified in Schedule 1 to which an exemption specified in regulation 4(a) or (b) applies; or
> (b)   any linseed residues
>
> otherwise than in accordance with the restrictions and requirements in Schedule 2.

Breach of the Regulations is made a summary offence with fines up to level 5 on the standard scale. The crop residues specified in Schedule 1 are cereal straw and stubble and the residues of oil-seed rape, field beans harvested dry and peas harvested dry.

The restrictions placed by Schedule 2 on crop burning in the exceptional cases permitted by regulation 4 are of two kinds. There are, first, distance limits to protect vulnerable objects and activities and, secondly, stipulations governing the conduct of the operation. The first four paragraphs of Schedule 2 include:

(a) a prohibition of burning from one hour before sunset to the following sunrise or on any Saturday, Sunday or bank holiday;
(b) a prohibition on burning if the area of cereal straw or stubble is more than 10 hectares and in other cases is more than 20 hectares;
(c) requirement for firebreaks of stated sizes around the area to be burned and also around any buildings or structures in the area;
(d) restrictions of crop burning in relation to its proximity to other areas of crop burning;
(e) restriction of cereal straw or stubble burning within 15 metres and of other residues within 5 metres of –
    (i)   trees,
    (ii)   hedgerows or fences in other occupation,
    (iii) electricity or telephone poles, pylons or substations;

(f) restriction of cereal straw or stubble burning within 50 metres or of other residues within 15 metres of –
  (i) residential building,
  (ii) thatched roofed structure,
  (iii) building or structure that could be set alight or damaged by heat from the fire,
  (iv) scheduled monument that could be ignited,
  (v) stack of hay or straw,
  (vi) accumulation of combustible material removed in making a firebreak,
  (vii) mature standing crops,
  (viii) nature reserve,
  (ix) building or structure containing livestock,
  (x) oil or gas installation on or above ground;
(g) restriction of crop residue burning less than 100 metres from –
  (i) motorway,
  (ii) dual carriageway,
  (iii) A road,
  (iv) railway line.

Where crop burning is to be undertaken, paragraphs 5 to 10 of Schedule 2 require that:

(a) all persons concerned in the burning be familiar with the contents of these regulations and the area to be burned is to be supervised by at least two responsible adults;
(b) between one and 24 hours' notice of the burning is to be given to –
  (i) environmental health department of the District Council for the area;
  (ii) occupiers of all adjoining premises;
  (iii) air traffic control of any aerodrome with a perimeter fence within 800 metres of the area to be burned;
(c) as preconditions of burning –
  (i) at least 1,000 litres of water in mobile container(s) with means of dispensing in a spray or jet at a rate of 100 litres per minute; and
  (ii) a minimum of five fire-beating implements;
(d) all associated vehicles to be equipped with a suitable and serviceable fire extinguisher;
(e) reasonable precautions be taken to prevent fire crossing a firebreak;
(f) burnt cereal straw or stubble ash to be incorporated into the soil within 24 hours of the commencement of the burning; or if likely to cause a nuisance, having regard to wind conditions, as soon as conditions allow.

ASBESTOS

The damage to the respiratory system caused by the inhalation of asbestos fibres is a matter of common knowledge. Equally, its widespread use before the danger became apparent in industrial and commercial applications has ensured that the environment within which most people live and work is likely to contain some of the material. In particular its heat resistant properties have ensured its popular use in the construction industry for insulation, lagging and fire retarding applications, in addition to its value as a general building material for guttering, tiles and cladding. Asbestos is most dangerous to health when fine particles are inhaled and lodge in the lungs. It is evident, therefore, that such asbestos-containing materials constitute the greatest risk when they are being worked and installed, or alternatively removed and disposed of; in short, when they are subjected to any process or treatment that sufficiently abrades the surface as to produce fine dust or fibres.

Environmental risks due to the handling of materials containing asbestos in both these situations are subject to control in the Control of Asbestos in the Air Regulations 1990.[55] Regulation 4 provides that:

55 S.I. 1990 No. 556; implementing in part Directive 87/217/EEC.

(1) Any person undertaking activities involving the working of products containing asbestos shall ensure that those activities do not cause significant environmental pollution by asbestos fibres or dust emitted into air; and
(2) Any person undertaking the demolition of buildings, structures and installations containing asbestos and the removal from them of asbestos or materials containing asbestos involving the release of asbestos fibres or dust into the air shall ensure that significant environmental pollution is not caused thereby.

For the purpose of these Regulations, regulation 1(3) provides that 'asbestos' means the following fibrous silicates – actinolite, amosite, anthophyllite, chrysotile, crocidolite or tremolite. The deficiencies of this provision are that the Regulations do not stipulate the authority responsible for enforcement and there is no guidance on the scope of 'significant environmental pollution'. Failing such legislative clarification, it is for the court to be satisfied on the matter, having regard, it is suggested, to the seriousness of the potential harm, the time the harmful particles may remain in the environment, the potential range of their distribution and the persons consequently at risk.

INFORMATION AND MONITORING

It is evident that controls in themselves and for their own sake are valueless. Unless, therefore, the extensive air pollution control structure is seen by the community and particularly by the persons on whom it bears to have discernible and worthwhile results, it will fall into disrepute and it, and legal control generally, will cease to attract the necessary support and goodwill to ensure achievement of its objectives. Establishing the need for controls on any given emissions and subsequent monitoring of their effectiveness, or lack of it, must therefore be an integral feature of any such pollution prevention mechanism. In addition to such self-evident merits the obligation of Member States to monitor the presence in the atmosphere of various gaseous pollutants is a Community requirement. Part V of the Clean Air Act 1993, entitled 'Information About Air Pollution' is directed to that end.

On the question of research and publicity, section 34 gives local authorities a broad range of powers, either on their own or with or by others, to investigate air pollution problems and then to publicise the issues and information through publications, lectures, films, exhibitions, pictures, models etc. There is a saving in this section governing disclosure of trade secrets without the written consent of the appropriate person, breach of which is actionable criminally or civilly against the authority, member or officer concerned.

The Act contains a number of detailed provisions concerned with the acquisition of information for different purposes and in differing contexts on pollution of the atmosphere. Section 35 as a general measure, enables local authorities to 'obtain information about the emission of pollutants and other substances into the air':

(a) by notice under section 36;
(b) by measuring and recording emissions; and
(c) by arranging for occupiers to measure and record emissions.

For the purposes of (b) above, an authority may use the powers of entry provided by section 56, subject to 21 days' written notice and to the right of the recipient to elect to provide the information himself as provided by section 36. The scope for a local authority to obtain such information about processes subject to IPC is restricted to the section 36 procedure, or investigation and research under section 34(1) without entering the premises. While operating these section 35 powers a local authority is required to consult representatives of businesses in the area, persons conversant with air pollution problems and those having an interest in local amenity on the general exercise of such powers and the way and extent to which the information is to be made publicly available.[56]

Under section 36, a local authority may, by written notice, require the occupier of any premises with the exception of private dwellings and caravans to provide within six weeks of the notice and by the means specified in it, information concerning the emission of pollutants and other substances into the air from the premises. In the case of premises subject to IPC, the authority is entitled only to information already being supplied to HMIP. Any notice under this section shall remain valid only for up to 12 months and may require periodic returns at no less than three-month intervals. Failure, without reasonable excuse, to supply the required information, or the supply of knowingly false information is a summary offence. 'Reasonable excuse' will include cases where the defendant has no control over the circumstances surrounding the alleged offence,[57] but will not include lack of finance.[58] Where a person is convicted of an offence under this section, the local authority may enter the premises for the purpose of obtaining the requisite information[59] and the restrictions on such action in section 35(2) do not apply.

There is in section 37 a right of appeal to the Secretary of State by a person served with a section 36 notice, or any other person with an interest in the premises on the grounds that the provision or publicising of the information will unreasonably prejudice some private interest or be contrary to the public interest, or alternatively that the required information is not readily available and cannot, without incurring undue expenditure, readily be collected. Appeals under this section are governed by the Control of Atmospheric Pollution (Appeals) Regulations 1977.[60] Information relating to any appeal in respect of a section 36 notice must be entered on the public register provided for by the Control of Atmospheric Pollution (Research and Publicity) Regulations 1977.[61] In addition to these powers exercisable at the discretion of the local authority, section 39 permits the Secretary of State, following consultation and subject to his payment of the capital costs, to issue directions requiring authorities to install and operate apparatus for measuring and recording air pollution and to transmit the resulting information to him.

As well as these general powers in sections 35 and 36, sections 10 to 13[62] also make provision for local authorities to obtain information on furnace plant and emissions to the air in specific circumstances. Section 10, applying to specific categories of larger plant, permits a local authority by notice to require the occu-

56 Section 35(4) and (5).

57 *Wellingborough BC v Gordon* [1991] JPL 874.

58 *Saddleworth UDC v Aggregate and Sand* (1970) 114 SJ 931.

59 Section 36(8) and (9).

60 S.I. 1977 No. 17.

61 S.I. 1977 No. 19; see below.

62 See Chapter 10 at p.269, 270.

pier to install and operate measuring and recording apparatus and notify the authority of the results obtained. This section makes no specific restrictions on the purpose of such demands or concerning the use of the information obtained. Under section 11, a local authority, either on its own initiative or at the request of the occupier of the building, has the power to make and record measurements of grit, dust and fumes emitted from furnaces. Section 12 also gives a local authority power to require from the occupier by notice 'such information as to the furnaces in the building and the fuel or waste burned in those furnaces as they may reasonably require ...'. The purpose of this requirement is limited to the performance by the authority of its duties under sections 5 to 11, i.e., to ensure that the individual plant is being operated within proper emission levels for grit and dust. Lastly, section 13, *inter alia*, applies the effect of those sections to outdoor furnaces.

The Secretary of State is given the power, following consultation with representative and knowledgeable persons, to make regulations prescribing the manner and methods by which local authorities are to perform their section 34(1), 35 and 36 functions relating to investigation, research and obtaining information about air pollution.[63] In particular, section 38(5) requires that registers maintained by local authorities under section 38(3)(d) shall be open to public inspection at the principal office of the authority free of charge at all reasonable hours, and facilities for obtaining copies are to be made available at reasonable cost. Consultation must be a genuine process rather than merely a matter of form[64].

The current regulations are the Control of Atmospheric Pollution (Research and Publicity) Regulations 1977[65] which are primarily concerned with the scope and procedure of notices issued under section 36. Regulation 6 does, though, require local authorities to maintain adequately indexed registers under these Regulations. Regulation 3 specifies the range of emissions from chimneys and flues that may be the subject of a notice as:

(a) sulphur dioxide or particulate matter derived from any combustion process where the material being heated does not contribute to the emission;
(b) any gas or particulate matter derived from any combustion process where the material being heated contributes to the emission;
(c) any gas or particulate matter derived from any non-combustion process or other similar industrial activity.

The core of the Regulations is to be found in regulation 4 which lists the information that may be required, whether by estimates or otherwise. The proviso to this requirement, in regulation 4(2), is that information on past emissions may only be required if it is already in the possession of the occupier of the premises concerned or is immediately available to him. Information, by regulation 4(1), may be required in relation to:

(a) sulphur dioxide emissions during any specified period –
    (i) aggregate duration of all discharges;
    (ii) from any specified chimney, flue or outlet, the temperature, efflux velocity, volume flow rates, and height above ground level of the discharge;
    (iii) aggregate quantity of sulphur dioxide ascertained either from calculation of the quantity of fuel burnt and its sulphur content or, if the local authority and occupier agree, by direct measurement;
(b) total emissions of particulate matter during any specified period –

63 Section 38(1) and (2).

64 See on this issue in Chapter 1.

65 S.I. 1977 No. 19; and see explanatory Circular 2/77.

(i) aggregate duration of all discharges;
(ii) from any specified chimney, flue or outlet, the temperature, efflux velocity, volume flow rates, and height above ground level of the discharge;
(iii) average concentration of particulates discharged in grams per cubic metre at standard temperature and pressure;[66]
(iv) aggregate quantity of particulates discharged during that period;

66 That is a temperature of 15 degrees Celsius and a barometric pressure of one bar.

(c) emissions of gases other than sulphur dioxide or of any specified particulate matter –
(i) aggregate duration of all discharges;
(ii) from any specified chimney, flue or outlet, the temperature, efflux velocity, volume flow rates, and height above ground level of the discharge;
(iii) average concentration of specified pollutants during the period;
(iv) aggregate quantity of specified pollutants discharged during the period.

Returning to the 1993 Act, a final section providing for the obtaining of information is section 58. A local authority is given the power by notice served on any person to require within the stipulated period or at stated times, specified information which it reasonably considers is needed for the purpose of any function under Parts IV or V of the Act. The Secretary of State may, by regulations, restrict the information obtainable under this section or specify its form. Failure to comply with such a notice, or making a false statement is a summary offence. The limitation here is that the authority has reasonably to consider that the information is necessary for the performance of its Parts IV or V functions; the decision of an authority being therefore challengeable on *Wednesbury* grounds.[67]

67 See at note 67 in Chapter 10; *Associated Provincial Picture Houses v Wednesbury Corporation* [1948] 1 KB 223; and see on the evidential issue, *Coleen Properties v Minister of H & LG* [1971] 1 WLR 433, CA.

There is here an extensive range of powers enabling local authorities to obtain information to facilitate the performance of their air pollution control functions. This information, while necessary for that purpose, may be of confidential concern or commercial value to the person originating it. It is therefore protected from unjustified disclosure by the authority and its officers, as well as by other third parties, by the terms of section 49(1). Categories of persons affected are not specified or, apparently, limited. It is sufficient that the information relating to a 'trade secret' has come into their possession 'by virtue of this Act'. Disclosure will be justified and therefore not restricted by this section if it is made:

(a) in the performance of a duty;
(b) in pursuance of section 34(1)(b);[68] or
(c) with the consent of the person having a right to disclose the information.

68 Section 34(1)(b) gives a local authority the power to publish information on air pollution problems.

The section protects information that is 'given to or obtained by' the person concerned, thus extending to material received passively and without resort to the formal procedures considered above.

10

Smoke Control

INTRODUCTION

The Clean Air Act 1993[1] consolidates and replaces with amendment:

- the Clean Air Acts 1956 and 1968,
- Part IV of the Control of Pollution Act 1974,
- Control of Smoke Pollution Act 1989,
- section 85 of the Environmental Protection Act 1990.

It is now therefore the principal measure dealing with atmospheric pollution from furnaces and heating plant and, with its attendant regulations, provides a comprehensive code dealing with the following:

Part I   Control of dark smoke emissions from chimneys and other sources.
Part II   Control and measurement of smoke, grit, dust and fume emissions; chimney heights.
Part III Creation and operation of smoke control areas.
Part IV   Additional and miscellaneous powers.

These matters will now be dealt with in turn. In considering these provisions it is to be remembered that, by section 41, Parts I, II, and III of the Act do not apply to prescribed processes for the purposes of IPC under Part I of the Environmental Protection Act 1990[2] from the date on which an authorisation was granted, refused or the appeal determined. Also, smoke emissions that are prejudicial to health or a nuisance may be dealt with under the statutory nuisance procedure in Part III of the Environmental Protection Act 1990.

DARK SMOKE EMISSIONS

Section 1 of the 1993 Act, re-enacting section 1 of the 1956 Act, creates two offences relating to the emission of dark smoke, section 1(1) providing that:

> Dark smoke shall not be emitted from a chimney of any building, and if, on any day, dark smoke is so emitted, the occupier of the building shall be guilty of an offence.

Section 1(2) is in similar terms and prohibits the emission of dark smoke from a chimney 'which serves the furnace of any fixed boiler or industrial plant'. Where in the opinion of an authorised officer[3] the offence has occurred the authority, as a necessary preliminary to proceedings under this section, is required by section 51(1) to notify the appropriate person in writing.[4] A potential problem with an offence of this nature occupying an indefinite period of time is to determine what constitutes one breach, and in particular when one offence has ended and another begun. The problem is resolved here by the inclusion of the limiting phrase

1 Operative date 27 August 1993; the antecedent Law Commission Report on the consolidation of this area of law is Law Com No. 209; Cm 1085.

2 As to which see in Chapter 2 at p.47.

3 Defined in section 64(1) as an officer authorised by the local authority in writing, either generally or specifically, to act in the specified matter.

4 Section 1(6).

'on any day' in the definition of the offence. A day is a period of 24 hours begin-ning at midnight[5] so, for example, one emission continuing over that time will constitute two offences.

A local authority may take action in respect of any smoke affecting its district even though originating outside,[6] and the terms of section 1 are applied to rail-way engines and vessels in all waters within the territorial limits respectively by sections 43 and 44. Crown premises are exempt, however, section 46(1) requir-ing the local authority, when an offence occurs, to report to the responsible Minister who 'shall inquire into the circumstances and if necessary employ all practicable means for preventing or minimising the emission'. Penalties for breach are, on summary conviction, for domestic premises, scale 3 on the standard scale and, for others, scale 5.[7] Under section 51(1) relating to chimneys, the appropriate person is the occupier of the building. Section 64(1) recognises that one building may be in more than one occupation, in which case the person having control of the part containing the relevant fireplace is responsible. As that last reference indicates, the question of occupation is related to a sufficient degree of control, either over the premises themselves or over the activities of persons thereon, although exclusive control is not necessary.[8] 'Occupier' also extends to a person having a licence en-titling them to possession.[9]

For the purposes of this section 'chimney' is defined as[10]:

includ[ing] structures and openings of any kind from or through which smoke, grit, dust or fumes may be emitted, and, in particular, includes flues, and references to a chimney of a building include references to a chimney which serves the whole or a part of a build-ing but is structurally separate from the building.

The scope of 'building' has yet to be considered in this context. However, other authority suggests that the term is to be given its ordinary meaning, Byles J describ-ing a building in *Stevens v Gourley* (1859)[11] as 'a structure of considerable size and intended to be permanent or at least to endure for a considerable time'. In the same case, concerning a wooden structure measuring 16 feet by 13 feet support-ed on timbers laid on the surface of the ground and intended to be used as a shop, Erle CJ said[12]:

... the structure was permanently built and reasonably calculated for the use of man; and though by the application of mechanical power a structure of considerable size may be removed, it does not therefore cease to be a 'building' within the meaning of the Act.

It may also require a roof.[13] In the planning context Lord Parker CJ said that[14]:

... when the Act defines a building as including 'any structure or erection and any part of a building so defined,' the Act is referring to any structure or erection which can be said to form part of the realty, and to change the physical character of the land.

Turning to the question of 'dark smoke', section 64(1) defines 'smoke' as 'includ[ing] soot, ash, grit and gritty particles emitted in smoke', that is the products of com-bustion. 'Dark smoke', by section 3(1), 'means smoke which if compared in the appropriate manner with a ... Ringelmann Chart would appear to be as dark as or darker than shade 2'. The standard Ringelmann Chart[15] consists of a cardboard sheet on which are printed five 101mm squares, four of which are cross-hatched by 20 horizontal and 20 vertical lines of progressively increasing thickness, so that in use and at the specified distance the cross-hatching merges into the white back-ground to produce, for each shade, a uniform grey. From shade 0, which is white

5 Section 64(1).

6 Section 55.

7 Section 37 of the Criminal Justice Act 1982.

8 See, e.g., *Wheat v E. Lacon & Co. Ltd* [1966] AC 552; *H & N Emmanuel Ltd v GLC* [1971] 2 All ER 835; *Harris v Birkenhead Corporation* [1976] 1 All ER 341.

9 *Stevens v London Borough of Bromley* [1972] Ch 400.

10 Section 64(1).

11 (1859) 7 CB (NS) 99 at p.112.

12 At pp.107–8.

13 *Per* Lord Esher in *Moir v Williams* [1892] 1 QB 264 at p. 270.

14 *Cheshire CC v Woodward* [1962] 2 AC 126 at p.135.

15 BS 2742C

each succeeding shade of grey from 1 to 4 has an increase in obscuration and therefore darkness of 20 per cent over the earlier shade. Ringelmann shade 2 therefore has a 40 per cent obscuration. Both the standard chart and the specified method of use are so cumbersome that it is questionable whether they are much used in practice, being substituted by the use of other forms of the chart.[16] This practice is recognised for the purpose of proceedings under the Act, section 3(2) providing that actual comparison of the smoke with the chart is not necessary. Also, of course, the visual assessment of dark smoke with the use of the chart at night presents certain difficulties. In such cases, and especially with larger plant, alternative evidence from, say, monitoring and recording apparatus in the furnace flues may be available.

The section 1(2) offence applies to 'fixed boiler or industrial plant', meaning boiler or industrial plant which is attached to a building or is for the time being fixed or installed on any land. This is a matter of fact and indicates a need for something more than the mere parking or stationing of plant on land, implying its established and settled siting though not necessarily permanence. In this case the person responsible is the person in possession. A person has possession of whatever is to his knowledge physically in his custody or under his physical control.[17]

Defences provided in section 1(4) against proceedings under this section are proof that the alleged emission was due to:

(a) lighting up a furnace from cold and that all practicable steps were taken to prevent or minimise the emission;
(b) failure of the furnace or connected apparatus that –
   (i) could not reasonably have been either foreseen or provided against, and
   (ii) the alleged emission could not reasonably have been prevented by action taken after the failure had occurred; or
(c) solely to the use of unsuitable fuel and that –
   (i) suitable fuel was unobtainable and the least unsuitable fuel which was available was used; and
   (ii) all practicable steps were taken to prevent or minimise the emission of dark smoke as a result of the use of that fuel,

or the alleged emission was due to a combination of two or more of those causes and the other conditions were respectively satisfied. It is also a defence to show, where appropriate, that the terms of section 51(1) have not been satisfied. 'Practicable' for the purposes of the section 1(4) defences means, by section 64(1),

> reasonably practicable having regard, amongst other things, to local conditions and circumstances, to the financial implications and to the current state of technical knowledge, and 'practicable means' includes the provision and maintenance of plant and its proper use.

There appears to be no obligation to notify reliance on any defence to the prosecution. As with other criminal proceedings, the standard of proof on the defence is not as onerous as that on the prosecution, being on a balance of probabilities.[18]

In practice it is impossible to operate furnaces without at times producing dark smoke, and in some circumstances it may be undesirable. The Act therefore provides for two forms of exemptions. Section 45(1)(a) gives local authorities the

16 See, e.g., the Miniature Smoke Chart, BS 2742.

17 *R v Maio* [1989] VR 281.

18 *R v Carr-Briant* [1943] KB 607; *R v Hudson* [1966] 1 QB 448.

19 S.I. 1958 No. 498, made under section 1(2) of the Clean Air Act 1956 and having effect under this present section of the 1993 Act by virtue of section 17(2)(b) of the Interpretation Act 1978.

20 S.I. 1958 No. 878.

21 'Vessel' has by virtue of section 11 of the Interpretation Act 1978, section 31(1) of the Clean Air Act 1956 and section 343(1) of the Public Health Act 1936, the meaning assigned by section 742 of the Merchant Shipping Act 1894, i.e., 'includes any ship or boat, or any other description of vessel used in navigation'.

power to exempt any chimney from the operation of section 1 for the purposes of research and investigation, subject to such conditions and for such period as it may specify. Alternatively, section 45(3) gives the Secretary of State power to make regulations prescribing periods for which the emission of dark smoke will be exempted from the prohibition. Such regulations are currently the Dark Smoke (Permitted Periods) Regulations 1958[19] and the Dark Smoke (Permitted Periods) (Vessels) Regulations 1958.[20] The former Regulations permit the emission of dark smoke and black smoke in the following terms, black smoke being smoke that is as dark as or darker than shade 4 on the Ringelmann Chart.

Dealing first with the regulations applicable to buildings, regulation 3(1) excludes from the operation of section 1, 'Emissions of dark smoke of not longer than 10 minutes in aggregate in any period of eight hours or, if soot blowing is carried out within such period, for not longer than 14 minutes'. Regulation 3(2) then provides for extensions of those times in the case of –
(i) a chimney serving two furnaces, to 18 and 25 minutes respectively;
(ii) a chimney serving three furnaces, to 24 and 34 minutes respectively;
(iii) a chimney serving four or more furnaces, to 29 and 41 minutes respectively.

Regulation 4 further provides that the Regulations do not authorise either the continuous emission of dark smoke for more than four minutes, unless caused by soot blowing, or the aggregate emission of black smoke for more than two minutes in any 30 minutes. By regulation 2(3), multiple furnaces in one boiler or unit of industrial plant discharging into the same chimney shall be deemed to be one furnace for the purpose of the Regulations.

The Vessels[21] Regulations, as may be expected, are designed to achieve similar aims, but necessarily in a wider range of circumstances. Regulation 3(1) therefore excludes from the scope of section 1 of the Act:

Emissions of dark smoke from a chimney of a vessel for not longer than the period specified in column (2) of the schedule ... in respect of the class of case specified in column (1); Provided that –

(a) continuous emissions of dark smoke caused otherwise than by soot blowing of a water tube boiler shall not exceed –
(i) in the case of classes 1 and 2, 4 minutes;
(ii) in the case of natural draught oil fired furnaces in class 4, 10 minutes; and
(b) in no case shall black smoke be emitted for more than 3 minutes in the aggregate in any period of 30 minutes.

The Schedule referred to in regulation 3(1) is reproduced below.

SCHEDULE

(1)	(2)
	Permitted period for
Class of Case	*Emission of dark smoke*
1. Emissions from a forced draught oil-fired boiler furnace, or an oil engine.	10 minutes in the aggregate in any period of two hours.
2. Emissions from a natural draught oil-fired boiler furnace, (except in the cases falling within class 4 below).	10 minutes in the aggregate in any period of one hour.

3. Emissions from a coal-fired boiler furnace:–
   a) when the vessel is not under way (except in the cases falling within class 4 below).   10 minutes in the aggregate in any period of one hour.
   b) when the vessel is under way.   20 minutes in the aggregate in any period of one hour.

4. Emissions from a natural draught oil-fired boiler furnace or a coal-fired boiler furnace in the following cases:–
   a) a vessel with funnels shortened for the purpose of navigating the Manchester Ship Canal;
   b) a tug not under way, but preparing to get under way or supplying power to other vessels or to shore installations;   20 minutes in the aggregate in any period of one hour
   c) a vessel not under way but using main power for the purpose of dredging, lifting, pumping or performing some other special operation for which the vessel is designed.

5. Emissions from any other source.   5 minutes in the aggregate in any period of one hour.

Regulation 3(2) stipulates that for the purposes of the Schedule a vessel is not under way when it is at anchor or made fast to the shore or bottom, and a vessel which is aground shall be deemed to be under way.

While section 1 of the 1993 Act prohibits the emission of dark smoke from chimneys, section 2, substantially re-enacting section 1 of the 1968 Act and section 2 of the 1989 Act, controls emissions from other sources in similar terms, section 2(1) providing that:

> Dark smoke shall not be emitted from any industrial or trade premises and if, on any day, dark smoke is so emitted the occupier of the premises and any person who causes or permits the emission shall be guilty of an offence.

Both the occupier and the person directly implicated may be liable for the one offence and, as with section 1 above, a necessary precondition to action by the authority is written notice under section 51 by the officer concerned. The scope of and the distinction between 'cause' and 'permit' has been considered in detail in Chapter 1. 'Industrial or trade premises', by section 2(6), means:

(a) premises used for any industrial or trade purposes; and
(b) premises not so used on which matter is burnt in connection with any industrial or trade process.

The scope of the term, is wide, being related to the purpose for which the premises are used[22]. For the purposes of this section, premises were held to include a demolition site in *Sheffield City Council* v *ADH Demolition* (1984).[23] The same case also considered that demolition was a 'trade process'. As is illustrated by this example, a primary aim of the section is to control burning in the open air in connection with a business, even if the burning happens, for example, on domestic premises. Activities such as scrap, tyre or car body burning will therefore be covered as well as building demolitions. By section 33 of this Act, cable burning to recover the metal may only be carried out lawfully as part of a process subject to IPC authorisation under Part I of the Environmental Protection Act 1990.

Unusually, the burden of proof is shifted to the defence by the terms and in the circumstances of section 2(3):

22 *Thames Water Authority* v *Blue & White Launderettes* [1980] 1 WLR 700, CA.

23 (1984) 82 LGR 177.

there shall be taken to have been an emission of dark smoke from industrial or trade premises in any case where –

(a) material is burned on those premises; and
(b) the circumstances are such that the burning would be likely to give rise to the emission of dark smoke,

unless the occupier or other person who caused or permitted the burning shows that no dark smoke was emitted.

The defences available in response to proceedings under this section are, by section 2(4):

(a) that the alleged emission was inadvertent; and
(b) that all practicable steps had been taken to prevent or minimise the emission of dark smoke.

As with section 1, it is also a defence to show that the local authority has not complied with the section 51(1) requirements. Also following the pattern of section 1, this section does not apply to emissions within regulations made by the Secretary of State and complying with stipulated conditions, if any. The currently applicable regulations are the Clean Air (Emission of Dark Smoke) (Exemption) Regulations 1969.[24] Regulation 3 provides that 'the emission of dark smoke caused by the burning of any matter prescribed in column 1 of Schedule 1 shall, subject to compliance with any conditions specified in column 2, be exempted from' section 2(1) of the Clean Air Act 1993. The schedule contents are as follows:

24 S.I. 1969 No. 1263.

Exempted Matter	*Conditions*
1. Timber and any other waste matter (other than natural or synthetic rubber or flock or feathers) which results from the demolition of a building or clearance of a site in connection with any building operation or work of engineering construction (within the meaning of section 176 of the Factories Act 1961).	A, B and C
2. Explosive (within the meaning of the Explosives Act 1975) which has become waste; and other matter which has been contaminated by such explosive.	A and C
3. Matter which is burnt in connection with: a) research into the cause or control of fire *or* b) training in fire fighting.	C
4. Tar, pitch asphalt and other matter which is burnt in connection wirth the preparation and laying of any surface, or which is burnt off any surface in connection with re-surfacing, together with any fuel used for any such purpose.	C
5. Carcases of animals or poultry which a) have died, or are reasonably believed to have died, because of disease; b) have been slaughtered because of disease; or c) have been required to be slaughtered pursuant to the Diseases of Animals Act 1950	A and C unless the burning is carried out on behalf of an inspector (within the meaning of section 84 of the Diseases of Animals Act 1950)

6. Containers which are contaminated by any pesticide   A, B and C
or by any toxic substance used for veterinary or
agricultural purposes; and in this paragraph
'container' includes any sack, box or receptacle of
any kind.

Condition A   That there is no other reasonable safe and practicable method of disposing of the matter.

Condition B   That the burning is carried out in such a manner as to minimise the emission of dark smoke.

Condition C   That the burning is carried out under the direct and continuous supervision of the occupier of the premises concerned or a person authorised to act on his behalf.

SMOKE, GRIT, DUST AND FUMES

The control and measurement of the emission of these materials is dealt with in sections 4 to 13 of Part II of the 1993 Act; sections 4, 5 and 13 restricting the discharge of smoke, grit and dust from furnaces, sections 6 and 8 requiring the fitting of arresting plant, and sections 10 and 11 dealing with measurement of emissions. As is to be expected, this legislation does not apply to circumstances already governed under other provisions, for example:

(a) processes designated as prescribed processes for the purposes of Part I of the Environmental Protection Act 1990 – see section 41;
(b) discharge of smoke, grit and dust from the combustion of mine or quarry refuse to which section 42 applies;
(c) smoke, grit or dust from railway locomotive engines – see section 43(5);
(d) smoke, grit or dust from any vessel – see sections 44(6) and 46(4);
(e) work within the Alkali, etc. Works Regulation Act 1906 – see section 66(1)(a) and Schedule 3, Part I, paragraphs 2 and 3.

Before considering the legal controls on these pollutants some identification or differentiation is perhaps desirable. With the exception of 'dust' they have all been defined in legislation as follows:

(a) Smoke is defined in section 64(1) of the Clean Air Act 1993 as including 'soot, ash, grit and gritty particles emitted in smoke'.
(b) Grit is defined in the Clean Air Act (Emission of Grit and Dust from Furnaces) Regulations 1971 as particles exceeding 76 microns in diameter.
(c) Fumes are defined in section 64(1) of the Clean Air Act 1993 as 'airborne solid matter smaller than dust'.
(d) British Standard BS3405 defines 'dust' as small solid particles between 1 and 75 microns in diameter.

Dealing with the provision of new non-domestic equipment, section 4(2) provides that:

No furnace shall be installed in a building or in any fixed boiler or industrial plant unless the furnace is so far as is practicable capable of being operated continuously without emitting smoke when burning fuel of a type for which the furnace was designed.

Section 4(6) extends the scope of this provision to the attachment to a building of a boiler or industrial plant that already contains a furnace, or the fixing or installing on land of any such boiler or plant. 'Furnace' is not defined for the purposes of this Act and its meaning has been considered by the courts only in the context of rating cases. In *British Steel Corporation* v *Pittock* (Valuation Officer) (1970)[25] the tribunal held that the furnace in question was the whole agglomeration of bricks, steel and parts, and as such, was a structure. Furnaces have been held to include cremators[26] and incinerators generally unless expressly excluded. A domestic furnace, by section 64(1), means any furnace which is:

(a) designed solely or mainly for domestic purposes; and
(b) used for heating a boiler with a maximum heating capacity of less than 16.12 kilowatts.

The requirement that fixed boiler or industrial plant is to be capable of smokeless operation is, as noted above, by section 4(6) extended to a boiler or industrial plant which is attached to a building or is for the time being fixed to or installed on any land. This definition seems wide enough to apply to a change of location or repositioning on the same site, making a further notification necessary. The Court of Appeal's view of 'attachment', formulated in the context of rating assessment, is that actual physical attachment is not a necessary feature and that the use and function of the premises are material considerations. In what is probably the leading case, *Tyne Boiler Works Co.* v *Overseers of Longbenton* (1886),[27] the question was whether boiler making machinery and plant used on the premises was the property of the appellants, or was annexed to and part of the soil or hereditaments and therefore the property of the freeholder. Lord Esher MR, after reviewing the earlier authorities, said[28]:

> I do not think that the Court meant by the word 'attached' that physical attachment should be the test, ... I believe the rule really to be that things, which are on the premises to be rated and which are there for the purpose of making, and which make the premises fit as premises for the particular purpose for which they are used, are to be taken into account in ascertaining the rateable value of such premises. Of course it is not all things on the premises, or that are used on the premises, which are to be taken into account; but things which are there for the purpose of making, and which do make them fit as premises for the particular purpose for which they are used. It seems to me that, when things are brought into that category, they would pass by demise of a premises as such as between landlord and tenant; ... Taking that to be the proper test and applying it to the question in this case, I should say, in accordance with the opinion of Patteson J,[29] with regard to each of the articles in question, that it is immaterial to inquire whether they are or are not physically annexed to the freehold, and that they, all of them, come within the rule as I have expressed it. They are all on the premises for the purpose of making and they do make them fit as premises for the purpose for which they are used, and therefore in arriving at the rateable value of such premises they must be taken into account.

Notice of the installation is to be given to the local authority and if, in addition, plans and specifications are submitted to and approved by the authority, the furnace shall be deemed to comply with section 4(2).[30] The note to section 1 on the scope of 'building' applies also to its use in this section. Failure to notify the local authority as required by section 4(1) attracts a fine on summary conviction up to level 3 on the standard scale, and a breach of section 4(2) up to level 5.[31] In contrast to the general prohibition in section 1 of the emission of dark smoke from all chimneys, this section requires that newly installed plant shall effectively be smokeless.

Section 5 creates two offences relating to the discharge of grit and dust from non-domestic furnaces.[32] First, the Secretary of State may, by regulation, prescribe

25 (1970) 16 RRC 374; (1970) RA 423, Lands Tribunal.

26 *Gudgion (Valuation Officer)* v *Croydon BC* 16 RRC 305; (1970) RA 423

27 (1886) 18 QBD 81, CA. Approved and applied by the House of Lords in *Kirby* v *Hunslett Union* [1906] AC 43.

28 At pp.91-2.

29 In *R* v *Haslam* (1886) 17 QB 220.

30 Section 4(1) and (3) respectively.

31 Section 37 of the Criminal Justice Act 1982.

32 Section 13 applies these provisions to outdoor furnaces.

limits on the rates of emission of grit and dust from furnace chimneys, in which case:

> If on any day grit or dust is emitted from a chimney serving a furnace to which this section applies at a rate exceeding the relevant limit prescribed under subsection (2), the occupier of any building in which the furnace is situated shall be guilty of an offence.[33]

33 Section 5(3).

Secondly, in the case of chimneys not covered by the regulations, section 5(5) stipulates generally that an occupier who 'fails to use any practicable means there may be for minimising the emission of grit or dust from the chimney', shall be guilty of an offence. Penalties, on summary conviction are up to scale 5 on the standard scale, and it is a defence to proceedings under section 5(3) to show that the best practicable means have been used to minimise the emission. It is also of course, by implication, a defence under section 5(5). The effect of section 13 is to apply sections 5 to 12 to the furnace of any fixed boiler or industrial plant as they apply to furnaces in buildings; in which case the person responsible is the person having possession of the plant instead of the occupier.

The applicable regulations within section 5(2)[34] are the Clean Air (Emission of Grit and Dust from Furnaces) Regulations 1971.[35] The Regulations make separate provision for 'Schedule 1 furnaces' and 'Schedule 2 furnaces', which are defined respectively as follows:

34 Made under section 2(1) o[f] the Clean Air Act 1968 and having effect under the presen[t] section by virtue of section 17(2)(b) of the Interpretation Act 1978.

(a) Schedule 1 furnace means a furnace of –
    (i) a boiler, or
    (ii) an indirect heating appliance in which the material heated is a gas or liquid; and where any such furnace falls also within the definition of 'Schedule 2 furnace', it shall be treated for the purposes of the Regulations as a Schedule 1 furnace.

35 S.I. 1971 No. 162.

(b) Schedule 2 furnace means a furnace –
    (i) of an indirect heating appliance, or
    (ii) in which combustion gases are in contact with the material being heated, but that material does not itself contribute to the grit and dust in the combustion gases.

It is also to be noted that Schedule 1 furnaces are rated by heat output, while Schedule 2 furnaces are rated by heat input. The Regulations do not apply to incinerators, that is appliances used to burn solid or liquid waste or refuse, whether or not the resulting heat is used for any purpose.[36] As with 'furnace', there is no definition of 'boiler' for the purposes of these provisions. A statutory definition did however appear in section 3 of the now repealed Boiler Explosions Act 1892, to the effect that a boiler was 'any closed vessel used for generating steam, or for heating water, or for heating any other liquids, or into which steam is admitted for heating, steaming, boiling or any other similar purposes'.

36 Regulation 6.

The key provision governing grit and dust emissions is to be found in the following terms in regulation 4:

> the quantities of grit and dust which may be emitted during any period from the chimney of a Schedule 1 furnace or a Schedule 2 furnace with a heat output or input which is within the highest and lowest values specified in column 1 of the relevant schedule shall not exceed the quantities prescribed by that schedule.[37]

37 Regulation 4(4) contains rules for applying the regulations to furnaces having rating values intermediate between two adjacent values i[n] column 1 of the schedules.

Furnaces falling outside the limits specified in the schedules are not therefore subject to stipulated emission periods but, as has been stated, will nevertheless come within the general requirement of section 5(5). The implication in the quotation from regulation 4 is that one chimney discharges from one furnace. This is not always or necessarily the case. To deal with the alternative, therefore, regulation 4(2) provides that:

where a chimney serves more than one furnace –

(a) if multiflue, each flue is to be taken as a separate chimney serving a separate furnace; and

(b) in any other case, to be taken as a single chimney serving a single furnace with a heat output or input equivalent to the aggregate of the furnaces concerned,

and any part which derives from a furnace to which these regulations do not apply shall be disregarded.

In applying the prescribed periods to furnaces, regulation 5 stipulates that:

the limits apply in respect of any period of standard operation, that is when it is operating –

(a) at or close to the loading to which it is normally subjected, or

(b) at any higher loading to which it is regularly subject for a limited time.

The contents of the schedules, which are largely self-explanatory, are as follows:

SCHEDULE 1
FURNACES RATED BY HEAT OUTPUT

Maximum continuous rating in pounds of steam per hour (from and at 100°C. (212°F) or in thousands of British thermal units per hour (1)	Maximum permitted quantities of grit and dust in pounds per hour	
	Furnaces burning solid matter (2)	Furnaces burning liquid matter (3)
825	1.10	0.25
1,000	1.33	0.28
2,000	2.67	0.56
3,000	4.00	0.84
4,000	5.33	1.12
5,000	6.67	1.4
7,500	8.50	2.1
10,000	10.00	2.8
15,000	13.33	4.2
20,000	16.67	5.6
25,000	20.0	7.0
30,000	23.4	8.4
40,000	30	11.2
50,000	37	12.5
100,000	66	18
150,000	94	24
200,000	122	29
250,000	149	36
300,000	172	41
350,000	195	45
400,000	217	50
450,000	239	54.5
475,000	250	57

Limitations on grit

In the case of a Schedule 1 furnace which burns solid matter, the prescribed quantities may not contain more than the following proportion of particles exceeding 76 microns in diameter, that is to say –

(a) 33% where the Maximum Continuous Rating does not exceed 16,800 pounds per hour of steam or16,800,000 British Thermal Units per hour or
(b) 20% in any other case.

SCHEDULE 2
FURNACES RATED BY HEAT INPUT

Heat input in millions of British thermal units per hour	Maximum permitted quantities of grit and dust in pounds per hour	
	Furnaces burning solid matter	Furnaces burning liquid matter
(1)	(2)	(3)
1.25	1.1	0.28
2.5	2.1	0.55
5.0	4.3	1.1
7.5	6.8	1.7
10	7.6	2.2
15	9.7	3.3
20	11.9	4.4
25	14.1	5.5
30	16.3	6.6
35	18.4	7.7
40	20.6	8.8
45	22.8	9.8
50	25	10.9
100	45	16
200	90	26
300	132	35
400	175	44
500	218	54
575	250	57

Limitation on grit

In the case of a Schedule 2 furnace which burns solid matter, the prescribed quantities may not contain more than the following proportions of particles exceeding 76 microns in diameter, that is to say –

(a) 33% where the designed heat input of the furnace does not exceed 25 million BTUs, or
(b) 20% in any other case.

The provision of arrestment plant to remove grit and dust from the flue gases of furnaces is required by sections 6 to 8 of the Act. Section 6 requires that non-domestic furnaces over specified sizes shall only be used if provided with grit and dust arrestment plant that has been approved by the local authority and which is properly maintained and used. Furnaces to be so equipped are those used:

(a) to burn pulverised fuel; or
(b) to burn, at a rate of 45.4 kg or more per hour, any other solid matter; or

(c) to burn, at a rate equivalent to 366.4 kilowatts or more, any liquid or gaseous matter.

The Secretary of State is given the power to change these limits 'as he thinks fit' by regulation, but their reduction requires the approval of Parliament.[38] Each daily breach constitutes an offence with penalties, on summary conviction, up to level 5 on the standard scale. The scope of the Secretary of State's discretion expressed in the phrase 'as he thinks fit' is not, as it appears, unrestricted or incapable of challenge. The exercise of such a power must be broadly within, and to achieve the purposes of, the statute concerned. If questioned, therefore, any particular decision will be assessed by the courts on the basis of its reasonableness in relation to the aims of these sections of the Act; referred to in administrative law terms as Wednesbury unreasonableness.

The provisions of section 6 are subject to two categories of exemption in section 7. By section 7(2), a local authority,[39] on the application of the occupier, may exempt a furnace from the operation of the section if it is satisfied that the emission of grit and dust will not be prejudicial to health or a nuisance if the furnace is used for a particular purpose without compliance. If the authority does not determine the application and notify the applicant within eight weeks the exemption shall be deemed to have been granted on the terms of the application. Refusal of an application is to be notified in writing with reasons, the applicant then having 28 days within which to appeal to the Secretary of State. The Regulations made for the purposes of section 6(1) and dealt with below also prescribe in Schedules 2 and 3, the form and particulars for applications to the local authority under section 7(2). The information required includes details of the applicant, the grounds on which exemption is claimed, the type and description of the furnace and its particulars, including maximum rating, type of fuel, rate of fuel consumption, method of firing, type of draught, production of grit and dust and pattern of operation.

The second form of exemption is as prescribed by regulations made by the Secretary of State under section 7(1). The current regulations, made under section 4(1) of the 1968 Act,[40] are the Clean Air (Arrestment Plant)(Exemption) Regulations 1969.[41] By regulation 3, 'furnaces in column 1 of Schedule 1 shall while used for a purpose set out in column 2 opposite that class be exempt from the provisions of [section 6 of the Clean Air Act 1993]'. Schedule 1 is as follows:

SCHEDULE 1
Exempted Furnaces

(1) Class of Furnace	(2) Purpose
1. Mobile or transportable furnaces	(a) Providing a temporary source of heat or power during any building operation or work of engineering construction (within the meaning of section 176 of the Factories Act 1961);
	(b) providing a temporary source of heat or power for investigation or research;
	(c) providing heat or power for the purposes of agriculture (within the meaning of section 109(3) of the Agriculture Act 1947.

38 Section 6(3); and see section 1(1) of the Laying of Documents before Parliament (Interpretation) Act 1948.

39 One must assume that the section should read 'the local authority'.

40 See note 34 above.

41 S.I. 1969 No. 1262.

2. Furnaces other than furnaces designed to burn solid matter at a rate of one ton an hour or more, which fall within any of the following descriptions and in which the matter being heated does not contribute to the emission of grit and dust :

(a) furnaces burning liquid matter, gas, or liquid matter and gas;

(b) hand-fired sectional furnaces designed to burn solid matter at a rate of not more than 25 pounds an hour for each square foot of grate surface;

(c) magazine type gravity-fed furnaces designed to burn solid matter at a rate of not more than 25 pounds an hour for each square foot of grate surface;

(d) furnaces fitted with an under-feed stoker designed to burn solid matter at a rate of not more than 25 pounds an hour for each square foot of the plan area of the combustion chamber;

(e) furnaces fitted with a chain grate stoker designed to burn solid matter at a rate of not more than 25 pounds an hour for each square foot of grate surface;

(f) furnaces fitted with a coking stoker designed to burn solid matter at a rate of not more than 25 pounds an hour for each square foot of the area covered by the fire bars excluding the solid coking plate.

Any purpose except the incineration of refuse

While section 6 applies to non-domestic furnaces over stated sizes burning all fuels, section 8 governs specified categories of domestic solid fuel burning furnaces. In those cases local authority approved arrestment plant is to be provided, maintained and used; contravention again being a summary offence carrying the same penalties as breach of section 6. The classes of furnace within section 8 are those used:

(a) to burn pulverised fuel; or

(b) to burn, at a rate of 1.02 tonnes an hour or more, solid fuel in any other form or solid waste.

'Domestic furnace' is defined in section 64(1).[42]

42 See above at p.263.

Both sections 6 and 8 require, in specified circumstances, the use of arrestment plant approved by the local authority. The terms of section 9 apply to the operation of such approvals, but not, it is to be noted, to local authority exemptions under section 7 which are dealt with in section 7(3) to (5). Here the authority is required to notify their decision in writing and, in the case of a refusal, to state its reasons. Should either the applicant or a person having an interest in the building for which the application is made be dissatisfied with the decision, they have a right of appeal within 28 days to the Secretary of State who may himself grant an approval.[43]

The measurement of emissions from furnaces in buildings is provided for in sections 10 and 11.[44] In the former case, applicable to larger plant, the local authority may require the occupier to undertake the measurement, while, under the broader operation of section 11, the occupier may also require the local authority to measure and record emissions from his plant. Section 10 gives a local authority the power to apply by written notice the provisions of section 10(2) to:

a furnace in a building used –

(a)   to burn pulverised fuel;
(b)   to burn, at a rate of 45.4 kilograms or more per hour, any other solid matter; or
(c)   to burn, at a rate equivalent to 366.4 kilowatts or more, any liquid or gaseous matter.

Such occupiers when so directed by the authority, are to comply with the requirements prescribed by regulations made by the Secretary of State as to:

(a) making and recording measurements from time to time of the grit, dust and fumes emitted from the furnace;
(b) making adaptations for that purpose to the chimney serving the furnace;
(c) providing and maintaining apparatus for making and recording the measurements; and
(d) informing the local authority of the results obtained from the measurements or otherwise making those results available to the authority.

The phrase 'from time to time' has been held to mean 'as the occasion shall arise' or 'as and when appropriate so to do'.[45]

The notice giving a direction applying section 10(2) to a furnace shall also notify the occupier of the terms of section 11(1) to (3).[46] A local authority representative is entitled to be present while such measuring is in progress. Penalties, by section 10(3), include a fine up to level 5 for failure to comply and a cumulative penalty for the duration of the failure in accordance with section 50. As with section 6, the Secretary of State is empowered to vary the furnace capacities subject to these provisions, but their reduction requires Parliamentary approval.[47]

In the case of any furnace to which the local authority has applied section 10(2) and which is used:

(a) to burn, at a rate less than 1.02 tonnes an hour, solid matter other than pulverised fuel; or
(b) to burn, at a rate of less than 8.21 Megawatts, any liquid or gaseous matter,

the occupier may request the local authority, by written notice, to make and record measurements of the grit, dust and fumes emitted from the furnace.[48] For the duration of the notice the authority shall maintain such records, and the occupier's obligations imposed by regulations under section 10(2) shall, with the exception of (b) providing for any necessary chimney adaptations, no longer apply.

The current regulations for the purposes of section 10(2)[49] are the Clean Air (Measurement of Grit and Dust from Furnaces) Regulations 1971.[50] Regulation 3 provides that where a local authority applies by direction the provisions of sec-

Footnotes:

43 Section 9(2) and (3).

44 The terms of sections 5–12 are applied to outdoor furnaces by section 13.

45 Halliday v Wakefield Corporation (1887) 57 LT 559 at pp.562 and 563, per Mathew J. and Re Von Dembinska, ex parte The Debtor [1954] 2 All ER 46 at p.48, [1954] 1 WLR 748, CA, per Evershed MR

46 Section 11(4).

47 Section 10(5).

48 Section 11(1) and (2).

49 Made under section 7(2) of the Clean Air Act 1956; see note 34 above.

50 S.I. 1971 No. 161, made under section 7(2) of the Clean Air Act 1956; see note 34 above.

tion 10(2) (as it is now) to a furnace, the occupier of the building containing the furnace shall comply, either himself or by another on his behalf, with the requirements of the Schedule to the regulations. The Schedule, in paragraph (1), requires that on receiving a minimum of six weeks' notice from the local authority the occupier shall, within the period specified in the notice, make the adaptations to the chimney and provide the apparatus necessary for making and recording the measurements by one of the procedures described in British Standard 3405: 1961, and thereafter maintain it in working order.

Having installed the equipment prescribed by paragraph (1) of the Schedule, paragraph (2) requires that, on receiving 28 days' written notice from the local authority, the occupier shall take and record measurements of grit and dust emitted from a furnace within the period specified in the notice,[51] giving the local authority 48 hours' written notice of the commencement of such measurements. The notice from the local authority may require the taking of measurements from time to time or at stated intervals, but generally only once in any three-month period. In complying with the requirement the occupier is to record and transmit to the authority within 14 days:

(a) the date on which any measurements were made;
(b) the number of furnaces discharging into the chimney on that date;
(c) the measurements in terms of pounds per hour of grit and dust emitted and the percentage of grit contained in the solids emitted.

The exercise by a local authority of its powers under sections 5 to 11 depends on the preliminary acquisition of the necessary information on furnaces, capacity, fuels and so on. To this end section 12 gives authorities the power to require occupiers 'to furnish to them, within fourteen days or such longer time as may be limited by the notice, such information as to the furnaces in the building and the fuel or waste burned in those furnaces as they may reasonably require', subject to summary proceedings on failure to comply or for supplying information known to be false in a material particular. Knowledge of the falsity of the information is a stipulated ingredient of the offence and must therefore be proved by the prosecution.[52] Knowledge for this purpose includes the state of mind of a person who shuts his eyes to the obvious,[53] and may include the constructive knowledge of a person who deliberately chooses not to enquire so as to remain in ignorance of what his enquiries would have revealed.[54] Mere neglect to make reasonable enquiries is not, however, in itself, equivalent to knowledge.[55] A statement may be false because of what is left out even though, on its terms, it is literally true.[56] Further, a particular may be material on the ground that it renders another statement more credible.[57]

CHIMNEY HEIGHTS

Apart from inducing air for combustion in natural draught furnaces, the height of a chimney has a direct bearing on the dilution and dispersal of the flue gases. Also, of course, and in close association with that function, an adequate height prevents the return of excessive quantities of grit, dust and fumes in the immediate vicinity. In consequence, chimneys of adequate height must be provided for furnaces. Section 14(2) of the Act requires that a furnace shall not be used in a building:

51 The procedure to be employed is that detailed in pp. 13 to 26 of P.G.W.Hawksley, S.Badzioch and J.H.Blackett, *Measurement of Solids in Flue Gases* (British Coal Utilisation Research Association, 1961).

52 See especially *Gaumont British Distributors Ltd* v *Henry* [1939] 2 KB 711, [1939] 2 All ER 808.

53 *James & Son Ltd* v *Smee* [1955] 1 QB 78 at p.91, [1954] 3 All ER 273 at p.278 per Parker J.

54 *Knox* v *Boyd* [1941] JC 82 at p.86; *Taylor's Central Garages (Exeter) Ltd* v *Roper* (1951) 115 JP 445 at pp,449, 450, [1951] WN 383 per Devlin J.

55 See *Taylor's Central Garages (Exeter) Ltd* v *Roper* above, and *London Computator Ltd* v *Seymour* [1944] 2 All ER 11, but note also *Mallon* v *Allon* [1964] 1 QB 385.

56 See *R* v *Kylsant* [1932] 1 KB 442, [1931] All ER Rep 179; *Curtis* v *Chemical Cleaning and Dyeing Co. Ltd* [1951] 1 KB 805 at p.808, 809, [1951] 1 All ER 631 at p.634, CA.

57 *R* v *Tyson* (1867) LR 1 CCR 107.

(a) to burn pulverised fuel;
(b) to burn, at a rate of 45.4 kg or more an hour, any other solid matter; or
(c) to burn, at a rate equivalent to 366.4 kg or more, any liquid or gaseous matter,

unless the height of the chimney has been approved for the purpose of this section by the local authority or the Secretary of State under section 15, and any conditions complied with. Section 14(4) applies a similar provision to a furnace serving 'any fixed boiler or industrial plant' unless it is exempted boiler or plant within regulations made by the Secretary of State under section 14(7). The persons responsible are respectively the occupier of the building and the person having possession. Failure in either case constitutes a daily offence actionable summarily.[58]

The relevant regulations for the purposes of section 14(7) are the Clean Air (Height of Chimneys) (Exemption) Regulations 1969.[59] By regulation 3, the prescribed purposes exempting chimneys serving new or enlarged furnaces connected with boilers or industrial plant from the height requirements of section 14 are:

(a) temporarily replacing any other boiler or plant which is –
    (i) under inspection, maintenance or repair,
    (ii) being rebuilt, or
    (iii) being replaced by a permanent boiler or plant;
(b) providing a temporary source of heat or power during any building operation or work of engineering contruction;[60]
(c) providing a temporary source of heat or power for investigation or research;
(d) providing products of combustion to heat other plant (whether directly or indirectly) to an operating temperature;
(e) providing heat or power by mobile or transportable plant for the purposes of agriculture.[61]

The approval procedure in section 15 provides for the granting of approval either with or without conditions relating to the rate and/or quality of emissions from the chimney. If the local authority refuses an application, or grants one with attached conditions, it shall so notify the applicant stating:

(a) the reasons for its decision; and
(b) in the case of a decision not to approve the chimney height –
    (i) the lowest height (if any) which it is prepared to approve without qualification; or
    (ii) the lowest height which it is prepared to approve if approval is granted subject to any specified conditions,
or (if it thinks fit) both.[62]

In such cases the applicant has a 28-day right of appeal to the Secretary of State against the local authority's decision; and in determining the appeal the Secretary of State may confirm the decision, cancel or amend any condition, or approve the height. The duty of the Secretary of State to notify the appellant is then identical to that of the authority earlier. The authority has four weeks within which to decide on the application, and on failure to do so unqualified approval is deemed to have been granted.[63]

The basis for the local authority's approval is, by section 15(2), that it is:

... are satisfied that the height of the chimney will be sufficient to prevent, so far as practicable, the smoke, grit, dust, gases or fumes emitted from the chimney from becoming

58 Fines up to level 5 on the standard scale.

59 S.I. 1969 No. 411, made under section 6(1) of the Clean Air Act 1968; see note 34 above.

60 Within the meaning of section 176 of the Factories Act 1961.

61 Within the meaning of section 109(3) of the Agriculture Act 1947.

62 Section 15(5).

63 Section 15(4).

prejudicial to health or a nuisance having regard to –

(a) the purpose of the chimney;
(b) the position and descriptions of buildings near it;
(c) the levels of the neighbouring ground; and
(d) any other matters requiring consideration in the circumstances.

Assistance in this determination, taking into account both the likely flue gas content and heights of surrounding buildings, is provided by the Third Memorandum on Chimney Heights.[64]

The purpose of the Memorandum is to provide a relatively simple method of calculating the approximate desirable height in normal circumstances, although such calculated height is to be regarded as a guide rather than as a mathematically precise decision. In consequence it may require modification in the light of particular local circumstances such as the presence of hills, valleys or other topographical features. The contribution that a given chimney is permitted to make to pollution in the atmosphere depends in part on existing pollution levels, chimneys in more highly polluted areas being required to discharge their contents at higher levels to secure greater dilution and dispersion. For this purpose the Memorandum divides areas into five categories related to background pollution levels:

A an undeveloped area where development is unlikely;
B a partially developed area with scattered houses;
C a built up residential area;
D an urban area of mixed industrial and residential development;
E a large city or urban area, of mixed heavy industrial and dense residential development.

Category C is to be regarded as normal, with adjustments of chimney height up or down as the area requires; thus chimneys having the same flue gas discharges will be highest in area E and lowest in area A.

The method in the Memorandum is applicable only to fuel burning plant with gross heat output of between 0.15 MW (150 kW) and 150 MW. Furnaces at the lower end of this range are outside the statutory requirement for local authority chimney height approval. In particular, the method does not apply to direct fired heating systems discharging into the space to be heated, gas turbines or incinerators.

The basis of the method can be summarised as follows:

(a) Determination of the minimum height for a chimney that will ensure adequate dispersal of sulphur dioxide and other products of normal combustion using formulae in the Memorandum. Note: calculations for Very Low Sulphur (VLS) fuels (i.e. < 0.04%) are different from those for normal sulphur fuels –
  (i) for VLS fuels the initial calculation depends on the maximum continuous rated heat input of the furnaces;
  (ii) for other fuels the initial calculation depends on the rate of emission of sulphur dioxide at the maximum heat input taking into account the type of area within which the chimney is situated.
(b) Then additional calculations may be necessary to take account of adjacent buildings and chimneys in determining the final required height.
(c) The calculations assume an adequate efflux velocity of the flue gases to prevent the plume flowing down the outside of the chimney.

64 Produced by the DoE (HMSO, 1981). The basis for the Memorandum is to be found in a paper by C.F. Barrett and S.C. Wallin entitled 'Determination of Chimney Heights: technical basis of the third edition of the DoE memorandum' in *Energy World*.

(d) Where there are several adjacent fuel burning plants in the same works the waste gases should normally be discharged through a common chimney, preferably multi-flued, producing a greater plume rise and reduced concentrations reaching the ground. Where several furnaces are served by one chimney or a cluster, the maximum sulphur dioxide emission rates (or for VLS fuels, the heat input rates) should be added in order to determine the chimney height.

Three primary principles to be observed in the operation of this method are that:

(a) a chimney should terminate at least 3 metres above the level of any adjacent area to which there is general access, e.g., roofs, openable windows;
(b) a chimney should never be less than the calculated uncorrected chimney height;
(c) a chimney should never be less than the height of any part of an attached building within a distance of five uncorrected chimney heights.

The Memorandum concludes, at paragraph 30, in the following terms:

> Those using the Memorandum should also bear in mind the following points:
>
> a. Although intermediate stages in the calculations should be performed to reasonable levels of accuracy the final result should normally be rounded to the nearest metre.
> b. The procedure is concerned only with normal emissions of gaseous pollutants; it does not deal with grit and dust or in the case of VLS fuels afford protection against excessive concentrations of carbon monoxide produced by inefficient combustion.
> c. The height of a chimney may be of considerable significance in the granting of planning permission for a new development and the relevant authorities should consider the issue together.
> d. There are circumstances in which the Memorandum will not provide adequate guidance, e.g., where a chimney is to discharge on a roof with complicated structures or in difficult topography or where there are a number of closely adjacent chimneys. Specialist advice should be sought in such cases.

Section 16 requires local authority approval, on the same criteria as section 15(2) above, of the heights of chimneys to new buildings or extensions, not being residences, shops or offices, and serving furnaces below the capacities covered by section 14. There are two significant limitations to be noted in the operation of this section. First, approval is required only where plans are deposited in accordance with building regulations, unlike section 14 which prohibits the use of any chimney without approval. Also, this section applies to a building 'outside Greater London or in an outer London Borough'. Rejection of the plans on this ground is to be notified to the applicant in the notice under section 16(6) of the Building Act 1984, there being a right of appeal to the Secretary of State.

It will have been noticed that section 14 is concerned with chimneys serving what might be called large industrial furnaces, while section 16 is limited to other industrial plant. Chimneys serving smaller, and essentially heating, units in houses, shops and offices are ignored. The contribution to pollution from such appliances may be considered to be limited, especially following the extensive application of the Smoke Control Area procedure now to be found in Part III of this Act and to be considered below. However, there will inevitably be circumstances where the proximity and size of buildings will cause problems with the dispersal of flue gases from neighbouring chimneys, whatever the nature of the buildings they serve. This problem is dealt with in section 73 of the Building Act 1984, which provides:

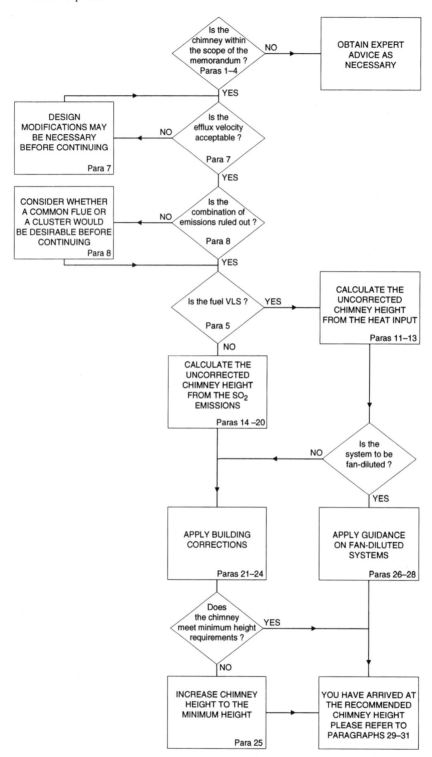

Figure 10.1 Procedure for using the Memorandum

(1) Where –

(a) a person erects or raises a building to a greater height than an adjoining building, and

(b) any chimneys or flues of an adjoining building are in a party wall between the two buildings or are 6 feet or less from the nearest part of the taller building,

the local authority may by notice –

(i) require that person, within a specified time, to build up those chimneys or flues, if it is reasonably practicable so to do, so that their top will be of the same height as the top of the chimneys of the taller building or the top of the taller building, whichever is the higher, and

(ii) require the owner or the occupier of the adjacent building to allow the first mentioned person to enter that building and carry out such work as may be necessary to comply with the notice.

The owner or occupier, on receipt of such a notice has, within 14 days of the date of service of the notice on him, the discretion to serve a counternotice on the first mentioned person and on the local authority to elect to do the work himself. He is then required to comply with the notice and may recover expenses from the other person. There is the normal right of appeal to the magistrates' court. Non-compliance is a summary offence with penalties up to level 1 on the standard scale, and the local authority may do the work in default.

65 S.I. 1991 No. 2768.

Further, Part J of Schedule I of the Building Regulations 1991,[65] applying to the construction of all chimneys irrespective of capacity, type or use requires that they shall be so installed that they:

(a) receive sufficient air for the proper combustion of the fuel and effective operation of the flue;

(b) are capable of normal operartion without the products of combustion becoming a hazard to health;

(c) are capable of normal operation without causing damage by heat or fire to the fabric of the building.

SMOKE CONTROL AREAS

Furnaces in large industrial plant are capable of burning even potentially smokey fuel smokelessly. They are therefore required to be operated so as not to emit excessive smoke, as considered above. Small domestic appliances, and in particular the open coal-burning fire cannot operate smokelessly. To achieve a clean, smoke-free atmosphere, therefore, the purpose of smoke control areas is to require all such small heating appliances within the designated area to be adapted or replaced to burn authorised, i.e., smokeless, fuel. The relevant legislation is now found in Part III of the Clean Air Act 1993, sections 18 to 29.

A local authority is given the power, in section 18, to declare by order any part of its district to be a smoke control area, and in so doing may make different provisions for different parts of the area, limit the operation of section 20 to specified classes of buildings, and exempt specified buildings or classes of buildings or fireplaces or classes of fireplaces either conditionally or unconditionally. Supplementary to this discretionary power of the local authority, the Secretary of State is given a power of direction by section 19, where, after consultation with the authority, he is satisfied that smoke abatement is necessary and the authority has not sufficiently used its section 18 powers. The authority is then required to submit proposals to the Secretary of State and implement them under his approval.

In exercising these powers the Secretary of State is required to consult the local authority, a process of substance rather than mere form.[66] Following the consultation, and as a product of it, he is then to be 'satisfied' of the two factors noted above. While this appears to be a purely subjective matter for the Secretary of State the grounds for and the legitimacy of the satisfaction can be challenged and assessed as to their reasonableness on what are generally referred to as *Wednesbury* principles. These are widely used as a ground of challenge in judicial review proceedings, and consequently are the subject of much judicial description and explanation. Lord Denning, in *Secretary of State for Employment* v *ASLEF* (No. 2) (1972),[67] to take one example, described the concept in the following terms:

> ... if the Minister does not act in good faith, or if he acts on extraneous considerations which ought not to influence him, or if he plainly misdirects himself in fact or in law, it may well be that a court would interfere; but if he honestly takes a view of the facts or of the law which could reasonably be entertained, then his decision is not to be set aside simply because thereafter someone thinks that his view was wrong.

The consideration of smoke control areas may be divided into two parts: their creation, and the obligations imposed on persons within an area once established. The rules governing the former are to be found in sections 24 to 26 and Schedules 1 and 2, and the latter in sections 20 to 23. As with other Parts of this Act considered above, these smoke control provisions of Part III do not apply to certain matters, including:

(a) prescribed processes within Part I of the Environmental Protection Act 1990;
(b) smoke etc. from the combustion of mine and quarry refuse within section 42;
(c) railway locomotive engines within section 43(5);
(d) vessels to which section 44(6) applies; and
(e) works governed by the Alkali, etc. Works Regulation Act 1906.

Smoke control order procedure

Dealing with the creation of an area, Schedule 1 of the Clean Air Act 1993 requires the local authority, prior to making the smoke control order under section 18(1), to publish in the *London Gazette* and in each of two successive weeks in a newspaper circulating in the area, a notice:

(a) stating that the authority proposes to make the order, and its general effect;
(b) specifying a place in the district of the authority where a copy of the order and any associated map or plan may be inspected free of charge at all reasonable times during a period of not less than six weeks from the date of the last publication of the notice; and
(c) stating that within that period any person who will be affected by the order may by notice in writing to the authority object to the making of the order.

The authority shall also display copies of the notice for the period in (b) above in sufficient conspicuous places in the area as it considers necessary to bring the proposal to the attention of persons who will be affected. 'Newspaper circulating in the area' includes both local and national papers, and apparently one which circulates among a limited class of persons rather than the public generally.[68] However, there appears to be at least a moral obligation on the authority to ensure that these

66 On consultation in the context of regulation making, see in Chapter 1 at p.18.

67 [1972] 2 QB 455.

68 *Re Southern Builders and Contractors (London) Ltd* (1961) *The Times*, 10 October; *R v Westminster Betting Licensing Committee, ex parte Peabody Donation Fund (Governors)* [1963] 2 QB 750.

stipulated forms of publicity in fact reach as wide an audience as possible. A period of 'not less than' excludes the date of the last publication of the notice.[69] If an objection is properly made the authority is required to consider it before making the order. The order will then, subject to a section 18(6) power of postponement, come into operation on the date specified in the order, being at least six months from the date on which it was made.

Either before or after the making of the order the local authority may, by section 24 and to secure compliance with section 20, serve a notice on the owner or occupier of a private dwelling requiring necessary adaptations. The provisions of Part XII of the Public Health Act 1936 governing appeals against and the enforcement of notices are applied here by section 24(2). The meaning of 'private dwelling' was considered in *McNair* v *Baker* (1904)[70] involving nuisance proceedings for the discharge of black smoke from the chimney of the St. James Club. The premises had been the French Embassy and consisted of domestic accommodation including dining rooms and bedrooms for both members and staff. Responding to the defence that as the premises were a private dwelling the statute did not apply, Lord Alverstone CJ said[71]:

> Apart from authority, it seems to me impossible to come to the conclusion that as a matter of law these premises are a private dwelling. We are not dealing with the construction of the premises, but with their user, and, having regard to the language of the section, I do not think it can be properly contended that premises so used are a private dwelling house.

The Act provides no specific guidance to determine when either the owner or occupier of a particular dwelling should be required to do the work. The strong implication of paragraph 1(4) of Schedule 2 supports the logical view that the owner be expected to undertake those works affecting the building structure and therefore forming part of the land, while the provision of moveable fittings should be the responsibility of the occupier; although the precise nature and terms of the occupation will govern the obligation in any particular case. That distinction is emphasised by the scope given to 'adaptation' in section 27(1), where it is said to mean the execution of works involved in:

(a) adapting or converting any fireplace;
(b) replacing any fireplace by another fireplace or by some other means of heating or cooking;
(c) altering any chimney which serves any fireplace;
(d) providing gas ignition, electric ignition or any other special means of ignition; or
(e) carrying out any operation incidental to any of the operations mentioned in paragraphs (a) to (d),

and being reasonably necessary to provide for cooking and heating without contravening section 20; the execution of works including the provision of fixed or moveable means of gas, electric or other means of ignition. To which section 28 adds that expenses include 'the cost of any fixed cooking or heating appliance ... notwithstanding that the appliance can be readily removed from the dwelling without injury to itself or the fabric of the dwelling'. What is 'reasonably necessary' has been said[72] to be a matter of fact for which supporting evidence will be required, an interpretation that may be taken to apply to the term in section 27(1). In deciding what works are reasonably necessary regard is to be had to the availability,

69 *R v Turner* [1910] 1 KB 346; Re Hector Whaling Ltd [1935] All ER Rep 302.

70 [1904] 1 KB 208, in proceedings under section 4 of the Public Health (London) Act 1891.

71 At p.212.

72 In *Coleen Properties v Minister of Housing and Local Government* [1971] 1 WLR 433, CA.

or availability otherwise than at a very high price, of any fuels that will be needed as a result of the works.[73] Should additional work be done that is not, in the opinion of the local authority, reasonably necessary for smoke control purposes, its cost is to be ignored in determining grant payments.[74]

Recognising that these provisions were introduced by the 1956 Act, it would seem reasonable to expect that houses built after that time would be constructed with smoke control requirements in mind, or at least would be fitted with modern, smoke-free heating and cooking appliances. Certainly it would be unreasonable to provide publicly funded grant aid for their subsequent conversion. Consequently, section 25 provides that the terms of Schedule 2 relating to expenditure apply only to what the section describes as 'old private dwellings', that is dwellings erected or created by conversion after 15 August 1964, i.e., the operative date of the preceding provision. Schedule 2 provides, in paragraph 1, that where the person concerned incurs relevant expenditure on the adaptation of an old private dwelling to the approval of the local authority, it shall repay to him either seven-tenths of the relevant expenditure or, at its discretion, all of it.[75]

Relevant expenditure, by Schedule 2, paragraph 1(2), is expenditure on adaptations in or in connection with old private dwellings which:

(a) is incurred before the coming into operation of the order and with the approval of the local authority given for the purposes of this paragraph; or

(b) is reasonably incurred in carrying out adaptations required by a notice given under section 24(1).

The local authority has discretion to approve expenditure after it has been incurred.[76] An authority also has the power, having regard to the likely lack of appropriate fuel in its area, to pass a resolution designating any class of heating appliance as being in its opinion unsuitable for installation in its area, and such appliance shall not be eligible for grant.[77] Special provisions delay payment of the grant in the case of moveable appliances provided by the occupier for two years and subject to their not by then having been removed.[78]

A local authority is also given the power, by section 26, to repay the whole or part of the expenditure incurred by the owner or occupier in the necessary adaptations to premises that are, by section 26(2):

(a) any place of public religious worship, either belonging to the Church of England or the Church in Wales, or that is certified as a place of religious worship;[79]

(b) any church hall, chapel hall or similar premises used in connection with any such place of public religious worship;

(c) any premises or part of any premises occupied for the purposes of an organisation which is not established or conducted for profit and whose main objects are charitable or are otherwise concerned with the advancement of religion, education or social welfare.

'Belonging to' has received judicial consideration only in the context of chattels and money,[80] so having limited bearing on the ownership of real property. It does appear from that judgement that the phrase is not a term of art but is to be given its ordinary meaning, which is wider than ownership. As to whether any building is a place of public religious worship, consecration is not of itself sufficient.[81] Conversely, a place may be one of public religious worship although only certain sections of the public are admitted.[82] The stipulation that the building is 'used'

---

73 Section 64(5).

74 Section 27(3).

75 Under paragraph 4(1) of Schedule 2 the Secretary of State has the discretion to reimburse to the local authority four-sevenths of its payments of that relevant expenditure. But now see Circular 9/93 on the withdrawal of Exchequer grant aid, with consequent reliance on Supplementary Credit Approvals.

76 Schedule 2, paragraph 1(5).

77 Schedule 2, paragraphs 2 and 3.

78 Schedule 2, paragraph 1(4).

79 On the certification of other than Anglican places of worship, see the Places of Worship Registration Act 1855. Certification is not conclusive as to whether a place is one of public religious worship – see *Rogers v Lewisham BC* [1951] 2 KB 768; 2 All ER 718, CA.

80 *Re Miller, ex parte Official Receiver* [1893] 1 QB 327 at pp.333, 334 CA.

81 *Oxford Poor Rate Case* (1857) 8 E & B 184.

82 *Stradling v Higgins* [1932] 1 Ch 143; [1931] All ER Rep 772.

83 *Yates (Revenue Officer for Burnley Assessment Area)* v *Burnley Rating Authority* (1933) 97 JP 226

84 *Schwerzerhof* v *Wilkins* [1898] 1 QB 640.

85 [1891] AC 531 at p.583, per Lord Macnaghten.

86 *Dingle* v *Turner* [1972] AC 601.

87 *Oppenheim* v *Tobacco Securities Trust Co. Ltd* [1951] AC 297.

88 *Gilmore* v *Coats* [1949] 1 All ER 848.

89 See per Lord Reid in *Scottish Burial Reform Soc.* v *Glasgow Corporation* [1968] AC 138 and also Recreational Charities Act 1958.

90 Section 51(1)(a).

91 Section 20(5), see note 31 above.

92 Section 20(4).

93 S.I. 1991 No. 1282 amended by S.I. 1992 No. 72 and S.I. 1992 No. 3148.

requires actual rather than potential use,[83] although temporary discontinuance of use will not prevent premises from being used within the meaning of the Act.[84]

The scope of charity, deriving from the definition or description in the preamble to the Statute of Charitable Uses 1601, was classified in *Commissioners for Special Purposes of Income Tax* v *Pemsel* (1891)[85] as consisting of trusts for the relief of poverty, for the advancement of education, for the advancement of religion and for other purposes beneficial to the community. To be charitable an activity must, with the exception of those within the first category,[86] be demonstrably for the public benefit.[87] In consequence some religious activities, essentially of a contemplative nature, have been held not to possess the necessary element of advancement or public benefit.[88] However, not all purposes beneficial to the community are thereby charitable. They must be within the range of objects in the 1601 preamble as extended by analogy and judicial interpretation.[89] As the matters specified in the final clause of section 26(2)(c) are charitable anyway, the extent to which the phrase extends the range of premises brought within the section is questionable.

Operation of smoke control areas

Turning now to the operation of a smoke control area following the making of the order, section 20 creates two offences. By section 20(1) the occupier is liable 'if, on any day, smoke is emitted from a chimney of any building within a smoke control area'. Similarly, section 20(2) provides that the person having possession is responsible where "smoke is emitted from a chimney which serves the furnace of any fixed boiler or industrial plant within a smoke control area'. A necessary preliminary to proceedings is written notice of the offence to the appropriate person,[90] the penalty on summary conviction being a fine up to level 3 on the standard scale.[91] It is a defence to show that authorised fuel was used at the time of the alleged emission[92] and, as with other offences under this statute, to show that the authority has not complied with section 51(1) imposing a duty to give written notification of the breach. Authorised fuel means a fuel declared so to be by regulations made by the Secretary of State under section 20(6). Many such regulations have been made under the 1956 Act, now consolidated in the Smoke Control Area (Authorised Fuel) Regulations 1991.[93] As is to be expected, authorised fuels are those that are capable of being burned without the emission of significant visible smoke. Such fuels fall into two groups. First, there are those that are naturally smokeless, i.e., gas and electricity, and a limited range of solid fuels with a low volatile content including anthracite, semi-anthracite and low volatile steam coal. Secondly, and more extensively, there is a wide and increasing range of proprietary solid fuels manufactured from coal, essentially by the removal of a proportion of its volatile content. The Regulations approve 25 to 30 such branded fuels, listing them by name, manufacturer, raw material used and indicating the manufacturing process. It is perhaps unnecessary in a work of this nature to include the regulation content in detail and a synopsis would be both impractical and valueless.

Section 20(3) exempts three circumstances where the restrictions will not apply to premises in a smoke control area. These are provided for in:

(a) section 18(2)(c) – specified buildings or classes of buildings or specified fireplaces or classes of fireplaces may be conditionally exempted from the operation of the order;

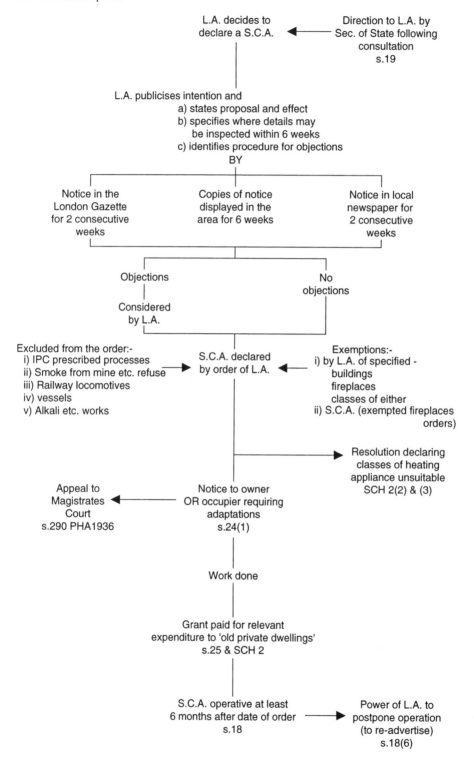

Figure 10.2 Smoke Control Area procedure

(b) section 21 – power of the Secretary of State by order to exempt any class of fireplace from the operation of section 20, on any specified conditions, if satisfied that they can burn other than authorised fuels without producing substantial quantities of smoke;

(c) section 22 – the Secretary of State has the power, if it appears necessary or expedient to do so, to suspend or relax the operation of section 20 in relation to the whole or any part of a smoke control area.

Under the preceding provision re-enacted by section 21, a large number of Smoke Control Areas (Exempted Fireplaces) Orders have been made.[94] Of these the first order may be noted as giving exemption to fireplaces designed to burn liquid fuel, i.e., oil. Other orders exempt a wide range of appliances to burn wood and various forms of wood waste as well as coal, with or without prior treatment. In all cases the exemption will apply only if the fireplace is burning the fuel for which it is designed and is installed and operated according to the maker's instructions. It may be noted at this point that the works of adaptation in the creation of a smoke control area which will rank for grant will largely be those involved in the fitting either of appliances capable of burning authorised fuel or of fireplaces exempted under the above orders. The third category of exemption, under section 22, is clearly an exceptional, emergency power and may be used, for example, for the duration of a temporary shortage of a particular authorised fuel. Where the Secretary of State exercises his section 22 power he may also suspend the operation of section 23(1), next to be considered. In such event the local authority has the responsibility, as soon as practicable after the making of the order, to bring its effect to the attention of the persons affected.[95]

Section 23 creates the offences of obtaining or selling for use in a smoke control area, solid fuel that is not authorised fuel. It will therefore be seen that the offences consequent upon the creation of a smoke control area extend back from the actual production of smoke to the possession by the potential user and to the sale by a retailer of unauthorised solid fuel. Specifically, section 23(1) stipulates that a person shall be guilty of an offence who:

(a) acquires any solid fuel for use in a building in a smoke control area, otherwise than a building or fireplace exempted from the operation of section 20;

(b) acquires any solid fuel for use in any, non-exempted, fixed boiler or industrial plant in a smoke control area; or

(c) sells by retail any solid fuel for delivery by him or on his behalf to –
   (i) a building in a smoke control area; or
   (ii) premises in such an area in which there is any fixed boiler or industrial plant.

Maximum fines are level 3 on the standard scale.[96]

'Retail', in the well-known case of *Chappell & Co. Ltd v Nestlè Co. Ltd* (1958),[97] was described in the following terms:

> The distinction appears to me to be between a sale to the trade on the one hand, and to the public, or, as Lord Dunedin puts it,[98] to the consuming customer on the other. A retail sale may take place in a number of ways. The commonest way no doubt is by a sale in a shop over the counter; but it may, and frequently does, take place by means of the post and other similar means. Again, a retail sale may be for cash or for credit, or may be in part exchange of other goods, as is frequently so in the case of motor cars. It was suggested at one stage of the argument that a sale could not be by retail if there were

94 S.I. 1970/615, as amended by S.I. 1974/855; S.I. 1970/1667, as amended by 1974/762; S.I. 1971/1265, as amended by S.I. 1974/762; S.I. 1972/438, as amended by S.I. 1974/762; S.I. 1972/955, as amended by S.I. 1974/762; S.I. 1973/2166, as amended by S.I. 1974/762; S.I. 1975/1001; S.I. 1975/1111; S.I. 1978/1609; S.I. 1982/1615; S.I.1983/277; S.I.1983/426; S.I. 1983/1018; S.I. 1984/1649, as amended by S.I. 1985/864; S.I. 1986/638; S.I. 1988/2282; S.I. 1989/1769; S.I. 1990/345; S.I. 1990/2457; S.I. 1991/2892; S.I. 1992/2811.

95 Section 22(3).

96 See note 31 above.

97 [1958] 2 All ER 155 at p.159 per Ormerod LJ.

98 In *Turpin v Middlesbrough Assessment Committee & Bailey* [1931] AC 451 at p.473.

conditions or restrictions attached to it. This would exclude from the definition sales by a co-operative society or by any dealer who sought to limit in any way the number or class of his customers.

The defence, provided in section 23(5), to a charge of selling is that the accused believed and had reasonable grounds for believing:

(a) that the building was exempted from the operation of section 20; or
(b) that the fuel was acquired for use in an exempted fireplace, boiler or plant.

Whether a person has 'reasonable grounds for believing' is the subject of some authority. In *IRC v Rossminster Ltd* (1980),[99] Lord Wilberforce said that 'The existence of this reasonable cause, and of the belief founded on it, is ultimately a question of fact to be tried on the evidence'. In the same case, Lord Diplock said[100]:

> These words appearing in a statute do not make conclusive the officer's own honest opinion that he has reasonable cause for the prescribed belief. The grounds on which the officer acted must be sufficient to induce in a reasonable person the required belief before he can validly seize and remove anything under the subsection.

In an earlier case, in the context of arrest without a warrant, Lord Wright said[101]:

> ... the inquiry is as to the mind of the chief constable at the time when he ordered the arrest, and it involves that it must be ascertained what information he had at the time, even though that information came from others. Of course, the information must come in a way which justifies him in giving it credit; the suspicion from which he must act, and, indeed, ought to act, in the course of his duty, must be a reasonable suspicion.

ADDITIONAL AND MISCELLANEOUS POWERS

In addition to its provisions governing the main categories of atmospheric pollution from premises as considered above, the Clean Air Act 1993, in Parts IV and VI, deals with a number of smaller but often equally intractable problems. These matters, now to be considered, include:

(a) sulphur content of fuel oil (section 31);
(b) cable burning (section 33);
(c) colliery spoilbanks (section 42).

Section 31 gives the Secretary of State the power by regulations to impose limits on the sulphur content of oil fuel which is used in furnaces or engines, for the purpose of limiting or reducing air pollution. As with the comparable provisions governing motor fuel, the penal provision is section 32(1), which makes an offence actionable summarily or on indictment, resulting in both cases in a fine.

The current regulations under section 31 are the Oil Fuel (Sulphur Content of Gas Oil) Regulations 1990,[102] giving effect to Directives 75/716/EEC and 87/219/EEC. Gas oil is defined in the same terms as apply to motor fuel,[103] and the Regulations are applied, by regulation 5, to any furnace or engine in Great Britain, except a furnace or engine used in a ship, or a diesel engine used to propel a motor vehicle. There are certain general exemptions essentially for manufacture, testing and experiment, and the Secretary of State may grant exemptions in particular cases for the period and subject to any conditions that are specified.[104] Regulation 3 stipulates that 'no person shall use, or cause or permit to be used,

99 [1980] 1 All ER 80 at p.84f.

100 At p.92j.

101 *McArdle v Egan* [1933] All ER Rep 611 at p.613b; and see also *Nakkuda Ali v Jayaratne* [1951] AC 66.

102 S.I. 1990 No. 1096.

103 See p.238.

104 Regulations 6 and 7 respectively.

in any furnace or engine to which these regulations apply, any gas oil having a sulphur content exceeding 0.3% by weight' when tested in accordance with regulation 4 which prescribes the method described in the Institute of Petroleum document entitled 'Sulphur in Petroleum Products by Energy Dispersive X-ray Fluorescence (Non-Dispersive X-ray Fluorescence)',[105] the results being interpreted in accordance with rules in BS 4306:1986 and ISO 4259-1979.

The practice of cable burning for the recovery of metal is an offence under section 33 of the 1993 Act and, following summary conviction, subject to a fine up to level 5 on the standard scale, unless it is an authorised process for the purposes of IPC or LAAPC under Part I of the Environmental Protection Act 1990.[106] For these purposes Schedule I to the Environmental Protection (Prescribed Processes and Substances) Regulations 1991 includes within Chapter 2 (Metal Production and Processing), 'Any process for ... recovering by ... the use of heat' a number of metals, and paragraph 2.2 includes non-ferrous metals. Conditions attaching to the authorisation may, or should, deal with the effective management of the toxic by-products of cable burning such as PCBs (polychlorinated biphenols).

The spontaneous combustion of refuse from mines and quarries may create a number of disparate problems, including the discharge of pollutants into the atmosphere. Section 42(2) therefore requires the owner of a mine or quarry from which coal or shale has been, is or is to be taken, to employ all practicable means:

(a) for preventing combustion of refuse deposited from the mine or quarry; and
(b) for preventing or minimising the emission of smoke and fumes from such refuse;

failure constituting an offence actionable summarily with a fine up to level 5 on the standard scale and cumulative penalties in accordance with section 50.

Before leaving this general area there are a number of administrative and operational provisions that deserve notice, although not conveniently finding a place in the consideration of the earlier substantive sections. First, where a body corporate is convicted of an offence under the Act that has been committed with the consent or connivance of, or which is attributable to the neglect of any director, manager, secretary or similar officer of the body corporate, section 52 enables that person also to be found guilty and punished accordingly. For these purposes knowledge of and agreement to a particular action amounts to consent[107] and a passive standing by or 'wilful blindness' is evidence of connivance.[108] A director is regarded as owing a duty to the company, including a common law duty of care,[109] although it may be that the more onerous obligations of the Company Directors' Disqualification Act 1986 may be held to apply in these circumstances.

Section 53 recognises that where the commission of an offence by a person under the Act is due to the act or default of some other person, that other person shall be guilty of the offence, whether or not proceedings are taken against the first person. This provision would appear to cover the uncertainties arising in the case of the employee exceeding his authority or disobeying instructions.[110] It would also meet the problems originating from various types of trespasser, assuming that they are discoverable. Turning to section 54, it may happen that to enable the use of a building by the occupier in conformity with the provisions of the Act some structural work is needed. Depending on the terms of the lease, such work may require the consent of the building owner. If that consent is not forthcoming this section empowers the county court, on an application from the

105 Published by the Institute of Petroleum as designation IP 336/81 (Reapproved 1986). Publications are obtainable from the Institute of Petroleum, 61 New Cavendish St., London W1M 8AR: tel. 0171 636 1004.

106 See Chapter 1, pp.47–61.

107 *Huckerby v Elliot* [1970] 1 All ER 189; *Bishopsgate Investment Management Trust v Maxwell* (No. 2) (1993) *The Times,* 16 February.

108 *Huckerby v Elliott,* ibid.

109 *Smith v Fawcett,* Re [1942] Ch 304.

110 *Tesco Supermarkets v Nattrass* [1972] AC 153.

occupier, to order in the terms they consider to be just, the doing of the work and recovery of the costs.

Local authorities are required in proper cases, as part of their functions under the Act, to report to the appropriate Minister emissions of dark smoke, grit and dust from Crown premises.[111] The Minister, following an investigation establishing the veracity of the complaint, shall 'employ all practicable means for preventing or minimising' the emissions, abating the nuisance and preventing their recurrence. By section 44(4), section 44 of the Act relating to vessels does not apply to vessels in, or operating for the purposes of the Royal Navy. This informal procedure is in substitution for coercive remedies which, by section 21 of the Crown Proceedings Act 1947, do not lie against the Crown.

The Secretary of State is given a very broad power, in section 59, to hold a public enquiry, either in relation to the operation of any provision of the Act or to preventing or dealing with air pollution at any place. Although discretionary, such enquiries will be governed by the Tribunals and Inquiries Act 1992.[112] The succeeding section 60 further gives the Secretary of State general coercive powers in respect of local authorities who, in his view, are failing to perform their functions under the Act; with the exception of declaration of smoke control areas.[113] He may, by order, declare the authority to be in default and specify the manner and times within which any stipulated duty is to be performed. On further failure to comply he may then by a further order transfer to himself those functions of the authority and recover from it the costs of performance.

111 Section 46.

112 See S.I. 1975 No. 1379 and also section 250(2) to (5)of the Local Government Act 1972.

113 See sections18 and 19(1); note the specific default provisions in section 19.

11

Noise

INTRODUCTION

While many material pollutants, because of their toxicity or volume, have far more serious or long-term environmental impact, noise, particularly in urban or industrial communities, is the factor most people identify as causing the greatest perceived deterioration in the quality of life. Certainly the number of noise related complaints continues to increase; domestic noise complaints to local authorities for the period 1992/93 showing a 20 per cent increase over the previous year. Further, the overall figure for all noise complaints of less than 1,000 per million of the population in 1978 had increased by 1992/93 to 4,400.[1] Although noise is therefore to be regarded as a serious pollutant, it and its perception exhibit characteristics not shared by other environmental pollutants. Some of those characteristics make the resolution of problems involving noise particularly intractable.

As the emphasis above implies, noise is the one pollutant considered exclusively in relation to its effect on people, i.e., on public health rather than environmental grounds.[2] Sound does of course affect other creatures in similar ways to its effects on people, but that aspect of the problem has yet to be the subject of practical concern or legal control. Another significant factor, bearing on the reception rather than the source of sound, is that unlike other senses hearing functions permanently even during sleep. No doubt there were solid evolutionary reasons for the operation of a sense capable of detecting possible danger at all times. When immediate physical safety is significantly less important than the reduction of stress and tension, though, the inability to control the sense of hearing is doubtless regarded by many as a serious developmental deficiency.

Noise is commonly described as unwanted sound, introducing as a further distinguishing element that of subjectivity. Although some noise is produced as an unsought and unwanted feature of certain activities or processes other forms – of which intruder alarms and amplified music are examples – are intentionally produced for their own sake. In this latter case, to describe the sound as unwanted and therefore 'noise' is to make a value judgement from one point of view. Any consequent remedial action therefore necessitates a balancing of conflicting interests and impartial, objective justification. Another consequence of the subjective aspect of the polluting nature of sound is that perception of it varies depending on circumstances, introducing a further variable into the judgement of its unreasonableness. The most obvious example of this variable perception is that between the level of sound that is tolerable by day and night.

The problem presented by these subjective variables was indicated by Lord Selbourne LC in *Gaunt* v *Fynney* (1872),[3] concerning an unsuccessful application for, *inter alia*, an injunction to restrain the owners of the adjoining silk mill from causing noise and vibration due to allegedly increased working:

1 1992/93 Annual Report of the Institution of Environmental Officers.

2 But see section 5(1) of the Civil Aviation Act 1982 below.

3 (1872) 8 Ch App 8, at pp.11 and 12.

A nuisance of this kind is much more difficult to prove than when the injury complained of is the demonstrable effect of a visible or tangible cause, as when waters are fouled by sewage, or when the fumes of mineral acids pass from the chimneys of factories or other works over land or houses, producing deleterious physical changes which science can trace and explain. A nuisance by noise (supposing malice to be out of the question) is emphatically a question of degree. If my neighbour builds a house against a party-wall, next to my own, and I hear through the wall more than is agreeable to me of the sounds from his nursery or music-room, it does not follow (even if I am nervously sensitive or in infirm health) that I can bring an action or obtain an injunction. Such things to offend against the law, must be done in a manner which, beyond fair controversy, ought to be regarded as exceptive and unreasonable.

Sound may affect people in a variety of ways. Noting first that it is a form of energy, prolonged exposure to sound of sufficient volume can cause physical damage in the form of noise-induced hearing loss. Those particular circumstances are generally confined to certain occupational situations which, coming within the area of employment law and industrial legislation, are outside the scope of this work. Other physiological effects produced as natural reflex responses to audible warning signals include muscle tension, acceleration or deceleration of the heart rate, general reduction in blood flow to the skin, changes in the secretion of saliva and gastric juice, and reflex movements of the gastro-intestinal tract. Prolonged exposure to intense noise may also have an identifiable effect on digestion. Disturbed rest and sleep, whether leading to actual awakening or not, may result in lack of concentration, irritability and reduced efficiency. Evidence, and indeed one's personal experience, also suggests that exposure to unaccustomed high levels of noise tends to change one's emotional responses, inducing agitation, irritation and short temper. Conversely, and to redress the balance, it is to be noted that the complete lack of sound for prolonged periods can itself be disturbing as inducing sensory deprivation.

A further way in which noise differs from other pollutants concerns waste. Many pollutants, being waste products, represent a financial loss, either through poor resource management or because they consist of materials that may not profitably be recycled. The classic example in the former category was probably the waste heat represented by the discharge of smoke from factory chimneys due to inefficient boiler operation. Noise, even when not specifically generated, represents such an insignificant fraction of the mechanical energy concerned that its control cannot be justified on purely economic grounds. The final characteristic peculiar to noise is that its impact is instantaneous, leaving no residues or other long-term effects as is common with many other pollutants.

Noise has been actionable at common law as a nuisance at least since the early seventeenth century. In his judgement in *William Aldred's Case*[4] Wray CJ enumerates various forms of nuisance, including a pig sty causing annoyance through stink and noise. The introduction of the statutory nuisance procedure in 1845, enforceable by local authorities by summary procedure in the magistrates' court, with subsequent re-enactments up to and including the Public Health Act 1936, did not extend to noise nuisances. The first legislative control appeared in the Noise Abatement Act 1960, which extended the statutory nuisance procedure of the 1936 Act to noise.[5] It also provided for a private procedure in the magistrates' court by three affected occupiers acting together, no doubt to exclude the individual crank or extremist. These provisions were re-enacted in the Control of Pollution Act 1974, omitting the need for action by three persons. The statutory

4 9 Co Rep 54; see also *Cristie v Davey* [1893] 1 Ch 316; 62 LJ Ch 439; *Leeman v Montagu* [1936] 2 All ER 1677; *Halsey v Esso Petroleum Co.* [1961] 2 All ER 145.

5 On nuisances, statutory nuisances and procedure, see Chapter 3.

nuisance procedure, further extended to cover street noise by the Noise and Statutory Nuisance Act 1993, is now to be found in Part III of the Environmental Protection Act 1990, while general noise control measures remain in the retained Part III of the 1974 Act.

It may be thought that noise *per se* being a significant issue for many people, and on that basis its origin being of less importance, the appropriate response would be to establish a generally applicable code of noise levels and limits as they bear on the hearer and irrespective of the source. Appropriate variations and exceptions for public utility, time of day or night and location relating to land use could be integrated into the scales. That has not been the approach to date, however. As will be seen in what follows, as each noise-producing source has been identified as a problem, so an applicable regulatory code has been produced for each, resulting in a multiplicity of disparate standards and enforcing procedures. Before embarking on a consideration of this hotchpotch some identification and explanation of the terms applicable to noise measurement and control may be desirable.

In spite of that concluding statement there is no method or equipment capable of measuring *noise*, which, as has been seen, implies a subjective element. Measurement is of *sound*, and that essentially of its volume. The unit of sound pressure level is the decibel (dB). The range of sound capable of reception by the human ear is very wide, being of the order of ten million million to one. Also, as a further complication, human hearing is non-linear, so that, for example, if sound pressure is doubled it will not sound twice as loud. For both of these reasons the decibel scale is logarithmic. A rule of thumb application of this, at first sight, confusing scale is that an increase of about 10dB produces an approximate doubling of loudness.

Another characteristic governing the perception of sound in addition to volume is its frequency, measured in Hertz (Hz). The range of frequencies audible to a young adult with normal hearing, i.e., the audio-frequency range, is 20 to 20,000Hz. With increasing age there is a progressive reduction in the upper limit to around 10,000 (10kHz). Perception over this range of frequencies is not equal, sensitivity being most acute in the 1,000Hz range, i.e., the frequencies of importance in speech intelligibility, and least acute at very low frequencies. The lowest sound pressure at any frequency that can be detected by a person with normal hearing is known as the threshold of hearing. As may be expected, that threshold level has very high values at the extremes of the audio-frequency range and low values indicating greatest sensitivity within the central, speech band.

In consequence, the measurement of sound to determine its likely effect on the hearer requires some frequency weighting. Although different weightings are used for different purposes, that most commonly used to approximate to the human ear is the 'A' weighting. Measurements using this scale are recorded and referred to as dB(A). A convenient definition of dB(A) is provided by the Control of Noise (Measurement and Registers) Regulations 1976,[6] although strictly only for the purposes of those Regulations: 'dB(A) is a measure of sound pressure level in decibels indicated by measuring equipment using A-scale frequency weighting (A-weighting).' The definition continues by specifying the particular measuring equipment, adding, 'as described in the British Standard Specification for a precision sound level meter which was published on 14th September 1967 under the number BS 4197: 1967 ...'.

Noise measurement as described above is appropriate for a given sound at a particular time. More often than not in reality, the nuisance effect of sound is affected both by fluctuating volume and duration. While these variables may be measured and recorded the result makes assessment and comparison difficult. The generally accepted alternative, therefore, is to measure the noise from a particular source as the equivalent continuous noise level (L_{eq}) measured in dB(A) over a stated period of time. The definition of L_{eq} is that level of continuous noise which has, over any defined period, the same energy content as the actual noise level during that period.[7] Department of the Environment Circular 2/76 notes that[8]:

> L_{eq} is a noise index which gives a reasonable indication of people's subjective reactions to most sources of noise. Its use in the United Kingdom has been endorsed by the Noise Advisory Council. Use of the equivalent sound level is recommended in connection with the environmental noise situation to which Part III of the Control of Pollution Act applies.
>
> ... In noise abatement zones the Control of Noise (Measurement and Registers) Regulations require the approval of the Secretary of State to be obtained before indices other than L_{eq} are used.

Such rationalisation of varying sound patterns has its uses, as has been suggested; however, depending on circumstances the result may need to be supplemented, for example by readings for maximum noise levels in the case of impulse noise. Lastly it may be noted that if the volume is great enough sound at frequencies below the audible range may be perceived as vibration. For purposes of legal control, therefore, noise is often defined to include vibration – see, for example, section 73(1) of the Control of Pollution Act 1974.

Detailed procedures for the assessment of industrial noise from fixed sources are to be found in BS 4142: 1990. The degree of detail prevents any comprehensive review of the contents here, but the two following paragraphs indicate its general purpose:

1. Scope

This BS describes methods for determining, at the outside of a building –

(a) noise levels from factories, including premises or fixed installations and sources of an industrial nature in commercial premises; and
(b) background noise level.

This standard also describes a method for assessing whether the noise referred to in (a) is likely to give rise to complaints from people residing in the building. The method is not applicable for assessing the noise measured inside buildings or for assessing noise in situations where the background noise level is very low, i.e., below an A-weighted sound pressure level of 30 dB.

8.1 General

For the assessment procedure, the likelihood of a noise provoking complaints, depends on its level relative to background noise level and whether or not it has certain audible characteristics. Other factors such as local attitudes to the premises in question may also have an effect but these cannot be included in the assessment procedure.

NOISE ABATEMENT ZONES

The ability to establish noise abatement zones gives a local authority, in this case a district council,[9] an anticipatory power to control noise. The purpose of a noise abatement zone is to stabilise noise levels from fixed premises and, in certain cir-

7 See, e.g., regulation 6(1)of the Control of Noise (Measurement and Registers) Regulations 1976, S.I. 1976 No. 37.

8 DoE Circular 2/76, 'Control of Pollution Act, Implementation of Part III – Noise' paragraph 16.

9 Section 73(1) of the Control of Pollution Act 1974.

cumstances, to secure their reduction. A major benefit in creating such a zone, therefore, is the ability to control noise without having to show that it is a nuisance. Conversely, by its nature the procedure is applicable only to permanently located noise sources, leaving the often acute impact of mobile noise to resolution by other remedies. Although the power may be used for the whole, or any part, of the authority's area its principal application would appear to be to control the effect of noise in predominantly residential areas. Although having evident value the power has been little used, due in large measure to the complexity of its procedures. For this reason the Noise Review Working Party in its 1990 Report recommended a Code of Practice for procedure in place of the current regulations. More recently the Batho Report[10] has considered this issue, as a result of which the procedures are expected to be simplified.

The provisions governing noise abatement zones are currently sections 63 to 67 and Schedule 1[11] of the Control of Pollution Act 1974.[12] Section 63 gives a local authority the power to designate by order, a 'noise abatement order', all or any part of its area as a noise abatement zone, the order specifying the classes of premises within the zone that are subject to control. Subject to the discretion of the authority, therefore, by no means all the premises in an area will be governed by the order. Schedule 1 provides the following procedure to make an order (and see Figure 11.1 p. 290):

Before making the order the authority shall serve a notice on all owners and occupiers of affected classes of premises in the proposed area and also publish in the *London Gazette* and in a local newspaper at least once in each of two successive weeks a notice that shall contain –

(a) a statement that the authority propose to make the order, and its general effect;
(b) the place where a copy of the order and any associated plan or map may be inspected free of charge for a period of at least six weeks from the date of last publication of the notice;
(c) a statement that within that period any person affected may object to the making of the order by notice in writing to the authority.

Should any objections be received, the authority is in general[13] required to consider them before making the order.

The order having been made, it must come into force on the date, being at least one month after the date of the making of the order, specified therein. This minimum period does not apply to orders revoking an existing order, or varying an order by excluding any specified class of premises. Also, if before the order is due to come into operation the authority by resolution postpones its operation and publicises that resolution in the press in the manner required of the original notice indicated above, the order shall come into operation on the date specified in the resolution.

After designation of a noise abatement zone, and while the order remains in effect,[14] the following provisions of the Control of Pollution Act 1974 govern its operation:

(a) section 64 (maintenance of a 'noise level register');
(b) section 65 (control of noise exceeding the registered level);
(c) section 66 (power to reduce noise levels);
(d) section 67 (determination of noise levels for new buildings).

The content and effect of these sections are now considered.

10 Report of the Government's Noise Review Working Party, 1990.

11 A new Schedule 1 has been substituted by Schedule 2 of the Local Government, Planning and Land Act 1980.

12 Brought into operation by the Control of Pollution Act 1974 (Commencement No. 4) Order 1975, S.I. 1975 No. 2118.

13 The authority may ignore objections in the two cases specified in paragraph 3(2) and, in the case of a variation or revocation order, in the circumstances in paragraph 3(3).

14 Section 63(3) gives the local authority the subsequent power to revoke or vary the order.

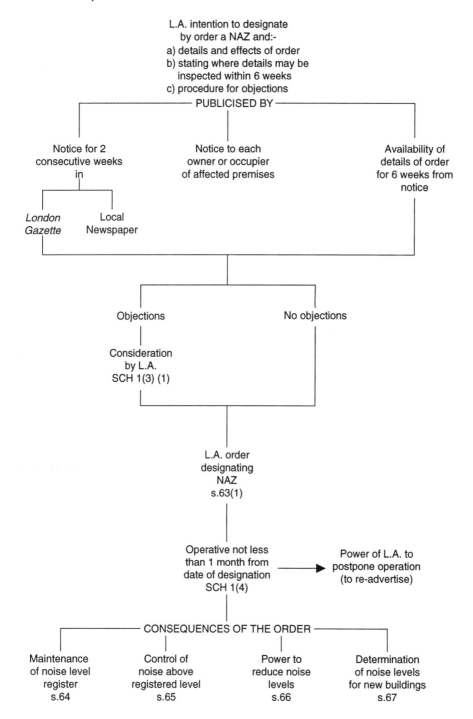

Figure 11.1 Noise Abatement Zone procedure

The noise level register

After designation of a noise abatement zone, section 64 of the 1974 Act requires the authority to measure the noise levels from all the premises of the classes specified in the order. Those measurements are then to be recorded in a 'noise level register'. In common with other public registers in the environment context, these are to be open to free public inspection at all reasonable hours. The authority is also to provide, on payment of reasonable charges, facilities for obtaining copies of entries in the register.

Entries on the noise level register are to show for each premises[15]:

15 Regulation 6(1) of the Control of Noise (Measurement and Registers) Regulations 1976, S.I. 1976 No. 37.

(a) the address or other sufficient identification;
(b) the particulars in regulation 6(2) below as appropriate;
(c) any cancellation or alteration, and the reason;
(d) the dates on which each entry is made.

The 1976 Regulations, regulation 6(2) requires that the record shall contain particulars of the methods employed to measure or calculate the noise level and the details of all relevant measurements and calculations, including:

(a) the location (including height) of each point at which the measurements were taken, or for which the calculations were made;
(b) relevant details of any equipment used for the purpose;
(c) the date on which each entry, cancellation or alteration is made.

A copy of the record is also to be served on the owner and occupier of the premises concerned. Any person so served is given a 28-day right of appeal to the Secretary of State against the record, and save for that right the validity or accuracy of any entry on the noise level register shall not be questioned in any proceedings. The significance of this first recorded measurement, and a primary reason for a right of appeal, is that it forms the standard against which future offences are to be judged.[16] The interest of the occupier of the premises producing the noise is therefore likely to be at variance with that of the authority. Equally, it is reasonable that once settled the registered noise levels should be accepted as authoritative and not be the subject of costly evidential dispute and argument in subsequent enforcement proceedings. If this is the thinking behind these provisions it is surprising, and indeed unusual, that some notification to the persons concerned of that right of appeal does not appear to be required.

16 See section 65.

In making the measurements it is for the authority to determine where they are to be made,[17] although the regulations next noted, which provide for methods of measurement, also offer guidance on this question. The methods of noise measurement for these purposes may be the subject of regulations by the Secretary of State, thus removing any scope for dispute. Current regulations for the purposes of section 64(8)(a) are the Control of Noise (Measurement and Register) Regulations 1976.[18]

17 Section 64(6).

18 S.I. 1976 No. 37.

Essentially, the Regulations provide that the methods of noise measurement in the scheduled memorandum to the Regulations are to be used to measure noise levels from classified premises[19] for the purposes of sections 64 and 66 of the Act. In cases where those measurement methods cannot be used the memorandum provides for calculation. In exceptional circumstances where neither measurement nor calculation according to those procedures is effective and on representations to him by the local authority, the Secretary of State may direct the use by the

19 Classified premises are, by regulation 2(1), premises of any specified class to which the noise abatement order applies.

authority of other methods as determined by him. The following extracts indicate the general approach of the memorandum.

Where to measure

Noise should be measured on a line (the noise control boundary) drawn so as to enclose all significant noise sources on the premises. In general the perimeter of the premises will be the appropriate line, but special factors (e.g. the presence of obstructions) may make it impracticable or inappropriate to measure the noise from the premises at the perimeter. The simplest situation is one where all the noise sources are close to the ground, where there is open land between the sources and the site perimeter and where the site perimeter is marked by fencing of open construction. In such circumstances it will be convenient to locate the measurement points around the perimeter at a height of 1.2 metres.

Determination of measurement points

The number and position of measurement points will be dictated by the degree of control proposed to be exercised over the level of noise from any premises. The most complete control will be obtained by a number of measuring points round the perimeter covering contiguous areas of noise source within an angle of between 45 and 65 degrees from each point.[20]

For rigorous control that basic coverage may need to be supplemented for a variety of reasons, for example where there is a permanent noise source, such as a ventilator, close to the perimeter, or where it is anticipated that new noise generating sources might be introduced in the future. Where the noise has noticeable pure tone (i.e., single frequency) components, standing wave patterns of noise (which are characteristically indicated by significant variations in noise level over short distances) may occasionally result. Where standing wave patterns are encountered, measurements made at fixed points on the boundary should be supplemented by a record of the maximum noise levels between the fixed positions.

It is essential that measurement points can be re-located for the purpose of future monitoring of noise levels. Hence it is important that a reliable way of noting the positions of points is used.

Where the perimeter comprises the external walls of a building flanking directly onto the highway, the noise control boundary must be outside the perimeter of the site. In this case the pavement width will probably limit the distance between the noise control boundary and the perimeter of the site, unless it is convenient to take measurements on the opposite sides of the surrounding roads. As a general rule more measuring positions will be required in such a case than where the external walls of a building do not flank directly onto the highway.

Height of measuring positions

As previously indicated the convenient height in a simple case would be 1.2 metres but the appropriate height at any particular point will depend on the circumstances.

For the maximum noise level emanating from the premises to be measured, the points from which noise is emanating should be visible from the measurement point. Where the site is enclosed by a wall or other sound-opaque structure at the perimeter, the measuring positions should normally be established at points high enough to measure the noise coming over the top of the wall.

When to measure

The aim should be to determine typical levels of noise from the premises. Measurements should therefore be made when activity is as near normal as possible. When making measurements the following situations should be borne in mind:–

(i) In some cases plant may be running below its maximum capacity for a long periods, e.g., 6 months or a year. If the registered noise levels are determined during this period a note should be made for inclusion in the noise level register that plant was operating below full capacity.

20 The memorandum explains the logic of these figures. It also provides practical illustrations and examples of the operation of the principles.

(ii) Noise levels at the perimeter of the premises may vary between summer and winter because doors and windows are left open in the summer in order to increase ventilation. Where doors and windows must be opened for ventilation the registered noise levels should be determined with them open.

For rigorous control of noise which varies throughout the day and between weekdays and the weekend the noise levels should be measured over appropriate day-time and night-time periods and registered accordingly, allowing separate control of noise levels over these periods. For less rigorous control the separate noise levels may be combined to form an equivalent noise level over a longer period.

Methods of measurement

The noise level to be measured at each measuring position is the equivalent continuous noise level (L_{eq}) measured in dB(A), over a stated period of time. Where appropriate (e.g., for impulsive noise), measurements of L_{eq} should be supplemented by measurements of the maximum noise level during the period.

No matter which measuring technique is used, the measurements should be carried out by competent staff and detailed records kept of the measurements, so that the techniques can be repeated during the different stages of noise monitoring and control. The acoustic performance of the measuring equipment must conform to the relevant standards, its calibration maintained and the overall acoustic performance checked before and after each measurement.

The effects of extraneous noise on the measurements should always be considered carefully. Measurements will not be affected where the extraneous noise is 10 dB(A) or more below the noise from the premises. Where extraneous noise dominates noise from the premises, and it is not possible to measure the noise in the way (previously) described, a calculation method should be used.

The memorandum then provides separate detailed procedures for the measurement of steady noise and varying noise levels. For this purpose a noise is deemed steady if fluctuations of the meter reading do not exceed plus or minus 4 dB(A).

Meterological conditions

The effects of meteorological conditions on sound propagation are complex, and are most marked when either the source or the receiver, or both, are close to the ground and when sound is propagated over large distances.

The memorandum then deals with –

(a) the effect of wind on sound propagation
(b) creation of noise at the microphone by strong winds
(c) the effect of a temperature gradient on sound propagation
(d) the influence on noise reception of a layer of snow.

Noise control

Returning to the 1974 Act, section 65 provides for the control of noise emitted from classified premises, section 65(1) stating that 'The level of noise recorded in the noise level register in respect of any premises shall not be exceeded except with the consent in writing of the local authority'. The emission of excess noise levels or the breach of a condition attached to a consent is therefore a summary offence. In addition to the section 74 penalties[21] on conviction, the magistrates' court may, if satisfied that the offence is likely to continue or recur, make an order requiring the execution of any works necessary to prevent it continuing or recurring. It may also, having heard the authority, direct it to do anything which it has the power to require the convicted person to do, either instead of or as well as imposing any requirement on that person.

1 Fine not exceeding level 5 on the standard scale and a daily penalty of £50 per day.

The authority's consent may be made subject to conditions specified in the consent and governing the amount by which the noise level may be increased, or the period for which or the periods during which, the level of noise may be increased. Particulars of the consent are to be recorded in the noise level register.[22] Any consent under this section is required to contain a statement to the effect that such consent of itself does not constitute a ground of defence against proceedings instituted under section 82 of the Environmental Protection Act 1990, i.e., statutory nuisance proceedings. If the authority does not respond to an application for a consent within two months of the application it is to be deemed to have refused it. An applicant is given a right of appeal to the Secretary of State either against the local authority's decision or, in the above circumstances, against its deemed refusal.

22 Section 65(2).

Noise reduction

Noise production in a noise abatement zone may not only be stabilised and controlled at existing levels; by section 66 the local authority also has power to reduce those levels subject to the criteria in section 66(1), which says:

> If it appears to the local authority –
>
> (a) that the level of noise emanating from any premises to which a noise abatement order applies is not acceptable having regard to the purposes for which the order was made; and
>
> (b) that a reduction in that level is practicable at reasonable cost and would afford a public benefit,
>
> the local authority may serve a notice on the person responsible.

There are therefore three criteria to be satisfied in deciding to serve a notice. It is also clear that an authority, in approaching the creation of a noise abatement zone, must identify with some degree of particularity the objectives intended to be achieved.

Section 66(2), (3) and (4) specify the matters that shall and may be included in the notice. First, the notice shall require the person:

(a) to reduce the level of noise emanating from the premises to such level as may be specified in the notice;
(b) to prevent any subsequent increase in the level of noise emanating from those premises without the consent of the local authority; and
(c) to take such steps as may be specified in the notice to achieve those purposes.

The notice shall also specify a time, not being less than six months from the date of service of the notice, within which the noise level is to be reduced to the specified level and, where the notice specifies any steps necessary to achieve that purpose, within which those steps shall be taken. In addition to these mandatory contents the notice may specify particular times, or particular days, during which the noise level is to be reduced, and may require the noise level to be reduced to different levels for different times or days.

Particulars of a noise reduction notice shall be recorded in the noise level register and shall have the effect of overriding any consent under section 65 permitting a higher level of noise emission. There is, as is to be expected, a standard right of appeal against the notice, in this case to the magistrates' court within three months of service. Contravention of the terms of a noise reduction notice without reasonable excuse is an offence subject to the penalties in section 74. Also, on the failure of the person served to comply with the terms of the notice, the local authority is given by section 69 the power to execute the works itself and to recover from that person the expenditure reasonably incurred in so doing.

In proceedings for an offence caused in the course of any trade or business, it is a defence to prove that the best practicable means had been used for preventing, or for counteracting the effect of, the noise. The scope of 'best practicable means' has been considered in Chapter 2. The meaning of 'trade or business' has received judicial consideration in other contexts. 'Trade' has been defined in the following terms:

> No doubt in many contexts the word 'trade' indicates a process of buying and selling, but that is by no means an exhaustive definition of its meaning. It may also mean a calling or industry or class of skilled labour.[23]

> A trade is an organised seeking after profits as a rule with the aid of physical assets.[24]

'Business' appears to be a wider term than trade, although it must be construed in its context. It has been said to mean ...

> almost anything which is an occupation, as distinguished from a pleasure – anything which is an occupation or duty which requires attention is a business.[25]

So professional activities would be included,[26] but purely domestic or recreational activities would not[27] and neither would an isolated transaction undertaken with no intention that it be repeated.[28]

Noise levels in new buildings

After the creation of a noise abatement zone any new buildings within the designated classes, or any brought in by a change of use, will of course be required to comply with the order, the necessary measurements and entry on the register being made. To this end section 66 applies, with the omission of subsections (1)(b) and (9) and with the substitution of three months as the time within which work to comply with the notice is to be completed.[29] The purpose and effect of section 67 is to allow anticipation of such use within the area of an existing noise abatement zone by the setting of noise levels before use commences. Section 67(1) states that:

> Where it appears to the local authority –
>
> (a) that a building is going to be constructed and that a noise abatement order will apply to it when it is erected; or
> (b) that any premises will, as the result of any works, become premises to which a noise abatement order applies,
>
> the local authority may, on the application of the owner or occupier of the premises or a person who satisfies the authority that he is negotiating to acquire an interest in the premises or on its own initiative, determine the level of noise which will be acceptable as that emanating from the premises.

The noise level so determined shall be entered on the register. The authority shall also notify the applicant, or owner or occupier, of its decision. The recipient then has a three-month right of appeal to the Secretary of State. Failure by the local authority to respond to an application within two months is to be taken as a decision by it not to make a determination, a consequence which is itself subject to appeal.

23 *Skinner v Jack Breach* [1927] 2 KB 220.

24 *Aviation & Shipping Co. v Murray* [1961] 1 WLR 974.

25 *Rolls v Miller* (1894) 27 Ch D 71, p.88.

26 See, e.g., *Re Wilkinson* [1922] 1 KB 584, P 587; *R v Breeze* [1973] 1 WLR 994.

27 See, e.g., *Abernethie v Keiman* [1970] 1 QB 10; *Town Investments v Dept of the Environment* [1976] 3 All ER 479 at p.496 CA.

28 See, e.g., *Re Griffin ex parte Board of Trade* (1890) 60 LJ QB 235 at p.237.

29 Section 67(5).

INSULATION AND COMPENSATION

The place and time to secure the reduction of noise, as is demonstrated in the fore-going part of this chapter, is at its source. Most effort is rightly directed to mini-mising unwanted sound production. When all that can reasonably be required in that respect has been achieved, though, there remain circumstances in which noise levels are produced of sufficient volume or duration to cause excessive disturbance to occupants of neighbouring buildings. In such cases the evident alternative or sup-plementary reduction measure is to prevent the ingress of noise by sound insulation.

Insulation

The provision of insulation in buildings that are recognised because of their loca-tion to be particularly vulnerable to chronic, excess levels of sound which for vari-ous reasons cannot be effectively reduced, may be assisted by grants. Before turning to those specific (and therefore limited) cases, though, the relevant provisions in the Building Regulations 1991 applicable to new dwellings generally (and irres-pective of their location) deserve notice. It is evident from their terms that the pur-pose of the Regulations is to reduce the transmission of sound from adjoining but separately occupied buildings or parts of buildings. There is no general require-ment that new buildings constructed for any purpose should be insulated against external noise.

In their introduction to the sound insulation provisions, the Regulations state that:

> There are two types of sound source: (1) airborne, such as speech and musical instru-ments (2) impact, such as footsteps, moving furniture etc. An airborne source sets up vibrations in the air, which in turn cause the surrounding elements to vibrate directly. These vibrations are passed on to adjoining elements in contact with them. All these el-ements cause the air in adjoining spaces to vibrate and thus noise is transferred. To achieve insulation this flow of energy, either direct or indirect (flanking) must be restricted.

In accordance with that division of source type, regulations E1, E2 and E3 pro-vide respectively for the transmission of airborne sound through walls, airborne sound through floors or stairs, and impact sound through floors or stairs. In each case the structure concerned is one which separates a dwelling from either another dwelling or from another part of the building not exclusively used with it, and in each case the regulations require that they be constructed so as to pro-vide resistance to the transmission of the specified type of sound.

Grants for insulation work may be available to protect against noise due either to the use of airfields or from public works. Also, in the latter case local author-ities may be authorised to do the work. Unlike the Building Regulation provisions just considered, the scope of these powers is not potentially confined to residences, although the current Noise Insulation Regulations 1975 (see below) applicable to public works are so restricted.

Aircraft noise

So far as aircraft noise is concerned, section 79 of the Civil Aviation Act 1982 gives the Secretary of State the power, if he considers 'that buildings near a desig-nated aerodrome require protection from noise and vibration attributable to the use of the aerodrome', to make by statutory instrument a scheme requiring the person managing the aerodrome to make grants towards the cost of insulating such buildings against noise. Prior consultation with the manager is a necessary precondition of the making of such a scheme. One may agree that as the airfield operator is apparently to finance these grants his views should reasonably be obtained prior to the scheme's inception. However, that requirement can produce only an unbalanced view of the need for, scope and consequent cost of the scheme. It may therefore be thought that equally cogent, though different, reasons could be advanced to justify consultation with the persons affected by the noise, or their representative local authorities.

The Secretary of State may specify the classes of buildings to which the scheme shall apply. Each scheme will be specific to a particular aerodrome and shall specify the:

(a) area(s) in which buildings will qualify for grant;
(b) persons to whom grant is payable;
(c) expenditure ranking for grant; and
(d) rate at which grants are to be paid.[30]

It may also:

(e) attach conditions to the payment of grant;
(f) require the manager to notify his reasons in the event of the refusal of an application;
(g) authorise or require local authorities to act as the manager's agents in operating the grant scheme;
(h) make different provision for different areas or circumstances.[31]

Public works

Part II of the Land Compensation Act 1973 gives the Secretary of State the power to make regulations governing the insulation of buildings affected by noise from public works. Disturbance may be caused by noise from the use of such works after construction and also, by entirely different forms and levels of noise, while they are under construction. Both situations are provided for. The scope of 'public works' for this purpose is '(a) any highway; and (c) any other works or land provided or used in the exercise of statutory powers'.[32]

By section 20(1):

> The Secretary of State may make regulations imposing a duty or conferring a power on responsible authorities to insulate buildings against noise caused or expected to be caused by the construction or use of public works or to make grants in respect of the cost of such insulation.

The current regulations made under this broad power, the Noise Insulation Regulations 1975,[33] are confined to the problems caused by highway noise. In considering the operation of the Regulations the meanings attached to the following terms are to be noted[34]:

> 'prevailing noise level' means the level of noise, expressed as a level of L10 (18-hour), one metre in front of the most exposed of any windows and doors in a facade of a building caused by traffic using any highway immediately before works for the construction of a highway or additional carriageway, or for the alteration of a highway, as the case may be, were begun;

30 Section 79(2).

31 Section 79(2) to (5).

32 Section 20(12), modifying section 1(3).

33 S.I. 1975 No. 1763.

34 All defined in regulation 2(1).

'relevant noise level' means the level of noise, expressed as a level of L10 (18-hour), one metre in front of the most exposed of any windows and doors in the facade of a building caused or expected to be caused by traffic using or expected to use any highway; 'L10' is the sound level in dB(A) which is exceeded for one-tenth of a period of one hour; 'L10 (18-hour)' is the arithmetic mean of all levels of L10 during a period from 0600 to 2400 hours on a normal working day ...

Regulation 3 provides that:

... where the use of a highway or additional carriageway first opened to public traffic after 16 October 1972 causes or is expected to cause noise at a level not less than the specified level, the appropriate highway authority[35] shall carry out or make a grant in respect of the cost of carrying out insulation work in or to an eligible building.

The 'specified level' means a noise level of L10 (18-hour) of 68dB(A), and a noise is at a level not less than the specified level if :

(a) the relevant noise level is greater by at least 1dB(A) than the prevailing noise level and is not less than the specified level; and
(b) noise caused or expected to be caused by traffic using or expected to use that highway makes an effective contribution to the relevant noise level of at least 1dB(A).

To determine whether the duty exists the necessary noise levels are to be ascertained in accordance with the advice and instruction contained in the technical memorandum entitled 'Calculation of Road Traffic Noise'.[36] The buildings eligible for this treatment are dwellings and other residential buildings not more than 300 metres from the nearest point on the newly constructed highway when completed. Excluded from this eligible category are any buildings that are or are liable to be the subject of a compulsory purchase order, subject to a closing or demolition order or within a clearance area. Also excluded are buildings that were first occupied after the 'relevant date', that is when the highway was first open to public traffic.[37]

In the performance of this duty the authority shall ascertain every building eligible for insulation work or grant under regulation 3 and identify them on a map or list, or both. Those documents shall then be deposited at the office of the authority, or the local authority agents,[38] nearest to the buildings concerned and there be available for public inspection during office hours and not later than six months after the highway was first open to public traffic, i.e., the relevant date.

As soon as the authority has deposited the documents in accordance with regulation 6 above, it shall make a written offer to the occupier, or to his immediate landlord or licensor, of every eligible building identified on the map or list. The offer shall, by regulation 8:

(a) identify the building to which it relates;
(b) offer to carry out or make a grant in respect of the cost of carrying out insulation work in or to every eligible room in the building;
(c) describe the work required to be carried out for this purpose;
(d) where the offer is made to the occupier, require him to notify his immediate landlord or licensor of the terms of the offer;
(e) where the offer is made to the landlord or licensor, require him to notify the occupier of the terms of the offer;
(f) set out the conditions in regulation 10 subject to which the offer is made;

35 By regulation 2(1) the highway authority who constructed, or proposes to construct, a highway or additional carriageway, or who altered or proposes to alter a highway.

36 HMSO, 1975.

37 Regulation 7.

38 Regulation 14 allows a local authority to act as agent for the appropriate highway authority 'in the discharge and exercise of its duties and powers under these regulations'.

(g) set out the restrictions on time of acceptance of the offer in paragraphs (4) and (7) of regulation 8.

An 'eligible room' for these insulation purposes means a living room or bedroom having an an externally opening door or window in the part of a building facade in respect of which the relevant noise level is not less than the specified noise level as indicated above. Where insulation work has been carried out in accordance with the requirements in the Schedule to the Regulations – 'the relevant specifications' – before an offer is made, a grant may be offered and paid to the person who incurred the cost. The regulation 10 conditions relate to access to the premises for the authority to carry out and/or inspect the work as the case may be, and, in the case of a grant, that the work be completed within 12 months from the date of acceptance.

Acceptance may be of the whole or part of the offer to do the work or make a grant, and is to be in writing either within six months of the date of the offer or within 12 months of the relevant date. If the offer is not accepted by the person to whom it is made within three months any other person to whom it has or could have been notified may accept it, and thereafter the person originally offered is no longer capable of accepting it. Where the offer is accepted by the landlord the work may be carried out notwithstanding lack of consent by the tenant. The amount of grant, by regulation 11, shall be equal either to the actual cost incurred by the claimant in carrying out the work or to the reasonable cost of the work, whichever is the less.

In the circumstances stipulated in regulation 3(1) the Regulations place a duty on the authority either to do the necessary work or to make a grant for its cost. In two other cases the Regulations allow the appropriate highway authority to carry out such insulation work or to make a grant towards the work at its discretion. First, by regulation 4, where its use causes or is expected to cause noise at a level not less than the specified level, the appropriate highway authority may carry out, or make a grant for, insulation work in the case of a highway –

(a) to which regulation 3 applies but before any regulation 8 duty has arisen;
(b) where the highway becomes a highway maintainable at the public expense[39] within three years of the relevant date;

39 Within section 295(1) of the Highways Act 1959.

The terms of the Regulations as already considered and subject to any necessary adaptations or modifications, apply. Secondly, regulation 5 provides a discretionary power to insulate against noise caused by the construction work. Where the appropriate highway authority considers that works for the construction of a highway cause or are expected to cause noise which will in its opinion seriously affect for a substantial period of time the enjoyment of an eligible building adjacent to the site on which the works are being carried out, but in respect of which no duty under regulation 3 or power under regulation 4(1) has arisen, it may carry out or make a grant towards the cost of carrying out insulation work in or to the building. The provisions of the Regulations apply so far as applicable, save that the time for acceptance is reduced to two months from the date of the offer.

The insulation work qualifying for action or grant under the Regulations is that complying 'with the relevant specifications' contained in the Schedule. While the subject matter of the schedule is too complex and detailed to justify inclusion here, its contents cover the following:

(a) Matters that shall be included, i.e. –
  (i) conversion or replacement of qualifying windows;[40]
  (ii) the provision as appropriate of sound attenuating ventilator units or air supply ducts;
  (iii) provision of combustion air for rooms containing appliances of differing capacities;
  (iv) the insulation of qualifying doors and door glazing;
  (v) ventilation provision for gas cookers.
(b) Matters that may be included, i.e. –
  (i) provision of insulation to non-qualifying doors and windows in eligible rooms;
  (ii) making good existing fabric and decorations affected by the carrying out of insulation work.

Compensation

The impact of noise will prejudicially affect the occupants of neighbouring properties in their use and enjoyment. For similar reasons it will affect the value of the land. Part I of the Land Compensation Act 1973 provides a scheme of compensation for the depreciation of the value of interests in land due to 'physical factors caused by the use of public works'. The payments are not therefore to compensate the current occupants for the annoyance and distress suffered from the noise and vibration. That is to be remedied, if at all, through reduction of emissions at source and insulation of the affected premises as already discussed.

The 'physical factors' referred to above are 'noise, vibration, smell, fumes, smoke and artificial lighting and the discharge on to the land in respect of which the claim is made of any solid or liquid substance'.[41] For purposes of section 1 'public works' are defined as:

(a) any highway;
(b) any aerodrome; and
(c) any works or land (not being a highway or aerodrome) provided or used in the exercise of statutory powers.[42]

The person entitled to the interest makes a claim by serving on the responsible authority[43] a notice with particulars of :

(a) the land in respect of which the claim is made;
(b) the claimant's interest and the date and manner on which it was acquired;
(c) the claimant's occupation of the land;
(d) any other interests in the land known to the claimant;
(e) the public works to which the claim relates;
(f) the amount of compensation claimed;
(g) any contiguous or adjacent land to which the claimant was entitled in the same capacity on the relevant date.

The claim period within which claims must be made[44] is the period of two years beginning on the expiration of 12 months from the relevant date.[45] In the case of a valid claim, the claimant is entitled, in addition to the compensation, to the costs of 'any reasonable valuation or legal expenses incurred by [him] for the purposes of the preparation and prosecution of the claim'.

40 Both 'qualifying windows' and 'qualifying doors' are defined in the Schedule at paragraph 1.

41 Section 1(2).

42 Section 1(3).

43 Under section 1(4), 'The responsible authority ... is, in relation to a highway, the appropriate highway authority and, in relation to other public works, the person managing those works'.

44 Save for earlier claims where the claimant has contracted to dispose of his interest or to grant a tenancy.

45 Section 3(1) and (2).

The 'relevant date' for determination of the commencement of the claim period is provided for in section 1(9), which states that:

Subject to section 9 below, 'the relevant date' in this Part of the Act means –

(a) in relation to a claim in respect of a highway, the date on which it was first open to public traffic;
(b) in relation to claims in respect of other public works, the date on which they were first used after completion.

Section 9 deals with the relevant date as it applies to alterations and changes of use, section 9(2) stating that it shall be:

(a) the date on which the highway was first open to public traffic after completion of the alterations to the carriageway;
(b) the date on which the other public works were first used after completion of the alterations; or
(c) the date of change of use,

as the case may be.

The key issue in respect of claims is of course the method of assessing compensation. The governing rules in sections 4 to 8, presented in simplified form, are:

(a) compensation is to be assessed by reference to prices current on the first day of the claim period;
(b) depreciation shall be determined by reference to the use of the works on the first day of the claim period, with any subsequent likely intensification;
(c) account shall be taken of the benefit of any statutory grant aided works that have or could have been carried out;[46]
(d) the interest subject to the claim shall be valued –
(i) as it subsisted at the date of service of notice of the claim,
(ii) in accordance with rules 2 and 4 in section 5 of the Land Compensation Act 1961,
(iii) if subject to a mortgage or contract made after the relevant date for the grant of a tenancy, as if it were not so subject;
(e) extensions or improvements after the relevant date shall be ignored in assessing the value of the interest;
(f) it shall be assumed that planning permission would be granted, subject to Section 5(3), for the land for development of the classes specified in Schedule 8 of the Town and Country Planning Act 1971 and for no other;
(g) compensation shall be reduced by an amount equal to any increase in the value of that or any contiguous or adjacent land in which the claimant has an interest attributable to the existence of, use or prospective use of the public works to which the claim relates;
(h) compensation shall only be payable on claims exceeding £50;
(i) payment having been made for depreciation of the value of an interest, no further compensation shall be payable in relation to the same works and the same land whether for the same or a different interest, with the exception of claims for the fee simple and a tenancy of a dwelling;
(j) where land in which the claimant has an interest is compulsorily purchased and whether or not any payment for injurious affection is made, compensation shall not be payable in respect of any land retained on a claim made after service of the notice to treat;[47]

46 Under section 15 of the Airports Authority Act 1965 or sections 20, 23 and 27 of the Land Compensation Act 1973.

47 Section 8(2)–(6) develop and qualify the relationship of compensation to compulsory purchase.

(k) compensation is not payable in respect of the same depreciation both under this Part of this Act and under any other enactment.

The rules in section 5 of the Land Compensation Act 1961 governing the assessment of compensation for compulsory purchase purposes, and applied here in (d)(ii) above, are:

(2) The value of land shall, subject as hereinafter provided, be taken to be the amount which the land if sold in the open market by a willing seller might be expected to realise.

(4) Where the value of the land is increased by reason of the use thereof or of any premises thereon in a manner which could be restrained by any court, or is contrary to law, or is detrimental to the health of the occupants of the premises or to the public health, the amount of that increase shall not be taken into account.

12

Noise Control

NEIGHBOURHOOD NOISE

The term 'Neighbourhood Noise' is used as a general, comprehensive phrase to cover the forms of noise that affect people in the domestic situation, with the exception of that from road traffic which is treated separately. The 1990 Report of the Noise Review Working Party[1] identified the sources of complaints within this broad category as follows:

1 Report of the Noise Review Working Party, 1990, HMSO, quoting the results of a BRE survey.

	%
Amplified music	34
Dogs	33
Domestic activities	9
Voices	6
DIY activities	5
Car repairs	3
Other	10

In considering legal remedies applicable to noise problems it is to be remembered that in many cases the statutory nuisance procedure in Part III of the Environmental Protection Act 1990[2] may be the most effective option. Also, of course, the individual affected retains a right of action to obtain civil remedies through private nuisance proceedings. Control over some types of noise may also be available in individual local authority areas under local byelaws. Section 235(1) of the Local Government Act 1972 gives authorities the power to 'make byelaws for the good rule and government of the whole or any part of the district or borough, as the case may be, and for the prevention and suppression of nuisances therein' – phraseology wide enough to cover various categories of noise. The Home Office has issued sets of Model Byelaws covering:

2 See chapters 3 and 4.

- Music near houses, churches and hospitals
- Playing of organs, wirelesses and gramophones
- Noisy hawking
- Unruly behaviour in places of public entertainment
- Noisy conduct at night
- Noisy animals.

Section 71 of the Control of Pollution Act 1974 gives the Secretary of State the power to prepare, approve and issue codes of practice giving guidance on appropriate methods for minimising noise, or to approve such codes issued by others. While, in common with all codes of practice, they have no legal authority *per se* they may be of evidential value in establishing the reasonableness or otherwise of an incident, and anyway provide approved guidance for the operation of such activities. Codes issued to date by the Department of the Environment and approved by the following Orders under this power, excluding construction noise which is dealt with separately below, are:

(a) Control of Noise (Code of Practice on Noise for Ice-Cream Van Chimes, etc.) Order 1981,[3]

3 S.I. 1981 No. 1828.

(b) Control of Noise (Code of Practice on Noise from Audible Intruder Alarms) Order 1981,[4]

4 S.I. 1981 No. 1829.

(c) Control of Noise (Code of Practice on Noise from Model Aircraft) Order 1981.[5]

5 S.I. 1981 No. 1830.

Further codes covering noise from audible bird scarers, clay pigeon shooting and off-road motorcycle sport are to be expected. The contents of the two former codes appear under their appropriate headings. A synopsis of the principal terms of the code appying to model aircraft follows:

Code of Practice on Noise from Model Aircraft

1. It is recommended that –
   (a) model aircraft are to be fitted with mufflers wherever practicable, except in the case of competitive flying;
   (b) except for competitive flying the maximum noise level should be no more than 82 dB(A) at 7 metres.
2. Where unmuffled flight causes substantial disturbance it should not be permitted.
3. Additional precautions may be necessary to limit model-flying noise heard by neighbours, that is –
   (a) separation distance
   (b) times of operation
   (c) numbers of model aircraft in operation simultaneously
   (d) barriers between flying site and noise sensitive premises.

An appropriate combination of these factors in each case to be agreed between the local authority and representatives of model-flyers.

4. The appendix to the Code provides a method of measurement of noise emitted by model aircraft.

Note – Legal Controls applicable to model aircraft include –

(a) Article 46 of the Air Navigation Order 1980 requires that a person shall not wilfully or negligently cause or permit an aircraft to endanger any person or property. That Article is the only part of the Order appying to model aircraft; the remainder, subject to exceptions by order of the Civil Aviation Authority, applies to aircraft weighing more than 5 kg (11.023 lb).
(b) A site used for model flying may in certain circumstances require specific planning permission – which may include conditions, *inter alia*, controlling noise.
(c) local authority byelaws may control model-flying on municipal land.

Loudspeakers

The use of loudspeakers in public places is governed by section 62 of the Control of Pollution Act 1974.[6] In spite of the general heading above, the section applies to all public places and is not confined to residential areas. Section 62(1) provides that:

6 Amended by section 7 of the Noise and Statutory Nuisance Act 1993.

a loudspeaker in a street shall not be operated –

(a) between the hours of nine in the evening and eight in the following morning, for any purpose;[7]
(b) at any other time, for the purpose of advertising any entertainment, trade or business ...'

The prohibition in the stipulated circumstances then is total, irrespective of volume. Possibly for that reason the section does not extend to speakers in hand-held radios playing music for pleasure. The person operating or permitting the operation of the loudspeaker commits the offence and, by section 74 as amended,[8] is liable on summary conviction to a fine up to level 5 on the standard scale. The meaning of 'permitting' has been considered in Chapter 1 in the context of 'cause or permit'.

The scope of 'street' for these purposes includes the highway and extends to 'any other road, footway, square or court which is for the time being open to the public'. The meaning of 'road', emphasising its essentially public nature, appears in the judgement of Lord Clyde in *Harrison* v *Hill* (1932)[9]:

It is plain from the terms of the definition, that the class of road intended is wider than the class of public roads to which the public has access by virtue of a positive right belonging to the public, and flowing either from statute or from prescriptive user. A road may therefore be within the definition (1) although it belongs to the class of private roads, and (2) although all that can be said with regard to its availability to the public is that the public 'has access' to it. ... I think also that, when the statute speaks of the public having 'access' to the road, what is meant is neither (at one extreme) that the public has a positive right of its own to access, nor (at the other extreme) that there exists no physical obstruction, of greater or less impenetrability, against physical access by the public; but that the public actually and legally enjoys access to it. It is, I think, a certain state of use or possession that is pointed to. There must be, as a matter of fact, walking or driving by the public on the road, and such walking or driving must be lawfully performed – that is to say, must be permitted or allowed, either expressly or implicitly, by the person or persons to whom the road belongs. I include in permission or allowance the state of matters known in right of way cases as the tolerance of a proprietor.

If the concluding phrase in the definition of 'street' may be taken to be synonymous with 'to which the public have access' it will include places to which the public have actual access by acquiescence or otherwise as well as by legal right, as considered in relation to roads. It was said in *Woods* v *Lindsay* (1910),[10] emphasising the general principle, that:

In construing the expression [public place] each statute must be considered by itself in the light of the expressions used therein and the evil which the statute seeks to check.

Two categories of exemption are to be found in section 62(2) and (3), covering respectively those operations that are totally exempt and those permitted between noon and seven in the evening if satisfying certain conditions. First, by section 62(2), loudspeakers used in the following circumstances are totally exempt from the section 62(1) prohibition:

(a) for police, fire brigade or ambulance purposes, by a water authority in the exercise of any of its functions, or by a local authority within its area;
(b) for communicating with persons on a vessel for the purpose of directing the movement of that or any other vessel;

7 Section 7 of the Noise and Statutory Nuisance Act 1993 gives the Secretary of State power to amend these times but not so as to extend into that prohibited period.

8 See sections 35, 37, 38 and 46 of the Criminal Justice Act 1982.

9 (1932)SC(J) 16; applied in *Buchanan* v *Motor Insurance Bureau* [1955] 1 All ER 607 concerning insurance following a road accident on Port of London premises accessible only by pass. See also *O'Brien* v *Trafalgar Insurance Co. Ltd* (1945) 61 TLR 225; *Thomas* v *Dando* [1951] 2 KB 620; 1 All ER 1010.

10 [1910] JC 88; for examples of places held to be 'public places' under various Acts see *R* v *Kane* [1965] 1 All ER 705; *Cooper* v *Shield* [1971] 2 QB 334; *Cawley* v *Frost* [1976] 3 All ER 744; *DPP* v *Vivier* [1991] 4 All ER 18.

(c) if the loudspeaker forms part of a public telephone system;

(d) if the loudspeaker –

    (i) is in or fixed to a vehicle, and

    (ii) is operated solely for the entertainment of or for communicating with the driver or a passenger of the vehicle or, where the loudspeaker is or forms part of the horn or similar warning instrument of the vehicle, solely for giving warning to other traffic, and

    (iii) is so operated as not to give reasonable cause for annoyance to persons in the vicinity;

(e) otherwise than on a highway, by persons employed in connection with a transport undertaking used by the public in a case where the loudspeaker is operated solely for making announcements to passengers or prospective passengers or to other persons so employed;

(f) by a travelling showman on land which is being used for the purposes of a pleasure fair;

(g) in case of emergency.

Car radios are therefore protected within subsection (2)(d), but only to the extent that they satisfy the requirements of (ii) and (iii).

Section 62(3) excludes the operation of section 62(1)(b), i.e., prohibiting the use of loudspeakers for advertising, when used between noon and seven in the evening on the same day if the loudspeaker:

(a) is fixed to a vehicle which is being used for the conveyance of a perishable commodity for human consumption; and

(b) is operated solely for informing members of the public (otherwise than by means of words) that the commodity is on sale from the vehicle; and

(c) is so operated as not to give reasonable cause for annoyance to persons in the vicinity.

The phrase 'reasonable cause for annoyance' appears in both subsections. On normal interpretation the term, with 'reasonableness' as the criterion, would appear to approximate closely to the standard applicable to nuisance. A further similarity with nuisance is the effect of malice or intention. In *Raymond v Cook* (1958),[11] concerning the breach of a byelaw prohibiting the use of 'any bell or other noisy instrument for the purpose of selling any article in any street or public place so as to cause annoyance to the inhabitants', Lord Parker CJ said:

> The proper approach to these cases is for the justices to ask themselves first, Was the instrument so noisy as to be calculated to annoy? On that, the facts may speak for themselves, or it may be necessary for them to hear evidence, albeit of only one person; but once they have come to the conclusion that the noise was calculated to annoy, then it is quite unnecessary for them to have any evidence as to who and how many people were in fact annoyed.

A local authority has the discretion under section 8 and Schedule 2 of the Noise and Statutory Nuisance Act 1993 to give its consent to the operation of a loudspeaker that would otherwise be in contravention of section 62(1) of the 1974 Act. As a preliminary to the use of this power the authority must by resolution apply Schedule 2 to its area; the schedule coming into force on the date specified, being at least one month from the date of the resolution.[12] Between the date of the resolution and its coming into force the authority is required to publish in a newspaper circulating in the area in two consecutive weeks a notice stating that

11 [1958] 3 All ER 407, at p.410; 102 Sol Jo 812.

12 Section 8(1) and (2).

the resolution has been passed and the general effect of Schedule 2. Having been adopted, Schedule 2 provides that:

(a) The local authority, on application by any person, may consent to the operation of a loudspeaker in contravention of section 62(1) of the 1974 Act, except in connection with any election or for the purpose of advertising any entertainment, trade or business.

(b) A consent may be granted subject to such conditions as the local authority considers appropriate.

(c) An application shall be in writing, shall contain such information as the authority may reasonably require and include a reasonable fee determined by the authority.

(d) An application shall be determined and notified to the applicant within 21 days of reception, including, where appropriate any conditions.

(e) In granting a consent the authority may publish a notice giving details of the consent in a local newspaper.

In the exercise of his power under section 71 of the Control of Pollution Act 1974, the Secretary of State has, by the Control of Noise (Code of Practice on Noise for Ice-Cream Van Chimes etc.) Order 1981,[13] approved a code for the operation of loudspeakers on ice-cream vans. A synopsis of its provisions follows:

13 S.I. 1981 No.1828.

Code of Practice on Noise from Ice-Cream Van Chimes

1. The general volume limit should be 80dB(A), although in narrow streets or where houses are close to the road a limit below 80dB(A) may be necessary.

2. Measurement by a meter conforming to BS 5969: 1981 (Type) set to A-frequency weighting and S-time weighting with the microphone at a height of 1.2 metres above ground and a distance of 7.5 metres from the speaker.

3. The passage of played music should last not more than 4 seconds.

4. Chimes should be played only once on the approach to each stopping place, never when the van is stationary and never at intervals of less than 3 minutes.

5. Chimes should never be played more often than once every 2 hours in a particular length of street, i.e., of 100–150 metres long.

6. Chimes should not be played in particularly sensitive areas and in particular not within 50 metres of –
   – a hospital or similar institution,
   – school during school hours,
   – place of worship on a Sunday.

Audible intruder alarms

The Noise and Statutory Nuisance Act 1993, section 9 and Schedule 3 provide an adoptive procedure for local authorities to deal with nuisance caused by noise from audible intruder alarms. Unlike the rest of the Act, those provisions will come into force on a day to be appointed.[14] The terms of section 62(1) of the 1974 Act make it clear that noise from loudspeakers in or attached to buildings does not come within its ambit, applying as it does to loudspeakers in streets. The currently available remedy therefore is by the statutory nuisance procedure in Part III of the Environmental Protection Act 1990 and subject to those criteria. In those proceedings the following Code of Practice may prove of evidential value in determining reasonableness for the purpose of establishing nuisance.

14 Section 12(2).

In the exercise of his power under section 71 of the Control of Pollution Act 1974, the Secretary of State has, by the Control of Noise (Code of Practice on Noise from Audible Intruder Alarms) Order 1981,[15] approved a code for the operation of such alarms. A synopsis of its provisions follows.

15 S.I. 1981 No. 1829.

Code of Practice for Audible Intruder Alarms
1. Installation and maintenance to be in accordance with BS 4737 (1977/78/79) Specification for Intruder Alarm Systems in Buildings.
2. Alarms should be fitted so that they are not automatically set off as a part of normal opening and closing procedures.
3. Where several are in close proximity, there should be means to identify which alarm is ringing, e.g., by a flashing light adjacent to the bell unit.
4. Alarms to be fitted with a cut-out device to stop ringing automatically after about 20 minutes from activation.
5. The alarm-holder should –
   (a) within 48 hours of installing or taking over an alarm, notify the police for the area in writing of the names, addresses and telephone numbers of at least 2 key-holders. The alarm-holder or a security firm may be nominated as key-holders.
   (b) at the same time, notify the local environmental health authority.

Entertainment noise

Noise may be produced from entertainment that is either public or private, each being subject to its own controls. Before reviewing those respective provisions, though, the scope and meaning of 'entertainment' requires consideration. While there appears to be no statutory definition of the term, it has received judicial commentary, notably in *Attorney-General* v *Southport Corporation* (1934).[16] The issue was whether payments by persons to gain access to an enclosure on the seafront where they could sit, consume refreshments and watch bathers in a public bathing lake were liable for entertainments duty within section 1 of the Finance (New Duties) Act 1916; in short, whether public bathing was 'entertainment'. Finlay J, with whose approach the Court of Appeal agreed, said[17]:

16 [1934] 1 KB 226.

17 At pp.233–4.

> I arrive at the conclusion that 'entertainment' means something in the nature of an organised entertainment, though not necessarily organised by the persons who are to receive payment for the seat, as is clearly shown by the illustration of the boat race or that of the Lord Mayor's Show. I do not think that where, as here, what is to be looked at is not anything in the nature of an organised entertainment, but is simply the spectacle of people bathing in an unorganised way for their own health and amusement, that can properly be said to be an entertainment.

The significant characteristic appears then to be that the activity is purposely organised with entertainment as one of its aims. So, for example, persons watching a working shepherd and his dog gathering sheep on a hillside are not seeing an entertainment, whereas the same people seeing the same man and dog doing the same thing in organised sheepdog trials probably are. Payment for admission, while indicative, is not, it is submitted, essential. The street entertainers in Covent Garden are still entertainers, irrespective of the proportion of the audience that fails to contribute to the collection.

Having identified the essential nature of entertainment, its scope is confined for these licensing purposes, in both the public and private context, to 'dancing, music

18 See respectively, Schedule 1, paragraph 1(2) of the Local Government (Miscellaneous Provisions) Act 1982 and section 2(1) of the Private Places of Entertainment (Licensing) Act 1967.

19 Paragraph 2(2) of Schedule 1 to the Local Government (Miscellaneous Provisions) Act 1982.

20 [1912] IR 327.

21 At p.336.

or any other entertainment of a like kind';[18] and in the public context only also 'includes, any public contest, exhibition or display of boxing, wrestling, judo, karate or any similar sport'.[19]

All that has been said in Chapter 3 concerning nuisance, reasonableness and give and take applies with particular emphasis to noise. That it can present especially acute problems for the reasons discussed in the introduction to the previous chapter, and because of the significant subjective element, is a matter of common experience. Nevertheless, the questions to be answered in relation to the assessment of the impact of entertainment noise on persons affected are the same as those for any other nuisance situation. In *New Imperial and Windsor Hotel* v *Johnson* (1912)[20] the proprietors of a hotel in Belfast applied for an injunction to restrain the defendant proprietor of tea-rooms and a restaurant on the opposite side of the street from using his premises for music, dancing etc., so as to cause a nuisance to the plaintiffs, their servants and guests. In granting the order, and in the course of a detailed and interesting review of the facts, Barton J said[21]:

> Among the noises which, if they do not cause substantial discomfort, residents in large industrial cities may have to put up with, is a certain amount of the noise which accompanies and is incident to the reasonable recreation of a crowded population. In the fashionable quarter of a city a similar discomfort is experienced at certain seasons, and within due limits, may have to be submitted to. The question in every such case, is whether such noises amount to a sensible or substantial interference with the comfort of neighbouring dwellers according to ordinary sober commonsense standards.

Public entertainment

22 The London Government Act 1963 governs both indoor and outdoor events in London and provides for a different range of conditions. Note that the penalty provisions of the London Act are amended by section 1(8) of this 1982 Act.

23 Section 1(2) – (6).

The licensing of public entertainments by local authorities outside London is provided for in Schedule 1 to the Local Government (Miscellaneous Provisions) Act 1982.[22] The schedule applies automatically to indoor events with the exception of music associated either with religious places or functions, or alternatively with entertainment in a pleasure fair. Paragraphs 3 and 4, which relate to open air events on private land, apply only where the local authority has adopted them by resolution. The adopting procedure, in section 1, is the same as that in section 8 of the Noise and Statutory Nuisance Act 1993 giving a local authority power to consent to loudspeaker noise, i.e., the paragraphs shall come into force on the date specified in the resolution, being at least one month from its date of passing.[23] Between the date of the resolution and its coming into force, and at least 28 days before that latter date, the authority is required to publish in a newspaper circulating in the area in two consecutive weeks a notice stating that the resolution has been passed and the general effect of the paragraphs.

Where the authority has adopted paragraphs 3 and 4, and for the purpose of licensing open air events, paragraph 3 identifies more specifically the activities subject to control, stipulating that:

(a) an entertainment is musical if music is a substantial ingredient;
(b) land is private if the public has access to it (whether on payment or otherwise) only by permission of the owner, occupier or lessee;
(c) the provisions do not apply to any of the following activities merely because music is incidental to them:

(i) garden fete, bazaar, sale of work, sporting or athletic event, exhibition, display or other function or event of a similar character, whether limited to one day or extending over two or more days, or
(ii) to a religious meeting or service;
(d) an entertainment held in a pleasure fair is excluded.

The terms, conditions and restrictions in licences granted under paragraph 4 for open air events may be imposed only for the following purposes:

(a) for securing the safety of performers and other persons present;
(b) for securing adequate access for fire engines, ambulances, police cars or other vehicles that may be required in an emergency;
(c) for securing the provision of adequate sanitary appliances and things used in connection with such appliances;
(d) for preventing persons in the neighbourhood being unreasonably disturbed by noise.

The general effect of the schedule is that the entertainments covered by paragraphs 1, 2, and 3 as indicated above are only to be provided in accordance with a licence (an entertainments licence[24]) granted or renewed under these powers by the appropriate authority. A licence may be granted in respect of one or more particular occasions or for a period of up to a year, may specify the entertainment(s) authorised and state the terms, conditions and restrictions to which they are subject. Power is provided to grant a provisional licence subject to confirmation, in respect of premises that are being constructed, extended or altered where the authority is satisfied that, if completed in accordance with the deposited plans, it would grant the licence. On completion according to the approved plans, and if satisfied that the licence is held by a fit and proper person, the authority shall confirm the licence.

An applicant for the grant, renewal or transfer of a licence is required to give at least 28 days' notice of his intention to the authority, chief police officer and the fire authority and provide with his application to the authority such information and give such further notices as the authority may by regulations prescribe. The applicant shall also pay the fee determined by the authority; except in the case of entertainments at places occupied in connection with a place of religious worship or at a village hall, parish or community hall or other similar building which are exempt. The authority may also remit the whole or part of the fee where in its opinion the entertainment is of an educational or similar character, or is given for a charitable or like purpose.[25] In considering the application the licensing authority may consult the other persons required to be notified.[26]

Having been granted, a licence may on application be renewed, varied, transferred or cancelled. Also, on the death of the holder, it is generally deemed to be transmitted to the person carrying on the functions to which the licence relates. In common with all such control procedures the applicant or holder, as the case may be, has a right of appeal against all those decisions of the authority for which applications to the authority may be made. The time for an appeal is within 21 days of notification to the appellant of the authority's decision, and having heard the appeal, the magistrates' court, or the Crown Court on subsequent appeal, may make whatever order it thinks fit.

A licensing authority may prescribe standard conditions applicable to all or any class of entertainments licence, and in such cases every licence or licence of that

24 Paragraph 22 of Schedule 1.

25 For the scope of 'charity' see at Chapter 10 p.279.

26 Paragraphs 6 and 7 of Schedule 1.

class shall be deemed to be granted, renewed or transferred subject to any standard conditions applicable to it unless they have been expressly excluded or varied.[27] A copy of the standard conditions is to be supplied on request and on payment of a reasonable fee.

There are clearly two types of offence contemplated within this schedule. First, the provision of an entertainment within these provisions without an applicable licence. In such a case any person concerned in its organisation or management or who 'knowing or having reasonable cause to suspect that such an entertainment would be so provided' allowed the place to be used or made it available is guilty of an offence. The penalty on summary conviction is a fine not exceeding £20,000 and/or imprisonment.[28] Secondly, the use of any licensed premises otherwise than in accordance with the terms and conditions of the licence. In this case the licence holder and any person who 'knowing or having reasonable cause to suspect that such an entertainment would be so provided' allowed the place to be used or made it available is guilty of an offence. The penalty on conviction is the same as in the first case and in addition the authority may revoke the licence. The Criminal Justice Act 1988 (Confiscation Orders) Order 1990[29] adds to the list of offences in Part I of that Act the two offences in paragraph 12 of Schedule 1 to the 1982 Act dealt with above, permitting magistrates to make confiscation orders under section 71 of the Criminal Justice Act 1988.

In order to ensure the due observance and operation of these licensing requirements rights of entry are given to appropriate officers, refusal without reasonable excuse to permit entry or inspection for these purposes being itself a summary offence. The rights of entry are for, *inter alia*:

(a) a constable or an authorised officer of the appropriate authority or of the fire authority to ensure that the licence terms, conditions or restrictions are being complied with, where they have reason to believe that an entertainment is being or is about to be given in a place in respect of which an entertainments licence is in force;

(b) a constable or an authorised officer of the authority authorised by a warrant granted by a justice of the peace where they have reason to suspect that an offence within the preceding paragraph is being committed.[30]

Private Entertainment

The Private Places of Entertainment (Licensing) Act 1967 governing these activities is an adoptive Act available to local authorities in London, or to those who already have powers under other legislation to licence public music and dancing. A necessary precondition to the exercise of control over noise from private parties and entertainments therefore is the prior adoption of the Act.

Section 2(1) provides that:

Where this Act applies no premises are to be used for dancing, music or any other entertainment of the like kind which –

(a) is not public within the meaning of the enactment mentioned in section 1(1) of this Act in force in that area;[31] but

(b) is promoted for private gain

except under and in accordance with the terms of a licence granted under this Act by the licensing authority.

---

27 Paragraph 11 of Schedule 1.

28 As amended by the Entertainment (Increased Penalties) Act 1990.

29 S.I. 1990 No. 1570; made under Schedule 4, Part II, paragraph 1 of the Criminal Justice Act 1988.

30 Paragraph 14 of Schedule 1.

31 The enactments referred to in section 1(1) and applicable to particular areas are section 51 of the Public Health Act Amendment Act 1890, the Home Counties (Music and Dancing) Licensing Act 1926, and paragraph 1 of Schedule 12 of the London Government Act 1963.

The broad effect of section 2(2) and (3) is to exclude from this requirement premises that are to be licensed under other statutes. Also, where a society either wholly established for purposes other than commercial gain or devoted to participation in or support of athletic sports or athletic games promotes an entertainment the proceeds of which are applied for the benefit of that society, the entertainment shall not be held to be promoted for private gain. 'Society' in this context embracing 'any club, institution, organisation or association of persons, by whatever name called, and any separate branch or section of such a club, institution, organisation or association'.

The procedural provisions in section 3 are broadly similar to those just considered in relation to public entertainment,[32] as is also the range and structure of appeals in section 5. The application for the grant, renewal or transfer of a licence is to be accompanied by the fee. A licence may be granted for the use of premises for all or any of the section 2 purposes and subject to the terms, conditions and restrictions specified therein. The maximum duration of a licence, subject to any specified shorter period, is one year.

It is apparent on their terms that the designation of the two offences in section 4 served as the progenitor of those in the 1982 Act dealt with above. The use of premises for an unlicensed entertainment for which a licence is required under the Act is an offence for which any person concerned in its organisation or management or who, 'knowing or having reasonable cause to suspect that such an entertainment would be so provided', allowed the place to be used or made it available is liable. Secondly, the use of any licensed premises in contravention of the terms and conditions of the licence is an offence for which the licence holder and any person who, 'knowing or having reasonable cause to suspect that such an entertainment would be so provided', allowed the place to be used or made it available is liable.

The penalties for these offences have been amended in the same way as those for public entertainment, the Entertainment (Increased Penalties) Act 1990 providing for a fine of not more than £20,000 and/or imprisonment. Likewise the Criminal Justice Act 1988 (Confiscation Orders) Order 1990[33] adds these two offences under section 4 to the list in Part I of Schedule 4 to the Criminal Justice Act 1988, being offences in respect of which magistrates may make confiscation orders.

Conclusion

It remains to emphasise what is perhaps already clear, at least by implication, in relation to the licensing provisions just considered applicable to both public and, where they apply, private entertainments. Attached conditions and restrictions may govern noise in respect to volume, duration and times of emissions. Further, past performance in this respect, for better or worse, may be a factor in the determination of future applications or renewals. As will have been noted, conditions attaching to public open air events by paragraph 4 include those 'for preventing persons in the neighbourhood being unreasonably disturbed by noise'.

Penalties available to the court have been significantly increased and may now act as a real deterrent, even having regard to the increased scale of and therefore income from such events. Supplementary to these specific criminal sanctions, section 222(1)(a) of the Local Government Act 1972 gives local authorities the power, where they consider it expedient for the promotion or protection of the interests of the inhabitants of their area, to 'prosecute or defend or appear in any legal pro-

32 See also, 'Joint Guidance Note on the Control of Noisy Parties' (Home Office and DoE, 1992).

33 See note 29.

ceedings and, in the case of civil proceedings, may institute them in their own name'. This provision enables local authorities, *inter alia*, to obtain injunctions to stop actual or anticipated public nuisances without the need to join the Attorney-General.[34] A particular advantage of this power in the present context is the availability of the interlocutory procedure to deal with anticipated events of a sufficiently disturbing nature.

CONSTRUCTION SITE NOISE

Noise caused by many of the processes and much equipment used in demolition, construction and civil engineering can be particularly intrusive. It may also continue for long periods and be extended by evening and night working. Other characteristics peculiar to noise from construction sites are emphasised in the Introduction to Part 2 of BS 5228: 1984:

> Construction and demolition works can pose different problems of noise control compared with most other types of industrial activity for the following reasons:
>
> (a) they are mainly carried out in the open.
> (b) they are of temporary duration although they can cause great disturbance while they last.
> (c) the noise they make arises from many different activities and kinds of plant and its intensity and character can vary greatly at different phases of the work.
> (d) The sites cannot be excluded by planning control, as factories can, from areas that are sensitive to noise.

Commenting on the control of construction site noise, Department of the Environment Circular 2/76[35] suggests:

> 29. Although the difficulties of exercising effective control over noise should not be underestimated, even a simple approach can achieve worthwhile results. It will often be sufficient to specify the noise level which may emanate from the site during different periods of day or night and on different days. Specifying a noise level in this way has the advantage of:
>
> (i) relating the noise limits directly to the degree of disturbance which is considered acceptable;
> (ii) enabling the noise levels to be monitored;
> (iii) giving contractors freedom to plan their work as they wish;
> (iv) enabling the limits to be specified early in the planning of the project.

Control of such excessive noise, either in advance or in response to an existing problem, is provided by sections 60 and 61 of the Control of Pollution Act 1974. For these purposes the range of activities covered is, by section 60(1):

(a) the erection, construction, alteration, repair or maintenance of buildings, structures or roads;
(b) breaking up, opening or boring under any road or adjacent land in connection with the construction, inspection, maintenance or removal of works;
(c) demolition or dredging work; and
(d) (whether or not comprised in paragraph (a), (b) or (c) above) any work of engineering construction.

Some of the terms used in that list have either received judicial consideration or are defined in the legislation. Authority suggests that 'building' is to be given its

34 See, e.g., *Solihull MBC v Maxfern Ltd* [1977] 2 All ER 177, 1 WLR 127; *Kent CC v Batchelor* (No. 2) [1978] 3 All ER 980, [1979] 1 WLR 213. On interlocutory relief in this context, see *Stoke on Trent City Council v B & Q (Retail) Ltd* [1984] Ch 1, [1983] 2 All ER 787.

35 DoE Circular 2/76 'Control of Pollution Act, Implementation of Part III – Noise'.

ordinary meaning, Byles J describing a building in *Stevens* v *Gourley* (1859)[36] as 'a structure of considerable size and intended to be permanent or at least to endure for a considerable time'. In the same case, concerning a wooden structure measuring 16 feet by 13 feet supported on timbers laid on the surface of the ground and intended to be used as a shop, Erle CJ said[37]:

> ... the structure was permanently built and reasonably calculated for the use of man; and though by the application of mechanical power a structure of considerable size may be removed, if does not therefore cease to be a 'building' within the meaning of the act.

It may also require a roof.[38] In the planning context Lord Parker CJ said that[39]:

> ... when the Act defines a building as including 'any structure or erection and any part of a building so defined', the Act is referring to any structure or erection which can be said to form part of the realty, and to change the physical character of the land.

A judicial interpretation of 'structure' appears in *Hobday* v *Nichol* (1944),[40] Humphreys J, with whom the other members of the court agreed, saying that:

> Structure, as I understand it, is anything which is constructed; and it involves the notion of something which is put together, consisting of a number of different things which are so put together or built together, constructed as to make one whole, which is then called a structure.

The phrase 'work of engineering construction' is stated by section 73(1) to mean 'the construction, structural alteration, maintenance or repair of any railway line or siding or any dock, harbour, inland navigation, tunnel, bridge, viaduct, waterworks, reservoir, pipeline, aqueduct, sewer, sewage works or gas-holder'.

Where a local authority believes that any of those works are being, or are about to be, carried on at any premises it may, by section 60(2), serve a notice imposing requirements on the way the works are to be carried out. Principles applicable to the service of notices generally were dealt with in Chapter 1, and section 60(3), governing their contents in these circumstances, stipulates that the notices may:

(a) specify the plant or machinery which is or is not to be used;
(b) specify the hours during which the works may be carried out;
(c) specify the level of noise which may be emitted from the premises in question or at any specified plant on those premises or which may be so emitted during specified hours; and
(d) provide for any change of circumstances.

While the enumerated factors are likely to cover the majority of construction noise problems they are not exclusive, the authority having discretion to deal with the particular circumstances of the case though going beyond those stated matters. Section 68 gives the Secretary of State a regulation-making power governing reduction of noise from plant or machinery and for limiting noise levels from construction plant or machinery. No such regulations have so far been made.

The section 60 notice is to be served on the person appearing to the authority 'to be carrying out, or going to carry out the works, and on such other persons appearing to the authority to be responsible for, or to have control over, the carrying out of the works'. This phrase, identifying two levels of relationship with the work in question, is wide enough to cover the main or management contractor, the works contractor and relevant subcontractors as well as the developer. Circular 2/76 recommends that normally notices issued before the work starts

36 (1859) 7 CB (NS) 99 at p.112.

37 At pp.107-8.

38 Per Lord Esher in *Moir* v *Williams* [1892] 1 QB 264 at p.270.

39 *Cheshire CC* v *Woodward* [1962] 2 AC 126 at p.135.

40 [1944] 1 All ER 302 at pp.303 and 304.

should be served on the promoter of the project (or his agent), and when the work has begun on the main contractor and relevant subcontractors. Adopting the terminology(and therefore presumably the meaning) of the statutory nuisance provisions, section 73(1) states that 'person responsible, in relation to the emission of noise, means the person to whose act, default or sufferance the noise is attributable'.[41]

In accordance with general principles and practice, section 60(7) gives the person served a 21-day right of appeal to the magistrates' court. Appeals are governed by section 70(1), (2) and (4), which apply the provisions of the Magistrates' Courts Act 1980 to these proceedings. Subsection (2) gives the Secretary of State the power to make regulations governing specified aspects of appeals. These are currently the Control of Noise (Appeals) Regulations 1975,[42] regulation 5 applying to section 60(7) appeals. In particular the regulation specifies grounds of appeal, which are that the:

(a) notice is not justified by the terms of section 60;
(b) notice or its procedure is defective;
(c) requirements are unreasonable or the authority has refused to accept reasonable alternatives;
(d) time(s) for compliance is/are inadequate;
(e) notice should have been served on someone else;
(f) notice might lawfully have been served on someone else as well;
(g) authority has not had regard to some or all of the subsection (4) matters.

Where the appeal is based on a procedural defect the court may dismiss it if of the opinion that the error was not material. In the case of an appeal on grounds (e) or (f), the appellant is required to serve a copy of his notice of appeal on the other person.

In taking or contemplating action under this provision, and as indicated in (g) above, an authority is to have regard to the section 60(4) matters, which are:

(a) the relevant provisions of any code of practice issued under this Part of this Act;

(b) the need for ensuring that the best practicable means are employed to minimise noise;

(c) before specifying any particular methods or plant or machinery, the desirability in the interests of the recipients of the notice in question of specifying other methods or plant or machinery which would be substantially as effective in minimising noise and more acceptable to them;

(e) the need to protect any persons in the locality in which the premises in question are situated from the effects of noise.

Section 60(4)(b) requires that the 'best practicable means' are to be employed. The general meaning given to that term in the environmental context has been considered in Chapter 2; however, it is specifically defined for the purposes of these noise provisions in section 72 of the Act, the respective subsections providing that:

(2) ...'practicable' means reasonably practicable having regard among other things to local conditions and circumstances, to the current state of technical knowledge and to the financial implications.

41 For the meaning of this expression, see in Chapter 3 at p.78.

42 S.I. 1975 No. 2116, as amended by S.I. 1990 No 2276.

(3) The means to be employed include the design, installation, maintenance and manner and periods of operation of plant and machinery, and the design, construction and maintenance of buildings and acoustic structures.

(4) The test of best practicable means is to apply only so far as compatible with any duty imposed by law, and in particular is to apply to statutory undertakers only so far as compatible with the duties imposed on them in their capacity of statutory undertakers.

(5) The said test is to apply only so far as compatible with safety and safe working conditions, and with the exigencies of any emergency or unforeseeable circumstances.

Failure to comply with the terms of a notice without reasonable excuse is, by section 60(8), an offence actionable summarily. Penalties on conviction are up to level 5 on the standard scale with further daily penalties of £50.[43] The provisions of section 87 apply to legal proceedings under this section; in particular to proceedings against bodies corporate, extending liability also to any implicated officers. It is a defence to these proceedings to show that the alleged contravention amounted to the carrying out of works in accordance with a consent under section 61. See Figure 12.1.[44]

43 Section 74.

44 Taken with approval from BS 5228: Part 2: 1984.

Prior consent

Whereas section 60 just considered gave the initiative to the local authority, section 61 enables the person undertaking the construction work to apply to the authority for prior consent. An application must be made at the same time as, or later than, the request for approval under building regulations and is to contain particulars of :

(a) the works, and the method by which they are to be carried out; and
(b) the steps proposed to be taken to minimise noise resulting from the works.[45]

45 Section 61(3).

Subject to the stated time constraints, there are evident advantages in as early an application as possible, and also in informal discussions before the formal application is made.

As BS 5228[46] makes clear:

46 BS 5228: Part 2: 1984, paragraph 4.5. Quoted with approval.

... the local authority's noise requirements may well affect both the tender and the contract price. It is therefore preferable that the local authority's requirements are made known before tenders are submitted. The best way of achieving this is for the person for whom the work is to be carried out to make the application to the local authority for a consent, before inviting tenders. ... When a person for whom construction work is to be carried out has sought and obtained consent from the local authority, the local authority's requirements should be incorporated in the tender documents so that tenderers do not base their tenders on the use of unacceptable work methods and plant.

As far as possible, a contractor should be allowed freedom of choice regarding plant and methods to be used but a local authority can, in consultation with the recipient of a consent, specify the type of plant or methods to be used with its consent. In addition to any approach made by a person responsible for construction work, a tenderer may also wish to apply to a local authority in order either to seek consent for the use of methods or plant in place of those specified in an earlier consent (or notice), or to satisfy himself that the detailed methods and plant that he had planned to use meet the conditions laid down.

On receiving an application the authority is required to give its consent if[47]:

47 Section 61(4).

(a) it considers that the application contains sufficient information,
(b) the works are carried out in accordance with the application, and
(c) it would not serve a notice under the preceding section,

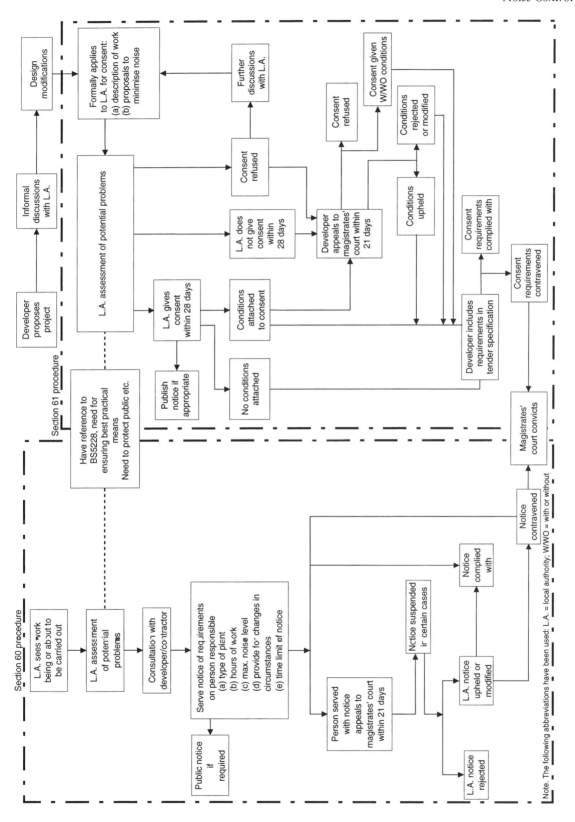

Figure 12.1 Procedures to control construction noise under the Control of Pollution Act 1974[44]

Note. The following abbreviations have been used: L.A. = local authority; W/WO = with or without

notifying the applicant of its decision within 28 days from receipt of the application. In giving its consent the authority is to have regard to the section 60(4) considerations and it may:

(a) attach any conditions to the consent; and
(b) limit or qualify a consent to allow for any change in circumstances; and
(c) limit the duration of a consent.

A consent given under this section is required to contain a statement that the consent of itself does not constitute a defence under the statutory nuisance provisions of Part III of the Environmental Protection Act 1990.[48] The local authority has the discretion, in granting its consent, to publish details of it in whatever way it considers appropriate.[49]

The failure to give consent within the stipulated period or at all or the attachment of a limiting or qualifying condition gives the applicant a right of appeal within 21 days to the magistrates' court. Such appeals are governed by the provisions of section 70(1), (2) and (4)[50] and regulation 6 of the Control of Noise (Appeals) Regulations 1975.[51] By the latter provision an appeal against a conditional consent may be on the ground that:

(a) any condition is not justified by the terms of section 61;
(b) there has been some procedural defect in connection with the consent;
(c) the requirements of the condition are unreasonable in character or extent, or are unnecessary;
(d) that any specified time(s) for compliance is/are not reasonably sufficient for the purpose.

The subsequent knowing or permitting the carrying out of work in contravention of a consent condition is a summary offence carrying the same penalties as section 60. Commentary on the scope of 'knowingly causing or permitting' is to be found in Chapter 1.

Codes of Practice

Section 71 gives the Secretary of State the general discretion to issue codes of practice giving guidance for the minimisation of noise generally, and section 71(2) requires that he shall approve a code of practice for the carrying out of section 60 works. The codes contained in Parts 1, 3 and 4 of BS 5228:1984 have been approved by the Secretary of State under this power in the Control of Noise (Code of Practice for Construction and Open Sites) Order 1984[52] and the Control of Noise (Code of Practice for Construction and Open Sites) Order 1987.[53]

The Standard, which amplifies and applies the terms of section 60, consists of:

Part 1 Code of Practice for basic information and procedures for noise control.
Part 2 Guide to legislation for noise control applicable to construction and demolition, including road construction and maintenance.
Part 3 Code of Practice for noise control applicable to surface coal extraction by opencast methods.
Part 4 Code of Practice for noise control applicable to piling operations.[54]

It is neither possible nor perhaps desirable in a work of this nature to include a comprehensive review of the document. The following extracts from Part 1 may, though, be noted as general guidance in approaching the question of construction

---

48 Section 61(9).

49 Section 61(6).

50 See their application to section 60(7) appeals above.

51 See note 14 above.

52 S.I. 1984 No. 1992.

53 S.I. 1987 No. 1730.

54 Other useful British Standards are: BS 661 Glossary of Acoustical Terms, BS 5930 Code of Practice for Site Investigations, BS 5969 Specification for Sound Level Meters; and see also ISO 1996 Acoustics – Description and Measurement of Environmental Noise, Part I, Basic quantities and procedures.

site noise. As well as their applicability to noise generated by construction work, these or similar factors may also be relevant to the assessment of other noise problems:

11. Criteria for setting noise control targets

It is not possible to provide detailed guidance for determining whether or not noise from a site will constitute a problem in a particular situation. However, a number of factors are likely to affect considerations of the acceptability of site noise and the degree of control necessary.

a)   **Site location.** The location of a site in relation to noise-sensitive development will be a major factor. The nearer a site is to noise-sensitive premises, the more stringent should restrictions be upon noise emanating from the site.

b)   **Existing ambient noise levels.** Experience of complaints about noise that has originated from new industrial sources indicates that the likelihood of complaint increases as the difference between the industrial noise and existing background noise increases. It is possible that a similar effect occurs with open site noise since the noise will, in general, be more noticeable in quieter areas. However, the relationship between response and noise level difference may well be different. For example, a greater difference may be tolerated when it is known that the operations are of short duration.

c)   **Duration of site operations.** In general, the longer the duration of noisy site operations, the more likely it is that the site noise will prove unsatisfactory. In this context, good public relations are important. Local residents may be willing to accept higher levels of noise if they know that such levels will only last for a short time. It is then important that noisy site operations are carried out according to a stated schedule.

d)   **Hours of work.** For any noise-sensitive building, some periods of the day will be more sensitive than others. For example, levels of noise that would cause speech interference in an office during the day would cause no problem in the same office at night. For dwellings, times of site operation outside normal weekday working hours will need special consideration. Noise control targets for the evening period in such cases will need to be stricter than those for the daytime and when noise limits are set the evening limit may have to be as much as 10dB(A) below the daytime limit. Very strict noise control targets should be applied to any site which is to operate at night. The periods when people are getting to sleep and just before they wake appear to be particularly sensitive. Site noise expressed as L_{Aeq} over 1 hour at the facade of noise-sensitive premises may need to be as low as 40dB(A) to 45dB(A) to avoid sleep disturbance.

e)   **Attitude to the site operator.** It is well established that people's attitude to noise can be influenced by their attitude to the source itself. Therefore noise from a site will tend to be accepted more readily by local residents if they consider that the site operator is doing all that he can to avoid unnecessary noise. The acceptability of the project itself may also be a factor in determining community reaction.

f)   **Noise characteristics.** In some cases a particular characteristic of the noise, for example the presence of impulses or tones, may make it less acceptable than might be concluded from the level expressed in terms of L_{Aeq}.

In many cases the identification of the problem will indicate the form of the remedy. Section five of the Standard considers noise control at source and in relation to its spread. Noise control at source may include:

(a)   substitution of alternative, less noisy plant;
(b)   modification of existing plant and equipment;
(c)   providing acoustic enclosures where reasonably practicable;
(d)   care in the siting and periods of use of noisy equipment and operations;
(e)   regular and effective plant maintenance.

Noise having been generated, methods of reducing its spread into the neighbourhood include:

(a) increasing the distance, if and when practicable;
(b) attenuation by screening barriers.

Appendices providing more detailed information and guidance in script, tabular and diagrammatic form include:

Appendix A Estimating noise from sites
Appendix B Noise monitoring
Appendix C Guide to sound level data on site equipment and site activities.[55]

The flow chart in Figure 12.2 for the prediction of site noise is reproduced from Appendix A where it is accompanied by a detailed discussion on its operation.

TRANSPORT NOISE

The forms of transport noise that are of most serious concern to people are those from road traffic and aircraft, the two categories to be dealt with here. While the latter may present far more acute problems to those affected by it, there can be no doubt that more people are more affected by the various types of noise generated by road vehicles. As the Noise Review Working Party said[56]:

> In terms of the number of people affected, road traffic noise is the most serious of all transportation noise problems. A moment's reflection will show why this should be so: roads are everywhere and pretty well unrestricted as to what may use them whereas railways and air traffic routes are limited and controlled.

Road traffic

The legal control of noise emissions from road vehicles operates within the same structure as the control of exhaust pollutants, i.e., the type approval of new vehicles and the construction and use regulations governing their subsequent use. That legal and enforcement structure, having been dealt with in the context of air pollution control, is not repeated now.[57] Within that structure the requirements applicable to noise emissions from vehicles are as follows.

Type approval

As with exhaust emissions, noise has been legislated for in a series of European Directives[58] that are now implemented in the United Kingdom for private and goods vehicles respectively by the Motor Vehicles (Type Approval) (Great Britain) Regulations 1984[59] and the Motor Vehicles (Type Approval for Goods Vehicles) (Great Britain) Regulations 1982.[60]

The current noise emission levels for that purpose are to be found in Annex I of Commission Directive 81/334/EEC, together with the application procedure, form of type approval certificate and, in particular, the test conditions and specifications. These last provide for the testing of moving and stationary vehicles, including the measuring apparatus, conditions of the test track, ambient noise, approach speeds at specified engine powers and calculation of the final result. The precise position of the recording microphones in relation to the moving vehicle is also stipulated.

55 More detailed information on this topic, from which much of Appendix C is drawn, is included in CIRIA Report 64, 'Noise from construction and demolition sites – measured levels and their prediction', available from CIRIA, 6 Storey's Gate Westminster SW1P 3AU.

56 1990 Report (HMSO), paragraph 4.2.

57 See Chapter 9 at pp.238–48.

58 These Directives are Council Directive 70/157/EEC, amended by Commission Directive 73/350/EEC, amended by Council Directive 77/212/EEC, amended by Commission Directive 81/334/EEC.

59 S.I. 1984 No. 981.

60 S.I. 1982 No. 1271.

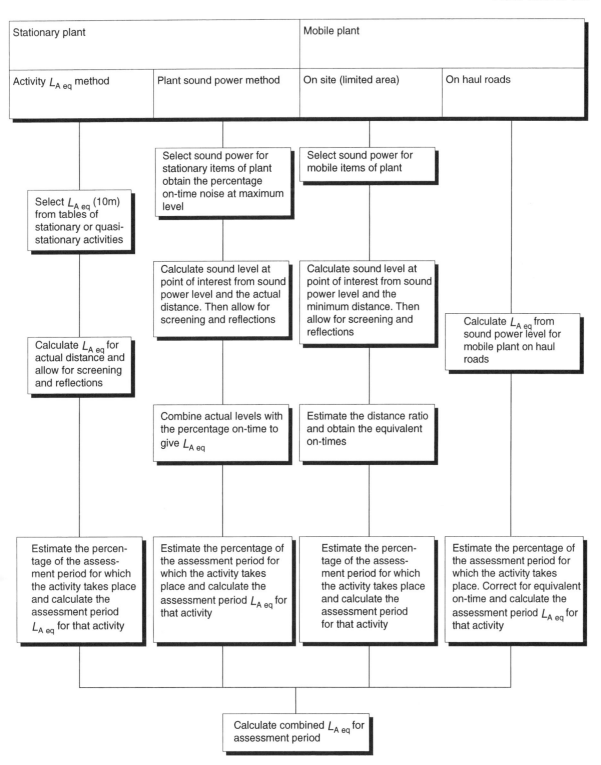

Figure 12.2 Flow chart for the prediction of site noise

Paragraph 5 of Annex I specifies the maximum sound levels for each class of vehicle when measured in accordance with the terms of the Annex and recorded in the test report and in a test certificate.[61] The sound levels for moving vehicles are as follows:

61 The form of test certificate is specified in Annex III.

Vehicle categories	Values expressed in dB(A)
Vehicles intended for the carriage of passengers, and comprising not more than nine seats including the driver's seat	80
Vehicles intended for the carriage of passengers, comprising more than nine seats including the driver's seat and having a maximum permissible mass not exceeding 3.5 tonnes	81
Vehicles intended for the carriage of goods, and having a maximum permissible mass not exceeding 3.5 tonnes	81
Vehicles intended for the carriage of passengers, comprising more than nine seats including the drivers seat and having a maximum permissible mass exceeding 3.5 tonnes	82
Vehicles intended for the carriage of goods and having a maximum permissible mass exceeding 3.5 tonnes	86
Vehicles intended for the carriage of passengers, comprising more than nine seats including the driver's seat and having an engine power equal to or exceeding 147 kW	85
Vehicles intended for the carriage of goods, having an engine power equal to or exceeding 147 kW and a maximum permissible mass exceeding 12 tonnes	88

Construction and use

Part K – Control of Emissions, of the Road Vehicle (Construction and Use) Regulations 1986[62] – specifies permissible sound levels from all classes of road vehicles. Regulation 55 provides for general noise limits, regulation 56 for agricultural vehicles and industrial tractors, regulation 57 for motorcycles, and regulation 58 for vehicles not covered by regulations 55 to 57. The provision governing motorcycles has subsequently been amended and is dealt with separately below.

62 S.I. 1986 No. 1078, implementing, for other than motorcycles, Community Directives 77/212/EEC, 81/334/EEC, 84/372/EEC and 84/424/EEC.

The general statement of principle in regulation 54 requires that the exhaust system of every vehicle propelled by an internal combustion engine is to be fitted with a silencer through which all exhaust gases are to pass. Such exhaust systems and silencers are to be maintained in good working order and are not to be altered to increase the noise made by the exhaust. Regulation 55 then applies detailed noise limits to the three classes of vehicles, having three or more wheels, in subparagraph (1) as follows:

(a) a vehicle, not falling within subparagraph (b) or (c), with or without bodywork;

(b) a vehicle not falling within subparagraph (c) which is –
    (i) engineering plant;
    (ii) a locomotive other than an agricultural vehicle;
    (iii) a motor tractor other than an industrial tractor or an agricultural motor vehicle;

(iv) a public works vehicle;

(v) a works truck; or

(vi) a refuse vehicle; or

(c) a vehicle which –

    (i) has a compression ignition engine;

    (ii) is so constructed or adapted that the driving power of the engine is, or by appropriate use of the controls can be, transmitted to all wheels of the vehicle; and

    (iii) falls within category 1.1.1., 1.1.2, or 1.1.3 specified in Article I of Community Directive 77/212.

These three categories of vehicles are individually provided for in the following table of sound level limits (see Table 12.1).

Exceptions not included within the scope of that regulation, nor the associated table, are the special cases falling within regulation 59, i.e., vehicles travelling to or from a noise testing centre, or alternatively those coming within regulation 55(2), i.e.:

(a) a motorcycle with sidecar attached;

(b) an agricultural motor vehicle which is first used before 1 June 1986 or which is not driven at more than 20 mph;

(c) an industrial tractor;

(d) a road roller;

(e) a vehicle specially constructed, and not merely adapted, for the purposes of fighting fires or salvage from fires at or in the vicinity of airports, and having an engine power exceeding 220 kW;

(f) a vehicle which runs on rails; or

(g) a vehicle manufactured by Leyland Vehicles Ltd and known as the Atlantean Bus, if first used before 1 October 1984.

A vehicle covered by this regulation is required to comply with the requirements of item 1, 2, 3 or 4 in Table 12.1 below, in that its sound level must not exceed the limit in column 2(a), (b) or (c) as the case may be when measured under the conditions specified in column 3 by the method specified in column 4 using the apparatus prescribed in paragraph (6).[63] Vehicles listed in column 2(a) are required to have exhaust silencers meeting the requirements specified in column 5, unless having less than four wheels or a maximum speed not exceeding 25 km/h, or listed in column 1(c), the exhaust silencer is required to meet the requirements specified in column 5.

The interpretation of Table 12.1 evidently requires detailed application of the terms of the Directives referred to therein, the vehicles covered by column 2(a), (b) and (c) being listed above. The conditions of measurement in column 3 make detailed provision for the test site and track, meteorological conditions, ambient noise and the condition of the vehicle. The method of measurement similarly covers the number and nature of tests, position of the microphones and conditions of operation including approach speed, operation of manual or automatic gearboxes and the interpretation of the results. Column 5 specifies construction provisions for exhaust systems containing fibrous materials.

Vehicles first used on or after 1 April 1990, unless equipped with five or more forward gears and having a maximum power to maximum gross weight ratio not

63 Regulation 55(6) stipulates the use of a sound level meter of one of the three following types:

(i) described in Publication 179 of the International Electrotechnical Commission, 1st or 2nd edition;

(ii) complying with the specification for Type 0 or Type 1 in Publication No 651 (1979) "Sound Level Meters" of the International Electrotechnical Commission

(iii) complying with the specifications of the British Standard Number BS 5969: 1981 which came into effect on 29 May 1981.

Table 12.1 Vehicle sound level limits (regulation 55(3))

1	2			3	4	5
	limits of sound level					
Item	*(a)* *Vehicle referred to in* *paragraph (1)(a)*	*(b)* *Vehicle referred to in* *paragraph* *(1)(b)*	*(c)* *Vehicle referred to in* *paragraph* *(1)(c)*	*Conditions of* *measurement*	*Method of* *measurement*	*Requirements for* *exhaust device*
1	Limits specified in paragraph 1.1 of the Annex to Community Directive 77.212	89dB(A)	82dB(A)	Conditions specified paragraph 1.3 of the Annex to Community Directive 77/212	Method specified in paragraph 1.4.1 of the Annex to Community Directive 77/212	Requirements specified in heading II of the Annex to Community Directive 77/212 (except paragraphs 11.2 and 11.5)
2	Limits specified in paragraph 5.2.2.1 of Annex I to Community Directive 81/334	89dB(A)	82dB(A)	Conditions specified in paragraph 5.2.2.3 of Annex I to Community Directive 81/334	Method specified in paragraph 5.2.2.4 of Annex I to Community Directive 81/334. Interpretation of results as specified in paragraph 5.2.2.5 of that Annex	Requirements specified in section 3 and paragraphs 5.1 and 5.3.1 of Annex I to Community Directive 81/334
3	Limits specified in paragraphs 5.2.2.1 of Annex I to Community Directive 84/372	89dB(A)	82dB(A)	Conditions specified in paragraph 5.2.2.3 of Annex I to Community Directive 84/372	Method specified in paragraph 5.2.2.4 of Annex I to Community Directive 84/372, except that vehicles with 5 or more forward gears and a maximum weight ratio not less than 75 kW per 1000kg may be tested in third gear only. Interpretation of results as specified in paragraph 5.2.2.5 of that Annex	Requirements specified in section 3 and paragraphs 5.1 and 5.3.1 of Annex I to Community Directive 84/372
4	Limits specified in paragraph 5.2.2.1 of the Community Directive 84/424	Vehicles with engine power – – less than 75 KW –84dB(A) – not less than 75 kW –86dB(A)	Limits specified in paragraphs 5.2.2.1 of Annex I to Community Directive 84/424	Conditions specified in paragraph 5.2.2.3 of Annex I to Community Directive 84/424	Methods specified in paragraph 5.2.2.4 of Annex I to Community Directive 84/424 except that vehicles with 5 or more forward gears and a maximum power to maximum gross weight ratio not less than 75 kW per 1,000 kg may be tested in 3rd gear only. Interpretation of results as specified in paragraph 5.2.2.5 of that Annex	Requirements specified in section 3 and paragraphs 5.1 and 5.3.1 of Annex I to Community Directive 84/.424

less than 75kW per 1,000kg, and being of a type for which a type approval certificate has been issued under the Type Approval (Great Britain) Regulations, are to comply with the requirements of item 4 of Table 12.1. Lastly, as an alternative to complying with this regulation, a vehicle may comply at the time of its first use with Community Directives 77/212, 81/334, 84/372 or 84/424.

Regulation 56 of the 1986 Regulations specifies noise limits for wheeled agricultural motor vehicles and industrial tractors first used on or after 1 April 1983 other than:

(a) an agricultural motor vehicle which is first used on or after 1 June 1986 and which is driven at more than 20 mph; or
(b) a road roller;

and save for the regulation 59 exceptions as noted above.

Paragraph (2) of Regulation 56 requires that when measured in accordance with the conditions and method specified in Annex VI of Community Directive 74/151 and using the apparatus stipulated in regulation 55(6), sound levels shall not exceed:

(a) vehicles with engine power of less than 65kW, 89dB(A);
(b) vehicles with engine power of 65kW or more and first used before 1 October 1991, 92dB(A);
(c) vehicles with engine power of 65kW or more and first used on or after 1 October 1991, 89dB(A).

By regulation 58 every wheeled motor vehicle first used on or after 1 April 1970 and not coming within regulations 55, 56 or 57 shall not exceed the maximum noise level appropriate to its class in Table 12.4 below when measured under the specified conditions using the prescribed apparatus. The 'specified conditions' for sound level measurement means the method described by the British Standard Method for the Measurement of Noise Emitted by Motor Vehicles, published on 24 June 1966 under the number BS 3425: 1966.

The 'prescribed apparatus' means a noise meter:

(a) which is in good working order and complies with the requirements laid down for vehicle noise meters in Part I of British Standard Specification numbered BS 3539: 1962, as amended by Amendment Slip No. 1, numbered AMD22, published on 1 July 1968;
(b) which has, not more than 12 months before the date of the measurement made in accordance with paragraph (1), undergone all the tests for checking calibration applicable in accordance with the Appendix to the said British Standard Specification; and
(c) in respect of which there has been issued by the National Physical Laboratory, the British Standards Institution or the Secretary of State a certificate recording the date on which as a result of those tests the meter was found to comply with the requirements of clauses 8 and 9 of the said British Standard Specification.[64]

64 Regulation 58(5).

The excepted circumstances or vehicles for which compliance is not required are, by paragraph (2), where the vehicle at the time of its first use complied with Community Directive 70/157, 73/350 or 77/212 or, in the case of an agricultural motor vehicle 74/151, or if it is:

(a) a road roller;
(b) a vehicle specially constructed and not merely adapted, for the purposes of fighting fires or salvage from fires at or in the vicinity of airports, and having an engine power exceeding 220kW;
(c) a vehicle propelled by a compression ignition engine and which is of a type in respect of which a type approval certificate has been issued under the Type Approval (Great Britain) Regulations;
(d) a motorcycle first used on or after 1 October 1980, with an engine capacity not exceeding 50cc which complies with the requirements specified in regulation 57(2); or
(e) an agricultural motor vehicle manufactured on or after 7 February 1975 which complies with the requirements specified in regulation 56(2).

Table 12.2 Maximum permitted sound levels

Class of vehicle	Maximum permitted sound level in dB(A)
Motor cycle of which the cylinder capacity of the engine does not exceed 50cc	77
Motor cycle of which the cylinder capacity of the engine exceeds 50cc but does not exceed 125cc	82
Motor cycle of which the cylinder capacity of the engine exceeds 125cc	86
Goods vehicle to which regulation 66 applies and which is equipped with a plate complying with the requirements of regulation 66 and showing particulars of a maximum gross weight of more than 3,560 kg	89
Motor car not being a goods vehicle of the kind described in item 4 above	85
Motor tractor	89
Locomotive	89
Agricultural motor vehicle	89
Works truck	89
Engineering plant	89
Passenger vehicle constructed for the carriage of more than 12 passengers exclusive of the driver	89
Any other passenger vehicle	84
Any other vehicle	85

Motor Cycles

Motor cycle noise can present particularly acute problems, either due to the nature of the vehicles themselves or because of the way they are used. The relevant legal controls are to be found in an amended regulation 57 of the Road Vehicles (Construction and Use) Regulations 1986[65] and in the Motor Cycles (Sound Level

65 S.I. 1986 No. 1078, amended by the Road Vehicles (Construction and Use) (Amendment) (No.3) Regulations 1989, S.I. 1989 No. 1865.

Table 12.3 Motorcycle sound limits (regulation 57(1A)

1	2		3	4	5
	limits of sound level				
Item	*(a)* *Vehicle referred to in* *paragraph (1)(a) or 2(a)*	*(b)* *Vehicle referred to in* *paragraph (1)(b) or 2(b)*	*Conditions of* *measurement*	*Method of measurement*	*Requirements for exhaust* *device*
1	73 dB(A)	Limits specified in paragraph 2.1.1 of Annex 1 to Community Directive 78/1015	Conditions specified in paragraph 2.1.3 of Annex 4 to Community Directive 78/1015	Methods specified in paragraph 2.1.4 of Annex 1 to Community Directive 78/1015. Interpretation of results as in paragraphs 2.1.5.2, 2.1.5.3 and 2.1.5.4 of that Annex	Requirements as specified in paragraph 3 at Annex 1 to Community directive 78/1015 except for sub-paragraph 3.2
2	73 dB(A)	First stage limits specified in paragraph 2.1.1 of Annex I to community Directive 87/56	Conditions specified in paragraph 2.1.3 of Annex I to Community Directive 87/56	Method specified in paragraph 2.4.1 of Annex I to Community Directive 87/56. Interpretation of results as in paragraphs 2.1.5.2, 2.1.5.3 and 2.1.5.4 of that Annex	Requirements specified in paragraph 3 of Annex I to Community Directive 87/56 except for sub-paragraph 3.2

66 S.I. 1980 No. 765, as amended by S.I. 1988 No. 1640; S.I. 1989 No. 713 and S.I.1989 No. 1591.

67 Defined in Schedule 9, paragraph 5.

Measurement Certificates) Regulations 1980.[66] The Motorcycle Act 1987 has yet to be implemented.

Subject to the regulation 59 exceptions, the present regulation 57 requires that mopeds[67] and other two-wheeled motor cycles, with or without a sidecar attached, and first used between 1 April 1983 and 31 March 1991 are to be so constructed that their sound levels conform to the limits specified in column 2 of item 1 or 2 of Table 12.2 when measured in accordance with the conditions and methods specified in columns 3 and 4. Motorcycle silencers are to meet the standards required in column 5. Such vehicles coming into use on or after 1 April 1991 are to comply with the limits in item 2 of Table 12.5. As an alternative to complying with these requirements, a motorcycle other than a moped may comply at the time of first coming into use with Community Directives 78/1015 or 87/56 if first coming into use between 1 April 1983 and 31 March 1991, or with Directive 87/56 if coming into use on or after 1 April 1991.

The interpretation of Table 12.2 obviously requires detailed application of the Directives referred to therein. Conditions of measurement in column 3 cover in detail the condition of the motorcycle, features of the test site, the track and the effects on sound emissions of the surroundings. Methods of measurement in column 4 specify the number and nature of the tests, the positioning of microphones and conditions of operation including use of gearbox, approach speeds and interpretation of the results. Comparable details are given for stationary tests. Column 5 is concerned with the construction and marking of exhausts if fitted with a silencer.

The Motor Cycles (Sound Level Measurement Certificates) Regulations 1980 and their amendments apply Council Directives 78/1015/EEC, 87/56/EEC and 89/235/EEC. Annex I to Directive 78/1015 as amended by the Annex to Directive 87/56, following very closely the procedures considered above for four wheeled vehicles, stipulates the measuring conditions, instruments and methods to be used for certification. The 1989 Directive, in Annex II, deals with original and replacement exhaust systems. These sound level certificates, in relation to sound from motorcycles, perform much the same function as type approval for motor vehicles generally. The preamble to the Directive states that their objectives are to set sound level limit values to improve the environment and to encourage technical development of less noisy motorcycles. The explanatory note to the 1980 Regulations says that the issue of sound level measurement certificates signifies that the specified types of motorcycles comply with the harmonised requirements specified in Directive 78/1015/EEC. Member States are required[68] to send copies of certificates within one month of issue to the competent authorities of other Member States; such certificates constituting proof for all Member States that the tests have been carried out and are not to be repeated.

Currently applicable sound level limits for different categories of motorcycles are now stipulated in Section 2.1.1.1 of the Annex to Directive 87/56 as follows:

68 Article 4 of 78/1015/EEC.

Annex to Directive 87/56/EEC

Motorcycle category by cubic capacity (in cm³)	Sound level limits in dB(A) and dates of entry into force for national type approval of motorcycle			
	First stage limits in dB(A)	Dates of entry into force for national approval	Second stage limits in force dB(A)	Dates of entry into for national approval
1. ≤ 80	77	1 October 1988	75	1 October 1993
2. > 80 ≤ 175	79	1 October 1989	77	31 December 1994
3. > 175	82	1 October 1988	80	1 October 1993

Aircraft

Control of aircraft noise is one of the matters dealt with in the Civil Aviation Act 1982. Aircraft cause noise problems while they are in the air and also when they are on the ground while running-up and testing engines and taxiing.[69] In the latter case noise production is likely to be more acute than in normal flight because of its proximity and duration. This characteristic of aircraft while on the ground also of course applies in some degree and for similar reasons during the approach to and departure from airfields. The operation of aircraft on and about airfields imposes responsibilities, reflected in the terms of the Act, on those concerned respectively with the management of the airfield and the aircraft. As well as the specific controls applicable at and about airfields for the reasons stated above, the Air Navigation (Noise Certification) Order 1986[70] requires as a condition of use that aircraft included in the order are to have a noise certificate. This issue will be dealt with first.

69 See, e.g., *Bosworth-Smith v Guynnes* (1920) 89 LJ (Ch) 368, which concerned the establishment during the First World War of a works for manufacturing and testing aeroplane engines in a quiet residential district.

70 S.I. 1986 No. 1304; made under sections 60, 61, 101 and 102 of the Civil Aviation Act 1982

Noise certificates

Article 5 of the 1986 Order prohibits an aircraft governed by the Order from landing or taking off in the United Kingdom unless there is in force in respect of the aircraft a noise certificate, issued either under the Order or by the competent authority of the country in which the aircraft is registered and which applies standards which in the opinion of the Secretary of State are substantially equivalent to those obtaining in the United Kingdom. Article 4 applies the Order to:

(a) every propeller driven aeroplane having a maximum total weight authorised of 5,700 kg or less;

(b) every aeroplane which is capable of sustaining level flight at a speed in excess of Flight Mach 1.0, being an aeroplane in respect of which applicable standards are specified in Article 6(9) of this Order;

(c) every aeroplane having an empty weight not exceeding 150 kg, a lifting surface area of not less than 10 square metres and a lifting surface loading not exceeding 10 kg per square metre at empty weight and which is designed to carry not more than two persons;

(d) every other aeroplane which in accordance with its certificate of airworthiness has a take-off distance required, at maximum total weight authorised on a hard level runway in still air in an International Standard Atmosphere at sea level, of more than 610 metres;

(e) every helicopter, being a helicopter in respect of which applicable standards are specified in Article 6(10) of this Order.

The Civil Aviation Authority shall issue a noise certificate in respect of any of the above aircraft on application, if satisfied that the aircraft complies with the standards specified in Schedule I of the Order as applicable to that type of aircraft and on provision of such evidence and the submission of the aircraft to such flying trials and tests as the Authority may require.[71] A noise certificate having been issued, it remains in force without limit of time.

Schedule I of the Order specifies the noise standards required of different classes of aircraft together with detailed testing and measuring procedures. The required noise standards are shown in diagrammatic form at Figure 12.4 below. The chart and the following comments present a broad, simplified view of the operation of the Order. In particular, the relationship between the size of the aircraft and the applicable noise level is more complex than can be represented in outline here. For their specific application to any given case, therefore, reference should be made to the terms of the Order.

The aircraft coming within each of the eight columns are specified in Article 6, a summary of which appears below. Article 6(11) stipulates that for the purpose of applying the table, where the interval between the application for an airworthiness certificate and its date of issue is more than five years the application shall be deemed to have been made five years prior to the date of issue.

(1) Column 1, Part I of Schedule I, applies to two classes of aircraft:

    (a) Aeroplanes having turbojet or turbofan engines, the subject of an airworthiness certificate applied for before 6 October 1977–Article 6(2);

    (b) Propeller driven aeroplanes having a maximum total weight authorised of more than 5700 kg being the subject of an airworthiness certificate applied for before 6 October 1977 and issued on or after 26 November 1981 or any such modification but excluding aircraft coming within column five – Article 6(6).

(2) Column 2, Part II of Schedule I, applies to two classes of aircraft:

    (a) Aeroplanes having turbojet or turbofan engines, the subject of an airworthiness certificate applied for on or after 6 October 1977 or to such a modification – Article 6(3);

71 Article 6(1).

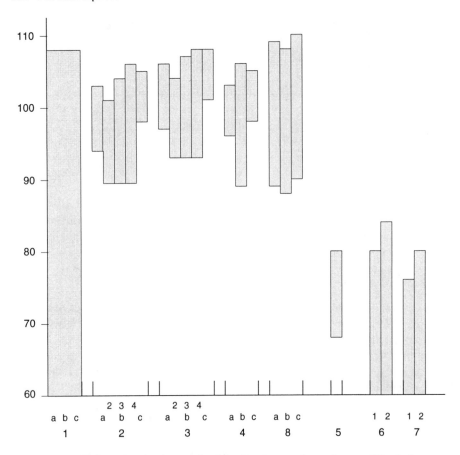

Figure 12.4 Noise standards required for the issue of a noise certificate to aeroplanes specified in Article 6

Note that : (a) columns 1, 2, 3, 4 and 8 are expressed in EPNdB
column 5 is expressed in dB(A)
columns 6 and 7 are expressed in LAX[72]

(b) where upper and lower figures are indicated the noise range between them covers weight
ranges as specified in the appropriate note below.

(b) Propeller driven aeroplanes having a maximum total weight authorised of more than 5,700 kg being the subject of an airworthiness certificate application on or after 1 Jan 1985 or such a modification – Article 6(7).

The five columns cover respectively aircraft of maximum total weight of –

    a   35,000kg or less to 400,000kg or more
    b2 48,125kg or less to 385,000kg or more
    b3 28,615kg or less to 385,000kg or more
    b4 20,234kg or less to 385,000kg or more
    c   35,000kg or less to 280,000kg or more

(3) Column 3, Part III of Schedule I, applies to aeroplanes having turbofan engines being a modification of a prototype as specified in (1) above – Article 6(4).

72 Article 3(1) of the Order defined these terms as:
'EPNdB' means the unit for expressing effective perceived noise level as specified in BCAR;
'dB(A)' means the unit for expressing A-weighted overall sound pressure level as specified in BCAR;
'LAX' means the A-weighted noise energy of a single aircraft noise event as specified in BCAR;
'BCAR' means the British Civil Airworthiness Requirements Section N – Noise Issue dated 10 November 1978 as amended by the Authority's Blue Paper N810 dated 12 January 1984 and by the Authority's Blue Paper N835 dated 12 June 1986.

The five columns cover respectively aircraft of maximum total weight of –
    a   35,000kg or less to 400,000kg or more
    b2 48,312kg or less to 325,000kg or more
    b3 34,000kg or less to 325,000kg or more
    b4 34,000kg or less to 325,000kg or more
    c   35,000kg or less to 280,000kg or more

(4) Column 4, Part IV of Schedule I, applies to propeller driven aeroplanes having a maximum total weight authorised of more than 5,700 kg – Article 6(5).
The three columns cover respectively aircraft of maximum total weight of –
    a 34,000kg or less to 384,666kg or more
    b 34,000kg or less to 358,906kg or more
    c 34,000kg or less to 384,666kg or more

(8) Column 8, Part VIII of Schedule I, applies to a helicopter the subject of an airworthiness certificate applied for on or after 1 August 1986 or a modification after that date or a modification of a helicopter that would have met the required standard applicable before 1 August 1986 and being a modification for which an airworthiness certificate was granted on an application made on or after 1 August 1986 – Article 6(10).
The three columns cover helicopters of maximum total weight of –
    788kg or less to 80,000kg or more

(5) Column 5, Part V of Schedule I, applies to propeller driven aeroplanes of maximum total weight authorised of 5,700kg or less and a propeller driven aeroplane of maximum total weight authorised of 6,500 kg or less being a modification of a prototype of maximum total weight authorised of 5,700 kg or less except aircraft subject to Article 4(c) – Article 6(8).
The weight range covered by the specified noise levels is –
    600kg or less to 1,500kg or more

(6) Column 6, Part VI of Schedule I, applies to an aeroplane within Article 4(c) registered in the United Kingdom before 1 April 1986 – Article 6(12)(a).
The maximum stated noise levels in columns 1 and 2 apply respectively to 1 and 2 seat aircraft.

(7) Column 7, Part VII of Schedule I, applies to an aeroplane within Article 4(c) registered in the United Kingdom on or after 1 April 1986 – article 6(12)(b).
The maximum stated noise levels in columns 1 and 2 apply respectively to 1 and 2 seat aircraft.

This consideration of the Order has so far omitted any reference to supersonic aircraft, because no applicable noise levels are specified. Article 6(9) provides that the standard to be applied to 'an aeroplane capable of sustaining level flight at a speed in excess of Flight Mach 1.0' and which conforms to a prototype for which an application for a certificate of airworthiness was applied for before 1 January 1975 and granted on or after 26 November 1981 or to a modification satifying the same criteria, is to be the noise level of the prototype when measured in accordance with paragraph 2 of Part I of Schedule I.

Columns 1 to 4 and 8 specify maximum noise levels for (a), (b) and (c). These are the points at which readings are to be taken for such aircraft and are identified in Article 2 as follows:

(a) on take-off, at a point on a line parallel to and 650 metres from the centre-line or extended centre-line of the runway where it appears to the Authority that the noise during take-off is greatest;

(b) on take-off, at a point on the extended centre-line of the runway, 6,500 metres from the start of the take-off run; and

(c) on the approach to landing at a point on the extended centre-line of the runway, 120 metres vertically below the 3 degree descent path.

In columns 2 and 3 the subdivisions of (b) into 2, 3 and 4 apply respectively to 2, 3 and 4-engined aircraft.

An aircraft is required to carry its noise certificate during flight, except that if the flight is beginning and ending at the same aerodrome it may be kept there. The certificate is then required to be produced by the commander of the aircraft within a reasonable time of being required to do so by an authorised person.[73] Subsequent articles of the Order provide for the revocation, suspension and variation of noise certificates and detail the offences, essentially in the nature of deception, relating to certificates. There is a right of access to aerodromes and other places for the Authority or for an authorised person to implement the terms of the Order, with the concomitant offence of obstruction, and Article 11 gives such persons the power to prevent an aircraft flying in breach of Article 5. The provisions of the Order apply to aircraft registered in the United Kingdom wherever they may be and to other aircraft when they are within the United Kingdom.[74] For the purposes of the Order, an 'authorised person' means any constable and any person authorised by the Authority either generally or in relation to a particular case or class of cases.

73 Articles 7 and 8 respectively.

74 Articles 17(1)(a) and (b).

CAA and Airport Management

The body having primary responsibility for the broad range of duties relating to securing the provision of and regulating 'air transport services which satisfy all substantial categories of public demand', and provided for in sections 2 to 4 of the 1982 Act, is the Civil Aviation Authority (CAA).[75] Subordinate to these primary functions, section 5(1) places on the CAA the duty

75 Section 7(3) establishes the CAA as a tribunal as specified in Schedule 1 of the Tribunals and Inquiries Act 1971.

in exercising any aerodrome licensing function in relation to any aerodrome to which this section applies, to have regard to the need to minimise so far as reasonably practicable –

(a) any adverse effects on the environment, and
(b) any disturbance to the public,

from noise, vibration, atmospheric pollution or any other cause attributable to the use of aircraft for the purpose of civil aviation.

The section applies to any aerodrome specified in an order made by the Secretary of State[76] for the purposes of the section. The scope of the CAA's licensing function under this section is determined by Air Navigation Orders made by the Secretary of State. This power, to determine the matters for consideration by the CAA in licensing or re-licensing an aerodrome, has yet to be used to include environmental factors.

76 Note that under this Act the term refers to the Secretary of State for Transport.

Ancillary to these powers and duties imposed on the CAA by sections 2 to 5, section 6(2) gives the Secretary of State an overriding power, after consultation with the CAA, to 'give it directions to do a particular thing which it has power to do or refrain from doing a particular thing, if the Secretary of State considers it appropriate to give such directions –

(c) in order to discharge or facilitate the discharge of an obligation binding on the United Kingdom by virtue of its being a member of an international organisation or a party to an international agreement; or
(d) in order to attain or facilitate the attainment of any other object the attainment of which is in his opinion appropriate in view of the fact that the United Kingdom is a member of an international organisation or a party to an international agreement; or
(f) in order to prevent or deal with noise, vibration, pollution or other disturbance attributable to aircraft used for the purpose of civil aviation ...'

The Noise Review Working Group cites as an example of the use of this power for environmental purposes, the ending of the Heathrow–Gatwick helicopter link.[77]

For the reasons briefly considered earlier, the operation of civil airfields will have an impact on, and therefore be of interest to, persons in their vicinity. To meet or indeed anticipate this concern, section 35 requires the person (other than the British Airports Authority) having the management of an aerodrome designated for the purpose of this section by the Secretary of State to provide:

(a) for users of the aerodrome,
(b) for any local authority (or, if the person having the management of the aerodrome is a local authority, for any other local authority) in whose area the aerodrome or any part thereof is situated or whose area is in the neighbourhood of the aerodrome; and
(c) for any other organisation representing the interests of persons concerned with the locality in which the aerodrome is situated,

adequate facilities for consultation with respect to any matter concerning the management or administration of the aerodrome which affects their interests.

Commenting on that provision, the Noise Review Working Group said[78]:

> At present all national and regional airports and some of the general aviation airfields, 47 in all, have been so designated. We were told that policy was to designate for consultation those airports with an annual turnover of more than £1m and to designate smaller aerodromes in response to representations where designation was likely to be helpful in alleviating local problems.

In addition to designated airfields, some others voluntarily provide consultation facilities. Most, however, do not.

Aircraft Noise

The control of aircraft noise is founded on sections 76 to 78 of the Civil Aviation Act 1982, their effect being to remove some common law remedies and replace them with controls in Air Navigation Orders. Section 76(1) removes liability in respect of trespass or nuisance 'by reason only of the flight of an aircraft over any property at a height above ground which, having regard to wind, weather and all the circumstances of the case is reasonable, or the ordinary incidents of such flight'. This protection is conditional on compliance with Air Navigation Orders, any

77 1990 Report; paragraph 4.31.

78 1990 Report; paragraph 4.30.

orders made under section 62[79] and the terms of section 81, which prohibits dangerous flying. The remaining provisions of the section are concerned with the consequences of material loss or damage caused by aircraft or things falling from them. The protection afforded by the section appears not to extend to nuisance caused by flights in the vicinity of a particular property. In *Roedene School Ltd* v *Cornwall Aviation Co. Ltd* (1926)[80] the school obtained an injunction to stop frequent, low level flights over and near to the school grounds.

Section 77(1) further provides that an Air Navigation Order may regulate the conditions under which noise and vibration may be caused by aircraft on aerodromes, and may provide in such cases that subsection (2) shall apply. That subsection stipulates that while such an Air Navigation Order is in operation and is complied with, 'no action shall lie in respect of nuisance by reason only of the noise and vibration caused by aircraft on an aerodrome'. The Air Navigation Order 1985[81] currently provides that:

> the Secretary of State may prescribe conditions under which noise and vibration may be caused by aircraft (including military aircraft) on Government aerodromes, aerodromes owned or managed by the Civil Aviation Authority, licensed aerodromes or aerodromes at which the manufacture, repair or maintenance of aircraft is carried out by persons carrying on business as manufacturers or repairers of aircraft.

In the exercise of that power conditions under which noise and vibration may be so caused are prescribed in the Air Navigation (General) Regulations 1981.[82] Those conditions, stipulated in regulation 12, are:

whether in the course of manufacture of the aircraft or otherwise

(a) the aircraft is taking off or landing; or
(b) the aircraft is moving on the ground or on water; or
(c) the engines are being operated in the aircraft
    (i) for the purpose of ensuring their satisfactory performance; or
    (ii) for the purpose of bringing them to a proper temperature in preparation for, or at the end of, a flight; or
    (iii) for the purpose of ensuring that the instruments, accessories or other components of the aircraft are in a satisfactory condition.

This exceptional and extensive immunity from the legal restrictions that bear on other activities warrants some justification, or at least explanation. The origin of that immunity is explained and its present validity assessed in this next extensive quotation from the Noise Review Working Group Report:

> 4.25 Any consideration of the problems caused by aircraft noise has to begin with a look at the present statutory position. Unlike other forms of traffic noise that which is caused by an aircraft is, so long as the Rules of the Air and Air Traffic Control Regulations and normal aviation practice have been observed, protected from action in respect of trespass or nuisance by sections 76 and 77 of the Civil Aviation Act 1982. We are not concerned with the question of trespass but we considered that the protection afforded by the Act against nuisance deserved some examination.

> 4.26 The provisions set out in sections 76 and 77 have a long history. The principle was first established in the Air Navigation Act 1920 and it has been carried through in all successive Acts up to the current Civil Aviation Act which received the Royal Assent in 1982. As we understand it the principle was introduced in 1920 in order to protect what was then a small but growing industry. For that reason the scope of sections 76

and 77 and their previous equivalents covers not only the flight of aircraft but also any measures associated with flight such as ground running and taxiing.

4.27   Seventy years on, not only is the air transport industry itself well established but non-commercial flying has grown to an extent which could scarcely have been imagined. There are now some 7,000 British-registered General Aviation aircraft flying from about 280 airfields in the UK. Most of these are used for private flying. The number of air movements is thus vastly greater than was the case when the Air Navigation Act was passed and it has been estimated that today's number of movements will itself be doubled by the end of the century.

4.28   With these considerations in mind the Working Party came to the view that the protection from action in respect of nuisance provided by section 76 of the Act is no longer appropriate. In particular we can see little justification for affording the same legislative protection to private and leisure flying as to the flying of commercial aircraft. We recognise that noise certification should mean the gradual phasing out of the older and noisier air transport aircraft but, because of the number of exemptions, certification is less effective in the case of smaller aircraft.

4.34   In our view the point has been reached – some would say long since passed – when the protection from action in respect of nuisance should no longer extend to all aircraft and when local authorities should be more closely involved in the control of noise and aircraft movements from airfields. As regards the first of these points we draw a distinction between commercial air transport and those aircraft used for private, business or leisure flying. The latter are in general much smaller than the air transport aircraft but in the area surrounding an airfield where there are large numbers of private, business and leisure aircraft flying relatively slowly and at lower levels, noise disturbance may be considerable. We therefore suggest that one way of changing section 76 so as to differentiate between commercial and non-commercial aircraft might be to provide that aircraft under a certain weight flying beyond the airspace customarily used within the aerodrome zone should no longer be exempt from action in respect of nuisance.

4.36   We also question whether it remains appropriate to exclude ground running, taxiing and other noise from static sources associated with flight from COPA's noise abatement procedures. These activities can be a serious source of noise nuisance. If the Air Navigation Order under section 77 of the Civil Aviation Act were to be modified so as to exclude from its scope the ground activities of aircraft the defence of best practicable means would still be available to the operators. Such a change would reinforce the importance the Government already attaches to consultation between the airport operator and the local authorities and residents.

Moving now from the exemptions granted to flying to the control of noise and vibration from aircraft, section 78(1) gives the Secretary of State the power by notice to prescribe requirements to be observed by an aircraft operator when taking off or landing at a designated aerodrome for the purpose of limiting or mitigating the effect of noise and vibration connected therewith. The notice imposes standards to be observed by aircraft using a particular airfield, and places responsibility on the person or company owning or operating the aircraft to secure compliance. On breach of the terms of the notice, and after giving the operator an opportunity of making representations which he is to consider, the Secretary of State may direct the manager of the aerodrome to withhold from aircraft of that operator such facilities for using the aerodrome as are specified in the direction. Aircraft noise and vibration is therefore subject to executive rather than legal control and on the initiative of the Secretary of State rather than of the person(s) affected.

In the context of noise control in the vicinity of airports the terms of section 78(3) are of particular importance, providing that:

(3) If the Secretary of State considers it appropriate, for the purpose of avoiding, limiting or mitigating the effect of noise and vibration connected with the taking-off or landing of aircraft at a designated aerodrome, to prohibit aircraft from taking-off or landing, or limit the number of occasions on which they may take off or land, at the aerodrome during certain periods, he may by notice published in the prescribed manner do all or any of the following, that is to say –

(a) prohibit aircraft of descriptions specified in the notice from taking off or landing at the aerodrome (other than in an emergency of a description so specified) during periods so specified;

(b) specify the maximum number of occasions on which aircraft of descriptions so specified may be permitted to take off or land at the aerodrome (otherwise than as aforesaid) during periods so specified;

(c) determine the persons who shall be entitled to arrange for aircraft of which they are the operators to take off or land at the aerodrome during the periods specified under paragraph (b) above and, as respects each of those persons, the number of occasions on which aircraft of a particular description of which he is the operator may take off or land at the aerodrome during those periods.

Considering the interpretation of this subsection, publication 'in the prescribed manner' means as prescribed in regulations made by the Secretary of State,[83] currently regulation 2 of the Civil Aviation (Notices) Regulations 1978.[84] Aerodromes may be designated for the purposes of sections 78 and 79 by an order of the Secretary of State under section 80. The Civil Aviation (Designation of Aerodromes) Order 1981[85] designates Heathrow, Gatwick and Stansted for the purposes of section 78, and Heathrow and Gatwick for the purposes of section 79. 'Taking off' is deemed to start when taxiing ends and power is applied for take-off,[86] and landing ends when the aircraft reaches the end of its landing run and begins to taxi.

Subject to certain specified exceptions[87] the aerodrome manager is to secure compliance with the notice, and in particular a person authorised by him has the power himself or through another, where he considers that an aircraft is about to take off in breach of the restrictions, to detain it for such period as he considers appropriate for preventing the contravention. In addition to those general enforcement powers exercisable by the aerodrome management, the Secretary of State is given a similar power to detain an aircraft.[88] These powers to prevent an aircraft from taking-off are, for obvious reasons, specifically excluded in the case of aircraft intending to land.[89] Before issuing a notice under this section the Secretary of State shall consult any body representative of aircraft operators using the aerodrome. The actual requirements of 'consultation' have been considered in Chapter 1.

As well as providing for control and restriction of aircraft noise by notice under section 78(3), section 78(6) enables the Secretary of State to give directions to the manager of a designated aerodrome for 'avoiding, limiting, or mitigating the effect of, noise and vibration connected with the taking-off or landing of aircraft at the aerodrome'.

Subordinate to these powers to control noise and vibration from aircraft, the section also provides for their monitoring. After consulting with the manager of a designated aerodrome the Secretary of State may by order require him to provide, maintain and operate in the vicinity of the aerodrome specified noise

83 Section 105(1).

84 S.I. 1978 No. 1303.

85 S.I. 1981 No. 651.

86 *Blankley* v *Godley* [1952] 1 All ER 436.

87 In subsections (4) and (5)(e) and (f).

88 Section 78(5)(c).

89 Section 78(5)(e).

measuring equipment. The order may also require access for the inspection of the equipment by a person on behalf of the Secretary of State and the making of returns to him of the resulting measurments.[90] Failure to comply with these requirements is a summary offence. The Secretary of State may also, either himself or through the CAA, remedy the failure, including where appropriate by the provision and operation of measuring equipment.

90 Section 78(8).

Part Four

WASTE MANAGEMENT

13

Waste Regulation

INTRODUCTION

Rubbish, like the poor, is always with us, the production of waste being an inevitable consequence of much human activity. As the number of people grows and their range of activity expands, so the quantity and variety of waste materials generated increase in proportion. Bingham LJ said:[1]

1 In *Leigh Land Reclamation* v *Walsall MBC* [1991] JPL 867.

> It is common knowledge that a modern community, particularly in an urban industrial area but also in the country, gives rise to a great deal of waste of all kinds. That waste has to be put somewhere, but a grave threat to health and general amenity would arise if the place and manner of its deposit were not subject to controls.

The need for controls stems from the essential feature of waste that it has no, or limited, value to the producer, who therefore has no incentive to treat it carefully but rather to give up possession and responsibility as quickly and cheaply as possible.

As an introduction to the law governing waste management and to put it in its practical context, reference may be made to passages from the 11th Report of the Royal Commission on Environmental Pollution.[2] In answer to the question 'Why is waste a problem?' they say:

2 'Managing Waste: The Duty of Care' Cmnd 9675, December 1985.

> 1.6 Waste and the activities associated with it can be harmful or undesirable in a number of respects:
>
> – as a hazard to human beings and other living organisms, e.g., by direct toxicity or through contamination of aquifers, water courses and land;
> – as a detractor from amenity and recreation, e.g., through visible, audible or odorous intrusion or through restricting the use of sites by chemical contamination or physical instability;
> – as a useless consumption of natural resources.

> Harm can be caused at any point during the production or disposal of waste – storage, transport, transfer, disposal – and subsequently, after deposition, harm can arise through matter given off or leached out, or where the waste is disturbed in such a way as to bring it into contact with the living environment.

The Report describes the 'Pollution Pathways' for each of the environmental media as follows:

> 1.8 Pollution or contamination of the ground and soil can be caused by wastes along four principal routes: deposition in landfills of toxic or hazardous wastes, which can seriously limit the sites' possible after-use; spreading on the ground of some treated wastes (e.g., water and sewage treatment residues), which can lead to a build-up of undesirable contaminants, such as heavy metals, in soils; the deposition of particulate emissions from waste incinerators; and the deposition on industrial sites of potential contaminants used in or generated by industry. Other nuisances or even health risks, such as vermin infestation and litter, can also occur when waste is disposed of to land.

1.9 Damage to the aquatic environment can arise through pollution of ground water, surface waters or the sea. The principal ways in which wastes can harm ground water are through contamination by liquids generated in or percolating through landfill sites (leachates) and through contamination from direct contact with liquid or solid wastes disposed of underground. Surface waters also can suffer pollution from landfill site leachates; from water running off landfill sites or mineral waste stockpiles; and from spillages, discharges, seepage and run-off of agricultural or industrial effluents to water courses ...

1.11 The atmosphere can be polluted by wastes or waste disposal in three main ways: dust and smells may be associated with municipal wastes during collection, transfer or disposal; gaseous or fine particulate emissions may escape from incinerators used to burn wastes; and explosive atmospheres can be generated by the accumulation of landfill gases caused by anaerobic decomposition of organic materials in landfill sites. The atmosphere is also the pathway for noise from waste disposal operations, which can detract from amenity.

Chapters 7 and 8 were concerned with liquid and water-borne wastes. The concern of this and the succeeding chapters is with the controls over the handling and disposal of this increasing volume of solid waste material. The magnitude of the problem is indicated by the statistics.[3] Total waste from all sources in the United Kingdom is estimated to be about 516 million tonnes per year. Of this some 140 million tonnes is controlled waste and about 2 to 2.5 million tonnes is special waste (see definitions below). Agriculture is considered to produce 250 million tonnes, and mining and quarrying 108 million tonnes. Of the controlled waste, 20 million tonnes is municipal or domestic waste; which is about one tonne of waste from each household per year. So far as disposal is concerned, currently about 86 per cent of controlled waste, including 90 per cent of domestic waste is landfilled and 4 per cent and 8–10 per cent respectively is incinerated. The remainder is dumped at sea[4] or disposed of in other ways. Of special waste, which includes hazardous, toxic and clinical wastes, 70 per cent is landfilled, 5 per cent is incinerated, 15 per cent is physically or chemically treated and the rest is dumped at sea. There appear to be no figures for the quantity of waste statistics produced each year.

In the past controls over this activity were conspicuous by their absence. Local authorities were made responsible for collecting house and trade refuse as it was then called.[5] What they did with it after collection was a matter for them, although the Town and Country Planning Act 1947 required planning permission for waste disposal sites. As authorities were permitted to charge for the collection of trade refuse there was a direct incentive for producers to find other, cheaper methods of disposal, giving rise to the familiar consequences of fly-tipping, dumping and uncontrolled burning, depending on the nature of the material, and causing environmental damage to land, water and air. The only controls over accumulations of rubbish were the statutory nuisance provisions considered in Chapter 4[6] and therefore limited to cases where the material was 'prejudicial to health or a nuisance' and also, of course, limited in practice to operating after the event when the damage had been done.

Public concern over the dumping of toxic waste in the Midlands produced the Deposit of Poisonous Wastes Act 1972,[7] effecting the first legislative control of waste disposal on land. It was thereunder an offence to deposit on land any poisonous, noxious or polluting waste in a manner likely to create an environ-

3 (1990) Digest of Environmental and Water Statistics, No. 13 and (1991) No. 14.

4 See in Chapter 7 concerning marine pollution.

5 See sections 72 and 73 of the Public Health Act 1936.

6 At p.97.

7 Repealed and replaced by the Control of Pollution (Special Waste) Regulations 1980, S.I. 1980 No. 1709.

mental hazard. The waste disposal authority or the water authority also had to be notified of the details of the waste. It is evident, and was confirmed in practice, that the sequence of operations from production via handling, storage and transport to disposal produced an unmanageable, and therefore uncontrollable, diffusion of responsibility. The method used to introduce order and responsibility to and for these activities was a system of licensing introduced in Part I of the Control of Pollution Act 1974. That system has been re-enacted and strengthened by Part II of the Environmental Protection Act 1990 which was, after a number of postponements and delays, brought into effect on 1 May 1994.

The scale of the waste disposal problem in the United Kingdom indicated by the statistics quoted above is indicative of the magnitude of the problem throughout the European Community. Also, of course, and apart from the intentional transfrontier shipment of waste, methods of disposal may produce air- and waterborne consequences that are not confined within national boundaries. Waste and its effective treatment is therefore seen by the Community as a European problem. In consequence a number of Directives have been adopted to harmonise the waste disposal policies of Member States and prevent the distortion of competition through the imposition of unequal waste disposal burdens. The 1989 'Community Strategy for Waste Management'[8] identifies five guidelines for any consideration of waste management:

(a) prevention;
(b) re-cycling and re-use;
(c) optimisation and final disposal;
(c) regulation of transport;
(d) remedial action.

The European Community's Fifth Action Programme on the Environment, 'Towards Sustainability'[9] reiterates this strategy and proposes a number of measures to promote it.

The 1975 Framework Directive[10] established general rules for waste management, including prevention, recycling and the harmless disposal of waste. It also provided for administration and a system of authorisations for operators. These provisions were amended by a 1991 Directive[11] to be implemented by Member States by 1 April 1993 and given effect to in the United Kingdom with the operation of Part II of the Environmental Protection Act 1990. That Directive defines waste as 'any substance or object ... which the holder discards or intends or is required to discard' and specifies 16 categories of waste. Further Directives cover a wide range of specific aspects of the industry and will be referred to as appropriate in the body of the chapter.

STRUCTURE AND AUTHORITIES

While many erstwhile local government functions have in the past 20 years or so been re-allocated to other agencies, responsibility for the handling and treatment of solid waste is still the responsibility of local authorities. With the creation of the Environment Agency, though, that body is expected to assume responsibility for the waste regulation function.[12] The handling and treatment of waste is divided into three separate activities and, in consequence, between three groups of authorities – waste regulation authorities, waste disposal authorities and waste

8 COM 89/934, dated 18 September 1989.

9 COM 92/23 final.

10 75/442/EEC.

11 91/156/EEC.

12 Statement of the Secretary of State, July 1992.

collection authorities – all being defined in section 30 of the Environmental Protection Act 1990 which reproduces the comparable terms of section 30 of the Control of Pollution Act 1974.

Waste regulation authorities

Waste regulation authorities, by section 30(1) of the 1990 Act, are in non-metropolitan counties the county councils, and in Wales and metropolitan counties the district councils. In the Greater London area the London Waste Regulation Authority is responsible, its composition including a member from each of the 33 constituent authorities.[13] In Manchester and Merseyside the responsible bodies are the Manchester and Merseyside Waste Disposal Authorities respectively, although to be known in the performance of this function as Waste Regulation Authorities.

The desirability of regional waste regulation has been recommended.[14] While initially rejecting the proposal, the Government has subsequently announced agreement with local authority associations on regional arrangements. Details have yet to be announced, but they would include the setting-up of a joint waste committee for each region and the establishment of a common approach to licensing and enforcement. The Government has further warned that should the voluntary arrangements fail to achieve the desired objectives of consistency, self-sufficiency and appropriate strategies, 'then the pressures for central government intervention would be difficult to resist'. The power for the Secretary of State to compel the creation of such regional authorities where he considers it advantageous is contained in section 31 of the Environmental Protection Act 1990. In such cases the Secretary of State may by order require two or more 'relevant authorities' to make joint arrangements for the discharge of waste regulation functions. The establishing order will, *inter alia*, specify the functions to be performed by the regional body, provide for the appointment to it of members of the relevant authorities and make necessary provision for staff, property and so on. The extent to which the development of this pseudo-voluntary structure will be affected by the creation of the Environment Agency referred to earlier remains to be seen.

The main functions of waste regulation authorities are[15]:

(a) waste management licensing (section 35);
(b) supervision of the duty of care as to waste (section 34);
(c) inspecting land before accepting surrender of licences (section 39);
(d) supervision of licensed activities (section 42);
(e) investigation of the need for arrangements for dealing with controlled waste arising within their area and preparation of disposal plans (section 50);
(f) powers to require the removal of waste unlawfully deposited (section 59);
(g) inspection of land for risks of pollution or harm to human health caused by gases or liquids arising from deposits of waste and action to avoid such pollution or harm (section 61);
(h) maintenance of public registers (section 64); and
(i) publication of annual reports (section 67).

Waste Collection Authorities

Section 30(3) of the Environmental Protection Act 1990 provides that waste collection authorities are the councils of districts or London Boroughs, the Common

13 See Part I of Schedule I to the Waste Regulation and Disposal (Authorities) Order 1985; S.I. 1985 No.1885.

14 See especially Report of the House of Commons Environment Committee, Toxic Waste (Session 1988–89, Second Report, February 1989), paragraphs 140–153.

15 See Stephen Tromans, *The Environmental Protection Act 1990; Text and Commentary* Sweet & Maxwell, London, 1991 pp.43-67.

16 See Tromans, *op. cit.* at
pp.43-68.

Council of the City of London, the Sub-Treasurer of the Inner Temple and the Under Treasurer of the Middle Temple. The main functions of those authorities are[16]:

(a) to arrange for the collection of household waste in their area (section 45);
(b) to arrange for the collection of commercial or industrial waste on request (section 45);
(c) to arrange for the emptying of privies or cesspools in their area (section 45);
(d) to determine the nature and source of receptacles in which household waste is to be placed for collection (section 46);
(e) to supply receptacles for commercial or industrial waste (section 47);
(f) to deliver for disposal waste collected to such places as the waste disposal authority directs (section 48);
(g) to carry out investigations as to appropriate arrangements for dealing with waste for the purpose of recycling and to prepare a statement of such arrangements (section 49); and
(h) to retain waste which the authority has decided to recycle and to make arrangements for its recycling (section 48).

The feature in this list requiring particular emphasis is that in relation to the first three functions a collection authority is to 'arrange for' its performance, indicating that the function is expected to be undertaken by a contractor. While the Act does not make this as explicit as the similar requirement in relation to disposal authorities, the implication is nevertheless clear.

Waste disposal authorities

Waste disposal authorities are, by section 30(2) of the Environmental Protection Act 1990, in England generally the county council or metropolitan district, and in Wales the district council. In Greater Manchester the disposal authorities are the district council for Wigan for its area and for the rest the Greater Manchester Waste Disposal Authority. The disposal authority for Merseyside is the Merseyside Waste Disposal Authority. For Greater London the relevant authority is:

(a) in the area of a London Waste Disposal Authority, that authority;
(b) in the City of London, the Common Council;
(c) in any other London Borough, the council of that borough.

Parts II, III, IV and V of Schedule I to the Waste Regulation and Disposal (Authorities) Order 1985 provide respectively for waste authorities serving the West, North, East London and Western Riverside areas, covering in all 21 boroughs. The remaining authorities, having responsibility for their own waste disposal, are mainly those in the south and south east.[17]

17 Westminster, Bexley,
Bromley, Croydon, Sutton,
Merton, Kingston-on-Thames,
Richmond-on-
Thames, Southwark,
Lewisham, Greenwich and
Tower Hamlets.

It will be apparent from the definitions that in the majority of cases the regulation and disposal functions are the responsibility of the same authorities. In such cases section 30(7) requires the authority to make administrative arrangements for separating the two functions. Details of those arrangements are to be submitted to the Secretary of State, who also has a power to give directions as to arrangements for separation. The reasons for the separation of these functions are self-evident but were stated by the Department of the Environment[18] in the following terms:

18 DoE Circular 10/91.

The administrative separation of regulation from disposal is ... intended to make it clear that decisions by a waste regulation authority about policies, standards and enforcement are to be taken free from pressures arising from the authority's position as a waste disposal authority. Waste regulation officers must be in a position to impose high environmental standards on the disposing of waste on behalf of the waste disposal authority as they would on other waste disposal contractors. ... The other purpose of separation is to increase public and industry confidence in waste regulation so that regulatory policies and practices can be seen to be directed solely towards achieving the highest practicable environmental standards in all waste management.

When the regulatory function is transferred to the Environment Agency this potential or apparent conflict of interest will be resolved.

The main functions of waste disposal authorities are[19]:

(a) formation of waste disposal companies and transfer of relevant parts of their undertakings to such companies (section 32);

(b) direction of waste collection authorities as to places to which collected waste is to be delivered (section 51(4)(a));

(c) arranging for the disposal of controlled waste collected in the area by waste collection authorities (section 51(1)(a));

(d) arrangement for the provision of places at which residents of the area may deposit household waste and for the disposal of waste so deposited (section 51(1)(b));

(e) arrangement for the provision of places where collected waste may be treated or kept prior to removal for treatment or disposal (section 51(4)(b));

(f) making payments to waste collection authorities for savings in disposal costs in respect of waste retained for recycling (section 52(1)); and

(g) waste recycling (section 55).

Waste disposal contractors

The 1990 Act requires waste disposal authorities, under the direction of the Secretary of State, to arrange for the performance of their disposal function by 'waste disposal contractors'.[20] Section 30(5) defines a waste disposal contractor as:

a person who in the course of a business collects, keeps, treats or disposes of waste, being either –

(a) a company formed for all or any of those purposes by a waste disposal authority whether in pursuance of section 32 ... or otherwise; or

(b) either a company formed for all or any of those purposes by other persons or a partnership or an individual;[21]

Existing disposal authorities, or their constituent authorities, may make arrangements either alone or with others to form a waste disposal company, to transfer to it, and thereafter cease to carry on, those functions and then to implement those proposals within a reasonable time.[22] Unless the Secretary of State is satisfied as to the adequacy of such arrangements, or if no such arrangements are made, he shall, under section 32(2), give directions to the authorities concerned requiring them to form, or to join in forming, waste disposal companies and transfer under a Schedule 2 scheme the relevant part[23] of their undertakings. The meaning and scope of 'company' is as defined by the Companies Act 1985, and section 32(7) and (8) provides that these waste disposal companies generally have the power to

19 See Tromans, *op. cit.* at pp.43–68.

20 Section 32.

21 'Company' has the same meaning as in the Companies Act 1985.

22 Section 32(3) and (5).

23 Defined in section 32(11).

engage in activities beyond the powers of waste disposal authorities, unless they are under authority control. In that case the authority must ensure that the company only engages in the disposal, keeping, treatment and collection of waste, and incidental activities.

Where a waste disposal authority forms a company for these purposes section 32(9) requires that it is to be an arm's length company for the purposes of Part V of the Local Government and Housing Act 1989. That Act, together with the Local Government Act 1986, largely implemented the recommendations of the Widdicombe Committee of Enquiry into the Conduct of Local Authority Business.[24] Sections 68 and 69 of the 1989 Act sub-divide local authority companies into local authority controlled companies, local authority influenced companies and companies in which the local authority has a minority interest. Section 68(1) specifies four ways in which a company may qualify as a local authority controlled company:

24 The Conduct of Local Authority Business: The Government Response to the Report of the Widdicombe Committee of Enquiry, 1988 Cm 433.

(a) subsidiary of the local authority by virtue of section 736 of the Companies Act 1985, which means:
 (i) the authority is a member of the company and controls the composition of the board of directors; or
 (ii) the authority holds more than half the nominal share value of the company's equity share capital; or
 (iii) the company is itself a subsidiary (by reason of (i) or (ii)) of a company which is a subsidiary of the authority;
(b) paragraph (a) does not apply but the local authority have power to control a majority of the votes at a general meeting of the company. This means, by virtue of subsection (3), control through either –
 (i) the holding of equity share capital by the authority, nominees or by persons whose shareholding is subject to the control or direction of the authority; or
 (ii) the holding of votes at a general meeting exercisable by the authority, or members or persons who vote under the instructions of the authority; or
 (iii) in a combination of these ways;
(c) paragraph (a) does not apply but the local authority have at that time power to appoint or remove a majority of the board of directors of the company; or
(d) the company is under the control of another company which is itself under the control of the local authority, i.e. in any of the ways stipulated above.

By section 73, where a company would not qualify as controlled by one local authority under these criteria but would if taken together with another authority or authorities, it is to be treated as local authority controlled.

In spite of this direct association, a controlled company may nevertheless rank as an arm's length company where it is distanced from the authority in the ways stipulated in section 68(6), i.e.:

25 By section 68(7) the Secretary of State has power to direct that any given removal be disregarded where he considers that it was not for the purpose of influencing the management of the company for other than commercial reasons.

Notwithstanding that a company may be a controlled company within this section, it may be an 'arm's length company' (for the purposes of Part V of this Act) for a particular financial year if, before the beginning of that year the local authority so resolve and the following conditions are satisfied throughout the year –

(a) each director is appointed for a fixed term of at least two years;
(b) no director has been removed by resolution under section 303 of the Companies Act 1985;[25]

   (c) not more than one-fifth of the directors have been members or officers of the authority;

   (d) the company has not occupied land in which the authority have an interest, other
than land for the best consideration reasonably obtainable;[26]

   (e) the company has entered into an agreement with the authority that the company will
use its best endeavours to produce a specified positive return on its assets;

   (f) the authority have not lent money to the company or guaranteed any sum borrowed
by it or subscribed for any securities in the company, except for the purpose of
enabling the company to acquire fixed assets or to provide it with working capital;

   (g) the authority have not made any grant to the company except pursuant to an agreement or undertaking preceding the financial year of the company in which it was made;

   (h) the authority have not made any grant to the company the amount of which is in
any way related to the financial results of the company in any period.

Section 70 specifies the rules governing a local authority's relationship and action in relation to their controlled companies and those under their influence. The section also empowers the Secretary of State to make provision by order for regulating, forbidding or requiring the taking of certain action or courses of action; thus providing the real substance of the regulatory code governing relations between authorities and these companies. It is the responsibility of authorities to ensure that they comply so far as practicable with such requirements, and if they fail to do so their payments to the company and any expenditure in contravention will be regarded as unlawful expenditure for the purpose of Part III of the Local Government Finance Act 1982,[27] carrying with it the sanctions of surcharge and disqualification.

Returning now to the Environmental Protection Act 1990, Schedule 2 contains provisions governing waste disposal authorities and companies. Part I of the schedule deals with transitional provisions, including Secretary of State directions, their contents, and consequences; paragraph 18 providing that 'A waste disposal authority shall ... so frame terms and conditions as to avoid undue discrimination in favour of one description of waste disposal contractor as against other descriptions of waste disposal contractors'. Part II is essentially concerned with contract tendering procedures and terms, and paragraph 20 provides that failure to observe the specified tendering procedure will make any resulting contract void. The actual requirements are comparable with those applicable to compulsory competitive tendering and are designed to secure sufficiently wide advertising of the proposed contract and equal and fair treatment of tenderers. In particular, both in inviting tenders and in awarding the contract, the waste disposal authority is required to disregard the fact that a contractor is or is not controlled by the authority. When preparing the terms and conditions of contracts for the keeping, treatment or disposal of waste a waste disposal authority must have regard to the desirability of including terms designed to, under paragraph 19:

   (a) minimise pollution of the environment or harm to human health due to the
disposal or treatment of the waste under the contract; and

   (b) maximise the recycling of waste under the contract.

In considering tenders the authority is entitled to have regard to the tenderers' acceptance or rejection of any such terms. Environmentally sound operation is therefore a material consideration in selecting tenders and not a form of improper discrimination.

26 See also section 123 of the Local Government Act 1972.

27 Sections 19 and 20.

Where the Secretary of State is proposing to issue a direction requiring transfer of the function to a company (LAWDC), notice of intention must be given to the authority who may make representations concerning either its contents or that, on the grounds in section 32(3), it should not be made at all. Paragraph 5 of the schedule provides that an authority so directed must form the company as one limited by shares and as a wholly-owned subsidiary[28] of the authority, or authorities, concerned. Also, the authority must resolve that, and ensure before the vesting date that, the company is an arm's length company and satisfies the requirements of section 68 (6)(a) – (h) of the Local Government and Housing Act 1989. Following formation the authority prepares a transfer scheme, requiring the Secretary of State's approval, for transfer to the company of property, rights and liabilities. While the authority may retain the freehold of waste sites and the ownership of plant and equipment used by disposal contractors, the Secretary of State will wish to ensure that the new company will be financially viable and that the arrangements are fair to existing private sector contractors.

In conclusion, it appears that the question for local authorities, subject to the Secretary of State's overriding power of direction, is whether to set up a LAWDC or to withdraw from operational activities. In the first case a further question concerns the extent of the authority's ownership and the consequent degree of control. While reduced control increases the company's freedom and range of commercial activity, it also carries the risk of exploitation of the authority at some future time.

CLASSIFICATION OF WASTE

Responsibility for the collection, handling and disposal of waste is determined in large measure by its type and contents. The category of any given waste will indicate its likely composition and therefore toxicity, and possibly its volume; factors of significance in its subsequent treatment. There is also a strong argument, in accordance with the 'polluter pays' principle, for placing responsibility, if only financial, for disposal with the producer, especially in the commercial and industrial context. Also, and potentially more, important is the question of when an article or material crosses the nebulous boundary from the useful to the useless and takes on the characteristics of waste. The general definition in section 75(2) of the 1990 Act provides that waste includes:

(a) any substance which constitutes a scrap material or an effluent or other unwanted surplus substance arising from the application of any process; and
(b) any substance or article which requires to be disposed of as being broken, worn out, contaminated or otherwise spoiled

but does not include a substance which is an explosive within the meaning of the Explosives Act 1875.[29] Section 75(3) then adds 'any thing which is discarded or otherwise dealt with as if it were waste shall be presumed to be waste unless the contrary is proved'. This will resolve the sort of situation presented to the Court of Appeal in *McVittie* v *Bolton Corporation* [1945].[30] Following destruction of a cinema by fire the local authority served a notice under section 58 of the Public Health Act 1936 requiring, *inter alia*, demolition and the 'removal of rubbish resulting from the demolition'. On the owner's default the authority cleared the site, also removing some machinery. The owner now sued the authority for con-

28 In accordance with section 736 of the Companies Act 1985.

29 'Explosive' is defined in section 3 of that Act as meaning –

(i) gunpowder, nitro-glycerine, dynamite, gun-cotton, blasting powders, fulminate of mercury or other metals, coloured fires or any other substance, whether similar to those mentioned above or not, used or manufactured with a view to produce a practical effect by explosion or a pyrotechnic effect; and
(ii) includes fog-signals, fireworks, fuses, rockets, percussion caps, detonators, cartridges, ammunition of all descriptions, and every adaptation or preparation of an explosive as above defined.

30 [1945] 1 All ER 379.

version of the machinery. He contended, and a majority of the Court of Appeal agreed, that the machinery could not be regarded as 'rubbish resulting from the demolition' that it retained its character as chattels and therefore remained his property. However, in his dissenting judgement, and anticipating this present statutory approach, Scott LJ said[31]:

31 At p.382a.

> I think anything left on the site of a building demolished under the default powers of this section which in fact results from the demolition is 'rubbish'. One test may be its function. All the machines about which the appellant complains, were there, not for their functional purposes, but merely as derelict appurtenances of the derelict building. ... The utter neglect of them by the appellant, I think, shows that he was treating them as mere scrap.

The, or a, problem in identifying waste is that, being apparently waste within the definition, it may then regain use and value and re-enter the commercial or industrial cycle. The question is, then, when or in whose opinion is the classification 'waste' to be applied to the given material? The courts have consistently held that the view of the person discarding it and the time at which it is discarded are the material considerations. Deputy judge P.J.Crawford QC, for example, said[32]:

32 *Berridge Incinerators* v *Nottinghamshire CC* 1987 (High Court, unreported but see DoE Circular 13/88 on The Collection and Disposal of Waste Regulations, paragraph 2.7).

> It is of course a truism that one man's waste is another man's raw material. The fact that a price is paid by the collector of the material to its originator is, no doubt, relevant, but I do not regard it as crucial. ... In my judgement, the correct approach is to regard the material from the point of view of the person who produces it. Is it something which is produced as a product, or even as a by-product of his business, or is it something to be disposed of as useless.

Earlier authority for the same view, and a useful factual example, is provided by *Filbey* v *Combe* (1837).[33] The parochial commissioners, by section 59 of the Metropolitan Paving Act,[34] had the power through appointed scavengers to 'take and carry away from the respective houses and premises of the inhabitants or occupiers their soil, ashes, cinders, rubbish' etc., the persons so appointed having the right and benefit in the material. The plaintiff brewers burnt coal to provide heat for brewing. Having been partially burnt in that process the residue was removed, mixed with dust and ashes and taken to other premises, where it was further burnt to heat water for cask washing and similar functions. The defendant scavengers had removed such partially burnt coal and ashes under their statutory powers and the plaintiff now sued to recover their value. In finding for the plaintiff Parke B, speaking of the statute, said[35]:

33 (1837) 2 M&W 677.

34 57 Geo 3 c29.

35 At p.683.

> I think it is clear, if you look at the whole context, that it applies to such things as are in the contemplation of the owner rubbish, and which he desires to dispose of in that character. If there be any other purpose to which the dust etc., can be applied, except treating it as merely rubbish, he has a right to do so, either where it is produced, or on any other premises. If it be combustible as fuel, he has a right so to use it on any premises he may have. The right of the scavenger only attaches when the owner has no use for the articles mentioned in the act except as rubbish.

This approach also broadly accords with the definition of waste in the EC Framework Directive on Waste[36] as 'any substance or object which the holder disposes of or is required to dispose of pursuant to the provisions of national law in force'.

36 75/442/EEC.

The Department of the Environment Circular[37] suggests the consideration of four questions from the point of view of the producer of the material to determine whether or not it is waste:

37 See note 32 above.

(a) Is it what would ordinarily be described as waste?

(b) Is the substance a scrap metal, effluent or other unwanted surplus?

(c) Is the substance or article required to be disposed of broken, worn out, contaminated or otherwise spoiled?

(d) Is the material being discarded or dealt with as if it were waste?

This really represents a detailed application of the statutory definition to resolve the question, as one would expect. Application of this approach in *Kent CC v Queenborough Rolling Mill Co. Ltd* (1991)[38] to material removed from a disused pottery found it to be waste, even after sorting and grading for use as filling material at a wharf. Pill J said:

38 (1991) 89 LGR 306, DC.

> In my judgement the purpose to which the material was put is irrelevant in the present situation. The nature of the material must first be considered at the time of its removal from the Stelrad site. The material had earlier been discarded and had lain on the site for many years. When removed from the site it was waste within the meaning of that word in section 30 [Control of Pollution Act 1974]. It bore the same quality when it was deposited at Coal Washer Wharf. The usefulness if it be so of the deposit as fill on the receiving site did not change the character of the material. Neither did the fact that the material was separated from other material before deposit deprive it of its identity as waste.

The Waste Management Licensing Regulations 1994[39] further provide that any reference in Part II of the Act to waste 'shall include a reference to Directive Waste'.[40]

39 S.I. 1994 No. 1056, Schedule ,4 paragraph 9 (1) and (2).

40 Categories of Directive Waste are listed in Part II of Schedule 4 to the 1994 Regulations; see below at note 55.

Waste within the above definition is subdivided for the purpose of regulation into:

(a) controlled;

(b) household;

(c) industrial;

(d) commercial;

(e) special.

These terms, with the exception of the last, are defined in section 75 of the Environmental Protection Act 1990. The statutory definitions of household, industrial and commercial waste are amplified by the Collection and Disposal of Waste Regulations 1988,[41] the Controlled Waste Regulations 1992[42] and the Waste Management Licensing Regulations 1994[43] which deal, *inter alia*, with classes or sources of waste where doubt concerning the appropriate category may exist or where its nature necessitates special treatment.

41 S.I. 1988 No. 819, amended by S.I. 1989 No. 1968.

42 S.I. 1992 No. 588.

43 S.I. 1994 No. 1056.

44 [1993] JUKELA 3 & 4, p.73 (26 February 1993)

Controlled waste is stated by section 75(4) to mean 'household, industrial and commercial waste or any such waste'. The scope of 'controlled waste' fell to be determined in *Thanet DC v Kent CC* (1993)[44] in the context of the appellant district council's collection of seaweed from holiday beaches and, after mixing with other material, its use on land as compost or fertilizer. The Divisional Court allowed the appeal, finding that the seaweed was not within any of the constituent categories of controlled waste or any combination or permutation of them, and that, being a penal statute, the term was to be construed restrictively. The Court also noted that the definition did not permit the inclusion of other distinct categories of waste on the *eiusdem generis* principle though having shared characteristics with those defined. Powers to add further categories by regulation had not been used to add seaweed. It would nevertheless appear that seaweed may be caught by the section 75(3) provision that 'Anything which is discarded or otherwise dealt with as if it were waste shall be presumed to be waste unless the contrary is proved'. The primary requirement that waste should derive from the application of a process is, however, lacking in the case of naturally occurring material. While the justices appear to have concluded that the collection and transport amounted to a process, the question was not argued on appeal. This decision suggests that any natural vegetation or soil cleared from land, or water, and deposited somewhere is outside the definition of controlled waste; except in the context of construction or engineering in which case it will be industrial waste.

Household waste is defined in section 75(5) as waste from:

(a) domestic property, that is to say, a building or self-contained part of a building which is used wholly for the purposes of living accommodation;
(b) a caravan (as defined in section 29(1) of the Caravan Sites and Control of Development Act 1960[45]) which usually and for the time being is situated on a caravan site (within the meaning of that Act);
(c) a residential home;
(d) premises forming part of a university, or school or other educational establishment;
(e) premises forming part of a hospital or nursing home.

This definition adds caravans to the previous Control of Pollution Act 1974 definition, thus resolving the problem revealed, for instance, in *Gordon* v *Kirkcaldy DC* (1990)[46] of whether a caravan could be included within the description of dwelling-house.

Schedule I of the 1992 Regulations, extending and developing the list in the 1988 Regulations, provides that waste produced from the following non-domestic premises is to be regarded as household waste:

(a) places of religious worship;
(b) premises occupied by charities;[47]
(c) land used with domestic property, a caravan or a residential home;
(d) private garage of less than 25 square metres or used for a private vehicle;
(e) private storage premises used for domestic articles;
(f) moored vessel used wholly as living accommodation;
(g) camp sites;
(h) residential hostels;
(i) prisons or other penal institutions;
(j) public meeting halls;
(k) royal palace;
(l) litter collected under section 89(2).

The Regulations[48] further provide that the following classes of waste, though produced from domestic premises, are not to be treated as household waste; the reason in each case, having regard to the nature of the material and consequent problems of disposal, being self-evident:

(a) mineral or synthetic oil or grease;
(b) asbestos; and
(c) clinical waste

45 Section 29(1) defines a caravan as 'any structure designed or adapted for human habitation which is capable of being moved from one place to another (whether by being towed, or by being transported on a motor vehicle or trailer) and any motor vehicle so designed or adapted, but does not include:
(a) any railway rolling-stock which is for the time being on rails forming part of a railway system, or
(b) any tent'.

46 [1990] SCLR 104.

47 For the meaning of 'charity' see Chapter 10 at p.279.

48 Regulation 4 of the 1988 Regulations and regulation 3 of the 1992 Regulations.

49 S.I. 1992 No. 588,
regulation 1.

Clinical waste is defined in the Controlled Waste Regulations 1992[49] as:

(i) any waste which consists wholly or partly of human or animal tissue, blood or other body fluids, excretions, drugs or other pharmaceutical products, swabs or dressings, or syringes, needles or other sharp instruments being waste which unless rendered safe may prove hazardous to any person coming into contact with it; and

(ii) any other waste arising from medical, nursing, dental, veterinary, pharmaceutical or similar practice, investigation, treatment, care, teaching or research, or the collection of blood for transfusion, being waste which may cause infection to any persons coming into contact with it.

Industrial waste is defined in section 75(6) of the Environmental Protection Act 1990 as meaning waste from any of the following premises:

(a) any factory (within the meaning of the Factories Act 1961);
(b) any premises used for the purposes of, or in connection with, the provision to the public of transport services by land, water or air;
(c) any premises used for the purposes of, or in connection with, the supply to the public of gas, water or electricity or the provision of sewerage services; or
(d) any premises used for the purposes of, or in connection with, the provision to the public of postal or telecommunication services.

Schedule 3 of the 1992 Regulations, amplifying and extending that of the 1988 Regulations, further provides that the following specified types or sources of waste are to be treated as industrial waste:

1 from premises other than a private garage used for maintaining vehicles, vessels or aircraft.
2 from a laboratory.
3 from non-factory workshops.
4 from premises of approved scientific research associations.
5 from dredging operations.
6 from tunnelling or excavating.
7 sewage from premises not on main drainage.
8 clinical waste from other than domestic premises.
9 from aircraft, vehicle or vessel not occupied for domestic purposes.
10 parts of aircraft, vehicle or vessel not household waste.
11 waste having been deposited on land, with contaminated soil.
12 leachate from a deposit of waste.
13 poisonous or noxious waste from specified processes.
14 from premises used for breeding, boarding, stabling or exhibiting animals.
15 waste oil, solvents or scrap metal, with specific exceptions.
16 litter collected from highways under section 879(2)(b).
17 imported waste.
18 tank washings or garbage landed in Britain.

The definition of 'factory' in section 175 of the Factories Act 1961 is long and detailed including a descriptive list of premises and activities that might be regarded as peripheral to the central definition. Essentially factories are premises, including open air premises, in which persons are employed in manual labour in the making, altering, repairing, ornamenting, finishing, cleaning, washing, breaking up, demolition or adapting for sale of any article; with the exception of such premises occupied by the Crown or other public authorities. In particular, and having regard to the wide definition of factory, the waste of various sorts from demolition and construction work is industrial and therefore controlled waste.

Commercial waste, by section 75(7) of the Environmental Protection Act 1990, means waste from premises used wholly or mainly for the purposes of a trade or business or the purposes of sport, recreation or entertainment, excluding:

(a) household waste;
(b) industrial waste;
(c) waste from any mine or quarry and waste from premises used for agriculture within the meaning of the Agriculture Act 1947; and
(d) waste of any other description prescribed by regulations made by the Secretary of State for the purposes of this paragraph.

Then, as with the other two specialised forms of waste, section 75(8) enables the Secretary of State by regulation to add or remove stipulated forms of waste from the definition; with the exception of (c) above which may not be removed. The subsection also provides that, subject to any regulations, sewage is not to be regarded as commercial waste. This definition therefore makes plain that commercial waste is the residual category, including all controlled waste that does not fall specifically within the other two categories.

Within the current regulations, the Controlled Waste Regulations 1992,[50] regulation 6 and Schedule 4 include as commercial waste that from offices, showrooms, hotels,[51] composite hereditaments used for trade or business, a private garage over 25 square metres or used for additional purposes, clubs, societies or associations conducted for the benefit of the members, courts, government and local government offices, corporate bodies, tents other than on camp sites, markets and fairs and waste collected under section 22(3) of the Control of Pollution Act 1974.[52]

The scope of 'trade or business' has been considered in the context of section 79(1)(d) of this Act concerning statutory nuisances,[53] as has the definition of 'mine or quarry'.[54] Section 109(3) of the Agriculture Act 1947 defines agriculture as including, 'horticulture, fruit growing, seed growing, dairy farming and livestock breeding and keeping, the use of land as grazing land, meadow land, ozier land, market gardens and nursery grounds, and the use of land for woodlands where that use is ancillary to the farming of the land for agricultural purposes ...'.

The three constituent categories of controlled waste just considered are further qualified in that regulation 22 of the Waste Management Licensing Regulations 1994,[55] adds a new regulation 7A to the 1988 Regulations providing that ' ... for the purposes of all the provisions of Part II of the Act, waste which is not Directive Waste shall not be treated as household waste, industrial waste or commercial waste'. Material will only be brought within any of those three definitions, then, where it is 'Directive Waste' as listed in Part II of Schedule 4 to the 1994 Regulations, which reproduces the list in Annex I to the Directive.[56] The definitions in the Act must now therefore be read in conjunction with that list:

SUBSTANCES OR OBJECTS WHICH ARE WASTE WHEN DISCARDED etc.
1 Production or consumption residues not otherwise specified in this Part of this Schedule.
2 Off-specification products.
3 Products whose date for appropriate use has expired.

50 S.I. 1992 No. 588.

51 As defined in section 1(3) of the Hotel Proprietors Act 1956.

52 This subsection gives a local authority power to arrange, by contract or otherwise, with the occupier of open land to which the public have access, not being a highway, for the cleaning of the land.

53 See at p.96 above.

54 See at p.104 above.

55 S.I. 1994 No. 1056.

56 This is Directive 75/442/EEC on waste as amended by Directives 91/156/EEC and 91/692/EEC.

4 Materials spilled, lost or having undergone other mishap, including any materials, equipment etc., contaminated as a result of the mishap.

5 Materials contaminated or soiled as a result of planned actions (e.g., residues from cleaning operations, packing materials, containers, etc.).

6 Unusable parts (e.g., reject batteries, exhaust catalysts, etc.).

7 Substances which no longer perform satisfactorily (e.g., contaminated acids, contaminated solvents, exhausted tempering salts, etc.).

8 Residues of industrial processes (e.g., slags, still bottoms, etc.).

9 Residues from pollution abatement processes (e.g., scrubber sludges, baghouse dusts, spent filters, etc.).

10 Machining or finishing residues (e.g., lathe turnings, mill scales, etc.).

11 Residues from raw materials extraction and processing (e.g., mining residues, oil field slops, etc.).

12 Adulterated materials (e.g., oils contaminated with PCBs, etc.).

13 Any materials, substances or products whose use has been banned by law.

14 Products for which the holder has no further use (e.g., agricultural, household, office, commercial and shop discards, etc.).

15 Contaminated materials, substances or products resulting from remedial action with respect to land.

16 Any materials, substances or products which are not contained in the above categories.

Taking the list as a whole, and particularly numbers 14 and 16, it is difficult to see exactly how it qualifies or limits the definitions. Anything deriving from the sources within each of the statutory controlled waste categories appears to be brought within this list, which to that extent elaborates on and illustrates forms of waste. Whether it does more will have to be seen.

The remaining category of waste listed initially and requiring consideration is special waste. Section 75(9) provides that the term means controlled waste 'as respects which regulations are in force under section 62'. Section 62(1) gives the Secretary of State a regulation-making power governing the treatment, keeping or disposal of waste if he 'considers that controlled waste of any kind is or may be so dangerous or difficult to treat, keep or dispose of that special provision is required for dealing with it'. Current regulations are the Control of Pollution (Special Waste) Regulations 1980[57] implementing the EC Directive on Toxic and Dangerous Waste.[58] Regulation 2(1) defines 'special waste' as any controlled waste which:

(a) consists of or contains any of the substances listed in Part I of Schedule I and by reason of the presence of such substance –
   (i) is dangerous to life within the meaning of Part II of Schedule I, or
   (ii) has a flash point of 21 degrees Celsius or less as determined by the methods and with the apparatus laid down by the British Standards Institution,[59]
     or

(b) is a medicinal product, as defined in section 130 of the Medicines Act 1968, which is available only in accordance with a prescription given by an appropriate practitioner as defined in section 58(1) of that Act.

The Secretary of State is given the power, in regulation 3(1), to extend the definition to categories of waste that, but for the fact that they are radioactive, would be controlled waste. The scope and content of this definition is considered in detail in Chapter 16.

57 S.I. 1980 No. 1709, amended by S.I. 1988 No. 1790.

58 78/319/EEC.

59 BS 3900: Part A, 8: 1976 (EN53).

Noting the scope of these constituent categories of waste, controlled waste may be regarded as including all waste with the exception of :

(a) waste derived from agricultural activities;
(b) mining and quarrying wastes; and
(c) radioactive wastes.

REGISTERS AND REGISTRATION

Public registers

Waste regulation authorities are required by section 64(1) of the Environmental Protection Act 1990 to maintain public registers of the information prescribed in regulations by the Secretary of State. Such registers, which may be in any form, are to be open to public inspection free of charge at all reasonable times and with associated facilities for copying, for which a charge may be made. The relevant provision is regulation 10 of the Waste Management Licensing Regulations 1994, which broadly amplifies the list of matters in section 64(1) and provides that such registers shall contain full particulars of:

(a) current or recently current waste management licences;[60]
(b) current or recently current applications for licences or for the transfer or modification of licences, including supporting and associated documents;
(c) notices under section 37 effecting modification of licences;
(d) notices under section 38 effecting the revocation or suspension of licences or imposing requirements on holders of licences;
(e) notices of appeal under section 43 with associated documents;
(f) details of any convictions of holders of licences under Part II of the Act;
(g) reports by the authority in the performance of any section 42 function;
(h) any monitoring information on the performance of licensed activity;
(i) any directions given to the authority by the Secretary of State under this Part of the Act;
(j) the authority's summaries of amounts of special waste produced or disposed of in its area;
(k) registers and records provided to the authority under regulation 13(5) or 14(1) of the Control of Pollution (Special Waste) Regulations 1980;[61]
(l) applications under section 39 for the surrender of licences, with details;
(m) written reports under section 70(3) by inspectors appointed by the authority.

60 By regulation 10(4) a licence is 'recently' current for a period of 12 months after it has ceased to be in force and applications are 'recently' current if relating to a licence which is current or recently current or, if rejected, for a period of 12 months after the date of notice of rejection.

61 S.I. 1980 No. 1709.

This required information is subject to three limitations in, respectively sections 65 and 66 of the Act and regulation 11. Under section 65, information is to be excluded from registers if, in the opinion of the Secretary of State, its inclusion would be contrary to the interests of national security. To this end he may give directions to authorities specifying the information to be excluded or to be referred to him for decision. Authorities are then required to notify the Secretary of State of any information that they exclude as a result of a direction. Further, any person who considers that any information should be excluded under this section may apply to the Secretary of State, who may notify the authority of the appropriate action.

Section 66 provides for the exclusion of confidential information, subsection (1) stipulating that the consent of the person concerned is required for the inclusion of information relating to the affairs of any individual or business that is commercially confidential and is not required to be included following a direction under subsection (7). That latter subsection allows the Secretary of State, on grounds of public interest, to authorise the inclusion of information on registers even though it is confidential. The section envisages two sequences of events giving rise to the issue and determination of confidentiality. First,[62] where a person supplies information in connection with an application for a licence or its modification, to comply with a licence condition or to comply with a section 71(2) notice,[63] he may apply to have the information excluded from the register on the ground that it is commercially confidential, either in relation to himself or another. The authority then has 14 days within which to make a determination; a failure so to do being regarded as a determination of commercial confidentiality. Alternatively,[64] if the authority receives information under any other Part II provision which it considers may be commercially confidential, it shall inform the person supplying it by notice that it will be included on the register unless excluded under this section and give him a reasonable opportunity of objecting to its inclusion and of making representations in support of that objection. If such representations are made the authority shall consider them in determining whether the information is commercially confidential. If the authority decides that the information is not commercially confidential, it shall delay entering it on the register for 21 days, within which time the person concerned has a right of appeal to the Secretary of State and, in the event of an appeal, until the appeal is resolved.[65]

Where information is excluded from the register on this ground it shall cease to be commercially confidential after four years, although the person concerned may apply for the information to remain excluded and the authority shall then again determine the matter. For these purposes information is to be regarded as commercially confidential 'in relation to any individual or person, if its being contained in the register would prejudice to an unreasonable degree the commercial interests of that individual or person'.[66] As has been said, the initial decision is for the authority. However, as with the exercise of discretionary powers by public authorities generally, these decisions may be challenged by judicial review on the grounds of unreasonableness or irrationality, bad faith and improper fettering.

Regulation 11 excludes two further categories of information from these section 64 registers. These are, first, information relating to any criminal proceedings before they are finally disposed of and, secondly, any monitoring information under (h) on the above list and any superceded information after four years from the time when it or the subsequent information was entered on the register.

Registration of Brokers

While the general waste management licensing structure provides the core control of the industry, and will occupy the next chapter, two ancillary functions are also made the subject of individual registration and are therefore to be dealt with here. First, registration of brokers of controlled waste is required by regulation 20 and Schedule 5 of the Waste Management Licensing Regulations 1994. Secondly, the Control of Pollution (Amendment) Act 1989 provides for the registration of carriers of waste, an activity that, because of a potential for generating damage and nuisance that has more often than not been realised in practice, has demanded the imposition of some measure of responsibility on its practitioners.

The duty of care requirement in section 34 of the 1990 Act applicable to persons having control of waste applies also to brokers.[67] Now, in addition to the

---

62 By section 66(2).

63 A section 71(2) notice may be served by the Secretary of State or the authority requiring any person to furnish the information specified in the notice.

64 By section 66(4).

65 Section 43(2) and (8) apply to these appeals.

66 Section 66(11).

67 See Chapter 14 at p.380.

waste management licence under section 33 applicable generally to persons handling controlled waste, regulation 20 of the Waste Management Licensing Regulations 1994[68] requires that any establishment or undertaking acting as a dealer and broker who 'arrange[s] for the disposal or recovery of controlled waste on behalf of another person' is to be registered. In spite of the subheading above, then, brokers as such do not require registration. These provisions only apply to an 'establishment or undertaking' that performs the broking function; but not if it is also licensed, or exempted, to carry out the disposal or recovery of waste or is registered as a carrier.[69] What is to be inferred from the use of the phrase 'establishment or undertaking' is difficult to see. Apparent attractions of the term are that it is very general in meaning and does not carry any burden of judicial commentary or authority. It may therefore be thought to embrace most, if not all, groups, bodies or organisations; a view supported by the specifically exempted establishments or undertakings noted below. The only apparent limitation to the term is that it would seem to be difficult to categorise an individual as an establishment or undertaking, although a person may engage in an undertaking.

It is in this latter sense that the term is used in the Radioactive Substances Act 1993, being defined in section 47(1) as including 'any trade, business or profession and, in relation to a public or local authority, includes any of the powers or duties of that authority, and, in relation to any other body or persons, whether corporate or unincorporate, includes any of the activities of that body'. Certain other bodies are also, by paragraph (4), exempt from this registration requirement, including:

(a) charities;[70]
(b) voluntary organisations within section 48(11) of the Local Government Act 1985;
(c) waste collection, disposal or regulation authorities;
(d) bodies applying before 1 January 1995, while the application is pending.

It has been seen that establishments or undertakings exempt from the waste management licensing requirement are nevertheless required to be registered.[71] No doubt for similar reasons the bodies exempted above, with the exception of the last, are required to be registered under regulation 12 of the Waste Management Licensing Regulations 1994[72] preparatory to arranging for the recovery or disposal of waste on behalf of another. Those bodies are to register with the waste regulation authority for the area in which they have their principal place of business and the authority shall enter on a register:

(a) the name of the establishment or undertaking;
(b) the address of its principal place of business;
(c) the address of any place at or from which it carries on its business.

Failure to register is a summary offence and registers are to be available for public inspection in the usual circumstances.

The enforcement and control provisions of the 1990 Act relating to the appointment of inspectors and the powers of entry and to obtain information apply here as they do to the Act. Breach of these obligations constitutes a summary offence attracting a fine up to level 5 on the standard scale. Schedule 5 governs registration, paragraph 2 of which places a duty on each waste regulation authority to establish and maintain a register of brokers of controlled waste[73] and to ensure

68 S.I. 1994 No. 1056.

69 Regulation 20(2) and (3).

70 For meaning of 'charity' see Chapter 10 at p.279.

71 See above.

72 S.I. 1994 No. 1056.

73 Registers shall also contain copies of applications (Schedule 5, paragraph 3(12)), details of appeals and the results (paragraph 3(15)), rejections of applications (paragraph 3(16)). Such matters may be removed from the register six years from the date the entry was made.

that it is open for public inspection at all reasonable hours free of charge and that copying facilities are available for a reasonable charge.

Applications for registration or renewal are to be made to the waste regulation authority for the area in which the applicant has his principal place of business and on the forms, or containing the information required by the forms, in the Schedule. The authority shall provide appropriate forms on request and shall charge fees for consideration of applications according to the scale in paragraph 3(11); the fee for a new application being £95. The information required includes, briefly:

(a) personal and business details, including the company name and, as the case may be, details of the directors or the partners. In the case of a partnership, all partners are to apply for registration and be registered;[74]

(b) details of any previous registration;

(c) any convictions of the applicant or other relevant person, for offences within regulation 3;

(d) details of any waste management licence or carrier registration.

The offences within regulation 3 are:

> section 22 of the Public Health (Scotland) Act 1897
> section 95(1) of the Public Health Act 1936
> section 60 of theTransport Act 1968
> sections 3, 5(6), 16(4), 18(2), 31(1), 32(1), 34(5), 78, 92(6), 93(3) of the Control of Pollution Act 1974
> section 2 of the Refuse Disposal (Amenity) Act 1978
> Control of Pollution (Special Waste) Regulations 1980
> section 9(1) of the Food and Environment Protection Act 1985
> Transfrontier Shipment of Hazardous Waste Regulations 1988
> Merchant Shipping (Prevention of Pollution by Garbage) Regulations 1988
> sections 1, 5, 6(9), 7(3) of the Control of Pollution (Amendment) Act 1989
> sections 107, 118(4), 175(1) of the Water Act 1989
> sections 23(1), 33, 34(6), 44, 47(6), 57(5), 59(5), 63(2), 69(9), 70(4), 71(3), 80(4) of the Environmental Protection Act 1990
> section 85, 202 or 206 of the Water Resources Act 1991
> section 33 of the Clean Air Act 1993.

The provisions of the Rehabilitation of Offenders Act 1974 relating to spent convictions apply.

The authority may refuse an application only where the procedure stipulated in paragraph 3 has not been followed, or where the applicant or other relevant person has been convicted of a relevant offence and the authority consider it undesirable for the applicant to be authorised to act as a broker. Such a refusal, with reasons, is to be notified to the applicant. An applicant has a right of appeal to the Secretary of State against a refusal, as he also has against either a failure to decide within the prescribed period or a revocation. Paragraph 6 governs the appeal procedure providing, *inter alia*, for contents of notice of appeal, notification of the authority by the appellant, the form of hearing and the Secretary of State's powers following the hearing.

On accepting an application, or following a successful appeal, the authority shall enter on the register in accordance with paragraph 4(1):

74 By paragraph 7(9) if any partner ceases to be registered or an unregistered partner joins the partnership registration automatically ends.

(a) the person and their registration number;
(b) date registration takes effect and expires;
(c) business name, address, phone and fax numbers and, if an individual, his date of birth;
(d) if a corporate body, the directors and officers;
(e) if a registered company, its registered number, and if incorporated outside Great Britain, its country of incorporation;
(f) details of any convictions for prescribed offences;
(g) if the applicant, or a company in the same group, is holder of a waste management licence or waste disposal licence, those details.

A copy of the entry shall then be supplied to the registered person free of charge, as shall a copy of any amended entry following renewal or notification of changed circumstances by the registered person as required by paragraph 4(6) and (7).

An authority may revoke a person's registration as a broker only if he, or another relevant person, has been guilty of a relevant offence and, in the authority's opinion, it is undesirable for the registered broker to continue to be authorised to arrange as a dealer or broker for the disposal or recovery of controlled waste on behalf of other persons. A registered broker may request the removal of his name from the register.[75] A registration or renewal shall generally be for a period of three years, there being special provisions to enable rationalisation of the registration periods of broker and carrier where both are held by the same person. The waste regulation authority is required, six months before the expiry date to so notify the broker and supply him with a renewal application. Where a renewal application is made within those six months the registration shall remain in force notwithstanding the passing of the expiry date until the application is withdrawn or accepted, or, where the authority refuses the renewal, until expiry of the appeal period or the applicant notifies his intention not to appeal.

75 Schedule 5 paragraph 7(4).

Registration of Carriers

The structure for control of the waste industry in the Control of Pollution Act 1974 exhibited a notable deficiency in that, being confined to operations occurring on licensed sites, it ignored the problems arising from and through the carriage of waste. Deriving from this uncontrolled transport of waste was the associated intractable problem of the casual dumping of waste on any available land, or fly-tipping. The first and current direct controls, that is apart from statutory nuisance or litter provisions, were enacted in the Control of Pollution (Amendment) Act 1989 and brought into operation on 1 April 1992 to give effect and meaning to section 34(3)(d) of the Environmental Protection Act 1990; that section being brought into operation on the same day.

Section 1 of the 1989 Act makes it an offence for

... any person who is not a registered carrier of controlled waste, in the course of any business of his or otherwise with a view to profit, to transport any controlled waste to or from any place in Great Britain.

In accordance with a general presumption of the criminal law and in the absence of any indication to the contrary in the provision, the necessary *mens rea* will be required to attach liability, in this case to the company or owner of the business concerned. The gap between the mind of the defaulting driver and that of his employer has to be bridged. The necessary implication of knowledge and there-fore responsibility, is achieved through section 33(5) of the Environmental Protection Act 1990, which provides that:

> Where controlled waste is carried in and deposited from a motor vehicle, the person who controls or is in a position to control the use of the vehicle shall ... be treated as know-ingly causing the waste to be deposited whether or not he gave instructions for this to be done.

The offence, which is actionable summarily,[76] is committed where the waste is transported in the course of a business or with a view of profit. This will exclude the householder taking his waste to the local tip or collection point. However, a business transporting waste derived from its commercial activities will be within the clause even though the transport of waste is not part of the business. Such businesses will include the producers of building and demolition waste. The extent to which the *de minimis* rule will apply, to say a sack of discarded office paper or stationery in the boot of an office manager's car, has yet to be determined.

Exceptions to the registration requirement are specified in section 1(2) and may be supplemented by regulations at the discretion of the Secretary of State. The statutory exceptions are the movement of waste within the same premises and the transport of waste into Great Britain before landing, or out of the country by air or sea. The current regulations, the Controlled Waste (Registration of Carriers and Seizure of Vehicles) Regulations 1991,[77] add the following further exceptions in regulation 2(1):

(a) waste collection authorities, waste disposal authorities and waste regulation authorities;
(b) the producer of controlled waste, except building or demolition waste;
(c) any wholly owned subsidiary of the British Railways Board that has applied for registration as a carrier of controlled waste;[78]
(d) a ferry operator in relation to carriage on the ferry of a vehicle carrying con-trolled waste;
(e) transport covered by the licensing provisions of Part II of the Food and Environment Protection Act 1985, including section 7 orders (sections 5 and 6);[79]
(f) a charity;[80]
(g) a voluntary organisation within section 48(11) of the Local Government Act 1985;
(h) a person having applied for registration before 1 April 1992 whose applica-tion is pending.

By regulation 2(2), building and demolition waste means 'waste arising from works of construction or demolition, including waste arising from works preparatory thereto' to which is now added 'construction includes improvement, repair or alteration'.[81]

It has been seen that establishments or undertakings exempt from the waste management licensing requirement are nevertheless required to be registered.[82] No doubt for similar reasons the bodies in categories (a), (c), (f) and (g) on the above list are required to be registered under paragraph 12 of Schedule 14 of the Waste Management Licensing Regulations 1994[83] if collecting or transporting waste on a professional basis and unless acting within the terms and conditions of a per-

76 Section 1(5).

77 S.I. 1991 No. 1624.

78 Amended by regulation 23 of the Waste Management Licensing Regulations 1994. The subsidiary is to be registered under paragraph 12 of Schedule 4 to those Regulations or have an application pending (dealing with registration of professional collectors and transporters of waste).

79 See on this at p.182 above.

80 For the meaning of 'charity' see Chapter 10 at p.279.

81 Added by regulation 10 of the Controlled Waste Regulations 1992, S.I. 1992 No. 588.

82 See above.

83 S.I. 1994 No. 1056.

mit. Those bodies are to register with the waste regulation authority for the area in which they have their principal place of business and the authority shall enter on a register:

(a) the name of the establishment or undertaking;
(b) the address of its principal place of business;
(c) the address of any place at or from which it carries on its business.

Failure to register is a summary offence and registers are to be available for public inspection in the usual circumstances.

The defences in section 1(4) broadly reproduce those in section 33(7) of the 1990 Act and include:

(a) that the waste was transported in an emergency of which notice was given, as soon as practicable after it occurred, to the disposal authority for that area;
(b) that the carrier did not know or reasonably suspect that what he was transporting was controlled waste and took all reasonable steps to ascertain whether it was such waste;
(c) that he acted under instructions from his employer.

In contrast to the scope of 'emergency' in the Act, which is limited to danger to the public, the meaning of the word is enlarged for present purposes to include 'serious danger to the public or serious risk of damage to the environment'. In such an event the use of an unregistered carrier may be necessary and may be used to avoid the risk. A further difference is in the employee's defence, which here merely requires that the defendant acted under his employer's instructions, thus omitting any additional requirement of knowledge or supposition that the act constituted an offence and so reducing its proof to a matter of fact and evidence.

The requirement of registration with disposal authorities to comply with section 1 as considered above is effected under regulations made by the Secretary of State within section 2. Matters to be covered by regulations are indicated in section 2(2) and (3) and are currently provided for in regulations 3 to 14 of the Controlled Waste (Registration of Carriers and Seizure of Vehicles) Regulations 1991.[84] Taking those regulations in order, regulation 3 requires authorities to keep registers of carriers of controlled waste, to ensure that they are open for free public inspection at all reasonable hours and that copying facilities are available at reasonable charges.

Applications for registration or for renewal are, by regulation 4, to be made to the authority in whose area the applicant has his primary place of business, using the form, or containing the information required by the form, in Part I of Schedule 2 and with the appropriate fee.[85] The required information includes:

(a) personal and business details, including the company name and, as the case may be, the directors or the partners. In the case of a partnership, all partners are to apply for registration and be registered;
(b) details of any previous registration;
(c) any convictions of the applicant or other relevant person, for offences within the regulations.

The offences[86] listed in the regulations are:

84 See note 77 above.

85 Currently £95 for an application and £65 for a renewal.

86 Note the exclusion of spent offences under the Rehabilitation of Offenders Act 1974.

section 22 of the Public Health (Scotland) Act 1897
section 95(1) of the Public Health Act 1936
section 60 of the Transport Act 1968
sections 3, 5(6), 16(4), 18(2), 31(1), 32(1), 34(5), 78, 92(6), 93(3) of the Control of Pollution Act 1974
section 2 of the Refuse Disposal (Amenity) Act 1978
Control of Pollution (Special Waste) Regulations 1980
section 9(1) of the Food and Environment Protection Act 1985
Transfrontier Shipment of Hazardous Waste Regulations 1988
Merchant Shipping (Prevention of Pollution by Garbage) Regulations 1988
sections 1, 5, 6(9), 7(3) of the Control of Pollution (Amendment) Act 1989
sections 107, 118(4), 175(1) of the Water Act 1989
sections 23(1), 33, 34(6), 44, 47(6), 57(5), 59(5), 63(2), 69(9), 70(4), 71(3), 80(4) of the Environmental Protection Act 1990.

Regulation 5 requires refusal of an application on procedural or substantive grounds, i.e.:

(a) for contravention of a regulation 4 requirement; or
(b) because the applicant or other relevant person has been convicted of a prescribed offence and in the opinion of the authority it is undesirable for the applicant to be authorised to transport controlled waste.

In this latter circumstance, where an offence was committed by some person other than the applicant, the authority, in accordance with section 3(6) of the Act, is to consider the extent to which the applicant 'has been a party to the carrying on of a business in a manner involving the commission of prescribed offences'. Should the authority decide to refuse the application, it is to notify the applicant of that decision, with its reasons. He then has a right of appeal under section 4(1) of the Act. Item (b) above and the section 3(6) qualification also, by regulation 10, govern the revocation of the registration. However, in the case of an appeal, and unlike the position in relation to the original application, the registration will remain in force until determination of the appeal.[87]

On accepting an application, or following a successful appeal, the authority shall enter on the register, as stipulated by regulation 6(1):

(a) the person and their registration number;
(b) the date registration takes effect and expires;
(c) business name, address, phone and fax numbers and, if an individual, his date of birth;
(d) if a corporate body, the directors and officers;
(e) if a registered company, its registered number, and if incorporated outside Great Britain, its country of incorporation;
(f) details of any convictions for prescribed offences;
(g) if the applicant, or a company in the same group, is holder of a waste management licence or waste disposal licence, those details.

The authority shall also issue free of charge a certificate of registration containing the Schedule 3 information, including name, registered number, business address and details, date of registration and expiry, and date of the last amendment. Under regulation 9, further copies are to be supplied on request and on payment. A reg-

87 Regulation 11(5).

istered person has a subsequent duty to notify the authority of any change of circumstances affecting the information on the register, with a comparable duty on the authority to amend the register and issue a new free certificate.[88]

Registration shall cease to have effect either if the registered carrier gives written notice requiring the removal of his name from the register,[89] or otherwise after three years from date of registration or renewal.[90] The authority is required to give the registered carrier six months' notice of the expiry with an application form for renewal. The registration then remains in force until either withdrawn or renewed if applied for within the six months, or until the period lapses. The registration of a partnership ceases if any partner ceases to be registered or if a non-registered person becomes a partner. When a registration ends[91] the authority is to record the fact in the register, the registered person then having a duty to return to the authority any certificate ceasing to have effect, with copies. Generally, entries shall be removed from the register six years after ceasing to have effect.

The control provisions applicable to the transport of waste are to be found in Chapter 15.

88 Regulation 8.

89 Section 3(2).

90 Regulation 11.

91 Either under regulation 11, or sections 3(2), 4(7) or 4(8) of the 1989 Act.

14

Waste Licensing

INTRODUCTION

1 'Managing Waste: The Duty of Care', Cmnd 9675, December 1985.

The 11th Report of the Royal Commission on Environmental Pollution,[1] at paragraph 1.12, provides a useful introduction to this subject:

> As far as their polluting effects are concerned, all forms of waste have one feature in common: waste, being no longer required by its owner, is consigned to the environment. By the act of consignment the waste may either find its final resting place, or it may pass into a state of transition – the waste stream. In either case, from the moment of consignment, it is a potential source of pollution, and this may largely be attributed to one or more of three features which many wastes share and which distinguish them from, for instance manufactured products – that waste is of little or no, or even negative, value; that there is often uncertainty about the composition of a waste; and that many waste streams exhibit a high degree of variability, both within and between loads. To prevent pollution from occurring there must be a secure waste stream, achieved through the exercise of a proper duty of care by producers, handlers and transporters of waste, and the ultimate means of disposal must be the best practicable environmental option.

The objectives in that final sentence may be regarded as the aim and purpose of the waste licensing process.

As has been indicated in introducing this subject, the most noticeable characteristic of early regulation was its absence. The handling, transport, storage and final disposal of waste were all equally regarded as the responsibility of the person having possession of it. The consequences can be envisaged. The remedy adopted by the Control of Pollution Act 1974 to remove the endemic laxity in the industry and attach responsibility to those engaged in its operation was to introduce a system of site licensing to regulate, initially, the disposal of waste. That original licensing structure has now been significantly strengthened and expanded by the implementation of Part II of the Environmental Protection Act 1990 and

2 S.I. 1994 No. 1056.

the introduction of the Waste Management Licensing Regulations 1994.[2] As well as disposal, the associated activities of handling, storage and treatment, which if improperly conducted may equally give rise to health, amenity and environmental problems, are now subject to regulation.

WASTE MANAGEMENT LICENSING

General licensing requirement

The requirement that activities relating to waste are to be licensed is to be found in section 33 of the Environmental Protection Act 1990, which provides that a person shall not:

(a) deposit controlled waste, or knowingly cause or knowingly permit controlled waste to be deposited in or on any land unless a waste management licence authorising the deposit is in force and the deposit is in accordance with the licence;

(b) treat, keep or dispose of controlled waste, or knowingly cause or knowingly permit controlled waste to be treated, kept or disposed of –

(i)   in or on any land, or

(ii) by means of any mobile plant,

except under and in accordance with a waste management licence;

(c) treat, keep or dispose of controlled waste in a manner likely to cause pollution of the environment or harm to human health.

Section 33(6) provides that 'a person who contravenes subsection (1) ... or any condition of a waste management licence commits an offence' which may be actionable summarily or on indictment.[3] The section continues, in subsections (2) and (3) respectively, to provide for two exceptions to this general licensing requirement. First, household waste from domestic premises treated, kept or disposed of within the curtilage of the dwelling by or with the permission of the occupier is excluded, although this exclusion does not extend to clinical wate, asbestos or any mineral or synthetic oil or grease.[4] Secondly, any categories prescribed in regulations made by the Secretary of State are excluded.[5]

This key section, forming the basis of the waste licensing and control structure, prohibits the deposit, treatment, keeping or disposal of controlled waste on land or by mobile plant unless authorised by a relevant waste management licence. As one would expect, the fact of re-enactment indicates and gives effect to a perceived need for reform. Practical experience in the operation of the Control of Pollution Act 1974 provisions revealed deficiencies, both of substance in the scope and application of the scheme to the full range of waste activities and procedurally.

The most apparent amendment is that indicated by a change of terminology, from 'waste disposal licence' in the 1974 Act to 'waste management licence', denoting a consequent increase in the range of the licensing process. A 'waste management licence' is defined in section 35(1) as a

> licence granted by a waste regulation authority authorising the treatment, keeping or disposal of any specified description of controlled waste in or on specified land or the treatment or disposal of any specified description of controlled waste by means of specified mobile plant

section 35(12) emphasising that such a licence may be either a 'site licence' or a 'mobile plant licence'. It will therefore be seen that any expansion in the range of activities to be licensed and implicit in the scope of waste management will be determined in part by the extent to which 'treatment' and 'keeping' add anything to 'disposal'.

By section 29(6), 'disposal' of waste includes its disposal by way of deposit in or on land. The terms 'disposal' and 'deposit' are evidently closely related but are not of course synonymous. In one sense the former word has a wider meaning than the latter, the deposit of waste on land in the context of landfill being merely one, though currently the commonest, method of disposal. Waste may of course be disposed of by other means such as incineration or by passing it on to another, as appears from the second of the cases now to be considered.

3 Section 33(9).

4 See Controlled Waste Regulations 1992, S.I. 1992 No. 588, regulation 3.

5 Section 33(4).

6 [1991] 2 Crim LR 298.

By the decision in *Leigh Land Reclamation Ltd* v *Walsall MBC* (1991),[6] 'deposit' had been confined to a final deposit on disposal, thus excluding intermediate stages or storage. This view has now been specifically disapproved in *R* v *Metropolitan Stipendiary Magistrate ex parte London Waste Regulation Authority* (1993),[7] the headnote reading:

7 [1993] 3 All ER 113, DC.

> the offence created by the 'deposit [of] controlled waste on any land,' was committed where waste was taken to a place from which it would later be transferred and was not restricted to final deposits or disposals since the purpose of the 1974 Act was to protect the environment from the consequences of dumping waste and it would unnecessarily erode the efficacy of the Act were it to be held that offences under section 3 could only be charged once the waste had reached its final place of deposit. Furthermore, on its ordinary meaning, 'disposal of' in the context of section 3(1)(b) implied 'getting rid of something' and did not import a final disposal, since an article could be regarded as being disposed of if it was destroyed or if it was passed on from one person to another.[8]

8 Section 3 of the Control of Pollution Act 1974 was the section re-enacted and amended by this section 33.

This latter definition is not only closer to normal usage but accords with its evident intended meaning in section 59.

It may perhaps be thought that this extended definition of 'deposit' has now been rendered superfluous by the inclusion within the current section 33 licensing provisions of 'keeping'. The terms do not however describe the same act. A deposit, as a single, finite action, will invariably precede the continuing process of keeping. Also, of course, the two activities may be performed by different persons, the waste being brought to and left at the site by someone other than the occupier who will be responsible for the subsequent keeping. Whether the two activities are undertaken by the same or different persons, the wording of the section makes it clear that each function constitutes a separate offence if unlicensed.

In the absence of statutory definition some consideration is required of the precise scope of 'keeping'; in particular, whether it is to be limited to an intentional or regular practice of storage or whether it may extend to a casual, individual deposit of waste for a limited time. Will any deposit of waste, however brief, constitute a keeping for licensing purposes? That it should not and that a line should be drawn having regard to the likely environmental consequences is indicated by the criteria in section 33(4) to be borne in mind by the Secretary of State in framing exclusionary regulations, i.e. that the waste is sufficiently small, temporary or innocuous as to warrant exclusion from the licensing requirement. That approach is also supported by a Canadian case which held that petrol remaining on premises for a short period due to an oversight was not 'kept' there.[9] It is also to be noted that the storage of household waste on the premises where it is produced is specifically exempted from the licensing requirement,[10] although whether this is due to its limited environmental impact or to the administrative burden of licensing every household is a matter for conjecture. Having regard to the common effect of these indicators and to the purpose of licensing, it would appear reasonable that in this context 'keeping' should not extend to the casual, isolated retention of innocuous waste for a strictly limited time.

9 *Blue* v *Pearl Assurance Co.* [1940] 3 WWR 13, at pp.19, 20.

10 Section 33(2), and see Collection and Disposal of Waste Regulations 1988,S.I. 1988 No. 819, regulation 9 and Schedule 6 paragraph 14.

So far as 'treatment' is concerned, section 29(6) provides that 'waste is 'treated' when it is subjected to any process, including making it re-usable or reclaiming substances from it'. Having regard to the range of processes that may be used in relation to the wide definition of waste in section 75(2), treatment would appear to cover all the activities from, say, baling or other preparation for transport or storage, through salvage or separation to destruction. The limiting requirement is that treatment is restricted to a process. This latter term received the attention of the House of Lords in *Nurse* v *Morganite Crucible Ltd* (1989)[11] concerning the prosecution of a company for breach of a duty to provide approved respiratory protective equipment where asbestos dust from a factory 'process' was liable to escape. The dust was produced during the demolition of equipment in the factory. In finding that such demolition was a process the Court held that:

> in the context of the Factories Act 1961 and the 1969 regulations the word 'process' was used in the broad sense of meaning any operation or series of operations to include an activity of more than minimal duration which had some degree of continuity or repetition of a series of acts.

Having regard to the similarity of purpose of this factory legislation and these environmental protection provisions, it is submitted that a correspondingly wide interpretation should be given to the word here. In further support for this view, for the purposes of the Clean Air Act 1968 'demolition' was stated to be a process within the phrase 'industrial or trade process' to apply the statute to the burning of rubbish on a demolition site.

In concluding this review of the meanings of these terms it is necessary to note the effect of paragraph 9(3) – (5) of Schedule 4 of the Waste Management Licensing Regulations 1994.[12] By paragraph 9(3), reference to the 'deposit' of controlled waste in or on land in sections 33(1)(a) and 69(2) of the Environmental Protection Act 1990 includes references to any operations listed in Parts III or IV of that Schedule involving such a deposit. Those two sections first prohibit the unlicensed deposit of controlled waste on land and, secondly, deal with powers of entry. Paragraph 9(4) provides that any reference to the 'treatment, keeping or disposal' of waste in sections 33(1)(b) and 69(2) shall be taken to be a reference to submitting controlled waste to any of the operations in Parts III and IV of the Schedule. Section 33(1)(b) prohibits the unlicensed treatment, keeping or disposal of controlled waste. Finally, paragraph 9(5) stipulates that any reference to the 'treatment, keeping or disposal' of controlled waste in sections 33(1)(c) and 35 shall include a reference to submitting controlled waste to any of the operations listed in Parts III or IV of Schedule 4. Section 33(1)(c) prohibits the treatment, keeping or disposal of controlled waste in a manner likely to cause pollution of the environment or harm to human health, and section 35 contains general provisions relating to waste management licensing.

It remains now to list the contents of Parts III and IV of the Schedule.

Part III of Schedule 4 lists the operations that are to be taken to constitute disposal:

1 Tipping of waste above or underground (e.g., landfill, etc.).
2 Land treatment of waste (e.g., biodegradation of liquid or sludge discards in soils, etc.).
3 Deep injection of waste (e.g., injection of pumpable discards into wells, salt domes or naturally occurring repositories, etc.).
4 Surface impoundment of waste (e.g., placement of liquid or sludge discards into pits, ponds or lagoons, etc.).
5 Specially engineered landfill of waste (e.g., placement of waste into lined discrete cells which are capped and isolated from one another and the environment, etc.).

11 [1989] 2 AC 692; 1 All ER 113.

12 S.I. 1994 No. 1056.

6 Release of solid waste into a water body except seas or oceans.

7 Release of waste into seas or oceans including seabed insertion.

8 Biological treatment of waste not listed elsewhere in this Part of this Schedule which results in final compounds or mixtures which are disposed of by means of any operations listed in this Part of this Schedule.

9 Physico-chemical treatment of waste not listed elsewhere in this Part of this Schedule which results in final compounds or mixtures which are disposed of by means of any of the operations listed in this Part of this Schedule (e.g., evaporation, drying, calcination, etc.).

10 Incineration of waste on land.

11 Incineration of waste at sea.

12 Permanent storage of waste (e.g., emplacement of containers in a mine, etc.).

13 Blending or mixture of waste prior to the waste being submitted to any of the operations listed in this Part of this Schedule.

14 Repackaging of waste prior to the waste being submitted to any of the operations listed in this Part of this Schedule.

15 Storage of waste pending any of the operations listed in this Part of this Schedule, but excluding temporary storage, pending collection, on the site where the waste is produced.

Part IV similarly lists activities that are to be regarded as waste recovery operations:

1 Reclamation or regeneration of solvents

2 Recycling or reclamation of organic substances which are not used as solvents

3 Recycling or reclamation of metals or metal compounds

4 Recycling or reclamation of other inorganic compounds

5 Regeneration of acids or bases

6 Recovery of components used for pollution abatement

7 Recovery of components from catalysts

8 Re-refining, or other re-uses, of oil which is waste

9 Use of waste principally as a fuel or for other means of generating energy

10 Spreading of waste on land resulting in benefit to agriculture or ecological improvement, including composting and other biological transformation processes, except in the case of waste excluded under Article 2(1)(b)(iii) of the Directive

11 Use of wastes obtained from any of the operations listed in paragraphs 1 to 10 of this Part of this Schedule

12 Exchange of wastes for submission to any of the operations listed in paragraphs 1 to 11 of this Part of this Schedule

13 Storage of waste consisting of materials intended for submission to any operation listed in this Part of the Schedule, but excluding temporary storage, pending collection, on the site where it is produced.

Where and to the extent that any of the operations in either of these lists includes or involves the deposit of waste, to that extent they will determine the meaning and scope of 'deposit'.

The meaning and scope of 'cause or knowingly permit' has been discussed in Chapter 1. This present statute, however, requires that the defendant should 'knowingly cause' as well as 'knowingly permit', clearly a narrower provision requiring more than the act alone. The precise scope and indeed location of the knowledge required in the case of a company charged with 'knowingly permitting' was considered by the Divisional Court in this context in *Ashcroft* v *Cambro Waste Products Ltd* (1981).[13] The defendants operated a waste disposal site under a disposal licence from the county council. At different times oil waste and bags of blue asbestos were deposited on the site without being covered with adequate material, and therefore in breach of conditions. The site foreman, who was responsible for the operation of the site but had no delegated management functions, was aware of the contravention of the licence conditions. The company director with overall responsibility for the site had no actual or constructive knowledge of the contraventions. The justices, considering that knowledge by the company was an essential element of the offence and that the foreman was not a directing mind of the company, dismissed the informations. The Court concluded, allowing the appeal by the prosecutor, that the offence in section 3(1) relating to the deposit of controlled waste on any land was committed unless such deposit was in fact in accordance with the conditions of a valid licence. Therefore, to establish the offence of 'knowingly permitting' it was for the prosecution to establish that the deposit had been knowingly permitted, but that it was unnecessary to prove knowledge of the breach of condition. It is sufficient then to establish knowledge of the fact of the deposit and additional evidence of knowledge that it was unauthorised or in breach of condition is unnecessary. This is evidently right. The alternative, where various levels of knowledge may be fragmented among a number of employees, as illustrated by these present facts, would make the imposition of liability on a defaulting company an uncertain business.

A further significant development, introduced by section 33(6), is that breach of any licence condition is now in itself an offence, whether or not it relates to the actual deposit, keeping or treatment of waste. In consequence, what might be thought of as peripheral, though nevertheless important, matters of general site management and subsequent maintenance will be more readily subject to control, provided that appropriate conditions were included in the licence. Establishing the breach of a condition is also likely to be a less onerous task for a waste regulation authority than that of proving that a defendant has deposited or knowingly caused or permitted a deposit. It is nevertheless apparent that the range of licence conditions directly affects the scope of control under the new licensing provisions. In determining the scope of conditions section 35(3) provides that they

may relate –

(a) to the activities which the licence authorises, and
(b) to the precautions to be taken and works to be carried out in connection with or in consequence of those activities;

and accordingly requirements may be imposed in the licence which are to be complied with before the activities which the licence authorises have begun or after the activities which the licence authorises have ceased.

This is clear and requires little explanation. It is common to find that before disposal operations commence preparatory works to prevent leaching into groundwater from a landfill site are necessary. The continuing obligations that may be imposed on operators of landfill sites after the site is completed and closed and

13 [1981] 1 WLR 1349.

14 *Cambridge Water Co. v Eastern Counties Leather plc* (1993) *The Times*, 10 December.

15 See section 6(2).

16 Section 35(7).

17 S.I.1994 No. 1056.

18 Guidance on licence conditions with examples and model conditions may be found in Waste Management Paper No. 4 on The Licensing of Waste Facilities, (HMIP) and Code of Practice for Liaison between the London Waste Regulation Authority and the London Boroughs on the Planning and Licensing of Waste Disposal Activities in London (July 1988).

19 Environmental Protection Act 1990 (London: Sweet and Maxwell, 1991) p.90.

20 Section 33(1)(b)(ii).

until the contents are stable and any impact on the surroundings has ceased, while constituting a necessary extension of control, may place heavy, long-term burdens on those operators. Also, as is indicated in a different context by the Cambridge Water case,[14] the progressively increasing environmental quality standards, stemming in part from the European Community, can be expected to increase such burdens.

The Control of Pollution Act 1974 listed a number of matters that may be the subject of conditions.[15] While that has not been repeated in this present statute the same range of conditions may no doubt be included at the discretion of the waste regulation authority and subject to the power of direction by the Secretary of State.[16] Section 35(6) gives the Secretary of State power to make regulations governing licence conditions. To that end regulation 13 of the Waste Management Licensing Regulations 1994[17] excludes conditions relating solely to securing the health of persons at work. The Secretary of State has indicated that while standards of waste handling and disposal need to be maintained, conditions should be reasonable in that they should:

(a) reflect the nature and scale of operations on and the circumstances of a particular site;

(b) afford adequate protection to local amenities from operations on the site; and

(c) not impose an unreasonable burden on the operator.[18]

Before leaving the question of licence conditions, it may be noted that the terms of section 35(4) stipulate that conditions may require the licensee to carry out works or do other things even though having no title or right to do so, and any person whose consent is required shall grant such rights in relation to the land as will enable the licence holder to comply with the licence conditions. On the face of it an otherwise uninvolved third party may therefore be faced with an obligation necessitating cost and disturbance and with no provision for consultation, compensation or right of appeal, such rights being limited, by section 43(1), to the applicant or to the holder, former holder or transferee of a licence. It is difficult to know what to make of, or indeed how to justify, such a draconian provision unless by recourse to the presumed overriding environmental need. It appears that any mitigation of its harshness can only be sought in the good sense of the authority responsible for imposing the conditions. In an attempt to find some rational interpretation or application of the provision, Tromans suggests[19] 'that the subsection simply allows the authority to make such consent a condition precedent of the licensed activities', but noting that 'while that interpretation seems more workable [it] could not be achieved without considerable violence to the actual words'.

The licensing scheme is also extended by the introduction of a 'mobile plant licence' for such plant used to treat, keep or dispose of controlled waste.[20] Section 35(12) defines 'mobile plant licence' as a 'licence authorising the treatment or disposal of waste by means of mobile plant'. The comparable provision in section 3(1)(b) of the Control of Pollution Act 1974 applied to plant or equipment whether mobile or not, used on land and therefore being included with other methods of disposal in the licence for that site. Under this provision it is the plant that is licensed, independently of its location. Subject to the power of the Secretary of State to make prescriptive regulations on the matter, 'mobile' plant is, by section 29(9), 'plant which is designed to move or be moved whether on roads or other land'. This is a question of fact, and whether it is designed to move or not is a different question from whether it is actually movable. 'Designed' may mean either an intention to that effect, or designed in structural or engineering terms.[21] Being mobile, the responsible licensing body is the waste regulation authority for the area in which the operator of the plant has his principal place of business.

In addition to the general prohibition on the unlicensed handling of controlled waste, section 33(1)(c) prohibits the treatment, keeping or disposal of controlled waste in a manner likely to cause pollution of the environment or harm to human health. On the assumption that the licence conditions may not anticipate every possible future eventuality, the mere unthinking conformity with the licence will no longer be enough. Now the essential underlying purpose of the legislation is secured by prohibiting *de facto* pollution, even in cases where licence conditions are satisfied. The 'environment' and 'pollution of the environment' are defined for this purpose respectively in section 29(2) and (3). The former provides that the 'environment consists of all, or any, of the following media namely land, water or air' and the latter that 'pollution of the environment' means pollution of the environment due to the release or escape (into any environmental medium) from:

(a) the land on which controlled waste is treated;
(b) the land on which controlled waste is kept;
(c) the land on which controlled waste is deposited;
(d) fixed plant by means of which controlled waste is treated, kept or disposed of:

of substances or articles constituting or resulting from the waste and capable (by reason of the quantity or concentrations involved) of causing harm to man or any other living organisms supported by the environment. It would seem that 'substances ... resulting from the waste' is wide enough to cover not only its original constituents but also products derived from the combination or interaction of different types of waste after deposit. Operators of disposal sites must therefore have regard to the possible consequences of mixing wastes during disposal, or indeed changes generated by the particular form or place of disposal.

As 'pollution of the environment' is defined to include the causing of harm to man, it is difficult to see what is added by 'harm to human health'. Indeed, 'harm to man' taken in conjunction with the escape of articles may be the wider term as embracing physical injury which has been excluded in the interpretation of health.[22] Both terms may be regarded as wider than 'public health' which refers to the health of society or a community at large and therefore may not extend to harm or danger to persons as individuals. That restriction no longer applies, and whether the discharged materials may cause risk of illness or injury to the public at large, to a neighbour, to an individual employee or to a visitor to the site or its locality, it will be caught by this provision. In relation to risk, it may be emphasised that both the definition of pollution of the environment and the section 33(1)(c) offence are framed in preclusive terms, it being unnecessary to show the occurrence of, or indeed to wait for, actual pollution. Whether an occurrence is likely imports an appropriate degree of possibility, it being equated with a 'reasonable prospect' of something happening.[23] In *R v Sheppard* (1980),[24] concerning the prosecution of parents for causing the death of their 16-month-old child by neglect, Lord Diplock said that 'The word is imprecise. It is capable of covering a whole range of possibilities from "it's on the cards" to "it's more probable than not"'.

21 *Wilson v West Sussex CC* [1963] 2 QB 764.

22 See per Lord Widgery CJ in *Coventry City Council v Cartwright* [1975] 2 All ER 99 at pp.102f and 104c.

23 Per James LJ in *Dunning v Liverpool Hospitals Board* [1973] 2 All ER 454 at p.460g.

24 3 All ER 899, HL.

The preceding discussion has been confined to the terms of section 33 and the requirement that activities involving controlled waste are to be authorised and controlled through the licensing structure. It will also be apparent that, referring to the definitions of the constituent categories of controlled waste, very little is excluded. Before proceeding to the mechanics of the licensing process, however, it may be observed that the handling of uncontrolled waste, that is waste from mines and quarries and from agriculture, is also subject to control. Section 63(2) provides that:

a person who –

(a) deposits any waste other than controlled waste, or
(b) knowingly causes or knowingly permits the deposit of waste other than controlled waste,

in a case where, if the waste were special waste and any waste management licence were not in force, he would be guilty of an offence under section 33 above shall, ... be guilty of that offence and punishable accordingly.

Offences concerning uncontrolled waste are therefore assimilated broadly to the unlicensed handling of special waste. Such action shall not be an offence where taken under the authority of any statute with the exception of planning provisions, whether under a consent, licence, approval or authority.

Section 63(1) also gives the Secretary of State the power, following consultation with such bodies as he deems appropriate, to make regulations applicable in a prescribed area applying the stated Part II provisions, modified if necessary, governing controlled waste to those categories.

Exemptions

Turning now to the exemptions from these licensing requirements, reference has already been made to that for household waste on the originating premises.[25] The other exemption, in section 33(3), is for cases prescribed in regulations made by the Secretary of State. In making such regulations he is to have particular regard to the exclusion of small, temporary or innocuous deposits, and also to cases for which adequate controls are provided under other provisions. The current exemptions are to be found in regulation 9 and Schedule 6 of the Collection and Disposal of Waste Regulations 1988,[26] the Disposal of Controlled Waste (Exceptions) Regulations 1991[27] and regulations 16 and 17 and Schedule 3 of the Waste Management Licensing Regulations 1994.[28] It will be seen that the 1994 Regulations provide for the same range of exemptions, with modifications, as the earlier instruments, although there is no indication that the earlier legislation is repealed. Indeed, as the 1994 Regulations amend those of 1988, the latter clearly remain in being.

Regulation 9(1) of the 1988 Regulations provides that, subject to paragraphs (2) and (3), Schedule 6 prescribes cases 'in which a disposal licence is not required for the deposit of controlled waste on land or for the use of plant or equipment for the purpose of disposing of such waste'. The two stipulated paragraphs respectively exclude cases where the presence of waste on land is liable to give rise to an environmental hazard within section 4(5) and exclude the operation of paragraphs 1–14, 16 and 17 of Schedule 6 where the waste is special waste. 'Special waste' is defined for these purposes in regulation 2(1) of the Control of Pollution (Special

25 See note 56 above.

26 S.I. 1988 No. 819; amended byS.I. 1989 No. 1968.

27 S.I. 1991 No. 508.

28 See note 2 above.

Waste) Regulations 1980.[29] The definition of 'environmental hazard' in section 4(5) of the Control of Pollution Act 1974 is not retained in the 1990 Act, nor is the term defined in any of the regulations. As the 1988 Regulations were made under the 1974 Act that statutory definition may perhaps still be applied. Should that be the case, the phrase is there defined as:

29 S.I. 1980 No. 1709; see at p.437–441 below.

(a) the presence of waste on land gives rise to an environmental hazard if the waste has been deposited in such a manner or in such a quantity (whether that quantity by itself or cumulatively with other deposits of the same or different substances) as to subject persons or animals to a material risk of death, injury or impairment of health or as to threaten the pollution (whether on the surface or underground) of any water supply; and
(b) the fact that waste is deposited in containers shall not of itself be taken to exclude any risk which might be expected to arise if the waste were not in containers.

While this definition has been repealed, it bears sufficient similarity to 'relevant objectives' in paragraph 4(1) of Part I of Schedule 4 of the Waste Management Licensing Regulations 1994 to have been its progenitor.[30]

30 See below at p.376.

Schedule 6 to the Regulations lists cases in which a disposal licence is not required. The list is divided into three parts:

1–17 deposit of waste on land,
18 disposal of waste by use of plant or equipment,
19–23 use of plant or equipment to deal with waste as prescribed by regulation 8, i.e., processing, use or storage.[31]

31 The methods prescribed by regulation 8 are listed in Schedule 5 of the Regulations.

A synopsis of the first part will sufficiently indicate its scope for present purposes, relating to the deposit of:

1 effluent or waste under a section 34 consent;
2 waste under a Part II Food and Environment Protection Act 1985 licence, and those covered by a licence exemption under section 7;
3 hardcore in association with construction on that site;
4 excavated material from peatworking, boreholes and excavations in connection with mineral extraction or water supply;
5 railway ballast and dredged material on adjacent land;
6 sewage sludge in a lagoon or container or on land for agricultural purposes;[32]
7 sewage from passenger rail vehicles or removable receptacles from other than domestic premises;
8 waste temporarily on the premises on which it is produced, including certain specified categories of special waste;
9 waste paper or rags with the approval of the occupier and pending disposal elsewhere.

32 Where waste is to be deposited on land, Schedule 6, paragraph 13(3) stipulates the information to be given to the disposal authority prior to the deposit.

The second part covers the disposal of waste as an integral part of the industrial process that produces it. The five processes in the third part of the schedule include –

19 Baling, compacting, pulverising or sorting waste on the premises on which it is produced.
20 Baling, sorting or shredding waste paper or rags.
21 Storing waste, including special waste of the categories specified in part 1, on the premises on which it is produced.

22 Incinerating waste, except special waste, on the premises on which it is produced in plant of a capacity less than 200 kg per hour.
23 Using waste oil as fuel to produce heat.

Licences under sections 5 and 6 of Part II of the Food and Environment Protection Act 1985 deal with the deposit of material at sea. Under those provisions licences are required for the deposit of substances or articles either in the sea or under the sea bed within United Kingdom waters from any vessels, aircraft, structures and so on, or anywhere in the sea or sea bed from such British owned vessels or structures. By section 7 the Ministers are given the power to specify by order operations:

(a) which are not to need a licence; or
(b) which are not to need a licence if satisfying conditions specified in the order.

33 S.I. 1985 No. 1699.

The current order is the Deposits at Sea (Exemption) Order 1985.[33]

The Disposal of Controlled Waste (Exceptions) Regulations 1991 exempt certain processes from the Part II requirements where, apart from final disposal by deposit in or on land, any deposit, disposal or dealing with controlled waste either:

34 See Environmental Protection (Prescribed Processes and Substances) Regulations, S.I. 1991 No. 472, at Chapter 2, p.49.

(a) is, or forms part of, a process designated under section 2(4) of the 1990 Act for central or local control[34] and authorised under section 6; or
(b) is listed in the Schedule as being or forming part of a process for the time being designated for local control.

As final disposal of controlled waste by deposit in or on land is specifically excluded from regulation under Part I of the Act, i.e., IPC authorisation, licensing under these provisions will apply to that part of any process. The Schedule referred to in (b) above lists the following processes within Part B of Schedule I to the Environmental Protection (Prescribed Processes and Substances) Regulations 1991, reproduced here in abbreviated form:

2 using straw, poultry litter or wood as fuel;
3 using tyres as a fuel;
4 operation, loading and unloading of a scrap metal furnace;
5 pulverising bricks, tiles or concrete;
6 depositing glass;
7 incinerating waste, depositing animal remains at an incinerator for burning and other operations ancillary thereto.

Regulation 16 of the 1994 Regulations excludes specified activities that are subject to control under other provisions and are therefore excluded from this licensing regime; while regulation 17 provides that, subject to certain qualifications in the regulation, the matters listed in Schedule 3 to the Regulations are also excluded from the licensing obligation. As has been said, these two regulations in effect repeat, extend and add detail to the terms of the regulations just considered.

Subject to the proviso that final disposal of waste by deposit in or on land is excluded, regulation 16(1) exempts from these licensing provisions:

(a) the recovery or disposal of waste under an authorisation granted under Part I of the Act where it forms part of a process designated for central control under section 2(4);
(b) the disposal of waste by incineration forming part of a process within Part B of Section 5.1 of Schedule I to the 1991 Regulations;

(c) the disposal of liquid waste under a consent under Chapter II of Part III of the Water Resources Act 1991 or under Part II of the Control of Pollution Act 1974; and

(d) the recovery or disposal of waste forming part of an operation being either –
  (i) the subject of a licence under Part II of the Food and Environment Protection Act 1985; or
  (ii) for which a licence as above would be required but for an order under section 7 of that Act.

By regulation 17, the activities listed in Schedule 3 are exempted from these licensing requirements. The Regulations, and especially the schedule, should be consulted for their detail. In considering the synopsis it is to be remembered that, as provided for in regulation 17:

(a) where appropriate an activity on land will be exempt only where the person concerned is entitled or has the authority of the occupier to so use the land;

(b) subject to stipulated exceptions, activities involving special waste will not be exempt;

(c) exemption will apply to the disposal or recovery of waste by an establishment or undertaking only if the type of waste and method of operation are consistent with the attainment of the 'relevant objectives';

(d) a container, lagoon or place is secure if reasonable precautions are taken to ensure that waste cannot escape and the public cannot gain access, and 'secure storage' is to be interpreted accordingly.

'Relevant objectives' are specified in paragraph 4(1) of Part I of Schedule 4 as:

(a) ensuring that waste is recovered or disposed of without endangering human health and without using processes or methods which could harm the environment, and in particular without –
  (i) risk to water, air, soil, plants or animals; or
  (ii) causing nuisance through noise or odours; or
  (iii) adversely affecting the countryside or places of special interest;

(b) implementing, so far as material, any plan made under the plan-making provisions.[35]

As a very brief synopsis of the 43 extensive, detailed paragraphs in Schedule 3 listing 'Activities Exempt From Waste Management Licensing' and to provide an indication of its content, there follows:

(1) storage and use of waste glass, up to 600,000 tonnes p.a.;

(2) operation under a Part I authorisation (i.e., IPC control) of a scrap metal furnace of up to 25 tonnes capacity;

(3) the secure storage and burning as fuel of straw, poultry litter, wood, tyres or manufactured fuel under a Part I authorisation;

(4) refurbishment of packing or containers, up to 1,000 tonnes per week;

(5) secure storage and burning of waste as fuel in an appliance of net rated thermal input of less than 0.4 MW and of waste oil as fuel in specified types of vehicles;

(6) the spreading on certain categories of land of a specified range of waste materials for agricultural or ecological improvement subject to certain limitations and controls and notification of the waste regulation authority;

35 The plan-making provisions, by paragraph 1 of Schedule 4, 'means paragraph 5 below, section 50 of the 1990 Act, and Part II of the Town and Country Planning Act 1990 ...'. Paragraph 5 provides for the preparation of offshore waste management plans.

(7) the recovery of sewage and septic tank sludge within the curtilage of a sewage works, including that from other works, up to 10,000 cubic metres p.a.;

(8) composting biodegradable waste at the place where it is produced or is to be used, up to specified maxima;

(9) the manufacture of board, bricks, blocks, roadstone, aggregate, soil or soil substitutes from waste from demolition, construction, tunnelling or other excavation work;

(10) the manufacture of finished goods from waste metal, plastic, glass, ceramics, rubber, textiles, wood, paper or cardboard;

(11) the benefical use of waste without further treatment;

(12) activities authorised under a licence granted under Articles 7 or 8 of the Diseases of Animals (Waste Food) Order 1973;[36]

(13) storage of specified categories and limited quantities of recyclable materials;

(14) storage on site of waste from construction and associated work for re-use on site;

(15) laundering or other cleaning of waste textiles preparatory to re-use;

(16) treatment and processing of wood and plant material up to 1,000 tonnes per week, for re-use;

(17) recovery and storage of silver from printing and photographic processing from up to 50,000 litres of waste per day;

(18) keeping and treatment of animal by-products in accordance with the Animal By-products Order 1992;[37]

(19) crushing, grinding or other size reduction of waste bricks, tiles or concrete under a Part I authorisation;

(20) deposit of waste and plant material from dredging of inland waters on the banks of such waters;

(21) recovery, disposal, storage, baling, compacting, crushing, shredding or pulverising of waste where it is produced;

(22) the incineration of waste where it is produced in an exempt incinerator for the purposes of Section 5.1 of Part I to the 1991 Regulations;[38]

(23) burning of wood and plant matter on the land where it is produced in connection with specified land use, e.g., woodland, parks, gardens, verges, recreation grounds, church yards or cemeteries;

(24) discharge onto the track of waste not exceeding 25 litres from a sanitary convenience or sink in a railway passenger vehicle;

(25) burial on the premises of contents of chemical and earth closets, up to 5 cubic metres p.a.;

(26) storage and disposal on site of peatworking waste;

(27) storage and disposal on site of spent ballast from rail and tramways, up to 10 tonnes per metre of track;

(28) deposit on site of material from mineral exploration boreholes, up to 45,000 cubic metres per hectare p.a.;

(29) temporary storage for up to seven days of garbage from ships in a harbour in accordance with the Merchant Shipping (Reception Facilities for Garbage) Regulations 1988[39] and similarly of tank washings in accordance with the Prevention of Pollution (Reception Facilities) Order 1984[40] (including special waste);

(30) burial of a dead domestic pet in the garden of the property where it lived;

36 S.I. 1973 No. 1936.

37 S.I. 1992 No. 3303.

38 See in Chapter 2, IPC control at p.50.

39 S.I. 1988 No. 2293.

40 S.I. 1984 No. 862.

(31) deposit or storage of samples of waste at the place where they are to be tested or analysed;

(32) the secure storage at a pharmacy of waste medicines for up to six months (including special waste);

(33) the storage in secure containers of non-liquid waste incidental to the collection or transport of waste, up to 50 cubic metres and for up to three months;

(34) the storage of waste, for up to 12 months, pending collection on the site where it is produced, with specific stipulations covering special waste;

(35) treatment, keeping or disposal of scrap metal or waste motor vehicles if carried on before 1 May 1994 and an application was made before that date for a disposal licence under Part I of the Control of Pollution Act 1974, while the application is pending (includes special waste);

(36) treatment, keeping or disposal of waste if carried on before 1 May 1994 and before that date no disposal licence was required under Part I of the Control of Pollution Act 1974 (includes special waste).

The assumption in these exempted cases is that for various reasons the full regulatory procedure consequent upon licensing is unnecessary. It is however desirable that the operation of exempted activities, and the identity of the persons responsible for them, should at least be known and recorded. It is for this reason that activities in Schedule 3 exempted from licensing are required, by regulation 18, to be registered with the appropriate registration authority. In some cases the activity is the subject of a licensing or registration requirement under other legislation. In those cases the appropriate registration authority will be that responsible body; which will usually be the local authority or the appropriate Minister. In all other cases the appropriate registration authority is the waste regulation authority.

The structure of registration presents some inherent inconsistency, in that regulation 18(1) makes the engagement of an establishment or undertaking in an exempt activity involving the recovery or disposal of waste without registration a summary offence. However, there is no overt obligation on such a body to seek registration. The corresponding duty, such as it is, placed on the registering authority is to enter the relevant particulars in the register if it receives written notice of them or otherwise becomes aware of them. There is an implication of, or at least the potential for, passivity on both sides. The risk of prosecution gives an operator an evident interest in ensuring registration. The process is informal in the extreme, though, and indeed may apparently occur even without the person registered knowing of it.

The particulars to be registered are:

(a) the name and address of the establishment or undertaking;
(b) the activity which constitutes the exempt activity; and
(c) the place where the activity is carried on.

As is usual, the register is to be available for free public inspection at all reasonable hours with copies at reasonable charges.

General defences

Returning to section 33 of the Environmental Protection Act 1990, subsection (7) lists the general defences to a prosecution under the section. The four defences in section 3(4) of the 1974 Act are here reduced to three, the claim that the defendant took all such steps as were reasonably open to him to ensure that the conditions were complied with being no longer available. Irrespective of the reasonableness or otherwise of the licensee's actions, therefore, the conditions either were or were not complied with. While such a claim is no longer relevant to conviction, though, it may still be material to sentencing. Of the retained defences, section 33(7)(b) and (c) correspond to section 3(4)(b) and (d) respectively, i.e., the defences of employer's instructions, subject to the proviso that the defendant had no reason to believe that the acts done constituted a contravention of subsection (1), and that the contravention arose from emergency action to avoid danger to the public. In the latter case the waste regulation authority is to be informed 'as soon as reasonably practicable'.

The first defence, in section 33(7)(a), is in simpler but wider terms than its predecessor, providing that the defendant 'took all reasonable precautions and exercised all due diligence to avoid the commission of the offence'. The presence of fault is therefore necessary to establish liability. What amounts to 'reasonable precautions' was considered by Lord Goff in *Austin Rover Ltd* v *H.M. Inspector of Factories* (1989),[41] albeit in the context of factory legislation:

> Where liability is imposed subject to the limited qualification 'so far as reasonably practicable,' the element of the likelihood of the risk eventuating is taken account of in the balancing exercise involved in deciding whether or not it was reasonably practicable to ensure the safety of the premises for the relevant use.

In undertaking this exercise it is of course difficult, but necessary, to surrender the clarity of vision derived from hindsight and consider the equation from the point of view of the reasonable man finding himself having to make such provision before the event. Concerning the 'due diligence' defence, Willmer LJ[42] has suggested that 'An obligation to exercise due diligence is to my mind indistinguishable from an obligation to exercise reasonable care'. In the same case Morris LJ[43] said: 'It seems to me that the question whether a carrier has exercised due diligence to make a ship seaworthy is primarily a question of fact. ... It must depend on the particular features and circumstances of each particular case'.

The second defence is that the defendant was acting under the instructions of his employer and neither knew nor had reason to suppose that the acts done by him constituted a contravention of subsection (1). The existence of the reason and of the supposition founded on it are matters of fact and therefore evidence. The grounds on which the defendant acted must be sufficient to induce in a reasonable person the required supposition.[44] Thirdly, it is a defence to show that the offence resulted from actions taken in an emergency in order to avoid danger to the public and that, as soon as reasonably practicable after they were done, particulars were furnished to the waste regulation authority. 'Reasonably practicable' has been said,[45] with particular reference to its use in safety legislation, to be:

> a narrower term than 'physically possible,' and implies that a computation must be made, before the breach complained of, in which the quantum of risk is placed in one scale and the sacrifice involved in the measures necessary of averting the risk (whether in money, time or trouble) is placed in the other, and that, if it be shown that there is a gross disproportion between them, the risk being insignificant in relation to the sacrifice, the person upon whom the obligation is imposed discharges the onus which is upon him.[46]

Earlier Lord Oaksey had said[47] that 'what is "reasonably practicable" depends upon a consideration whether the time, trouble and expense of the precautions

41 [1989] 3 WLR 520 at p.527 HL.

42 In *Riverstone Meat Co.* v *Lancashire Shipping Co.* [1960] 1 All ER 193 at p.219h.

43 At p.199a.

44 See especially *McArdle* v *Egan* (1933) 150 LT 412, All ER Rep 611, CA; *Nakkuda Ali* v *Jayaratne* [1951] AC 66, PC.

45 Halsbury's Laws of England, vol. 20 (4th edn), paragraph 553.

46 See, e.g., *Edwards* v *NCB* [1949] 1 KB 704 at p.712, 1 All ER 743 at p.747, CA; *McCarthy* v *Coldair Ltd* [1951] 2 TLR 1226, CA; *Marshall* v *Gotham Co. Ltd* [1954] AC 360 at p.373, 1 All ER 937 at p.942, HL.

47 In *Marshall* v *Gotham Co. Ltd* [1954] AC 360.

suggested are disproportionate to the risk involved'. As a concluding general principle, it is to be remembered that the standard of proof required of the defence in criminal proceedings is not as onerous as that on the prosecution, being discharged by satisfying the court on a balance of probability rather than beyond reasonable doubt.[48]

48 See *R* v *Carr-Briant* [1943] KB 607, 2 All ER 156; *R* v *Dunbar* [1958] 1 QB 1, [1957] 2 All ER 737.

The duty of care

A major problem in the handling and disposal of waste in the past was the ease with which the material and responsibility could be disposed of, whether by fly-tipping or by delivery to an indifferent vehicle operator who himself found the cheapest convenient site on which to dump it. Loss of possession, however it was achieved, carried with it total relief from any concern over the waste's subsequent fate or consequences. In a significant addition to the preceding control structure the Environmental Protection Act 1990 seeks to create a proper sense of responsibility in persons involved in the handling of waste by imposing on them a statutory duty of care. The value, or indeed necessity, of such an approach was advocated in the 11th Report of the Royal Commission on Environmental Pollution[49]:

49 Managing Waste, The Duty of Care', Cmnd 9675, December 1985.

> 3.3 Because of the particular characteristics that distinguish wastes from manufactured products and other articles of value, it may be necessary to change the constraints which govern the fate of wastes in the environment, if we wish to see a reduction in pollution. ... The objective of such changes must be to ensure the long-term integrity and security of the waste stream – a term which we use to mean the life history of an item of waste from the point at which it originates to the point at which it ceases to be waste or is finally disposed of.

> 3.4 The first task is for society to identify where the responsibility lies for ensuring that wastes are properly handled and disposed of. In our judgement this must rest with the individual or organisation who produces the wastes. The producer incurs a duty of care which is owed to society, and we would like to see this duty reflected in public attitudes and enshrined in legislation and codes of practice.

Adopting this approach, section 34(1) of the 1990 Act provides that:

... it shall be the duty of a person who imports, produces, carries, keeps, treats or disposes of controlled waste or, as a broker has control of such waste, to take all such measures applicable to him in that capacity as are reasonable in the circumstances –

(a) to prevent any contravention by any other person under section 33 above;
(b) to prevent the escape of the waste from his control or that of any other person; and
(c) on the transfer of waste to secure –
   (i) that the transfer is only to an authorised person or to a person for authorised transport purposes; and
   (ii) that there is transferred such a written description of the waste as will enable other persons to avoid a contravention of that section and to comply with the duty under this subsection as respects the escape of waste.

Persons involved in the 'waste stream' not only have a duty of care for their own activities, but are hereby constituted their brother's keepers. They have a statutory duty, so far as reasonable, to assist others to meet their obligations, to ensure that they do so, and especially to provide the necessary information to discharge those obligations. Responsibility therefore does not end when control of the waste is surrendered. With the exception of the domestic householder,[50] the duty extends to all those importing, producing, carrying, keeping, treating or disposing of con-

50 Section 34(2).

trolled waste. Further, the duty extends to 'brokers' who have been described as 'Those that contrive, make, and conclude bargains and contracts between merchants and tradesmen for which they have a fee or reward'.[51] The limitation in this case is that a duty of care applies only to the extent that the broker has control of the waste and, in common with other forms of brokerage, there will doubtless be many cases where that will not apply.

'Authorised person' for the purposes of transfer in section 34(1)(c)(i) is defined in section 34(3) as:

(a) a waste collection authority;
(b) the holder of a waste management licence under section 35 or a disposal licence under section 5 of the Control of Pollution Act 1974;
(c) persons exempted from the licensing requirements by regulations under section 33(3);
(d) a registered carrier of controlled waste under section 2 of the Control of Pollution (Amendment) Act 1989;[52]
(e) persons exempt from registration as a carrier by section 1(3) of the 1989 Act.

As an alternative to delivery to such an authorised person the duty of care may be satisfied within section 34(1)(c) by transfer for 'authorised transport purposes' which, by section 34(4), includes movement within the same premises or into or out of Great Britain before arrival at its destination, or after leaving the final point of export. For the purposes of these provisions 'transport' means,[53] 'in relation to any controlled waste, includ[ing] the transport of that waste by road or rail or by air, sea or inland waterway but does not include moving that waste from one place to another by means of a pipe or other apparatus that joins those two places'. Waste disposed of through the Garchey system, a waste disposal unit in a sink or similar facility is therefore, and obviously, excluded. Failure to discharge this duty of care in its various forms may result in summary or indictable proceedings and, in either case, a fine.[54]

The Secretary of State is given powers in support of this duty of care requirement, first, in section 34(5), to make regulations governing the making, keeping and provision of documents ancillary to and as a record of the subsection (1) transactions. The present regulations are the Environmental Protection (Duty of Care) Regulations 1991.[55] They require that the communication of the written description of the waste for the purposes of section 34(1)(c)(ii) shall be accompanied by a 'transfer note' completed and signed on behalf of the transferor and the transferee, stating:

(a) the identity and quantity of the waste, if in a container the kind of container, and the time and place of transfer;
(b) names and addresses of the parties;
(c) whether the transferor is the producer or importer of the waste;
(d) if transfer is to a person for authorised transport purposes, which of those purposes;
(e) the category of person in the Table to the Regulations applicable to the transferee and the provision of the additional information required by that Table.[56]

Both parties are to keep copies of written descriptions of the waste and of the transfer note for two years after the transfer and, in response to a written notice from the waste regulation authority, to supply copies of such documents as required in the notice within a stipulated period of not less than seven days.

51 *Per* Alderson B in *Milford* v *Hughes* (1846) 16 M&W 174 at p.177.

52 See above p.360.

53 Section 9 of the Control of Pollution (Amendment) Act 1989.

54 Section 34(6).

55 S.I. 1991 No. 2839.

56 Essentially in the stipulated cases the transferee is required to identify the authority with whom he is licensed or registered.

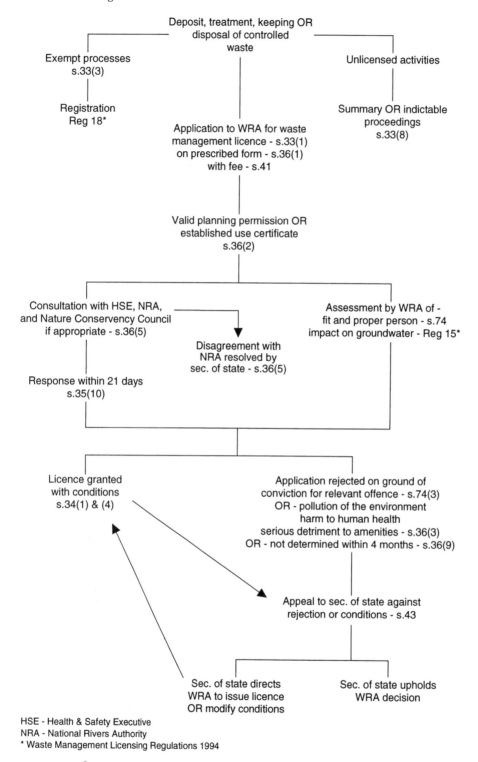

Figure 14.1 Waste management licence applications: Environmental Protection Act 1990, Part II

57 As to proper consultation, see in Chapter 1 at p.18.

58 Section 34(7).

59 Section 34(10).

60 S.I. 1980 No. 1709.

While the regulation-making power is discretionary, the Secretary of State has a duty, after proper consultation,[57] to issue a code of practice of guidance on the discharge of the duty of care.[58] In common with all such codes it has no legal authority but, depending upon the particular circumstances, the terms of the code may be of evidential value in determining whether the duty of care requirement has been satisfied. Further, where the court considers that a provision of the code is relevant to any question arising in the proceedings, it is required to take it into account in determining the matter.[59] A code of practice has been issued by the Department of the Environment and the Welsh Office containing detailed guidance on satisfying the duty of care requirement and the action to be taken when it is suspected that waste does not correspond to the purported description or is being handled incorrectly. A complementary joint circular, essentially for local authorities, on the operation of the duty of care requirement has been issued by the Department of the Environment (19/91), the Welsh Office (63/91) and the Scottish Office (25/91). It may be noted in conclusion that the duty of care applies to the Crown, including government departments. It also applies to the handling, transport and so on of special waste, in addition that is to the provisions of the Control of Pollution (Special Waste) Regulations 1980.[60]

Consequential licensing matters

Sections 35 to 44 of the 1990 Act, dealing with consequential licensing matters, are modelled on and follow closely the equivalent sections 5 to 10 of the Control of Pollution Act 1974. However, the experience gained in the latter's operation is reflected in a number of amendments and additions that serve to make waste licensing more effective as a control process. Licences are to be granted, by section 35(2), in relation to activities on land, to the occupier, and in the case of mobile plant, to the operator. Applications are to be made, in the first case, to the waste regulation authority for that area, and in the second, to the waste regulation authority for the area in which the operator has his principal place of business.[61]

61 Section 36(1).

As with the Control of Pollution Act 1974 provisions, prior planning approval is required in the form either of planning permission or an established use certificate.[62] When a licence application is received and the authority proposes to issue a licence it is first required to refer the proposal to the NRA and the Health and Safety Executive. If the land which is the subject of the application is protected land under section 28(1) of the Wildlife and Countryside Act 1981, the proposal is also to be referred to the Nature Conservancy Council.[63] These bodies have 21 days from notification within which to reply and the authority is required to consider any representations they may make. Should the NRA either oppose the issue of the licence or disagree with the proposed conditions, the dispute is to be submitted to the final decision of the Secretary of State.[64]

62 As to certificates under section 27 of the Town and Country Planning Act 1971, see *R v Bradford-upon-Avon UDC ex parte Boulton* [1964] 1 WLR 1136. There are three cases where planning permission is not required: uses commenced prior to 1 July 1948; uses within a special or general development order; use of Crown land.

63 But see section 131(3).

64 Section 36(5).

The grounds for rejecting an application for a licence, by section 36(3) and subject to the applicant being a fit and proper person, are that rejection is necessary to prevent:

(a) pollution of the environment;
(b) harm to human health; or
(c) serious detriment to the amenities of the locality.

Where an appropriate planning approval exists the prevention of 'serious detriment to the amenities of the locality' requirement is deemed to be satisfied.[65] The

65 Section 36(3).

meaning of 'amenities' received judicial consideration in *Cartwright* v *Post Office* (1968)[66] concerning, in the planning context, the routing of overhead telephone wires. Willis J said:

66 [1968] 2 QB 439 at p.456b.

> ... I am quite satisfied that the Post Office proposals will involve no depreciation in the value of the land, nor will they result in any significant reduction in its amenity, if I rightly understand that word as referring to its visual appearance and the pleasure of its enjoyment.

Similarly in *Re Ellis and Ruislip-Northwood UDC* (1920),[67] Scrutton LJ said 'The word "amenity" is obviously used very loosely; it is, I think, novel in an Act of Parliament, and appears to mean "pleasant circumstances or features, advantages"'. Both 'pollution of the environment' and 'harm to human health' have been considered in relation to section 33(1)(c) above. Should the authority have made no response within a period of four months, or any longer period agreed between the parties in writing, the application is deemed to have been rejected.

67 [1920] 1 KB 343 at p.370.

Fit and proper person

A particularly significant additional factor for the licensing authority's consideration is that the applicant is to be 'a fit and proper person'. In granting a disposal licence under the preceding 1974 Act provisions the authority could have no regard to the suitability or otherwise of the person responsible for the operation; a serious lacuna in any regulatory structure, and especially for such an environmentally sensitive activity. As the Royal Commission on Environmental Pollution noted in its 11th Report[68]:

68 'Managing Waste: The Duty of Care', Cmnd 9675, at paragraph 8.41.

> As the law stands at present, waste disposal authorities must grant site licence applications if planning permission exists for the use of the site for waste disposal and if water resources and public health are not threatened. This means that they cannot refuse a licence even to applicants whom they know to be unsuitable, perhaps as a consequence of enforcement action at another site, provided they satisfy these conditions. The introduction of some concept of good repute or professional competence, comparable to that used in operator licensing, would enable waste disposal authorities to take account of the qualifications and previous conduct of applicants when determining site licence applications.

The meaning and scope of 'fit and proper person' is to be found in section 74 which provides that:

(2) Whether a person is a fit and proper person to hold a licence is to be determined by reference to the carrying on by him of the activities which are or are to be authorised by the licence and the fulfilment of the requirements of the licence.
(3) ... a person shall be treated as not being a fit and proper person if it appears to the authority –
   (a) that he or another relevant person has been convicted of a relevant offence;
   (b) that the management of the activities which are or are to be authorised by the licence are not or will not be in the hands of a technically competent person; or
   (c) that the person who holds or is to hold the licence has not made and either has no intention of making or is in no position to make financial provision adequate to discharge the obligations arising from the licence.

'Fit and proper', then, is to be determined initially in relation to the particular activities to be carried on, their extent and degree of risk. As Rhodri Price Lewis

69 [1992] JPL 303 at p.306.

notes in this context[69]: 'Clearly it is one thing to be entrusted with the operation of a small mobile plant – it is quite another to have the responsibility of running a big landfill site taking toxic chemical waste'. The assessment of 'fit and proper' is further to be determined by reference to the three criteria in section 74(3). Whether these are exclusive or whether the licensing authority may have regard to other matters has yet to be determined. In the absence of authority and in accordance with general principles of statutory interpretation, it may be assumed that the statement of these express factors without any concluding general inclusive phrase will serve to exclude any potential, implied terms. It was of course open to Parliament to include a suitable omnibus phrase to that effect had it been so minded. It is also to be recalled that the absence of a 'fit and proper person' test in the earlier legislation was seen as a serious deficiency in practice requiring statutory remedy and not as a matter to be left to the discretion of licensing authorities. If this view is not correct and licensing authorities do have a wider discretion than that legislated for, such discretion will be limited by and to the aims and purposes of the statute.[70]

70 See, e.g., *Mixnams Properties Ltd* v *Chertsey UDC* [1965] AC 735.

The first ground for the rejection of an appplication, in section 74(3)(a), is that the applicant or other relevant person has been convicted of a relevant offence. Section 74(7) specifies the circumstances in which a person is to be regarded as having been convicted of a relevant offence, the purpose being to 'pierce the veil' and identify the person actually at fault where a corporate body was convicted. They include:

(a) a person who commited a relevant offence either while employed by the present or proposed licence holder or while a partner in a business a member of which partnership was the present or proposed licence holder;

(b) the present or proposed licence holder was a director, manager, secretary or similar officer of a corporate body and that body was convicted of a relevant offence;

(c) the present or proposed licence holder is a body corporate and a director, manager, secretary or similar officer either has been convicted of a relevant offence or held a similar position with another company so convicted.

This is a paraphrase of the statutory provision, which nevertheless indicates that a conviction is applicable if it occurs in the context of current employment or while a partner in a business another partner of which was the actual or proposed licence holder. Parts (b) and (c) are complementary, providing that a conviction will apply where the applicant is either the company or one of its specified officers and it was the other party that was convicted.

Having clarified this particular limited question, no guidance is given to the scope or meaning of 'relevant person'. Section 74(5) gives the Secretary of State power to issue guidance to waste regulation authorities concerning the operation of this section, which they are required to follow, and it may be that such guidance will identify categories of personnel who are to be regarded as relevant persons for these purposes. One may expect that they will at least include the persons listed in (b) and (c) above. Whether they will be limited to the 'controlling minds' of the company or extend to employees engaged in the practical on-site operations, for instance the site manager or foreman, awaits determination, either by ministerial guidance or judicial decision. That the fitness of such persons bears directly on the effective day to day conduct of the operation, making their competence relevant in any assessment of future performance, is beyond dispute.

Section 74(6) gives the Secretary of State a regulation-making power to determine, *inter alia*, what shall constitute relevant offences within section 74(3)(a). In the exercise of that power regulation 3 of the Waste Management Licensing Regulations 1994 lists as relevant offences for this purpose those under the following enactments:

(a) section 22 of the Public Health (Scotland) Act 1897;
(b) section 95(1) of the Public Health Act 1936;
(c) section 3, 5(6), 16(4), 18(2), 31(1), 32(1), 34(5), 78, 92(6), or 93(3) of the Control of Pollution Act 1974;
(d) section 2 of the Refuse Disposal (Amenity) Act 1978;
(e) the Control of Pollution (Special Waste) Regulations 1980;
(f) section 9(1) of the Food and Environment Protection Act 1985;
(g) the Transfrontier Shipment of Hazardous Waste Regulations 1988;
(h) the Merchant Shipping (Prevention of Pollution by Garbage) Regulations 1988;
(i) section 1, 5, 6(9), or 7(3) of the Control of Pollution (Amendment) Act 1989;
(j) section 107, 118(4), or 175(1) of the Water Act 1989;
(k) section 23(1), 33, 34(6), 44, 47(6), 57(5), 59(5), 63(2), 69(9), 70(4), 71(3) or 80(4) of the 1990 Act;
(l) section 85, 202 or 206 of the Water Resources Act 1991;
(m) section 33 of the Clean Air Act 1993.

In conclusion it is to be noted that the provisions of the Rehabilitation of Offenders Act 1974 apply to convictions for the purposes of section 74.

The second element in determining whether a person is 'fit and proper' for these licensing purposes is technical competence. To this end section 74(3) provides that 'a person shall be treated as not being a fit and proper person if it appears to the authority ... (b) that the management of the activities ... are not or will not be in the hands of a technically competent person'. This wording emphasises that, in this respect, the fitness of the organisation or person applying for the licence depends on the ability of the particular individual responsible for or in control of the operation or site that is the subject of the application. This evident clarity may be obscured in practice in two distinct ways. First, management may be, and often is, the responsibility of more than one; the person on the ground with apparent authority being restricted by decisions taken by others. Also it is inevitable that eventually, and usually sooner rather than later, the person identified in the application and having the necessary attributes is moved to some other role and replaced by another who has not, and who possibly could not stand the same scrutiny.

As with the identification of 'relevant offences', section 74(6) permits the Secretary of State to make regulations determining the qualifications and experience that will satisfy this requirement. Regulation 4(1) of the Waste Management Licensing Regulations 1994 specifies what shall amount to technical competence in relation to different types of facility and operation by reference to certificates of particular levels awarded by the Waste Management Industry Training and Advisory Board as follows:

Type of facility	Relevant certificate of technical competence
A landfill site which receives special waste.	Managing landfill operations: special waste (level 4).
A landfill site which receives biodegradable waste or which for some other reason requires substantial engineering works to	1. Managing landfill operations: biodegradable waste (level 4); or
protect the environment but which in either case does not receive special waste.	2. Managing landfill operations: special waste (level 4).
Any other type of landfill site with a total capacity exceeding 50,000 cubic metres.	1. Landfill operations: inert waste (level 3); or
	2. Managing landfill operations: biodegradable waste (level 4); or
	3. Managing landfill operations: special waste (level 4);
A site on which waste is burned in an incinerator designed to incinerate waste at a rate of more than 50 kg per hour but less than 1 tonne per hour.	Managing incinerator operations: special waste (level 4).
A waste treatment plant where special waste is subjected to a chemical or physical process.	Managing treatment operations: special waste (level 4).
A waste treatment plant where waste is subjected to a chemical or physical process and none of the waste is special waste.	1. Treatment operations: inert waste (level 3); or
	2. Managing treatment operations: special waste (level 4).
A transfer station[71] where – (a) biodegradable, clinical or special waste is dealt with; and (b) the total quantity of waste at the station at any time exceeds 5 cubic metres.	Managing transfer operations : special waste (level 4).
A transfer station where - (a) no biodegradable, clinical or special waste is dealt with; and (b) the total quantity of waste at the station at any time exceeds 50 cubic metres.	1. Transfer operations: inert waste (level 3); or
	2. Managing transfer operations: special waste (level 4).
A civic amenity site.[72]	Civic amenity site operations (level 3).

[71] A 'transfer station' means a facility where waste is unloaded in order to permit its preparation for further transport for treatment, keeping or disposal elsewhere: regulation 4(3).

[72] By regulation 4(3), 'a civic amenity site' is a place provided under section 1 of the Refuse Disposal (Amenity) Act 1978 or by virtue of section 51(1)(b) of the 1990 Act.

These provisions do not apply to a facility used exclusively for a scrap metal business or for dismantling motor vehicles. Regulation 5 contains transitional provisions. Where a person has applied to the Board for a certificate and has within the preceding 12 months acted as manager of such a facility, he shall be treated as technically competent for facilities of the types covered by such certificate until 10 August 1999. Alternatively, where a person is 55 or over on 10 August 1994 and has had five years' experience in the previous 10 years as manager of a facility within the Table, he shall be regarded as technically competent in relation to facilities of the types within a certificate for that level.

The third and final requirement in establishing the suitability of an applicant to be a licence holder within section 74 is financial competence. Unlike the two earlier criteria which apply also to appropriate employees, this requirement applies exclusively to the applicant or licence holder, be they a person or a company. It must be seen that they have, and will make available, the necessary resources to 'discharge the obligations arising from' the activities to be licensed. This will of course include meeting any licence conditions, the terms of planning consents and any aftercare or restoration requirements. Again, the guidance issued under section 74(5) may include these matters as well as indicating what is to be regarded as adequate financial provision. It may be assumed that generally the resources of the licence holder will require some form of support in the nature of a guarantee, bond or insurance provided, depending on its nature, either from within the industry or by the financial market. The difficulty, and therefore a major inhibiting factor for financial institutions, is not only to assess the potential risks over a given time scale in any particular case but also to gauge likely future trends and obligations to be imposed by, no doubt, increasingly stringent regulation. It is finally to be noted that this section 74 'fit and proper person' concept applies not only to the assessment of an applicant for grant of a licence under section 36 but also to the revocation and suspension of licences under section 38.[73]

73 See sections 38(2) and (6).

Licensing Procedure

In relation to the licensing procedure, including that for subsequent variations, revocations and so on, section 44 makes it an offence for a person knowingly or recklessly to make a statement which is false in a material particular. For this purpose knowledge includes constructive knowledge, a person deliberately refraining from enquiring because they might not wish to know the answer being deemed to have that knowledge.[74] However, mere neglect to discover what could have been found out by making reasonable enquiries will not constitute knowledge.[75] The meaning of 'recklessness' in criminal law has received much and differing consideration. The statement of the principle by Lord Diplock in *R v Caldwell* (1982) may now, though, be regarded as authoritative for this present purpose.[76] He said:

74 See *Knox v Boyd* [1941] JC 82 at p.86; *Taylor's Central Garages (Exeter) Ltd v Roper* (1951) 115 JP 445 at p.449 per Devlin J.

75 See *Taylor's Garages* above.

76 [1982] AC 341 at p.354f; [1981] 1 All ER 961 at p.967.

> In my opinion, a person charged with an offence under section 1(1) of the Criminal Damage Act 1971 is 'reckless as to whether any such property would be destroyed or damaged' if he (1) does an act which in fact creates an obvious risk that property will be destroyed or damaged and (2) when he does the act he either has not given any thought to the possibility of there being any such risk or has recognised that there was some risk risk involved and has nonetheless gone on to do it.

Turning now to the phrase 'false in a material particular', a statement may be false in its terms and also because it is misleading even though factually true. In *R v Kylsant* (1932)[77] a company prospectus, though accurate as far as it went, was held to be untrue because what was omitted created an entirely false impression of the state of the company. Commenting on 'material particular' Tromans says[78]:

77 [1932] 1 KB 442; [1931] All ER Rep 179.

78 *Op. cit.*, note 19, p.103.

> This suggests that the statement must relate to matters which would have the tendency, or natural and probable result, of inducing the authority to act on the faith of it in such a way as might affect the outcome of the decision. It does not appear to be an ingredient of the offence that the authority should actually have relied on the statement or that it should actually have influenced the decision, if any.

One thinks in this context of statements concerning, for example, relevant convictions or technical competence in establishing that the applicant or an employee is a 'fit and proper person'.

Groundwater protection

The disposal of waste by landfill presents two potential forms of pollution hazard. There are, those associated with the activity itself, including noise, vibration, dust, vermin and so on. Also there is the pollution of groundwater due to the leaching of constituents of the waste from the landfill site. The likely harm will depend on the nature and toxicity of the materials deposited. The duration of the risk will be governed by the quantity of dangerous materials and the patterns of groundwater flow.

Directive 80/68/EEC on the protection of groundwater places on Member States the duty to prohibit the direct discharge of List I substances to groundwater and, subject to prior investigation, to limit the direct discharge of List II substances and the indirect discharge of List I and II substances into groundwater so as to avoid pollution by these substances. Article 1.2 defines these terms as follows:

(a) 'groundwater' means all water which is below the surface of the ground in the saturation zone and in direct contact with the ground or subsoil;
(b) 'direct discharge' means the introduction into groundwater of substances in lists I or II without percolation through the ground or subsoil;
(c) 'indirect discharge' means the introduction into groundwater of substances in lists I or II after percolation through the ground or subsoil.

79 Paragraph 3, and see W.O. 34/90.

80 S.I. 1994 No. 1056.

Circular 20/90[79] suggested that waste regulation authorities should review disposal licences for landfill sites involving the disposal of wastes containing substances within List 1. This issue has now been legislated for in the extensive regulation 15 of the Waste Management Licensing Regulations 1994.[80] Before issuing a waste management licence for:

(a) disposal that may lead to an indirect discharge of a List I or List II substance into groundwater; or
(b) direct discharge into groundwater of a List I or a List II substance,

the regulation authority must first ensure that a prior investigation is undertaken of the proposed activities and, secondly, that the groundwater quality will undergo requisite surveillance. 'Prior investigation' is stated in paragraph (2) to include hydrogeological examination of the area, the possible purifying powers of the soil and subsoil, and the risk of pollution and alteration of the quality of the groundwater from the discharge. It shall also establish whether the discharge of the substances into groundwater is a satisfactory solution from the point of view of the environment. Licences authorising such discharges shall be granted for a limited period only and shall be reviewed at least every four years. This regulation is stipulated to apply, with necessary modifications, to the review of disposal licences under Part I of the Control of Pollution Act 1974.

Having regard to the results of the prior investigation, any authorisation that the authority decides to issue shall include as applicable the conditions and comply with the criteria in paragraphs (4)–(7) which provide, in synopsis, that:

(a) In relation to the discharge or access of a List I substance into groundwater permanently unsuitable for other uses a licence may be issued only if the authority is satisfied that –

(i) its presence in groundwater will not impede the exploitation of ground resources; and

(ii) precautions to protect other aquatic and eco-systems are taken.

(b) Where the waste regulation authority is satisfied that the subject groundwater is not permanently unsuitable for other uses it shall only issue a licence with conditions that precautions to prevent discharges into it of List I substances are taken.

(c) Where applicable a licence shall only be issued subject to conditions requiring precautions for preventing groundwater pollution by List II substances.

(d) In the case of licences for the discharge of List I and II substances to groundwater, conditions shall specify –

(i) place of discharge;

(ii) method of discharge;

(iii) essential precautions to be taken having regard to the nature of the effluents and of the receiving environment;

(iv) maximum quantity of substances in any specified period;

(v) monitoring arrangements for effluent discharges;

(vi) arrangements for monitoring groundwater quality.

The Annex to Directive 80/68/EEC contains the two Lists as follows:

LIST I OF FAMILIES AND GROUPS OF SUBSTANCES

List I contains the individual substances which belong to the families and groups of substances enumerated below, with the exception of those which are considered inappropriate to list I on the basis of a low risk of toxicity, persistence and bioaccumulation.

Such substances which with regard to toxicity, persistence and bioaccumulation are appropriate to list II are to be classed in list II.

1. Organohalogen compounds and substances which may form such compounds in the aquatic environment
2. Organophosphorus compounds
3. Organotin compounds
4. Substances which possess carcinogenic mutagenic or teratogenic properties in or via the aquatic environment[81]
5. Mercury and its compounds
6. Cadmium and its compounds
7. Mineral oils and hydrocarbons
8. Cyanides

81 Where certain substances in list II are carcinogenic, mutagenic or teratogenic, they are included in category 4 of this list.

LIST II OF FAMILIES AND GROUPS OF SUBSTANCES

List II contains the individual substances and the categories of substances belonging to the families and groups of substances listed below which could have a harmful effect on groundwater.

1. The following metalloids and metals and their compounds:

1. Zinc	11. Tin
2. Copper	12. Barium
3. Nickel	13. Beryllium
4. Chrome	14. Boron
5. Lead	15. Uranium

6. Selenium	16. Vanadium
7. Arsenic	17. Cobalt
8. Antimony	18. Thallium
9. Molybdenum	19. Tellurium
10. Titanium	20. Silver

2. Biocides and their derivatives not appearing in list I.

3. Substances which have a deleterious effect on the taste and/or odour of ground-water, and compounds liable to cause the formation of such substances in such water and to render it unfit for human consumption.

4. Toxic or persistent organic compounds of silicon, and substances which may cause the formation of such compounds in water, excluding those which are biologically harmless or are rapidly converted in water into harmless substances.

5. Inorganic compounds of phosphorus and elemental phosphorus.

6. Flourides.

7. Ammonia and nitrites.

Continuing Licensing Functions

While a waste management licence is in force it will be subject to variation within the terms of section 37. This section provides for three initiatives leading to variation of a licence. First, the waste regulation authority may at its own discretion modify the conditions of a licence to the extent that it thinks desirable and provided that it is unlikely to require unreasonable expense on the part of the licence holder. This is of course a matter of judgement for the authority which, being grounded on 'reasonableness', may as in similar contexts be challenged on *Wednesbury* principles.[82] Secondly, within the same section 37(1), the licence holder may himself apply for modification of the conditions. If the application produces no response within two months of its receipt it is to be presumed to be rejected. Lastly, in section 37(2), the authority shall modify the licence conditions, except where it revokes it entirely, to the extent necessary in the authority's opinion to ensure that the authorised activities do not cause pollution of the environment or harm to human health, or become seriously detrimental to the amenities of the locality affected by the activities. These are of course the same grounds on which the original application may be rejected under section 36(3) and, being reproduced here, recognise that circumstances may change during the currency of the licence. From the time that these Environmental Protection Act 1990 provisions came into operation, all existing disposal licences are to be treated as site licences and subject to the provisions of this Act.[83] Notification of a variation is to be by notice served on the licence holder stating the time when the modification is to take effect.

In any particular case the Secretary of State has the power, in section 37(3), to direct an authority concerning the modifications to be made to a licence, the authority having a duty to give effect to the direction. Any modifications of licence conditions, however initiated, are to be preceded by consultation with the specified bodies as required by section 36(4)–(8) and (10) for issue, so far as the authority considers appropriate having regard to the particular modification.

While a licence is in force the waste regulation authority may by notice revoke it in whole or in part[84] if it considers that:

(a) its continuation would cause pollution of the environment or harm to human health or be seriously detrimental to the amenities of the area; and

[82] *Associated Provincial Picture Houses v Wednesbury Corporation* [1948] 1 KB 223.

[83] Section 77(2).

[84] Section 38(4) and (3).

(b) modification of the licence conditions will not resolve the threat;

or alternatively that the licence holder has ceased to be a fit and proper person due to conviction for a relevant offence. It may similarly revoke a licence in part where the licence holder has ceased to be a fit and proper person because the management of the activities has ceased to be in the hands of a technically competent person. In partially revoking a licence under section 38(3) the waste regulation authority is to specify those requirements which are to continue to bind the licence holder. The same power is not of course available where a licence is fully revoked under section 38(4), implying that such entire revocation will be possible only where there are no continuing or long-term consequences to the environment from those licensed activities. The strong implication is therefore that partial revocation is likely to be the norm. The authority has an additional power of revocation by notice on the failure of a licence holder to pay any prescribed fees or charges imposed under section 41.

The waste regulation authority has the power in section 38(6) to suspend by notice any of the licensed activities for the period stipulated where it appears that the management of those activities has ceased to be in the hands of a technically competent person, or that serious pollution of the environment or serious harm to human health has resulted from or is about to be caused by the activities and continuing those activities will continue or cause that serious damage. With the suspension, or at any time while it is in operation, the authority may require the licence holder to take any measures to deal with or avert the pollution or harm, and failure to comply constitutes a criminal offence. The emphasis on seriousness indicates that this power is for use only in such situations that present an emergency or real danger.

A licence holder had the option, under section 8(4) of the Control of Pollution Act 1974, of notifying the authority that he no longer required the licence, to return it and therefore, in effect, at his own discretion, to walk away from any present or future responsibilities for the site. A significant strengthening of the licensing structure has been made in this respect in that, by section 39, a licence having been issued, it may be surrendered only with the approval of the licensing authority. Application for surrender must be made according to regulations made by the Secretary of State and with the prescribed fee.[85] Regulation 2(2) of the Waste Management Licensing Regulations 1994 provides that applications for surrender of licences are to be made in writing and subject to certain qualifications, to include the information and be accompanied by the evidence prescribed in Schedule 1. In its turn Schedule 1 requires:

(a) the full name and address and, as applicable, phone, fax and telex numbers of the holder and any agent;
(b) the number of the site licence and the address and description of the site;
(c) a detailed map showing the location of the site and of the various activities on it;
(d) a description of the activities carried on involving the treatment, keeping or disposal of controlled waste, an indication of when they were carried on and an estimate of the total quantities of different types of waste dealt with at the site;
(e) where the site is a landfill or lagoon –

85 See generally on the question of fees at p.395 below.

(i) engineering works carried out to prevent or minimise pollution of the environment or harm to human health, or of restoration on completion of the works;

(ii) geological, hydrological and hydrogeological information for the site;

(iii) monitoring data on surface or groundwater quality that could be affected by the site and on the production of any landfill gas or leachate, and information on the physical stability of the site;

(iv) records and plans relating to the deposit of any special waste;

and estimates of total quantities of different types of waste, differentiating between biodegradable, non-biodegradable and special waste;

(f) where the site is not a landfill or lagoon –

(i) details of the contaminants likely to be present and the nature of different types of waste dealt with at the site;

(ii) a report showing results of sample analysis in such numbers as to provide a reliable indication of the location of likely contaminents together with the locations and numbers of samples;

(g) any other information the applicant wishes the authority to take into account.

On receiving an application the authority is to inspect the site, if appropriate, and may request further information from the licence holder. Acceptance or rejection of the application depends upon the authority's opinion on whether the condition of the land, resulting from its use for waste treatment, disposal etc., will cause pollution of the environment or harm to human health.[86] Where it proposes to accept surrender the authority is first required to refer the proposal to the NRA, consider any representations from it and, if it disapproves of surrender, the matter may be referred for the decision of the Secretary of State. Formal recognition of surrender is by issue of a 'certificate of completion' stating that the authority is satisfied that the land is unlikely to cause the pollution or harm already referred to. The certificate is sent with the notice of the authority's decision and its issue determines the licence. Lack of response from the authority for three months implies rejection of the application.

Transfer of a licence within section 40 may occur whether or not it is partly revoked or suspended. Both parties to the transaction are to make a joint application to the authority in accordance with regulations made by the Secretary of State, with the old licence and the prescribed fee. Regulation 2(5) of the Waste Management Licensing Regulations 1994 stipulates that an application for transfer, in writing, is to include the information prescribed by Schedule 2, that is to say:

1 the full name and address and, as applicable, phone, fax and telex numbers of the holder;

2 the number of the waste management licence and, except for mobile plant, the address and description of the location of the subject premises;

3 in the case of mobile plant, sufficient information to identify the plant;

4 where the transferee is an individual, his name, age , address etc;

5 where the transferee is a company or other body corporate, details of the company, its registered address and the personal detrails of each director, manager, secretary or other similar officer;

6 where the transferee is a partnership, details of the partnership and the full name and address and age of each partner;

86 Section 39(6).

7 the transferee's business name, if different from the name mentioned above;
8 where the transferee has appointed an agent to deal with the transfer, details of the agent;
9 details of any conviction of the transferee or other relevant person;
10 the name of the person who is to manage the licensed activities, including information to establish that he is a competent person;
11 the financial provision the transferee has or proposes to make to meet obligations arising from the licence;
12 any other information which the applicant wishes the authority to take into account.

If the authority is satisfied that the transferee is a fit and proper person within section 74 it shall effect the transfer by endorsing the licence with the name and particulars of the proposed transferee. Again there is a period, in this case two months, beyond which silence is deemed to imply rejection of the application. Lastly it is to be noted that with the operation of Part II of the 1990 Act existing disposal licences are to be treated as site licences and will in consequence be subject to these procedures governing variation, revocation, suspension, surrender and transfer.[87]

87 Section 77(2).

A right of appeal to the Secretary of State is provided in section 43 for a person affected by a decision of the authority following an application for any of the purposes in sections 36 to 40; with, of course, the exception where the authority is acting under his direction. The Secretary of State is given a wide discretion in dealing with an appeal, which is to be on documentary submissions unless either party requests an oral hearing, that in turn being either public or private. Sections 43(4) to (7) specify in particular cases the interim effect on the authority's decision of the pending appeal. In the case of a variation or revocation the appeal renders the change ineffective until it is resolved or withdrawn, but it will not affect a suspension which takes effect pending determination of the appeal. Section 43(8) provides for regulations governing the timing and form of appeals and the manner in which they are considered. The current provisions are to be found in regulations 6 to 9 of the Waste Management Licensing Regulations 1994.[88]

88 S.I. 1994 No. 1056.

Those regulations provide that for the purposes of appeals under either section 43 or section 66(5), notice is to be in writing and is to include:

(a) a statement of the grounds of appeal;
(b) the application and supporting documents;
(c) documents relevant to the particular appeal;
(d) the appellant's preference for the appeal to be by hearing or on written representations.

Copies of the notice of appeal and associated documents are to be served on the waste regulation authority. The time limits for appeals are, generally, six months from the date of the decision appealed against and, in the case of a section 66(5) appeal, 21 days from notification of the determination. The Secretary of State has a discretion in the first case to extend the period. The person hearing an appeal under section 43(2)(c) shall report to the Secretary of State with his conclusions and recommendations, or alternatively his reasons for not making recommendations. The Secretary of State, or any other person determining the appeal, is to notify the appellant in writing of the decision with reasons and, in the former case, with a copy of the report of the hearing. Copies of such documents are also to be sent to the waste regulation authority.

On resolution of an appeal the authority is required to implement the Secretary of State's decision. As well as the hearing of appeals and the prescribing of controlling regulations, there is a general power in many of these licensing provisions for the Secretary of State to direct the decision of the authority in a particular case, with a consequent duty on the part of the authority to implement or accept that direction.

The Secretary of State, with Treasury approval, is to make and periodically revise a charging scheme of fees to be paid to waste regulation authorities for applications for the issue, surrender and transfer of licences, for variation of conditions and in respect of the subsistence of licences.[89] This represents a major change from the Control of Pollution Act 1974 structure which made no provision for the financing of the considerable work load represented by the processing of applications and the initial and subsequent routine inspections of sites. The reasoning behind the introduction of a charging scheme was explained by the Earl of Arran in the following terms[90]:

> The charges for licences are intended to meet the estimated costs of waste regulatory activity for authorities taken as a whole. We are committed to introducing a national scale of charges, so the differences between authorities in the amount of resources they devote to waste regulation – which has been the subject of intense criticism – do not exacerbate the difference in costs of disposal in the areas of the good and not so good authorities. This inevitably means that costs of individual authorities will not necessarily be matched exactly by the revenue from licensing. However, for those authorities not currently providing the required level of regulation, the extra income will provide the resources to allow them to do so. We will of course keep the level of charges under review and will consult local authorities and industry on the level at which they should be set.

He went on to indicate that these charges would cover the costs of inspecting and monitoring, but not the costs of prosecution which, if successful, would be met by costs awarded by the court. As, by virtue of section 77(2), existing disposal licences issued under the earlier Act are to be treated hereafter as site licences within the 1990 Act, it would seem that they too will be liable for continuing subsistence charges.

Section 42 places a general duty on licensing authorities to oversee activities of licence holders and to ensure that any conditions are complied with. Following the issue of a licence and for its duration the waste regulation authority shall inspect and oversee as necessary the licensed operations to ensure that:

(a) they do not cause pollution of the environment or harm to human health or serious detriment to the amenities of the locality; and

(b) the licence conditions are complied with.[91]

If it appears to the authority that any of the licensed activities is likely to cause pollution of water, it must consult the NRA. Depending on the nature of the default, section 42 offers the authority two remedies for breach of a condition in addition to prosecution within section 33(6). Where it appears to a duly authorised officer of the authority that an emergency within subsection (1) requires it, the authority may do any necessary work on land or in relation to any plant or equipment and recover any consequent expenditure from the licence holder.

89 Section 41(1) to (3).

90 Hansard HL vol. 522, col. 35.

91 Section 42(1).

Alternatively, where the waste regulation authority considers that a condition is not being complied with, it may, following warning and sufficient time to remedy the defect, require the licence holder to comply within a stipulated time. Should he then fail to do so the authority may revoke or suspend the licence or, as the case may be, the relevant part of it.[92] These powers are similar to but in addition to those in section 38. The Secretary of State is given the power in section 38(7) to issue directions to a waste regulation authority in relation to a licence granted by it, the authority then having a duty to observe its terms.

92 Section 42(6)

15

Waste Treatment

COLLECTION

Household Waste

A waste collection authority has the duty, under section 45(1)(a) of the Environmental Protection Act 1990, to arrange for the collection of household waste in its area. The two exceptions to this general obligation are (i) where in the opinion of the authority the waste's location is so isolated or inaccessible that the cost of collecting it would be unreasonably high, and, (ii) where the authority is satisfied that adequate arrangements for disposal can be made by the person having control of the waste. This collection service is to be provided free of charge save for those cases prescribed in regulations, and in such cases the duty to arrange for collection shall not arise until the person having control requests collection. The wording of the section does not clearly indicate at what stage or stages a request is to be made in the event of a regular service. It would however appear reasonable and logical for one initial request to be made, at which time the level of charges and time for payment would be determined.

The categories of household waste for which charges may be made are to be found in regulation 4 and Schedule 2 of the Controlled Waste Regulations 1992,[1] the collecting authority having the discretion whether to impose a charge in any given case. The inevitable consequence of imposing charges is of course that people are encouraged to seek other, invariably less satisfactory methods of disposal, ultimately placing a heavier cost on the authority than any charges initially remitted. Schedule 2 lists the following matters:

(a) any article of waste exceeding 25 kg in weight;
(b) any article of waste unable to fit into –
    (i) a receptacle for household waste provided within section 46, or
    (ii) where no such receptacle is provided, a cylindrical container 750 mm in diameter and 1m in length;
(c) garden waste;
(d) clinical waste from a domestic property, a caravan or moored vessel wholly used for living accommodation;
(e) waste from a residential hotel, residential home or premises forming part of a university, school or other educational establishment or part of a hospital or nursing home;
(f) waste from domestic property or a caravan used in the course of a business for the provision of self-catering holiday accommodation;
(g) dead domestic pets;
(h) any substances or articles which by virtue of a notice of the collection authority under section 46, the occupier may not put into a receptacle for household waste;

1 S.I. 1992 No. 588.

(i)   litter and refuse collected under section 89(1)(f);
(j)   waste from domestic property forming part of a composite hereditament;[2]
(k)   any mineral or synthetic oil or grease;
(l)   asbestos;
(m) waste from a caravan which is not allowed to be used for human habitation throughout the year;
(n)   waste from a camp site, other than from domestic property on the site;
(o)   waste from premises occupied by a charity and wholly or mainly for charitable purposes, unless falling within paragraph 1 of Schedule 1.[3]
(p)   waste from a prison or other penal institution;
(q)   waste from a hall or other premises used wholly or mainly for public meetings;
(r)   waste from a royal palace.

2 The definition of composite hereditament in section 64(9) of the Local Government Finanace Act 1988 applies: 'a hereditament is composite if part only of it consists of domestic property'.

3 For the meaning of 'charity', see Chapter 10 at p.279.

Material collected in accordance with section 45 powers belongs to the collecting authority, by subsection (9), and may be dealt with accordingly; subject only to that authority's general duty in section 48 to deliver it for disposal to places designated by the disposal authority. While collecting authorities have the responsibility to 'arrange for' the service, it will be recalled that the actual function is expected to be performed by contractors. The contractor will therefore be in possession of the material as agent of the collecting authority who will have ownership, presumably until delivery to the disposal site. The purpose of subsection (9) is to resolve an issue that has caused considerable argument, and indeed litigation, in the past, although having regard to previous disputes it may be suggested that the provision does not go far enough.While ownership is established following collection, just as much contention has been generated over title to articles after they have been discarded, placed in bins whether belonging to the householder or the authority, or come into the possession of employees engaged in collecting.

Probably the leading case in which the Divisional Court considered these matters was *Williams* v *Phillips, Roberts and Phillips* (1957).[4] The Corporation had an agreement with its dustmen that proceeds from the sale of refuse were to be divided proportionately between the parties. Refuse, including wool and rags, was collected and placed in sacks on Corporation dustcarts. Subsequently it was sold by the appellants instead of being handed over to the Corporation. The Court decided that:

4 (1957) 41 Crim App R 5.

(a)   refuse had not been abandoned by owners of premises when placed in dustbins, but had been put there for the specific purpose of its being collected and taken away by the local authority;
(b)   the refuse passed into the constructive possession of the local authority as soon as it was placed in its carts;
(c)   there was abundant evidence of *animus furandi* on the part of the appellants in view of their knowledge, therefore they were properly convicted of larceny.

In his judgement Lord Goddard CJ added:

(d)   until taken away by the local authority the refuse remained the property of the depositor: on collection it becomes the property of the local authority;
(e)   agreement has no great bearing on the commission of a criminal offence, except to establish honesty or dishonesty.

5 [1948] 1 All ER 860 at p.862.

The view expressed in (d), that items even though discarded remain the property of the occupier while on his land, is supported in *Hibbert* v *McKiernan* (1948),[5] concerning the ownership of lost golf balls. Lord Goddard CJ stated the general principle in sufficiently wide terms to apply to discarded waste, saying:

> Every householder or landowner means or intends to exclude thieves and wrongdoers from his property, and this confers on him a special property in goods found on his land sufficient to support on indictment if the goods are taken therefrom, not under a claim of right, but with a felonious intent.

6 (1854) 6 Cox 284 at p.288.

In the earlier case of *Reed and Another* (1854)[6] Lord Campbell said that 'The constructive possession of the master need not be distinct from the actual possession of the servant'. These views have been implemented in the terms of section 45(9). The 1957 decision offers useful guidance on the complementary question of ownership before collection.

While material discarded as waste may generally be treated as such, there is some authority that some articles, though placed among waste and apparently discarded but which are clearly not waste – for instance because of their value and also perhaps because of their distinct and different nature – will not be regarded as waste. Even though collected and removed, therefore, such property may be recovered by the original owner. In *Thomas* v *Greenslade* (1954),[7] the plaintiff owner of a pile of scrap metal paid a dealer £1 to remove it. Unknown to the plaintiff there was among the iron a box containing 1,452 National Savings Certificates. The dealer was required in these proceedings to return them to the plaintiff. In similar circumstances a collecting authority would appear to have the duty to make reasonable enquiries to endeavour to establish ownership and return the property.

7 (1954) *The Times*, 6 November.

Pending periodic collection, household waste has to be stored on the originating premises. Having the duty to collect, the waste collection authority is entitled to stipulate by notice the type and number of storage receptacles[8] to be used, including:

8 For these purposes 'receptacle' is defined, in section 46(4), to include a holder for receptacles

(a) their size, construction and maintenance;
(b) location and access for emptying purposes;
(c) placing on the highway for emptying;
(d) substances or articles that may or may not be put into receptacles or compartments and the precautions to be taken in respect of particular substances or articles;
(e) the steps to be taken by occupiers of premises to facilitate the collection of waste from the receptacles.

9 Section 46(5).

10 *Mayor of Wandsworth* v *Baines* [1906] 1 KB 470.

The requirement in (c) above must have the prior consent of the highway authority and arrangements concerning liability for damage arising out of the receptacles being so placed must have been made.[9] A receptacle placed on a highway otherwise than in accordance with arrangements made under this subsection will constitute an unlawful obstruction.[10] The power in section 46(1) to require receptacles is to be exercised reasonably, including the provision of separate containers or compartments for waste that is to be recycled and waste that is not. The notice, while covering those aspects of storage provision, does not necessarily place the obligation to provide on the occupier. Section 46(3) offers the authority a number of alternatives in relation to the responsibility for provision, including:

(a) by the authority, free of charge;
(b) by the authority, on either one or periodic payments by, and with the agreement of, the occupier;
(c) by the occupier, if he does not enter into an agreement under (b) within a specified period;
(d) by the occupier.

A significant change from previous legislation is that as an alternative to provision by the authority, the responsibility for providing waste containers rests solely with the occupier. The authority is therefore no longer faced with the choice of requiring provision by either the owner or occupier of the premises, and, thankfully, the associated case law can be ignored. Failure to comply with a requirement of a notice is a summary offence, subject of course to a right of appeal within 21 days of either the end of the period in (c) above or of receipt of the notice. The grounds of appeal are that either the requirement is unreasonable, or that the receptacles in which household waste is placed for collection from the premises are adequate. Pending determination of the appeal the requirement shall be of no effect.

In order to empty containers the authority may demand that they be placed on the highway, or the collectors may need to gain access to the premises. In the latter case refusal to permit access or removal, even without violence, will amount to an obstruction.[11]

11 *Borrow* v *Howland* (1896) 60 JP 391.

While there is a statutory duty on collection authorities to provide a collection service for household waste, disposal authorities are given the complementary power in section 51(1)(b) of providing places to which residents of the area may bring and leave their household waste. Such provision is to satisfy the following criteria, that is, it is to be:

(a) situated either within the area or otherwise reasonably accessible to its residents;
(b) available for the deposit of waste at all reasonable times;
(c) available for the deposit of waste free of charge to the residents;

although arrangements may restrict specified places to specified descriptions of waste. The availability of such places to residents free of charge may be extended to other persons for the deposit of household or other controlled waste subject to such conditions, including payment, as the authority determines.

That the placing of containers in public locations for the reception of waste under this, and indeed any other, power carries with it the potential for obstruction and damage to third parties is self-evident. The providing authority will therefore be liable in accordance with general negligence principles in such circumstances. Such liability is not necessarily or completely discharged on initial installation but imposes a continuing obligation to be aware of and respond to changing conditions, as may be required. In *Morrison* v *Sheffield Corporation* (1917)[12] the defendant local authority had planted trees on the highway, surrounded by spiked metal guards. Subsequently, under the Defence of the Realm Regulations, the chief constable required that all street lights be extinguished at a certain hour. The plaintiff suffered serious injury while using the street on a dark night. In finding the local authority liable Pickford LJ said[13]:

12 [1917] 2 KB 866.

13 At p.872.

> We start with the fact that the place was safe under ordinary conditions, and it is said
> that there was no obligation on the defendants to see that it did not become a danger in

the altered conditions. I do not agree with that contention; I think there was an obligation on the defendants to take reasonable care to see that it was not a danger under the altered conditions. ... It is said that our decision will involve a hardship on local authorities and will impose on them an obligation to guard or to paint every post and kerb, but in truth it only imposes an obligation to take reasonable care that what they have put in the roadway shall not become a nuisance and a danger under altered conditions.

Commercial and industrial waste

Section 45(1)(b) of the 1990 Act places a duty on waste collection authorities, if requested by the occupier of premises, to arrange for the collection of commercial waste. If it is so requested by the occupier the authority may arrange for the collection of industrial waste, with the consent of the waste disposal authority. In the performance of the collection function, and having regard to the scope of each definition, it is significant to note the gradation of responsibility attaching to household, commercial and industrial waste respectively. In the first case the collection authority has a duty to collect. In the second case the duty arises only when a request has been made. Finally, in relation to industrial waste, the authority is given a discretion to collect after a request has been made. The grading of these obligations strikes a balance between social necessity on the one hand, and the burden and costs of treating potentially complex and harmful materials on the other.

Concerning the matter of cost, the person requesting collection may be liable for a reasonable charge to the collection authority for collection and disposal;[14] implying consultation with and payment to the disposal authority of an appropriate portion of the sum. Conversely, a waste collection authority is given a discretion[15] to contribute towards the cost of providing or maintaining plant or equipment to deal with commercial or industrial waste before collection. One thinks in this context perhaps of baling machinery to facilitate collection and transport of bulky waste.

A waste collection authority may, under section 47, on request and for a reasonable charge, supply receptacles for commercial or industrial waste that it has agreed to collect; although it has power to remit the charge in the case of commercial waste. Alternatively, the authority may require by notice the occupier of premises to provide a reasonable type and number of receptacles for the storage on the premises of commercial or industrial waste. This power is conditional on the authority being of the opinion that such waste on the premises will be of a kind which, if not stored in receptacles of a particular type, is likely to cause a nuisance or to be detrimental to the amenities of the locality.[16] The matters that may be covered by such a notice are identical to those five items listed above in connection with household waste. Also identical to the comparable matters in section 46 are offences and appeals.

DISPOSAL

The meaning of 'disposal' has already been considered in the context of the licensing process. The term is defined in section 29(6) of the Environmental Protection Act 1990, the operations constituting disposal are listed in Part III of Schedule 4 of the Waste Management Licensing Regulations 1994,[17] and the latest judicial

14 Section 45(4).

15 In Section 45(8).

16 Section 47(2).

17 S.I. 1994 No. 1056.

view of its meaning is to be found in *R* v *Metropolitan Stipendiary Magistrate ex parte London Waste Regulation Authority* (1993).[18] This collectively wide-ranging view of disposal is designed for and meets the needs of the control process. For the present purposes of exposition, though, it is convenient to distinguish between, on the one hand, disposal as the final removal of material from any utilitarian use and, on the other hand, recycling, which serves to re-introduce waste material into the commercial stream with all the environmental benefits that flow therefrom.

The European Directive on waste[19] associates with disposal the requirement that the process be environmentally sympathetic. Article 4 provides that:

> Member States shall take the necessary measures to ensure that waste is disposed of without endangering human health and without harming the environment, and in particular:
>
> without risk to water, air, soil and plants and animals,
> without causing a nuisance through noise or odours,
> without adversely affecting the countryside or places of special interest.

Being in possession of the waste collected under section 45, the question of disposal concerns the collection authority as well as the disposal and regulation authorities. In metropolitan areas and in Wales, the collection and disposal authorities are of course the same. A collection authority is required, by section 48(1), to deliver to the places directed by the disposal authority for disposal the waste collected by them. As an exception to this general duty the collection authority may make arrangements for recycling household or commercial, but not industrial, waste, in which case it is to so notify the disposal authority. However, where the disposal authority has an arrangement with a contractor for the recycling of any waste it may object to the recycling proposals of the collection authority, and to the extent of the objection those proposals shall cease to be available to the collection authority.

Waste regulation authorities are charged with the duty in section 50 of preparing waste disposal plans,[20] a role that under section 2 of the 1974 Act was the responsibility of the disposal authority. The consequent changes in emphasis and function of the new plans were indicated by Lord Reay for the Government in the following terms:

> The first point to make is that although the name, waste disposal plan, is unchanged, the content of these new waste disposal plans should be quite different from the plans that have been compiled up to now. Current waste disposal plans are compiled by waste disposal authorities. They tend to be operational documents detailing what the authority does at its own sites with household waste. That is not the intention of our new waste disposal plans.
>
> In future waste disposal plans will be compiled by regulation authorities. They will identify the current and projected amounts of waste arising in the area. The plan will match those arisings to existing and planned disposal facilities and will identify future needs for new facilities. They will also set out the regulation authority's policies for waste disposal and recycling. Disposal plans will focus on additional disposal facilities which will be needed in the future. In that way they will act as a guide to investment by waste disposal contractors, who will actually provide the necessary facilities.[21]

The approach of the regulation authority and the content of the plan are stipulated in section 50(1) and (3) respectively. In preparing the plan the authority is to:

(a) investigate the present and future arrangements needed for treating and disposing of controlled waste produced in its area so as to prevent or minimise pollution of the environment or harm to human health;

(b) decide what arrangements in (a) above are required and how it should discharge its licensing functions;

(c) prepare a statement (the plan) of the arrangements made and proposed by waste disposal contractors for the treatment or disposal of waste;

(d) conduct periodic investigations to determine the need for changes in the plan; and

(e) make any appropriate consequent modifications to the plan.

In preparing or modifying the plan the authority is to have regard both to the likely cost of the arrangements and to their likely beneficial effects on the environment.

The authority is required to include in the plan, by section 50(3):

(a) the kinds and quantities of controlled waste which the authority expects to be –
  (i) situated in,
  (ii) brought into,
  (iii) taken for disposal out of,
  (iv) disposed of in,
  its area during the period specified in the plan;

(b) the methods (and their respective priorities) by which in the opinion of the authority controlled waste in its area should be disposed of or treated during that period;

(c) the authority's policy for the discharge of its licensing function and relating to any guidance issued by the Secretary of State;

(d) the sites and equipment that persons will, or will be expected to, provide for disposing of controlled waste; and

(e) the estimated costs of the proposals in the plan.[22]

The remaining subsections of section 50 are concerned with procedural matters, and in particular consultation and publicity. By section 50(5) preparation of the plan, or its modification, is to be preceded by consultation with:

(a) the NRA;

(b) waste collection authorities for the area;

(c) in Wales, the county council for the area;

(d) where the plan proposes disposal or treatment in the area of another regulation authority, that authority;

(e) persons who in the opinion of the authority are, are likely to be or are representatives of persons, engaged by way of trade or business in the disposal or treatment of controlled waste in the area of the authority;

What is implied by 'consultation' and the expectation that an authority's opinion be 'reasonable' have both been considered earlier.[23] In the case of (d) above, the proposals to be included in the plan require the consent of the other authority or, failing that, of the Secretary of State. Before finally determining the content of the plan or modification, a draft shall be sent to the Secretary of State so that he may ensure compliance with section 50(3) and, if necessary, give directions to that end. The Secretary of State is also given the power, to overcome any excessive delay

22 Section 50(3) gives the Secretary of State the power by regulations to modify the content of plans. No such regulations have yet been made.

23 See respectively in Chapter 1 at p.18 and Chapter 10 at p.276.

on the part of an authority in the preparation of the plan, by direction to require performance by a specified time of any duty under this section.

Also, as a preliminary to preparation of the plan or a sufficiently significant modification, the authority shall adequately publicise its proposals in the area. The public is then also to be given opportunities of making to the authority representations on the proposals, which are to be considered and, if appropriate, incorporated in the plan. When the authority has finally settled the contents of the plan or modification, it shall take the steps necessary in its opinion to give adequate publicity to it in its area and send a copy to the Secretary of State.

The disposal functions of waste disposal authorities are stated in section 51(1) to apply to the controlled waste collected in their areas by waste collection authorities and to the household waste deposited by residents of the areas at places provided for that purpose.[24] In either case disposal is to be by means of arrangements with waste disposal contractors. In the performance of these two functions disposal authorities are given, in sections 51(4) and (5) respectively, two separate sets of duties. First, in respect of the disposal of controlled waste they:

24 See under collection of household waste at p.400 above.

(a) shall give directions to the waste collection authorities in their area as to the persons to whom and the places at which the waste is to be delivered;
(b) may arrange for the provision by waste disposal contractors of places at which waste may be treated or kept prior to removal for treatment or disposal;
(c) may make available to contractors plant and equipment to enable the keeping or treatment of waste prior to removal for disposal or to treat waste to facilitate its storage or transport;
(d) may make land available to contractors to enable them to treat, keep or dispose of waste thereon;
(e) may contribute towards the costs incurred by producers of commercial or industrial waste in providing plant or equipment for dealing with such waste before it is collected; and
(f) may contribute to the similar costs of providing or maintaining pipes or associated works connecting with pipes provided by a waste collection authority within their area.

The comparable duties in subsection (5) relating to household waste left by residents at collection points, are that the authority:

(a) may arrange for the provision of places at which waste may be treated or kept prior to removal for treatment or disposal;
(b) may make available to contractors plant and equipment to enable the keeping or treatment of waste prior to removal for disposal or to treat waste to facilitate its storage or transport;
(c) may make land available to contractors to enable them to treat, keep or dispose of waste thereon.

The powers in (c) and (d) of the first list and (b) and (c) of the second to provide plant, equipment or land to contractors necessarily permits disposal authorities to own such property.

The duty to dispose of waste, involving as it does potentially offensive materials and processes, can be a source of objection to those in the vicinity. The obligation to perform that function may not, however, be used to justify or excuse causing offence; it being well established that the performance of a duty imposed

25 (1915) 84 LJ KB 1734.

by statute cannot, of itself, be a defence to nuisance proceedings. In the present context the court, in *Priest* v *Manchester Corporation* (1915)[25] held that the conveyance of land to the local authority for the tipping of refuse does not impliedly authorise the local authority to tip refuse in such a way as to cause a nuisance on the adjoining land when such tipping can be done without causing the nuisance. The court left open the associated question, whether in the event of it being impossible to use the land for tipping without creating a nuisance the local authority would be so authorised. The facts here concerned the tipping of material which due to its size and impervious nature caused rainwater to run off onto an adjoining street, eroding its surface and causing a danger to passers-by. These issues would now doubtless be resolved, or at least considered, at the planning stage, but the principle still holds good. That the performance of a statutory duty is a sufficient defence when it necessarily leads to the infringement of another's rights is well established in other contexts; see, for example, dicta of Lord Dunedin in *Manchester Corporation* v *Farnworth* (1930).[26]

26 [1930] AC 171; see Chapter 3 at p.83.

The obligation on authorities to use contractors to carry out the disposal function does not absolve them from responsibility for its effective and proper performance. In the event of harm or loss to others occasioned by such operations both the authority and the contractor may be liable. However, a person engaging an independent contractor does not have the same degree of control over his actions as does an employer over those of an employee. In apportioning responsibility for the consequences of actions of an independent contractor. Therefore, it is necessary to determine the relationship of the particular action to the attainment of the statutory purpose. While the authority will retain liability for the consequences of those activities of the contractor necessarily attendant upon the discharge of the statutory duty, it will not be responsible for the results of what has been referred to as 'casual or collateral' negligence.

So much appears from the decision of the Court of Appeal in *Robinson* v *Beaconsfield RDC* (1911).[27] The local authority had a contract with Hook for the emptying of cesspools. The agreement made no provision for the disposal of the contents after emptying, Hook being instructed by the council surveyor to deposit them where they would not be a nuisance. The plaintiff now alleged deposit of sewage on his farm land without permission and close to his tenants' houses, causing a nuisance. In holding the authority as well as the contractor liable the Court adopted the statement of principle of Lord Blackburn in *Dalton* v *Angus* (1881)[28] in which his Lordship said:

27 See at Chapter 3 note 81.

28 6 App Cas 740 at p. 829.

29 (1840) 6 M & W 499.

> Ever since *Quarman* v *Burnett*[29] it has been considered settled law that one employing another is not liable for his collateral negligence unless the relation of master and servant existed between them. So that a person employing a contractor to do work is not liable for the negligence of that contractor or his servants. On the other hand, a person causing something to be done, the doing of which casts on him a duty, cannot escape from responsibility attaching on him of seeing that duty performed by delegating it to a contractor. He may bargain with the contractor that he shall perform the duty and stipulate for an indemnity from him if it is not performed; but he cannot thereby relieve himself from liability to those injured by the failure to perform it.

The Court noted further that:

> Lord Blackburn in this passage contrasts a contractor's negligence, which he calls 'collateral', with failure on the part of a contractor to perform the duty of his employer. For

the first the employer is not liable; for the second he is, whether the failure is attributable to negligence or not

In support of their decision, Buckley LJ noted that in this case the contract was only for emptying and carting away. On that ground also, therefore, responsibility for disposal remained with the local authority.

Another useful formulation of the same principle, although in the context of road works and danger to the public, is to be found in *Penny* v *Wimbledon UDC* (1899).[30] A.L. Smith LJ, adopting the statement of Bruce J at first instance, said:

> The principle of the decision, I think, is this, that when a person employs a contractor to do work in a place where the public are in the habit of passing, which work will, unless precautions are taken, cause danger to the public, an obligation is thrown upon the person who orders the work to be done to see that the necessary precautions are taken, and that, if the necessary precautions are not taken, he cannot escape liability by seeking to throw the blame on the contractor'. I agree with this entirely, but would add as an exception the case of mere casual or collateral acts of negligence, such as that given as an illustration during the argument – a workman employed on the work negligently leaving a pickaxe, or such like, in the road. I cannot hold that leaving heaps of soil in the road, which would by the very nature of the contract have to be dug up and dealt with, is an act either casual or collateral with reference to the contract.

RECYCLING

The common characteristic of waste is that it has no value to the person having possession of it. Indeed, the need to secure its disposal may involve expense. This burden may be reduced by giving back to waste material, or some elements of it, some value by removing it from the waste stream and re-introducing it to commercial use. As well as offering immediate benefit to the producer the re-use of waste assists in the reduction of energy costs in the production of new materials and of the increasing costs of disposal.

As an indication of the potentially available forms of such re-use the 11th Report of the Royal Commission on Environmental Pollution[31] notes that:

> If material in the waste stream can be used without significant alteration it may then be considered suitable for *reuse*. Returnable bottles are an example. Alternatively waste materials may be recycled as raw materials for the same sorts of products: waste paper for paper manufacture; cullet for glass manufacture; oil for re-refining, and so on. A further option is that the waste material can be reclaimed as the raw material for some new product or use, such as the manufacture of compost or waste derived fuel; the recovery of energy as heat or electricity from the mass incineration of wastes is also a form of reclamation.

As may be expected, therefore, the European Directive on waste[32] requires in Article 3 that 'Member States shall take appropriate steps to encourage the prevention, recycling and reprocessing of waste, the extraction of raw materials and possibly of energy therefrom and any other process for the re-use of the waste'.

That recycling, however virtuous as a concept, is not an end in itself but must be assimilated to general industrial and commercial needs has to be recognised. Recycling targets originally set by EC Environment Ministers involved specific percentage figures for the recovery and recycling of packaging within five- and ten-year periods. However, Germany's experience with its DSD scheme, in which

30 [1899] 2 QB 72 at p.76.

31 'Managing Waste: The Duty of Care', Cmnd 9675, December 1985, paragraph 5.2.

32 75/442/EEC.

far more material was collected than the industry could cope with, has induced a more flexible approach. The target now is for a 60 per cent recovery rate for packaging within five years, with national flexibility for re-use, recycling and so on within that 60 per cent figure.[33]

33 *Environmental Health News*, vol. 8, no. 43 dated 29.10.1993.

As is to be expected, therefore, one finds in the Part II provisions of the Environmental Protection Act 1990 a clear predisposition in favour of recycling as the preferred method of waste disposal. Recognising that the earlier materials to be recycled are removed from the waste stream the lower the cost is likely to be, the Act places primary responsibility for the process on waste collection authorities. Just as regulation authorities are required to develop disposal plans so, by section 49, waste collection authorities are required to produce waste recycling plans. The terms of the section have close similarities with those for waste disposal plans in section 50. Section 49(1) requires collection authorities, in respect of household and commercial waste in their areas, to:

(a) investigate appropriate arrangements for dealing with waste by separating, baling or otherwise packaging it for recycling;
(b) decide what arrangements are required for that purpose;
(c) prepare a statement (the plan) of the arrangements made and proposed by the authority and others for dealing with waste in those ways;
(d) conduct periodic investigations to determine the need for changes in the plan; and
e) make any appropriate consequent modifications to the plan.

In preparing or modifying the plan the authority is to have regard both to the effects such arrangements are likely to have on the amenities of the area and to the costs or savings attributable to the arrangements.

The authority is required to include in the plan, by subsection 49(3):

(a) the kinds and quantities of controlled waste which the authority expects to –
    (i) collect,
    (ii) purchase,
    (iii) process as in (1)(a) above,
in its area during the period specified in the plan;
(b) the arrangements it expects to make with waste disposal contractors for waste recycling during that period;
(c) the plant and equipment which the authority expects to provide under sections 48(6) or 53; and
(d) the estimated costs or savings attributable to the recycling proposals in the plan.

A copy of the draft plan is to be sent to the Secretary of State so that he may be assured that the section 49(3) requirements are satisfied. In that regard he may issue directions to the authority, which then has a duty to comply with them. On final determination of the plan contents the collection authority shall:

(a) take adequate steps to publicise it in their area; and
(b) send copies to the waste disposal and regulation authorities for that area.

The collection authority shall keep a copy of the plan and any modifications available for public inspection at all reasonable times free of charge, and supply a copy of the plan on payment of a reasonable charge. The Secretary of State is also given the power, to overcome any excessive delay on the part of an authority in the preparation of the plan, by direction to require performance by a specified time of any duty under this section.

Before leaving the topic of disposal plans, it is to be noted that the section 50 powers of disposal authorities incorporate a recycling element. In including in its disposal plan the methods and priorities by which controlled waste in its area should be disposed of or treated, the authority is to give priority, where reasonably practicable, to recycling waste.[34] In support of this obligation, subsection (7) requires a disposal authority in preparing or modifying its disposal plan to consider, in consultation with waste collection authorities in its area and others:

(a) arrangements that may reasonably be made for waste recycling;
(b) provisions to be included in the plan for that purpose.

Collection authorities are given express powers in connection with recycling in sections 48, 52 and 55. It scarcely needs to be said, though, that these powers are not concerned with recycling *per se*, which is a matter of commercial rather than legal potential. These enabling powers are to allow public authorities concerned with the handling of waste to separate out and redirect appropriate components for further commercial use as an alternative to disposal.

By section 48(6), a waste collection authority[35] may provide plant and equipment for the sorting and bailing of waste that it decides to retain for recycling under subsection (2). Subsection (8) then gives the authority the discretion to allow others to use such equipment, or specifically to provide plant and equipment for such use, and provides that:

(a) a reasonable charge shall be made for its use, unless the authority considers it appropriate not to;
(b) no charge is to be made in respect of household waste;
(c) anything delivered in the use of these facilities shall belong to the authority.

Both disposal and collection authorities are given, slightly differing, powers for recycling waste by section 55. By section 55(2), a disposal authority may:

(a) make arrangements with disposal contractors for them to recycle the waste received by the authority either under section 51(1) or by agreement;
(b) make arrangements with disposal contractors for them to use waste for the purpose of producing heat or electricity or both;
(c) buy or otherwise acquire waste with a view to its being recycled;
(d) use, sell or otherwise dispose of any such waste or anything produced from it.

A waste collection authority may similarly, by section 55(3):

(a) buy or otherwise acquire waste with a view to recycling it;
(b) use or dispose of, by sale or otherwise, waste belonging to the authority or anything produced from it;

So far as waste 'belonging' to the authority is concerned, section 45(9) provides that 'anything collected under arrangements made by a waste collection authority under this section shall belong to the authority and may be dealt with accordingly'.

As has been seen, and as one would expect from their designations, waste collection authorities are responsible for collection and disposal authorities for dis-

34 Section 50(4).

35 Section 48(7), if the waste collection authority is also a waste disposal authority it may only undertake this function through an arrangement with a waste disposal contractor.

posal of controlled waste. To the extent that the burden of these statutory duties is reduced or performed by others in recycling a proportion of that waste, section 52 makes provision for equivalent financial compensation. Section 52(1) to (4) provide respectively that:

(1) where a collection authority retains collected waste for recycling, the disposal authority shall make payments to it representing its net saving of expenditure on disposal costs;

(2) where a disposal authority arranges collection points for the receipt of waste, the collection authority shall make payments to it of sums representing its net saving of expenditure on collection;

(3) where a person other than a collection authority collects waste for recycling, the disposal authority for that area may make payments to him representing its net saving of expenditure on disposal costs;

(4) where a person other than a collection authority collects waste for recycling, the collection authority may make payments to him of sums representing its net saving of expenditure on collection.

A significant distinction in emphasis is to be observed in the obligation to pay these 'waste recycling credits'. As between public authorities, sections 52(1) and (2) require that compensatory payments shall be made. So far as third parties are concerned, who are likely to be operating on a commercial basis anyway, the authorities are given a discretion in sections 52(3) and (4) whether to make payments. Baroness Blatch offered further reasons for the distinction[36]:

36 *Hansard*, HL, vol. 522, col. 363.

> When [*local authorities*] have identified all those bodies undertaking recycling in their area, they may decide that it would not be desirable for credits to be paid in every case. There may be instances where economies of scale make it more appropriate for the waste collection authority to undertake recycling rather than it being done by voluntary bodies. There may be other cases where a number of bodies are undertaking similar schemes in the same area. It would not necessarily be appropriate for an authority to be required to pay recycling credits to a number of competing schemes in the same area, particularly where some of the schemes yielded only small quantities of waste. Giving disposal authorities discretion to pay credits will allow them to make sensible judgements about the type of third party recycling scheme which should be encouraged in their area.

In spite of the cogency of such arguments the Secretary of State has, in section 52(5), the power by regulation to impose on waste disposal authorities the duty to make the subsection (3) payments.

The meaning of 'net saving of expenditure' in the case of disposal and collection authorities is dealt with respectively, in sections 52(6) and (7). In the former case, relating to disposal authorities, it means the amount of expenditure which the authority would, but for the retention or collection, have incurred in having it disposed of, less any amount payable to the authority by a person in consequence of the retention or collection for recycling of the waste. Similarly, in respect of collection authorities, it is the amount of expenditure which the authority would have incurred if it had had to collect the waste. The actual determination of a waste disposal authority's net saving of expenditure for the purposes of section 52(1) and (3) is according to the principles contained in regulations made by the Secretary of State under section 52(8), such regulations being the Environmental Protection (Waste Recycling Payments) Regulations 1992.[37] The saving shall be:

37 S.I. 1992 No.462.

... half the expenditure which it would have incurred in disposing of the waste at a cost per tonne equal to its average cost per tonne at the relevant time of disposing of similar waste using its most expensive disposal method unless it can be shown that its net saving of expenditure is a higher amount, in which case it shall be that amount'.[38]

Factors to be taken into account in determining the average cost are, in connection with that waste:

(a) the value of any assets used in connection with disposal, including land;
(b) any site operating expenditure in connection with disposal;
(c) any transport costs in connection with disposal;
(d) any expenditure incurred in concluding the use of the disposal site;
(e) any other expenditure incurred in relation to the waste.

Where it is not reasonably practicable to make a determination under regulation 2(2) the Schedule to the regulations provides substitute figures.

Lastly, section 52 makes provision for financial redress in two further cases. By section 52(9) a collection authority is to pay the disposal authority the reasonable cost of disposing of commercial and industrial waste collected in its area, thus separating the functional and financial responsibility. Secondly, and recollecting the duty on the collection authority to deliver waste to the place specified by the disposal authority, where such place is unreasonably far from the collection authority's area the disposal authority shall make a reasonable contribution to the additional cost.[39]

TRANSPORT

National

Registration of carriers of waste under the Control of Pollution (Amendment) Act 1989 has been considered above.[40] Founded on that structure is control of waste transport in practice, section 5 providing that where it reasonably appears to a duly authorised officer of a regulation authority[41] or to a constable that controlled waste is being or has been transported in contravention of section 1(1) (i.e., by a person who is not registered), he may:

(a) stop and search the vehicle;
(b) require production of the certificate of registration;[42]
(c) test or take samples of anything found.

The power to stop a vehicle on a road is restricted to a constable in uniform. Once the vehicle is stopped either official may implement the section 5 provisions. Where the carrier is unable to produce an authority forthwith he shall produce or send it to the principal office of the authority within seven days.[43] For this purpose a copy of the certificate of registration provided under regulation 9 of the Controlled Waste (Registration of Carriers and Seizure of Vehicles) Regulations 1991 No. 1624 shall constitute such authority. Offences under this section are either intentional obstruction or failure, without reasonable excuse, to comply with a lawful requirement. These breaches must also occur in the context of the transport of controlled waste to or from places in Great Britain. Fly-tipping and other waste-related offences may also lead to loss of the goods vehicle operator's licence under section 69 of the Transport Act 1968.[44]

38 Regulation 2(2).

39 Section 52(10).

40 See Chapter 13 at pp.360–4.

41 Changed from 'disposal authority' by section 162(1) and Schedule 15, paragraph 31(1) of the Environmental Protection Act 1990.

42 Or alternatively evidence that registration is not required.

43 The Controlled Waste (Registration of Lorries and Seizure of Vehicles) Regulation 1991 No. 1624.

44 See Environmental Protection Act 1990, Schedule 15, paragraph 10.

Section 6 provides an additional restricted power to seize vehicles and their contents under a warrant issued to a disposal authority by a justice of the peace, which may be executed either by a duly authorised officer of the disposal authority or by a constable. The warrant, which remains in force until executed, is issued on a sworn information that:

(a) there are reasonable grounds for believing that –
   (i) an offence under section 3 of the Control of Pollution Act 1974 has been committed;[45] and
   (ii) that vehicle was used in the commission of the offence;
(b) proceedings for that offence have not yet been brought; and
(c) the authority has failed, after taking prescribed steps, to ascertain the name and address of any person able to provide the prescribed information about who was using the vehicle when the offence was committed.

The 'prescribed steps' for the purposes of (c) above are specified in regulation 20 of the Controlled Waste (Registration of Carriers and Seizure of Vehicles) Regulations 1991[46] by which the regulation authority is to:

(a) obtain information concerning the keeper of the vehicle from –
   (i) if registered in Great Britain, the Secretary of State for the Environment,
   (ii) if registered in Northern Ireland, the Secretary of State for Transport,
   (iii) if foreign registered, the chief constable for the area where the offence was committed;
(b) serve notice on any person it considers able to provide information as to the person using the vehicle at the relevant time under section 71(2) of the Environmental Protection Act 1990 requiring the name and address of that person.

The attempt to obtain the necessary information to allow conventional enforcement action is thus a necessary precondition to this draconian process of last resort.

The subsequent treatment of the seized property, including its removal, return or disposal, may be provided for by regulations made by the Secretary of State under sections 6(5) to (7). The current provisions are to be found in regulations 21, 22 and 23 of the Controlled Waste (Registration of Carriers and Seizure of Vehicles) Regulations 1991. Regulation 21 provides that, following seizure, the vehicle and contents may be removed by being driven, towed or otherwise reasonably removed, using any necessary steps to facilitate that purpose. The regulation recognises that separate removal of the vehicle contents may be necessary and is therefore authorised where:

(a) it is reasonable to do so to facilitate removal of the vehicle;
(b) there is good reason for storing them at a different place from the vehicle;
(c) their condition requires that they be disposed of without delay.

Property seized under section 6 may be returned, unless disposed of under regulation 23, to a person who:

(a) produces satisfactory evidence of his entitlement and identity; or
(b) if acting as agent of another, of that person's identity and entitlement and of his authority;
(c) in the case of a vehicle, produces the registration book.

45 That is, prohibition on the unlicensed disposal of waste; now section 33(1) of the Environmental Protection Act 1990.

46 S.I. 1991 No. 1624.

Proof of entitlement to the vehicle generally implies entitlement to its contents; subject to sufficient proof of another's claim. In the event of more than one claim the authority is to determine the better entitlement on the basis of the evidence submitted.

The regulation authority is given power under regulation 23 to sell, destroy or deposit at any place property seized under section 6 if:

(a) it has advertised in a local newspaper notice of the details, circumstances of the seizure, the procedure for a claim and the intention of the authority to dispose of the property;

(b) it has served a copy of the notice on –
 (i) the person served under section 71(2) of the 1990 Act;
 (ii) the chief constable for the area;
 (iii) the Secretary of State for Transport;
 (iv) Hire Purchase Information plc.

(c) 28 days has expired from publication of the notice under (a) above and there has been no request under regulation 22, or the condition of the property requires it to be disposed of without delay.

Following disposal of a vehicle the authority is required to notify the parties at (ii) to (iv) above. The proceeds of sale are to be used to meet any expenses of the authority in performing section 6 functions, and then in meeting any claim by a person providing satisfactory evidence of entitlement under regulation 22 if the property had not been sold.[47] The implication in the possibility of a surplus to meet claims from erstwhile owners is that the authority may use the proceeds of sale only to meet the expenses attendant upon that transaction, rather than those arising from the performance of its section 6 functions generally.

Two provisions in section 7 are worth noting in conclusion. Section 7(5) provides that where the commission of an offence is due to the act or default of another, that other shall also be guilty of the offence; and a person may be charged and convicted under this subsection whether or not proceedings for the offence are taken against any other person. Section 7(6) deals with corporate bodies, providing that where an offence has been committed by such a body, but with the consent or connivance of or with neglect on the part of any director, manager, secretary or similar officer of the body, that person as well as the body corporate shall be guilty of the offence.

European Community

Controls on the shipment of waste within, into and out of the European Community came into operation on 6 May 1994. These controls are to be found in Council Regulation (EEC) No. 259/93, ('the Waste Shipments Regulation' or 'the Regulation'), which is directly applicable without transposition into national legislation, and, to supplement the Regulation within the United Kingdom, the Transfrontier Shipment of Waste Regulations 1994.[48] As their titles indicate, they bear very close similarities in operation and effect to the Order and Regulations of 1988 which applied to hazardous waste[49] and which they now replace.

The Waste Shipments Regulation gives effect to the Basle Convention on the Control of Transboundary Movements of Hazardous Wastes and their Disposal (the Basle Convention),[50] which itself provides an international structure of envi-

47 Regulations 24 and 25.

48 S.I. 1994 No. 1137; and see DoE Circular 13/94.

49 See in Chapter 16 at p.441.

50 Presented to Parliament in March 1990, Cm 984 (HMSO).

51 Of 15 December 1989.

ronmental controls on movements of waste and to which the United Kingdom and the European Community became parties on 8 May 1994. The Regulation also gives effect within the European Community to the Lomè IV Convention,[51] requiring the prohibition of exports of hazardous wastes from the Community to approximately 70 African, Caribbean and Pacific countries.

To facilitate the movement of waste for the purpose of recovery within the OECD, that body has produced a supplementary agreement under Article 11 of the Convention, the OECD Decision on the Control of Transfrontier Movements of Waste Destined for Recovery Operations (the OECD Decision).[52] That decision classifies wastes commonly subject to recovery into three lists, reflecting their hazardous nature – green, amber and red.

52 Organisation for Economic Co-operation and Development: C(92)39/Final, adopted by the Council on 30 March 1992. Amended by Decision C(93)74/Final, adopted by the Council on 23 July 1993.

Green list wastes, by far the largest group, are subject only to normal commercial controls. To indicate the range of material included, the extensive list contains the following subdivisions:

A   Metal and metal-alloy wastes in metallic, non-dispersible form.
B   Other metal bearing wastes arising from the melting, smelting and refining of metals.
C   Wastes from mining operations: in non-dispersible form.
D   Solid plastic wastes.
E   Paper, paperboard and paper product wastes.
F   Glass waste in non-dispersible form.
G   Ceramic waste in non-dispersible form.
H   Textile wastes.
I   Rubber wastes.
J   Untreated cork and wood wastes.
K   Wastes arising from agro-food industries.
L   Wastes arising from tanning and fell-mongery operations and leather use.
M   Other wastes.

The movement of red list waste for recovery is subject to the same controls as is the transport of such waste for disposal. Red list materials are:

(a)   Wastes, substances and articles containing, consisting of or contaminated with polychlorinated biphenyl (PCB) and/or polychlorinated terphenyl (PCT) and/or polybrominated biphenyl (PBB), including any other polybrominated analogues of these compounds, at a concentration level of 50 mg/kg or more.
(b)   Wastes that contain, consist of or are contaminated with any of the following:
    (i)   any congener of polychlorinated dibenzo-furan,
    (ii)   any congener of polychlorinated dibenzo-dioxin.
(c)   Asbestos (dusts and fibres).
(d)   Ceramic based fibres similar to those of asbestos.
(e)   Leaded anti-knock compound sludges.
(f)   Waste tarry residues (excluding asphalt cements) arising from refining, distillation and any pyrolitic treatment.
(g)   Peroxides other than hydrogen peroxide.

Amber list waste products are subject to a more simplified control procedure, reflecting their reduced potential for harm in comparison with those on the red list. There is a total of 72 materials and classes on this list, representative examples being:

- Ash and residues of zinc, lead, copper, aluminium and vanadium
- Municipal waste combustion residues
- Lead-acid batteries, other batteries and accumulators
- Waste oils, mixtures and emulsions
- Waste reprographic and photographic chemicals
- Asphalt cement wastes
- Galvanic sludges
- Hydrogen peroxide solutions
- Arsenic and mercury waste and residue
- Explosive wastes, when not subject to other specific legislation
- Leaded petrol (gasoline) sludges
- Chlorofluorocarbons
- Halons
- Metal shredding fluff
- Brake and antifreeze fluids
- Sewage sludge
- Household wastes
- Wastes from the production and preparation of pharmaceutical products
- Acidic and basic solutions

The Regulation deals with the transfrontier shipment of all waste for disposal, with the exception of :

(a) operational waste from ships and off-shore oil platforms,
(b) civil aviation waste,
(c) radioactive waste as defined in Directive 92/3/EURATOM,
(d) green list wastes.[53]

Movements of waste within an individual Member State are, under Article 13, to be governed by an appropriate system established by that State. That does not prevent a Member State adopting this trans-Community procedure for its internal use if it so chooses. In the United Kingdom control is exercised under the Control of Pollution (Amendment) Act 1989 considered above, and the Control of Pollution (Special Waste) Regulations 1980;[54] see also section 34 of the Environmental Protection Act 1990 imposing a duty of care.

Summarising the principles of this new system, the Department of the Environment Circular says, at paragraph 12:

> The new transfrontier control system is based on 'prior informed consent'. It requires notification where appropriate to the competent authorities of dispatch, destination and transit, using a consignment note containing prescribed information. Only when consent has been given by the relevant authorities may the waste be shipped (this is what is meant by references to shipments being 'allowed'). The competent authorities must also be notified by the consignee when the waste has been received and, later, receive certification that it has been disposed of or recovered.

The concept of 'competent authorities' is fundamental to the system of waste shipment control, it being left to individual Member States to identify their own competent authorities. In the United Kingdom waste regulation authorities (WRAs) have been designated for that purpose. In relation to imports the competent authority of destination is the WRA for the area in which the waste is received, and for exports from the United Kingdom it is the WRA for the area where the waste is

53 The possible exceptions where green list wastes may be covered are:

(a) if the EC determines that the waste exhibits any hazardous characteristics, Article 1(3)(c);
(b) where, exceptionally, a Member State wishes shipments of such waste to be controlled for environmental or public health reasons, Article 1(3)(d);
(c) if a non-OECD country wishes categories of green list waste to be controlled, Article 17.

54 S.I. 1980 No. 1709; and see in Chapter 16 at p.435.

55 Regulation 3 Transfrontier
Shipment of Waste Regulations
1994; S.I. 1994 No. 1137.

56 Regulation 4 of the 1994
Regulations.

57 Council Directive
75/442/EEC.

58 DoE Circular 13/94;
paragraphs 25, 28 and 31
respectively.

produced or collected before transport.[55] The Basle Convention, and therefore the Regulation, requires that the competent authority of transit (i.e., for the purposes of movement of shipments of waste through a State) shall be a single body. The Secretary of State is therefore designated as the competent authority for transit in the United Kingdom.[56] With the eventual transfer of the waste regulation function from local authorities to the anticipated Environment Agency one may assume that it will assume that role. The creation of an Environment Agency as presently envisaged will also resolve any problems of communication that may now arise between WRAs as waste disposal licensing agencies and HMIP as the authorising body for such facilities coming within the Integrated Pollution Control (IPC) (or local authorities and LAAPC) provisions of Part I of the Environmental Protection Act 1990.

This Regulation adopts the definitions of 'waste' and 'disposal' from the Framework Directive on Waste.[57] Article 1(a) of that Directive provides that '"waste" means any substance or object which the holder disposes of or is required to dispose of pursuant to the provisions of national law in force'. Article 1(b) similarly defines 'disposal' as meaning:

– the collection, sorting, transport and treatment of waste as well as its storage and tipping above or under ground,
– the transformation operations necessary for its re-use, recovery or recycling.

Bearing in mind the differing procedures attaching to shipment of waste for disposal or recovery, the peculiarity of this definition is that it includes recovery within disposal.

The terms 'shipment', 'consignment' and 'environmentally sound management' though frequently appearing in the Regulation are not defined in it but are considered in the DoE Circular.[58] 'Shipment', it suggests, may be taken to mean the movement by land, sea or air of waste from its place of original production (or in the case of waste from various producers, the place where the waste is collected) to the place of its recovery or disposal. 'Consignment' may be regarded as a quantity of waste that is intended to be, is being, or has been transported from one State to another without its being divided or added to. It will be the subject of one notification, Article 29 prohibiting the mixing of wastes which are the subject of different notifications.

'Environmentally sound management' of wastes must be interpreted according to the type of shipment involved, its intended destination and the process for which it is destined. Regulation 11 of the Transfrontier Shipment of Waste Regulations 1994 requires the Secretary of State to prepare a waste management plan in accordance with Article 7 of the Framework Directive on Waste, setting out his policies on the import and export of waste for recovery or disposal. That plan will contain guidance on the meaning and application of that principle. So far as the import of waste into the United Kingdom for recovery or disposal is concerned, the fundamental requirement is that the facility is licensed or authorised to deal with the proposed wastes.

The transactions for which the Regulation specifies control procedures, together with the applicable Articles, are as follows:

Articles	Shipments within the Community
3–5	Shipments between Member States for disposal, including transit through one or more Member States, and for single or multiple consignments.

6–9	Shipment between Member States of amber list waste for recovery, including transit through one or more Member States, and for single or multiple consignments.
10	Shipment between Member States of red list waste (and waste not yet assigned to an Annex) for recovery, including transit through one or more Member States.
12	Shipments between Member States for disposal or recovery with transit via third States.

Exports from the Community

14–15	Export from the Community for disposal.
16–17	Export from the Community to and through OECD countries of amber list waste for recovery.
16–17	Export from the Community to and through OECD countries of red list wastes (and wastes not yet assigned to an Annex) for recovery.
16–17	Exports from the Community to non-OECD countries of amber, red and unassigned waste for recovery.

Imports into the Community

19–20	Imports of waste into the Community for disposal.
21–22	Imports of waste into the Communbity for recovery from and through countries to which the OECD Decision applies.
21–22	Imports into the Community of waste for recovery from non-OECD countries.

Transit through the Community

23	Transit through the Community of waste from outside for disposal or recovery outside the Community, excluding recoverable wastes shipped to and from OECD countries.
24	Transit of waste for recovery from and to an OECD country.
25(2)–26(2)	Re-shipment of waste.

At first, and perhaps subsequent, sight these provisions appear complex and possibly confusing. They are certainly detailed. Examination reveals, however, that, as may be expected from their general similarity of purpose, the procedures, though reproduced for each situation with necessary amendments to meet differing circumstances, all have a broad common structure. In consequence the procedure for the first operation, shipments between Member States for disposal, will now be considered in sufficient detail to provide an understanding of the process; followed by the major variations applicable to other procedures.

Shipments between Member States for disposal, (Articles 3–5)

(a) Notifier to have a contract with the consignee[59] which must provide for:
    (i) notifier to take back the waste if the shipment is not completed as planned or if effected in violation of the Regulation,
    (ii) consignee to certify as soon as possible or at least within 180 days that the waste has been disposed of in an environmentally sound manner.
(b) Competent authority of dispatch issues on request consignment note[60] blanks to notifier.

59 These terms are defined in Article 2 of the Regulation.

60 The EC has yet to adopt a standard consignment note as provided for in Article 42 of the Regulation. Until then the note adopted under Directive 84/631/EEC and used for the Transfrontier Shipment of Hazardous Waste (the TFS Document) will continue to be used – see Article 42(2). Forms are obtainable by competent authorities from HMIP, Room P3/019, 2 Marsham St, London SW1P 3EB.

(c) EITHER – notifier informs the competent authority of destination

OR – competent authority of dispatch decides to transmit notifications and notifier supplies consignment note and documents to that authority. Within three days competent authority of despatch notifies competent authority of destination with copies to competent authorities of transit (if any) and consignee with acknowledgement to the notifier, or if there are objections, so informs the notifier; in which case the process terminates.

(d) Within three working days competent authority of destination informs the notifier of its decision, with copies to other concerned competent authorities.

(e) Other competent authorities then have 20 days following dispatch of acknowledgement to raise and inform the notifier of any reasoned objections, lay down conditions or request additional information.[61]

(f) In the absence of objections competent authority of destination to give its authorisation between 21 and 30 days of dispatch of acknowledgement, by stamping the consignment note.

In the case of multiple shipments the procedure to this point is to be performed once prior to the first shipment. Separate movement/tracking forms are then to accompany individual shipments.[62]

(g) Before the shipment leaves the United Kingdom, notifier is to obtain a certificate from the competent authority of dispatch in accordance with regulation 7 of the Transfrontier Shipment of Waste Regulations 1994.[63]

(h) Three working days prior to the shipment notifier to send to all competent authorities concerned copies of the completed consignment note, including dates of shipment.[64]

(i) Copy of the consignment note (the tracking document) to accompany the shipment. All parties – notifier, carrier, consignee – to complete, sign and retain a copy.

(j) Within three working days of receipt of the waste consignee to send copies of the completed consignment note to notifier and all concerned competent authorities.

(k) As soon as possible, and not later than 180 days following receipt of the waste, consignee to send certificate of disposal to notifier with copies to concerned competent authorities.

(l) Upon receipt of certificate of disposal by notifier, the financial guarantee shall be released or returned.

Waste for recovery (Articles 6–12)

(a) Competent authorities have 30 days from date of dispatch of acknowledgment within which to object to the shipment; but may consent within that period.

(b) Competent authorities have 20 days from date of dispatch of acknowledgment within which to lay down conditions governing transport of the waste within their jurisdiction.[65] Conditions are to be notified in writing to the notifier and entered on the consignment note, with copies to other competent authorities.

(c) Tacit consent is given if there are no objections within 30 days, such consent expiring after one year.

61 Article 4(3)(a) gives Member States the power to 'prohibit generally or partially or to object systematically to shipments of waste'. Such measures are to be notified immediately to the Commission which will inform Member States.

62 'Multiple shipments' apply where waste having the same physical and chemical characteristics is shipped periodically to the same consignee following the same route. The maximum period over which shipments can be made under a general notification is one year.

63 S.I. 1994 No. 1137. The certificate certifies the authority's satisfaction that a financial guarantee or equivalent insurance exists in respect of the costs of shipment and disposal or recovery and satisfying the requirements of Article 27 exists.

64 Article 3(5). The completed consignment note will provide full details of the source, composition and quantity of the waste and the producer(s)' identity; routing and third party insurance; measures to ensure safe transport and satisfy any transport conditions; identity of the consignee, location and details of authorisation of the disposal centre; disposal operations – see Annex II[(a)] of Directive 75/442/EEC.

65 Article 7(3) and (4) specifies the scope of conditions and objections respectively.

(d) Competent authorities with jurisdiction over specific waste recovery facilities may decide not to object to shipments to them of certain types of waste. Commission to be provided with details of the facility and types of waste; they in turn are to notify other competent authorities in the Community and the OECD Secretariat.

(e) Shipments of Annex IV waste (red list) or unassigned waste for recovery are subject to the Articles 6–8 procedure, except that the written consent of competent authorities is required before commencement of the shipment (see (e) and (f) above).

(f) Article 11 specifies the information to accompany shipments of Annex II (green list) waste to assist tracking, which information is to be treated confidentially.

(g) In the case of shipments between Member States with transit through other Member States, Articles 3–10 apply and, by Article 12, the notifier is to send a copy of the nofication to the competent authority of the third State(s). The competent authority of destination shall receive their consent before giving its authorisation.

Exports of waste from the Community (Articles 14–18)

(1) For disposal:
   (a) Article 14 prohibits all exports of waste for disposal except to EFTA countries which are parties to the Basel Convention.
   (b) Exports of waste to EFTA countries are also banned –
      (i) where the country of destination prohibits import of such waste or has not given written consent to the import of that specific waste;
      (ii) if the competent authority of dispatch in the Community has reason to believe that the waste will not be managed in accordance with environmentally sound methods.

The competent authority of dispatch is to require that waste exported to EFTA countries is to be managed in an environmentally sound manner during shipment and in the State of destination.

   (c) The competent authority of dispatch has from 61 to 70 days from the date of acknowledgment to decide whether to authorise shipment, with or without conditions, or to refuse it. Competent authorities of dispatch and transit have 60 days to raise objections based on Article 4(3) (i.e., to implement the principles of proximity, priority for recovery and self-sufficiency at Community and national levels in accordance with Directive 75/442/EEC) and to request additional information.

   (d) on the incorrect issue of the certificate of disposal with the consequent release of the financial guarantee, the consignee is to bear all the costs of the return of the shipment to the jurisdiction of the competent authority of dispatch and of its disposal.

   (e) The competent authority of transit may not impose more stringent conditions than those applying to shipments of waste within its jurisdiction.

   (f) A specimen of the consignment note shall be delivered by the carrier to the last customs office of departure when the waste leaves the Community. They shall then sent a copy to the competent authority which issued the authorisation.

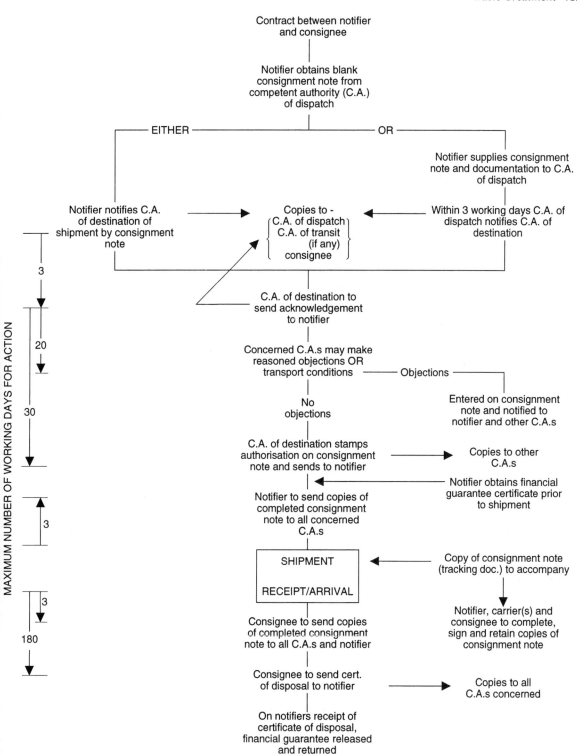

Figure 15.1 Shipments between member states for disposal

(g) If after 42 days of the waste leaving the Community the authorising competent authority has not received notification from the consignee of his receipt of the waste, it shall so inform the competent authority of destination. Similar action shall be taken if it does not receive from the consignee the certificate of disposal within 180 days.

(2) For recovery:
  (a) All exports of waste for recovery are prohibited except those to –
    (i) countries to which the OECD decision applies;
    (ii) other countries which are parties to the Basle Convention, and/or with which the Community or the Community and its Member States have concluded bilateral or multilateral or regional agreements in accordance with Article 11 of the Basle Convention and paragraph 2,[66] or with which individual Member States have concluded bilateral agreements prior to the operation of this Regulation.
  (b) Exports of waste to those paragraph (a) countries shall also be prohibited–
    (i) where that country prohibits the import of such wastes; or
    (ii) where it has not given its consent to their specific import;
    (iii) if the competent authority of dispatch has reason to believe that the waste will not be managed in an environmentally sound manner in that country.
  (c) The competent authority of dispatch is to require that any waste for recovery authorised for export be managed in an environmentally sound manner during shipment and in the State of destination.
  (d) Provisions concerning the competent authorities of dispatch and transit only apply to those within the Community.
  (e) Stages (f) and (g) in export for disposal apply here also.
  (f) Exports of red list and unassigned wastes to and through OECD countries for recovery requires that prior consent of the competent authorities concerned be provided to the notifier in writing before shipment.
  (g) Competent authorities of dispatch and transit within the Community may only raise reasoned objections in accordance with Article 7(4), rather than Article 4(3) in relation to disposal in (c) above.[67]

Imports of Waste into the Community (Articles 18–22)

(1) For disposal
  (a) All imports of waste for disposal are prohibited except those to –
    (i) EFTA countries which are parties to the Basle Convention;
    (ii) other countries which are parties to the Basle Convention, and/or with which the Community or the Community and its Member States have concluded bilateral or multilateral or regional agreements in accordance with Article 11 of the Basle Convention guaranteeing that recovery is carried out at an authorised centre and in an environmentally sound manner, or with which individual Member States have concluded bilateral agreements prior to the operation of this Regulation.[68]
  (b) The procedure is comparable with that for export for disposal.
  (c) Prior to the transaction the notifier must have obtained from the competent authority of destination in the United Kingdom a certificate in accord-

66 Article 16(2) requires that these agreements shall guarantee an environmentally sound management of the waste in accordance with Article 11 of the Basle Convention with specific coverage of certain matters.

67 The Article 7(4) grounds of objection include: compliance with Directive 75/442/EEC, Article 7; contrary to national laws relating to environmental protection, public order, safety or health; notifier or consignee have been guilty of illegal trafficking; shipment conflicts with international convention obligations; ratio of recoverable waste does not justify recovery on economic and environmental grounds.

68 In this latter case certain restrictions and limitations apply. In exceptional cases Member States may conclude such agreements after the date of application of the Regulation.

ance with regulation 7 of the Transfrontier Shipment of Waste Regulations 1994, certifying the adequacy of the financial guarantee.

(d) A specimen of the consignment note shall be delivered by the carrier to the customs officer of entry into the Community.

(2) For recovery
    (a) All imports of waste for recovery are prohibited except those to –
        (i) countries to which the OECD decision applies;
        (ii) other countries which are parties to the Basle Convention, and/or with which the Community or the Community and its Member States have concluded bilateral or multilateral or regional agreements in accordance with Article 11 of the Basle Convention guaranteeing that the recovery is carried out at an authorised centre and in an environmentally sound manner, or with which individual Member States have concluded bilateral agreements prior to the operation of this Regulation.
    (b) Procedure for the import of amber and red list wastes is essentially the same as for shipments between Member States.
    (c) For amber and red list wastes, and those not yet assigned, the consignment note is issued by the competent authority of dispatch in the OECD country of export.

Transit of waste through the community (Articles 23–24)

(1) Generally:
    (a) For transit shipments the last competent authority of transit in the Community is required to co-ordinate the responses of the others to notification and shall also –
        (i) issue the consignment note,
        (ii) receive notification by consignment note,
        (iii) notify shipment consents to other competent authorities,
        (iv) receive notification of the shipment's arrival at its destination.
    (b) Specimen of the consignment note to accompany each shipment.
    (c) Specimen of the consignment note to be supplied by the carrier to the customs officer of departure when the shipment leaves the Community.
    (d) When the shipment has left the Community, the customs officer of departure shall send a copy of the consignment note to the last competent authority of transit within the Community.
    (e) Within 42 days after leaving the Community the notifier shall certify to the competent authority that it has arrived at its intended destination.

(2) From and to an OECD country for recovery:
    (a) Consignment note is issued by the OECD country of dispatch
    (b) All competent authorities of transit within the Community to be notified by the consignment note.
    (c) Shipments may only proceed in the absence of objections from competent authorities of transit.
    (d) In the case of red list and unassigned waste, shipment requires prior written consent.

A number of essentially administrative provisions of general application are to be found in Articles 25 to 44. Some of particular importance deserve notice. Article

33(1) authorises a competent authority to charge its appropriate administrative and supervisory costs, including those for any analyses and inspections, to the notifier. Where a shipment, having received consent, cannot be completed in accordance with the terms of the consignment note or contract, the competent authority of dispatch within 90 days of such notification shall ensure that the notifier returns the shipment to its jurisdiction unless satisfied that it can be disposed of or recovered in an alternative and environmentally sound manner.[69]

A shipment shall be deemed to be illegal traffic if effected[70]:

(a) without notification to all competent authorities concerned,
(b) without their consent in accordance with the regulations,
(c) with consent obtained through falsification, misrepresentation or fraud,
(d) which is not specified in a material way in the consignment note,
(e) which results in disposal or recovery in contravention of Community or international rules,
(f) or contrary to Articles 14, 16, 19 or 21.

Depending on the responsibility for the illegal traffic being that of the notifier or consignee, the competent authority of dispatch or destination shall enforce against that person environmentally sound return and disposal or recovery methods within 30 days of receiving notification of the illegality.

Member States are required to take appropriate legal action to prohibit and punish illegal traffic, so, in addition to the remedial action under regulations 8 or 9 dealt with below, regulation 12 provides that contravention of the Regulation so that the shipment is deemed to be illegal traffic is an offence. Further offences within regulation 12, which are generally actionable summarily or on indictment with penalties of a fine up to the statutory maximum and/or two years' imprisonment, are:

(a) breach of a condition governing transport, disposal or recovery;
(b) failure to send a certificate of disposal or recovery within the set time limit, or the sending of a certificate false in a material particular;
(c) contravention of regulation 7 (requiring financial guarantees);
(d) the supply of false information to a competent authority to obtain a regulation 7 certificate;
(e) the mixing of wastes subject to different notifications during transit contrary to Article 29;
(f) shipping of waste from the United Kingdom without having entered into a prior contract with the consignee;
(g) the shipping of waste to which Article 11 applies from the United Kingdom without the accompanying information required by that Article;
(h) failure to comply with a regulation 8(2) or 9(2) notice;
(i) the intentional obstruction of an inspector or other authorised person while acting under regulations 9 or 10.

The due diligence defence applies generally to these offences. In appropriate cases it is also a defence to prosecution for breach of a condition to show that the breach was in response to an emergency.

The powers of a competent authority of dispatch or destination to secure by notice, in the former case, the return of waste to the United Kingdom and, in the latter, its disposal or recovery, in an environmentally sound manner are to be

69 Article 25.

70 Article 26(1).

found respectively in regulations 8 and 9. By regulation 8(2) a notice served on the notifier shall require the return of the waste to an area within the United Kingdom specified in the notice by a date also so specified. Comparably, regulation 9(2) provides for the service of a notice on the consignee 'to ensure the disposal or recovery of waste in an environmentally sound manner in accordance with the notice and by a date specified in the notice'. In both cases the date is to provide a reasonable time for compliance.

On failure of the notifier to comply with the notice under regulation 8 the competent authority of dispatch may act as his duly authorised agent to effect the return of the waste to the United Kingdom and to fulfil its obligations under Arts 25(1) or 26(2). To that end the notifier shall provide such information and assistance as the authority may reasonably request in writing.

1 Appointed under section 8(3) of the Environmental Protection Act 1990.

Should the consignee fail to comply with a notice under regulation 9 an inspector[71] acting on behalf of the authority may take such necessary action within regulation 9(6) as is needed to effect the disposal or recovery of the waste and fulfil the obligations of the authority under Article 26(3). The subsection (6) powers available to an inspector are, on the production of his authority, to:

(a) enter any land that he reasonably believes to be necessary and take with him—
   (i) any other duly authorised person and, if apprehending serious obstruction, a constable; and
   (ii) any required equipment or materials;
(b) make such examination and investigation as may be necessary;
(c) remove, or arrange for the removal, of any waste from the land for the purpose of its disposal or recovery;
(d) dispose of or recover, or arrange for the disposal or recovery, of waste.

To achieve those authorised purposes the consignee shall provide such information and assistance as the authority may reasonably request in writing.

2 Regulation 10(1); "customs officer" is defined in the Customs and Excise Management Act 1979.

3 Giving effect to Article 7 of Council Directive 75/442/EEC.

When requested by a competent authority of dispatch or destination, and to facilitate the performance of their duties under the Regulation, a customs officer may detain for not more than three working days the waste specified in the request.[72]

Regulation 11[73] requires the Secretary of State to prepare a waste disposal plan 'which shall contain his policies in relation to the import and export of waste for recovery or disposal into and out of the United Kingdom'. Provisions preventing the import or export of wastes for disposal shall be in accordance with the Article 4 principles.

ENFORCEMENT AND CONTROL

Enforcement

Common experience indicates that while the designated waste authorities have responsibility in law for the handling and disposal of waste, many persons in possession of waste will seek to circumvent, in a variety of more or less satisfactory ways, those formal processes and costs. As well as having their own individual roles in respect of waste treatment, therefore, those authorities are also given enforcement functions over casual and unauthorised waste operations. These additional functions are now to be considered.

Both waste regulation and waste collection authorities are given the power, in section 59 of the Environmental Protection Act 1990, to deal with the unauthorised deposit of controlled waste in their areas; that is, deposits in breach of section 33(1) or 'fly-tipping'. The enforcement procedure here exhibits close similarities to the statutory nuisance procedure in Part III of the Act, a significant distinction being that in this case the authority is given a discretion whether to take action on discovering a contravention. By section 59(1), if controlled waste is deposited in or on any land in its area the authority may by notice require the occupier to do either or both of the following, that is:

(a) remove the waste from the land within a specified period not less than a period of 21 days beginning with the service of the notice;
(b) take within such a period specified steps with a view to eliminating or reducing the consequences of the deposit of the waste.

For this purpose 'land', by section 29(8), 'includes land covered by waters where the land is above the low water mark of ordinary spring tides', thus necessarily extending these control powers to the dumping of waste into streams, ponds, water filled quarries and so on. Failure, without reasonable excuse, to comply with the notice is a summary offence with liability to fines up to level 5 on the standard scale and to further fines of an amount equal to one-tenth of level 5 for each day on which the failure continues after conviction.

The minimum 21 day period is to provide time for, *inter alia*, an appeal to the magistrates' court. Pending determination of an appeal the terms of the notice are of no effect, and in modifying the requirements or dismissing the appeal the court may extend the period within which the terms of the notice are to be satisfied. There is a general power in the court to modify the notice requirements or dismiss the appeal. However, it shall quash the requirement if satisfied that:

(a) the appellant neither deposited nor knowingly caused or knowingly permitted the deposit of the waste; or
(b) there is a material fault in the notice.[74]

Matters pertaining to the contents and service of notices have been dealt with in Chapter 1,[75] and the scope and meaning of 'deposit' and 'knowingly cause or knowingly permit' in the context of licensing in the previous chapter.[76]

In addition to enforcement through prosecution, authorities are given two alternative remedies involving what might be called direct action. First, where a person has failed to comply with a notice requirement, the authority may do the stipulated work and recover the costs reasonably incurred.[77] The availability of this remedy makes the original framing of the notice requirements particularly important, the authority being expressly limited to the recovery of the reasonable expenses of doing those notified works, whatever remedial work may in fact prove necessary.

Alternatively, section 59(7) gives an authority remedial powers independent of the notice procedure. If it appears to the authority that waste has been deposited in or on any land in contravention of section 33(1) and that:

(a) in order to prevent pollution of land, water or air or harm to human health it is necessary that the waste be forthwith removed or other steps be taken to eliminate or reduce the consequences of the deposit or both; or

74 Provisions governing appeals are to be found in section 59(2)–(4).

75 See at pp.20–4.

76 See at pp.367 and 370 respectively.

77 Section 59(6).

(b) there is no occupier of the land; or

(c) the occupier neither made nor knowingly permitted the deposit of the waste;

the authority may remove the waste from the land or take other steps to eliminate or reduce the consequences of the deposit or, as the case may require, to remove the waste and take those steps.

In taking this action an authority is entitled to recover the costs necessarily incurred either, in the case of section 59(7)(a), from the occupier, unless he proves that he neither made nor knowingly caused or knowingly permitted the deposit of the waste or, in any other case, from any person who deposited or knowingly caused or knowingly permitted the deposit of any of the waste.

While section 59 deals with fly-tipping, section 60 prohibits unauthorised sorting, that is, without the consent of the relevant person. Section 60(1) provides that:

No person shall sort over or disturb –

(a) anything deposited at a place for the deposit of waste provided by or with the approval of a waste collection or disposal authority or by another local authority or person;

(b) anything deposited in a public or private receptacle for waste provided by or with the approval of a waste collection or disposal authority, a parish or community council or the holder of a waste management licence; or

(c) the contents of any receptacle for waste which under sections 46 or 47 is placed on a highway for emptying."

This provision provides comprehensive cover of material in landfill sites, treatment and storage facilities, public litter bins and refuse containers while placed in public areas to await collection. An offence under this section is punishable on summary conviction by a fine up to level 3 on the standard scale. In some circumstances this activity will necessarily also involve trespass and may lead to theft. In support of this latter view, the 1990 Act emphasises that waste in the possession of waste authorities is to be regarded as belonging to them.[78]

For the purpose of legitimising the sorting of waste, the right to do so, or relevant consent, may be granted by:

(a) in the case of (a), the authority, contractor or other person who provides the place for the deposit of the waste;

(b) in the case of (b), the authority, contractor or other person who provides the receptacle for the deposit of the waste;

(c) in the case of (c), the person either having the right to the custody of the receptacle or the function of emptying such receptacles.

It has been seen that conditions under the new waste management licensing structure may, and indeed should, extend the operators' responsibility to aftercare of landfill sites. Depending on the nature of the material deposited and the characteristics of the site, its contents may continue to present a source of risk to the surrounding environment, whether by methane gas production or the leaching of pollutants into groundwater, for some considerable time.[79] While a site licence is in force the responsibility for observing any conditions in the operation of the site rests of course with the licence holder subject to the section 42 supervisory control of the regulation authority. When tipping is completed and the site closed, even though some licence conditions remain in force, the operator will have departed and will in consequence have other priorities.

78 See, e.g., sections 45(9) and 59(7).

79 See generally on this question HMIP Waste Management Paper No. 27, 'The Control of Landfill Gas'; DoE Planning Circular 17/89,' Landfill Sites: Development Control' (W.O.38/89).

To meet the problems that may be produced in these circumstances waste regulation authorities are given the duty, in section 61, of causing their areas 'to be inspected from time to time to detect whether any land is in such a condition, by reason of the relevant matters affecting the land, that it may cause pollution of the environment or harm to human health'. This duty to inspect remains for the authority's 'period of responsibility' for the land, which extends from the time at which the condition of the land first appears to the authority to be such that it may cause pollution of the environment or harm to human health until the authority is satisfied that no such pollution or harm will be caused by reason of the relevant matters affecting the land.[80]

80 Section 61(4) and (6).

The purpose of inspection, then, is to determine the potential for environmental harm of the 'relevant matters' affecting the land. These are, by section 61(2), the concentration or accumulation in, and emission or discharge from, the land of noxious gases or noxious liquids caused by deposits of controlled waste on land. 'Land', as was seen in the context of section 59, includes land covered by water. 'Pollution of the environment' is specifically defined for the purposes of waste disposal in Part II of the Act as meaning:

> ... pollution of the environment due to the release or escape (into any environmental medium) from ... (c) the land in or on which controlled waste is deposited, ... of substances or articles constituting or resulting from the waste and capable (by reason of the quantity or concentrations involved) of causing harm to man or any other living organisms supported by the environment.[81]

81 Section 29(3).

Noting that in the same section 'environmental medium' is defined to include land, and having regard to the purpose of this section, it would seem a reasonable presumption that the phrase extends to emissions or discharges into neighbouring land as well as into air and water.

Though the section heading and main aim of the provision is directed to landfill sites, the actual wording is clearly wide enough to cover all locations where controlled waste has been dumped and seepage of solid or liquid substances into the soil or water has occurred or may be anticipated. Waste regulation authorities thus appear to have a general supervisory responsibility for at least the more grossly contaminated land, if attributable to controlled waste, extending for the duration of the risk.

If on inspection it appears to the authority that the condition of the land due to the relevant matters is such that pollution or harm is likely to be caused, the authority shall do any necessary works and take such other steps (whether on the affected or adjacent land) as appear to the authority reasonable to avoid the pollution or harm. Where in the opinion of the authority the condition of the land is likely to lead to pollution of water, it has a duty to consult the NRA on the action it proposes to take.[82] The authority is then given a discretion to recover all or part of the reasonable costs of the work from the owner of the land unless it has accepted the surrender of the relevant waste management licence under section 39. In exercising this discretion it is to have regard to any hardship that may be caused to the land owner. There is here, then, a specific power to deal with contaminated land originating from landfill of waste. The deficiency of this section is that it has yet to be implemented.

82 Section 61(7) and (5).

The last statutory power of enforcement in the Act itself, is to deal with emergency circumstances of serious danger. Where an inspector finds on any premises he has power to enter,[83] any article or substance which he has reasonable cause

83 As to which, see duties to inspect and powers of entry below at p.429.

to believe, in the circumstances in which he finds it, is a cause of imminent danger of serious pollution of the environment or serious harm to human health, he may, by section 70(1), seize it and cause it to be rendered harmless (whether by destruction or otherwise). Prior to its being rendered harmless, if practicable to do so and if, in the case of an article, it forms part of a batch of similar articles, the inspector shall take a sample of the substance or article and give to the responsible person at the premises a sufficiently identified portion of the sample.

When the object or material has been seized and rendered harmless the inspector is required to prepare a signed report giving particulars of the circumstances in which it was seized and dealt with; one copy of which is for the responsible person at the premises where the material was found and one for the owner of the material, if different from the person at the premises. Intentional obstruction of an inspector in the performance of these functions is a summary or indictable offence. These are evidently special powers designed to be used in circumstances where the imminent risk of serious damage demands an immediate response. Where such emergency powers are used the circumstances must clearly warrant them, and the procedure by and through which they are justified is to be meticulously observed.

Control

In support of the enforcement duties just considered, authorities and their officials are given a range of powers necessary to enable their performance. These responsibilities fall largely, but not entirely, on waste regulation authorities and cover:

(a) the appointment of inspectors;
(b) inspection of premises;
(b) powers of entry;
(c) obtaining of information;
(d) annual reports.

The keeping of, and access to, public registers has already been considered in the context of licensing. The matters listed above have now to be dealt with.

Waste regulation authorities may appoint, and terminate the appointment of, sufficient suitably qualified inspectors as they consider necessary to perform the functions under Part II of the Act in their area.[84] In the performance of their functions inspectors are relieved from personal civil or criminal liability if the court is satisfied that the act was done in good faith and that there were reasonable grounds for doing it.

The general duty to inspect is to be found in paragraph 13(1) of Schedule 4 of the Waste Management Licensing Regulations 1994,[85] which provides that:

> Any establishment or undertaking which carries out the recovery or disposal of controlled waste, or which collects or transports controlled waste on a professional basis, or which arranges for the recovery or disposal of controlled waste on behalf of others (dealers or brokers), shall be subject to appropriate periodic inspections by the competent authorities.

The identity of the competent authority is determined by the particular function and is specified in Table 5 in Schedule 4 as follows:

84 Section 68(3).

85 S.I. 1994 No. 1056.

Competent authorities (1)	Specified functions (2)
Any planning authority.	The taking of any specified action.
A waste regulation authority, the Secretary of State or a person appointed under section 43(2)(b) of the 1990 Act.	Their respective functions under Part II of the 1990 Act in relation to waste management licences, including preparing plans or modifications of them under section 50 of the 1990 Act.
A disposal authority or the Secretary of State.	Their respective functions under Part I of the Control of Pollution Act 1974 in relation to disposal licences and resolutions under section 11 of that Act.
A licensing authority or the Ministers.	Their respective functions under Part II of the Food and Environment Protection Act 1985, or under paragraph 5 below.[86]
An enforcing authority, the Secretary of State or a person appointed under section15(3)(b) of the 1990 Act.	Their respective functions under Part I of the 1990 Act in relation to prescribed processes except when – (a) the process is designated for local control; and (b) it is an exempt activity carried out subject to the conditions and limitations specified in Schedule 3.
The National Rivers Authority or the Secretary of State.	Their respective functions in relation to the giving of consents under Chapter II of Part III of the Water Resources Act 1991 (offences in relation to pollution of water resources) for any discharge of waste in liquid form other than waste waters.

86 Paragraph 5 is concerned with the preparation of offshore waste management plans by licensing authorities.

The functions referred to in the Table do not include the production, amendment etc., of subordinate legislation authorised by statutory instrument. In discharging their functions relating to the recovery or disposal of waste, competent authorities are required to have regard to the relevant objectives, these being, by paragraph 4 of the Schedule:

(a) ensuring that waste is recovered or disposed of without endangering human health and without using processes or methods which could harm the environment and in particular without –
   (i) risk to water, air, soil, plants or animals; or
   (ii) causing nuisance through noise or odours; or
   (iii) adversely affecting the countryside or places of special interest;
(b) implementing, so far as material, any plan made under the plan-making provisions.

Paragraph 2(3) rationalises the functions of the responsible authorities in situations where these powers coincide with those under Part I of the Act (IPC).

The existence of a duty to inspect necessarily requires a right of access, for which provision is made in the extensive powers of entry provisions of section 69. The section does not indicate the inspectors empowered by these provisions. However, as the preceding section deals specifically with the appointment of inspectors by the Secretary of State and waste regulation authorities, they at least may be regarded as the intended categories. By the terms of the section an inspector may, on production (if so required) of his authority, exercise any of the subsection (3) powers in relation to the range of premises in subsection (2) for the purpose of :

(a) discharging any functions conferred or imposed by or under Part II on the authority or the inspector;
(b) determining whether or how such a function should be discharged; or
(c) determining whether any relevant provision is being complied with.

These three objectives, albeit widely drawn, identify the grounds and consequently determine the legitimacy of entry. Entry to premises, or parts of premises, that is not protected by statutory authority is of course unlawful and constitutes a trespass.[87]

87 See general discussion of this topic in Chapter 1 at p.24.

The property in respect of which these powers may be exercised includes:

(a) land or vessels in, on or by means of which controlled waste is being or has been deposited, treated or disposed of;
(b) land or vessels in, on or by means of which controlled waste is believed on reasonable grounds to be or have been deposited, treated, kept or disposed of;
(c) land believed on reasonable grounds to be affected by the deposit, treatment, keeping or disposal of controlled waste on other land.

The extensive list of powers granted to an inspector in subsection (3) makes any view of section 69 as merely a 'power of entry' section inadequate in the extreme. The powers available in pursuit of the subsection (1) objectives, i.e., essentially the oversight of controlled waste operations, are:

(a) entry of premises at any reasonable time that he believes it is necessary for him to enter, or at any time if in his opinion there is an immediate risk of serious pollution of the environment or serious harm to human health;
(b) to take with him on entering the premises –
  (i) any person authorised by the authority and, if apprehending serious obstruction, a constable;
  (ii) any equipment or materials required for the purpose of the entry;
(c) to make such examination and investigation as may be necessary;
(d) to direct that the premises, or any part, or anything in them, shall be left undisturbed for as long as necessary for the purposes of (c) above;
(e) to take such measurements, photographs and recordings as he considers necessary for the purposes of (c) above;
(f) to take samples of any articles or substances found on the premises and of air, water or land in , on or in the vicinity of the premises;
(g) to dismantle or subject to any process any article or substance found on the premises which appears to him to have caused or to be likely to cause pollution of the environment or harm to human health, but not so as to damage or destroy it unless that is necessary;
(h) to take possession of and detain any article or substance in (g) above for as long as is necessary to –
  (i) examine it or do anything else authorised under that paragraph,
  (ii) ensure that it is not tampered with before completion of his examination,

(iii) ensure that it is available for evidence in any proceedings under this Part;

(i) to require any person to answer questions pertaining to his examination or investigation under (c) and sign a declaration of the truth of the answers;

(j) to require the production of, or extracts from, records required to be kept under this Part, or that it is necessary for him to see for the purposes of his examination or investigation under (c) and inspect and take copies of such material;

(k) to require any person to afford him such facilities and assistance within their control or responsibility as are necessary to enable the inspector to exercise any of these powers.

Where an inspector proposes to take action under (g) above, he shall first consult persons he considers appropriate to ascertain any possible dangers in those proposals, and the responsible person on the premises is entitled, at his request, to be present while that action is undertaken.[88] On taking possession of an article or substance under (h) above the inspector shall leave a notice giving sufficient particulars to identify it and of his authority for taking it, either with a responsible person or, if that is not practicable, affixed conspicuously to the premises. Further, if it is practicable, he shall take a sample and leave a sufficiently identified portion of it with a responsible person at the premises.[89] No answer required under (i) shall be admissible in evidence against that person in any proceedings.

It is a summary offence punishable by a fine up to level 5 on the standard scale to fail without reasonable excuse to comply with any requirement imposed under this section, to prevent any other person from appearing before or answering any question required by an inspector or intentionally to obstruct an inspector in the exercise of his powers and duties.[90] The requirement to produce information and records does not extend, by virtue of subsection (11), to documents protected by legal professional privilege. This principle covers confidential communications between a client and his legal adviser made for the purpose of obtaining or giving legal advice. Such privilege extends to advice from salaried legal advisers[91] but not from non-legal professional advisers.

Waste regulation authorities are given the power, in section 71(2)(b), to facilitate the discharge of their Part II functions, to require by notice any person to provide the information specified in the notice that the authority reasonably considers it needs in the form and within the time stipulated. A person who fails without reasonable excuse to comply with such a requirement, or who makes any statement which he knows to be false or misleading in a material particular, or who recklessly makes a statement which is false or misleading in a material particular may be liable summarily or on indictment. On the meaning of 'reckless' Lord Diplock said in *R* v *Caldwell* (1982)[92]:

> In my opinion, a person charged with an offence under section 1(1) of the Criminal Damage Act 1971 is 'reckless as to whether any such property would be destroyed or damaged' if he (1) does an act which in fact creates an obvious risk that property will be destroyed or damaged and (2) when he does the act he either has not given any thought to the possibility of there being any such risk or has recognised that there was some risk risk involved and has nonetheless gone on to do it.

This statement of principle may be regarded as authoritative for present purposes.

In conclusion here, section 67 requires waste regulation authorities to prepare and publish for each financial year a report on the discharge by the authority of

88 Section 69(6) and (5).

89 Section 69(7).

90 Section 69(9).

91 *Crompton (Alfred) Amusement Machines* v *Commissioners of Customs and Excise* (No. 2) [1972] AC 405.

92 [1982] AC 341 at p.354f; [1981] 1 All ER 961 at p.967.

its functions under Part II of the Act. The reports are to include information on:

(a) licences applied for, granted, in force, modified, revoked, suspended, surrendered or transferred during the year and appeals made against decisions in respect of them;

(b) the authority's exercise of its section 42, 54, 61 or 62 powers;

(c) implementation of the authority's section 50 plan, with special reference to recycling of waste;

(d) number and description of prosecutions under Part II; and

(e) costs incurred and income received in the discharge of these Part II functions.

Each report is to be published within six months of the end of the applicable year and a copy is to be sent to the Secretary of State. Not only will such reports publicise performance and standards, thus helping to concentrate the mind of the authority, but by virtue of subsection (4) the reports will provide a means of monitoring performance in relation to EC Directives.

POWERS OF THE SECRETARY OF STATE

Sufficient has been said in this and the previous chapter to establish that the summit of the present waste licensing and control structure is occupied by the Secretary of State, being given statutory responsibility for general oversight and the necessary powers to perform that function. His regulation-making powers have been referred to in the treatment of the regulations concerned, as have some other functions in their appropriate context. The purpose now is to identify and review the general range of his functions in a reasonably comprehensive fashion, giving particular attention to those not previously considered.

The Secretary of State has general responsibility to settle appeals from decisions concerning licences. A right of appeal is provided in section 43 for a person affected by a decision of the authority following an application for any of the purposes in sections 36 to 40; with, of course, the exception where the authority is acting under his direction. The Secretary of State is given a wide discretion in dealing with an appeal, which is to be on documentary submissions unless either party requests an oral hearing; that in turn being either public or private. Section 43(8) provides for regulations governing the timing and form of appeals and the manner in which they are considered.[93]

93 Regulations 6–9 of the Waste Management Licensing Regulations 1994, S.I.1994 No. 1056 are dealt with in Chapter 14 at p.394.

The Secretary of State is given the duty, after consultation with representative bodies, of producing and subsequently revising a Code of Practice on the duty of care requirement imposed by section 34(1) on any person who imports, produces, carries, keeps, treats or disposes of controlled waste or, as a broker, has control of such waste.[94] The purpose of the Code is to provide practical guidance on how to discharge that duty of care. It has been seen that in issuing, and renewing, transferring etc., waste management licences the determination of the applicant as a 'fit and proper' person is of prime importance. In making this determination waste regulation authorities have a duty to have regard to any guidance issued to them by the Secretary of State.[95] Section 41 gives the Secretary of State the power, with the approval of the Treasury, to issue a charging scheme prescribing the fees to be charged for licences.[96]

94 Section 34(7) and (8).

95 Section 74(5).

96 See in Chapter 14 at p.395.

While public authorities are given a number of duties in the performance of their Part II functions, many sections contain powers that may be exercised if, and how, the particular authority chooses. In many of these cases, however, the Secretary of State is empowered to issue directions to the authority, thus precluding the exercise of that discretion and securing the implementation of central rather than local policy. Such powers of direction include:

- section 31(1) – formation of regional waste regulation authorities;
- section 32(2) – formation of waste disposal companies;
- section 35(7) – terms and conditions to be included in a waste management licence;
- section 37(3) – modification of licence conditions;
- section 38(7) – revocation and suspension of licences;
- section 49(7) – time within which waste recycling plans are to be produced;
- section 50(11) – time within which waste disposal plans are to be produced;
- section 65(2) – exclusion of information from public registers;
- section 66(7) – inclusion of commercially confidential information on registers.

Those powers of direction just considered concern the performance by public authorities of their statutory powers. Two powers of direction of an entirely different order are provided for in section 57. Under section 57(1) the Secretary of State may by notice in writing, direct the holder of a waste management licence 'to accept and keep, or accept and treat or dispose of, controlled waste at specified places on specified terms'. Similarly by section 57(2), he may direct 'any person who is keeping controlled waste on any land to deliver the waste to a specified person on specified terms with a view to its being treated or disposed of by that other person'. The procedure may therefore be used in individual cases with respect to the production of waste with certain characteristics, or alternatively in relation to one particularly hazardous or dangerous consignment. The stipulation that failure to observe either direction constitutes a summary offence,[97] thus creating criminal offences, emphasises that these powers of direction are legislative in nature and are to be used in emergency situations, or where action by consent or agreement proves not to be possible.

It will be seen that the two provisions may be used if necessary to deal with the two parts of the same event. The person having possession of the specified kind or consignment of waste is required to deliver it to a stated person or place, and may be required, in accordance with the polluter pays principle, to pay the costs of disposal. A similar direction then requires the recipient to deal with it at a specified place or in particular ways. Accepting that a direction under this section imposes obligations supported by criminal sanctions, it is strange to find that by section 57(6) compliance with such a direction will justify breach of other legal duties only if they have been specified in regulations by the Secretary of State. No such regulations appear to have been made, indicating perhaps the perceived exceptional nature of this power and the likelihood of its use.

Earlier reference has been made to the section 68 power of waste regulation authorities to appoint inspectors. Subsection (2) similarly authorises the Secretary of State to appoint and terminate the appointment of inspectors, under whatever title he deems suitable, to assist him in the performance of his Part II functions. The expectation is that such appointments will be made to the regional offices of HMIP. Within the terms of section 68 the Secretary of State also has the function of keeping under review the performance of waste regulation authorities. A sig-

97 Section 57(5); fines up to level 5 on the standard scale.

nificant part of this duty will no doubt be satisfied through the annual reporting requirement of section 67. However, it may be that (particularly being found in the same section) a primary function of this central inspectorate will be oversight of regulation authorities.

Within the section 71 powers the Secretary of State may, for the discharge of his functions under Part II, by written notice require, by subsection (1), a waste regulation authority to provide specified information relating to the performance of its functions. Further, by subsection (2), he may similarly require any person to supply such information specified in the notice as he reasonably considers he needs, in the form and within the time specified in the notice. Failure, without reasonable excuse, to comply with a subsection (2) requirement, or the making of a statement known to be false or misleading in a material particular, or recklessly to make such a statement is an offence punishable summarily or on indictment with penalties up to a maximum of a fine and two years' imprisonment.

Lastly, in reviewing these powers of the Secretary of State reference should be made to his default powers under section 72 where in his view a waste regulation authority has failed to discharge any particular functions or any class of functions as required by Part II. In such cases he shall make an order declaring the authority to be in default and directing the authority to perform any function specified in the order and stipulating the manner and time of such performance. Should the authority fail to observe the terms of the order the Secretary of State may either enforce the order by mandamus or, by another order, transfer to himself any or all the functions specified in the earlier order together with such property, rights, liabilities and obligations of the authority as he considers appropriate. The expenses incurred in performing those functions may be recovered from the authority on whose behalf they were carried out.

16

Hazardous Waste

INTRODUCTION

As a large proportion of waste can be regarded for practical purposes as inert, the major disposal problem is related to its bulk. What applies in this respect to disposal applies equally to its handling, transport and so on. However, because industry produces and uses an increasing number of substances that are harmful to living organisms it is inevitable that they also will enter the waste stream, either as by-products of production or at the end of their commercially useful life. The treatment, handling and disposal of such hazardous materials requires an additional level of supervision and control to ensure that their potential to cause environmental damage is not realised.

The preliminary question in dealing with this issue is to define and identify the substances and materials that are regarded as sufficiently dangerous to warrant special treatment. The difficulty is compounded in that materials may be more or less dangerous depending on their concentration, quantity or association with other substances. Emphasising both the acute and chronic aspects of danger, hazardous wastes have been defined by the World Health Organisation as those

... wastes which present either –

(1) short-term hazards, such as acute toxicity by ingestion, inhalation or skin absorption, corrosivity or other skin or eye contact hazards or the risk of fire or explosion;
(2) long-term environmental hazards including chronic toxicity upon repeated exposure, carconogenicity (which may in some cases result from acute exposure but with a long latent period), resistance to detoxification processes such as biodegradation, the potential to pollute underground or surface waters or aesthetically objectionable properties such as offensive smells.

The approach adopted by the first legislation in this field, the Deposit of Poisonous Waste Act 1972, was to identify and list those wastes that were regarded as presenting no dangerous environmental or health problems. Any substances or materials not listed were 'notifiable wastes' to be treated as hazardous. The lack of precision and the open-endedness of this approach produced sufficient difficulties to prompt a change in the 1980 Regulations (below) to an inclusive approach, by listing those wastes warranting control because of their nature or effects. The remaining problem not yet tackled by legislation, much less resolved, is that relating to the production of dangerous materials from the mixing of innocuous substances. Commenting on this issue the Select Committee on Science and Technology[1] said:

Hazards, moreover, arise not only from dangerous substances, whether listed or not, but also from the synergistic effects of substances which in themselves are relatively harmless, e.g., the reaction of a dilute acid with a sulphide producing hydrogen sulphide

1 House of Lords Select Committee on Science and Technology 1980–81 Report, Hazardous Waste Disposal, 3 vols (HMSO), paragraphs 13 and 14.

gas. Synergistic effects are not always predictable and give rise to concern about the possible mobilisation around the environment of toxic substances or even the formulation of new ones. This is one of the factors making the accurate identification of wastes a vital precondition of safe disposal. The multitude of different wastes, including several that are specific to one producer only and the prevalence of mixed waste streams mean that hazard assessment for individual wastes often depends on judgement on the spot, taking account of the nature of the wastes, the disposal method proposed and, in the case of landfill, the nature of the site.

It may be that, having regard to the final point, the wide diversity of possible products makes any comprehensive legislation on the question impracticable, leaving control to be applied through specific licence conditions in each case.

The meaning of 'special waste' was considered in the context of controlled waste in Chapter 13 and is repeated here. Section 75(9) of the 1990 Act provides that the term means controlled waste 'as respects which regulations are in force under section 62'. Section 62(1) gives the Secretary of State a regulation-making power governing the treatment, keeping or disposal of waste if he 'considers that controlled waste of any kind is or may be so dangerous or difficult to treat, keep or dispose of that special provision is required for dealing with it'.

2 S.I. 1980 No. 1709, amended by S.I. 1988 No. 1790.

3 78/319/EEC.

Current regulations are the Control of Pollution (Special Waste) Regulations 1980,[2] implementing the EC Directive on Toxic and Dangerous Waste.[3] Regulation 2(1) defines 'special waste' as any controlled waste which:

(a) consists of or contains any of the substances listed in Part I of Schedule I and by reason of the presence of such substance –
 (i) is dangerous to life within the meaning of Part II of Schedule I, or
 (ii) has a flash point of 21 degrees Celsius or less as determined by the methods and with the apparatus laid down by the British Standards Institution;[4] or

4 BS 3900: Part A, 8: 1976 (EN53).

(b) is a medicinal product, as defined in section 130 of the Medicines Act 1968, which is available only in accordance with a prescription given by an appropriate practitioner as defined in section 58(1) of that Act.[5]

5 Procedures for assessing the status of a particular waste are to be found in Waste Management Paper 23, 'Special Wastes: a technical memorandum providing guidance on their definition' (HMSO).

6 See sections 9(1) and 30(5) of the Radioactive Substances Act 1960.

The Secretary of State is given the power, in regulation 3(1), to extend the definition to categories of waste that, but for the fact that they are radioactive, would be controlled waste.[6]

For the purposes of the Medicines Act 1968, section 130 provides that:

(1) Subject to the following provisions of this section, in this Act 'medicinal products' means any substance or article (not being an instrument, apparatus or appliance) which is manufactured, sold, supplied, imported or exported for use wholly or mainly in either of the following ways, that is to say –

 (a) use by being administered to one or more human beings or animals for a medicinal purpose;
 (b) use, in circumstances to which this paragraph applies, as an ingredient in the preparation of a substance or article which is to be administered to one or more human beings or animals for a medicinal purpose.

(2) In this Act a 'medicinal purpose' means any one or more of the following purposes, that is to say –
 (a) treating or preventing disease;
 (b) diagnosing or ascertaining the existence, degree or extent of a physiological condition;

  (c) contraception;

  (d) inducing anaesthesia;

  (e) otherwise preventing or interfering with the normal operation of a physiological function, whether permanently or temporarily, and whether by way of terminating, reducing or postponing, or increasing or accelerating, the operation of that function or in any other way.

The remaining subsections ((3)–(10)) amplify and particularise in the application of the definition to particular contexts. Section 58(1), in relation to 'appropriate practitioners', gives the Ministers the power to specify by order:

... the descriptions or classes of medicinal products ... and in relation to any description or class so specified, the order shall state which of the following, that is to say –

(a) doctors,

(b) dentists, or

(c) veterinary surgeons or veterinary practitioners

are to be appropriate practitioners for the purposes of this section.

Section 58(2) then stipulates that such medicinal products are to be sold by retail only in accordance with a prescription given by an approved practitioner.

The substances listed in Part I of Schedule I to the 1980 Regulations are:

Acids and alkalis
Antimony and antimony compounds
Arsenic compounds
Asbestos (all chemical forms)
Barium compounds
Beryllium and beryllium compounds
Biocides and phytopharmaceutical substances
Boron compounds
Cadmium and cadmium compounds
Copper compounds
Heterocyclic organic compounds containing oxygen, nitrogen or sulphur
Hexavalent chromium compounds
Hydrocarbons and their oxygen, nitrogen and sulphur compounds
Inorganic cyanides
Inorganic halogen-containing compounds
Inorganic sulphur-containing compounds
Laboratory chemicals
Lead compounds
Mercury compounds
Nickel and nickel compounds
Organic halogen compounds, excluding inert polymeric materials
Peroxides, chlorates, perchlorates and azides
Pharmaceutical and veterinary compounds
Phosphorus and its compounds
Selenium and selenium compounds
Silver compounds
Tarry materials from refining and tar residues from distilling
Tellurium and tellurium compounds

Thallium and thallium compounds
Vanadium compounds
Zinc compounds

For the purposes of the definition waste is to be regarded as 'dangerous to life' by paragraph 1 of Part II of Schedule I, if:

(a) a single dose of not more than 5 cubic centimetres would be likely to cause death or serious damage to tissue if ingested by a child of 20 kg body weight or

(b) exposure to it for 15 minutes or less would be likely to cause serious damage to human tissue by inhalation, skin contact or eye contact.

Part II then elaborates on particular aspects of this definition, including the approach to assessing the effects of ingestion. For the purposes of (a) above, if the waste is in such a form that either the ingestion of less than 5 cubic centimetres is not possible or there is no risk that a toxic constituent could be assimilated if the waste were to be ingested, then it is not to be regarded as dangerous to life. In relation to samples of mixed waste, paragraph 4 provides that 'waste is to be regarded as dangerous to life if a sample of 5 cubic centimetres taken from any part of a consignment falls within either of the descriptions in paragraph 1 of this schedule'.

This definition of special waste, with its subordinate qualifications and commentary, is to say the least complicated. Some simplification through a structured approach to the application of the definition is provided diagramatically in Waste Management Paper 23,[7] reproduced in Figure 16.1. The diagram offers a logical approach to the assessment of the status of a given waste according to the defined criteria. The question order does not relate to their importance, but provides the quickest approach to a reasoned decision.

SPECIAL WASTE

As has been seen, the Control of Pollution (Special Waste) Regulations 1980,[8] together with the amending Control of Pollution (Special Waste)(Amendment) Regulations 1988,[9] are authorised under section 62 of the Environmental Protection Act 1990, the 1980 regulations superceding sections 3 and 4 of the Deposit of Poisonous Wastes Act 1972. The definition of special waste in the 1980 Regulations makes clear that it is controlled waste. The waste management licensing requirements considered in Chapter 14 will therefore apply here as to other categories of controlled waste. In particular, any necessary forms of treatment, protection or monitoring in relation to its longer-term effect on the environment following disposal may be the subject of conditions in the site licence. The purpose of these Regulations, indicated by the phrase in section 62(1) 'dangerous or difficult to treat, keep or dispose of that special provision is required for dealing with it', is to secure control of and responsibility for those activities associated with the passage of such harmful materials between production and final disposal, i.e., the 'dealing with it'. The method used is, by a system of consignment notes, to ensure that each person having possession of the material knows precisely what its characteristics are and has responsibility for the competence of the person to whom it is transferred. These in the past have represented the two major areas of uncertainty in the handling of dangerous waste – that the operator could plead ignorance of any potential haz-

7 See note 5 above

8 S.I. 1980 No. 1709.

9 S.I. 1988 No. 1790; and see DoE Consultation Paper, ' Special Waste and the Control of its Disposal, February 1990; reviewing the regulations preparatory to their re-issue'.

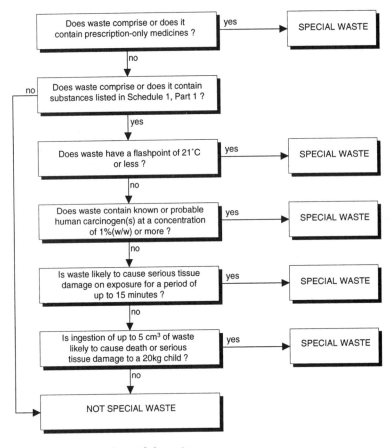

Figure 16.1 Assessment of special waste

ard associated with its composition and, having disposed of it who knows where, that he was effectively absolved from any further responsibility.

Part II of the Regulations imposes duties in respect of consignment notes on producers, carriers and importers and exporters of special waste.[10] Before special waste is removed from the premises where it is produced the producer is required to prepare six copies of the consignment note[11] and complete parts A and B. This document, serving to identify the quality and quantity of the waste, thereafter accompanies it, shedding copies to concerned parties as the consignment proceeds to its destination. The first copy is to be sent to the disposal authority for the area in which the waste is to be disposed of, to arrive between three days and one month before the waste leaves the producing premises.[12] For this purpose a copy of the note will be deemed to be properly sent if posted to arrive in the normal course of post within the stipulated time limits.

Before the waste is removed from the producer's premises the carrier is to complete part C of the note and the producer completes part D. The producer then retains one copy of the note on which parts A, B, C, and D have been completed. If the waste is to be disposed of in the area of an authority different from that in whose area it was produced, the producer shall send a copy to the authority for his own area. All the remaining copies go to the carrier who hands them on to the

10 It appears that this procedure may be due for some simplification in the government's deregulation legislation.

11 The form of the consignment note is to be found in Schedule 2 of the 1980 Regulations. The producer may prepare fewer than six copies if he has reasonable grounds to suppose that a smaller number will be needed.

12 In calculating this period weekends and public holidays are to be excluded. On the duration of a month, see in Chapter 1 on the question of notices, at p.22.

disposer with the consignment of waste. The disposer then completes part E and returns one completed copy to the carrier, sends one copy to the disposal authority for the area in which the waste was produced, and retains the final copy. This procedure does not apply to disposal authorities who both collect and dispose of special waste within their own area. It would appear, however, that where disposal occurs in another area, and to facilitate proper monitoring, this consignment note procedure will apply. Also, these record-keeping requirements do not apply to waste disposed of by pipeline or within the curtilage of the premises at which it is produced. By regulation 7[13] the same procedure applies to persons importing special waste into Great Britain as it applies to producers, and to exporters from Great Britain as it applies to disposers. This is now subject to the amendments in regulation 18 of the Transfrontier Shipment of Waste Regulations 1994[14] to avoid overlap between the control procedures governing domestic and transfrontier movements of waste.

This procedure applies to ensure effective monitoring of individual consignments of special waste. It may therefore prove unreasonably cumbersome, and indeed unnecessary, in the case of routine production of consistent waste. In such cases the disposal authority is given the power in Part III of the Regulations, by a written direction to any named producer or disposer and in respect of any special waste produced in its area, to substitute for the documentary procedure required by regulations 4 and 6 a requirement to supply consignment notes to that authority and other disposal authorities at intervals not exceeding 12 months. In exercising this discretion the disposal authority is to 'have regard to the frequency at which consignments of special waste having a similar composition are transferred for disposal to the same site'. Where such regular consignments are disposed of in the area of another authority, it is to be consulted and its views considered in making any direction. The purpose here, then, is solely to simplify administration in the provision of copies to the authority. The consignment note procedure still applies to accompany transactions between the operating parties.

Where these circumstances arise a producer or disposer of special waste may request the disposal authority in writing to make a direction under regulation 9. If the authority refuses or fails to respond within two months, such failure constituting a deemed refusal, the applicant may appeal to the Secretary of State.[15] By regulation 12, where a direction is in existence the named producer or disposer shall prepare a three-monthly forecast of the special waste the removal or disposal of which he expects to notify at the end of the three-month period in accordance with the direction. He shall then supply copies of the forecast to the disposal authority who made the direction and also, if the waste is to be disposed of in a different area, to that other authority. Where waste materially different from that forecasted is to be removed or disposed of notification of that change shall be provided to the authority to whom the original forecast was sent.

Registers of copies of consignment notes are to be kept by carriers and, copies of notes of consignments of special waste produced and disposed of at each site by producers and disposers respectively. Producers and carriers are to keep such records for a minimum of two years from the date of removal of the consignment. The register at the disposal site is to be kept until the disposal licence is surrendered or revoked and then is to be given to the disposal authority for the area. Where disposal is by deposit on land the following additional information is required by regulation 14:

13 Substituted by regulation 3 of the Control of Pollution (Special Waste)(Amendment) Regulations, S.I. 1988. No. 1790.

14 S.I. 1994 No. 1137.

15 Regulation 11; written notice of appeal to be given within six months of the date of refusal or deemed refusal.

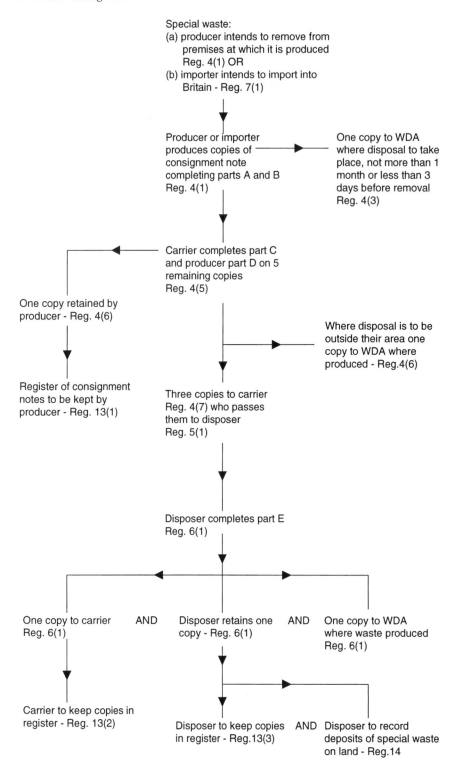

Figure 16.2 Disposal of special waste: general procedure

(a) the location of each deposit on a site plan, either marked with a grid or provided with translucent overlays showing deposits in relation to the contours of the site;

(b) a description of the deposit by reference to the consignment note, except where disposed of by pipeline or within the curtilage of the producing premises or by a disposal authority in its own area when description shall be by reference to a record of the composition of the waste and the date of its disposal;

(c) in the case of liquid special wastes discharged without containers into underground strata or disused workings, a record of the quantity and composition of the waste so discharged.

It is the responsibility of the disposal authority for the area to ensure that the records required by these Regulations are properly maintained.

The Secretary of State is given a power of direction in relation to the disposal of consignments of special waste. A direction may require either the holder of a waste management licence or the disposal authority to accept and dispose of the specified special waste at the place and on the terms stated in the direction. Those terms may provide for payment to the recipient of the direction. Except in an emergency, these directions are to be preceded by a minimum of 28 days' notice to the person concerned to enable representations to be made and considered.

Failure to comply with these Regulations is an offence actionable summarily or on indictment and punishable by fine and up to two years' imprisonment. Failure to comply with a regulation 15 direction will amount to a summary offence attracting a fine up to £400. A general defence to proceedings under these Regulations is that the defendant took all reasonable precautions and exercised all due diligence to avoid the commission of such an offence by himself or any person under his control. In respect of offences relating to the provision and supply of copies of consignment notes, it is a further defence for the person charged to show that he could not reasonably have complied because of an emergency and that he took all reasonable steps to ensure that the necessary copies were completed and supplied as soon as practicable after the event.

TRANSFRONTIER SHIPMENT OF HAZARDOUS WASTE

16 S.I. 1988 No. 1562.

The Transfrontier Shipment of Hazardous Waste Regulations 1988[16] implemented Directive 84/631/EEC as amended, on the supervision and control within the European Community of the transfrontier shipment of hazardous waste. As may be deduced, the sphere of operation of these Regulations, and therefore their purpose, was similar to, though on a wider scale than, those concerning special waste considered above. Those 1988 regulations have been repealed with effect from 6

17 S.I.1994 No. 1137.

May 1994 by the Transfrontier Shipment of Waste Regulations 1994[17] and subject to the transitional provisions in regulation 21 of those Regulations. These latter Regulations, together with the EC Waste Shipments Regulation, implement the Basle Convention, providing a code governing the transfrontier shipment of all, or most, forms of waste and are dealt with in Chapter 15.

18 Presented to Parliament in March 1990, Cm 984 (HMSO).

The Basle Convention on the Control of Transboundary Movements of Hazardous Wastes and their Disposal,[18] Article 13, dealing with the transmission of information, provides in paragraph 1 that:

The Parties shall, whenever it comes to their knowledge, ensure that, in the case of an accident occurring during the transboundary movement of hazardous wastes or other wastes or their disposal, which are likely to present risks to human health and the environment in other States, those States are immediately informed.

Subsequent paragraphs require the Parties to the Convention to inform each other, through the Secretariat, of changes to their national structure and procedures for handling hazardous wastes, including in particular:

(a) the designation of competent authorities;
(b) national definition of hazardous wastes,
(c) refusal of consent to the import of hazardous waste for disposal.

Parties are also required to transmit through the Secretariat to the Conference of the Parties an annual report on the operation of the Convention and stipulated information and statistics on hazardous waste operations.

CONTAMINATED LAND[19]

Land becomes more or less contaminated by the use to which it is put, and depending on the concentration and toxicity of any substances intentionally or casually placed on the land during use or for disposal. The duration of contamination will also depend on the concentration of the materials, together with their quantity and resistance to degradation. Because of the widespread and, in the past, uncontrolled nature of land use, the actual amount of land presently affected and the degree of contamination are matters for conjecture. Government estimates are that 65 per cent of derelict land (i.e. approximately 27,000 ha) should be regarded as potentially contaminated.[20] This is undoubtedly a conservative or optimistic assessment. The opposite view holds that all land subjected to industrial use is likely to be in some degree contaminated. The difficulty here, of course, is that there is no accepted definition or consensus on the meaning of 'contamination' for this purpose.

A definition offered by the Department of the Environment in 1983 is:

> Land which, because of its former use, now contains substances that present hazards likely to affect its proposed form of redevelopment, and which requires an assessment to determine whether a proposed development should proceed or whether some form of remedial action is required.

The significant feature of this definition, which would not be accepted by everyone, is that whether land is contaminated is to be determined in relation to its current or immediately projected use. On that basis there can be no contaminated land *per se*. An alternative and more positive approach would be to identify contaminated land on the basis of a general or accepted definition, possibly with categories reflecting levels of contamination. Its appropriate use, or the action needed to fit that land for a particular use, would then arise as a later question. The one, and fatal, deficiency of such an approach is the cost of implementing it.

The NRA regard as 'contaminated sites' those previously used for gas works, landfill sites, chemical works, heavy industry, waste lagoons, mining, waste disposal, sewage treatment works and oil refineries.[21]

Also, considering sources of contamination, the Royal Commission on Environmental Pollution has said that[22]:

19 See generally on this topic 'Contaminated Land', Report of the House of Commons Environment Committee, chairman Sir Hugh Rossi MP (Session 1989-90, First Report, 170 I-III) and the Government response of July 1990 (Cm 1161).

20 Quoted by Stephen Hawkins,' Clean-up of Contaminated Land: An Assessment of the Mechanisms Available' [1992] JPL 1119.

21 NRA, 'Policy and Practice for the Protection of Groundwater, Draft for Consultation; C. Contaminated Land', October 1991.

22 11th Report, 'Managing Waste: The Duty of Care' Cmnd 9675, December 1985, paragraph 2.48.

Land may become contaminated for a variety of reasons, but the following are the most common categories:

(i)   derelict former industrial sites (e.g., gas works and sewage works);
(ii) former waste tips within the boundaries of defunct processing plants;
(iii) abandoned stores of materials (not necessarily wastes during the active life of the stores); and
(iv) disused waste disposal sites.

The problem is that even where such sites can be identified the nature of the contaminants is usually unknown. The mere location and identification of the substances involved through sampling and analysis will therefore in itself entail considerable cost even before any remedial work is contemplated.

Section 143

To identify and define the problem, section 143 of the Environmental Protection Act 1990 authorises the Secretary of State to make regulations specifying contaminative uses of land and prescribing the form of registers and the particulars to be included in them. Local authorities would then have the responsibility of maintaining such registers with the stipulated particulars and making them available to public inspection free of charge and with copying facilities at reasonable charges. While there is an implication, or at least an understanding, that the registration obligation would impose an active responsibility to identify such sites, the section merely provides, in subsection (3), that the duty on the authority is 'to compile and maintain the register from the information available to the authority from time to time'. The intention therefore appears to be that the register will gradually develop over a period of time through the accumulation of information from a variety of (trustworthy) sources, but occasioning a minimum of expensive fieldwork by the authority. On this matter Lord Hesketh said, in introducing the clause in the House of Lords[23]:

> As a result of our own pilot studies and several pilot registers by local authorities we have concluded that suitable registers can be compiled from desk studies of historic land-uses from which the potential for contamination might be inferred and further investigated where necessary, but without placing onerous responsibilities of judgement on those compiling the registers.

Such a register, at least in concept, would therefore appear to offer merely one far from comprehensive or authoritative source of information for persons having an interest in the land. In reality, and however incomplete it may be at a particular time, its status as an official public register would give it authority, both as to what it does and does not contain.

With the publication of draft regulations in 1992 the uncertainties became more uncertain, generating increasing criticism, particularly from land owners and local authorities. While access to this type of information would clearly be of considerable value to intending purchasers and developers it could cause corresponding detriment to existing land owners, even though that was not the Government's intention. The Minister of State for the Environment and Planning said, in announcing this provision[24]:

> We envisage that these registers will identify sites of potential contamination, based on past land use. In this way, they will provide a means of alerting interested parties to the

23 *Hansard*, HL, vol. 520, cols 2268–9 (5 July 1990).

24 DoE News Release No. 279, 30 April 1990.

potential for contamination so that, where necessary, more detailed site surveys can be undertaken. At the same time, I want to ensure that we avoid extending planning blight in those areas of the country with a legacy of industrial land use.

To summarise the major grounds of criticism and concern, then, it may first be noticed that the declared objective of the exercise is to identify land that at some time has been subjected to 'contaminative use' – a term defined in section 143(6) as meaning 'any use of land which may cause it to be contaminated with noxious substances'. The inclusion of land on the register does not therefore mean that it is contaminated, much less that it is sufficiently seriously affected to pose a danger to subsequent users. A past use that raises the possibility of contamination is enough to warrant inclusion. The purpose is to put enquirers on notice and to prompt investigation. It may also be that, following Lord Hesketh's view quoted above, the Government were of the opinion that it would be easier and cheaper for local authorities to identify a past contaminative use than any current level of contamination. In reality, and even before they have been inaugurated, the registers are commonly referred to as registers of contaminated land, with all the connotations and implications attaching to the term. Although, in large measure in response to these fears of landowners, introduction of the regulations has been delayed, the inevitability of some system of monitoring or recording, whether due to United Kingdom or European initiative, has begun to create the planning blight disavowed by the Minister. At least, searches prior to purchase are beginning to ask questions in appropriate circumstances. A major, undesirable consequence is of course to increase the attraction for development of green field sites over the redevelopment of derelict land.

A further ground of objection is the absence of any system of grading or quantification of contamination. All land appearing on the register and being impliedly 'contaminated' is, so to speak, tarred with the same brush; or at least will encourage a prospective purchaser to think so. Also, once a given site is placed on the register there is no procedure for removing it if and when it is cleaned-up. Lastly, it has to be noted that this registration procedure has no direct connection with any remedial works. As Hawkins notes[25]:

> Whilst the presence of land on the register may trigger a more detailed examination of the condition of that land, whether it is in fact contaminated and the nature of that contamination, knowledge of that contamination is merely a necessary first step for clean up. Thereafter whether land will be cleaned up will depend on either a legal liability to do so or the prospect of achieving a financial advantage if the land is cleaned up.

25 Stephen Hawkins 'Clean-up of Contaminated Land: An Assessment of the Mechanisms Available' [1992] JPL 1119 at p.1126.

The likelihood is that the stimulation will be commercial rather than legislative.

While regulations are indefinitely postponed, that they will eventually appear should be regarded as inevitable, even though long delayed. Almost equally inevitable is the provision of a definition of contamination that is confined to the more serious contaminants or levels of pollution and that any subsequent reduction of the contamination will be included on the register, thus answering two of the current critisisms. When such regulations appear, though, they will, as has been said, have no direct impact on the removal of contamination from identified sites.

The further consideration of contaminated land now will therefore review the legal powers that may be used to secure its cleansing. It is important here to bear in mind that these powers were all enacted for other purposes and, to the extent

26 Richard Stein, 'Cleaning up Contaminated Land' *Environmental Health*, vol. 102/06 June 1994, p.146.

that they achieve this objective, clean-up is subordinate to their primary function. In this context Stein[26] points out that:

> Most of the statutory powers which may assist in the clean-up of contaminated land require that the contamination is likely to lead to some actual harm, e.g., harm to human health or safety; escape of pollutants into water or onto other land, or pollution of the environment. The mere existence of contamination on the land itself does not trigger any kind of liability requiring the land to be cleaned up unless the particular requirements of one of the statutory provisions is met.

Currently, therefore, securing the cleansing of contaminated land through legal procedures may be regarded as a by-product of the attainment of other environmental objectives, which will of course significantly affect the scope and nature of the particular procedures.

In contemplating the use of a statutory power for what might be called a peripheral purpose, it is important to bear in mind the well-established principle of administrative law that a power designed to achieve a particular objective is to be used solely for that purpose. In short, it is an abuse of power, or alternatively evidence of bad faith, to misuse a statutory power to achieve an unauthorised or *ultra vires* purpose. These provisions are therefore to be applied for their intended purpose and any ancillary benefit accepted as a bonus. While the distinction is not entirely clear cut it is convenient to divide these provisions into two categories: (i) those that are primarily concerned to prevent contamination occurring, and (ii) those that may be applied to remedy existing contamination.

Prevention of contamination

As may be supposed, the powers available to prevent land contamination are those governing the treatment and disposal of waste, and have therefore been considered under that head. Of primary importance, section 33(1) of the 1990 Act makes it an offence to deposit or to treat, keep or dispose of controlled waste in or on any land without or contrary to the terms of a waste management licence, or to treat, keep or dispose of controlled waste in a manner likely to cause pollution of the environment or harm to human health.[27] The determining criteria, therefore, are either the applicable licence conditions, or the causing of pollution or harm to health. Contamination *per se* is not then sufficient, although it may of course be argued that a deposit that does not produce any polluting effect is scarcely contaminating. The other severe limitation of this provision, to be expected from its context, is that the potentially wide category of contamination deriving from the storage of non-waste materials preparatory to use is not covered.[28]

27 See in Chapter 14 at p.365.

28 But see Planning (Hazardous Substances) Act 1990.

Where any controlled waste has been deposited in or on any land in contravention of the section 33(1) prohibition, section 59 gives the waste regulation or collection authority the power, by notice, to require the occupier of the land to do either or both of the following within the period stated, being not less than 21 days:

(a) remove the waste from the land;
(b) take the specified steps to eliminate or reduce the consequences of the deposit of the waste.

It may be, and in relation to fly-tipping probably will be, the case that the occupier will not be responsible for the unlawful deposit. In that event he is given a defence in an appeal to the magistrates' court that he neither deposited nor knowingly caused or knowingly permitted the deposit of the waste.[29] Otherwise, failure to comply with the notice is a summary offence attracting a fine up to level 5 on the standard scale and a daily penalty of one-tenth of level 5 for each day the offence continues after conviction. In the event of non-compliance the authority may, under section 59(6), do the necessary work and recover from the person served with the notice the costs reasonably incurred. The scope and interpretation of 'knowingly cause or knowingly permit' has been considered in the context of water pollution.[30]

As an alternative to the basic section 59 procedure, subsection (7) authorises the authority to act directly to remove the waste deposited in contravention of section 33(1) or to reduce its consequences, without the prior service of a notice. This procedure is available where:

(a) immediate removal of the waste or other action is necessary to remove or prevent pollution of land, water or air or harm to human health, or to eliminate or reduce the consequences of the deposit; or
(b) there is no occupier of the land; or
(c) the occupier neither made nor knowingly permitted the deposit of the waste.

In this case also the authority may recover the costs reasonably incurred in the work either, in (a), from the occupier, unless he proves that he neither made nor knowingly caused or knowingly permitted the deposit of the waste, or, in any case, from the person who deposited or knowingly caused or knowingly permitted the deposit of any of the waste.[31]

A further provision attaching responsibility for damage consequent upon a section 33(1) or section 63(2)[32] offence is to be found in section 73(6), which provides that:

Where any damage is caused by waste which has been deposited in or on land, any person who deposited it, or knowingly caused or knowingly permitted it to be deposited, in either case so as to commit an offence under section 33(1) or 63(2) above, is liable for the damage except where the damage –

(a) was due wholly to the fault of the person who suffered it; or
(b) was suffered by a person who voluntarily accepted the risk of the damage being caused;

but without prejudice to any liability arising otherwise than under this subsection.

The defences available in a prosecution under section 33 apply also to these proceedings. For these purposes 'damage' is defined in section 73(8) as including 'the death of, or injury to, any person (including any disease and any impairment of physical or mental condition)' and 'fault' has the same meaning as in the Law Reform (Contributory Negligence) Act 1945.[33]

The definition of 'damage' serves to extend the term. It will therefore cover damage to property and other legal rights. The effect of the phrase 'is liable for the damage' is to attach civil liability for the losses or injury consequent upon the criminal offences. The wording of the provision confines available civil remedies to damages compensating for past injury. Future harm cannot therefore be anticipated by injunction. The exceptions in section 73(6)(a) and (b) apply respectively the contributory negligence principles of the 1945 Act and the tort principle of *volenti non fit injuria* to these actions. The whole question of civil liability for the

29 Section 59(3).

30 See in Chapter 7 at p.162.

31 Section 59(8).

32 Offences relating to other than controlled waste.

33 Section 4 of that Act provides that 'fault means negligence, breach of statutory duty or other act or omission which gives rise to liability in tort or would, apart from this Act, give rise to the defence of contributory negligence'.

consequences of waste handling and disposal is currently the subject of EC proposals.[34]

Remedy of past contamination

34 Proposal for Directive on civil liability for damage caused by waste; submitted 18 September 1989, COM (89) 282 final SYN 217 (OJ 1989 C. 251, p.3).

In so far as contamination may, if it is known about, affect the subsequent use of land, and as proposed land use is a matter for planning approval, it is evident that the former should influence the latter. The aim of Circular 21/87, 'the Development of Contaminated Land', is to encourage the re-use of urban land and thereby protect the Green Belt and countryside. It necessarily emphasises, though, that contamination, actual and potential, is a material consideration for the determination of planning applications. Specialist advice is available from the Interdepartmental Committee on the Redevelopment of Contaminated Land (ICRCL) which publishes periodical guidance notes on particular types of contamination.[35]

35 ICRCL Guidance Notes, published by the DoE, include: Notes on the redevelopment of landfill sites, ICRCL 17/78; Notes on the redevelopment of gasworks sites, ICRCL 18/79; Notes on the redevelopment of sewage works and farms, ICRCL 23/79; Notes on the redevelopment of scrap yards and similar sites, ICRCL 42/80; Guidance on the assessment and redevelopment of contaminated land, ICRCL 59/83; Notes on the fire hazards of contaminated land, ICRCL 61/84.

Whether and the extent to which a contaminated site is cleaned up ultimately depends on the developer, the nature of the contamination and the sensitivity of the proposed use. Toxic contamination of the subsoil will be of greater concern if the projected use is for a pre-school playgroup or horticulture, for example, than if the site is to be concreted over for a car park. The planning authority, in granting permission, has the discretion in appropriate cases to attach conditions requiring that soil samples be taken, and if contamination is revealed that it be remedied before redevelopment is carried out. The decision on the economic justification of such an exercise, though, will be for the developer, who may feel that the consequent costs warrant the use of another site. The failure of a future use is likely in the planning context to delay or prevent any reduction of the contamination.

In addition to the planning controls considered above that may be activated in response to a planning application and are therefore initiated by the land owner, the Town and Country Planning Act 1990 empowers the local planning authority to take action in respect of 'land adversely affecting amenity of neighbourhood'. It may be emphasised again in this context, though, that such land 'adversely affecting amenity' is not necessarily synonymous with contaminated land. Further, even in those sites where the two issues coincide the remedying of the amenity problem may not involve or require the removal of the contamination. Nevertheless, in many cases there will doubtless be a sufficient concurrence of pollution, nuisance and aesthetic problems that the resolution of the latter is likely to secure some amelioration of the former.

Where it appears to the local planning authority that the amenity of a part of its area or of an adjoining area is adversely affected by the condition of land in its area, section 215(1) and (2) gives it the power to serve a notice on the owner and occupier requiring them to remedy the condition of the land as specified in the notice. The period specified in the notice for completion of the work is to commence at least 28 days after service. As originally framed in section 65 of the 1971 Act this power was confined to 'any garden, vacant site or other open land'. 'Open land' was narrowly defined, the Court of Appeal in *Stephens* v *Cuckfield RDC* [1960][36] holding that a car breaker's yard that was open to the air and not built on but was fenced, was not open land. The scope of this present power now extends to 'any land'.

36 [1960] 2 QB 373.

The apparently wide application of the section is limited in practice, though, by the second of the grounds of appeal listed in section 217(1), which are:

(a) that the condition of the land does not affect the amenity[37] of any part of the local planning authority's area;
(b) that the condition of the land is attributable to, and such as results in the ordinary course of events from, the carrying on of operations or a use of land which is not a contravention of Part III (planning control);
(c) that the requirements of the notice exceed what is necessary to achieve its purpose;
(d) that the period specified in the notice for carrying out the work is insufficient.

37 For the meaning of 'amenity' see Chapter 14.

The, or a major, consequence of ground (b) would appear to be to confine the use of the section to waste, derelict or development land when that amenity-damaging use has ceased. In such cases, though, the present owner or occupier on whom is cast the burden of clearing up the offensive conditions may not be the person responsible for causing them. While this is of course immaterial to the operation of the section, the persons currently in place being responsible, it is, so far as actual rather than legal responsibility is concerned, unfortunate. Also, it emphasises the benefit to purchasers of instituting a comprehensive investigation of the property before purchase. The disparity between causation and ultimate responsibility in such circumstances does appear to be recognised and something of a solution offered by section 219(2), which provides that where, following service of a section 215 notice, expense is incurred by the owner or occupier in complying with it, or the owner pays any expenses of the local planning authority in doing the work, those sums 'shall be deemed to be incurred or paid for the use and at the request of the person who caused or permitted the land to come to be in the condition in which it was when the notice was served'. The inference is then that the costs of cleaning up the site, if the initiative is from the authority rather than a whim of the present owner, are recoverable as a civil debt.

Challenge to the terms of the notice, either by the person served or any other person having an interest in the land, on the abovementioned grounds is exclusively by appeal to the magistrates' court, such issues not being open to question in any other proceedings; including their use as a defence to prosecution. Failure to comply with the terms of the notice is a summary offence attracting fines up to level 3 on the standard scale. Further, by section 219(1), if the notice is not complied with within the period specified in the notice, as may be extended, the local planning authority who served the notice may enter the land and do the work and recover from the owner the expenses reasonably incurred in so doing.

Closely associated with planning controls in practice are building controls. The Building Regulations 1991[38] have a limited concern with contaminated land in two respects. Regulation 4(1) provides that 'Building work shall be carried out so that ... (a) it complies with the relevant requirements contained in Schedule 1'. That schedule contains the substance of the building control provisions and includes:

38 S.I. 1991 No. 2768.

A2 The building shall be constructed so that ground movement caused by –
    (a) swelling, shrinkage or freezing of the subsoil; or
    (b) land-slip or subsidence (other then subsidence arising from shrinkage), in so far as the risk can be reasonably foreseen,
will not impair the stability of the building ...
C2 Precautions shall be taken to avoid danger to health and safety caused by substances found on or in the ground to be covered by the building.

A2 does not of course apply to contaminated land *per se,* and the precautions are concerned with the load-bearing properties of the subsoil rather than its composition. However, to the extent that landfill sites or made-up ground may contain contaminants the two issues may be so inextricably interrelated that the one will be influenced by the other. It is C2, though, that applies directly, even though tentatively, to the composition of the subsoil. The harm sought to be guarded against is 'danger to health and safety', making this clearly a public health rather than an environmental provision. Also, and having in mind the purpose of the Regulations, the health and safety to be protected from the substances in the ground must be that of the occupiers and users of the building. A further and more serious limitation, even given the narrow environmental aims of these Regulations, is that the precautions may only apply to 'the ground covered by the building'. Being found in a penal provision these words are to be interpreted restrictively. In the nature of things, and except for the most acute cases, the normal site preparation and building structure can be expected to achieve that objective. Depending on the use of the building, it would appear that the state of the surrounding land not built on is likely to present more of a hazard to health.

Waste regulation authorities are given the duty, by section 61(1) of the Environmental Protection Act 1990,[39] of causing their areas 'to be inspected from time to time to detect whether any land is in such a condition, by reason of the relevant matters affecting the land, that it may cause pollution of the environment or harm to human health'. The purpose of inspection is to determine the potential for environmental harm of the 'relevant matters' affecting the land. These are, by section 61(2), the concentration or accumulation in, and emission or discharge from, the land of noxious gases or noxious liquids caused by deposits of controlled waste on land; which includes land covered by water. 'Pollution of the environment' is specifically defined for the purposes of waste disposal in Part II of the Act as meaning:

> ... pollution of the environment due to the release or escape (into any environmental medium) from ... (c) the land in or on which controlled waste is deposited, ... of substances or articles constituting or resulting from the waste and capable (by reason of the quantity or concentrations involved) of causing harm to man or any other living organisms supported by the environment.[40]

Though the section heading and main aim of the provision are directed to landfill sites, the actual wording appears wide enough to cover all locations where controlled waste has been dumped and seepage of solid or liquid substances into the soil or water has occurred or may be anticipated. Waste regulation authorities thus appear to have a general supervisory responsibility for at least the more grossly contaminated land, if attributable to controlled waste, extending for the duration of the risk.

If on inspection it appears to the authority that the condition of the land due to the relevant matters is such that pollution or harm is likely to be caused the authority shall do any necessary works and take such other steps (whether on the affected or adjacent land) as appear to the authority reasonable to avoid the pollution or harm. Where in the opinion of the authority the condition of the land is likely to lead to pollution of water it has a duty to consult the NRA on the action it proposes to take.[41] The authority is then given a discretion to recover all or part of the reasonable costs of the work from the owner of the land unless it has accepted the surrender of the relevant waste management licence under section 39. In exercising this discretion the authority is to have regard to any hardship that may be caused

39 See also in Chapter 15 at p.426.

40 Section 29(3).

41 Section 61(7) and (5).

to the land owner. There is here, then, a specific power to deal with contaminated land originating from landfill of waste – a major category of such contamination. The real deficiency in the operation of this section is that it has yet to be implemented.

A common problem associated with contaminated land is the leaching of substances into groundwater and thence into other supplies. The NRA is given the power, by section 161 of the Water Resources Act 1991, to take direct action itself to prevent or remedy the pollution of controlled waters and recover the reasonable costs of such action from the person responsible.[42] Where the Authority considers that any poisonous, noxious or polluting matter or any solid waste is likely to enter, or to be or to have been present in, any controlled waters it is empowered to carry out works and operations to prevent such entry or to remove, dispose of, remedy or mitigate any pollution so caused. Under section 161(1) the preventative action is available where such matter 'appears likely to enter' any controlled waters. This is a matter of fact and judgement but implies an appropriate degree of proximity, in both time and space. These powers are not expressly stated to be of an emergency nature. However, the absence of any prior notification requirement, coupled with the right to recover costs, indicates that a factor in the judgement may be the anticipated inadequacy, either because of lack of time or co-operation, of other enforcement action.

Material dumped on land that is 'prejudicial to health or a nuisance' may be dealt with by the local authority under Part III of the 1990 Act as a statutory nuisance.[43] While again this provision is not directed to the issue of contaminated land as such nor to environmental consequences, there will be circumstances where the deposited material will be contaminating and the nature of the prejudice or nuisance will be coextensive with environmental damage. The matters stated by section 79(1) to be statutory nuisances include, '(e) any accumulation or deposit which is prejudicial to health or a nuisance'. Where the local authority becomes aware of such circumstances it is required to remedy them by the service of an abatement notice and summary proceedings if necessary. The authority is given the discretion, as well as or instead of such proceedings, to do the necessary remedial work itself and to recover the costs from the person by whose act, default or sufferance the nuisance arose or was caused.

Contaminated land and derelict land, while not synonymous terms, conceptually cover a large area of common ground, so to speak. As was suggested initially, one view is that derelict land, by that very fact, will necessarily be contaminated. Be that as it may, and the issue finally turns on the interpretation of 'contaminated', initiatives to remedy and restore derelict land may be accepted as likely to make a positive contribution to resolving the problem of contaminated land. In consequence the availability of grants towards the regeneration of derelict land provided for in the Derelict Land Act 1982 now deserve consideration. By section 1, the Secretary of State is given discretion, with Treasury consent, to pay grants in respect of relevant expenditure incurred in reclaiming, improving or enabling the bringing back into use of:

(a) land which is derelict, neglected or unsightly; and
(b) in relation to a local authority in whose area it is situated, land which is not derelict, neglected or unsightly but is likely to become so by reason of actual or apprehended collapse of the surface as the result of the carrying out of relevant operations which have ceased to be carried out.

42 Section 161(3).

43 See further on this issue in Chapter 4 at p.97.

Relevant operations are, by section 1(11), 'underground mining operations other than operations for the purpose of the working and getting of coal, or of coal and other minerals worked with coal, or for the purpose of getting any product from coal in the course of working and getting coal'. The Secretary of State has discretion over the manner, amount, time and conditions to be attached to such payments. For these purposes 'relevant expenditure' is that incurred with the approval of the Secretary of State in connection with:

(a) the carrying out for reclaiming, improving or bringing back into use of any works on that or other land;
(b) the carrying out of a survey of the land to determine whether such works should be undertaken; and
(c) in relation to a local authority, the acquisition of land for that purpose.[44]

44 Section 1(3).

The amount of grant, provided for in section 1(5) and (6), is determined according to whether the land is or is not in a development area or intermediate area. The Secretary of State has the power, by order, to declare that any particular land is to be treated as if in such an area, and it is then to be known as a derelict land clearance area.

The specific reference to local authority action in section 1 is explained in section 3 of the 1982 Act which, in substituting a new section 89(2) of the National Parks and Access to the Countryside Act 1949, gives a local authority the power in relation to land satisfying the section 1(a) and (b) criteria above, to carry out such works on that or other land as appear expedient to reclaim, improve or bring the land back into use.

As a conclusion to this consideration of contaminated land it may be reiterated that the measures just reviewed are not intended for or primarily directed to the remedying of such contamination. Any improvement is therefore to be regarded as, at best, a by-product of the achievement of the statutory objective. It may therefore be appropriate to conclude as Hawkins does[45]:

45 *Op. cit.*, note 25, at p.1127.

> Ultimately, contaminated land will only be cleaned up if someone has the duty to do so (either because of a statutory duty on a public authority or legal liability upon an owner or person responsible) or if the owner can see economic advantages flowing from the clean up. The United Kingdom system does not in any satisfactory manner provide the certainty and clarity whereby this 'carrot and stick' approach has any real prospect other than in exceptional circumstances of causing clean up of contaminated land.

17

Radioactive Waste

INTRODUCTION

Radioactivity

Although radioactivity is a subject that is broadly understood by most people, its terminology and principles are less familiar in detail. While this is a law textbook, a consideration of the legal controls on the treatment and disposal of radioactive waste may usefully be preceded by a brief review of the subject, if only to put the basic terminology into context. The following treatment of the subject is extracted from Chapter II of the 6th Report of the Royal Commission on Environmental Pollution, 'Nuclear Power and the Environment'.[1]

1 Cmnd 6618, September 1976.

Radioactivity is the emission of certain radiations by the nuclei of unstable atoms. An atom consists of a central nucleus which contains almost all the mass of the atom and which electrically is positively charged, and a surrounding cloud of planetary electrons of very little mass which are negatively charged. Normally an atom is electrically neutral, the central positive charge on the nucleus being exactly balanced by the negative charges on the electrons. In the course of chemical or physical processes it is common for atoms to gain or lose one or more of their planetary electrons without affecting the charge of the nucleus, and thereby to acquire an overall negative or positive charge respectively: in such a condition the atom is referred to as an 'ion' and the process is called 'ionisation'.

The atomic nucleus is a compact blob of extremely dense matter which may be considered to consist of a mixture of two kinds of similar particles – protons and neutrons. Between neutrons and protons in close contact there are very strong forces, the so-called nuclear forces, which are capable of binding them together into a stable nucleus in spite of the electrical repulsion which exists between the protons. The stability, however, depends upon a rather precise ratio of neutrons to protons. If there are too many or too few neutrons the nucleus will be unstable and will remedy the situation by spontaneously changing the ratio. This may be done in one of two ways, depending on the precise nucleus concerned, and producing an emission of either alpha- or beta-particles (alpha- or beta-radioactivity). The process of going from a less stable to a more stable state releases energy. This energy is used in propelling the alpha- or beta-particles which are therefore emitted from the atom with considerable speed. Some of the excess energy may also appear in the form of gamma-rays, which are electromagnetic radiations similar to X-rays but usually of shorter wavelengths, and which like X-rays are also ionising.

Atoms of the same chemical element always have the same number of protons in their nucleus, and hence the same number and configuration of orbiting electrons. But they may have different numbers of neutrons. Such different atoms are called 'isotopes' of the element, indicating that they have the same place in the periodic table. They also have identical chemical properties. They are written, e.g., strontium-90, connoting that the strontium nucleus (which has 38 protons) has 52 neutrons, making a total of 90 'nucleons'. Some isotopes are stable, others such as strontium-90 emit radiation and are called 'radioisotopes'. A substance containing unstable atoms is described as radioactive and, as has been seen, may emit four kinds of radiation: alpha, beta, gamma, and if fission occurs, neutrons. The individual processes by which radioactive atoms approach stability by emitting radiation occur completely at random and are independent of all physical and chemical circumstances; the process can neither be advanced or delayed by man.

There is, however, for each particular type of radioisotope, a definite characteristic rate at which the atoms will disintegrate or 'decay': this is measured by its physical 'half-life', that is, the time in which one half of the atoms will decay. The half-life may be a fraction of a second or it may be millions of years, but it is always the same for a given isotope. After one 'half-life' the amount of radioactivity from the given nuclei will be halved, and after a second half-life it will be halved again, and so on. Thus the radioactivity will never reach zero, though after sufficient half-lives it will become negligible. In theory of course radioactivity will reach zero when the last nucleus disintegrates.

The four kinds of radiation differ in their powers of penetration and in their interactions with the materials through they pass. They are listed in the Table [below]. Alpha-particles are relatively slow-moving and lose their energy in a short distance. They are able to penetrate only a few tens of millimetres of air and are easily stopped by a sheet of paper. However, because they leave a short but dense trail of ionisation in the matter through which they pass, they can cause more damage in living tissue than particles of longer path length. Nuclei emitting only alpha-particles are biologically ineffective unless they are taken into the body. This may be by inhalation, ingestion, or at the site of an open wound. Both alpha- and beta-particles, especially the latter, may also emit gamma-radiation.

Electrons, or beta-particles, vary widely in their energy and it is less easy to specify a range for their effect. Beta-particles lose most of their effect if shielded by say a few millimetres of perspex. Thus nuclei which are 'beta-emitters' are again of particular danger if taken into or onto the surface of the body. In practice, however, many 'beta-emitters' also emit very penetrating gamma-radiation which, like X-rays, can pass easily through matter, and thus irradiate the whole body. Living cells require to be shielded from gamma-radiation by considerable thicknesses of heavy materials such as lead or concrete. Reactors, for example, are usually surrounded by a 'biological shield' several metres thick.

Neutrons, because they are electrically uncharged, are slowed down only by direct collisions with nuclei. After they have lost most of their energy by making many such collisions they will be absorbed into a nucleus, which thus becomes a higher isotope of the same element and will often be radioactive. Since nuclei are very small compared with atoms, and neutrons uncharged, collisions happen infrequently. Neutrons may therefore penetrate matter to considerable depths before absorption takes place. When a neutron strikes a nucleus, some of its energy will be transferred to the nucleus which therefore recoils. Being electrically charged and massive the recoiling nucleus creates dense ionisation over a short distance like an alpha-particle does. This is why neutrons, although they do not themselves cause ionisation, are so damaging to living tissue – and indeed, to solid matter such as fuel elements and their cladding. When neutrons are eventually absorbed, moreover, intense gamma-radiation is usually emitted by the absorbing nucleus and this, too, is ionising.

The different types of radiation

Type	Particle	Stopped by
Alpha	Helium – 4 nucleus (Heavy, +ve charge)	A few cm of air: 40mm tissue
Beta	Electron (Light, –ve charge)	A few mm of plastic: 40mm tissue
Gamma	Photon (Electromagnetic radiation)	Progressive attenuation especially by heavy nuclei: e.g., 40mm of lead reduces to 1/10
Neutrons	Neutron (Heavy, uncharged)	Progressive attenuation especially by light nuclei: e.g., 0.25m of water reduces to 1/10

In considering radioactivity and possible radiation doses associated with radioactive material, including waste, it is important to realise that any radiation thereby received would be additional to the radiation that is already received from a range of other sources by the general population. Particular groups within the population will of course by subjected to increased doses through, for example, employment or medical procedures. Radiation doses from man-made sources are no different in character from naturally-occurring ones, although they may affect particular parts of the body rather than the body as a whole.

Dose rates of ionising radiation received by an average member of the population in the UK[2]

	Bone marrow mrem/yr	Reproductive cells: genetically significant dose (GSD) mrem/yr
Naturally ocurring:		
From cosmic rays	33	33
From soil and airborne	44	44
Within the body (mainly potassium-40)	24	28
	101	105
Manmade:		
Medical, diagnostic X-rays	32	14
Medical, radiotherapy	12	5
Medical, radioisotope use	2	0.2
	46	19
Fallout from bomb tests	6	4
Occupational doses (other than from nuclear power)	0.4	0.3
Nuclear power industry	0.25	0.2
Miscellaneous (mainly occupational doses)	0.3	0.3
	7	5
	154	129

2 6th Report of RCEP, Cmnd 6618, September 1976, at paragraph 43.

S.I. 1986 No. 1082.

The United Kingdom is committed to the adoption of SI units (International System of Units) established for use in all branches of science. The Units of Measurement Regulations 1986[3] made pursuant to section 2(2) of the European Communities Act 1972 give effect to that obligation. The SI unit for the quantity of radioactivity is the becquerel (Bq). It is defined as a unit of activity equal to one nuclear disintegration per second. The becquerel has replaced the curie (Ci) which was based on the activity of one gram of radium. There are 37,000 becquerels to a microcurie. The SI unit for the quantity of absorbed radiation dose is the gray (Gy). It has replaced the rad. One gray is equal to 100 rads. The quantity absorbed dose is multiplied by modifying factors characteristic of the type of radiation in order to generate a quantity dose equivalent which takes into account the different effectiveness of the various ionising radiations in causing harm to tissue. In the old system of units, the unit of dose equivalent was the rem. In the SI system the gray is related to the new unit of dose equivalent, the sievert (Sv), in exactly the same way. One sievert is equal to 100 rems.

Relationship between SI units and non-SI units

Physical quantity	SI unit	non-SI unit	Relationship
Activity	becquerel (Bq)	curie (Ci)	$1\ Bq = 2.7 \times 10^{-11}\ Ci$ = 27 pCi $1\ Ci = 3.7 \times 10^{-10}\ Bq$ =37 GBq
Absorbed dose	gray (Gy)	rad (rad) 1 rad = 0.01 Gy = 10 mGy	1 Gy = 100 rads
Dose equivalent	sievert (Sv)	rem (rem)	1 Sv = 100 rems 1 rem = 0.01 Sv = 10 mSv

Prefixes for SI units

Factor	Prefix	Symbol	Factor	Prefix	Syumbol
10^{12}	tera	T	10^{-3}	milli	m
10^{9}	giga	G	10^{-6}	micro	μ
10^{6}	mega	M	10^{-9}	nano	n
10^{3}	kilo	k	10^{-12}	pico	p

In concluding this brief general review of the subject one may note the following definitions from the Glossary of Terms attached to 'A Guide to the Administration of the Act', i.e., the Radioactive Substances Act 1960 (the Guide)[4]:

This Guide, which is pplicable to the 1993 Act with mended section numbers, may e found as an Appendix to hat Act in Current Law tatutes.

Radiation   The process of emitting energy as waves of particles. The energy thus radiated. Often used for 'ionising radiation'.

Ionisation   The process by which a neutral atom or molecule acquires an electric charge.

Ionising radiation   'Radiation' that produces 'Ionisation' in matter, e.g., alpha particles, beta particles, gamma rays, X-rays and neutrons.

Management of Radioactive Waste

An introduction to this subject may conveniently be taken from 'Radioactive Waste Management',[5] which at paragraph 8 says:

5 Cmnd 8607, July 1982.

> Techniques have been developed to detect and measure extremely low levels of radioactivity and a great deal is known about the pathways of radioactive substances in the environment, which are what would determine the likely consequences of disposal. An estimated 78 per cent of the radiation received by the population of the United Kingdom is from natural sources, and a further 21 per cent from medical uses. The amount received from all other uses is very small, about 1 per cent, and the amount caused by the discharge of radioactive wastes to the environment is only 0.1 per cent of the total. Proposals to bury radioactive wastes have to be viewed in the perspective of the very large amounts of radioactivity already present in the ground in the form of naturally-occurring radioactive substances.

As a basis for controlling exposure of persons to ionising radiation the National Radiological Protection Board has accepted the system of dose limitation recommended by the International Commission on Radiological Protection (ICRP) in 1977.[6] The Guide, in appplying those recommendations to the management of radioactive waste in the United Kingdom, identifies the objectives, in paragraph 46, as:

6 'Recommendations of the International Commission on Radiological Protection' (ICRP Publication 26). Expanded in ASP2 NRPB; Advice to the Expert Group reviewing the White Paper Command 884, 'The Control of Radioactive Wastes' (HMSO). Note: the ICRP membership is appointed by the International Congress of Radiology on the basis of their individual scientific reputations. It operates independently of governments and is answerable to the International Congress of Radiology.

(a) that all practices giving rise to radioactive wastes must be justified, i.e., the need for the practice must be established in terms of overall benefit;

(b) radiation exposure of individuals and the collective dose to the population arising from radioactive wastes shall be reduced to levels which are as low as reasonably achievable, economic and social factors being taken into account;

(c) the average effective dose equivalent from all sources, excluding natural background radiation and medical procedures, to representative members of a critical group of the general public shall not exceed 5mSv[7] (0.5 rem) in any one year.

7 mSv = millisievert.

The expectation is that the application of these principles will produce for an individual a lifetime whole body dose equivalent not exceeding 70 mSv (7 rem). What applies to the human population in respect of exposure to radiation applies in broadly similar terms to other living organisms. The ICRP's view in its recommendations is therefore that the protection arrangements adopted for man will generally provide sufficient protection for other species. However, the Guide takes the view that in considering dose levels to organisms it is enough to restrict exposure at the 'population' rather than the 'individual' level.

In 1992 the National Radiological Protection Board published new objectives for land-based disposal, including the following recommendations:

(a) Future generations should not be subjected to risks which would be considered unacceptable today, i.e., people alive at any time in the future should be given a level of protection at least equivalent to that accorded to members of the public alive now.

(b) The radiological risk from one disposal facility to the most exposed group of people should not exceed a risk of serious health effects in the individuals or their descendants of 1 in 100,000 per year.

(c) The radiological risks to members of the public should be as low as reasonably achievable, economic and social factors being taken into account.

The treatment appropriate to any given radioactive waste will be determined largely by the strength or quantity of radioactivity emitted. On this basis such waste is divided into four categories[8]:

(a) Very-low-level: waste of sufficiently low radioactivity that it can be disposed of by normal 'dustbin' disposal without the need for authorisation.

(b) Low-level: wastes with a low level of radioactivity which can be disposed of by existing routes, the arrangements depending on the particular level and type of radioactivity.

(c) Intermediate-level: wastes which at present can be safely stored but for which disposal facilities are not at present available and which do not fall within the next category.

(d) Heat-generating (or High-level): wastes in which the temperature may rise significantly as a result of rapid radioactive decay, so that this factor has to be taken into account in designing disposal facilities. In the UK these are the highly active liquid residues arising from the first stage of the reprocessing of spent reactor fuel.

The following extract consisting of paragraphs 50 to 57 of the Guide deals with the general principles and practices for the disposal of solid waste and will serve as an introduction to the provisions of the 1993 Act. The Guide also deals in some detail with disposal practices for liquid wastes and atmospheric discharges, demolition and other high volume wastes, and the trench burial and sea disposal of solid wastes.

50. Where it can safely be done it is desirable to use conventional methods of waste disposal such as discharge to sewers or disposal on local authority refuse tips and this has been the practice since the first authorisations were issued. Among the factors taken into account are the nature and amount of radioactive waste and the facilities available locally. For example, the extent to which disposal can safely be made into the sewers will depend, among other things, on the volume of flow in sewers and where the sewage effluent is finally discharged. In the case of solid wastes the suitability of local authority refuse tips will depend on the nature of the tip and the amount of non-radioactive material available to cover the solid wastes. Each authorisation requires separate consideration; that is done on a case by case basis, taking into account the particular circumstances.

51. Some low level radioactive wastes are not suitable for local disposal. Arrangements known as the National Disposal Service have been made by the Department of the Environment under section 10 of the 1960 Act for dealing with these wastes. UKAEA and British Nuclear Fuels Ltd (BNFL) accept wastes whose disposal via the service is permitted under an authorisation. The waste is generally either buried in trenches at the BNFL site at Drigg or suitably packaged by UKAEA and disposed of at sea in the Atlantic at a depth generally in excess of 4,000 metres of water in accordance with internationally agreed conditions. Section 10(3) of the Act allows reasonable charges to be made for this service.

52. Where disposal routes are available they should be used to the full for disposal of current arisings and backlogs of the appropriate types of waste in order to prevent the unnecessary accumulation of waste requiring storage and surveillance at production sites. The disposal routes currently available are described below. In all cases it is desirable that the disposal arrangements adopted for a particular kind of waste should not be more elaborate than the characteristics of the waste actually require. The development of fur-

8 'Radioactive Waste Management' (1982) Cmnd 8607. Amended by 'Radioactive Waste: The Government's Response to the Environment Committee's Report' (1986) Cmnd 9852.

ther disposal routes will be the responsibility of the Nuclear Industry Radioactive Waste Executive (NIREX) based at Harwell.

Disposal Practices – solid wastes

Very low level wastes
53. Very low level solid waste, less than 0.4 Bq/g and organic solvent waste containing only carbon-14 or tritium at total concentration of less than 4 Bq/ml can be exempted from consideration under the Act. A Low Activity Substances Exemption Order, which will cover both substances and wastes and will comply with the EC Directive, will be made.

Low level waste in domestic refuse
54. Small amounts of solid radioactive waste are authorised for disposal with ordinary refuse. The limits for such 'dustbin disposals' are:

(a) 400 kBq in any 0.1 cu metre and:
(b) 40 kBq per article.

However where the radioactive content is due solely to the presence of carbon-14 and/or tritium, those limits are relaxed to 4,000 kBq in any 0.1 cu metre and not more than 400 kBq in any one item. A volume of 0.1 cu metre is taken to be the equivalent of one dustbin. Alpha emitters and strontium-90 are usually excluded from dustbin disposals. Dustbin disposals under these conditions present no hazard either to the refuse collectors or at the disposal site.

Incineration
55. This method of disposal is useful for wastes which are obnoxious or biologically toxic, and is sometimes advisable simply because the wastes concerned are combustible or inflammable. It often has the advantage of reducing the volume of solid waste ultimately requiring disposal, but on the other hand it suffers from the potential disadvantages that the radioactivity (from nuclides other than tritium and carbon-14) may be concentrated in the ash. Where the quantity and nature of the radionuclides and the throughput of ash production of the incinerator are known authorisations for disposal in this way are generally given on a case by case basis, taking all the local circumstances into account. However it is usual to permit disposals of up to 4 MBq a day of the commonly used tritium and carbon-14 without this detailed examination. Conditions concerning safe disposal of the ash are laid down, where necessary, in the authorisation for disposal of the waste to the incinerator, rather than in a separate authorisation.

Special precautions disposals
56. Within certain limits and provided that special precautions are observed, solid wastes which are too radioactive for dustbin disposal may be disposed of at suitable landfill sites. The appropriate precautions are specified in the authorisation for disposal. The ones usually employed are –

(a) waste shall be conveyed to the disposal site in a sealed, plain, unlabelled plastic or multi-layer paper sack, in a closed metal bin;
(b) at the disposal site the sack shall be removed from the bin and placed either at the foot of the tipping face or in a hole dug for it, and immediately covered with inactive refuse to a depth of not less than 1.5 metres.

The usual limits are that no one sack shall contain more than 4MBq of radionuclides of half life greater than one year and 40 MBq of others, except that where the radioactive content is due solely to the presence of carbon-14 and/or tritium the limit is 200MBq per sack. There may be a further restriction of not more than 400 kBq of long lived activity in relation to any one article in the waste, where the activity is not due to carbon-14 or tritium.

57. Authorisations for special precautions disposals are only granted where the disposal will be at sites with the necessary characteristics and after consultation with the appropriate public and local bodies. The Act allows the disposal authority to make a charge for special precautions disposals.

RADIOACTIVE SUBSTANCES ACT 1993

Scope of the Act

In approaching this area of control it is to be observed that the material under consideration is 'radioactive' and 'waste'. In the operation of regulations applying specifically to the first characteristic it is necessary to make provision for the assimilation or exclusion of the body of law governing waste generally. Section 78 of the Environmental Protection Act 1990 therefore provides that none of the provisions of Part II of that Act dealing with waste disposal applies. Also, subject to any modifying regulations made by the Secretary of State, the pollution provisions of the Water Resources Act 1991 do not apply to radioactive waste. The current regulations applying specified sections of that Act to radioactive waste are the Control of Pollution (Radioactive Waste) Regulations 1989.[9] Regulation 3 provides that the sections listed in the Schedule 'shall have effect, without modification, in relation to any radioactive waste as they have effect in relation to any effluent or other matter or substance which is not radioactive waste'. The Schedule lists the particular sections of the Water Act 1989, but the corresponding sections in the 1991 Act are sections 82, 84–88, 92, 99, 161, 190, 202, 203, and 213.

The principal statute concerned with the treatment and disposal of radioactive waste is now the Radioactive Substances Act 1993, consolidating the 1960 Act and Part V and Schedule 5 of the Environmental Protection Act1990. This Act replaces, with some modification, the 1960 statute, which was based on recommendations in the White Paper, 'Control of Radioactive Wastes'.[10] In accepting the report of the expert panel set up in 1956 to advise on the Control of Radioactive Wastes, and which was appended to the White Paper, the Government stated that:

> An important section of the panel's report is concerned with the standards by which the discharge of radioactive waste should be controlled. These standards are not immutable; they will be subject to review from time to time in the light of advice received from international and national advisory bodies. Neither will they provide a charter for the discharge of radioactive waste at will, provided that the discharges remain within specified upper limits; it is the essence of the prudent system of control that discharges should be kept not only within the upper limits of safety, but as far below them as can reasonably be achieved.

It is evident from its title that the Act has a broad scope, controlling the handling of radioactive substances and materials generally. The present concern, though, is with those provisions bearing on 'radioactive waste', a term which by section 2 of the Act:

... means waste which consists wholly or partly of –

(a) a substance or article which, if it were not waste, would be radioactive material, or
(b) a substance or article which has been contaminated in the course of the production, keeping or use of radioactive material, or by contact with or proximity to other waste falling within paragraph (a) or this paragraph.

9 S.I. 1989 No. 1158.

10 Published in November 1959; Cmnd 884.

'Waste' is defined for the purposes of this Act in section 47(1) as including:

any substance which constitutes scrap material or an effluent or other unwanted surplus substance arising from the application of any process, and also includes any substance or article which requires to be disposed of as being broken, worn out, contaminated or otherwise spoilt

Section 47 (4) supplements that definition in adding:

Any substance or article which in the course of the carrying on of any undertaking, is discharged, discarded or otherwise dealt with as if it were waste shall, for the purposes of this Act, be presumed to be waste unless the contrary is proved.

The phraseology of these statements, emphasising as it does the view of the owner or user of the material, accords with the judicial view of waste considered in the general context of waste regulation in Chapter 13. Section 47(1) also provides that 'substance means any natural or artificial substance, whether in solid or liquid form or in the form of a gas or vapour'.

'Contamination' in the radiological context is defined in section 47(5) in the following terms:

Any reference in this Act to the contamination of a substance or article is a reference to its being so affected by either or both of the following, that is to say –

(a) absorption, admixture or adhesion of radioactive material or radioactive waste, and
(b) the emission of neutrons or ionising radiations,

as to become radioactive or to possess increased radioactivity.

The expression 'radioactive material' appearing in the definition above is itself defined in section 1(1) for the purposes of the Act as meaning 'anything which, not being waste, is either a substance to which [the] subsection applies or an article made wholly or partly from, or incorporating such a substance'. The subsection is then, by subsection (2), stipulated to apply to substances of either or both of the following descriptions:

(a) a substance containing an element specified in the first column of Schedule 1, in such a proportion that the number of becquerels of that element contained in the substance, divided by the number of grams which the substance weighs, is a number greater than that specified in relation to that element in the appropriate column of that Schedule;
(b) a substance possessing radioactivity which is wholly or partly attributable to a process of nuclear fission or other process of subjecting a substance to bombardment by neutrons or to ionising radiations, not being a process occurring in the course of nature, or in consequence of the disposal of radioactive waste, or by way of contamination in the course of the application of a process to some other substance.

Section 1(5) gives the Secretary of State the power, by order, to change what constitutes radioactive material by amending, varying or adding to Schedule 1. The power has not so far been used.

SCHEDULE 1

SPECIFIED ELEMENTS

Element	Becquerels per gram (BQ G^{-1})		
	Solid	Liquid	Gas or vapour
1. Actinium	0.37	7.40×10^{-2}	2.59×10^{-6}
2. Lead	0.74	3.70×10^{-3}	1.11×10^{-4}
3. Polonium	0.37	2.59×10^{-2}	2.22×10^{-4}
4. Protoactinium	0.37	3.33×10^{-2}	1.11×10^{-6}
5. Radium	0.37	3.70×10^{-4}	3.70×10^{-5}
6. Radon	–	–	3.70×10^{-2}
7. Thorium	2.59	3.70×10^{-2}	2.22×10^{-5}
8. Uranium	11.1	0.74	7.40×10^{-5}

The control of radioactive waste disposal and of its accumulation for disposal is through a system of authorisations. While this 'authorisation' procedure governs the handling of radioactive waste, the storage and use of radioactive material is subject to control through 'registration'. The section 47(1) definition of 'disposal' for the purposes of this Act is very wide, providing an equally comprehensive control structure. Disposal,

> in relation to waste includes its removal, deposit, destruction, discharge (whether into water or into air or into a sewer or drain or otherwise) or burial (whether underground or otherwise) and 'dispose of' shall be construed accordingly'.

This authorisation structure, centred on sections 13 and 14, is comparable with that for waste management licensing dealt with in Chapter 14.

By section 13(1,) a person may only 'dispose of any radioactive waste on or from any premises which are used for the purposes of any undertaking carried on by him, or cause or permit any radioactive waste to be so disposed of' only in accordance with an applicable authorisation, unless he is covered by an exemption. Knowledge or reasonable grounds for believing that the material is radioactive waste is a necessary element of the offence. 'Premises' includes any land, whether covered by buildings or not, including any place underground and any land covered by water. 'Undertaking' is defined in section 47(1) as including 'any trade, business or profession and, in relation to a public or local authority, includes any of the powers or duties of that authority, and, in relation to any other body or persons, whether corporate or unincorporate, includes any of the activities of that body'. The scope of the phrase 'cause or permit' has been discussed in Chapter 1.[11] The requirement for an authorisation is extended by section 13(5) to premises situated on a nuclear site but which have ceased to be used for the purpose of the licensee's undertaking. The power of the Health and Safety Executive to attach conditions to nuclear site licences with regard to the discharge of substances on or from such a site is without prejudice to this subsection.[12]

Two additional offences are created by the succeeding subsections of section 13. Section 13(2) provides that a person shall not dispose of any radioactive waste arising from the operation of any mobile radioactive apparatus kept by him, or

11 See at p.30.

12 Section 4 of the Nuclear Installations Act 1965.

cause or permit any such radioactive waste to be disposed of except in accordance with an applicable authorisation. Similarly, section 13(3) prohibits a person who in the course of an undertaking receives radioactive waste for the purpose of disposal by him, from so disposing of it without an authorisation where he knows or has reasonable grounds for believing it to be radioactive waste. However, there is no need for an authorisation under this subsection where the disposal is already the subject of an authorisation under subsections (1) or (2). 'Mobile radioactive apparatus' is defined by section 3 to mean:

> any apparatus, equipment, appliance or other thing which is radioactive material and –
> (a) is constructed or adapted for being transported from place to place, or
> (b) is portable and designed or intended to be used for releasing radioactive material into the environment or introducing it into organisms.

To conclude the range of activities requiring an authorisation, section 14 makes it an offence for a person, except in accordance with an authorisation, to accumulate any radioactive waste on any premises used for the purposes of an undertaking, or to cause or permit such accumulation, knowing or having reasonable grounds for believing it to be radioactive waste. This provision does not apply to accumulations either in circumstances to which section 13 applies or on nuclear sites.[13] For the purposes of this section the accumulation of radioactive material for at least three months is to be presumed to be, first, radioactive waste and, secondly, accumulated with a view to its disposal; authorisation under section 14(1) will therefore be required. Nuclear sites, which are licensed under the Nuclear Installations Act 1965, are defined in section 47(1) of the present Act to mean:

[13] Section 14(2) and (3) respectively.

(a) any site in respect of which a nuclear site licence is for the time being in force; or
(b) any site in respect of which, after the revocation or surrender of a nuclear site licence, the period of responsibility of the licensee has not yet come to an end.

A nuclear site licence is required, by section 1(1) of the 1965 Act, for the installation or operation of:

(a) any nuclear reactor (other than comprised in a means of transport); or
(b) any other installation of such class or description as may be prescribed, being an installation designed or adapted for –
  (i) the production or use of atomic energy; or
  (ii) the carrying out of any process which is preparatory or ancillary to the production or use of atomic energy and which involves or is capable of causing the emission of ionising radiations; or
  (iii) the storage, processing or disposal of nuclear fuel or of bulk quantities of other radioactive matter, being matter which has been produced or irradiated in the course of the production or use of nuclear fuel.

Before moving on to consider the exemptions, it may be useful to summarise the range of activities involving radioactive waste that require authorisation under these provisions:

(a) disposal on or from premises where used, including removal;
(b) disposal from operation of mobile radioactive apparatus;
(c) disposal of waste received in the course of an undertaking;
(d) accumulation of waste from other sources.

The operations or activities of mobile apparatus for which registration is required are:

(a) testing, measuring or otherwise investigating any of the characteristics of substances or articles; or

(b) releasing quantities of radioactive material into the environment or introducing such material into organisms.[14]

In addition to the exemption in section 14 for nuclear sites, section 15 makes provision for further exemptions from those authorisation requirements. By section 15(1), the disposal or accumulation of radioactive waste arising from clocks and watches does not require an authorisation. However, this exemption does not extend to waste arising on the premises at which clocks and watches are manufactured or repaired by a process using luminous material. Section 15(2) gives the Secretary of State the power, by order, to exclude any descriptions of radioactive waste from any of the provisions of sections 13 or 14, either absolutely or subject to limitations or conditions.[15]

Enforcing authorities

Control under the 1993 Act is exercised by the Secretary of State for the Environment and, in the case of disposals of radioactive waste on or from premises of the UKAEA (United Kingdom Atomic Energy Authority) and sites licensed under the Nuclear Installations Act 1965, control is exercised jointly with the Minister of Agriculture, Fisheries and Food (the Minister). To secure the performance of these functions, section 4 gives the Secretary of State the power to appoint inspectors and a chief inspector. Inspectors appointed under this provision may also act for the purposes of IPC under Part I of the Environmental Protection Act 1990. HMIP therefore currently performs both roles.[16] Section 4(6) gives inspectors thus appointed the power to conduct proceedings in magistrates' courts for offences under the Act, and section 38 effectively restricts to them the institution of prosecutions. Similar powers of appointment are given to the Minister by section 5 in respect of his functions under the Act.

The control provisions of the Act are a matter for central rather than local government. However, local public bodies clearly have an interest in the accumulation and disposal of radioactive waste in their area. As the Guide points out by way of example, the Fire Services need to know the whereabouts of radioactive materials to enable them to take appropriate precautions in emergencies. If, therefore, in considering an application for an authorisation under section 13, it appears to the chief inspector, or in appropriate cases the chief inspector and the Minister, that the disposal of the radioactive waste is likely to involve the need for special precautions to be taken by 'a local authority, a relevant water body or other public or local authority', they shall consult with such bodies before granting the authorisation.[17] A relevant water body, by section 47(1), means in England and Wales, 'the National Rivers Authority, a water undertaker, a sewerage undertaker or a local fisheries committee'. The meaning and requirements of effective consultation have been discussed in Chapter 1. Even where consultation is not required, the Guide suggests that the Secretary of State or the Minister will consult the relevant authorities 'where it seems appropriate to do so'. Where the local body must take special precautions in disposing of radioactive waste it has the power under section 18(2) to make a charge for so doing.

14 Section 9(2).

15 Statutory instruments currently in force for England and Wales are –
(S.I. 1962 No. 2646)
(S.I. 1962 No. 2648)
(S.I. 1962 No. 2649)
(S.I. 1962 No. 2710)
(S.I. 1962 No. 2711)
(S.I. 1962 No. 2712)
(S.I. 1963 No. 1831)
(S.I. 1963 No. 1832)
(S.I. 1967 No. 1797)
(S.I. 1980 No. 953, as amended by S.I. 1991 No. 477)
(S.I. 1985 No. 1047)
(S.I. 1985 No. 1048)
(S.I. 1985 No. 1049)
(S.I. 1986 No. 1002, as amended by S.I. 1992 No. 647)
(S.I. 1990 No. 2512)

16 Information on the activities of HMIP in relation to radioactive substances can be found in the Fifth Annual Report, for 1991/92.

17 Section 18(1).

The division of responsibility for radioactive and non-radioactive material is emphasised in section 40, which provides that in the discharge of their functions under the statutes listed in Schedule 3 the responsible authorities shall take no account of 'any radioactivity possessed by any substance or article or by any part of any premises'. For the purposes of those specified statutory functions, therefore, all material whether radioactive or not is to be treated in the same way; leaving responsibility for any radioactive characteristics and consequences with those having the necessary expertise and experience to deal with it. The statutes there listed include amending legislation and delegated legislation authorised by those provisions. Local Acts relating to, or giving local or public authorities powers in respect of, waste disposal or accumulation, or to substances that are a nuisance or prejudicial to health, noxious or polluting or similarly described are also governed by this provision.

The statutes listed in Part I of Schedule 3, applying to England and Wales, are:

(a) Sections 48, 81, 82, 141, 259, and 261 of the Public Health Act 1936.
(b) Section 10 of the Clean Air Act 1956.
(c) Section 5 of the Sea Fisheries Act 1966.
(d) Section 4 of the Salmon and Freshwater Fisheries Act 1975.
(e) Section 59 of the Building Act 1984.
(f) The Planning (Hazardous Substances) Act 1990.
(g) Part III of the Environmental Protection Act 1990.
(h) Sections 72, 111 and 113(6) and Chapter III of Part IV of the Water Industry Act 1991, and paragraphs 2 to 4 of Schedule 8 to that Act so far as they re-enact provisions of sections 43 and 44 of the Control of Pollution Act 1974.
(i) Sections 82, 84, 85, 86, 87(1), 88(2), 92, 93, 99, 161, 190, 202, 203, and 213 of and paragraph 6 of Schedule 25 to the Water Resources Act 1991.
(j) Section 18 of the Water Act 1945 so far as it continues to have effect by virtue of Schedule 2 to the Water Consolidation (Consequential Provisions) Act 1991 or by virtue of provisions of the Control of Pollution Act 1974 not having been brought into force.

Authorisation procedure

The procedure for the grant of authorisations is contained in section 16 of the 1994 Act. Applications[18] for authorisation of the activities specified in sections 13 and 14 are made to and the authorisation granted by the chief inspector, unless the application relates to radioactive waste from a nuclear site in which case the authorisation is to be granted jointly by the chief inspector and the appropriate Minister. A copy of the application shall be sent to each local authority in whose area the radioactive waste is to be disposed of or accumulated. If the application is not determined within four months the applicant may treat it as refused and act accordingly.

An application shall be accompanied by the prescribed fee. Section 43 gives the Secretary of State, with Treasury approval and in appropriate cases the consent of the Minister, the power to make a charging scheme covering, *inter alia*, fees for authorisation applications, variations and providing for the impostion of annual subsistence charges. By section 43(4) the purpose of the scheme is to cover the expenditure of the chief inspector and the Minister in exercising their functions under the Act. The present scheme is set out in the Fees and Charges for Radioactive

18 Application forms are available from the Department of the Environment, Room 502, Romney House, 43 Marsham St., London SW1P 3PY.

Substances Act Regulation 1993–1994.[19] To determine the applicable fee, premises are allocated to one of four bands:

(a) Bands 1 and 2 cover British Nuclear Fuels plc. at Sellafield and other major nuclear power stations which are charged on an individual time spent basis.
(b) Band 3 includes those premises which dispose of or accumulate radioactive waste and are authorised under sections 13 and 14, e.g., hospitals or university laboratories. These are subject to an application or variation fee of £1,385 and an annual subsistence fee of £820. In some cases the annual subsistence fee is reduced to £80 per authorisation.
(c) Band 4 premises are those registered under sections 7 or 10 for keeping or using radioactive material and are not therefore of present concern.

The grant of an authorisation may be for radioactive waste generally, or for one or more descriptions of radioactive waste as specified in the authorisation. It may also be subject to such limitations and conditions as the granting authorities deem suitable. The Secretary of State is given the power in section 44 to establish general limitations or conditions. When it is proposed to impose limitations or conditions the person directly concerned must be given a hearing by a person appointed by the Secretary of State. The chief inspector has the power following grant of an authorisation, at any time to revoke it or to vary it by attaching limitations or conditions, or by revoking or varying those that already apply.[20]

In those cases where the chief inspector and the Minister act jointly to:

(a) refuse a section 13 authorisation; or
(b) attach limitations or conditions to an authorisation; or
(c) vary an authorisation otherwise than by revoking a limitation or condition; or
(d) revoke such an authorisation,

the person directly concerned and such local authorities or other persons whom the Secretary of State and that Minister consider appropriate may be afforded the opportunity of a hearing before the decision is made.[21] The same opportunity is to be given to a person served with a section 21 or section 22 notice by the Minister, in this case after service.

The similar wording of the corresponding 1960 Act section was the subject of judicial consideration in *R v Secretary of State for the Environment, ex parte Dudley MBC* [1990] JPL 683.[22] The case concerned an application for judicial review by the local authority, of a decision by the Minister to grant an authorisation permitting the disposal of radioactive waste in its area. The applicant company had not asked for a hearing. The question for the Court was whether, in granting an authorisation to the company, the Secretary of State was under a duty to consider whether the local authority should be given an opportunity of a hearing; something he had not done. The Court held that the Secretary of State was entitled to have a policy that unless the applicant requested one, other relevant persons would not be given an opportunity for a hearing except in exceptional circumstances. Nevertheless, the Court also held that the Secretary of State should have considered the question of whether a local authority that was opposed to an application should be given the right to a hearing, whether or not the applicant had asked for one.

When an authorisation is granted, the chief inspector shall provide the applicant with a certificate containing all the material particulars of the authorisation.

19 A copy of the scheme may be found as Appendix 6 to the Act in Current Law Statutes.

20 Section 17.

21 Section 28(1).

22 (1990) 90 JPL 683, DC.

He shall also send a copy to each local authority in whose area the radioactive waste is to be disposed of or accumulated and to each of the public or local authorities that were consulted in relation to the application; unless the Secretary of State has directed under section 25 that knowledge of the authorisation be restricted on grounds of national security. Generally an authorisation shall take effect not less than 28 days after it has been sent.

Authorisation having been granted, the person authorised has a duty under section 19 to keep a copy of the certificate displayed so as to be conveniently accessible to persons visiting the premises and who may be affected by those matters. Following authorisation, the chief inspector may by notice specify in relation to site or disposal records the period for which they are to be retained following cessation of the activities regulated by the authorisation, or that in the event of cancellation or revocation of the authorisation or cessation of the regulated activities copies be delivered to him.[23] For this purpose section 20 defines 'records' as those required to be kept by virtue of conditions attached to the authorisation, 'site records' as records relating to the condition of the premises on which those activities are carried on, and 'disposal records' to mean records relating to the disposal of radioactive waste on or from the premises on which the activities are carried on.

The Environmental Protection Act 1990[24] introduced wider provisions relating to public access to documents in keeping with the general tenor of that Act and in accordance with Community developments. Those obligations are now re-enacted in section 39 of this 1993 Act. First, section 39(1) requires the chief inspector to keep copies of :

(a) applications made to him under the Act;
(b) documents issued by him under the Act;
(c) other documents sent to any local authority due to a direction of the Secretary of State; and
(d) records of convictions as may be prescribed by regulations.

Copies of those documents are to be made available to the public, with the exception of those that relate to 'any relevant process or trade secret' or in respect of which the Secretary of State has issued a direction restricting access on grounds of national security. The regulations applicable to (d) above are the Radioactive Substances (Records of Convictions) Regulations 1992[25] which prescribe the information to be made available to the public. In relation to each conviction that information comprises the details of the offence; the name of the offender; the date of the conviction; the penalty imposed; and the name of the court. Spent convictions under the Rehabilitation of Offenders Act 1974 must be removed from the register.

The same section imposes a similar duty on local authorities in respect of documents sent to them under the Act, unless directed by the chief inspector that a document or part of one is not to be made public. Directions may only be given to prevent the disclosure of relevant processes or trade secrets and may apply generally, to specified classes of documents, or to particular documents or parts. Copies of documents knowledge of which should be restricted on grounds of national security are not supplied to local authorities. The public's right of access includes free inspection at all reasonable times and the obtaining of copies on payment of a reasonable fee. The explanatory Circular[26] emphasises that this public

---

23 Section 20.

24 Schedule 5, paragraph 15; and see DoE Circular 21/90, 'Local Authority Responsibilities for Public Access to Information under the Radioactive Substances Act 1960 as Amended by the Environmental Protection Act 1990', amended by DoE Circular 22/92.

25 S.I. 1992 No. 1685.

26 *Op.cit.*, note 24 above.

right of access and inspection applies only to documents sent to local authorities after 1 January 1990. No documents supplied before that date are to be made available. Following the implementation of the 1990 Act the chief inspector, and where appropriate the Minister, progressively reviewed all such documents and issued fresh copies where appropriate. A document is to be kept by a local authority for four years after it ceases to have effect.

Carrying on a section 13 or section14 activity without an authorisation, or failing to comply with a limitation or condition or failing to comply with a term of a notice served under section 21 or section 22 are offences actionable summarily or on indictment with punishment up to five years' imprisonment, or a fine of £20,000 or both.[27] HMIP's summary prosecution of Nichols Institute Diagnostics in April 1993 provides an illustration of the operation of these provisions. The defendants imported diagnostic kits from the USA, some of which contained radioactive trace elements, and in particular Iodine 125 and Tritium. To use the material the company required registration under the 1960 Act, and its accumulation in any quantity or its disposal was the subject of an authorisation under the Act. HMIP inspectors visited the site in July 1992 and found an accumulation of Liquid Iodine 125 in excess of its authorisation. Further, some of the material had been received before its registration date in April 1991. While there was no danger to public safety there were clear breaches of the legislation. The defendants pleaded guilty and were fined £10,000 and ordered to pay the prosecution costs of £2,726.

Contravention of the section 19 duty to display the certificate of authorisation, the damaging or defacing of such documents, and the failure to comply with the requirements of a section 20 notice are similarly constituted summary or indictable offences by section 33, but with appropriately lower punishment maxima.

27 Section 32.

Enforcement

The 1993 Act provides the chief inspector, or, in appropriate cases, the chief inspector and the Minister, with two enforcement powers. The breach or anticipated breach of a limitation or condition in an authorisation or registration may be remedied by the 'enforcement notice' procedure in section 21, while 'prohibition notices' under section 22 are for use where the chief inspector considers that there is 'imminent risk of pollution of the environment or of harm to human health' through the activities controlled by the Act relating to radioactive material or waste. These powers to regulate operations involving radioactive material were introduced by section 102 of the Environmental Protection Act 1990.

Enforcement notices are required by section 21(1) and (2) to:

(a) state that the chief inspector is of the opinion that a person to whom registration under section 7 or 10 relates, or to whom an authorisation was granted under section 13 or 14 –

    (i) is failing to comply with any limitation or condition subject to which the registration or authorisation has effect, or

    (ii) is likely to fail to comply with any such limitation or condition,

    he may serve a notice under this section on that person;

(b) specify the matters constituting the breach or making a breach likely;

(c) specify the necessary remedial action and the period within which they are to be taken.

The wording of the subsection emphasises that these matters are mandatory, failure to comply therefore providing a ground of challenge to the validity of the notice.[28] Where copies of the authorisation were sent to any public or local authorities under section 16(9)(b), they are also to be sent a copy of the notice. Examples of early enforcement notices[29] include that served on Lucas Aerospace for failing to notify loss of radioactive sources, failure to implement security measures previously requested by an inspector, and for having more radioactive sources than was permitted by the company's registration. Another notice was issued to a hospital in Chelmsford which was no longer incinerating its radioactive clinical waste but accumulating it. The notice required the hospital to recommence incineration.

Prohibition notices governing situations where 'the keeping or use of radioactive material or of mobile radioactive apparatus, or the disposal or accumulation of radioactive waste, by a person in pursuance of a registration or authorisation ... involves an imminent risk of pollution of the environment or of harm to human health', are to contain the following information[30]:

(a) the chief inspector's opinion;
(b) the matters giving rise to the risk involved in the activity, the steps that must be taken to remove the risk and the period within which those steps must be taken; and
(c) direction that the registration or authorisation shall, until the notice is withdrawn, wholly or to the extent specified in the notice cease to have effect.

Service of a prohibition notice is sanctioned whenever the necessary conditions exist and irrespective of whether the particular activity complies with any limitations or conditions attached to a registration or authorisation. When satisfied that the risk specified in the notice has been removed the chief inspector shall by a further notice withdraw the prohibition notice.[31] As with enforcement notices, copies of the prohibition notice and notification of its withdrawal are to be sent to any public or local authority that recieved a copy of the original registration or authorisation. Failure to comply with the terms of either a section 21 or a section 22 notice is a criminal offence under section 32, attracting the penalties noted above.

These enforcement powers presuppose the necessary antecedent authority to enter and inspect premises. Those section 32(1) rights in respect of, *inter alia*, premises for which authorisations have been issued and 'for the purposes of the execution of this Act' are to:

(a) enter at reasonable times, or in the case of an emergency at any time, applicable premises, with such equipment as the inspector may require;
(b) carry out tests and inspections, take photographs and obtain and take away samples as the inspector may consider necessary or expedient;
(c) direct that the whole or any part of the premises, or anything in them, is to be left undisturbed for as long as reasonably necessary for the purpose of any tests or inspections; and
(d) require the occupier or any other person with duties on the premises to provide facilities and assistance and information relating to the use of the premises, or to permit the inspection of relevant documents as the inspector may require, and in the case of answers to questions to sign a declaration of the truth of those answers.[32]

28 *Miller-Mead* v *Minister of Housing and Local Government* [1963] QB 196 at p.226; see in Chapter 1 at note 53.

29 HMIP Fifth Annual Report for 1991-1992 (HMSO).

30 Section 22(3).

31 Section 22(7).

32 These powers are restricted in respect of UKAEA premises that have been declared to be prohibited places for the purposes of the Official Secrets Act 1911; see section 6(3) of the Atomic Energy Authority Act 1954.

Entry is conditional on the production, if requested, of written evidence of the inspector's authority.

In addition to those powers applicable to authorised premises, section 31(4)(b) gives an inspector a more circumscribed right of access to any premises where he has reasonable grounds for believing that radioactive waste has been or is being disposed of or accumulated and, in relation to such premises, the right to exercise the subsection (1) powers. The general nature of those powers is restricted in that they may only be exercised either with the consent of the occupier, or under the authority of a warrant or in the case of an emergency.[33] The issue of a warrant for these purposes is provided for in Schedule 2. A justice of the peace is to be satisfied on sworn information in writing that admission is reasonably required to exercise powers conferred by the Act and:

33 Section 31(6); this restriction does not apply to premises that have been but are no longer the subject of an authorisation (section 31(7)).

(a) that admission to the premises for those purposes was sought –
    (i) in the case of section 31(1) premises, after not less than 24 hours' notice had been given to the occupier, or
    (ii) in the case of other premises, not less than seven days' notice had been given; or
(b) that admission in the case of an emergency was sought and refused; or
(c) that the premises were unoccupied; or
(d) that an application for admission would defeat the object of the entry.[34]

34 Schedule 2, paragraph 3.

Once granted, a warrant remains in force until its purpose has been achieved. An emergency is deemed to exist where the person seeking entry has reasonable cause to believe:

(a) that circumstances exist which are likely to endanger life or health; and
(b) that immediate entry to the premises is necessary to verify the existence of those circumstances or to ascertain their cause or to effect a remedy.[35]

35 Schedule 31(11).

Complementary to these rights of entry, section 35 makes it an offence for any person intentionally to obstruct an inspector in the exercise of section 31 powers, or to refuse or without reasonable excuse fail to provide facilities or assistance or information, or to permit any reasonable inspection. On conviction summarily or on indictment a fine up to £5,000 may be imposed. Powers of entry and the meaning of 'obstruction' are dealt with generally in Chapter 1.

Rights of access and inspection by public officials allied to the power to obtain information and see documents exposes the person or organisation subject to those procedures to the risk that information of commercial value or processes unique to them will be revealed, and possibly thereafter passed to third parties. The disclosure of such trade secrets is prohibited by section 34. It is an offence for a person to disclose 'any information relating to any relevant process or trade secret used in carrying on any particular undertaking which has been given to or obtained by him under this Act'. The exceptions are if the disclosure of the information is:

(a) with the consent of the person concerned;
(b) in accordance with a direction of the Secretary of State;
(c) in connection with the execution of the Act; or
(d) for the purposes of legal proceedings arising out of the Act.

For these purposes the section states that 'relevant process means any process applied for the purposes of, or in connection with, the production or use of radioactive material'. As with most offences under this Act, this disclosure is actionable summarily or on indictment, with penalties up to two years in prison, or a fine of £5,000 or both.

Appeals

A person applying for or who is granted an authorisation, i.e., 'the person directly concerned', has a right of appeal to the Secretary of State against a refusal of an application, any limitations or conditions, or its revocation or variation.[36] Section 26(2) gives a similar right of appeal against section 21 and section 22 notices. These rights of appeal are from decisions or actions of the chief inspector alone, no such appeals lying from joint decisions of the chief inspector and the Minister under section 16(3) or against notices served by the Minister. Also, of course, there is no right of appeal against an action of the chief inspector pursuant to a direction of the Secretary of State under sections 23 or 24.

The appeals procedure is found in section 27 and the Radioactive Substances (Appeals) Regulations 1990,[37] a synopsis of which now follows. The appellant must give written notice to the Secretary of State with a full statement of the case, copies of all supporting documents and a statement of his preference for determination of the appeal either by a hearing or by written representations. That notice is to be given within two months of the notification to the appellant of the decision or action challenged, or of the date on which the application is deemed to be refused for non-determination. In the case of a revocation of an authorisation the period for appeal is 28 days and the fact of appeal serves to suspend the revocation until determination of the appeal.

Having received notice of appeal the Secretary of State will send a copy of the notice, details of the case and the appellant's preference for the form of appeal to the chief inspector. He shall also notify any public or local authorities who were consulted in the authorisation process, giving them 21 days within which to make any representations 'with respect to the subject-matter of the appeal'. The Regulations are silent on the person having the final decision on the form of appeal, although the wording of regulation 5(1) implies that the appellants choice of written representations is decisive. The form of both procedures is stipulated in the Regulations.

In determining an appeal, the Secretary of State, by section 27(4):

(a) may affirm the decision;

(b) where the decision was a refusal of an application, may direct the chief inspector to grant the application;

(c) where the decision involved limitations or conditions attached to an authorisation, may quash those limitations or conditions wholly or in part; or

(d) where that decision was a revocation of an authorisation, may quash the decision;

and in the case of (b) (c) or (d), may give directions to the chief inspector as to the limitations and conditions to be attached to the authorisation. The Secretary of State shall also notify the appellant in writing of his determination and of his reasons. If the appeal was by way of hearing the appellant shall also be provided with a copy of the report of the person who conducted it. Copies of those documents shall also be sent to the chief inspector and to any authority to whom he gave notice of the appeal.

36 Schedule 26(1).

37 S.I. 1990 No. 2504; HMIP have produced a guidance note which amplifies the regulations and is based on the planning appeals structure. The guidance note is available from HMIP on request.

Secretary of State's powers

As was noted in dealing with enforcing authorities, control under the Act is given to the Secretary of State but is exercised in practice by HMIP. The power given to the Secretary of State by section 4 of the 1993 Act to appoint inspectors for the purposes of this Act has already been noted. While this gives the inspectorate, and particularly the chief inspector, general day to day executive control, the Secretary of State retains a number of residual powers through which he may direct or override those of the inspectorate.

Powers of direction under section 23(1) and (2) may be exercised in relation to an authorisation under either section 13 or section 14 to require the chief inspector to refuse or to grant an application, to attach any specified limitations or conditions, to vary an authorisation or to cancel or revoke (or not to cancel or revoke) an authorisation. The Secretary of State may also direct the service of notices under sections 21 and 22 in specified terms. Directions may also require the chief inspector to send to specified local authorities such written particulars relating to authorisations as may be stipulated. As an alternative to that section 23 power of direction in respect of individual authorisations, section 24 enables the Secretary of State to require the chief inspector to refer to him for determination either applications of a particular description or any particular application. In the latter case, relating to an individual application, the Secretary of State may cause the holding of a public enquiry.[38]

On grounds of national security the Secretary of State has the power, in section 25(2), to direct the chief inspector to restrict the knowledge of any particular application or description of application for authorisation under sections 13 and 14, or of any authorisation or description of authorisation under those sections. In such cases the chief inspector shall not send copies of documents to public or local authorities as required by section 16. This same power may be exercised jointly by the Secretary of State and the Minister of Agriculture, Fisheries and Food in relation to nuclear sites.

Should the Secretary of State consider that adequate facilities are not available for the safe disposal or accumulation of radioactive waste he may provide, or arrange for the provision of, such facilities.[39] Exercise of this power is to be preceded by consultation with the local authority for the area and also with other public or local authorities (if any) as appear to him to be proper. On the meaning of 'consultation' in this context see the discussion in Chapter 1. The Secretary of State has the ancillary power to determine the level of charges to be made for the use of facilities provided under this section. Supplementary to these general powers, section 30 enables the Secretary of State, in relation to any particular case of radioactive waste where he is satisfied that the waste ought to be disposed of, but that because the premises are unoccupied, or the occupier is absent or insolvent, or for any other reason it is unlikely that the waste will be disposed of unless he uses these powers, to dispose of that waste as he thinks fit. He may then recover the reasonable costs of disposal from the occupier or, if the premises are unoccupied, from the owner[40] of the premises.

38 In such cases the provisions, suitably modified, of section 250(2) to (5)of the Local Government Act 1972 apply.

39 Section 29(1).

40 For this purpose 'owner' is as defined in section 343 of the Public Health Act 1936, i.e., the person receiving or entitled to receive the rack rent of the premises.

Appendix
Environment Agency

ORIGINS

- In July 1991, the Government expressed its intention of setting up a national Environment Agency – consultation paper in Oct 1991.
- Proposed operative date of 1995 delayed by Treasury pressure – now Spring 1996
- DoE report in July 1994 on possible structures (five alternatives) with an advisory committee to oversee its creation and operation.

DRAFT ENVIRONMENTAL AGENCIES BILL

Introduced by SoS on 13 Oct 1994 – i.e. 'agencies' envisages one for England and Wales and one for Scotland. Proposed agency to be formed from the merger of HMIP, NRA, and waste regulation function of LAs.

Its structure approximates very closely to that of the NRA, being a non-departmental public body sponsored by the DoE. Its Board will consist of 8–15 members, all appointed by and responsible to Ministers. Day to day operations will be the responsibility of a Chief Executive appointed by the Board with the approval of the Secretary of State.

Its responsibilities are intended to include:

1 IPC authorisations under Part I of EPA 1990.
2 Disposal and storage of radioactive waste.
3 Control of water pollution and abstraction.
4 Management of water resources and fisheries.
5 Conservation and enhancement of inland and coastal waters.
6 Regulation of treatment, storage, disposal and transport of controlled waste.
7 Various DoE functions, e.g. assessment of chemicals under EU law, technical guidance on waste and contaminated land, co-ordination of national radiation monitoring scheme.

Points to note:

1 Moving waste regulation from local authorities; lack of accountability
2 The cost benefit assessment. The bill requires the Agency to *'take into account the costs which are likely to be incurred, and the benefits which are likely to accrue'* in considering whether, or how, to exercise a power. However this duty will not apply if it would be unreasonable for the Agency to comply with it *'in view of the nature or purpose of the power or in the circumstances of the particular case'*. NRA has expressed particular concern over this provision and is seeking assurances from the government that the duty only applies to strategic and policy issues rather than day to day issues. Is that too optimistic? Note scope for challenge by judicial review in the operation of this principle.
3 Conservation duties. The original clause requiring the Agency to *'have regard to the desirability of'* conserving and enhancing natural beauty and wildlife was criticized and has been strengthened to impose a duty to further the conservation and enhancement of natural beauty and the conservation of flora, fauna and geological or physiological features of special interest.
4 It appears likely that these provisions will form part of a larger Environment and Countryside Bill, incorporating other environmental matters, e.g.

(a) contaminated land, identification and clean-up
(b) pollution from abandoned mines
(c) statutory plans for packaging waste recovery
(d) protection of hedgerows
(e) establishment of independent national park authorities.

5 The Agency, or its reputation, will stand or fall in almost direct proportion to the adequacy of its funding. (On this see the government's record e.g. in relation to the Crown Prosecution Service and the Child Support Agency.) Already this year's budget to HMIP has been severely cut, requiring staff reductions.
6 The Agency's limited role has already been criticised e.g. the CIEH has argued that it should be responsible for co-ordinating green policies within all government departments.

MANAGEMENT STATEMENT

A draft management statement was published with the draft bill, outlining:

– the Agency's aims, objectives, duties and powers
– the policy background of its work
– responsibilities of its Board and Chief Executive
– relationship with Ministers, government departments and other bodies.

The overall aim of the Agency is stated to be–
'that it should help to promote sustainable development through high quality, integrated environmental protection, management and enhancement.'
In support of this aim, six main objectives are specified for the Agency:

1 To provide effective environmental protection, management and enhancement, particularly in ways which take account of impacts on all aspects of the environment.
2 To impose the minimum burden on industry and others consistent with the above, by developing single points of contact through which industry and others can deal with the Agency.
3 To operate to high professional standards, based on the best possible information and analysis of the environment and of processes which affect it.
4 To organise its activities in ways which reflect good environmental practice and provide value for money for those who pay its charges, and for taxpayers as a whole.
5 To provide clear and readily available advice and information on its work.

6 To develop a close and responsible relationship with the public, local communities and regulated organisations.

AGENCY ADVISORY COMMITTEE

The composition of this nine-strong body has recently been announced. The committee will advise Ministers on the formation of the Agency and is expected to form the core of the Board. The committee's composition (its chairman is Lord de Ramsey, an East Anglian landowner) has already been criticized by the Institute of Waste Management for its lack of members with any experience of or expertise in waste management issues.

AREAS OF DOUBT AND UNCERTAINTY

1 Regional committees to be established, but no indication of their function.
2 The management statement recognises the need for close liaison with local authorities in areas such as air pollution control, planning, waste, contaminated land. However there is no indication of the method of such co-operation.
3 No indication of the detailed internal structure of the Agency. Should regional boundaries follow river catchment areas as currently applied by the NRA or local authority boundaries as used by HMIP and waste regulation authorities?
4 A further question concerns the merit of a broad separation of function between the 'regulatory' i.e., pollution control, and the 'operational' i.e., all others. The NRA considers that such a division would be highly artificial, unsatisfactory and costly as the functions are mutually supportive. Conversely HMIP consider that such a separation is crucial if the Agency is to avoid apparent conflict of interest and consequent public suspicion.
5 So far no attention appears to have been given to the continuity of functions between the existing bodies and the Agency. Unless this question is resolved the resulting uncertainty is likely to hinder the work of the present bodies over the next year.

Index